SO-AII-488

PENGUIN BOOKS

DANGEROUS PILGRIMAGES

Malcolm Bradbury is a novelist, critic, television dramatist and part-time Professor of American Studies at the University of East Anglia. He is author of six novels: *Eating People is Wrong* (1959); *Stepping Westward* (1965); *The History Man* (1975), which won the Royal Society of Literature Heinemann Prize and was adapted as a famous television series; *Rates of Exchange* (1983), which was shortlisted for the Booker Prize; *Cuts: A Very Short Novel* (1987); and *Doctor Criminale* (1992). All are published by Penguin. His critical works include *The Modern American Novel* (1984, revised 1992), *No, Not Bloomsbury* (essays, 1987), *The Modern World: Ten Great Writers* (Penguin, 1989), *From Puritanism to Postmodernism: A History of American Literature* (with Richard Ruland; Penguin, 1993) and *The Modern British Novel* (Penguin, 1994). He has also edited *The Penguin Book of Modern British Short Stories* (1988) and *Modernism* (with James McFarlane; Penguin, 1991). He is the author of *Who Do You Think You Are?* (Penguin, 1993), a collection of seven stories and nine parodies, and of several works of humour and satire, including *Why Come to Slaka?* (Penguin, 1992), *Unsent Letters* (revised edition, Penguin, 1995) and *Mensonge* (Penguin, 1993). He has written several television 'novels', including *The Gravy Train* and *The Gravy Train Goes East*, and adapted several other television series, including Tom Sharpe's *Porterhouse Blue*, Kingsley Amis's *The Green Man* and Stella Gibbons's *Cold Comfort Farm*.

Malcolm Bradbury lives in Norwich, travels a good deal, and in 1991 was awarded the CBE.

MALCOLM BRADBURY

DANGEROUS PILGRIMAGES

TRANS-ATLANTIC MYTHOLOGIES
AND THE NOVEL

PENGUIN BOOKS

To Jasmine

PENGUIN BOOKS

Published by the Penguin Group
Penguin Books Ltd, 27 Wrights Lane, London W8 5TZ, England
Penguin Books USA Inc., 375 Hudson Street, New York, New York 10014, USA
Penguin Books Australia Ltd, Ringwood, Victoria, Australia
Penguin Books Canada Ltd, 10 Alcorn Avenue, Toronto, Ontario, Canada M4V 3B2
Penguin Books (NZ) Ltd, 182–190 Wairau Road, Auckland 10, New Zealand

Penguin Books Ltd, Registered Offices: Harmondsworth, Middlesex, England

First published by Martin Secker and Warburg Ltd 1995
Published in Penguin Books 1996
3 5 7 9 10 8 6 4 2

Copyright © Malcolm Bradbury, 1995
All rights reserved

The moral right of the author has been asserted

Printed in England by Clays Ltd, St Ives plc

Except in the United States of America, this book is sold subject
to the condition that it shall not, by way of trade or otherwise, be lent,
re-sold, hired out, or otherwise circulated without the publisher's
prior consent in any form of binding or cover other than that in
which it is published and without a similar condition including this
condition being imposed on the subsequent purchaser

Emperors and kings, dukes and marquises, counts, knights, and townsfolk, and all people who wish to know the various races of men and peculiarities of the various regions of the world, take this book and have it read to you.

The Voyages of Marco Polo

"And where?" cried Tom, "Oh where will you go?"
  "I don't know," he said, "Yes, I do. I'll go to America."
  "No, no," cried Tom in a kind of agony. "Don't go there. Pray don't. Think better of it. Don't be so dreadfully regardless of yourself. Don't go to America!"

Charles Dickens, *Martin Chuzzlewit* (1844)

"Ah, off to Europe!" Hudson exclaimed with a melancholy cadence as they sat down. "Happy, happy man!"

Henry James, *Roderick Hudson* (1876)

Presently he heard footsteps approach and, without moving, could see they were a woman's. Feet, ankles, calves came progressively into view. Like every pair in the country they were slim and neatly covered. Which came first in this strange civilization, he wondered, the foot or the shoe, the leg or the nylon stocking? Or were these uniform elegant limbs, from the stocking-top down, marketed in one cellophane envelope at the neighbourhood stores? Did they clip by some labour-saving device to the sterilized rubber privacies above?

Evelyn Waugh, *The Loved One* (1948)

Contents

Acknowledgements

This book has been a good while in the making. I am grateful to many people who, over the years and in different ways, helped me write it. I had help from a number of writers who gave me their personal accounts of transatlantic or expatriate experience in different eras: Ezra Pound, T. S. Eliot, Malcolm Cowley, Vergil Thompson, William Carlos Williams, Glenway Wescott, Robert M. Coates, Harold Loeb, Alfred Kreymborg, Allen Tate, Merrill Moore, John Hawkes, Gore Vidal, Leslie Fiedler, Joseph Heller, Raymond Federman, William Gass, John Barth, David Lodge, Martin Amis, Ian McEwan, Clive Sinclair, Edmund White, and many more. I interviewed some of these in the BBC's New York studios for a Third Programme documentary on American writers in Paris in the Twenties, *Paris France* (broadcast 19 February 1960), and I am greatly indebted to the producer, Christopher Holme, and Lilian Lang of BBC New York. At Yale I had great help from Norman Holmes Pearson, Donald C. Gallup, and the staff of the Sterling Memorial Library; at Harvard from Harry Levin, and the staff of the Widener Library. At Manchester Marcus Cunliffe, especially, and Geoffrey Moore gave invaluable direction and guidance. So did Howard Temperley, with whom I taught a special subject at UEA on some aspects of this topic. I have also explored it with many other people, and there are many other important debts: to Daniel Aaron, Harry Allen, Harold Beaver, Millicent Bell, Christopher Bigsby, William Brock, Hans Bungert, Christopher Butler, William Van O'Connor, Howell Daniels, Leon Edel, John H. Elliott, John Fletcher, Winfried Fluck, Mick Gidley, Arnold Goldman, Iain Hamilton, Ihab Hassan, Gerhard Hoffmann, Richard Hoggart, Eric Homberger, Heinz Ickstadt, Anthony Kenny, Brian Lee, William Leuchtenburg, Lawrence Levine, Paul Levine, André Le Vot, Jay Martin, Leo Marx, Helen McNeil, Peter Mayer, Jeffrey Meyers, Eric Mottram, Herbert Nicholas, Henry Dan Piper, Jack Pole, Richard Ruland, Irving Sablosky, Raymond Seitz, Barry Spacks, Patricia Meyer Spacks, Cushing Strout, Werner Sollors, Tony Tanner, Anthony Thwaite, Frank Thistlethwaite, Alan Trachtenburg, Brom Weber and Heide Ziegler, all of whom added to my ideas.

Elements of the argument have appeared here and there in other forms, and

I have drawn somewhat on some of my previous publications. This includes two pamphlets, *The Outland Dart: American Writers and European Modernism* (London, The British Academy, 1978); *The Expatriate Tradition and American Literature* (British Association of American Studies, Pamphlet No. 9, 1982), and a fair number of essays, including "American Realism and the Romance of Europe: Fuller, Frederic, Harland," *Perspectives in American History*, IV (1970) (written with David Cheshire); "Dangerous Pilgrimages, 1, 2 and 3," in *Encounter* (December 1976; February 1977; May 1977); and "Second Countries: The Expatriate Tradition in American Writing," *The Yearbook of English Studies* (Summer 1978). I have also drawn on my editorial introductions to editions of the following: Washington Irving, *The Sketch Book of Geoffrey Crayon, Gent.* (London, Everyman, 1993), Nathaniel Hawthorne, *The Blithedale Romance* (London, Everyman, 1993), Nathaniel Hawthorne, *The Marble Faun* (London, Everyman, 1994), and Stephen Crane, *The Red Badge of Courage* (London, Everyman, 1992); also F. Scott Fitzgerald, *The Great Gatsby* (London, Everyman's Library, 1991) and Ernest Hemingway, *A Farewell to Arms* (London, Everyman's Library, 1993).

I have been grateful for scholarships from the English-Speaking Union and the British Association for American Studies, which enabled me first to research this material in the USA. Though the book started life a good time ago at Indiana, Yale and Harvard, it was lately completed when I was Senior Visiting Research Fellow at St John's College, Oxford. I warmly thank the fellows and the President, Bill Hayes, for the ideal circumstances of its finishing. From the very beginning, when we first met in the research shelving of the Nottinghamshire County Library, my wife Elizabeth has been a fundamental support in researching this book, and I am most of all grateful to her.

Introduction

It's a well-known fact that the wide Atlantic Ocean, which, according to your viewpoint, either links or separates the continents of Europe and America, has generated a roaring trade not just in gold and silver, slaves and sugar, cotton and crack, Scotch and Bourbon, the Rolling Stones and Madonna, but a stranger and more elusive commodity: images. From the Age of Discoveries on, when Europeans boldly sailed where none had gone before, and found the peoples who were there already, explorers and colonists, pilgrims and traders, immigrants and expatriates, traders and tourists have shuttled across its width, in both directions; and today it is the busiest of the world's international routes in goods and human traffic. But these explorers, migrants and travellers have long been drawn not only by realistic needs and interests – the search for freedom, the hope of opportunity, the hunger for wealth – but by an elaborate and dense body of notions that seated themselves first in the European, and then later in the American, mind. Encrusted round the many actual voyages, from the first dangerous adventures of exploration and settlement to the jumbo shuttles that now link Heathrow and Kennedy, Schiphol and Dulles – voyages that have narrowed the ocean down from months to weeks, weeks to days, days to hours, so that now, flying westward, you can arrive before you leave – there have been even more journeys of the imagination, a flourishing traffic in fancy, fiction, dream and myth. Over the centuries one of the most important trades has been in mutual fantasy, the barter of myths and illusions: American Dreams, American Nightmares, European Fantasies. On the one hand the Wild West, the thunderous Pacific, the Chisholm Trail and Route 66, Cape Kennedy and the Astronauts; on the other the Sistine Chapel and Dracula's castle, thatched cottages and cream teas, Paris in the spring. No matter that their feet were locked in place in the weaving sheds of Manchester or the rolling mills of Pittsburgh: Europeans looked across the Atlantic and dreamt of freedom, a land of opportunity and the fresh start, and Americans, looking the other way, dreamt of bucolic villages and ancient customs, and longed for "history" – precisely what they or their forebears had so often crossed the Ocean to escape.

This is the transatlantic refraction, sometimes called the Grand Alliance or the Special Relationship: because what has gone into the traffic exceeds most mythologies of voyage, adventure and contact, because of its vast economic and political consequences, its massive impact on modern world history. It's a highly ambiguous trade, and has been carefully cultivated by the exploiters of such things: sponsors of exploration, justifiers of colonization and conquest, traders and politicians, shipmasters and railroad barons, speculators in cheap land and employers hunting cheap labour, tourist agencies and airlines, boosters, advertisers, media image-makers. The great transatlantic bridge is of enormous political and economic significance, and has everything to do with the destiny and evolution of the modern world. The American way has been one of the great historical options – and for many more people than Europeans. And none of it is new. Once it had been discovered by the world outside, America came to seem for many people nothing less than the model of the future or progress itself. "The discovery of America, and that of a passage to the East Indies by the Cape of Good Hope, are the two greatest and most important events recorded in the history of man," wrote Adam Smith in *The Wealth of Nations*. "Two new worlds have been opened to . . . industry, each of them much greater and more extensive than the old one."

It was perhaps ironic that Smith's great work of political economy appeared in 1776: the year America, or a significant northern part of it, declared its independence of Europe, or rather Britain, and became the world's First New Nation. But with American Independence – later echoed in the Revolution in France, the independence revolutions of Latin America – the contact did not wane, despite those who wished it to do so ("England to Europe, America to itself!" pronounced Tom Paine, the renegade Thetford staymaker and revolutionary, who himself soon returned to Europe). Indeed it increased, and grew ever more complex, as the rising western empire entered history, began more and more to shape it, and finally took a major place in the larger affairs of the world. It has since intervened in the destiny of many nations and peoples, deeply affected the pattern of human migration and settlement, generated much of human invention and technological progress, and presided over the fortunes and the disasters of the modern world economy, to the point where modernization and Americanization have come to seem almost the same thing. In the last half-century the choice between America and the Soviet Union, capitalism and communism, materialistic individualism and totalitarian Marxism, became the essential political choice of the age – between two divergent principles of modernization, two fundamentally different versions of historical destiny. Even today, when the New World Order has turned into the New World Disorder, when America shifts its attention to the Pacific Rim and NAFTA, and Europe looks with hope or anxiety toward its own new-forging identity, the symbol of the New World retains its global power and influence.

But an essential part of its importance and its fascination – this is my theme in this book – is that it has also involved the higher myth-makers: the philosophers, the cosmographers, and the fantasists, the poets, the playwrights and the novelists. Beyond all matters of conquest and world politics, power and economics, there has always been a mythic surplus: of tales and fantasies, dreams and mythologies. They belong in the province of human desire; many millions have gone to America in search of a fictional dream. But they also belong in the province of art, the realm of image and fiction. Such fictions existed from the beginnings. It has been fairly argued, by the Mexican historian Edmundo O'Gorman, that America was not discovered (it was there already, with its own dense culture and history) but invented – and invented in the image of its inventor, the Renaissance mind of Europe. The invention went back, in fact, to classical times, when the notion of an unknown world to the west which might begin history over again – a New World, in short – came into being. In medieval thought – in the imaginary voyages of Sir Thomas Mandeville, for instance – the idea of the undiscovered land in the west revived and took on new importance as part of humanism. And these historic and often illusory notions were carried by the first explorers – the Columbuses, Raleighs, Vespuccis, Frobishers, Magellans, and Cabots – and planted on the lands they found, mapped and claimed. For the peoples already here, nothing except the European invasion itself was new. But for Europeans old dreams and ideas were being confirmed or disproved, and the mythology was tested anew in every new voyage, adventure, encounter, conquest. American dreams as well as European greeds accompanied the first discoveries and settlements. Fantasies of quite extraordinary wonders – Cities of Gold, Fountains of Eternal Youth, the Terrestrial Paradise – as well as desire for conquest and possession drove the Spanish *conquistadores* as they plundered in the "golden lands" of South America. Biblical notions of the return to the Promised Land as well as religious persecution guided the Pilgrim Fathers, as they sought to found their City Upon a Hill. Utopian images of liberty and freedom, the arcadian birthright, as well as famine and repression impelled the many millions of Europeans who, in their "huddled masses," risked the stinking two-week voyage across the Ocean to Ellis Island to begin the "new life" in the new world. No less remarkable fantasies of futurist cities and scientific discovery, the "shape of things to come," as well as Nazi, Bolshevik and Fascist persecutions brought the European *émigrés* of the 1930s who helped transform the scope and prospects of American culture in the postwar world.

"In the beginning, all the world was America," wrote John Locke, following out the familiar notion that the land to the west represented nothing less than the world's lost Golden Age. Through classical, medieval, Renaissance, Enlightenment, Romantic and modernist thought, this idea has remained. The European voyage to America was a revelation, a fresh triangulation on the world. Adam Smith wrote his noted book partly in response to an essay competition set by the French *philosophe* and former Jesuit, the Abbé Reynel – who had asked his fellow philosophers to write a useful number of words dealing with the question of whether the discovery of America had been helpful or harmful to mankind. For generation after generation, this was a question many in Europe (then the presumed home of mankind) continued to ask, as the nature of the dream or expectation changed. For Hegel, America was "the land of the future, where, in the ages that lie before us, the burden of the world's history shall reveal itself." For Marx and Engels, it was the site where at last the victory of the proletariat would be ensured, the world historical process come to fruition. For Sigmund Freud, it was a disastrous Oedipal adventure, surely invented by a malevolent Providence, for no human being would invent it – but this did not prevent America from becoming a Freudian wonderland, the ultimate, ideal, narcissistic homeland of the Viennese talking cure. From the eighteenth century onwards, many Europeans went to America – as did Alexis de Tocqueville in the 1830s – to see "more than America," which in de Tocqueville's case meant no less than the spirit of modern democracy, which the age of President Andrew Jackson was putting on anxious world display. From the 1850s on, the great bogey, "Americanization," or in other words technical modernization, was already a matter of concern in Europe. Meantime, in an age of vast demographic movement, many migrant narratives recounted both the trials of the passage and the wonders of the American Dream in the pioneering spaces that lay across the seas and over the American plains. Increasingly curious Europeans travelled to the United States not simply to see its famous natural wonders – Niagara Falls and the Mississippi Valley, the wide prairies and the Pacific Coast – but its human ones, no less extraordinary than those that confronted Columbus or Cortez. Here, it was told, were novel cities that showed scarcely a trace of the past, amazing inventions and technologies, the McCormick reaper and the telephone, the street car, the automobile, the airplane, the space shot, the hula hoop, Madonna and Michael Jackson: here was modernity itself. Indeed, as, after the age of Revolutions, the idea of the modern came to obsess Europe and the wider world, it was always to possess a powerful American dimension. Art Nouveau, Bauhaus, Futurism, Constructivism and Cubism – all looked across the ocean to America, not just for new kinds of cities but new kinds of people to put into them. Le Corbusier remarked on the way American necessities compelled a changed, functional kind of engineering which shows "the way to create plastic facts, clear and limpid, giving rest to our eyes and to the mind the pleasures of geometric forms." America became an appropriate subject-matter for the modern arts themselves, for Dvořák and Picasso, Stravinsky and Léger, Diaghilev and Mondrian, Mayakovksy and Cocteau, Čapek and Debussy, Maeterlinck and Milhaud (and wasn't the skyscraper the ultimate cube of Cubism?). Then came the one great popular image-technology America made its own – the movies, the films – which, often thanks to European actors and directors, carried American myths and fantasies, often of Europe, back into every corner of the world.

It was never necessary to visit America in order to imagine it, to have a share in the fantastic American dream, or toss in terror with the American nightmare. During the Renaissance age of discoveries, Brave New Worlds filled the stuff of European painting and literature. In the eighteenth century, philosophers in the European courts and capitals solemnly debated the nature of the New World – Utopia, Atlantis – as they sought to devise the "natural" form of human existence: the "social contract." America, it has been fairly said, has never been a real place – not even to Americans themselves. "The European visual image of America was created largely by artists who never went there," says Hugh Honour in his catalogue to a splendid Bicentennial exhibition on the topic, illustrated with the work of Holbein, Rubens, Tiepolo, Goya, Delacroix, Doré, and many more, from early fantasies through to the Modernist age. The same was true in literature: Tasso, Ronsard, Montaigne, Spenser, Shakespeare, Donne, Marvell, Hobbes, Pope, Prévost, Rousseau, Diderot, Schiller, Goethe and the Romantic poets in general wrote of America without crossing the Ocean Sea. Imaginary Americas prospered quite as well, often better, than did the real one, and showed that what was at stake were not the strict realities or hard facts of history, but the mind's eternal fascination with images of strangeness and otherness. In his novel *Amerika* (post., 1927), Franz Kafka invented an entirely convincing America without troubling to go there, or doing much more than reading the many immigrant fictions that had spread for a couple of centuries through Europe, and then subjecting them to the enormities of his own pained and modern imagination. "It had taken me some forty years to invent Russia and western Europe, and now I was faced with the task of inventing America," said Vladimir Nabokov, explaining the problems of writing his *émigré* novel *Lolita* (1955). Nabokov did, by necessity, go there; but America nonetheless remained a trope of the literary imagination, as he made clear in *Ada* (1969), a book set at the mysterious transatlantic Ardis Hall, "built on the eminence of old novels," where one imaginary geography is superimposed on top of another. The tale is set on a distorted American soil, but the distances are measured in Russian versts, the characters defined with Russian patronymics.

But nor was it necessary for the American to go to Europe in order to imagine it. "Have you been in England, sir?" asks the young Martin Chuzzlewit (in Charles Dickens' novel of that name, published in 1842) of an American General who firmly insists Queen Victoria lives in the Tower of London. "In print I have, not otherwise," replies the General, and it was evidently quite enough. By now, the traffic had become completely two-directional. No sooner was the American Revolution completed than it grew clear that the New World needed an Old one quite as greatly as the Old World needed the New. The new American people might have been through a fundamental rite of passage, an

Atlantic death and rebirth, a physical and now a political severance, from which had been created a new society, a new identity, a new psychology, a new history. But all this depended on contrast and complementarity, on Oedipal formation, on measuring out the way the child differed from the parent or the New World from the Old. Americans, looking westward, had to think of Europe to triangulate their own situation against the wilderness, the savage, the Pacific. Newly positioned in history, they required the credit of origins and a past, and these they ascribed back to Europe, therefore reserving the new life and the great historical future for themselves. The Europe they imagined was not so much a nation, or a even complex of nations. It was an idea, an opposite, a polar contrast. If America was the newborn child of history, Europe was the presumed parent. If America was the world's rising western empire, Europe must be the falling one. If America was, as Hegel claimed, "the land of the future," Europe must be the world of the past. If America was the place where, as Tocqueville proclaimed, "everything is in constant motion," Europe must be the continent of fixity and continuity. In the transatlantic narrative, Europe thus became past to America's present, civilized to America's primitive and pristine, poetic to America's practicality, decadent to America's promise, experienced, or even corrupt, to America's inno- cence. With improved travel opportunities – the regular sailing packet from 1816, first-class cabins from 1827, the fifteen-day steamship passage from 1840 – Americans, like their eighteenth-century British predecessors, began to take the Grand Tour, and later on the package. Just as Europeans had "invented" America – that is, laid a myth and a meaning over what was there already – so Americans now began inventing Europe.

In fact, as time went on, it came to seem that in the American mind there was an eternal corner reserved for notions of Europe, otherwise the "Old World." It was a vague, only half-defined cluster of nations, kingdoms, bishoprics and principalities, filled with castles and peasants, old folkways and despotic customs, Gothic darkness and cultural density – on the downturn of history, yes, but still somehow needed for remembrance, ancestral regard, a myth of origins. Like America itself, it was much more an idea than a real place, a generalized image rather than a spot on the map, and one thing it did was to help define what made American existence and character so different. Meantime, for those who actually lived in Europe, America more than any other country or continent refracted their "Europeanness" back to them. Other nations and continents had seen Europe, or Christendom, as a frontierless and seamless whole. But few people in Europe, unless they had the ambitions of a Charlemagne or a Napoleon, thought of it that way. Americans generally understood the basic differences between the European powers: Britain was the parent overthrown, France the revolutionary ally, Italy the seat of Catholicism, Greece the classical source of democracy. But they also perceived a broader Old World to set against the New. Often it remained largely in the realm of fantasy: the powers of industrialism, the energies of historical change, the development of liberal institutions were often scarcely noticed. Nor was the fact that, though America was the first New Nation, there were actually many much newer ones (Belgium was founded in 1830, unified Italy in 1870, Germany became a nation in 1871), and much of the European idea and panoply of the nineteenth-century nation state emerged long after the foundation of the USA. To Americans the people in Europe were Europeans, though few citizens in few nations or fiefdoms really thought of themselves as that. They were Friesians or Moldavians, Franconians or Frankfurters, Walloons or Neapolitans, Cornishmen or Welshmen, at most Britons or Frenchmen. Still, when a good many of them sailed the Atlantic as emigrants, joined the American melting-pot, and looked back to consider where they came from – then they, or some of them, also felt that Europe was where they had their origins. "The mind of Europe," so often sought by many European intellectuals, and still an obscure object of desire for the makers of the present-day European union, was, for most people, in most centuries, at the most a vague abstraction. Nowadays, as they wave their blue twelve-starred flags and sing "The Ode to Joy," the movers and shakers of the European Community, the "New Europe," should feel very grateful to the refraction back from America, which did nearly everything to get them this far.

And so, over time – as America, or some of it, turned from *terra incognita* to gold mine, from gold mine to colony, from colony to nation, from nation to industrial power and then world superpower; and as Europe, or some of it, turned from colonizer to oppressive parent, from oppressive parent to cultural exporter, from cultural exporter to a "banquet of initiation," as Henry James put it, and then a battlefield and a ruin and at last to a significant, uncertainly-united contemporary power bloc – the doubled transatlantic refraction became a powerful, a

fundamental, a shaping fact of history. But it also became a fundamental narrative, a story of two poles of the imagination and two
related and yet deeply different visions of the world. A complex and
wonderful traffic in dreams, images, myths and fantasies developed,
and the twin terms "America" and "Europe" became elements in a
dialectic that, like most dialectics, moved on through history, and
ever-deeper into its own complexity. And between the imaginative
poles there passed the travellers, many of them artistic ones – the
"passionate pilgrims," as Henry James called them. European writers
– British, French, Spanish in particular – from Columbus, Cortez and
Raleigh onward travelled to America, and not only to record it but to
imagine it more deeply; by the nineteenth century these travellers'
tales and imaginings were a staple of the European book market,
feeding the American Dream. And even before the Revolution
American writers and artists began going to Europe, back, it seemed,
to the source of the arts. By the second half of the nineteenth century
the phenomenon of American artistic expatriation was so common
that "literary absenteeism" actually became a political issue: the
artistic wanderings were considered to be going the wrong way,
against the great, defining tide of migration and history. "It's a
complex fate, being an American, and one of the responsibilities it
entails is fighting against a suspicious valuation of Europe," Henry
James wrote, and spent most of his writing life in Europe, doing just
exactly that. He also thought the fate was special – "No European is
obliged to deal in the least with America" – but this was surely wrong.
Obliged or not, many European writers did so. Some of them, just like
James himself, became artistic migrants to the other continent, and
some returned home again to tell the tale, or never physically went at
all. But, as a result, a great mutual trade developed. Writer influenced
writer, image influenced image, book influenced book. Something like
a common narrative began to unravel, a huge fictional story of the
transatlantic world as it moved through history and sensibility (I have
tried to follow it in this book). James himself wrote what he called the
"international novel," which was actually the transatlantic novel. But
he was one of the best of many. The importance of the common story
went even further, for the traffic in artistic exile brought about the
formation of a new kind of international literary community. It was a
community of exiles and expatriates, of bohemians and wanderers.
From it came many of the most important of our art-movements: the

spirit of romanticism, the spirit of international realism, the spirit of experimental modernism.

And modernity itself was always a part of the story. From the London Great Exhibition of 1851 onward, America and modernity became closely associated: and it was the powers of modernity – the industrial and technological revolutions, their inventions and skills and their consequences – that kept the fates of Europe and America close together. By the dawn of the twentieth century, America was no longer the terrestrial paradise, the land of pioneers and Indians. It was, on the northern continent at least, the land of new cities, skyscrapers, assembly-lines, labour-saving devices, mass consumption and radical invention. It had pioneered the age of mechanical reproduction, and this had profound consequences not just for history but for the entire, enveloping nature of modern culture and the arts. Architecture, design, painting and literature responded to the enormity, which was transforming the world on both sides of the Ocean. Futuristic cities came off the architectural drawing boards; skyscraper towers entered the frame of Cubist paintings; there was even a new popular art-form developed from mechanical reproduction: film, as much a European as an American area of technical and artistic invention until the European industry in effect collapsed and left the way for Hollywood in the crisis of 1914. In the story of the modernization of the Western imagination, this was a crucial phase. If Europe represented the forms of an older type of culture, itself disssolving under the powerful pressures of the modern, America was quick to develop the new popular culture, and fill it with its own images and iconographies. The transatlantic refractions that had been for so long part of the traffic were easily digested into the medium. They had to a considerable degree become a common folklore already. But now they became a universal popular mythology – of cowboys and Indians, gangsters and criminals, jazz and ragtime, Le Drugstore and Kentucky Fried Chicken on the one hand, but also castles and ruins, English milords and romantic French lovers, the Beatles and Carnaby Street, the Rue de Rivoli and the Colosseum on the other. Today, as the Marxists say, it is no accident that London Bridge now stands rebuilt in the Arizona desert, that Russian radios play American songs, or Italian studios make spaghetti Westerns, that Americans eat hamburgers, and Hamburgers eat hot dogs. Disneyland in Florida is filled with models of the same castles, kings and princesses America was created to overthrow; Europe's Disneyland ("Here you leave today and enter a world of history, discovery, and ageless fantasy!") has meantime the cowboys and Indians, the talking ducks and laughing mice, that Europeans affect to despise but have in fact digested into their consciousness. When we think of our times as "postmodern," what we generally mean is this sense of ever-refracted, depthless, despatialized history, this sphere of random and pluralistic quotation, this merging of myths and motifs that suggests we live in a culture beyond culture. Our transatlantic images have become global icons, part of a complex mythology far beyond our disentangling, the content and the very form of pastiche Superculture itself. In our age of mass culture and virtual reality, we now take images, icons, for the illusory things they are. They are commodities, identities, not facts but refractions, not realities but simulacra, the stuff of late modern style itself. In short, they are fictions – and indeed the French philosopher and intellectual "terrorist" Jean Baudrillard has described America as the model postmodern nation which has "opened a true fictional space" in which we now all live.

So this is a book about fictions: fictions that are in history and are about real things, but which have been raised up a little apart from them, as have the very ideas of America and of Europe itself. It is in fictions that many of our truly essential stories are told, many of our essential desires and dreams expressed. And all this has been plain enough in the transatlantic traffic. But this is also a book about *fiction* – the novel, the literary form that has always most interested me. The novel and America have long had intimate connections. Both were born from the enquiries of the Renaissance imagination, when adventure and discovery, humanism and experiment, became central to Western activity. The early novels were generally adventures, traveller's tales, journeys through society or real or fantastic geography. Frequently they pretended to be true while insisting they were false, or imagined – the persisting paradox of fiction. Time and again they turned toward America, the great site of modern voyage. America itself was slow to develop the novel; the Puritans distrusted it, and in Latin America the Spaniards, some of the chief inventors of fiction, banned it for centuries. But after the War of Independence, when there really was a novel American story to tell, the form began to prosper, and from then on the novel filled with transatlantic mythologies. European writers wrote of America, American ones of Europe. Writer influenced writer, and the images and motifs passed back and forth across the water. That process is my chief theme in this book. Some of the transactions were based on real journeys, but certainly not all. As with Charles Dickens' American General, many of the great voyages in the transatlantic mythology (Poe's *The Murders in the Rue Morgue* (1845) and Kafka's *Amerika* (1927) are just two of many) occurred in print, and not otherwise. They still became part of the greater fictional truth. From the time of Walter Raleigh or Chateaubriand to that of Thomas Pynchon and Martin Amis, the fictive transaction has continued, back and forth. What's more, it has not simply shaped the subject-matter of the novel, but its form, its voices, its techniques, its mythic aims. So it has widened our conception of fiction itself. When I think of myself as a novelist, I think of myself as working in a transatlantic space; in that I'm far from alone. If the novel is a form of discovery, then one emblem of that is America or the New World itself. V. S. Naipaul has suggested that perhaps it is, of all forms, the novel that has come nearest to managing the mixture of realities, myths and cultural possibilities through which we try to find our own writerly way into the future of history and experience. Now, in a multi-cultural, international world where there are so many forms of human imagination to include, so many tales to tell, this multi-angled aspect of fiction is of ever greater value. As American, Caribbean-American, Indian- and Latin-American writers continue their quest into their plural continent, and as European writers look ever more deeply into the fast-changing state of their own, it is ever worth reminding ourselves of the strong transatlantic thread that runs through the history of fictions, and the great shaping of the modern novel.

This book has a very personal origin. In the mid-Fifties, I travelled, a young postgraduate student with a brand-new thesis under my arm, across the Atlantic to the United States. Travel in Europe was difficult, but intellectual and academic contacts with America were growing fast. This was the time of the Fulbright Generation; young writers and teachers like myself went to the United States, crisscrossing with American academics bound for Europe to teach Henry James in Paris or Hawthorne in Rome. American literature, like American power, was prospering in Europe, and European readers and writers were nodding in recognition. I went as a graduate student to Indiana University, in the cornfields of the Midwest, teaching the arts of underlining and the comma to classes in Freshman Composition, enrolling in classes in American literature and the new *terra incognita* of Creative Writing.

Almost inevitably, I started work on an Anglo-American novel, born out of my own seemingly individual encounter between European innocence and American experience. The book, called *Stepping Westward*, kept me busy as I shuttled the Atlantic over several more years of transatlantic travel, and came out at last in 1965. Writing it, though, I grew ever more interested in the long-standing refractive relationship between European and American writing, ever more fascinated by the large number of writers who had made the transatlantic journey in both directions, and written about it. I started exploring in detail the literary migrations and fictional imaginings, the international myth and the midatlantic kitty, that have made up the dangerous pilgrimages of my title. I have gone on pursuing the topic ever since, and much of my fiction and critical writing has been shaped in one way or another by it. In this great pursuit, I have had the help of very many people on both sides of the Atlantic, as the list of acknowledgements makes clear. But I must again mention three people in particular. One is the late Marcus Cunliffe, who really set me off on the journey. Another is my former colleague H. C. Allen, who then widened my historical sense and extended my interest. And the third is my wife Elizabeth, who has accompanied and supported me for much of the way on this very pleasant dangerous pilgrimage.

Malcolm Bradbury
Norwich and Oxford, 1994

ONE

The Primeval Fields of Nature:
Chateaubriand, Cooper
and the transatlantic novel

I.

"*Bien sur!* He invented America; a very great man," says Mademoiselle Noémie Nioche, a cunning little copyist in the Louvre in Paris, at the start of Henry James' *The American* (1877) – the story of an innocent Western businessman, very aptly called Christopher Newman, who is making the reverse journey, and trying to find his American passage through the "great world" of Europe. The "he" Mlle Nioche is talking about is Christopher Columbus. And, give or take an explorer or two, an interpretation or two, in fact a name or two (Christopher Columbus was also Cristoforo Columbo and Cristobal Colón), the clever French copyist is perfectly right. Everyone knows Columbus did not discover America. It had been around a very long time, lived in by many peoples, developed major civilizations, like the Aztec and the Mayan, and voyagers from Europe had undoubtedly set foot there before. But on the famous third voyage of 1498 he not only set foot on continental American soil, but invented it, adding to the existing maps a whole "New World." He also invented Europe too, turning the present "known world" into the "Old World." He invented, of course, a great deal else: the length of time he took on his passage, the cannibal customs of the natives he found, the rich promises of gold, the easy access to the spices of Cathay. Travellers' tales are always rich in fictions; those of the New World were generally more fictional than most. "Everything on this side of the Gulf was real, everything on that side was fantasy": so V. S. Naipaul comments on Sir Walter Raleigh's reports on the discovery of Guiana in 1595, which seemed to confirm the existence of El Dorado.[1]

[1] See V. S. Naipaul, *A Way In the World: A Sequence* (London, Heinemann, 1994), as well as his *The Loss of Eldorado* (London, Heinemann, 1969).

The fact remains that all this stimulated that age of mental and global discovery we call the Renaissance, as the news, the treasures, the imperial expectations, the fictions and wild illusions began to flourish back in Europe. So, of course, did much else; the imperialism, exploitation, colonialism, genocide that followed the moment of finding and naming. As the recent anxious, ambiguous Columbian ceremonials of 1992 reminded us, five hundred years ago Columbus, through the vividness of his record, and the magic power of the treasures and trophies he brought home, caught an entire continent thousands of times vaster than his imaginings in the grid of European naming. A new age of transatlantic contacts and conflicts, dreams and disasters started, which transformed the historical future and reshaped the human imagination. For good or ill, and whether in bitterness, in guilt or in hope, we live now in a post-Columbian – a post-Colon-ial – world.[2]

It was ironic, then, that the continent Columbus invented did not come to bear his name, or only small bits of it did. For in 1507, one year after his disappointed, unhappy death in chains (for most of the early explorers, like Raleigh, who penetrated Trinidad, Guiana and Venezuela, American dreams generally brought tragic disappointments), the young Lorrainian geographer Martin Waldseemüller, stimulated by the discoveries into doing what we do with these things, make maps, speculatively drew his version of the distant "newfoundeland," identifying it as the "fourth part of the globe." He then called it for the first time "America," after someone else's explorer, Amerigo Vespucci. Columbus had shown the world was round, but Vespucci had revealed a vast continent that doubled the globe's size and destroyed all previous maps. Thereafter two vast stories unfolded side by side. One was the European exploration and conquest of the American continent, a tale of discovery, destruction, conquest, crime

---

[2] As J. H. Elliott puts it in his invaluable short study, *The Old World and the New, 1492–1650* (Cambridge, Cambridge University Press, 1970; rev. ed., 1992): "The [1992] anniversary has, not surprisingly, prompted a vigorous debate over the whole record of European conquest and settlement, and a general reassessment of the historical relationship of Europe and America, the Old World and the New. The Western triumphalism that surrounded the 1892 celebrations has now been replaced by defensiveness, self-condemnation, and doubt. It is clear that a major change has occurred in its perception of its relationship with the non-European world as the curtain is finally rung down on an age of empire, and a very different phase of world history is symbolically inaugurated."

and a vast migration of peoples and cultures. The other, just as important, was the steady assimilation of America into the consciousness of Europeans, so that their world and culture changed vastly too. The crucial fact is that, as the Mexican historian Edmundo O'Gorman tells us in his splendid book *The Invention of America*, the America or Americas we know today were named, plotted and mapped by European inventors, who imprinted their European conceptions on American facts. So to this day, America is, as O'Gorman notes, the greatest example of the Supreme Fiction, a classic instance of the nominalist's, and the novelist's, point that "the being of things is not something they contain within themselves, but something that is assigned or granted to them."[3] This is still quite clear in the writing of V. S. Naipaul, whose work has been an endless fictive exploration of what he calls this "wiped-out world" where El Dorado was endlessly being won and lost, or in the current vigour of Latin-American fiction, the kind we call "magic realism." It is somehow appropriate that the novel, forbidden as a form for three hundred years in South America by the Spanish Inquisition, should be a chief means for exploring, through its magical and folkloric histories, a continent that constantly seems to resist its own naming, is always dissolving into strangeness, and still remains eternally in the process of being invented by the human imagination. America, as O'Gorman says, was plotted and named in the spirit of its inventor. But that inventor was never Columbus alone; he too became a fiction. It was rather the medieval and Renaissance mind of Europe itself, which provided him with the ideological and imaginative baggage he carried in his head, and then imprinted onto his version of the continent. Like his fellow discoverers who sailed the eastern coasts of the western continent in search of a passage, he arrived with a fully-developed mythology of the unknown world he was expecting to find. Fact persistently contradicted fiction.

[3] Edmundo O'Gorman, *The Invention of America: An Inquiry into the Historical Nature of the New World and the Meaning of its History* (Bloomington, Ind., Indiana University Press, 1961). And Marcus Cunliffe has also argued that for most Europeans America has never existed but been "a theorem, a symbol, a Never-Never Land," then adding that for most Americans it has never existed either, since the images Europeans projected on America have also become American self-images: "America has never been a 'real,' finite place to Americans themselves." See Marcus Cunliffe, "Europe and America, Transatlantic Images, 1," in *Encounter*, December 1961; the essay is reprinted, revised, in Marcus Cunliffe, *In Search of America: Transatlantic Essays, 1951–1990* (New York, Westport, London, Greenwood Press, 1991).

These were not the Indies. Nor, of course, was the vast pole-to-pole continent virgin land. Major civilizations had developed large parts of the continent, had shaped its landscape, worked its agriculture, developed its irrigation, founded cities, even deposited behind them remarkable ruins that showed the greater cycles of history had not passed them by. But the very name we give to these civilizations and monuments – "Pre-Columbian" – shows how the power of naming, the force of language following the force of arms, lay with the new discoverers, who let America into history. A continent that had long survived contentedly out of history now became America – a point of intersection between a great pre-existent world and a potent Renaissance imagination, which imprinted new meanings on everything that has happened on the continent since.

It imprinted new meanings on everything that has happened since in the Old World too. But America existed in Europe long before it was discovered. "When a European sets out on his first journey to America he knows, or thinks he knows, not only where he is going but what he will find when he arrives. So did Columbus"; thus begins Hugh Honour's book *The New Golden Land* (1976), a wonderful textual and visual cornucopia of the rich imagery and mythology that has surrounded the transatlantic relation from, and even before, the fifteenth-century voyages of discovery through to our present day.[4] The fact was that, a long time before the fact of America was known to Europeans, it was a governing idea or myth – a classical, a medieval, then a Renaissance dream, a notion of the still uncomplete globe and what it might promise, a great undiscovered continent to the west. From as early as Plato on the speculation prospered. Here might be Atlantis, Avalon, Eldorado, the Hesperides, the Promised Land, the New Eden, the Golden Age reborn, or Paradise renewed. It might be "virgin land" (as it turned out, it both was and wasn't), or a world of great cities of gold and fountains of eternal youth. Its natural wonders would be strange, its people innocent and novel. Perhaps there would be gods or demi-gods, men with their heads in their chests, creatures known only in mythology, or primal and innocent types of social

---

[4] See Hugh Honour, *The New Golden Land: European Images of America from the Discoveries to the Present Time* (New York and London, Pantheon, 1976). Honour wrote the book to coincide with the American Bicentennial in 1976, and organized a remarkable art exhibition on the subject. See his catalogue, *The European View of America* (Washington and Cleveland, 1975), cited in my introduction.

organization – the life of the "Golden Age" that Sir Thomas More speculated on in his famous book of 1515, *Utopia*. In one Christian version, which Columbus himself carried as he searched over voyage after voyage for the western route to the Indies and Cathay, the place he was seeking was none other than the Earthly Paradise itself, the place where the world began and would end. Earlier voyagers had sought it in the Holy Land; others thought it might be in Cathay. It was for Cathay Columbus still thought he was headed when, on the third voyage, he set foot on what he at last came to suspect might be an American mainland. He was, of course, looking for power and wealth for the new Spain of the Catholic Kings, who were freeing Iberia from the eastern Moors in the same year, 1492, Columbus first opened the New World to the West. But he was also looking for the New Heaven and the New Earth, and God, he reassured his royal Spanish patrons, had "showed me the spot where to find it." Ideas of paradise and the Golden Age filled his first reports, and those of most of the other explorers who followed.[5]

From this point on, "America" was to become a constant testing-place for the myths Europeans already had of it. Many of the confusions persisted in the face of fact, and later explorer-conquerors like Cortez and Diaz continued to express their discoveries, their first encounters with the inhabitants, their aims of conquest in the mythic tropes of the poets and utopians. The confusion of Orient and Occident persisted; only slowly did it grow clear that the western continent was a vast landmass obstructing and not opening the passage to India. The new continent confirmed many previous notions, even while it disconfirmed others. There were really wonders: gold, savages (noble or ignoble?), beasts never before recorded. There was pristine nature, strange springs and fountains, strange and innocent societies, Edenic bliss. There was also death, disease, rapine, slaughter, and bullion for the European coffers. Profit as well as Paradise, conquest as well as

[5] Columbus recorded his discoveries in *Christopher Columbus: Four Voyages to the New World*, trans. R. H. Major (London, 1847; repr. New York, 1961). On Columbus and the first discoverers see S. E. Morison, *Admiral of the Ocean Sea: A Life of Christopher Columbus* (2 vols, Boston, 1942) and his *The European Discovery of America: Vol. 1: The Northern Voyages* (New York, 1971) and *Vol. 2: The Southern Voyages* (New York, 1974). For a contemporary revisionist view, see Kirkpatrick Sale, *The Conquest of Paradise: Christopher Columbus and the Columbian Legacy* (New York and London, Knopf, 1991). And also see German Arciniegas, *America in Europe: A History of the New World In Reverse* (San Diego, Harcourt Brace Jovanovich, 1986).

Canaan, drew the explorers, discoverers, *conquistadores*, missionaries and settlers over the so-called Ocean Sea.[6] The wonders and the profits spread through Europe, and began to transform the European mind and imagination itself, as well as its religion, its politics, its economics. Historians still argue by how much, but there can be no doubt that the Americas vastly shaped the formation of that age of adventure and humanism, profit and colonialism we call the Renaissance. Though many resisted, Europeans were forced to see that the world around them was not already in their grasp, complete and God-given, but had distant frontiers, prospects, alternatives; the reshaping of European experience that followed was one of the motors of modern history and adventure. As banks and palaces rose on the bullion brought home by the trading galleons, cities like Seville grew rich and powerful on the New World trade – starting in Europe itself a new if later much-troubled Golden Age. Meanwhile in nearly all the European languages the reports came back, of wonders seen, new lands charted, dangers risked and profits or empires taken; this is some of our earliest American literature. Trophies, treasures and tributes, even representative "savages," were brought back to the courts of Europe for inspection. In a long process of discovery, exploration and anxious self-analysis, the New World began to take its place in the fate, fortunes and imagination of the Old.[7]

2.

"Raise your spirits . . . Hear about the new discovery!" announced Peter Martyr to the grandees of Spain in 1493, reporting that Columbus had returned safe and sound: "he says he has found marvellous things, and he has produced gold as proof of the existence of

[6] There are many important treatments of the myth of America, but especially see Howard Mumford Jones, *O Strange New World: American Culture, The Formative Years* (New York, Viking, 1964), Charles Sandford, *The Quest for Paradise: Europe and the American Moral Imagination* (Urbana, Ill., University of Illinois Press, 1961), and Hoxie N. Fairchild, *The Noble Savage* (New York, 1941).

[7] For a sceptical view of some of this, see J. H. Elliott, *The Old World and the New*, cited above. Elliott notes that for all the profound transformation there was also a rejection of the New World, and a resistance to its meanings: "It is as if, at a certain point, the mental shutters came down; as if, with so much to see and absorb and understand, the effort suddenly becomes too much for them, and Europeans retreat to the half-light of their traditional mental world."

mines in those regions." Soon, across the Mediterranean and the Holy Roman Empire, the records were being written, and the discovery of the "Indies" was being called "the greatest event in the history of creation." "I saw the things which have been brought to the King from the new golden land," reported the great humanist painter, Albrecht Dürer of Nuremberg, in 1520, as he looked in Aachen at the extraordinary tributes from Cortez and Montezuma King Charles V displayed as he toured triumphally across Europe on his enthronement as Holy Roman Emperor. "All the days of my life I have seen nothing that gladdened my heart so much as these things . . ."[8]

The great shiver of wonder that spread through Europe as the frontiers of the world expanded, its secrets of nature and culture were disclosed to European eyes, satisfied many mythological expectations. Here was the space-age adventure of the day, a remaking of the world's meaning, a fresh start to history. So, increasingly, the American wonders from the "new golden land" transfigured the content of the European imagination, rich as it was already in arcadian dreams of a Golden Age, a new exploration of human possibility. "Luther and Columbus appeared; the whole universe trembled, and all Europe was in commotion," wrote the Abbé Reynel in the no less tumultuous 1770s. In writers from Tasso, Ariosto and Montaigne to Spenser and Shakespeare, Drayton and Marvell, in painters from Dürer to Rubens and Tiepolo, the new mythology flourished. Sir Thomas More, in his *Utopia* of 1515, drew on Vespucci's southern voyages to invent his ideal if very mechanical future world, starting a fashion that has not ceased. Montaigne's essays in the 1580s celebrated an allegorized New World of people "fashioned very little by the human mind, and . . . still very close to their original naturalness" – Noble Savages, in short – and even called cannibalism, now considered a typical New World custom, a reasonably innocent pastime when compared with European follies and savageries. Shakespeare borrowed from Montaigne when he wrote *The Tempest* (1611), his magical hymn to art and the "brave new world," filled with pastoral dreams, humanist hopes, and moral contradictions, a work which anticipated, as one critic has said, "the moral topography of the American imagination."[9] Andrew Marvell

---

[8] Quoted in Hugh Honour's marvellous study, *The New Golden Land: European Images of America from the Discoveries to the Present Time*, cited above.
[9] Leo Marx, *The Machine in the Garden: Technology and the Pastoral Ideal in America* (New York and London, Oxford University Press, 1967), Chap. 2.

looked west and celebrated a new world of rich natural abundance, John Donne prospected a sexual newfoundeland, Michael Drayton hailed a new Golden Age. Here too, you could say, was American literature, much of it the project of the pure and excited European imagination.[10]

In fact, each to its taste, every major European nation or empire distilled its own version of the New World, their accounts reflecting not just national temperament and religious belief but what part of the great pole-to-pole continent they had penetrated. For the Renaissance, there were already many Americas: Catholic and Protestant, tropical or arctic, populous or unsettled, redemptive or threatening, barbarous or utopian, wild or innocent. The Spanish New World was the world of the savage, the Indian, cities of gold, the earthly paradise, conquest, tribute and bullion; the great adventurers were Columbus and the seafarers, but also Cortez and Diaz, the *conquistadores*. For Portugal the New World meant the adventures of their great explorer-navigators, Vasco da Gama and Magellan. For the French it meant nothing less than a new instance of human civilization, very possibly founded on rationalist principles. Their great explorers in the north were men like Jacques Cartier and Samuel Champlain, always closely followed by the missionaries. The British, entrepreneurial if not Thatcherite even then, preferred mercantile dreams, voyages that emphasized the opening of new sea-passages and the eventual prospects of trade and "planta-tion," or settlement. Thoughts shifted from harrying the Spanish empire to setting up one of their own; as Edward Hayes argued in 1583, "the countreys lying north of Florida [sought by the French], God hath reserved the same to be reduced unto Christian civility by the English nation." Now the journeys of Cabot and Hawkins, Drake and Raleigh were recorded in Richard Hakluyt's huge *The Principal Navigations, Voyages and Discoveries* (1589–1600), one of the great texts of the Elizabethan age, stories that were then to be embellished and made far more marvellous in Samuel Purchas's *Pilgrimages* (1625) and subse-quent volumes. These fables were still effective two centuries later, helping for instance to shape Coleridge's "The Ancient Mariner"

---

[10] For fuller details, see A. L. Rowse, *The Elizabethans and America* (London, Macmillan, 1959), Louis B. Wright, *The Elizabethans' America* (Cambridge, Mass., Harvard University Press, 1965), and Harry Levin, *The Myth of the Golden Age in the Renaissance* (Bloomington, Ind., Indiana University Press, 1969).

(1798), that great voyage-myth of the now post-Renaissance and Romantic imagination.

So even the sober Protestant British created and developed their New World myth, which became one of the foundations of Elizabethan and Jacobean nationhood and sensibility. When, in 1607, Captain John Smith participated in the early near-disastrous British settlement on the northern continent, at Jamestown, Virginia, and then went on to map and name the decidedly chilly and seemingly unparadisial coast of what he called "New England," he wrote a decidedly restrained record. He emphasized the importance of hard fact and detailed accounting, ever urging the crucial claims of "plantation" ("What so truely suits with honour and honesty as the discovering things unknown: erecting towns, peopling countries, informing the ignorant, reforming things unjust, teaching virtue; and gain for our native mother country a kingdom to attend her?"). Yet even Smith was by no means averse to a romantic tale or two. In his various accounts of the dangerous Virginian adventures – ranging from his early *True Relation of Virginia* (1608) to his *General History of Virginia* (1624), and so from troubled first landing to real and successful settlement – he gave a wonderfully graphic account of the charming Indian princess, Pocahontas, who intervened to rescue him from death at the hands of her tribe and her father, the chief Powhatan. British readers no longer needed to look to the French; they had now acquired their first truly Noble Savage. Married to John Rolfe, converted to Christianity, Pocahontas became England's most celebrated Indian. She came to Britain in 1616, to public fascination, only, alas, to die one year later, in sombre Gravesend. Three years after that, the Pilgrim Fathers, driven from the Anglican Church for their purist ways, and guided across the dangerous ocean by "wonder-working providence," found landfall in a snowstorm at Plymouth Plantation. A new mythology began, rooted in the Puritan view of the Bible. By 1630 Massachusetts Bay Colony had been founded – a City upon a Hill, Beacon to the world, a millennial sign of the birth of a new age. In several different senses, these Puritan colonists brought the word along with them. They carried not only the Bible, their eternal guide, but also the printing press; soon the first American books were appearing on American soil. The works this small devout band of settlers on the chilly North Atlantic coast published from 1640 on were largely religious and devotional tracts, emphasizing the wonder-working mission, and drawing on Genesis and Exodus to explain the passage to the Promised Land. Often held to be the first American literature, they were only another small part of the great American story now being told, mostly by adventurous travellers, to fascinated European readers hungry to know the lesson of the "new world."

For even in the less exotic northern half of the great "new" continent there were different, contrasting tales to tell. In a great swathe behind coastbound "New England," the French explored "New France." Gradually they reached through the hinterland, opening up the imperial route that would eventually lead right down from the cold plains of Canada to the tropics of Louisiana, by way of the Great Lakes and the long valley of the Mississippi. This was a different, lusher, un-Puritan North America, with remarkable natural wonders, not least the extraordinary Niagara Falls. The French had a different and in many ways closer contact with the Indians: in 1604 the explorer Samuel de Champlain, pioneering down the St Lawrence River for his New France, published his *Des sauvages: ou, voyage de Samuel Champlain de Brouage fait en la France nouvelle*, while various Jesuit missionaries recorded their endeavours to convert these same "*sauvages*." Though they wandered much the same lands as the British, the French missionaries and explorers read American nature and Indian life with a very different map, stoking, as you would expect from the French, the fires of a new philosophical debate at home. By the eighteenth-century Enlightenment, Voltaire and Rousseau were seriously debating the nature of the "noble savage," seeking to read from primal Indian experience the ideal social contract, a triumph of humanity and reason over the pre-existing social institutions. Rousseau and Montesquieu identified the American Indian with "natural man," "the very youth of the world." Voltaire – later followed by Buffon and De Pauw – countered by viewing them as degenerate creatures, and Buffon claimed American nature itself was distorted by the endemic corruption of the New World. Even though French influence in the northern continent now began to decline, these arguments never lost their power. They duly attracted post-Puritan Americans like Benjamin Franklin and Thomas Jefferson, those colonial *philosophes*, stoking the notions of Deism, social democracy and Revolution that, at the close of the eighteenth century, turned the whole world upside down. America, in short, still remained within the framework of the arguments and expectations that shaped the thoughts and arts of the Old World –

which in turn had enormous influence on the fate and fortunes of the New.[11]

3.

The transatlantic connection, as the Abbé Reynel and Adam Smith said, had enormous influence on the destiny of modern economic and political history itself. But it no less shaped the history of the modern imagination, and above all the shape and theme of one of its most interesting artistic forms, the novel. It was itself a Renaissance literary genre that was, as its name implies, as original as the New World itself. "Between the novel and America there are special and intimate connections," Leslie Fiedler has claimed. "A new literary form and a new society, their beginnings coincide with the beginnings of the modern era and, indeed, help define it."[12] The point Fiedler is making is that both the New World and the new genre, born in and from the Renaissance, drew on a fresh kind of imagination, exploratory, sceptical, and mercantile, that came from the Americanizing age. And it is certainly true that the form we still call "novel" was bred in a time when the imagination grew more investigative, sceptical, mercantile and material, when accounts of common individual experience and tales of travel and adventure became the key matter of stories. But the connection goes further. By the conventional view, the novel started – like the Discoveries themselves – in Spain: a new Spain that had been transformed, enriched, mercantilized, filled with wonder by its New World trade. The first great novel we acknowledge is Miguel de Cervantes' *Don Quixote* (1605, 1615), a tale of comic adventures written by a soldier-adventurer who had lost a hand in the battle of Lepanto, and then seen his Spain change from romantic idealism to new mercantilism, a fresh religious intolerance, and a loss of its old chivalry. His great comic epic tells the story of an old gentleman who, soaked in the stories of ancient knight-errantry, sets out to preserve the Golden Age in the new age of iron and the commonplace. Cervantes parodies

---

[11] On this whole topic, see Stephen Greenblatt's fascinating *Marvellous Possessions: The Wonder of the New World* (Oxford, Clarendon Press, 1991).

[12] Leslie Fiedler, *Love and Death in the American Novel* (New York, 1960; London, rev. ed., Cape, 1967). This is a brilliant study of the importation of the novel form into America, noting its deep dependence on the Gothic tradition.

the courtly past, but mocks the commonplace present, and so produces two contesting versions of the life of adventure and "errantry." So he produced what Michel Foucault once declared the first work of modern literature. As Milan Kundera has splendidly put it: "As God slowly departed from the seat whence he had controlled the universe and its order of values, told good and evil, and given a sense to each thing, then Don Quixote came out of his mansion and was no longer able to recognize the world. In the absence of the supreme arbiter, the world suddenly appeared a fearsome ambiguity . . . Thus was born the world of the Modern Era, and with it the novel – the image and model of that world – sprang to life."[13]

Certainly the spirit of what Cervantes had created – a comic picaresque epic which was also a story of encounter with the modern world – spread across Europe. It had a special appeal in Britain, where in the eighteenth century it acquired the form of the "burgher epic," the expression of an age of pragmatism, humanism and mercantilism. Daniel Defoe, a merchant adventurer and inveterate traveller, borrowed picaresque methods to tell his tales of contemporary experience and adventure, often leaving it obscure whether his tales were really fact or fiction. His great, self-reliant hero in *Robinson Crusoe* (1721) finds himself stranded on a desert island with one companion, the exemplary Noble Savage, to whom he usefully teaches the European rules of Protestant individualism and material survival. Two later stories, *Moll Flanders* and *Colonel Jack* (both 1722), are also picaresque stories of entrepreneurial success. Both, notably, have episodes set in the Virginia colonies, where the scandalous but successful Moll Flanders actually makes her fortune through good eighteenth-century sexual and economic management; some thought the book was meant as propaganda for the colonies. In fact American scenes quite often entered the pages of the emerging British novel. Jonathan Swift's remarkable dystopian satire, *Gulliver's Travels* (1726), draws, of course, on the travel tale for its form, following the popular fashion for such works. And Swift too picked up on the American motif; Brobdingnag, in the Second Book, is set on a vast tract protruding from

---

[13] Milan Kundera, "The Novel and Europe," *New York Review of Books*, 19 July 1984. According to Michel Foucault, *Don Quixote* is the first modern novel because "in it language breaks off its old kinship with things and enters into that lonely sovereignty where it will appear in its separated state, only as literature"; it reads the world as a text. The argument is in Michel Foucault, *The Order of Things* (London, 1970).

the northwest coast of America. Tobias Smollett – who translated *Don Quixote* into English – borrowed Cervantes' picaresque form for his many novels of travel and adventure, and one of them, *Humphrey Clinker* (1771), contains stories about American Indians. Indeed American subjects were becoming commonplace in not just British but European fiction: in Diderot, for example, or Saint-Lambert's sentimental tale *Les Deux Amis, conte iroquois* (1770), a high-minded representation of male friendship among the noble redskins which Diderot parodied. And the theme would flourish right through the nineteenth century, in Dickens and Thackeray, for instance, and so onward, as we shall see, into the fiction of our own day.[14]

But if European fictions were beginning to travel, in imagination at least, toward America, there was no great evidence that the new form was attracting writers in America itself. The Spaniards banned the novel in Latin America, but it attracted little respect in North America either. The Puritans distrusted all false fictions, and even the Americans of the eighteenth-century Enlightenment suspected the novel as a European indulgence. Jefferson doubted it, Noah Webster declared it encouraging to vice. As a result pre-Revolutionary America produced almost no fiction of its own, and it was not until the end of the eighteenth century that the form started to develop on American soil – so that, as Fiedler has to admit, the emergence of American fiction is really "an event in the history of the European spirit – as, indeed, is the very invention of America itself." When the American novel did begin to appear, it thus largely took the form of the Gothic novel or the historical romance, two influences that remain heavily imprinted on American fiction to this day.[15] Nowadays it is Charles Brockden Brown, the Godwinite publisher from Philadelphia who is usually acknowledged as the founding father of American fiction, with works like *Wieland: An American Tale* (1798) and *Edgar Huntly* (1799), and he

[14] Two interesting studies of this are Robert B. Heilman, *America in English Fiction, 1760–1800* (Baton Rouge, La., Louisiana State University Press, 1937), and J. M. S. Tompkins, *The Popular Novel in England, 1770–1800* (London, Constable, 1932).
[15] On the early American novel, see Richard Chase, *The American Novel and Its Tradition* (Garden City, N.Y., Doubleday, 1957); Daniel Hoffman, *Form and Fable in American Fiction* (New York, Oxford University Press, 1961); Joel Porte, *The Romance in America* (Middletown, Conn., Wesleyan University Press, 1969); Henri Petter, *The Early American Novel* (Columbus, Ohio, Ohio State University Press, 1971); William C. Spengemann, *The Adventurous Muse: The Poetics of American Fiction, 1789–1900* (New Haven/ London, Yale University Press, 1977); and Robert Clark, *History, Ideology and Myth in American Fiction, 1823–52* (London, Macmillan, 1984).

looked to the spirit of Gothic (itself very European, as its name says) as the appropriate American form. "America has opened new views to the naturalist and politician, but has seldom furnished themes to the moral painter. That new springs of action and new motives to curiosity should operate; that the field of investigation opened to us by our own country should differ essentially from those which exist in Europe, may readily be conceived," he noted patriotically in the preface to *Edgar Huntly*, adding: "Puerile superstition and exploded manners, Gothic castles and chimeras, are the materials usually employed toward this end. The incidents of Indian hostility, and the perils of the western wilderness, are far more suitable; and for a native of America to omit these would admit of no apology." Brown did not omit these things, but set them in a world where strange European secret societies like the Illuminati, and strange mysteries like mesmerism and ventriloquism, also flourish. Shifting Gothic myth from the haunted European castle to the haunted American forest, or the streets of the American city, Brown is an important originator. The vein of fiction he opened would go on to shape the work of Edgar Allan Poe and Hawthorne, and twentieth-century novelists like William Faulkner and John Hawkes; his impact, as devourers of Gothic American fictions well know, is with us still. Similarly James Fenimore Cooper, the first truly important American novelist, often seen as the American Scott, would transfer to the frontier the apparatus of the European romance. But standing at the start of the American novel is another writer, far less well-remembered, perhaps because he is not American, nor even British, at all. For the fact is that it was a melancholic young French writer from Brittany, who spent only five crucial months of his long life in the United States, who wrote what is surely the first truly remarkable American novel.

4.

In 1791, François Auguste René de Chateaubriand, a gloomy young vicomte from St Malo in Brittany, travelled to America on what he claimed was an official mission from France to explore the Northwest Passage. Chateaubriand belonged to the age of three revolutions – the American, the French, and the Romantic – and, on both sides of the Atlantic, he had come to know a changed new world. Influenced by what had happened in the new United States, the French Revolution had started two years before, even beginning the calendar anew. Now it was the time of the Reign of Terror, and this was probably what Chateaubriand was actually escaping; many French aristocrats and anti-Jacobins (not least the great chef Brillat-Savarin) found their way to America at this time. By this date America had slowly completed its own Revolution. The thirteen former British colonies, cramped along the Eastern seaboard, had succeeded, with much trouble, in ratifying their democratic constitution only three years earlier, and now they were the world's first New Nation. America now represented a great Romantic and libertarian principle; but it was a romanticism yet to be written. In this new historical world the invention of America began over again; it was a nation, a land and landscape with its image of society yet to be formed, its identity still to be forged, and its distinctive imagination created. Its promise was great, its destiny high, its wonders sublime, its landscape novel. In the same year Chateaubriand made his mysterious journey, the most notable American travel book of the age, William Bartram's *Travels in East and West Florida*, came out. It suggested the wonder of the American Romantic sublime, and its potential significance for the new Romantic imagination. Not surprisingly, it had enormous impact on the work of British and European Romantic poets, especially Coleridge, who were looking to the sublime promises of nature for an explanation of the world and the transcendental powers of the imagination.[16]

Chateaubriand thus came to a land and a nation where the now native Anglo-Americans were taking control of a continent they had only just started to populate; so the spirit of exploration was in the air. In the closing years of the Revolutionary War, Thomas Jefferson (who would become the third US president in 1800) had been the popular American ambassador in Paris. Thanks to Franklin and Jefferson, most of the French thinkers of the day, like Diderot, had welcomed the American revolution and grown newly interested in American matters, so shaping their own destinies. It was therefore appropriate that it was

---

[16] William Bartram's *Travels through North and South Carolina, Georgia, East and West Florida, the Cherokee Country, the Extensive Territories of the Muscogulges, or Creek Confederacy, and the Country of the Choctaws: Containing an Account of the Soil and Natural Productions of these Regions, together with Observations on the Manners of the Indians* (Philadelphia, 1791). John Livingstone Lowes gives a brilliant exposition of the impact of this book on Coleridge in *The Road to Xanadu: A Study in the Ways of the Imagination* (Boston, Houghton Mifflin, 1927; rev. ed., 1955), and it played a central role in the international romanticization of the American landscape.

in Paris Jefferson published his *Notes on the State of Virginia* (1785), with its great dream of the yeoman farmer, the freeman on the new land. He also set out to interest the French in the idea of exploring and opening a land-route from "Louisiana" – the French name for the central Mississippi Valley region, the American heartland they had contested with the British and had now largely ceded to Spain – out to the Pacific North-West, a Northwest Passage. This is very possibly the project that Chateaubriand had been sent out to America to pursue. But this was not how things turned out, for in these troubled and dangerous times he was also pursuing a different fascination, and chasing an imaginative adventure that was founded on the French heritage so powerfully imprinted on the American continent, and now under threat in the Age of Revolutions. After all, from the close of the sixteenth century to the Seven Years' War, the French had held mastery of the inner heartland, three times as large as the area held by the thirteen British colonies. They made their alliances and treaties with the Indians, developed their institutions and their missions, spread their Catholic faith. French explorers, from Cartier to La Salle, had opened and mapped the entire central region down from cold Canada to the lush Bay of Mexico. French Jesuit missionaries had described the customs of the Indian tribes of the interior, and converted many to their faith. French travellers from Samuel de Champlain to Louis Hennepin (*Description de la Louisiane* (1683)) celebrated the extraordinary landscape of these inner regions, so different from the New England and Virginian coast. They recorded the extraordinary wonder of Niagara Falls, one of the world's great new natural glories, and the fascinating lushness of that great artery river the Mississippi, the world's longest and most crooked river, linking north to south – and "well worth reading about," as Mark Twain, that son of the great river, was to say a century later in his *Life on the Mississippi* of 1883.[17]

French America had always been written about in a voice quite different from that of the British-descended colonials, who concentrated on trade, improvement, settlement. It was a lush region of nature, forested and tropic, and a romanticized version of the American

---

[17] On French-American cultural relations, see Howard Mumford Jones, *America and French Culture, 1750–1848* (Chapel Hill, University of North Carolina Press, and London, Oxford University Press, 1927), Elizabeth Brett White, *American Opinion of France, from Lafayette to Poincaré* (New York, Knopf, 1927), and Durand Echeverria, *Mirage in the West* (Princeton, Princeton University Press, rev. ed., 1968).

natural sublime had already had considerable impact on French philosophy, literature and the imagination. Now, though, the great French age was dying or dead. With the defeat of Montcalm at Quebec in 1759, and then the Treaty of Paris of 1763 which ended the Seven Years' War, Canada had been handed to the British, while control of the Mississippi had now largely passed to Spain. Still, when Revolution for American Independence came in 1776, it was – thanks chiefly to the political skills of Franklin and Jefferson – strongly supported by the French. The surge of libertarian feeling it released quickly passed through Europe, and shaped the formation of the radical new Romantic imagination. America – a New Nation born in nature but now inheriting history – took on a fresh complexity of meaning, a new mythological function, to do now not with imperial power but with liberty and equality. Not only the French felt its effects; libertarians everywhere celebrated the outcome. For William Blake, it meant nothing less than the beginnings of the millennium itself; his poem "America" (1793) celebrates both the restoration of "what the Ancients call'd the Golden Age," and also an era of libertarian release when "even the doors of marriage are open." For young British romantics, America became a landscape of new dreams, the land of a restored primal nature, the space for new freedom. Coleridge, Southey and Charles Lamb dreamt of creating a Pantisocracy, "Heaven on Earth," a Utopian society consisting of twelve men "of good education and liberal principles," with the same number of ladies, where even the cat would be called sister, on "the banks of the Susquehanna." The poetry of Wordsworth, Coleridge, and Thomas Campbell began to fill with Indian laments, dreams of "stepping westward." The French Revolution was itself a product of many of these Romantic dreams, though its blood and terror would sour most of them. But, for the moment, as the eighteenth century closed, America represented to the world's reforming spirits the ideal fulfilment of the best Enlightenment principles, in fact the nature of Romanticism itself.

So it can only seem appropriate that three of the most important books that celebrated the new, Enlightenment American spirit were to be written by Frenchmen, who saw America in their own light and through distinctively French preoccupations and discourse. Hector St John de Crèvecoeur came to "New France" in 1755 with the French army, and was wounded serving under Montcalm in Canada. Then, suddenly changing name and identity, he settled as a farmer in Upper

New York State, and became a model American colonial. Crèvecoeur was always an ambiguous figure, a European gentleman masquerading as an American son of the soil; a Loyalist in the Revolution, who then became a friend of Jefferson. Forced to flee during the War of Independence, he made his way to Britain, where he published, for British readers, what is surely the strongest and most vivid account of the independent yeoman spirit of Jeffersonian democracy: his famous *Letters from an American Farmer* (1782). Crèvecoeur revamped the work for French publication in 1784, and throughout Europe it became unsurprisingly a prodigious success. Crèvecoeur adopted the guise of a bluff American farmer ("Farmer James"), but he thought in the manner of the French *philosophes*. His America was a Golden Age world, but his idyll is destroyed by the Revolution, which sets settler against settler and Indian against white. And yet somehow the heart of the idyll remains, above all in its great evocation of the "new man."[18] "What then is this American, this new man?" he asked, and answered: "*He* is an American who, leaving behind him all his ancient prejudices and manners, receives new ones from the new mode of life he has embraced, the new government he obeys, and the new rank he holds." And if Crèvecoeur celebrated the American "new man," it was another Frenchman, Alexis de Tocqueville, who, fifty years further on, when the world order had deeply changed, celebrated and examined the new type of political order these new men had created for themselves. Travelling to America in the 1830s to see "more than America" (in fact to examine the American prison system) he produced his remarkable study *Democracy in America* (1835), a work of powerful political analysis about the workings and psychology of the democratic system that affected European thought and institutions throughout the rest of the century.

Midway between the two of them there arrived Chateaubriand, on his mysterious five-month American voyage of 1791. He too came to see "more than America," though what he actually did over those months remains to this day highly obscure – mostly because the many memoirs he wrote about this crucial journey, which he reflected on again and again over the rest of his life, give us almost comically contradictory accounts. He certainly did not find the missing Northwest Passage, but

[18] See Marcus Cunliffe (ed.), *The Divided Loyalist: Crèvecoeur's America* (London, Folio Society, 1978), and his essay "Crèvecoeur Revisited" in *In Search of America: Transatlantic Essays, 1951–1990* (New York, Westport and London, Greenwood Press, 1991).

then he seems not to have looked especially hard. He appears to have called on George Washington, but most probably when he was out. He visited the great symbol of the American natural sublime, Niagara Falls, and almost came to grief there; his horse, startled by a rattlesnake, nearly went over the edge, but then managed, he claimed, a prodigious if not folkloric leap backwards. He certainly travelled down the main artery, from the Great Lakes via the Upper Hudson River across to the Mississippi, and got down as far as Florida. He saw his travels as no less exotic, and quite as deeply felt, as those of his predecessors the great French explorers. He was steeped in the arguments of the *philosophes*; he had read his Rousseau – in fact he described himself as at the time a "disciple of Rousseau," though he later changed his mind – but also his Buffon, and it was the great eighteenth-century border between civilization and primitivism that fascinated him most. Above all there were those "savages" about which all of them, from Champlain on, had written. He paid special attention to the life and customs, the mind and sensibilities of the Indians, those mournful, philosophical, displaced "children of nature," whose feelings and ways surely revealed the prospects, the temper and the spirit of the great Golden Age.

While he was still in America, he began to plan a great work in the French spirit – nothing less than an "epic of natural man," to be called *Les Natchez*, this being the name of one of the Indian tribes closest to the French. This would turn into a lifetime project, a great discourse, a text of massive length and multiple form he would develop, rewrite, sub-divide and reconstruct through most of the rest of his days. It would appear over many years as personal memoir, philosophical specula-tion, travel-text, natural history, anthropological record, epic cele-bration, poem, work of fiction. Carrying the beginnings of the story with him, Chateaubriand ended his tour after five months and went back to the chaos of France, which he had doubtless been trying to evade. He married (unhappily) and joined the pro-Royalist army fighting the Jacobins. As a result, in 1793, he was forced into exile in England, and here wrote his *Essai sur les révolutions* (London, 1797), a work that expresses his bitter reaction against the Revolution, and marks his break with the spirit of Rousseau and his speculative return from Deism to the fold of Christianity. And here too – in Kensington Gardens, he tells us – he separated out from the larger project (most of which would not be published for thirty years) two episodes, written in the manner of fiction, and called *Atala* and *René*. He returned to Paris in 1800, leaving the main manuscript behind in Britain. The next year, in 1801, he published *Atala*, to sudden and enormous acclaim ("It is then my public career began"); and a year later the companion piece, *René*, came out as part of the contents of a larger work, *Génie du Christianisme*, a poetic and romantic vision of religious feeling. These two imaginative tales can be linked together and regarded as single piece of fiction, a notable American novel; they have been published that way since. But *Atala* remains the more important of the two. It was, in effect, the founding text of melancholic French Romanticism, as Goethe's *The Sorrows of Young Werther* (1774) was in Germany, Byron's *Childe Harold* (1812) was in Britain. All these works are dark with Romantic sorrows; all acquired a continuous and developing existence in the life of their authors, as part of a personal and philosophical autobiography told over a lifetime of radical transformations. Chateaubriand's own chameleon political allegiances changed several times; he became a diplomat for Napoleon in Rome and Switzerland, fell out with him, and served various successor regimes, finally becoming most famous for his travels in the Middle East.

Yet, throughout all this, he returned again and again to his American tale. *Les Natchez* came out at last in 1825, his *Travels in America* told another version of the story in 1827, and he revisited his American experience once more in his autobiography *Mémoirs d'outre-tombe* (*Memoirs from Beyond the Tomb*, Paris, 1849–50). The web of melancholic mystification he built round the whole youthful adventure even affected the manuscripts themselves. As Michel Butor explains in his essay "Chateaubriand and Early America," he provided them with a miraculous history – there are various versions of the loss of the manuscripts, their recovery, even their role in protecting him from a bullet on the battlefield, which in turn construct a confusing ambiguity about the actual meaning of the stories themselves.[19] Later versions of the text change the spirit of earlier ones, partly in response to the shifting historical and political circumstances of his changeable age,

---

[19] "Chateaubriand and Early America," trans. Derek Coltman. In Richard Howard (ed.), *Inventory: Essays by Michel Butor* (London, Cape, 1970). Butor also published a wonderful novel, or "stereophonic text," called *6,810,000 Litres d'eau par seconde* (1965), translated as *Niagara* (1970), which incorporates segments from *Atala*. Other important studies of Chateaubriand are André Maurois, *Chateaubriand: Poet, Statesman, Lover* (London, 1958), and George D. Painter, *Chateaubriand: A Biography* (London, 1970).

partly because Chateaubriand was an obsessive rewriter and self-recreator. But, Butor suggests, the ambiguity goes far deeper. These American and Indian experiences rested at the very centre of Chateaubriand's intellectual and emotional life, making him a writer whose consciousness was burdened, burned, by the fundamental contrasts he had read there: nature and civilization, solitude and society, instinctive religion and revealed Catholic faith. So, as with so many treatments of America from European writers, these stories are deeply imprinted with European psychological and political obsessions, dominated by the polarities of French discourse. Atala – the heroic Indian woman – would always be the central figure, a mythic character who became of fascination to the entire age. But the chief theme is the debates (and likewise the male bonding, the essential friendship) between two men, the brave, stoic Indian Chactas and the melancholy European white man who comes to his tribe, René (i.e. Chateaubriand). As Chactas usefully explains, a "strange fate" has drawn them together: "I see in you the civilized man who has become a savage; you see in me the savage man whom the Great Spirit (I know not why) has wished to civilize." Both are speakers in the familiar debates of the European *philosophes*, here renegotiated for the age of European Romanticism. But these are also debates about the underlying myth of America itself – one reason why *Atala*, above all, deserves to take its proper place in the making of American, and transatlantic, fiction, in which it was to play a key part. Another is that, for all its complicated and cosmopolitan origins, *Atala* surely has good claim to be thought of as the first American novel.

5.

Atala is a tale set in the past, in the middle of the seventeenth century and at the beginning of the eighteenth, in the fading French empire of North America; in fact the book is partly an act of mourning for its demise. In consequence it excludes nearly all social or political detail, and is set in a wonderland of nature – as a good part of early American literature would prove to be. The setting is that "delightfully beautiful country, called by the people of the United States the New Eden, and named by the French, musically, Louisiana." And the book is made dense with a wealth of Edenic associations, rooted in a landscape of great rivers, rich swamps, dark forests, and Indian settlements, where "grace is always welded to splendour." It opens with a lush, half-fanciful evocation of the "primeval fields of nature" on the two contrasting banks of the lower Mississippi, where "one can see bears drunk with grapes unsteady on the branches of the elm trees; caribou bathe in the lake; black squirrels caper in the thick foliage; mocking birds, Virginia doves bigger than the sparrow, alight on the grass red with strawberries . . ." It ends with a visit to the falls at Niagara ("with awesome pleasure I contemplate this spectacle"), so celebrating the great natural wonder that would put America firmly into the world map of the romantic sublime. Finely done, this is a realm of visual and emotional excess which the prose can only stylize, civilize, Europeanize (vines "jump from the maple to the tulip tree, forming a thousand grottos, a thousand arches, and a thousand porticos"). Everything is vividly described, enriched with exotically observed detail, dressed with European comparisons (the Mississippi is "the Nile of this wilderness"), given a sombre dignity. This a New World brightly and marvellously seen, but it is filled with the thoughts, needs, desires and images of the Old.

Against this backcloth, in a sequence of highly stylized scenes, the sentimental and mournful story, of Indian love, honour and religious faith, is posed in classical style. When Chactas, the great blind chief of the Indian tribe the Natchez, is introduced, he is a neo-classical figure. His credentials are gentlemanly and impeccable; no noble savage could come nobler or better-connected. "Not only were the forests of the New World filled with his sorrows, but he had borne them to the shores of France," we are told, "During his life he spoke with the great men of this century, attended the Court functions at Versailles, was present at the tragedies of Racine and the funeral orations of Bossuet." Though Chactas has suffered badly through his capture at the hands of the French, he still loves and admires them. It seems entirely reasonable that he is seen in the light of the highest classical lore (his sufferings are compared to those of Oedipus), that he interprets the story of his life in the language of Western rationalism, indeed of a poeticized version of Western Christianity, rather than in anything distinctively "Indian," and that he appears as a tribal version of a French *philosophe*. When in 1725 a gloomy young Frenchman, René, "driven by his passions and sorrows," arrives with the tribe, he is adopted by Chactas, and married to an Indian girl. It is to him that Chactas tells his tale, which is itself a classical tragedy, decorated however with great detail about Indian life and customs, set in the most splendid of landscapes. It is an exotic story of love and faith; it is also an erotic story, emphasizing the high-minded French passions of two noble lovers, Chactas and Atala, and their struggles between love and religious duty. "Great passions are solitary," Chactas explains to René, "and when you bring them into the wilderness, you bring them to their natural home."

There is little wonder that, for many Europeans, the story of Chactas and Atala became the exemplary Indian tale. Chactas recounts how, when young, he was defeated in battle by the Muskogee Indians, befriended by a Spaniard, Lopez, and educated in European ways. Attempting to return to his tribe, he is captured by the Muskogees, who mean to kill him, until (in a clear echo of the Pocahontas tale) he is saved at great risk by Atala, the chief's daughter, who has been Christianized by her mother. Indeed she is the ideal romantic combination; she has both a strong Catholic faith and "a certain virtuous, passionate air the charm of which it was impossible to resist." They flee together, and, though Atala is tempted to return to her "natural" tribal ways by various strongly presented rituals of Indian love and motherhood ("What could prevent her being charmed by nature?"), she continues to assert her Catholic faith and her trust in its Virgin Queen. The still not yet fully Europeanized Chactas is impressed: "I have marvelled at this religion which, opposing its might against the torrent of the passions, alone is enough to conquer them when everything favours them: the secret of the woods, the absence of men, and the faithfulness of shadows." Captured again (an opportunity for Chateaubriand to record the Indian Feast of the Dead), Chactas is rescued for a second time by Atala, and he realizes that she loves him. He now sees her as "an incomprehensible being," eternally divided between love and religion ("you either had to adore her or to hate her"), and perceives a great inner war between savagery and civilization is tearing at her soul. Their sorrows heighten their love, and, lost in the middle of a dramatic storm, they come very close to consummating their passion. But first Atala tells Chactas her story; it emerges that she is the daughter, by an Indian mother, of Lopez, Chactas' Spanish benefactor.

Just as they come to the very brink of sexual fulfilment, they are found and "rescued" by a remarkable Jesuit hermit called Father Aubry, a "man of ancient days," an "old spirit of the mountain." He takes Chactas off to his missionary village, which he finds a perfect kingdom – a Christianized Indian paradise, "the most touching blending of social and natural life." Now he begins to feel the "charm of religion," but, returning to Atala, he finds her dying by her own hand. Her love for Chactas has threatened the religious vow of virginity she has taken in childhood. Theology here grows a little obscure, since Father Aubry appears to justify her choice of suicide, explaining the sorrows of the world – suffering, boredom, and infidelity – that would have been consequent on her expulsion from Paradise had she broken her virgin vows ("This coffin, a nuptial bed which you have chosen, will never be dishonoured, and the embraces of your heavenly husband will be without end"). As Atála dies, in a touching scene, she symbolically hands over her crucifix to Chactas. Chactas and Aubry bury her under a "natural bridge" (there was a famous one on Jefferson's estate which Chateaubriand probably had in mind), in a complicated and allegorical mixture of Christian and natural ceremony. Christianity and nature, love and self-sacrifice, savagery and civilization, here meet and unite at last.

The story has an important coda. It is rounded off by a contemporary narrator (Chateaubriand?), who makes what has become the statutory American visit, to Niagara Falls. Here by the torrent he finds the last miserable members of the Natchez tribe. Their fate has been tragic; they have been driven off their lands first by the French, and then by the Virginians. Now the end of the tribe, the last of the Natchez, is near. From a mourning Indian woman, with her dead child in her arms, he learns the rest of the tale. Chactas was captured by the French, then returned to his tribe, where he adopted René, who is the grandfather of the mourning Indian woman. But both Chactas and René were eventually massacred by the French, and Father Aubry by the Cherokees. The great Golden Age is gone, and the tribe will not survive the consequences. The modern narrator draws a tragic lesson, that all, civilized and savage, live in eternal exile ("Man, you are but a hasty dream, a vision of sorrow; you exist only as misery; you are something only by the sadness of your soul and the eternal melancholy of your thought!") His own fate, then, is no different, and he identifies with the fate of the Indians. "Unfortunate Indians whom I have seen wander in the wilds with the ashes of your ancestors, you who have offered me hospitality in spirit of your misery – I could not return your kindness today, for I wander like you at the mercy of men, and less fortunate in

37

my exile, for I do not carry with me the bones of my ancestors." The dying Indians, the despondent European, fate and natural glory are thus romantically posed forever against the tumble of the great Falls.

To this twice-tragic tale, the shorter narrative *René* – in which René in turn tells his story to Chactas and a handy French mission priest, Father Souel – forms a natural companion piece, giving the tale a European dimension. René is a passionate, melancholic, world-weary European, a prototype of the romantic French intellectual, who has, after many travels and travails, not least in his own spirit, come to the Indian lands to find solitude. After the death of his father in France, his family has broken up, and so he wanders, a saddened traveller in exiled *Weltschmerz*, through the Piranesian ruins of Europe. He visits Greece and Rome, Sicily and Caledonia, all key landscapes of gloomy Romanticism, finding a haunted world where "past and present are incomplete statues": the past bears the burden of the ages, the revolutionary present has not reached the point of real progress. Mourning the decline of France from its seventeenth-century glories ("From the height of genius, from respect for religion, from perfection of manners, everything suddenly degenerated to wit, godlessness, and corruption"), he comes to bemoan the vanity of all human wishes, the exile of the contemporary spirit. Though all this is set nearly a century before, it is plainly a fable for the age of the French Revolution, when history runs amiss, empires collapse, exile is everywhere, everything falls to ruin and can be seen only in the gaze of melancholy contemplation. René decides to withdraw from life, cultivates solitude, considers suicide. His only remaining affection is for his sister Amelia, but she suddenly retreats into a convent. It becomes clear that this is because she feels an incestuous love for her brother – a clear parallel to the story of Chactas and Atala, who share, in effect, a common parent in Lopez. Like Atala, she sacrifices herself to the vows of her faith, the duties of self-sacrifice. Her head shaved, she passes symbolically through the tomb into faith and eternal chastity. "For the most violent love, religion substitutes a kind of burning chastity in which lover and virgin find fulfilment," she explains to René in a letter. René sails for America and seeks out the Indians, looking for salvation in the solitary wilderness. But the mission priest rebukes him: "Solitude is evil for him who does not live with God." Finally learning that "there is happiness only along common paths," the two men of sorrows, Chactas and René, meet, the civilized savage and the primitivized European sophisticate.

Chactas adopts René, and both of them find in the sacrifice of their two women a crucial lesson in faith, social duty, natural stoicism, and eternal melancholy. "It is said that, encouraged by the two old men, [René] returned to his [Indian] wife, but found no happiness," the story concludes. "He died a short time afterward with Chactas and Father Souel, in the massacres of the French and Natchez in Louisiana. The rock is still pointed out where he went to sit and gaze at the fires of sunset."

6.

In Europe, the moving and tragic story of Atala, a plaint for a dying Golden Age, proved a prodigious success. It was a perfect myth for the troubled years after the French Revolution, when empires were tumbling and turning, history falling into ruin, faith fading, the age of Napoleonic secularization come, and *Weltschmerz* was the order of the day. Chateaubriand had first meant his tale as a celebration of the noble savage in a world of innocent nature, but since the bloodbath of the Revolution nature now seemed imbued with guilt, innocence with tragedy. But even in tragedy nobility survived; the savage became that much more noble, even learning and teaching the lessons of Christianity, and so reconciling, as their author put it, "the harmonies of the Christian religion with the scenes of nature and the passions of the human heart." Still, it was not just the story's religious lesson but its vivid and moving depiction of the lost and noble Indians and their dying empire that won the hearts of the time. The dispossessed noble savage became a widespread motif, somehow uniting American disasters and European woes. The Atala vogue spread quickly across Europe. Imitations of Chateaubriand's book poured from the presses. It was transferred to the stage and set to music, finding its most famous expression in Verdi's romantic opera *Atala*. Atala herself, the noble Chactas and the heroic missionary Père Aubry all became popular icons, depicted in statuary, pottery and little wax dolls. The sacrificial death of Atala became a great painterly subject, and Duret's sculpture of the philosophic Chactas a European symbol for the Indian's tragic demise. In his "The Last of the Natchez," Delacroix depicted a famous version of the book's final scene, the Indian mother mourning her dead child, though he strangely omitted one essential feature of the subject, the romantic and tragic sublimity of Niagara Falls. But when Gustave Doré provided magnificent illustrations for the book, he added to the human figures the dense wonders of American nature, and included a powerful representation of the greatest natural symbol of all, the Falls. Here everything was united; the tumbling torrent, expressing nature's power, the mournful figures beside it, dwarfed by its cosmic force. Imbued with Christian feeling and pagan celebration, classic tragedy and romantic exoticism, the Noble Savage reached apotheosis. As the Indian began to expire in fact, pushed onto marginal lands by the great migration, growing beggarly and depraved as his culture was destroyed, he, and she, became an icon of the European imagination, moving out of history and fact into fictive and mythic space. It was a myth that was to continue into popular culture, finding a debased form in the circus-like "Western" displays of "Buffalo Bill" at the end of the century.

In Chateaubriand's sad Indian tales it was also possible to read a further meaning. For these are also fables of the relationship between European and American history at a crucial, indeed revolutionary, time in both. They are tales of two continents caught at different stages of development, though what Chateaubriand saw on both sides of the Atlantic were two empires both falling into ruins. As he says of René's wanderings: "The past and the present are incomplete statues: one has been drawn all mutilated from the debris of the ages; the other has not yet achieved the perfection of the future." Unlike American writers, who naturally felt compelled to write patriotically of their nation's new destiny, Chateaubriand could see two old empires, one European and one Indian, sharing a common decline. Thus his Indians are not simply noble savages but European citizens of the world, like René and the author, and they together mourn their tragic demise beside that great cosmic flood, the Niagara Falls.[20] Both draw out stoicism, melancholy, and sublime pathos – the sensibility of those agonized by the changing, destructive cycles of the age. In this sensibility Chateaubriand was not alone; in fact the preoccupation with the ruins of empire was everywhere in Europe, part of the great "Europe-weariness" that culminated in Edward Gibbon's *Decline and Fall* – the first volume of which came out, like Adam Smith's great work, in the Revolutionary

[20] For the powerful role of Niagara Falls in the iconography of America, see Elizabeth McKinsey, *Niagara Falls: Icon of the American Sublime* (Cambridge, Cambridge University Press, 1965).

year of 1776. This was the age of universal ruins; indeed in the same year, 1791, as Chateaubriand's American visit, another notable French visitor to America, Count Constantine Volney, who likewise wrote of American nature and recorded Niagara Falls, published his great study *Ruins*, a work about the mouldering of civilizations, the collapse of empires, the fall of eternal things into decay. The book, translated by Thomas Jefferson and the Francophile poet Joel Barlow, attracted great attention in the United States, not least because it reinforced the myth that as European empires fell into ruin a new stage of civilization was emerging in America. The myth of the "course of empire" depended on the well-established notion that culture passed through cycles of change, from the savage through the pastoral to the civilized and then the desolate, and that the rhythm of empire moved from east to west. This view went right back to the early Discoveries, but it now had a fresh appeal for Americans, creating their western "empire." On the other hand, the French had good reason to think of America as an empire in decay; it was becoming clear that the days of French "Louisiana" were numbered. Even so, they did not fail to leave behind in the new nation their sensibility, their sense of noble sublimity, their awareness of the great cycles of human and political change. In doing that, they invested the American landscape with the spirit of Romantic imagination, and the need to write of nature and civilization, wilderness and the dying Indian empires, the complex and ambiguous materials of the American sublime. These would be themes the early writers of the New Nation would take up and transform when they, in turn, began trying to write America's unwritten narrative and its place on the stage of history.

Meantime, the days of France's American empire were numbered indeed. In 1801, the year of *Atala*'s publication, Napoleon ambitiously re-acquired the Louisiana lands from Spain – and this could well have been one of the several reasons for the book's first success. But with ambitions all over Europe and expanding ones in the "Orient," the Middle East, where he found ruined grandeurs with which to decorate his new imperial age, his American empire declined in importance. So came one of the biggest bargains in history, the "Louisiana Purchase." In 1803, determined to embarrass the British, he signed away the French territories to Jefferson, who was now the American president. Despite some constitutional opposition, he purchased Louisiana and parts of Florida from the French for the sum of 60 million francs, or 15 million dollars, the price of a modest office block in contemporary New York or a cheap movie. The New Nation immediately tripled in size, and became a power with a manifest western destiny. Jefferson lost no time in exploiting his purchase, and westward expansion immediately resumed, along with the quest for the Northwest Passage to the Pacific, which had ostensibly brought Chateaubriand to America in the first place. Meriwether Lewis and William Clark were sent to scout the northern segment, heading for the West Coast via the Oregon Trail; Zebulon Pike set off to explore the Southwest toward Colorado, also trying to open a way to the Pacific. The tale of the Mississippi Valley and the West which Chateaubriand had so exotically recounted in French was now expressed in another language, English, and in quite different discourses: the languages of the explorer, the engineer, the naturalist, the scientist, the tactician, the merchant. In 1810 Pike published his *Account of Expeditions to the Sources of the Mississippi*; and in 1814 Lewis and Clark brought out the journals of their famous expedition of 1804–6 as the *History of the Expedition to the Sources of the Missouri*. An old quest was satisfied; on 7 November 1805, the records show, Lewis and Clark found what Jefferson had been after from the beginning, the Northwest Passage: "Great joy in camp we are in *view* of the *Ocean*, this great Pacific Ocean which we have been so long anxious to See." From that moment on, American writing, American painting, American science all had a new subject, a new landscape, a manifest destiny of their own. Writers and painters – including another Frenchman, the painter-ornithologist John James Audubon – as well as prodigious frontiersmen like Davy Crockett now began plotting the golden west; the books quickly multiplied. "Until the cession of Louisiana to the American government . . . Chateaubriand had peopled it with beings of his own creation, and had pictured it to our imagination, as the region of romance," observed a reviewer of one such book, Timothy Flint's *Recollections of the Last Ten Years* (1826), about the settlement of the Mississippi Valley. But now, he said, "The scene is changed, and we are introduced to the rough, but frank and hospitable, backwoodsman, with his rifle in his hand, his dogs at his heels, 'all girt for the chase' . . . The preachers, the lawyers, the great and little men of the West, the Indian, the negro, the fantastic, the venerable chronicler of 'the olden time,' the fresh and lovely 'rose of the prairie,' successively pass in review before us."[21]

[21] Quoted in Stephen Fender, *Plotting the Golden West: American Literature and the Rhetoric of the California Trail* (Cambridge, Cambridge University Press, 1981).

And what of Chateaubriand? Reconciled to the age of Napoleon, and following his master's changing imperial dreams, he was soon taking his distinctive melancholic imagination to cultures and ruins elsewhere. Napoleon had decided to found his empire not on the American model, but on a quite different one, that of Egypt and the Pharaohs; these were the lands where he had enjoyed some of his greatest military triumphs. So, like so many nineteenth-century French writers, from Volney to Lamartine and Rimbaud, Chateaubriand, ever a follower of the powerful image, turned his eyes to the Orient, to find a new wonderland of the imagination. In 1810 he published an account of his travels through Palestine and Egypt, quite as romantic as his accounts of Louisiana. Here too were historical sublimity, melancholic sensations, dying empires, sublime views, ancient ruins, ages that needed to be redeemed, both by the Christian and the poetic, dreaming, myth-making imagination. As Edward Said observes in his splendid and influential study, *Orientalism*, Chateaubriand was a key figure in creating the Orient as a romantic possession of the European imagination. In his vision of the "Orient" he reconstructed much what he had found in Louisiana, moving from the monuments of nature, Indian culture, geology and ruin he had found in the New World to the monuments of Pharaonic civilization and ancient grandeur that lay in a world even older than the Old one. As in Louisiana, he concerned himself not with present realities but something more obscure, historic, derived from the power of sensibility: "*j'allais chercher des images; c'est tout,*" he said. Now his belief in the redemption afforded by Christianity was secure, and what was left was a poetic sense of landscape, history, religion and sentiment. As Said says, what Chateaubriand imposed on blanked-out Oriental landscape and society was above all his own poetic self, a self that was part of a new Napoleonic colonization, a fresh imperial age. In the cycle of Empires, the age of ruins, the European imagination was beginning to change its investments, and create imaginative frontiers elsewhere. The process of colonial "invention" began over again, with, as Said points out, fundamental political consequences for our own times. And in that complicated traffic, the Romantic shaping of our imaginative geography, Chateaubriand, the sad viscount from Brittany, in his disoriented romantic world, undoubtedly played a central, and controversial, part.[22]

[22] See Edward Said's brilliant book *Orientalism* (New York, Pantheon, and London, Routledge, 1978; paperback, 1985), espec. pp. 171–5.

7.

The tale of Chateaubriand's remarkable American novel does not end there. With the Louisiana Purchase, and the vast expansion of American destiny, cries for an original American literature soon arose again. American magazines filled with articles explaining what the new literature should contain: the sublimity of American nature, the commanding power of the wilderness, the grandeur of exploration, the tales of Indian history, the spectacles of American wildlife – crocodiles to katydids – and the expansive, expansionist spirit of America's own romanticism. "The materials are rude, yet talent only is wanting to mould and animate them," instructed William Tudor in 1815. It all proved easier said than done. Writers emerged, the tale of the new land and its new history came to be written. But its authors were soon lamenting their difficulties, as they compared their fates with those of their European counterparts. In America there were no established poetic myths, no patrons, no copyright protection, no true critics, not even enough readers. For those who attempted to write fiction, there was a "poverty of materials," an "absence of forms." "There are no annals for the historian; no follies . . . for the satirist; no manners for the dramatist; no obscure fictions for the writer of romance," James Fenimore Cooper explained apologetically to his European readers in his *Notions of the Americans* (1828). "There is no costume for the peasant (there is scarcely a peasant at all), no wig for the judge, no baton for the general . . . However useful and respectable all this may be in actual life, it indicates but one direction to the man of genius . . ." The direction Cooper had in mind was to take the boat to Europe, which is where he wrote this book. For by now American writers (like American painters) were already beginning to take the path of expatriation. There rests, though, an enormous irony in Cooper's comments. The truth was that, over more than thirty novels, Cooper himself would explore, in nearly all the forms he said were unavailable to American writers, nearly all the things he claimed were absent from American life. In fact it was Cooper (only rivalled by Charles Brockden Brown) who would prove the true founding father, the great inventor and mapper of a native American fiction.[23]

[23] On the American myth of the West, see Henry Nash Smith, *Virgin Land: The American West as Symbol and Myth* (Cambridge, Mass., Harvard University Press, 1950); R. W. B. Lewis, *The American Adam: Innocence, Tragedy and Tradition in the 19th Century* (Chicago,

For this he was ideally placed. Born in 1789, right after the Revolution ended, he was the son of a Federalist judge, William Cooper, who had taken control of large tracts of the wilderness land that now opened up in Upper New York State. His lands were close to Niagara Falls, by Lake Otsego, on the upper springs of the Susquehanna: this meant, in other words, that Cooper, who was brought here at the age of one, had actually grown up on Chateaubriand's frontier. These were strategic and much disputed lands, formerly Indian possessions, long fought over between British and French, and between the Revolutionaries and the Loyalists, from whom some of the land was confiscated. George Washington had himself visited, seen that the lands offered an opening to middle America, and advised their development, or "improvement." Judge Cooper was one of the largest developers; indeed it became his boast he had put more land under the plough than any American. He was himself the author of a book, *A Guide to the Wilderness* (1810) – a wilderness he was determined to tame, "improve," by bringing in pioneers. He created a settlement that took his own name, Cooperstown, attracting settlers from New England and Pennsylvania, French from Louisiana or fleeing the Reign of Terror. Within forty years his patch of wilderness had become a patch of busy roads, farms, schools, manufactures, law offices, taverns, print-shops, "academies and minor edifices of learning," as James Fenimore explained when he wrote a highly Oedipal novel about it all, *The Pioneers: Or, the Sources of the Susquehanna* (1823), the story of a forty-year process of clearing that he had witnessed season by season and stage by stage, from the first year of his life.

The Pioneers was Cooper's third novel, and the book where he lays down the central themes of his fiction. It is said that he started writing fiction to pay his debts, and on a dare from his wife, when he claimed he could write a novel as good as the one he was reading. In fact his first novel, *Precaution* (1820), is a very pallid Jane Austen imitation, a

Chicago University Press, 1955); Frederic I. Carpenter, *American Literature and the Dream* (New York, Philosophical Library, 1955); Edwin Fussell, *Frontier: American Literature and the American West* (Princeton, Princeton University Press, 1965); Tony Tanner, *The Reign of Wonder: Naïveté and Reality in American Literature* (Cambridge, Cambridge University Press, 1965); Richard Slotkin, *Regeneration Through Violence: The Mythology of the American Frontier, 1600–1860* (Middleton, Conn., Wesleyan University Press, 1973), and Christopher Mulvey, *Anglo-American Landscapes: A Study of 19th Century Anglo-American Travel Literature* (Cambridge, Cambridge University Press, 1983).

"respectable moral tale," which he published at his own expense and attempted to pass off as a British work. Then, more profitably, he turned for a model to Walter Scott, and wrote *The Spy* (1823), an historical romance set in the Revolutionary War. Notably, it reaches its climax – just like *Atala* – with a death at Niagara Falls. But *The Pioneers* is the first great book, a book about the great encounter of nature and culture, paradise and progress, the dying past and the bursting present. Here nature confronts culture, Eden meets busy change. Judge Cooper is in it, not too heavily disguised as Judge Temple. He pioneers in lands that have belonged to the Loyalists, but there is an even older title: that, again, of the Indian tribes, who were dispersed after the French and Indian Wars of 1763. Now, in 1793, Judge Temple comes into conflict with the remnant of those times. There is the sad Indian, John Mohegan, and there is also a ragged old scout from the old wilderness, from the days when the land was still "the second paradise," and not under individual ownership. At the end of the tale we see this man, effectively expelled from this disappearing frontier and moving west – an ambiguous figure, "foremost in the band of Pioneers, who are opening the way for the march of the nation across the continent." The scout is in other words that Romantic figure the "borderer," the wild huntsman between two civilizations, who makes friends with the Indians, adopts their ways and attitudes, and expresses the spirit of free American nature. His name is Natty Bumppo, also known as "Leatherstocking"; he was to become the most famous character in all early American literature.

When Cooper began his novel, Natty Bumppo seemed to be just one more character in the complex gallery of human types who make up his variegated pioneers of American settlement. By the end of it, he has plainly taken a central place in Cooper's imagination. He was to become the subject of four more novels – "The Leatherstocking Saga" – and a world-class mythic hero. He no doubt owes a lot to Davy Crockett, the famous frontiersman, and to the many tales and legends that now began to pour out of the West. But in Cooper's version he bears a larger burden. He may seem yet another type of pioneer, a stage in the general march of civilization; but he is also a man dispossessed, in mournful withdrawal from its increasingly ruinous shadows. He embodies a different cycle of experience from the others who are "opening the way for the march of the nation across the continent." He expresses the timeless natural rhythms of the land, and is trained by the

Indians in the lasting ways of the forest, the code of the hunter and the trapper. He stands eternally on the cusp of history, threatened, stage by moving stage, by the advance of a "civilization" Cooper gradually comes to see as no finer, and probably more ruinous, than the primal world it replaces. For, like Chateaubriand's novel, or for that matter the paintings of Thomas Cole, Cooper's saga too is about the hopes and ironies of the "course of Empire" – the grand transitions of human culture through stage after stage, from the primitive to the civilized, hunter to farmer, farmstead to city, and from the high civilization to imperial decline and ruin.

In the second Leatherstocking story, *The Last of the Mohicans* (1826), Cooper took the history backwards by forty years, to 1757. The Indians still live like feudal princes, disputing territory among themselves, but are still in possession, the French and Indian Wars are in train, Natty is in his prime – until the great disaster of which the book tells us begins. But it was with the third Leatherstocking novel, *The Prairie* (1827), that Cooper began most powerfully to explore the grand historical rhythms and the mythic force of his theme. This book is set right on the cusp in 1803 – exactly at the time of the Louisiana Purchase, which, as he says, "gave us sole command of the great thoroughfare of the interior [the Mississippi], and placed the countless tribes of savages, who lay along our borders, entirely within our controul . . ." Americans are now tracking west, into the arid prairies west of the great river. This is "the march of civilization," which, Cooper writes, "has a strong analogy to that of all coming events, which are known to 'cast their shadows before'. The gradations of society, from that state which is called refined to that which approaches as near barbarity as connexion with an intelligent people will readily allow, are to be traced from the bosom of the states, where wealth, luxury and the arts are beginning to seat themselves, to those distant, and ever-receding borders which mark the skirts, and announce the approach, of the nation, as moving mists precede the signs of day." But Cooper is by no means celebrating the process, for Natty has taken refuge here to stay ahead of civilization's march. Now old and decrepit, the pioneer has ended up like Wordsworth's "Leechgatherer," an ancient, eternal figure on the bleak and denuded prairie. He has made Pawnee friends, and in the book he debates and challenges the codes of settlement, society and science that are transforming the old Indian lands across the nation, and turning the Indians into "straggling tribes." The book closes with his death, and his part-Christian, part-Indian funeral, and his great cry: "If it was given to me to choose my time and place again . . . I would say, twenty and the wilderness!" So, as Cooper explains in his preface, we see him to the last, "dying as he had lived, a philosopher of the wilderness, with few of the failings, none of the vices, and all the nature and truth of his position."

By *The Prairie*, Cooper had distilled a deeper meaning for Leatherstocking, and a place for him both in myth and in the large history of Indian and white America. But it is of great importance that Cooper wrote most of this story not in the trans-Mississippi lands where it is set. In fact he did not write it in America at all; the book was completed in Paris. For, on 1 June 1826, when he had just finished his sixth novel, *The Last of the Mohicans*, and begun to acquire an international reputation, Cooper set off, with wife, five children, and a nephew, on a Grand Tour of Europe, intending to take in not just the most familiar countries but Scandinavia, Russia and Egypt. Such ambitious travels by American writers and artists were now becoming more common, as, feeling the limitation of opportunities at home, they looked across the ocean to Europe.[24] Cooper was a keen and vigorous traveller, just like his contemporary, Washington Irving. His aims at first seemed similar. "The European who comes to America plunges into the virgin forest with wonder and delight, while the American who goes to Europe finds his greatest pleasure, at first, in hunting the memorials of the past," he explained, and he proved himself a rapturous tourist and a devotee of the sublime. But, far more than Irving, he was fascinated by contemporary politics and institutions, by historical change and the great structural transformations now taking place in the European social order: Europe was a place not just of landscapes and ruins, a timeless romance, but a world of complicated manners, forms, institutions. Paris fascinated him, with its republican inheritance, its political activity, its social complexity, its literary atmosphere, a vivid

[24] Thus Washington Irving went in 1818, John Neal in 1823, Cooper and Longfellow in 1826, N. P. Willis in 1832, Ralph Waldo Emerson and Oliver Wendell Holmes in 1833. They went for many different reasons – sometimes journeys of youthful self-education, *Wanderjahre*; some for an American version of the grand tour; some to protect literary copyrights; some to link their fortunes with those of European writers; most to compare American and European culture and society. The tours often ended with divided loyalties, split obligations. Orie Long, *Literary Pioneers: Early American Explorers of European Culture* (Cambridge, Mass., and London, Harvard University Press, 1935), examines the detail.

city attractive to American literary visitors. Joel Barlow had come after the Revolution, and become a French deputy for a time; he died on American government business during Napoleon's retreat from Moscow. Irving had visited in 1804, George Ticknor in 1819, Longfellow came at the same time as Cooper, starting a fundamental tradition of American literary pilgrimage. Here Cooper could discuss international affairs with General Lafayette, or meet his admired Balzac (and on one occasion Walter Scott). He was there over another period of revolutionary transformation, witnessing the 1830 Revolution which established Louis-Philippe as citizen-king, and opened the age of the "career open to talents," the basis of modern France. He took it as his role to explain American democracy to Europeans, meantime judging the new American order against the best of the social and political institutions he found in Europe. The wide range of his writing over this period, from travel writing to social polemic, from frontier novels to romances of European history, pays testament to the enormous range of his curiosity, the value of his expatriation, his powerful sense of transatlantic comparison, his internationalism.

Now his literary task seemed to change. He had to explain America to the Europeans, and the Europeans to America. In doing so he had become an international writer. He continued work on *The Prairie*, now mythicizing Leatherstocking (in *The Pioneers* essentially a realistic figure) from a European and romantic distance. The book done, and Leatherstocking's tale told, at least for the moment, he turned to European subjects. He wrote three historical romances –*The Bravo* (1832), *The Heidenmauer* (1832), and *The Headsman* (1833) – which are far more than evocations of the past, but explorations of the very meaning of democracy. Each is set at a crisis moment in the European past when oligarchy and democracy contend: "the drift of the book is political," he noted in the preface to *The Bravo*. Republican novels, they also attack republican crimes, from crass social levelling to slavery. They are also works of perspective, seeing his themes as an exploration of a world-historical process in which the American experience was one more instance. The promises and problems of modern republican democracy are there in all his novels; they would become central to his work when he returned home from Europe, after seven years, in 1833. He had now come to believe in the French "career open to talents," the ideal of the non-hereditary gentleman, the meritocrat. He saw the writer as a philosopher who stood beyond society to criticize it, from a position that was not national but international, and he began to write what has been called the "international novel," in which the institutions of Europe and America are compared. In *The Monikins* (1835) he satirizes both Britain (Leaphigh) and America (Leaplow), hierarchy and levelling. *Homeward Bound* and *Home As Found* (both 1838) are two devastating and satirical novels about Jacksonian levelling, America judged from the standpoint of a civilized international group of travellers. Sharp, exacting insights into American life, they are critical texts, founded on a fondness for an ideal democracy. Europe had led Cooper to re-perceive America. In one generation, Washington Irving (of whom more in a moment) had invented a fresh psycho-geography for the American mind, a romantic and eternal Europe to set against the plain American present; Poe had begun to imagine a world of dark European Gothicism and a terror not of Germany but the soul; and Cooper had created a Europe that made a political, moral and mythical contrast to the new Jacksonian America. In the event, he was reviled for it; the American press went for him bitterly when he returned home.

But – as his French contemporaries, who had hailed him, so clearly saw – his greatest achievement was the invention of Natty Bumppo, Leatherstocking, the half-Indian, half-Christian hero of the wilderness, seen in youth and age, in the age of tribal innocence and new American empire-building. An admiring Balzac described him as "a magnificent moral hermaphrodite, between the savage and civilized states." And by the time of *The Prairie*, Natty has become something new. He was not now the scraggy-necked old hunter of *The Pioneers*, nor even the vigorous near-Indian of *The Last of the Mohicans*. He was a great Romantic ancient, indeed a true *philosophe*, an heir to the tradition of Chateaubriand, posed against a grand wilderness landscape that truly reflected him. (Balzac also admired Cooper's distinctive power of pictorializing American nature: "This is the school that literary landscape painters ought to study; all the secrets of the art are there.") It was no wonder that Cooper had not yet done with Leatherstocking. He returned to him in two further novels, *The Pathfinder* (1840) and *The Deerslayer* (1841), and was planning a sixth when he died in 1851. Ever since coming home in 1833, he had become an unpopular writer in his own land. His expatriation was resented, and he found himself bitterly at odds with his American public over his Europeanized, very critical, "aristocratic" view of American society and Jacksonian democracy. Nonetheless his varied, plentiful fiction, set on land and sea, in west and east, in America and Europe, in the past and the present, shaped and guided the forms and themes of the many American novels, or romances, that began to appear over the next several decades. Near the end of his life, he predicted that if anything survived from his writings, it would be his Leatherstocking Tales. They did, not only in American literature but in the European and the world imagination.

Cooper, a remarkable writer who never really gets his due, influenced a good deal more than the destiny of the American novel. Throughout the nineteenth century his works were to be widely imitated, and illustrated, right across Europe. They became boys' books for men too that belonged to an age of empires and adventures, of dark forest paths and glittering lakes and mysterious tribes that summoned up noble expectations. There was eventually a French Cooper, Gustave Aimard – author of *Les Trappeurs de l'Arkansas* (1858) and fifty or so more Paleface and Redskin romances about the mythic West of the world imagination. Then there was the German Cooper, Karl May, who from 1875 produced a massive sequence of stories about the dying red tribes, about Shatterhand and Winnetou, decked out alike with neo-Wagnerian motifs and Western lore; they famously stirred the Aryan imagination of Adolf Hitler, and they are still read today. (The Karl May Museum in Bamburg is filled with the trophies of May's avid acquisition of Indian and frontier artefacts, which are still fondly collected in Europe.) In Britain the imperial tales of Rider Haggard and Rudyard Kipling show a plain debt to Cooper. And in the United States, as time passed, and the Indians were driven from their lands and slaughtered, the Western became an essential domain of popular mythology. The Beadle Dime Novels soon developed the tradition of the popular Western; the genre increased rather than diminished in popularity when the frontier officially closed in 1893, America became the land of cities and technology, and "Buffalo Bill" paraded the sad remnants of Indian times and the "Old West" in his circus-like spectaculars. Thus the Course of Empire goes. So, detached from their historical, cultural and political origins, set apart from the cycle of empires and the wonder of ruins, paleface and redskin, cowboy and Indian, frontiersman and savage, Leatherstocking and Chingachgook, entered the universal mythological world of the dime novel, the comic, the boys' book. Niagara Falls, once a great ruinous wonder of nature, turned into America's favourite honeymoon spot; Louisiana became the home of jazz; the prairie, with its log cabins and sod huts, turned into the typical place of settlement. When the movies started, the Western and all that went with it – cowboys and Indians, wigwams and missions, trappers and settlers, forests, mesas, cactus and the sublime American landscape – became perhaps their most powerful and universal myth. Between them, Chateaubriand and Cooper, writing the gloomy romantic history of a revolutionary age, had created something new. They had constructed a mythic fund, more than European, more than American, a transatlantic, indeed a global, version of the primeval fields of nature, the world of twenty and the wilderness, but also of an eternal residual guilt. The Western was America, but it would not have flourished as it did without the Eastern – the struggle of the European mind in its encounter with the other and the wilderness.

TWO

Storied Associations:
Washington Irving goes to Europe

I.

As his proud first name suggests, Washington Irving was born in Revolutionary times. In fact he was born on 3 April 1783, right after the Treaty of Paris which brought the War of Independence to a close. Colonial times were over, and the world's first "New Nation" was emerging into the light of historical day. Irving thus belonged to the first generation of those who could really call themselves "Americans." And when, growing up in post-colonial New York, the "Knicker-bocker" city, with its famous Dutch heritage, he decided to become a writer, he inevitably became part of the first generation of a real or national "American literature." Urged on by the magazines, this dream of a new literature became a powerful notion for independent times. It was not surprising that, when independence from Britain had not just been declared but won, after a war of seven bitter years, cries for an equal literary independence quickly emerged, and Americans now started looking around for the poets, the playwrights, the essayists and the novelists who would declare and celebrate it. "America must be as independent in *literature* as she is in *politics* – as famous for arts as for arms," pronounced Noah Webster, the great dictionary-maker and patriot, in 1789. And he set off, through his dictionaries, to forge a distinctive American language and spelling in which that new demo-cratic, original literature might now be written.

But not everyone was so sure. Philip Freneau, the Philadelphia poet and patriot, had fought in the Revolution and proudly celebrated in verse "The Rising Glory of America," but he was one of many to sound a note of caution. A political and a literary independence were, he warned, two different things: "the first was accomplished in about seven years, the latter will not be completely effected, perhaps, in as

53

many centuries." And the forging of an original American literature, in a brand-new nation that had been for 150 years a British colony, was still founding its cultural and intellectual institutions, and had not stopped looking to Britain and Europe for most of its ideas, arts and books, was never going to be a simple task. There was, for the moment at least, no powerful tradition, no real store of myth or legend, no independently American way of writing. There was no literary class and culture, no real literary patronage, no copyright protection for authors, and – despite Webster's heroic claims – no distinctive literary language. And all this, especially after the bitternesses of the War of 1812, the British magazines and quarterly reviews were very ready to point out. The campaign for a distinctive American literature, the natural instinct to inflate modest talents into great native geniuses, the mood of epical heroism, soon came in for their thundering mockery. "The Americans have no national literature, and no learned men," declared *The British Critic* in 1818. "But why should Americans write books, when a six weeks' passage brings them, in their own tongue, our sense, science and genius, in bales and hogsheads? Prairies, steamboats, gristmills, are their natural objects for centuries to come," asked a splendidly condescending Sydney Smith in *The Edinburgh Review* in the same year. The "paper war" across the Atlantic had begun. Two years later, in 1820, Smith was back on the attack: "In all four quarters of the globe, who reads an American book? or goes to an American play? or looks at an American picture or statue?" he demanded, as over the water the clamour for an American literature rose yet again.

Yet later that year the mood would suddenly change. In the very same *Edinburgh Review*, the formidable Scots critic Francis Jeffrey was to be found hailing "a very remarkable publication" as the first work of American literature truly deserving of praise. It was, he said, "the foundation of a chaster and better school," which would "form an era in the literature of the nation to which it belongs." The book was *The Sketch Book of Geoffrey Crayon, Gent.*, the author was the youthful Washington Irving, and the work went on to transform British and international attitudes toward American writing and writers. Irving became for a spell the one well-known American writer, was duly hailed as the father of American literature, and in the larger world he stood for what the American imagination could now achieve. This, it may be said, was not an entirely enviable role. Not all the British critics thought so well of him, and to some of them he was known as "Addison and water." Nor did all his fellow Americans. There were, after all, rivals for the office: Charles Brockden Brown from Philadelphia, a generation older, had brought European Gothic to the new American plains and cities. There was James Fenimore Cooper, "the American Scott," Irving's contemporary and greatest competitor, who could fairly challenge his fame. Some Americans thought that, in writing to please the complaining British, Irving had betrayed his origins; others suspected his taste for foreign travels and foreign forms. And these arguments have gone on ever since. Irving's reputation has gone up and down, as different generations have gone on disputing what American literature is and where it comes from, something they are still busily doing, with deep deconstructive passion, as I write. In Britain, Byron admired him for his sensibility, but Hazlitt found him pallid, "gay but guarded." Dickens was influenced by him, and he was read as a model of prose in British schools, though Lockhart advised him to stick to American scenes and pumpkin pies. In the United States, he finally became a hero to his age, but a generation on Emerson dismissed him, along with most writers of his era, as simply "picturesque." By the end of the nineteenth century he had come to stand for the "Genteel Tradition" – the "paleface" Europeanized tradition of American writing that the feisty new "redskins" of writing, like Walt Whitman, wanted to overturn, and mostly did. So it goes on; the arguments hang on to this day. Irving is still there, but he remains an uncomfortable antecedent of the wealth of American literature that was, as Herman Melville was to foresee, duly read in all the four quarters of the globe.

Still, as America's first professional writer (first to make a living by the pen), the inventor of Rip Van Winkle, the chief founder of the Columbus legend, the inventor of America's literary Europe as well as an early writer-explorer of the American West, and the pioneer of American literary Romanticism, Washington Irving is not easily dismissed. Nor is the writer who can be said to be founder of the great "international theme" in American literature, the originator of the transatlantic dimension to American letters to which nearly every significant American writer – Cooper and Irving, Longfellow and Poe, Hawthorne and Melville, James and Twain, Wharton and Stein, Eliot and Pound, Hemingway and Fitzgerald, Baldwin and Pynchon – has contributed, to the point where it still remains an essential dimension of the American tradition. Irving was a writer who knew he was at the beginning of things, and who saw the American author had a complex task to perform. He needed to define what was national, and what was international, what was regional and what cosmopolitan, what was American and what was European, for the purposes of art. He confronted the classic difficulty, which outlasted the nineteenth century, of adapting, teasing, reshaping, rejecting the European literary heritage, and making from it a fresh American sensibility. Irving was born on two cusps. One was the transformation from colony to nation, historical isolation to modern political identity – the transformation through which his most famous hero, Rip Van Winkle, sleeps his twenty-year sleep. The other was the great transformation of art, feeling and sensibility which took the Western arts and their underlying ideas from a Neo-Classical to a Romantic age, from the age of rule, convention and universality to the age of poetic subjectivity and originality. And there was every good reason why, in the civic new democracy of the United States of America, founded on Deist dreams and Athenian models, Classical models had a special appeal, and the Romantic movement was slow to penetrate; in fact it did not come in full flood until the 1840s, with Transcendentalism. But America was also born in the spirit of Romanticism, with its feeling both for landscape and popular nationhood. Romanticism was a new spirit in history that reconstructed history, looking back to the national and regional past, seeing writing as born from the speech of the people, the genius of the place, the funds of its folklore, the strength of its legends. Nationality and internationality were the important issues of the day, and where more so than in the first New Nation – which knew it embodied the Romantic principle, but still had to learn how to write of it.

The task was to learn how, and to do him justice Irving did exactly that, forging, over the years, a complicated, evasive, plural and international literary identity. At first, a young lawyer-writer working in the New York press, he was "Jonathan Oldstyle," a name that reveals all; he was willingly writing in the mannered way of Addison and the eighteenth-century British essayists. A little later he was the satirical "Launcelot Longstaff," and soon he was "Diedrich Knickerbocker," the quaint historian of the Dutch-American past, recalling, or rather inventing, the absurd wonderful legends of old Knickerbocker New York. Then, when he crossed the ocean to develop his literary career in Britain and other parts of Europe, he became "Geoffrey Crayon, Gent.," a wandering amateur artist carrying his literary easel and everywhere sketching the quaint and the strange. Quite often these identities mixed, one mask to be laid on top of another. True, this was probably the opposite to the great cult of originality and sincerity of many of the European Romantics. Still, the destination was Romanticism, and he was to be guided on his way by many of its great progenitors: Scott and Byron, Tieck and Jean-Paul and Hoffmann and de Navarrete. Two different sensibilities, even two different cultural ages merged in him. Out of them Irving made something distinctive, complicated, refractive, a romantic expatriation that constantly looked back and forth between the world of Europe and his own native land. And, as the triumphant reception of *The Sketch Book* showed, Europe wanted what he had to offer: a romantic account of its own history, seen from the standpoint of the shifting present, presented by a New World traveller come to claim a heritage in the Old. And America wanted it too; the Old World could now lend a vital bloodline to the New.

But the most important thing of all is that Irving invented – with all the novelty of a new, young American vision casting its curious gaze across the Atlantic distance – a quite new imaginary geography, a whole idea of Europe and its signification, that has had enormous cultural and political meaning ever since. If Americans still frequently trace their imaginative origins back to a Europe from which some of them never came, if America still draws heavily on European folklore, if the myths of Towers of London and dark German forests still have power in Arizona and California, all that has something to do with the spirit of Irving. And if Europeans know that European is what they actually are, if today there is something called a Euro-community and even a Euro-imagination, that owes something to Irving too. Irving stood at the beginning of something that would really come to be called American literature. For good or bad, he took it off on a journey of wandering cosmopolitanism, of transatlantic myth-making, of strangely mirrored and refracted internationality that, for all the challenges that have been put to it (no more so than today), it has never entirely lost. He was the first real American literary expatriate: not, like Cooper, falling out of love with his own country; not like James, determined to find and capture the cultural and artistic densities that were missing at home; not, like Gertrude Stein, hoping to take command of the whole great campaign of artistic innovation; not, like Eliot, looking to take up the mantle of the European; not, like Pound, trying to forge a new *paideuma* of culture, art, politics and history. His was an amiable voyage of the imagination, designed to cause no great offence to Europeans or to his own compatriots. His spirit was ambassadorial, and in Britain, France, Germany and Spain he made his own special relationships, becoming, finally, an Ambassador himself, the American Minister in Madrid. But his real relation was to Europe as a whole, picturesque, romantic, poetic, its history always overshadowing its present reality. For his readers in the New World it provided a land of old origins, a legendary past, in which they could and did delight. But, transferred and transcribed, it also promised to that rising New World a legendary present and a future, which they could, and did, delight in too.

2.

Irving was the late, youngest, eleventh child of a successful Scots Presbyterian merchant with a transatlantic import-export business who had settled in colonial America in 1763. He was born in New York City, lively, busy, commercial, aspiring, and, after the Revolution, seriously challenging Philadelphia for economic, cultural and political domination. The Knickerbocker city, an old Dutch settlement bought from the Indians, and occupied by the British during the Revolutionary War, was turning into a booming centre of trade with the best harbour on the coast. In the 1780s it was briefly the national capital, before the honours passed for a while to Philadelphia; then matters were settled by the building of a brand-new city on the quiet Potomac which happened to bear the same name as Irving himself; in 1800 Washington became the nation's capital. Over the new century other honours began passing on too; for much of the nineteenth century it was Boston that would be the nation's cultural and intellectual "hub." But in Irving's youth New York was perhaps the liveliest literary and political city – and, training for the law, Irving also turned to cultural and literary pursuits. He wrote for his brother Peter's newspaper the *New York Morning Chronicle*, producing witty newspaper reports on social events and fashions under his Addisonian pseudonym, "Jonathan Oldstyle, Gent.," which showed him to be a typical *New Yorker* correspondent of his day. Then in 1804, in the Napoleonic era, he went to Europe, on the first of three visits that would each, in their own way, change his life. He was twenty-one, and in physical and emotional ill-health, and his brothers were worried for him. They paid for what was in effect the American variant on the Grand Tour, and sent him off on a trip that would eventually last for eighteen months. In mid-May he left by sailing ship from New York, and landed at Bordeaux on 1 July. Then, frequently in company with other Americans, he travelled through France and Italy to Sicily, where, as if things were not exotic enough already, his ship was stopped and ransacked by pirates. He took the way back through Switzerland to Paris, the Low Countries, and finally reached London. "The Sunrise was beautiful, the atmosphere pure and serene, and I could scarcely believe it was the Island of Smoak & Fog that I saw before me," he said of his English arrival. England did not entirely please, however; it was short on romantic sensations, and the people seemed haughty toward Americans ("I had expected to be delighted on finding myself in England – that my heart would expand, my feelings all fly out to hail my kinsmen – quite otherwise . . . I look about me with distrust"). And then it was home on a sailing ship journey that took fifty-two days, a clear and revealing sign of the distance in space and time that separated "commonplace" America from "poetic" Europe.[1]

For a young and literary American, this was all a deeply formative experience. It was also a training in what would become, recognizably, the Irvingesque sensibility, the sensibility of the romantic American literary traveller. His brothers had pressed him to take the trip seriously, and he did, keeping a full record, which he used for letters home and then wrote up as a journal. He consulted his guides and his guidebooks, used his letters of introduction, and made many drawings as well as notes. The tradition was clear; this was a sentimental journey in the Sternean fashion. "I look with an eye to the *picturesque*," he notes, surveying the walls of Mons. "I am once more venturing my *life & fortunes* on the 'vasty deep' speeding away to Sicily the Island of fable and romance," he writes home. "Accustomed to our *honest* American hills & dales where *stubborn fact* presides and checks the imagination in

[1] Irving's accounts of his travels are to be found in various volumes of Henry A. Pochmann (ed.), *The Complete Works of Washington Irving* (28 vols, Madison, Wisconsin, University of Wisconsin Press, 1969–). The chief life is Stanley T. Williams, *The Life of Washington Irving* (2 vols, New York, Oxford University Press, 1935). Also see William Hedges (ed.), *The Old and New World Romanticism of Washington Irving* (Westport, Conn., Greenwood Press, 1986), Jeffrey Rubin-Dorsky, *Adrift in the Old World* (Chicago, University of Chicago Press, 1988), and Joy S. Kasson, *Artistic Voyagers* (Westport, Conn., Greenwood Press, 1982).

its wandrings you may conceive with what enthusiasm I haste to those 'poetic fields' where fiction has shed its charm o'er every scene." In Italy he finds "despotic corruption" and "miserable indigence," but he always emphasizes – as later in *The Sketch Book* – the poetry Europe, thanks to its distance, difference and antiquity, spreads over everything, or rather that the modern romanticizing imagination learns to spread over it: "There is a poetic charm (if I may so express myself) that diffuses itself over our ideas in considering this part of the globe," he notes of Italy. "We regard everything with an enthusiastic eye – thru a romantic medium that gives an illusory tinge to every subject . . . A delicious mistiness is spread over the scene that softens the harshness of particular objects – prevents our examining their forms too distinctly – a glow is thrown over the whole that by blending and softening and enriching – gives the landscape a mellowness – a sweetness – a loveliness of coloring – not absolutely its own, but derived in a great measure from the illusive veil with which it is o'erspread." Elsewhere he says that the days of romance are over ("The Gods are tired of us heavy mortals and no longer admit us to their intimacy"), but our consolation is "to wander about their most frequented haunts and endeavour to make up by imagination the want of the reality" – a task he would dedicate himself to in his later adult writings, to very great effect.

Back in New York in January 1806, Irving knew himself a writer, and over the next nine years he constructed a significant literary reputation among the emerging "Knickerbocker" school of writers now flourishing in the city; it included James Kirke Paulding, Fitz-Greene Halleck and Joseph Rodman Drake. They engaged in political controversy, borrowing the styles of the eighteenth-century wits in a time when classical manners indeed still prevailed in writing, art and public architecture, but they also took a lively interest in the Romantic movement emerging in Britain, and made heroes of Byron, Shelley, Scott and Thomas Campbell. With Paulding and his brother William, Irving involved himself in the publication of a group of witty, gossipy satirical essays, the *Salmagundi* papers, subtitled *The Whim-Whams and Opinions of Laurence Longstaff* (1807–8). Then in 1809, when he was still only twenty-six, he published, under the elaborate, quaint pen-name of "Diedrich Knickerbocker," his cod *History of New York: From the Beginning of the World to the End of the Dutch Dynasty*, a "comic history of the city." Filled with mock-learning, literary parody, strange characters and legends, it vividly pictorialized the region's Dutch past. A delightful, much under-estimated book, it is probably New York's first real story, the tall tale of a distinctive mercantile city and section of America that was Dutch before it was British, Native American before it was Dutch. Irving had found his "region"; it stretched from Manhattan up the wooded banks of the great Hudson River, where Henry Hudson had sailed in 1609 looking for a Northwest Passage for the Dutch East India Company, leaving Dutch traces everywhere. Irving's writing, comic but celebratory, led in turn to the celebrations of the region in the paintings of the Hudson River School. In a preface he later added to the book, Irving explained what he then thought the task of the American writer was: it was "to clothe home scenes and places and familiar names with those imaginative and whimsical associations so seldom met with in our own new country, but which live like charms and spells about the cities of the old world." It was whimsy, and it worked; the book won him immediate success and the admiration of British contemporaries like Scott and Byron, some of whom always thought it his best. But above all it now raised the prospects of a serious literary career and an international reputation, perhaps helpfully financed by the family's thriving transatlantic import-export business, in which he had now become a partner.

3.

Then, though, came the great interruption: renewed war with Britain. The War of 1812, during which the United States invaded and torched in Upper Canada, and the new Capitol in the new city of Washington was burned down by British troops, brought a renewal of recent transatlantic cultural hostilities. Irving felt patriot enough to give up his writing and serve briefly as an aide-de-camp to Governor Daniel Tomkins, joining in the conflict in Canada. But the serious crisis was the threat to the family business, which had bases in Liverpool and Birmingham, and was at risk on both sides of the water. After hostilities ceased, Irving sailed again to Europe – on a voyage that would eventually last seventeen years, and turn him into "Geoffrey Crayon" and a famous writer. On 15 May 1815, he sailed for Liverpool on the *Mexico*. The main intention was to rescue the affairs of the family business and resume the transatlantic trade. But personal depression, a romantic disappointment, and his rising literary ambition also fuelled the voyage. "Travelling is a convenient alternative to resort to, when we begin to grow sated by the objects around us, and require to be stimulated by novelty and variety," he told a friend. "I always keep it in view as a kind of succedaneum for matrimony, and promise myself in case I am not fortunate enough to get happily married to console myself by ranging a little about the world." Despite the recent hostilities, there was, he found, a desire for reconciliation, and he was received with great warmth in Britain: "I am delighted with England," he noted. "The country is enchanting and I have experienced as yet nothing but kindness and civility." However this was to prove a very different visit from the romantic, youthful tour of ten years before, when Europe glowed before him. His plans for further travels in Europe were trimmed when it grew plain that the business was in serious difficulties, and for the next two years, until the final bankruptcy, he had to devote himself unwillingly to commercial affairs in Liverpool and Birmingham. "It was my lot almost on landing in Europe, to experience a reverse of fortune, which cast me down in spirit, and altered the whole tenor of my life," he would explain.

But Irving had not set aside his literary intentions, and when the crisis came he turned once more to writing, "to reinstate myself in the world's thoughts." He travelled widely round Britain, and the experiences of these Regency and Georgian years are to be found in *The Sketch Book*, and successor volumes like *Bracebridge Hall* (1822) and *The Crayon Miscellany* (1835). He was hardly the only American artistic expatriate around at the time. In August 1817, in London, he made contact with the group of American expatriate painters, who had gathered there in the wake of the great earlier expatriates, Benjamin West and John Singleton Copley. There had been an American colony of painters in London right through the Revolution (West, who became president of the Royal Academy, painted for George III even as he celebrated American victories) and the artistic traffic had never ceased. In fact, as the great expatriate Henry James observed, it was these early painters who, "amid difficulties and dangers, set the example and made out the road."[2] The present-day group included the painter-poet

---

[2] Henry James, *William Wetmore Story and His Friends* (2 vols, 1903; reissued London, Thames and Hudson, 1957). West's students included John Trumbull, Gilbert Stuart, Robert Fulton (inventor of the submarine), Mather Brown and William Dunlap. There are details in R. B. Mowat, *Americans in England* (London, Harrap, 1935), and Lewis Einstein, *Divided Loyalties: Americans in England During the War of Independence* (Boston, Houghton Mifflin, 1933). As James indicates, the writers who came to Europe were often following in the footsteps of the painters, and as these increasingly moved toward Italy so did literary interest.

Washington Allston, author of the novel *Monaldi* (written 1822, published 1841), Gilbert Stuart Newton, and Charles Robert Leslie, who became a close friend and appears in "The Wife," one of *The Sketch Book* essays. Irving loved the company of painters, and had aspired to be one himself. At the same time, he also met many of the important figures of the British Romantic movement – Coleridge, Thomas Campbell and Byron's publisher John Murray, the key to his later literary success – and found his New York fame had gone ahead of him. He also made a month's tour of Scotland, was warmly received in Edinburgh, and met Samuel Rogers and Francis Jeffrey (who would review him so well in *The Edinburgh Review*). And above all he went, as all American literary tourists did, to Abbotsford, home of Walter Scott, who welcomed him with the greatest warmth: "the glorious old minstrel himself came limping to the gate." The two found much in common – Scots ancestry, antiquarian interests, concern with regional writing and legend, a love of a new, nationalistic historical romanticism. Irving celebrates and ritualizes this momentous visit in his essay "Abbotsford," collected in *The Crayon Miscellany*, seeing it as his true introduction to Romanticism. And, as Scott brought out Irving's romantic instincts, Scotland brought out the Irvingesque mood; he granted the scenery could be misty and monotonous, but "such has been the magic web of poetry and romance thrown over the whole, that it had greater charm than the richest scenery I beheld in England." Scott encouraged him to read the German romantic and folktale writers, like Schiller, Wieland, the Grimm brothers and Tieck, starting a folkloric quest that would enthrall Irving for years. "This was to be happy," Irving noted of the meeting, "I felt happiness then."

Irving had also found another revolution: in the nature of the literary profession itself. For, in the age of Romanticism, the marketplace was expanding. Writers, free of the age of the patron, were living by writing at last, working directly for publishers, soliciting fond readers. Returned to Birmingham and Liverpool, he set about amassing the materials of *The Sketch Book*, hoping to make his escape from business and bankruptcy problems (in fact the firm failed in 1818). "I shall be able, I trust, now to produce articles from time to time that will be sufficient for my present support, and form a stock of copyright property," he explained to his brother, who secured him a post as clerk in the American navy: "To carry this into better effect it is important for me to remain a little longer in Europe . . . Do not, I beseech you, impute my lingering in Europe to my indifference to my own country or my friends. My greatest desire is to make myself worthy of the good-will of my country, and my greatest anticipation of happiness is the return to my friends." Irving here had a serious point. Copyright law, and the London publishing boom, meant he was better off in Britain, where he could hold onto British rights and contracts as long as he had residence, and where, as Byron showed, writers could sometimes make a good literary living. Irving had first meant his book for the American market, and in its first form *The Sketch Book* appeared in seven paperbound numbers in the USA (appropriately, given its most famous story, from the firm of C. S. Van Winkle) in 1819–20. But unauthorized British reprints soon appeared (it was a transatlantic custom), so – as he tells the story in the British 1848 edition – he approached Murray with an extended two-volume British version. Murray did not judge it commercially profitable, but Irving now had useful friends. He sent the manuscript to Scott, who replied offering him support and the editorship of a new weekly periodical in Edinburgh, a generous offer Irving politely rejected ("I am as useful for regular service as one of my own country Indians, or a Don Cossack"). He decided to publish at his own expense; however no sooner had the first volume appeared in 1820 than the printer went bankrupt. Scott not only helped ensure some favourable reviews, but got Murray to take it over: "Thus under the kind and cordial auspices of Sir Walter Scott, I began my literary career in Europe." The two-volume *Sketch Book*, with its shadowy author, "Geoffrey Crayon, Gent.," only identified as author of *The History of New York*, appeared. And the anonymous author's plea for "courtesy and candour" from the reviewers was more than satisfied. The book was an enormous triumph, and proved one of Murray's most successful titles. Irving was received everywhere, fêted in society in London and Paris, went "hand-in-glove with nobility and mobility." The fame was international; he became the best-known, best-rewarded, exemplary American writer.[3]

---

[3] The fuller tale is told in Harris McClary, *Washington Irving and the House of Murray; Geoffrey Crayon Charms the British, 1817–1856* (Knoxville, University of Tennessee Press, 1969).

4.

Irving's great success is striking because in manner *The Sketch Book* is a self-consciously modest work, almost teasingly set before the public. It is presented in the rough manner of the tourists' sketch book, not as a work of finished portraiture: "As it is the fashion for modern tourists to travel pencil in hand, and bring home their portfolios filled with sketches, I am disposed to get up a few for the entertainment of my friends. When, however, I look over the hints and memorandums I have taken down for the purpose, my heart almost fails me at finding how my idle humour has led me aside from the great objects studied by every regular traveller who would make a book." As we have it, it holds thirty-four sketches, "miscellaneous, and written for different humours": travel sketches, sentimental pieces, essays of opinion, folktales. The largest number deal with English life and scenes: Westminster Abbey, Stratford-upon-Avon, English village life, the English Christmas. Others gently establish the author as an American, concerned about the state of Anglo-American relations and the difficulties of writing about his own country. What holds the entire miscellany together is the character of "Geoffrey Crayon," the modest traveller with a "rambling propensity" and a taste for the out-of-the-way, a sketch artist who is "always fond of visiting new scenes, and observing strange customs and manners." "Crayon" is a curious figure, a composite who somehow reaches out to serve both a British and an American readership: a travelling American but with some peculiarly British qualities, as his designation "Gent." suggests. He is the eighteenth-century sentimental traveller, heir to Addison, Steele, and the British essayists; but he is also the nineteenth-century romantic wanderer seeking poetic and picturesque sensations not available in his rawer transatlantic world. He is the artistic amateur, wandering with his portable sketch-pad and hunting in every nook and cranny that could call forth a sensation and a "sketch." But he is also the carefully masked figure whose shadowy face yields in turn to other masks, including "Diedrich Knickerbocker," and who is a very carefully constructed literary character, a multi-faced persona.

From the start Irving creates him carefully, providing an "author's account of himself," defining his sensibility. "Crayon" is a curious American of melancholic and meditative disposition, evidently disappointed in love, and with a "roving passion." He loves the natural treasures of his own country, but has always hoped to wander the larger globe. He is drawn toward Europe, and especially Britain, "the land of my forefathers," which has a special lure and a peculiarly romantic role to perform in his world. "Crayon" is hunting the past in order to venerate it, record the sensations it stimulates. What's more, in discovering the "romance" of Europe, he is filling both an imaginative and a political breach:

> But Europe held forth all the charms of storied and poetical association. There were to be seen the masterpieces of art, the refinements of highly cultivated society, the quaint peculiarities of ancient and local custom. My native country was full of youthful promise: Europe was rich in the accumulated treasures of age. Her very ruins told the history of times gone by, and every mouldering stone was a chronicle. I longed to wander over the scenes of renowned achievement – to tread as it were in the footsteps of antiquity – to loiter about the ruined castle – to meditate on the falling tower – to escape in short, from the commonplace realities of the present, and lose myself among the shadowy grandeurs of the past.

It's a skilful contrast. For Irving is parcelling out the elements of American and European difference in terms that seem favourable to each side – so that, as one critic has said, his work has "a quaint Janus-faced quality, a tendency to look both ways across the Atlantic at once." To America he grants all the grandeur of new, unwritten, sublime nature; this was the view of it held by most Americans and many Europeans. To Europe (he incorporates Britain in it) he grants "storied association," in every sense of the term; it is "history," "chronicle," and source of poetic stimulus – the same notions of the world of the imagination he had set down in his early travel journals. All this comes from ruin and decline – "the ruined castle," "the falling tower" – seen as objects of art and meditation, as well as "ideas of order, of quiet, of sober well-established principles, of hoary usage and reverend custom," which seem to pervade everything he observes. Wakes, fairs, the English Christmas, the life of inns and stagecoaches, become the key materials of his sketches, which are studied, as he says, not with the eye of a philosopher, "but with the sauntering gaze with which humble lovers of the picturesque stroll from the window of one print shop to another."

This may be quaint, but it is not merely quaint. Just like Chateaubriand in America, Irving is looking for some of the essential sensations of a transitional and revolutionary age. Volney's *Ruins*

(1791) had associated mouldering civilization with political and imperial decline. Irving associates it with the spirit of art and poetry itself, and this is plainly intentional. In a difficult political situation, Irving was writing in a healing, apolitical mode, though with a few hints toward the importance of politics. What he had to offer was a refined and generous sensibility, ever turning awkward issues into poetry, myth, legend. In the essay "The Voyage" he explains his meditative sensibility, and his desire to close one page of life so he can open another. "Roscoe" takes William Roscoe, a leading Liverpool banker and liberal political figure of the day, "born in the very market place of trade," says Irving, but dignifies him as a neo-classical image of life's mutability. In the splendid tale "Rip Van Winkle" he comically revives his previous literary identity as "Knickerbocker,"and claims Dutch New York as yet another place of legend. It's only in the fifth essay, "English Writers on America," that he addresses political issues and cultural antagonisms, implicitly comparing the criticisms of the many English travellers to America – who instead of judging philo-sophically and reporting graphically on "a country in a singular state of moral and physical development," give prejudiced and misleading accounts in their books – with his own poetic approach to travel-writing. The task, as he makes clear, is, in a time of political change and conflict, to create a romantic perception – or, as he put it himself, of "looking at things poetically rather than politically."

But the truth was, of course, that the Britain Irving had come to was by no means simply a land of "neat cottages," "mouldering ruins," "village churches." The Industrial Revolution was driving onward, peasants were being driven from the land into milltowns and cities, there was much social protest and hunger for reform, and a growing sense of political disorder. The cities where Irving spent nearly all his time in Britain, Liverpool and Birmingham, were centres of trade, nests of urban problems, places of poverty, and homes to liberal and radical dissent. Irving knew that very well, but it was never his theme. The William Roscoe essay, about a liberal reformer, scarcely mentions his political role; he is drawn in statuesque portraiture, as a classical hero in a landscape of mutability, ruin and antiquity. As there is little sign of industrial revolution or social upheaval in the world Irving "sketches," there is also no suggestion that the Britain that is America's past could also well be America's future – as its industries grew, its cities crowded with migrants, and the age of nature, the frontiersman and the

Jeffersonian farmer gave way to the age of masses, machines and social disparity and conflict. These were in fact the themes behind Cooper's novels, now just starting to appear as Irving published; one thing that is Romantic about them is that they depict the pressures on timeless natural America, and the dying of the day of Leatherstocking. Clearly what Irving chooses to neglect is as important as what he chooses to perceive. But that is the point: in Irving's view, an age of change, reform, revolution, deep historical unease, needed to acquire a romantic sense of history. He turned Europe's Romanticism right back on itself, and found instead the history, even the "ruin," Britons and Europeans were coming to crave and cultivate as the brazen age of industrialism developed. So it was an age already fading or gone that Irving sketched, along with a timeless, apolitical "rambling propensity" that helped in the seeing of it.

The fact was that Irving was constructing an important mythology which would have enormous influence on European and American writing, and the transatlantic theme that would long continue to connect the two. According to this myth, which was not novel to Irving alone, America becomes the land of progress and the future, a land of sublime nature and unwritten romanticism. Europe becomes the world of the past, of ivy-clad ruin, of legend and poetry. Irving puts this even more plainly in the preface to his next book, *Bracebridge Hall* (1821):

> Having been born and brought up in a new country, yet educated from infancy in the literature of an old one, my mind was early filled with historical and poetical associations, connected with places, and manners, and customs of Europe, but which could rarely be applied to those of my own country. To a mind thus peculiarly prepared, the most ordinary objects and scenes, on arriving in Europe, are full of strange matter and interesting novelty. England is as classic ground to an American, as Italy is to an Englishman; and old London teems with as much historical association as mighty Rome.

For Irving England – and later Europe in general – is shaped as the repository of a literary sensibility, "Romance," still not yet fully available in the United States. And his remarkable success was to invest Britain – almost for the first time, and with the happy consent of its citizens – with just the kind of poeticized antiquarian fascination eighteenth-century British travellers had so often conferred on Rome. Behind this lay fairly clear implications, drawn out in a number of the books of the time (like Volney's *Ruins*). Once again the great cycle of

Empire was turning. It ran from rise to fall, from innocent and pastoral natural beginnings, through civilization, and then to the age of ruin and decay – but it was just this that generated poetry, art, romantic feeling. America was still in the first stages, Europe was reaching the last. All this became the stuff of a new American Grand Tour, and Irving's skill was to draw out the associations connected with this, charmingly doing for Britain what earlier travellers had done for Athens and Rome. So, in classical fashion, *The Sketch Book* acknowledges the "ancient tie of blood," the labyrinthine quaintness of the English cities ("a realm of shadows, existing in the very centre of substantial realities"), the strange power of rural custom ("the beautiful and simple hearted customs of rural life which still linger in some parts of England"), the eternal stabilities of the countryside, the geniality of British squire-archical life, the "timeless" life of the village church ("It is a pleasing sight of a Sunday morning . . . to behold the peasantry in their best finery, with ruddy faces and modest cheerfulness, thronging tranquilly along the green lanes to church"). It builds a climate, and out of it can be constructed an entire and now very familiar landscape: Westminster Abbey, the Boar's Head Tavern, Stratford-upon-Avon ("I had come to Stratford on a poetical pilgrimage"), Dr Johnson's Lichfield, and other places associated with poetic virtue or literary achievement, or sanctified by antiquity and indeed decay – the ruined castle, the falling tower, the crooked byway, the British picturesque. The resulting sensations are both touristic and poetic, sentimentally graceful and always vivid, and flattering to British readers. Yet, like much in Romanticism, they are also touched with irony, or a hint of super-session. And in one essay, aptly called "John Bull," Irving offers signals of the modern change the new American order might exert, the historical promise it could one day claim, the notion of supersession.

5.

But there was another task *The Sketch Book* had to perform – and from Irving's point of view it was to become the most important. The question remained of just how to poeticize bare, plain, young American life. America needed a legendary past of its own, and in building the book Irving went on to provide one. In fact the reason the volume is most remembered now is that it contains two of the great ur-stories of

American literature – "Rip Van Winkle," and "The Legend of Sleepy Hollow." Both are attributed to the records of his familiar old antiquarian narrator, Diedrich Knickerbocker, and described as oral legends of American life. But, manipulating his mouthpieces, Irving also deviously indicates that they are not; nor are they. Scott's advice to Irving to look to German folktale had not been wasted. Both of the stories have German originals. "Rip Van Winkle" has its original source not, as is hinted, in the more obscure Rothbart, but in the German folktale "Peter Klaus" (which was later to be translated into English by none other than William Roscoe). "The Legend of Sleepy Hollow" draws for its details on a German folktale to be found in various anthologies of the day. There is a third legend or ghost story in the volume, "The Spectre Bridegroom," which comes from a popular German ballad "Lenore," but for his retelling Irving more conventionally choses to retain, if teasingly, the German setting and atmosphere.[4]

Irving's crucial decision was to shift his two stories into the American landscape, rather than simply retelling them as his version of old German tales. It was this act of appropriation that rendered them great American folktales, read as such to this day. If the New Nation thought it lacked history and legend, Irving was redeeming the lack. He chose his settings carefully, shifting the tales to the sleepy Dutch-American villages along the Hudson River valley which he, as Diedrich Knickerbocker, had already used in his *History of New York*. Here, as he carefully explained in "The Legend of Sleepy Hollow":

> ... population, manners and customs remain fixed; while the great torrent of migration and improvement, which is making such incessant changes in other parts of this restless country, sweeps by them unobserved. They are like those nooks of still water which border a rapid stream, where we may see the straw and bubbles riding quietly at anchor, or slowly revolving in their mimic harbour, undisturbed by the rush of the passing current.

And here too literature could occur, folklore develop, timeless Europe feed its stories into timebound new America. What's more, in shifting the setting, Irving also shifts his tales into a new historical world, and so entirely changes their meanings. For now in the background Irving sets the bustle of events, the pressure of change, the revolutionary transformation from colony to nation. Rip Van Winkle sleeps his

---

[4] The details of this are to be found in Walter A. Reichart, *Washington Irving and Germany* (Ann Arbor, University of Michigan Press, 1957).

twenty-year sleep right through the Revolution – to find, on his return to the village, that the old timelessness has gone. Bustle and disputation have arrived (they did), the Liberty pole has replaced the great tree that used to shelter the "quaint Dutch inn" (now the "Union Hotel"), and on the inn-sign the head of King George has become General Washington. Rip is asked to decide whether he is Federal or Democrat, and treated as a traitor until he tells his story. This allows him (and his author) to overcome accusation and defeat change by becoming a maker of legends, a teller of tales about timeless times, before the Revolutionary War. If Rip deceives time by making legend, Ichabod Crane in "The Legend of Sleepy Hollow" is in turn deceived by the legends told to him. He is something of a rationalist, but he does know and believe another source of American legend, the Puritan witchcraft tales of Cotton Mather. So he succumbs to the region's "marvellous tales of ghosts and goblins, and haunted fields and haunted brooks, and haunted houses," which again draw on situations (Major André, the Hessian soldier) taken from the Revolutionary War. But, once again, history freely moves from politics to legend. And Ichabod Crane's story, like that of Rip, itself becomes a local legend, to be gathered up by "Diedrich Knickerbocker" – whose presence puts everything into a quaint comic frame where the very relationship between truth and fiction becomes refracted and obscure.

Critics have sometimes complained that Irving chose to escape into legend in order to avoid history, and to some degree this is both true and self-confessed. And yet, of course, the reasons the stories, like most mythic tales, have lived so well is precisely that Irving lets them survive as legend or fantasy while successfully transporting them over the Ocean into the distinctive world of the new American culture and its shaping age of history. Rip is no European peasant; he becomes an intrinsically American figure, the rogue boy-man ever in flight from shrewish women and work. Ichabod Crane is the calculating Yankee, Brom Bones the not-so-simple frontiersman. And above all the spirit of German mysticism and gloom disappears. Irving rejects the Gothic of witchery or psychic terror, the uncanny psychological disturbance of Charles Brockden Brown's American Gothic, or the mortal horror of Edgar Allan Poe. His are comic, teasing, unreliable tales, their truth and moral left deliberately obscure, their trickery made plain. Irving makes a Euro-American world where history is arrested, stories abound, and all narrators are masked and untrustworthy tricksters.

But plain Yankee common sense dispels Gothic unreason, and ghosts are deceptions; meantime the real deceiver is the storyteller himself. Yes, they are "magic moonshine," as Irving said: peaceable tall tales, aspiring to myth but also to fictionality, entirely in tune with American comic scepticism. At the same time, along with the Indian pieces also included in the volume, they wrote up America for the international imagination. Indeed they mattered as much to British readers as they did to Americans themselves.

The truth was that, timing matters perfectly, Irving evolved an ideal voice, and gave transatlantic writing a mirrored image that would live long in the cultural imagination of the future. And there *was* a substantial political meaning. Now Anglo-American relations were improving, the "Battle of the Quarterlies," the transatlantic "paper war" between the critics, was fading. What was more, with the development of a regular sailing packet service after 1816, Europe and America were coming physically as well as politically closer. Europeans were travelling increasingly to America, and they were also ready to read new "American" authors – even as those authors tried to construct their own tentative, difficult, original relationship with the current English and European literature. "Geoffrey Crayon" was just the good-humoured ambassador, the multi-angled literary voice, the age needed. In a time of shifting history and sensibilities on both shores, *The Sketch Book* gave each side of the Atlantic what it wanted most. It associated America with progress and promise, though also with an "all-pervading commonplace" which Irving nonetheless turned into a timeless space for folklore and a new sense of history to evolve in. And it associated Europe with past splendours, exotic decay, poetic fascination, moral feeling, granted it those dark forests of the imagination and of national feeling that brought Romanticism into being. While the European imagination busily pastoralized America as the garden of Eden, the land of wide prairie and open frontier, Irving pastoralized Europe as a kind of Arcadia in a state of Piranesian ruin, rich in chronicle, set beyond change, hoary with age, dense with the lives and the customs of the past. These two versions of picturesque complemented each other perfectly, and marked a new stage in Anglo-American Romanticism which is still not forgotten.

In fact the England – and later on the Europe – Irving invented was one for which many, from nineteenth-century politicians to modern airlines, travel companies and tourist boards, have very good reason to be grateful. Hazlitt summed it up: "He takes Old England for granted as he finds it described in our stock-books of a century ago – gives us a Sir Roger de Coverley in the year 1819, instead of the year 1709; and supposes old English hospitality and manners, relegated from the metropolis, to have taken refuge somewhere in Yorkshire, or in the fens of Lincolnshire." Yes, it was an England already fading as he observed it, but then he observed it precisely because it was fading, passing into the realm of the picturesque – a half-mythic land of stagecoaches and ivy-covered cottages, festive Christmases and forelocked peasants, high church spires and quaint crooked byways, to be discerned somewhere beyond the smoke of the new industrial cities. But images have power. Not only did he establish a route for the travelling imagination, a fundamental geography of Westminster Abbey and Stratford-upon-Avon, Lichfield and Edinburgh that would be travelled by countless American tourists, passionate pilgrims *via* American Express, but what he saw was soon imbibed into the British national self-image. With his distinctive, backward-glancing American imagination for what Hawthorne – one of his many successors in transatlantic travel – would call "our Old Home," Irving saw England as it had never quite been seen before. What he "sketched" would strongly affect Charles Dickens – whose early novels imbibe the Irvingesque British past of Christmases and stagecoaches even as they begin to confront the enormous social changes, the crowded fogbound cities, and the hard times of the Victorian age. And it would no less shape the vision of American traveller-writers yet to come: Longfellow and Hawthorne, Melville and Henry James, with their "romantic travellers" and "passionate pilgrims," "ancestral footsteps" and "international scene." When Hawthorne noted in the preface to his Italian novel *The Marble Faun* (1860) that "Romance and poetry, ivy, lichens and wall-flowers, need ruin to make them grow," or when James remarked on the American complex fate ("one of the responsibilities it entails is fighting against a superstitious valuation of Europe"), they were still writing in the Irvingesque tradition, and often travelling with Irving's sketch-book still in hand.

6.

Irving's success was enormous; *The Sketch Book* was indeed one of the great publishing triumphs of the Romantic period. "It is true, he brought no new earth, no sprig of laurel gathered in the wilderness, no red bird's wing, no gleam from crystal lake or new discovered fountain (neither grace nor grandeur plucked from the bosom of this Eden-state like that which belongs to cradled infancy)," Hazlitt wrote in 1829, incidentally displaying his own folkloric version of the pastoral America, "but . . . we saw our self-admiration reflected in an accomplished stranger's eyes; and the lover received from his mistress, the British public, her most envied favours." A large literary career now lay open before Irving; but also a hard choice of literary identity. He could stay a fêted guest of British society, could return proudly home to the States, or continue to indulge his "rambling propensity" elsewhere in Europe. The first did not entirely satisfy; while he enjoyed his reputation, he did not quite wish to become a British writer. Yet living as a writer in the USA seemed self-evidently impossible, as he explained to his friend Breevort: "I can only say that I see no way I would be provided for – not being a man of business, a man of Science, or in fact anything but a mere *belles lettres* writer." He chose to continue his European travels and writings, while acknowledging "I do not wish to remain long enough in any place in Europe to make it my home." This choice would define the shape of his life for the following fourteen years. He moved on to Paris, and spent a happy social year there. Then he returned to London for the publication of further English essays and sketches, *Bracebridge Hall*. But he sensed he had begun to exhaust his English materials, and went on to Germany. In 1822 we find him travelling the Rhine, explaining "I meant to get into the confidence of every old woman I met with in Germany and get from her, her budget of wonderful stories." Scott's advice to him that Germany was the root-forest of romanticism and folklore had evidently not been wasted.

Perhaps more usefully, he went for thirteen months on a great *Wanderjahr* through the German cities, to Munich, Vienna and Dresden – capital of the Kingdom of Saxony and the great centre of German romanticism, "a place of taste, intellect, and literary feeling," as he said. There was now a strong interest in things German, especially in Schiller, Goethe, Wieland and Klopstock, among readers British and American. What is more, a new generation of American historians, Ticknor, Edward Everett, Joseph Cogswell and George Bancroft, was now coming to study historical method in the great

German universities. Wintering in Dresden, Irving was made welcome at the Saxon court, met Tieck and other German writers, and took an interest in the Romanticism of *Sturm und Drang*. He turned to opera, and worked on English translations of the libretti of Weber's *Der Freischütz* and *Abu Hassan*. When, in 1824, he published *Tales of a Traveller* his "German book" (though its stories are also set in England, France and Italy), it was clear that Geoffrey Crayon, Gent., was now a serious wanderer through all of Europe, gathering up a folkloric landscape of old German ghosts and hauntings, Italian *banditi*, the terrors, castles and quaint peasantry of dense Gothic mysticism, all reported in the sceptical and sometimes over-comic tone of the sophisticated American traveller. But the British reviewers who had first praised him now attacked him, as reviewers do, finding the spirit of his new book far too literary, its romantic feeling too bland. Tastes and sympathies were already beginning to change, and Irving's widened view of Europe, his rather weary note ("I am an old traveller; I have read somewhat, heard and seen more, and dreamt more than all"), and his love of fanciful legend and literary hoaxes were beginning to separate him from his British audience.

Even so, Irving's great mapping of Europe was nowhere near done. For tastes were changing yet again, as fashionable and historical interest began to move southward, toward Spain. The American West was opening up, and historians were beginning to look back from the western plains and deserts and the old Spanish settlements they found there to the first explorers and discoverers of the Old World. George Ticknor, the professor of Belles Lettres at Harvard, came to Spain, working on his history of Spanish literature. He in turn guided William Hickling Prescott to undertake his great work on Iberia; in 1826 he began his famous *History of the Reign of Ferdinand and Isabella*, published eleven years later, and would follow this with his noted histories of the conquest of Mexico and of Peru. Meanwhile, back in Paris between 1823 and 1826, Irving was growing bored. He had worked on his German sources, developed his opera translations, but the poor reputation of his last book depressed him. Suddenly, in a ceremonial change of interests, he set aside his German material, even handing over his German phrasebook and Italian grammar to a friend. He started taking lessons in Spanish, and read Calderón and Arab history. Then he arranged an invitation from the new American Minister in Spain, his friend Alexander Hill Everett. In February 1826, after three years of Paris, he announced his decision: "I am on the wing for Madrid!" After England, after Germany, Irving was now ready to start creating his third Europe.

Given Irving's temperament, it is no surprise that the first thing he found in Spain was a new spirit of romance. Spain proved at once a joyous new dimension to his vision of Europe; here he found more than anywhere the sensations he craved. "The Spaniards seem to surpass even the Italians in picturesqueness; every mother's son of them is a subject for the pencil," he wrote to Leslie in delight. Everett wanted him to translate Martin Fernandez de Navarrete's *Collection of the Voyages of Columbus*, but the volume consisted mainly of source materials, details of the voyages themselves, and struck him as dreary. But he was lodging with Obadiah Rich, an American who had one of the best Hispano-American collections in Europe. With the help of this, he decided to embellish de Navarrete's Columbus story for American readers, and render it as an epical romance. It proved the perfect subject, the ideal myth. Irving's famous version of the Columbus legend, *The Life and Voyages of Christopher Columbus*, appeared in New York and London in 1828, and was translated in France, Germany, Italy and Spain itself. It went through several versions, and did much to restore not just Irving's but Columbus' international fame. American writers and political mythmakers had treated Columbus before; Joel Barlow had given him epic treatment in *The Columbiad* (1807), for example. But Irving's version was grander – a great historical romance about a near-mythic American hero, based on documentary sources, but turned toward the legendary. Columbus was a "poetic" figure, and the Spain he departed was a "waking dream." So the romance of the New World was spun out of the misty poetry of the Old. For a nation still looking for a history and in search of some sturdy and monumental heroes, and trying to map out a significant past that, with expansion into the Western and Pacific territories, now needed to incorporate not just Britain but Spain, Columbus proved the perfect icon. It was Irving who put him firmly into the pantheon of American heroes – where he survives, admittedly somewhat shakily, still. Painters, sculptors, and other national mythmakers soon picked up on the heroic figure, and Irving had helped create yet another national legend.

Meantime Irving went ever deeper into Spanish materials, making contact with Spanish writers, and travelling widely. His romantic feelings were reinforced by a visit to Granada, another great site of the mythic year of 1492, when the Moors were expelled from Spain and Columbus set sail. Above all there was the old Moorish citadel, the Alhambra: "The evening sun shone gloriously upon its red towers as we approached it, and gave a mellow tone to the rich scenery of the vega. It was like the magic glow which poetry and romance have shed over this enchanting place." Out of this came *A Chronicle of the Conquest of Granada* (1829), history made legend, as Irving, who had firmly linked America to romantic Spain, traced the history yet further back, into the story-filled Arab world. The thrill was so great that Irving took up residence within the Alhambra itself, explaining:

> From earliest boyhood, when, on the banks of the Hudson, I first pored over the pages of old Gines Perez de Hytas's apocryphal but chivalresque history of the civil wars of Granada, and the feuds of its ancient cavaliers, the Zegries and the Abencarrages, that city has ever been a subject of my waking dreams; and often have I trod in fancy the romantic halls of the Alhambra.

Now he lived there, as he told Breevort, as if "I am spellbound in some fairy palace." He found himself "in the midst of an Arabian tale, and shut my eyes as much as possible, to everything that should call me back to every-day life." The residence gave him *The Legends of the Alhambra* (1832), surely the lushest of his works. As he had in Britain, and then in Germany, Irving had found a perfect American past, storyladen and yet somehow historyless. This was the high point of his romantic self-investment in Europe, "nestled in one of the most remarkable, romantic and delicious spots in the world." He had only one complaint to offer: "The sole fault was that the softness of the climate, the silence and serenity of the place, the odour of flowers and the murmur of fountains had a softening and voluptuous effect that almost incapacitated me for work." But such is the price of paradise.

By now he had become the perfect literary ambassador to Europe, in all its rich, different, romantic variety. It was perhaps both appropriate and romantically sad that his delicious, "voluptuous" residence now ended. President Andrew Jackson acknowledged his importance by offering him the post of First Secretary to the American Legation back in London. Such political patronage was one of the few and possibly the more enlightened rewards the American system could offer. In fact a significant number of writers – Hawthorne, Melville, William Dean Howells and James Russell Lowell – not only depended on but were cosmopolitanized by it. Irving took up this none-too-demanding office in 1829, and his role as what has been called "ambassador to the old world" began.[5] He found himself restored to British literary life, in the scene where it had all really started; Oxford awarded him an honorary degree. But this was a different and tenser age, a time of Chartist agitation, and the timeless British past now felt much further distant. In any case Spain was now his chief material; in London he completed what he called his "Spanish sketch book," the romanticized and dreamlike *The Legends of the Alhambra*, and it came out in 1832. This was a famously troubled year – in Britain the radical year of the Reform Bill, in the United States the Jackson administration entered its second term. Irving decided to end his seventeen-year expatriation at last, and return home to the States. He experienced a homecoming quite unlike that of James Fenimore Cooper, who on his homecoming in the following year would be attacked violently in the press for his European expatriation. Irving, though, was fêted on arrival in New York City, as the greatest American writer of the day. The city gave him a public dinner in the City Hall, where he spoke warmly of the unique attractions of his nation, promising to remain in his own land for life. He had written to Breevort: "The fact is, the longer I remain away from home the greater charm it has in my eyes and all the coloring that the imagination once gave to distant Europe now gathers about the scenes of my native country." But he also confided that he expected to become like Rip Van Winkle in his own country:

> I shall return home and find all changed, and shall be sensible how much I have changed myself. It is this idea which continually comes across my mind, when I think of home, and am continually picturing to myself the dreary state of a poor devil like myself, who, after wandering the world among strangers returns to find himself a still greater stranger in his native place.

His fears were understandable. He had won his literary and popular success, but left behind the imaginative things that had provided it. Whatever the reasons – professional, sentimental, emotional – for his long foreign residence, it had formed him as a writer, and exposed him to a European way of forming his art. He had always insisted on his Americanness, which indeed had provided him with a detachment ever

[5] George S. Hellman, *Washington Irving, Esquire: Ambassador at Large from the New World to the Old* (New York, A. A. Knopf, 1925). Also see Claude Bowers, *The Spanish Adventures of Washington Irving* (Boston, Houghton Mifflin, 1940).

important for the tone of his writing. His note was that of the universal stranger, the traveller moving through other people's arts and dreams. Still, perhaps now it was Europe that was commonplace, and America romantic. He moved to Tarrytown on the Hudson, to a house appropriately called Sunnyside, living among the people whose folklore he had composed. But soon the "rambling propensity" returned, and he took the new Grand Tour to the expanding American West, the land of "manifest destiny," which writers like his rival Cooper had already made a scene of romance. But American romance was also the old American actuality ("Good lord deliver me from the all pervading commonplace which is the curse of our country," he had once noted in Paris), and, as he had half-feared, his imagination did really not catch fire. His *A Tour of the Prairies* (1835) is a wooden book, and the other work of these Sunnyside years – *The Crayon Miscellany* (1835), which contains both European and American material; *Astoria* (1836), a commissioned hype of John Jacob Astor and his western mercantile adventures in the fur trade; *The Adventures of Captain Bonneville* (1837), another biography of Western adventuring – lacked the famous Irving glow. The landscape of Western adventure never seized him as Europe had, or as it seized Cooper. It seemed that the author who could best write the Eastern could not write the Western, the writer who found poetic romance in Europe could not construct the neo-romantic actuality of the half-recorded, under-poeticized world of the West. Nathaniel Hawthorne later reflected that the plain American present suppressed the imagination, and always needed the leaven of solitude and romance. Like Hawthorne, Irving evidently needed his "magic moonshine," which he found best in Europe or the Hudson River backwaters. He had been right; like his own hero Rip Van Winkle, who escapes politics and petticoat government by returning to tales of the legendary past, Irving needed storied and legendary associations that America still could not quite provide.

7.

Alas, Europe, it seemed, no longer provided them either. For in 1842, when he was now fifty-nine, and the leading American writer who had just welcomed the visiting leading British writer, Charles Dickens, to New York, Irving made his third European visit. This time he journeyed not as an aspiring man-of-letters, but as diplomatic eminence: the Tyler Administration had made him Minister Plenipotentiary to the Court of Spain. The new visit started off in Britain, where he was presented to Queen Victoria, and France, where he met King Louis-Philippe. It was a grand, distinguished return to the places of his young imagination, and yet, he confessed, "It is wonderful how much more difficult it is to astonish or amuse me than when I was last in Europe. It is possible I may have gathered wisdom under the philosophic shades of Sleepy Hollow, or may have been rendered fastidious by the gay life of the cottage [Sunnyside]; it is certain that, amid all the splendours of London and Paris, I find my imagination refuses to take fire, and my heart still yearns after dear little Sunnyside." Once in Spain, Irving found the romance of current events – especially that of the "little queen," Isabella the Second – did begin to engage him. But, he said, he saw Spain "much more in its positive light than I did sixteen or seventeen years since, when my imagination still tinted and wrought up every scene." "Positive" here means "ordinary"; he was no longer the curious traveller with the rambling propensity, but an official and very public presence. He served four years of office with distinction, but refused to renew it, and returned with relief to Sunnyside, to work on his last major project, a life of the George Washington after whom he had been named.

When he came back to America, that too was in a new era: the age of what F. O. Matthiessen has called "the American Renaissance." A new Romanticism, philosophical as Irving's never was, had taken over American literature, with the work of Emerson, Thoreau, and the Transcendentalists. The ambiguous relation of actuality and romance was being probed in art by Hawthorne and Melville. In 1849 Melville published his novel *Redburn*, in which a young American sailor, Wellingborough Redburn, sails to Liverpool, where Irving had spent much time. He is seeking the romantic England of his father's guidebooks, which are written in the spirit of Irving. He learns a lesson:

> The world, my boy, is a moving world; it's Riddough's Hotels are forever being pulled down; it never stands still . . . And, Wellingborough, as your father's guide-book is no guide for you, neither would yours . . . be a true guide for those who come after you. Guide-books, Wellingborough, are the least reliable books in all literature; and nearly all literature, in one sense, is made up of guide-books . . . Every age makes its own guide-books, and the old ones are used for waste paper.

There seems little doubt that the guidebooks that so disillusion Wellingborough Redburn are books such as Irving's own. Yet that is not quite the end of the story. Certainly Irving had imagined and romanticized a Europe that, even as he visited it, was already slipping away back into the past, and the realm of legend and fantasy. But the hauntings he constructed never fully departed from the American literary and popular sensibility. And many more Americans than the young Redburn travelled to Europe with their Irvingesque visions, and followed the guiding maps of feeling and landscape they constructed. Emerson and Hawthorne went to England, and amended Irving's vision with their own later commentaries, Emerson in his more critical *English Traits* (1856) and Hawthorne in his *Our Old Home* (1863). More intensely, Henry Wadsworth Longfellow set off on his academic and literary travels on the European continent, recording his intense and romantic experience in *Outre-Mer: A Pilgrimage Beyond the Sea* (1835), a work that was meant as a rewriting of Irving's *Sketch Book* ("I am also writing a book – a kind of Sketch-Book of France, Spain and Italy"). But he was particularly taken by Germany, about which he wrote a romance in the spirit of Goethe's *Wilhelm Meister*; called *Hyperion* (1839), it was the ultimate, extreme story of the American hero in the soulful world of German romance. Numerous travellers made their way to Spain, and followed Irving in reporting the exotic world of Moorish history and legend. Irving had begun work on a map that others would soon fill out.

And, as the travellers and writers came, it soon became clear that, as so often with literary imaginings, the images Irving had constructed not only shaped New World experience but also cast their meanings over the life and writings of the Old World itself. British writers were shaped by Irving's tales, and not only Charles Dickens but others took their sense of the national past and its heritage of literary sensibility from him. The comic reworkings Irving made of German folktale influenced later German writers. Irving's romantic Spain, above all his Columbus, had a great impact on Spanish self-mythologization, and does so to this day. But perhaps what is most important is the sheer largeness and completeness of Irving's imaginative geography of the European world in total. When the New World was discovered, and the discoverers and then the immigrants went West, Europe became the Old World. Many of the migrants rejected it for a time, but then they began to look back to what lay behind – at monasteries and marketplaces, princes and prelates, ghosts and ancestral secrets, the ruined castle and the falling tower. It was, perhaps, a world that made up for what had happily been discarded: wars and battles, famine and persecution, the conflict of tribes and cultures. But it served a necessary function; Europe became an American myth. America was for the present, Europe for the past, suggested Irving. America for innocence, Europe for experience, suggested Henry James. Two weeks in the European wonderland, with bathroom and bidet, offered American Express. The Americans came, and there they found it all much as Irving had said. There were castles and monasteries, Moorish palaces and strange German inns, picturesque ruins and storied associations, along with unnecessary and foolish wars, undrinkable water, and a mysterious mishmash of languages, cultures and ethnicities who all hated and seemed to think they were different from each other, when it was clear they were very much the same.

It took the Old World to construct the New, narrate it into existence, name its places, shape its geography, find its discourse. And it took those who settled in the New World then to look back on, rediscover, narrate and name the Old. Irving played a key part in the traffic, providing the American sentimental traveller, always hungry to cast on Europe's very moving world the idealized stillness of sensation and poetry. He was the kind of American writer who wrote best abroad (as many would), found his art, poetry and stimulus elsewhere, drawing his large legendary map of Stratford-upon-Avon and Wesminster Abbey, Heidelberg and the Rhine Valley, Madrid and the Alhambra. He began to narrate Europe to itself, and at the same time ask fundamental questions about the sources and resources of the American imagination, the wellsprings of American art, and the relation of that art to American plainness and democracy. Yes, it was indeed an imaginary geography, never quite a real world; but it is of just such things that fictions and histories too are made. Looking to invent the most useful story for the New World, Irving effectively and poetically constructed the Old World, otherwise known as "Europe." It went on existing through the generations, and it still exists today, as an aspiring and growing political entity, though still a fiction like any other. The crucial point was that the two worlds were each mythically dependent on the other, and that both, by refraction, acquired a new shape, a wholeness, a common interconnectedness, that they would not have had without the transatlantic traffic. Neither was ever quite the real world, but the images became realities as, once constructed, they continued to feed the imaginative life of the other.

THREE

Blowing up the 'Merrikins:
Charles Dickens and the regeneration of man

I.

"It's a complex fate, being an American, and one of the responsibilities it entails is fighting against a superstitious valuation of Europe," Henry James, one of the great figures of the transatlantic traffic, would famously write in a youthful letter of 1871. Yet, he complained, "no European is obliged to deal in the least with America." This seems a strange opinion, and he must have changed it later, since many of his novels – from *The Europeans* (1878) to *The Golden Bowl* (1904) – depict Europeans doing just exactly that. For the fact of the matter was that, whether obliged or not (and during the course of the nineteenth century, for a variety of potent political reasons, many Europeans felt very obliged to deal with America), a great many writers and thinkers did deal with America. From the moment it was founded, the first New Nation played a large role in the workings of the European mind. European writers like Goethe and Balzac dreamt of American opportunities. Innumerable visitors crossed the Atlantic not simply to see its natural wonders – Niagara and the Mississippi Valley, the Spanish West and the Pacific Coast – but its human ones: its new cities, democratic institutions, modern inventions. In arts and sciences, politics and business, trade and invention, changing political dreams and social expectations, America and all it stood for was a constant theme in the great debates of the age.[1] As conditions and speed of travel improved over the course of the century, as the immigrant numbers grew, as American visitors came again and again to Europe, not just to

[1] For accounts of this, see H. S. Commager (ed.), *America in Perspective: The United States Through Foreign Eyes* (New York, Random House, 1947), and Marvin Fisher, *Workshop in the Wilderness: The European Response to American Industrialization, 1830–1860* (New York, Oxford University Press, 1967).

see the Old World but proclaim the progress of the New, the process of contact and interdependence intensified; by the time James wrote his novels they had become a common phenomenon of the age. But what is true is that, as times changed and development accelerated, as America ceased to be a pastoral wonderland and became a power in history, as cities rose everywhere, communications improved, canals and then railroads began to link the country, and the country itself spread ever further west, the image of America became very different – to Americans themselves, of course, but to Europeans too. It began to lose its Golden Age innocence, and become a central player in the age of machines and development. Its social institutions and its democratic principles became a hope or a threat to many in Europe with this or that interest to pursue. When, just after the mid-century, when the developmental Victorian age was well under way, the nation itself split in two, and the Civil War began, there was, in Europe, a great taking of sides. And when the nation pulled itself together again, exploiting all its military and industrial strength and formidable resources, it no longer seemed, whether at home or abroad, the same America, but a massive new industrial power pulling Western history along on its tail.

By this time it was clear that the old Utopia of the European (and American) imagination was going. The city was now more important than the frontier, the factory more significant than the farmstead, the machine more important than the mission, and many meanings had to be re-written. As the Centennial Exhibition held in Philadelphia in 1876 displayed, the New Nation had begun in one spirit, the spirit of the Enlightenment, and then turned into something very different. The land of the Indian and the Jeffersonian yeoman farmer, Crèvecoeur's "new man," had become the land of the steam locomotive, the McCormick reaper, soon the skyscraper. Within fifty years after Independence the drift of this change could already be seen. In the 1820s Cooper was reporting the end of the age of the free frontiersman. In the revolutionary 1830s de Tocqueville was reporting on the growth of the institutions of a mass democracy, including the growth of a scurrilous press. By the 1840s the hoot of the Boston locomotive was interrupting Henry David Thoreau as he sat immersed in nature beside (sometimes in) Concord's Walden Pond. Before too long the steam-train was puffing across the prairies, through the Rockies, coast to coast, first servicing the war itself and then linking the nation, tying the West into the national economy. It was opening the Pacific, depositing immigrants and settlers, creating towns, turning Indians into railside beggars, pulling new territories into the Union, creating military-like systems and strategies, defining the very rules of time. Population, material resources, economic power and technological invention grew, like the cities and their skyscrapers; and it now was clear growth was the American way. Similar processes were transforming the economies, the cities, the infrastructures of European societies as well, bringing them into a formidable competition of industrial and technical development. Steam and cities, iron and steel, made each world look across the Ocean at the other, as they considered what the power and direction of the future was likely to be. Still, by the last quarter of the century, it was clear that America was running ahead.

In fact from the end of the Revolution on the New Nation had begun to depart the realm of pastoral and enter history, had ceased to be virgin land and become the beacon of the future. This was how its revolutionary heroes, like Franklin, Washington, and Jefferson, were represented to the world: "Our national birth," explained *The Democratic Review* in the late 1830s, "was the beginning of a new history . . . which separates us from the past and connects us with the future only." This increasingly was the transatlantic myth to which Europeans responded, positively or negatively. America became Hegel's "land of the future where, in the ages that lie before us, the burden of the world's history shall reveal itself," or Friedrich Engels' "more favoured soil . . . where no medieval castles bar the way, where history begins . . ." The Romantic myths many Europeans had celebrated – Blake and Schiller in their poetry, Goethe in *Wilhelm Meister's Travels* (1821, 1829), for instance, where he shows a band of German immigrants seeking a new start free from the harms of Europe in America's open and natural space – changed, and often grew a little sour. Most of the Romantic poets had announced their Jacobin and their paradisial enthusiasms, and imagined happy American freedoms, social, political and sexual, for themselves in a cabin on the banks of the Susquehanna. Others, like John Keats, whose brother lost a fortune in a far from gilt-edged American investment, began to change their view: "Their bad flowers have no scent, birds no sweet song, / And great unerring Nature once seems wrong," he complained, presenting the negative view of nature's Utopia. Thomas Moore set off to see the "elysian Atlantis, where persecuted patriots might find their visions realized," only to find himself far from content with the elysium he found there: "In all these flattering expectations I find myself completely disappointed," he wrote.

He was not alone. Despite the difficulties of travel, European visitors were soon travelling in significant quantities to post-Revolutionary America. Many had access to a publisher, and books about the American tour became a staple of the market. Travelling with open notebook, they stared down at the great torrent of Niagara, examined the American prison system, visited the swamplands of the Mississippi Valley, looked at the sad fate of the Indians, considered the phenomenon of slavery, reported on American domestic manners ("spitting"), and reflected what American political institutions and social habits might mean not so much for the destiny of the New World as for the future of the Old. As Washington Irving indicates by his comments in *The Sketch Book* as early as 1819–20, quite a few of these early reports by British travellers already inclined toward the disappointed and the negative. As time went on, records of American travels – and then, increasingly, reports for those who were prospective immigrants – started to pour off the European presses in ever greater numbers; indeed this became one of the most popular genres of the day. More than two hundred books of travels by British writers appeared in England between 1815 and the Civil War, as American travels became a familiar, and profitable, literary trope.[2] The British were particularly regular visitors, not surprisingly, since they felt a strong (if often condescending) sense of common identity, and quite a number had (like Keats' brother) speculated in various American commercial projects – some of them, as it turned out, decidedly dubious. It was not too surprising that a fair number of these reports were disapproving. The image of America had been built so high that many visitors could not but be dissatisfied with the reality. The cocky and confident air of the Americans, these "new men," was not to everyone's taste, and, in return, one thing American democratic spirits particularly failed to appreciate was the note of British condescension. But a good deal more was at stake. America had been founded, according to Tom Paine, as a

2 Studies of this include Jane Louise Mesick, *The English Traveller in America, 1785–1835* (New York, Columbia University Press, 1922), Max Berger, *The British Traveller in America, 1836–1860* (New York, King and Staples, 1943), Allan Nevins, *America Through British Eyes* (New York, Oxford University Press, 1948), and Richard L. Rapson, *Britons View America: Travel Commentary, 1860–1935* (Seattle, University of Washington Press, 1971).

political model to the world, a lesson to mankind. So, like de Tocqueville, many travelled to America to see more than America, just as after the Russian Revolution many travelled to Bolshevik Russia, seeking to consider whether this exemplary new order was the age's utopia, or its dystopia. British and European opinion split on the question, generally along political lines. Already in the eighteenth century political thinkers like Hobbes and Locke, Voltaire and Rousseau, had quarrelled over whether America represented a perceived advance on European institutions. In the political order of the nineteenth, when European systems were themselves confronting the challenge of democracy or radical social transformation, such questions took on an even more complex and dangerous meaning.

Both the ideal and the actuality of America became important to the debates and political disagreements of Europe. And nowhere more so than in Britain, where the rise of Chartism and reform, of radicalism and protest, seriously upset the reigning political order. For Chartist and reforming minds, America represented the Land of Liberty, the Beacon of Freedom, the place of the regeneration of man. In the wake of Tom Paine, it became a known haven for radicals and republicans. William Cobbett lived there for a time, Cobden and Bright became known in Parliament as the members for the United States. It was a place of social experiment and new communities, Owenites and Fourierites, a liberal paradise – until, as the century went on, and the engines of capitalism seemed to gather in the United States, it shifted in meaning, and turned into the land of Robber Barons, trusts, conglomerates and union-busting. Meanwhile, for conservatives, and a good many of the rising and entrepreneurial middle classes, it looked less like the future paradise than the dangerous example: "The current sets in strong and fast from the Transatlantic shores, and the old bulwarks are fast giving way before its fury," warned *Blackwood's Magazine*. The argument was to turn. By the late years of the century, it was conservatives who were admiring America, venerating what Anthony Trollope described as its "wonderful contrivances," and reading in the fortunes of the two nations a common Anglo-Saxon destiny. America always was, and remains, an ambiguous image for Europeans, and other peoples elsewhere. And, like most forms of reflection, refraction and triangulation, the image of a place elsewhere is generally and finally used for the better understanding of ourselves.

In an interesting brief article Marcus Cunliffe once drew up a handy list of some of the dominant images Europeans, over time, have held of America.[3] There was America the Earthly Paradise; America the land of the Noble Savage; America the Beacon of Liberty; America the Land of the Future; America the Fate of Europe, and so on. Each one of these notions, he notes, soon acquired an archetypal or mythic quality, the power to outlast any particular political situation or historical moment. What is more, each heroic image also soon acquired its negative version, its contradiction, its counter-proposition. The Earthly Paradise, the American Utopia, also became the Paradise of Fools, Lubberland, the Kingdom of Cockaigne, Big Rock Candy Mountain, where foolish people thought the ice-cream grew on the trees, and life was easy. The Noble Savage quickly found his counterpart in the Ignoble Savage, the cannibal, the soulless brute, the raider, and then, later on, the cultureless and historyless American tourist raiding Europe with his shorts, his chewing-gum and his Kodak. The image of America as Land of Liberty found its opposite in the notion of America as the Land of Licence, Libertinism, and Lunacy (later this was largely narrowed down to the image of California). The notion of America as Hegel's Land of the Future, and so as Europe's promised hope, was balanced by the notion of America as history's great warning, Europe's threatened fate. If there was, in Europe, an American dream, there was equally an American nightmare, and the one could quickly turn into the other, or external perceivers could see America as a mixture of both. Cunliffe also remarks not just on the power of these images, but the amount of fictionality and mythicization involved in their making. For most Europeans, he says, America was never finally a real place, but "a theorem, a symbol, a Never-Never Land." And in consequence, he adds, even for Americans America was never a fact either, but a myth, an image, and a Dream. All this suggests, perhaps, why for even literary travellers of goodwill the actual visit to mythic America was apt to prove a mystification, an ambiguity, or even a bitter disappointment – as on many famous occasions it did.

[3] Marcus Cunliffe, "Europe and America: Transatlantic Images, 1," *Encounter*, December 1961 (this and a parallel article by Melvin Lasky were reprinted as *Encounter Pamphlet* 7 (London, Encounter, 1962), and another version appeared in Cunliffe's *In Search of America: Transatlantic Essays*, cited above. There is a valuable exploration of these various images both in literature and in art in Hugh Honour, *The New Golden Land*, cited above (p. 17).

2.

It was in the 1830s the issue reached its greatest intensity, and for good reason. In Britain, with Chartist and Corn Law agitation, and pressure for suffrage, the decade was one of disorder and political conflict. In the United States, too, there was a new climate; this was the aggressive, populist, egalitarian age of Jacksonian democracy. Few British conservatives forgot that, in 1828, as radical movements and campaigns grew at home, the chairs and punchbowls of the White House had been smashed by supporters at the inauguration of General Andrew Jackson, "Old Hickory," the plain man out of the West. America appeared to be reform-land itself. Radical movements on both sides of the Atlantic seemed to be linking hands: the anti-slavery movement, the communitarian movement of Robert Owen and others, setting up their utopian villages, farms and factories on the edge of the frontier, and other radical causes like universal suffrage, republicanism, Fenianism, socialism, and feminism, passed back and forth across the Ocean. It was exactly at this time of disturbing transatlantic political change, in 1831–2, that the French aristocrat Alexis de Tocqueville – following in the footsteps of Crèvecoeur, Condorcet, Volney and Chateaubriand – went to America to "see more than America." In fact like other European visitors, he went to inspect and analyse the image of democracy itself, "with its inclinations, its character, its prejudices and its passions." "In order to learn what we have to fear or hope from its progress . . . I have turned my thoughts to the Future," he explained. His analysis in *Democracy in America*, published in Europe in two volumes in 1835 and 1840, observed that "equality of condition" and "sovereignty of the people" were the two essential American facts from which all others derived. His portraits of a new order of life, which displayed the age of the mass, or what he called the "Anglo-American condition" of the human being lost in the crowd, confirmed some in their political hopes, and others in their worst fears. The book was immediately translated into English, and to enormous effect.[4]

---

[4] For fuller details of all this, see G. D. Lillibridge, *Beacon of Freedom: The Impact of American Democracy upon Great Britain, 1830–1870* (Philadelphia, University of Pennsylvania Press, 1955), Frank Thistlethwaite, *The Anglo-American Connection in the Early Nineteenth Century* (Philadelphia, University of Pennsylvania Press, 1959), and H. C. Allen, *Great Britain and the United States: A History of Anglo-American Relations, 1783–1952* (London, Odhams, 1954). Also see Christopher Mulvey, *Anglo-American Landscapes: A Study of Nineteenth Century Anglo-American Travel Literature* (Cambridge, Cambridge University Press, 1983).

Meantime the many British travellers to America, their journeys now aided by improvements in travel and growing transatlantic contacts, were also multiplying their reports. A good number were by novelists, and many were as highly worrisome to the anxious British middle classes as they were angering to their American readers. In 1829 Captain Basil Hall published his critical study *Travels in the United States*, a tale of a bitterly disappointed journey through the democratic American wonderland, and a good many similar works appeared throughout the disordered 1830s. Quite the most famous record was by Mrs Frances Trollope, mother of the novelist Anthony, as well as being quite a novelist herself. The adventurous Mrs Trollope cannot be said to have been a disinterested reporter. When her irritable lawyer-husband began to lose his London clients, and the family fortunes started to fail badly at home, she decided to risk her life and fate – and that of three of her children – in the Utopia of the New World. She herself was lured there by just such another of these travellers' reports, Frances Wright's warmly affirmative *Views of Society and Manners in America* (1821). Wright was a charismatic, freethinking Scot, whose book (and her other charms) had won her the attentions of the French General Lafayette, who had fought in the American Revolution, and who travelled with her through the United States, describing her as his "ward." A Utopian and Owenite reformer, she then went bravely on to found an experimental colony, Nashoba, near Memphis in Tennessee, where she purchased slaves and sought to educate them for freedom. She regularly returned to Europe, where she and Frances Trollope became good friends. In 1827, as her troubles mounted, Mrs Trollope, taken with Wright's striking dreams, decided to accompany her across the water and try the charms of this jungle Utopia, taking the seven-week passage to New Orleans and then the steamboat voyage up the Mississippi. Alas – like so many Utopias –the reality of Nashoba proved very different from the initial descriptions. Indeed, "one glance sufficed to convince me that every idea I had formed of the place was as far as possible from the truth," Mrs Trollope recorded. "Desolation was the only feeling . . ." There was little wonder; the isolated colony was hardly built, there was very little to eat, malarial disease raged, and the venture was just reaching the point of failure; Wright would soon ship her former slaves off to Haiti, and take up the lecture-circuit instead. In fact the situation closely resembles that endured by the young Martin in Dickens' *Martin Chuzzlewit*, and Dickens' account surely owes much to Mrs Trollope's story. Cutting her losses, she next decided to move on up the Mississippi to Cincinnati, Ohio, following out a second ambition that had lured her to the New World. What she proposed was nothing less than to open up a refined fancy-goods bazaar out on the Ohio frontier, to sell British wares to the natives. The Gothic bazaar and cultural centre she had designed and erected as a palace for the refinement of Cincinnati became one of the great monuments of the city, known as "Trollope's Folly." So it was, for this venture too failed, when she wildly overspent, caught malaria, and the British goods her husband shipped out to her proved to be trinkets and trash. There was only one thing left for her to do: tour further in the United States, see the obligatory Niagara, return to Britain, and write a book about the experience.

So Mrs Trollope had a good deal of disappointment to purge when, in 1832, the year of the Reform Bill, she published her *Domestic Manners of the Americans* – which broadly took the view that they really didn't have any. Her book – very vivid and very successful, restoring her fortunes, for the moment at least – is a story both of utopian expectations and commercial fancies sadly dashed on the chaotic, cultureless American frontier. It also presented a disturbing wealth of what were now becoming increasingly familiar complaints from British travellers – about spitting, heavy drinking, lack of personal privacy, dull uniformity, provincialism, the rudeness of servants, the degradation of the frontier, above all about the "peculiar institution" of slavery, which succeeded in offending or upsetting even conservative visitors to America. "I suspect that what I have written will make it evident I do not like America," she noted, as, given her social and financial misfortunes, she felt she had reason to do. Though she admired much in the civilized East, she made plain her feelings about the general populace: "I do not like their principles. I do not like their manners. I do not like their opinions." When, thirty years later, her son Anthony visited America during the Civil War that brought the peculiar and depressing institution of slavery to an end, he sought to make some filial amends for this famous account in his own much warmer traveller's report, *North America* ("It has been the literary ambition of my life to write a book about the United States"). As he tried to explain, his mother had written always as a woman, describing "with a woman's light but graphic pen, the social defects and absurdities which our near relatives had adopted into their domestic life," but not really regarding it part of her task to consider "those political arrangements which had produced the absurdities she saw." However, in the age of Andrew Jackson, a "citizen-king" in France, and the British Reform Bill, it was just these political implications that were easily deduced by English and European readers; this was the nature of the "democracy" the age was now discussing. Of course, back across the Atlantic, Mrs Trollope's first disappointed book caused great offence, generating much abuse and many bitter parodies. But it set her off as a writer, and among the many books she went on to publish several were novels with American settings, including *The Refugee in America* (1832), and her anti-slavery, anti-lynch-law novel *The Life and Adventures of Jonathan Jefferson Whitlaw, or Scenes on the Mississippi* (1836), which compares very well with Harriet Beecher Stowe's much later *Uncle Tom's Cabin* (1852).[5]

However, the influential, critical, refined Mrs Trollope was but the first of a gathering swarm. Between 1834 and 1836 the high-minded reformer, abolitionist, novelist and political economist Harriet Martineau spent two years in the United States, even including in her itinerary a visit to "Trollope's Folly" in Cincinnati, with its Gothic windows, Grecian pillars, and Turkish dome: "The bazaar is the great deformity of the city," she reported. Her account of her experiences, *Society in America* (1837), was generally appreciative of American political institutions, but she too found a good many causes for moral disappointment, above all in the South. Then in 1837 to 1839 Captain Frederick Marryat – the noted novelist and author of *Mr Midshipman Easy* (1836) and *Children of the New Forest* (1847), as well as other books for children, some with American settings – spent two years in the United States and Canada, travelling widely (he too visited "Trollope's Folly," which he found splendidly preposterous). In 1839 he published his *Diary in America, With Remarks On Its Institutions* – another highly critical text which argued that American populist democracy had led to an irresponsible press and great political corruption. Here the political aim was clearly acknowledged; it was, he said, to do "serious injury to the cause of democracy." Again the Americans protested, and in no quiet fashion. This time Marryat was hanged in effigy, and his book was burned in public. Altogether, American tales were becoming a serious business, as more and more

5 For the story of Mrs Trollope and her American experience, see Johanna Johnston, *The Life, Manners and Travels of Fanny Trollope: A Biography* (London, Constable, 1979).

British writers realized. They stirred up fierce transatlantic and international controversy, and became central to the political debate of the day. But they were also becoming an important part of the literary marketplace – as Tony Weller in Dickens' *Pickwick Papers* (1836–7) has already realized, when he advises Mr Pickwick to escape Mrs Bardell by decamping across the Atlantic, "and then let him come back and write a book about the 'Merrikins as'll pay all his expenses and more, if he blows 'em up enough."

In truth, the troubled 1830s represented probably the lowest point in the entire transatlantic debate. The "blowing up of the 'Merrikins" reflected the social and political contracts between social Europe and frontier America, but also bitter anxieties about the political and social changes that were also reshaping Europe at the dawn of Queen Victoria's reign. As time went on, relations and reports would greatly improve, not least in the sober, considered commentaries of writers of the next generation, like William Makepeace Thackeray and Anthony Trollope, both of whom spent a significant time in the United States, and both of whom used the experience in their fiction – Thackeray in *The Virginians* (1857–9) and Trollope in *The American Senator* (1877). It was notable that many of these travelling commentators were also novelists, often hoping to find in their American experiences an original subject for their fiction. In the ingenious argument of his book *Imagining America* (1980), Peter Conrad proposes it was exactly this that became part of the problem. These British writers, he argues, were trying to draw American experience, society and nature within the social codes and moral sensibilities of Victorian fiction. Hence it was the dis-ordered, unstructured character of American social institutions, the informality of American customs, the indescribability of American nature and the chaos of settlement that struck them most. It was as if, for the European writer of fiction, with distinct expectations of society and human behaviour, America re-ordered the very stuff of the novel itself: tradition, custom, manners, institutions, hallowed associations, ideas of form, sublimity and proportion, the relation of past to present, landscape, time, the notion of human character and the nature of the English language. America, it was already widely acknowledged, not least by American writers themselves, was a world hard to write, a land and nation half uninscribed. For socially concerned British novelists, it acquired a character of permanent unreality, a climate of eternal decomposition. "For the Victorians, America is unreal and imaginatively unavailing," Conrad claims. "For their successors [British and European], its unreality is its imaginative attraction."[6] In fact, he says, America was a challenge to their whole social idea of the European novel itself. This argument is ingenious indeed. And, true or not, it does seem to have some appropriateness to the most important and interesting encounter that came between a British novelist and the whole idea of America. For it was at the start of the next decade, when Charles Dickens went to the United States on a triumphal literary tour, that the real crisis came – and it would prove one it took Americans, and Dickens himself, a very long time to forget.

3.

It was over the 1830s that Charles Dickens surged into fame, to become nothing less than the wonder-writer of his day. In 1836 the young parliamentary and political reporter who sat in the House of Commons to witness the machinations of the Reform Bill and observe the new political age coming into shape published his first book, with drawings by Cruikshank, and an Irvingesque title. *Sketches by "Boz"* collected the vivid comic portraits of London life he had been contributing to newspapers and magazines over the two previous years. "Sketches" they were – exactly observed scenes from the daily world, intended to accompany an engraver's comic drawings at a time when caricature had become a central public form. They were so successful that Dickens was invited to write the text for the illustrated *The Pickwick Papers* (1836–7), a work of comic good feeling that made reviewers compare it with Washington Irving for its portraits of stagecoaches, Christmas celebrations and country life – though it also had a sharp edge of political satire. The book was self-creating, growing in size and scope as its readers fell in love with the episodes. Everyone, it seemed, loved the round Mr Pickwick and Sam Weller, his Sancho Panza and sidekick, Cockney London in full voice. Dickens' career as a comic inventor was made, and as the Victorian age started he was already being hailed as its chief novelist and recorder. He soon signed contracts for five more novels, which were to command his time, and create his fame, over the following five years. The importance of what Dickens was doing for the

6 Peter Conrad, *Imagining America* (London, Routledge, 1980).

beginning Victorian age is best made plain by Raymond Williams. "It was not society or its crisis that produced the novels," he says of the dawning of early Victorian fiction, in which Dickens was central. "The society and the novels – our general names for those myriad and related primary activities – came from a pressing and varied experience which was not yet history; which had no new forms, no significant moments, until these were made and given by direct human actions."[7] What we now call the Victorian novel was a new invention, built with the energy and change of the new Victorian order. And at the heart of that was the energetic young Dickens, who over the next years produced – at the most enormous writing speed, and through the journalistic mechanism of publication by serial monthly parts – *Oliver Twist* (1838), *Nicholas Nickleby* (1838–9), *The Old Curiosity Shop* (1840–1) and *Barnaby Rudge* (1841), all five of them finished before he was thirty.

But now, these contracts completed, Dickens felt it was time for a pause. He wanted to fulfil a long-standing dream: and it was nothing less than to go to America. He persuaded his publishers to finance a sabbatical year off that would provide him with another book, possibly recalling the advice his Tony Weller had given to Mr Pickwick. However, nothing suggests that when the journey was planned Dickens had any intention of "blowing up the 'Merrikins." Indeed it was quite the reverse. America was his Utopia, and a trip to the United States, the land of freedom and the regeneration of man, was something that, as a sentimental radical, he had long looked forward to. His fame there had already grown massive, though it was sadly and annoyingly true it had been won largely through pirated editions that brought him no financial reward at all. But, famously, American readers had waited at the New York pierhead, shouting to incoming ships to find out if Little Nell was dead. Now, he was given to understand, they waited just as excitedly for him. Washington Irving had sent him a letter of invitation, telling him a visit from him would be a public triumph of a kind never before seen. Dickens accepted warmly, writing back to say he was at last on his way to "the soil I have trodden in my day-dreams many times and whose sons (and daughters) I yearn to know and be among." "I am still haunted by visions of America, day and night," he wrote to his British friend John Forster, just before setting out. He prepared

---

[7] Raymond Williams, *The English Novel from Dickens to Lawrence* (London, Chatto and Windus, 1970).

intensively, reading through a large pile of the books – Captain Basil Hall's, Mrs Frances Trollope's, Captain Marryat's, and more – in which recent British travellers had set down their records. These were the very books he had mocked in *Pickwick Papers*. And he was determined to correct their negative and supercilious reports, not to repeat them.

When, therefore, he sailed off in 1842 for an extensive tour in the States, there was every reason on every side, not least his own, to suppose his responses would be in the affirmative. On 2 January 1842 – never the best time of year for a transatlantic sea-voyage – he and his wife set sail from Liverpool aboard one of the earliest steamships, the *Britannia*. After ploughing the ocean and briefly snagging on a mudbank, they made landfall at Halifax, Nova Scotia, where Dickens was greeted with a remarkably warm reception: the first of many. They sailed on south to Boston, where the reception was formidable. So it was throughout the USA; great crowds showed up everywhere, lining the streets, cheering him at the theatre, and throughout his American journeying his reception outshone even what Irving had promised. At first everything went wonderfully well. The reception accorded to the young British novelist (Dickens was still only thirty) affirmed he was a literary lion, indeed the most famous writer of his day. America loved him, society loved him, and he was so in demand he had to hire George W. Putnam as his social secretary. He liked New England. He was a writer of reforming, benevolent, populist inclinations, always concerned with social issues, and so he looked around the schools, prisons, orphanages, the model industrial mill-town of Lowell. He generally found them good, models of sensible Utopianism, and thought the charities and public institutions of Boston as near perfection as wisdom, benevolence and humanity could make them. He admired American cities, and he was delighted by the New England landscape.

He equally liked the intelligent, intellectual Americans he met. He had arrived at the start of an expansive time in American literature, the era of what F. O. Matthiessen called "the American Renaissance," which had New England as its reforming, abolitionist heartland, and Boston as its capital – the cultural hub of the nation, the place where, it was said, you could not shoot an arrow in any direction without bringing down a writer. The star of Transcendentalism was rising, radical and utopian sentiment was increasing, the nation was confidently expanding westward. Boston was "culture," and Americans across the continent were looking to culture, which was spread through Lyceum lectures and the visits of dignitaries like himself. The great "Boston Brahmins" welcomed him, and the academics of Harvard, and he found "a whole Pantheon of better gods." Henry Wadsworth Longfellow – the poet and scholar who had written his own "sketchbook" record of his own deeply romantic European tour in *Outre-Mer: A Pilgrimage Beyond the Sea* (1833, 1835), and then developed this into a novel of the birth, through Europe, of the romantic artist in *Hyperion* (1839) – was particularly generous, as he was famous for being ("This forenoon fourteen callers, thirteen of them English," he once noted in his journal).[8] The two men became friends, and not much later Longfellow was visiting Dickens back in London. Meanwhile just that year Ralph Waldo Emerson published his influential essay "The Transcendentalist," describing Transcendentalism as "Idealism as it appears in 1842," and Dickens declared that if he lived in Boston he would have been a Transcendentalist. He also observed the American passion for lectures: "Devotions and lectures are our balls and concerts," Martin Chuzzlewit will later learn in the crucial novel of that name. In New York the acclaim was even greater, and certainly noisier; indeed there had been nothing like it. Washington Irving greeted him and toasted him warmly at a great civic dinner, and "Boz Balls" were held in his honour. He went to Philadelphia, and Washington, and was received by the President, John Tyler, becoming the object of all Washington's attention. He went south to Richmond, where he saw and was troubled by slavery, travelled west by steamboat down the Ohio River to Cincinnati, and then went on down the Mississippi to Saint Louis, the furthest point of his journey, and his nearest access to the West and the frontier.

It was, indeed, a triumph – and yet somehow, somewhere, the great and splendid visit to his American Utopia began to go wrong. His letters home began recording it. He wrote celebrating the American virtues; Americans, he said, are "friendly, earnest, hospitable, kind, frank, very often accomplished, far less prejudiced than you would

8 *Outre-Mer*, consciously modelled on Irving's *The Sketch Book*, is the tale of a tour of the Mediterranean countries by a "pilgrim" devoted to soul-nourishment. The "pilgrim" notes: ". . . to my youthful imagination the Old World was a kind of Holy Land, lying afar off beyond the blue horizon of the ocean." *Hyperion*, the product of Longfellow's second European visit as a scholar to Germany, is the story of a young man's total immersion in the spirit of German romanticism, based on Goethe's *Wilhelm Meister*. This was a work much admired in its day.

suppose, warm-hearted, fervent, and enthusiastic . . . chivalrous . . courteous, obliging, disinterested . . ." However, this letter suddenly and surprisingly goes on to say: "I think it impossible, utterly impossible, for any Englishman to live here, and be happy." What so upset Dickens' first American visit has never really been satisfactorily explained. He was young, new to his fame, and possibly in some ill-health. There is no doubt he was socially and physically over-used, like many a literary lion on many a celebrity tour, constantly tuft-hunted and intruded on. He was treated by some Americans as pure carnival entertainment, and an intrusive press expected him to answer questions on every social and political issue of the day. Moreover, as James Fenimore Cooper had found on his unhappy return to his own country, the "free" American press was growing ever more populist, and ever more famous for its scurrility. There had been the earlier British visitors, who had rewarded American hospitality with critical reaction; there were several political controversies simmering in Anglo-American relations, and a quarrel brewing between the countries over possession of the Oregon Territory. There was a good deal of pro-Irish Home Rule feeling, and a strong, "Jacksonian" levelling spirit at work; all in all, this was a time when a representative British visitor could come to feel uncomfortable. Travelling onward, he became more and more aware of the power of commercialism and political nepotism, leading to what seemed to him (and others too) a corruption of public life. And then, perhaps most importantly, Dickens decided to raise on his tour the whole vexed question of International Copyright, which not only meant that American publishers were free to pirate books by British writers, but that American writers were deeply disadvantaged in the marketplace (as Cooper, too, had pointed out). Dickens, as a bankrupt's son, had learned to be firm over money, and he insisted on raising the matter in most of his public speeches. This was thought inhospitable and venal by the no less venal American press, who began attacking and vilifying him for it. "You must drop that, Charlie, or you will be dished; it smells of the shop-rank," wrote a Boston paper. This growing press hostility was certainly one of the things that marred his tour: "I vow to Heaven that the scorn and indignation I have felt under this unmanly and ungenerous treatment have been to me an amount of agony such as I have never experienced since my birth," he wrote bitterly home in a letter.

But there was more to it still. Even the respect and adulation he met with, the constant pressure of celebrity, evidently an American speciality, began to displease him. "I can do nothing that I want to do, go nowhere I want to go, and see nothing that I want to see . . . ," he complained, "I have no rest or peace, and am in a perpetual worry." In another letter he noted: "I am sick to death of the life I have been living here – worn out in mind and body – and quite weary and distressed." But the disappointment became more than that with an over-demanding and physically damaging tour. Indeed it became quite fundamental, a bitter reaction to America itself. "This is not the republic I came to see," he wrote to his friend Macready. "In everything of which it has made a boast – excepting its education of the people and its care for poor children – it sinks immeasurably below the level I had placed it upon . . . A man who comes to this country a Radical and goes home with his opinions unchanged must be a Radical on reason, sympathy and reflection, and one who has so well considered the subject that he has no chance of wavering." This was serious stuff; Dickens till now had largely identified with radical attitudes and the Chartist view of America as the land of the modern freedoms, and these feelings had very significant consequences for his general political opinions. His comments make it clear he did not see himself as this kind of fixed and eternal Radical, but as a man humanistically and sentimentally concerned by the sufferings, disappointments and con-tradictions he saw round him in contemporary society. Like many of the confused visitors to Stalin's Russia, so often divided between what they believed they should affirm and what they had actually seen or discovered, Dickens looked, considered, and found he could not simply accept or fall in love with the real America he saw in 1842. He increasingly began to notice contradiction, cant and hypocrisy in American ways. Of course Americans celebrated the brotherhood of man, but they did seem to spend much of their time celebrating entrepreneurialism and commercial advantage. They were avid demo-crats, but everyone seemed to have some form of suspect title (Professor, General). They claimed freedom of speech, but they expressed it through the instrument of a salacious gutter press. They declared they invited criticism and free speech, but they really expected flattery. They were dedicated to the principle of "equality of con-dition," yet in the Southern states they practised slavery. They saw man as a free, regenerated hero in nature, but they were making him into a creature of the machine. They lived in the world of Eden, but what made Eden work was – in a notable phrase Dickens himself invented – the Almighty Dollar.

Many of these contradictions had, of course, been observed by American writers themselves, and were matters of critical concern. But the adverse comments of a foreign visitor had never been especially welcome; and American sensibilities were growing ever more touchy on the matter of British condescension. Still, the adulation continued, and his unhappiness intensified. In retrospect, it now seems very likely that what he sensed was some deep and fundamental change within himself, a troubled realization that his own Utopian idealisms were no longer agreeable to him. In the end he cut short his intended six-month American tour, and decided to spend the final month in British Canada. It was a post-American relief, and he was able to thrill more than usual to the transcendental wonder of Niagara Falls ("Then, when I felt how near to my Creator I was standing, the first effect, and the enduring one – instant and lasting – of the tremendous spectacle was Peace, Peace of Mind, Tranquillity, Calm Recollections of the Dead, Great Thoughts of Eternal Rest and Happiness: nothing of gloom or Terror. Niagara was at once stamped upon my heart, an Image of Beauty"). But above all he was longing to go home ("home home home," he wrote), realizing that he no longer felt his American sympathies, that his real nature was deeply English. At last he sailed from New York aboard an American sailing ship, the *George Washington*, and landed with a sigh of relief in Liverpool on 29 June. Many reasons have been given for what went wrong on the famous American tour: perhaps it was the sudden break in his literary production, perhaps the sheer physical exhaustion of a man who thought himself inexhaustible, perhaps the realization that fame and celebrity have their darker side, perhaps it was a mental crisis amounting to a near nervous breakdown. Whatever the reason, the episode had been a crisis, and one that hit him hard. It changed his feelings about himself, and society; it changed the tenor of his writing, which moved into a new and darker phase, where the awareness of cant, hypocrisy and selfishness is intensified. The comic note of the first five novels darkens from this point, and the spirit of his social criticism changed. And, as Peter Ackroyd notes in his biography, his very understanding of character seems to have been deepened: "Dickens' American journey had been a journey toward himself." Something was wrong with Utopia, and Dickens did not take long to make that very clear.

4.

The consequences of Dickens' American visit were soon apparent. The trip took part in the first half of 1842; by October he had already completed and published his record of the tour, *American Notes for General Circulation*. There were several cunning puns in the title, for here Dickens had found the perfect image for the America of the day. American notes – banknotes, credit, the paper dollar – were still much in dispute. Andrew Jackson had come to office on his campaign against the "Monster Bank," the notion of a National Bank and a common American currency, in fact the transition into the high era of American capitalism. The Almighty Dollar was the Ecu of its day, and just as suspect. In fact the 1830s in America had been a Thatcher-like era of "reckless banking," of speculation and over-extended lines of credit; this led to a major slump in 1837, and so to a general feeling about the unreliability of all "American notes." As for "general circulation," that no doubt referred to the American custom of literary piracy – to which his own new book, as he very well knew, would immediately be subjected, without his permission or profit. It was, of course. *American Notes* quickly went into general circulation in the United States and caused enormous outrage. The (Anglophobe) editor of the *New York Herald*, James Gordon Bennett, clearly didn't like it, declaring Dickens "the most trashy . . . the most contemptible" of British visitors, "the essence of balderdash, reduced to the last drop of silliness and inanity." Even some of the British reviewers were unhappy. In fact the book, though it is in the tradition of negative record, and is strongly critical of the belief among many Americans that theirs was a great successful social experiment and a perfect republic, was neither entirely hostile, nor completely unfair in its judgements. It has all Dickens' comic brightness, and expresses all his passionate regard for America as it best aspired to be. It shows his deep interest in America's reforming institutions and intellectual achievements, and many thoughtful Americans would appreciate its attack on the press and slavery; it venerates the American intellectual classes, though it's disturbed by their willing deference to the mass and to commerce. In the preface to a later edition, Dickens explained, "Prejudiced, I have never been otherwise than in favour of the United States." But it breached some implied rule of American hospitality, and no book more soured literary relations between the countries, as well as between Dickens and his American readers.

There was more to come. For, that book finished, he now began on his next and sixth novel, *The Life and Adventures of Martin Chuzzlewit*.[9] Dickens started the new novel in the November of 1842, and it began appearing in monthly parts in 1843–4. He set to work, it seems, with a returned good humour, and with a comic, and parodic, vigour. He intended to write the book to a clear plan, advancing far less spontaneously than before, with a carefully worked-out scheme. "I have endeavoured in the progress of this Tale, to resist the temptation of the current Monthly number, and to keep a steadier eye upon the general purpose and design," his preface explained when the work came out in book form in 1844. He also firmly emphasized the book's central theme – "to exhibit in a variety of aspects the commonest of all the vices; to show how Selfishness propagates itself; and to what a grim giant it may grow, from small beginnings." He first meant the whole book to be set in England, an England of greed and selfishness; the primary landscape of the book is still the countryside around Salisbury and the City of London, a London dominated by the strange bulk of the Monument, which casts its shadow right across the tale. In spirit the book was notably different from the five novels that had gone before. Martin Chuzzlewit the younger is a highly imperfect hero, and hardly a central character in the way earlier young Dickensian heroes had been. The hypocritical Mr Pecksniff, the murderous Jonas, the splendid comic invention of Mrs Gamp, and the gentle Tom Pinch all come out as stronger figures, though the young Martin is the picaresque hero whose adventures shape the story. The book starts on a very parodic literary note, cleverly mocking the great genealogies of noble British families with which so many novels begin – for this too is, as the longer title for the monthly parts says, a book about "who inherited the Family Plate, who came in for the Silver Spoons, and who for the Wooden Ladles." There is an insistent tone of social satire and inner parody new to his work, as well as a deepened seriousness that has made modern critics consider it amongst his finest novels.

Perhaps this change in tone and attitude was felt by his readers, perhaps his absence from the marketplace had a price, perhaps

9 The story of Dickens' troubled American visit is vividly told in Peter Ackroyd, *Dickens* (London, Sinclair-Stevenson, 1990). Also see Edgard Johnson, *Charles Dickens: His Tragedy and Triumph* (London, 1953). And also Charles Dickens, *American Notes for General Circulation* (London, Penguin English Library, 1972), with its useful introduction by John S. Whitley and Arnold Goldman.

American Notes had done him harm. At any rate Dickens soon learned to his dismay that monthly sales of the book had badly dipped – down to twenty thousand copies, compared with the hundred thousand once reached by *The Old Curiosity Shop*. But, since he was still writing the novel as the monthly parts came out, he still had time to revise the plan, and try and recapture his audience. This, it seems, was the point when he decided to give the book a sharp change of direction, and send his imperfect hero, the young Martin Chuzzlewit, off to America. There is no doubt the decision shifted the thrust of the book, and to this day some critics think it distorts it. But the American segments are not just a skilful use of his recent visit, but also a response to the central theme, which in any case had probably come to him as a result of his transatlantic experiences. Even for Dickens, the novel is a long one, and in total proportion the American segment is relatively brief. And it does follow consequentially from the main picaresque line of the story. When Martin is dispossessed by his guardian (the older Martin), cast out by the plotting Mr Pecksniff, and deprived of the girl he loves, he has little else to do but behave like an eighteenth-century hero, and go off to seek his fortune. At the same time he is a flawed hero in a comic and satirical plot, guilty of impetuousness and selfishness, inability to acknowledge misfortune or recognize his moral link with others: it is comedy that suggests he can be finally returned to good fortune once his follies have been purged. But above all Martin has that familiar Dickensian quality, great expectations, which make his heroes think they are men of rank while they live in poverty, and sets them chasing false financial dreams and speculations. And at this time, for Dickens, great expectations put in peril had one natural destination, the United States. The American passages are entirely consistent with the "selfishness" theme, selfishness being the real serpent in Eden, and they provide a fable for the inner development of selfish Martin himself.

5.

Fortunately, they also do something else, providing us with the densest and most significant treatment of the American theme we can find in any nineteenth-century British novel. The episode starts when Martin makes his "desperate resolution" to go to America. From the start the omens look grim. His overly cheerful servant and Sancho Panza, Mark

Tapley, agrees to accompany him, explaining that he needs some real disaster in order to make his unrelieved cheerfulness into real virtue, and he takes it for granted that this is a journey to misfortune, a "very likely place for me to be jolly in." On the cart to London he hears about "Lummy Ned," who went to the States, made a fortune, and lost it next day in "six-and-twenty banks as broke." His friend Tom Pinch warns him of the dangers – "Don't be so dreadfully regardless of yourself. Don't go to America!" – and so does Mary, the girl he loves. The grim sea-voyage by "the fast-sailing line-of-packet ship, 'The Screw,'" introduces him to the world of immigrant expectations, no less deluded than Martin's even greater ones. Dickens makes a fine comic scene of that classic moment, the arrival in the New World. Landing in New York, he is greeted by newsboys ("Here's this morning's New York Sewer! . . . Here's this morning's New York Stabber . . . Here's the papers, here's the papers!"). He is asked, even before he lands, how he likes the country, and advised of the promise of the new nation and the imminent demise of his own. He is warned that success and rank now only depend on intelligence and virtue, which can be measured by dollars: "Martin was very glad to hear this, feeling well assured that if intelligence and virtue led, as a matter of course, to the acquisition of dollars, he would speedily become a great capitalist." Soon he is introduced to various oddly down-at-heel successes of noisy, paper-filled New York City, each of whom professes deep egalitarianism but bears some title ("there were no fewer than four majors present, two colonels, one general and a captain . . . There seemed to be no man without a title: for those who had not attained to military honours were either doctors, professors, or reverends"), and each of whom is presented to him as "one of the most remarkable men in our country." Within pages, Dickens has dickensianized the whole American world.

Critics have often complained of a marked tonal difference between the British and American parts of the book, and the different kind of characterization used. Peter Conrad puts it plainly: "The English characters are poetic fantasists, their American counterparts prosaic ranters. The English have too much character, and are immured in monomania; the Americans have no character at all, and hope to borrow some from the institutions to which they adhere." In fact they are mostly types, journalists, politicians, republican bores, tricksters and operators of the timbre of Major Pawkins, who

In commercial affairs . . . was a bold speculator. In plainer terms he had a most distinguished genius for swindling, and could start a bank, or negotiate a loan, or form a land-jobbing company (entailing ruin, pestilence, and death, on hundreds of families), with any gifted creature in the Union. This made him an admirable man of business. He could hang around a bar-room, discussing the affairs of the nation, for twelve hours together; and in that time could hold forth with more intolerable dullness, chew more tobacco, smoke more tobacco, drink more rum-toddy, mint-julep, gin-sling, and cock-tail, than any private gentleman of his acquaintance. This made him an orator and a man of the people.

No doubt there is a difference, though the themes of the American episodes and characterizations perfectly match the events of the British chapters, with which they are always cross-cut. Mr Pecksniff is another money-hungry hypocrite, creator of a false prospectus, a maker of deceits; Jonas Chuzzlewit is involved in a corrupt joint stock company, and on his way to becoming a murderer. But what is true is that, where Pecksniff is part of a much larger, humanly very varied British scene, and his faults are highly personal, the American characters tend to be caricatures, quickly caught types all bearing a family resemblance to each other (as Conrad puts it, Dickens suggests that when you've seen all Americans, you've seen one). For all his vivid love of particular detail, Dickens is clearly interested in generalizing about American failings, and this part of the book is heavy with direct authorial commentary. With the clear exception of Mr Bevan, the one virtuous and self-critical American, the characters are mostly examples of the corruption of the American Dream itself, each of them wrapping themselves in the flag to disguise their various dishonesties. So corrupt politicians are described as an expression of "the Spirit of Republicanism"; commercial trickery is seen as American industriousness and energy; snobbery and tuft-hunting are hidden under claims of "brotherly love and natural equality"; behind the Spirit of Freedom is the fact of slavery. Above all, as in *American Notes*, there is the Almighty Dollar, the greatest corruption of American possibilities.

In developing all this, Dickens chooses to relate Martin's voyage to an insistent satire on American contradictions – the fundamental difference that existed, as it always had, between the American Dream and the actuality. It was this that led to American complaints that the book was unduly acrimonious. Acrimonious it is; Dickens regularly comments authorially on the corrupting power of commerce and the dollar ("Make commerce one huge lie and mighty theft. Deface the banner of the nation for an idle rag; pollute it star by star; and cut out stripe by stripe as from the arm of a degraded soldier. Do anything for dollars! What is a flag to *them*!"). Mark must learn that pursuit of money does not bring happiness, especially when it is represented as advancing the cause of mankind. In a novel about hypocrisy, Dickens endlessly multiplies examples of its American brand (slavery disguised by appeals to "Liberty and Moral Sensibility," and so on). But what really affronted Americans was that, where in depicting English life he shows selfishness as part of a larger picture, seeing it as an individual rather than a national distortion, in the American sections he displays selfishness and hypocrisy as part of a collective national "cant." So he speaks of the "cant of a class, and a large class" of Americans, who "avow themselves senseless to the high principles on which America sprang, a nation, into life," and so put "in hazard the rights of nations yet unborn, and the very progress of the human race." Apart from Mr Bevan, Martin meets no examples of the happier facets of American life, or the positive side of American institutions – as Dickens in fact had on his own visit. What's more, it was also very clear that, with characteristic Dickensian extravagance, the great English celebrity was taking very considerable satirical advantage of his own American experience. Martin is consistently treated *as* a celebrity, even though Dickens was, and Martin is not. He constantly attends levees, great scenes of speech-making, meetings with literary figures. There are regular attempts to solicit his support and patronage ("In literature or art; the bar, the pulpit, or the stage; in one or other, if not all, I feel certain to succeed," writes one supplicant). He is repeatedly challenged (as Dickens himself was) for his British condescension, his European guilt and corruption, his refusal to celebrate American life before he has seen it, his failure to proclaim American ingenuity, heroism, grandeur, cunning, glory and virtuous innocence. Evidently Dickens was extravagantly purging, through the form of comedy, the more absurd aspects of what he felt he had suffered himself.

But the story never loses sight of its mythic direction. From the start we know Martin is on a deluded quest: the pursuit of money at any price. It's also clear that the voyage is his purgatory, or, as Dickens says, his "education," through which he learns himself and human nature. Beyond the satirical detail and bitter commentary, we can see his journey falls into four distinct stages: the introductory experiences in New York City; the midway episode in the National Hotel and the

Eden Settlement Office; the disastrous purgation in the communitarian experiment of Eden itself; the journey homeward, with Martin in changed heart. Because the story is picaresque, some of the episodes, characters and examples of American boasting ("Our fellow-countryman is a model of a man, quite fresh from Natur's mould . . . Rough he may be. So air our Barrs") are over-repetitious. But others are superb satire, especially on the great American culture-hunger. And behind it is the deeper theme – Dickens' darkly comic version of the mythic journey westward, the search for innocence, paradise and, of course, wealth. Like many heroes and discoverers in this traffic before him, Martin is making his journey not just to mid-America, but to the millennial, prelapsarian Utopia it stands for, the place of eternal American innocence, where all shall be well and all manner of things shall be well.[10] Dickens was not the only writer to look sceptically at this guiding American myth; Hawthorne and Melville did the same; in fact it is one of the repeated ironies that runs through American literature. But he was the most blatantly satirical, the frankest and funniest ironist of Utopia, the glorious dream-land that has urged on the human mind so often, and so often been found at odds with human nature and simple common sense.

What is so striking about the American part of *Martin Chuzzlewit* is that Dickens clearly knew this Utopian lore very well, and everything that went with it: the terrestrial paradise, the virgin land, the redeeming frontier, eternal perfection, the communal Utopia, the American Adam, the myth of the renewed Golden Age, the land of New Harmony in the West. He had done his homework on the sceptical British travellers' tales and the many immigrant tracts. He also knew the Eden myth of Chateaubriand, to whom he alludes directly. Martin has trained with Mr Pecksniff as an architect; architecture, or the making of the good and harmonious community, is a main theme of the book – in fact of all his novels. It is not surprising that before long he is

[10] There are several classic and important studies of this fundamental American motif. R. W. B. Lewis, *The American Adam: Innocence, Tragedy and Tradition in the Nineteenth Century* (Chicago, University of Chicago Press, 1955), notes that in the mid-nineteenth century "the image contrived to embody the most fruitful contemporary [American] ideas was that of the authentic American as a figure of heroic innocence and vast potentialities, poised at the start of a new history . . . It was an image crowded with illusion . . ." His book is a study of how, among the leading American writers, the image was both affirmed and tested. Also see Harry Levin, *The Power of Blackness: Hawthorne, Poe, Melville* (New York, Vintage, 1958).

offered "a reasonable opening in Eden," the new settlement on the banks of the Mississippi which, when inspected on the map in the Eden Settlement Office, is a flourishing, architectural city in the wilderness. In fact it is the American Dream itself: "What are the great United States for, sir," asks General Choke, offering him this opportunity of paradise, "if not for the regeneration of man?" Negative warnings are plain. Mr Scadder, the agent, is a man with two distinct sides to his face, and the prototypical American confidence man, as well as a version of the grim figure from fairy tale who lures innocents to misfortune. Mark Tapley is warned that "nobody as goes to Eden comes back a-live"; the ferry-boat that takes them onward is like Charon's boat; the landscape they sail through is half-growing, half-decaying. Eden (based, in fact, on Cairo, Illinois) not surprisingly proves a half-derelict settlement, like "the grim domains of the Giant Despair." ("The waters of the Deluge might have left it but a week before: so choked with slime and matted growth was the hideous swamp that bore that name.") Agriculture has virtually ceased, the cabins are in a state of collapse, and (Dickens comes back to his central metaphor, money and national credit) "the most tottering, abject, and forlorn among them was called, with great propriety, the Bank, and National Credit Office. It had some feeble props about it, and was settling deep down in the mud, past all recovery."

Yet decaying Eden actually *does* provide for the regeneration of man. Martin falls ill of the prevailing fever, goes through a dark night of the soul, comes close to death. When the same thing happens to Mark Tapley, who has lovingly nursed him, he begins to learn the lesson of his own selfishness: ". . . the curtain slowly rose a very little way; and Self, Self, Self, was shown below." As he comes to understand: "Eden was a hard school to learn such a lesson in; but there were teachers in swamp and thicket, and the pestilential air, who had a searching method of their own." The lesson is that man cannot be regenerated from without, by sinless nature. Here the blight outside is the mirror of the blight within: "he felt and knew the failings of his life, and saw distinctly what an ugly spot it was." As Martin becomes aware of his real disease, selfishness, the chain of humanity begins to reform. He recrosses America (more social satire) and sails for England, leaving America behind with an image of its phoenix-like redemption and promise – he sees the nation itself "springing from the ashes of its faults and vices, and soaring up anew into the sky." The myth is clear.

Through the degenerate Utopia, the false terrestrial paradise, Martin has been regenerated: "So low had Eden brought him down. So high had Eden raised him up." His fortunes end reasonably happily, in one of those communitarian new families, half inside, half outside the social order, that so often replace the harsh institutional family in Dickens' novels. Utopia lies not in some arcadian paradise but in a middle settlement, in natural human communities and inside the human heart.

In *Martin Chuzzlewit*, according to Peter Conrad, Dickens is overthrowing the key American myth of redemptive Eden: "his imagination, like his finest characters, is abnormal, improper, comically unregenerate . . . Hence, when America constitutes paradise, Dickens longs for the fall." Another way of saying this is to note that Dickens is treating the American Edenic pastoral with a historical doubt and moral scepticism also apparent in some of his finest American contemporaries. Dickens, we should not forget, was attentive to the spirit and direction of current American literature. Significantly, he takes the trouble to insert, in the course of Martin's return journey, a brief satiric episode where he meets two L.L.s, Literary Ladies, Miss Toppit and Miss Codger. The ladies are part of an important new American phenomenon; they are Transcendentalists (" 'Mind and matter,' said the lady in the wig, 'glide swift into the vortex of immensity. Howls the sublime, and softly sleeps the calm Ideal, in the whispering chambers of the Imagination. To hear it, sweet it is. But then, outlaughs the stern philosopher, and saith to the Grotesque, "What ho! arrest for me that Agency. Go, bring it here!" And so the vision fadeth.' ") This is much to the point: Dickens had considerable sympathies with Transcendentalist thought (he had said if he lived in Boston he would have been a Transcendentalist), shared its philanthropic bias, anti-utilitarianism and anti-mechanism, its assault on the life of quiet desperation. But he was no pure idealist, drawn to the new equation of Soul and Oversoul. Like Carlyle, the friend to whom he dedicated *Hard Times*, he shared Transcendentalism's hope but distrusted its ethereal detachment from the realm of hard fact ("You seem to me in danger of dividing yourselves from the Fact of this present Universe, in which alone, ugly as it is, can I find any anchorage," Carlyle wrote to *his* friend, Emerson). Like many British comic novelists (it is notable that many British novelists, past and present, writing about America have been comic novelists), he was an empiricist – an observer of the contradictions and self-deceits of human nature, an ironist, distrustful of grand trips into the empyrean. And if his American visit seems to have had one effect above all others, it was to turn him further away from abstract idealism toward a darkened humanism and scepticism, qualities that seem essential to the maturity and greatness of his later works. Dickens had, in fact, applied to his American experience that vein of comic, sceptical realism for which, for good or bad, British fiction was to be famous. And why not? When the idealists and utopian dreamers among us rise up, as they so often do, with their transcendental wonderlands, there is much to be said for the spirit of irony.

6.

There is another very important aspect to the American scenes of *Martin Chuzzlewit*; the impact of America not just on Dickens' view of human nature but on his basic fictional style. It is a well-known fact that Dickens' portraits of English life, especially in the early works, feel modern but are frequently not quite contemporary, and allude to an older order. In the English sections of *Martin Chuzzlewit*, the journey from Salisbury to London, taken several times in the story, is done by stagecoach or cart, never by train. Offices are old and musty, and though there is contemporary bustle the flavour of past life persists, emblemized by the shadow of the Monument that falls across the book. By contrast the America of his novel is a contemporary place, present American fact constantly swamping the older American dream. The American world he creates is modern, commercial, industrial, mechanical – far more so than it is in most of the American novels published around the same date. It is a world where the press runs the show, the speculator is in charge, the machine is dominant over nature – where, as de Tocqueville put it, "everything is in constant motion." If the British and American chapters do show a marked difference in style, as the critics say, this is one essential reason. Cross-cutting as he does between British scenes and American ones, the contrast comes over with a particular sharpness, as when, for example, we cut from the sound of someone knocking at Pecksniff's very rural door to the sound of "an American railway train at full speed." The futuristic engines of the present are ever at work in America: the steamboat and the locomotive. "How the wheels clank and rattle, and the tram-road shakes, as the train rushes on! And how the engine yells, as if it were lashed and tortured like a living labourer, and writhed in agony," he writes, adding: "A poor fancy; for steel and iron are of infinitely greater account, in this commonwealth, than flesh and blood." Dickens may resent the triumph of Emerson's "things in the saddle," and it is the engine of the present that dehumanizes; the America that dreams of pastoral is no longer a pastoral land, is the America of "the machine in the garden,"[11] to which his American contemporaries were only just starting to respond. Yet what he resists emotionally he responds to imaginatively, with a deep change of imagery and language, yielding to the pressure of stylistic stress and strain. Critics still argue about whether Dickens' American scenes were "necessary." But they were certainly necessary if Dickens was to explore how, in the fast-changing world of iron and steel, Carlyle's age of men "grown mechanical in heart and head," he was to write a new kind of novel. Dickens' American scenes signal a deep change in the fiction of the 1840s on both sides of the Atlantic as, with the old utopias going, writers were learning to write of an age not in pastoral stasis but rapid mechanical change.

And in his next book, *Dombey and Son* (1846–8), a novel of the teeming and changing modern city, Dickens did exactly that: with it we now feel ourselves to be fully in the world of the Victorian novel. The 1840s were the founding era of a new kind of fiction, right across Europe, as the times changed their vision of life. In the fiction of Dickens, Thackeray, Mrs Gaskell, Disraeli and the Brontës in Britain, Stendhal, Balzac and Flaubert in France, Gogol, Pushkin and Dostoevsky in Russia, the form begins to open out to an age of growth and contradiction: to teeming cities and their lower depths, to crime and poverty, to crowds and strange impressions, to interweaving, contradictory, polyphonous voices, to the sound of the crowd, the beat of the engine, the hum of the factory, the clank of the machine. And so, if in a different way, it does in the American fiction of the same decade – above all in the work of Hawthorne and Melville, the two essential

11 On the emergence of this theme in American literature in the 1840s, see Leo Marx, *The Machine in the Garden: Technology and the Pastoral Ideal in America* (New York, Oxford University Press, 1964), which follows out the process of the incorporation of the machine, most familiarly typified by the railway locomotive, into the pastoral and arcadian myth of America.

novelists of the period. Their work is far less obsessively social than that of most of their European contemporaries, and preserves more of that tradition of romance represented by Cooper and his successors. Hawthorne constantly professed his distrust of "the Present, the Immediate, the Actual," and his faith in the "Imaginary"; Melville in *The Confidence Man: His Masquerade* (1857), a book about national deception that owes not a little to Dickens, noted: "It is with fiction as with religion; it should present another world, and yet one to which we feel the tie." Yet the note of modern industrializing change visibly runs through the writing of both of them. Hawthorne wrote of the difficult relation of the deformities of the human heart, the world of what he called, in *The Blithedale Romance* (1853), "self, self, self" (it is not the only Dickensian echo in the novel), and the need to form a magnetic chain of being. Melville, initially a writer of Polynesian pastoral, wrote of an arcadian and natural world that was dying, and an age of industrialism and moving history that was taking its place. Both came to challenge the pastoralizing, regenerative myth so important to American sensibility, to test the idea of the American Adam in his eternal innocence, to see that that age of nature was becoming the age of the machine, to find a blackness, or blankness, hidden in American dreams. At a different level both took the mythology that Dickens had explored and caricatured, and the modern process he saw in train, and gave it the shape of an American tragedy.

The fact is that, in deciding to take *Martin Chuzzlewit* off in the American direction, Dickens created a radically fresh note in fiction, as well as a remarkable if bitterly critical portrait of an emblematic land. The book's tone, its comic attack, even its note of utopian disappointment, shaped many later European writers in their treatment of America; it even entered the tone of the fiction Americans wrote themselves. The book is – of course, like all books – a period piece, about Chartist and early-Victorian illusion and disillusion with a particular American moment, but it was a moment when America was discovering something new about itself and its relation to history. Then, with the Civil War, and the technological innovation it stimulated both at the time and in the age that followed, America changed; and to itself and to those in Europe who followed its fate it came to stand for something quite different. It was no longer a pastoral dream but an industrial one, no longer a land of individualistic enterprise but of corporate activity. It was no longer associated with a pristine past, but with a modernized future. The age of pastoral Edenic dreams and the high American romance was largely over and done. Transcendentalism too had passed away, and most of its writers with it. Now the machine dominated, and the locomotive, clanking and rattling, rushed right across the interlinked continent. As for the new American writing of the day, that was now couched far less in the language of arcadian romance, more in that of chastened realism. And Dickens' vision, slipping away into history, became less of an affront, more the vivid record of a crux in American historical development.

7.

In the winter of 1867-8, just twenty-five years after his first visit, Charles Dickens visited America again. The time was the immediate aftermath of the Civil War, and that terrible conflict had in fact delayed a tour he had long had in mind. It was a very different event, at a very different time. America had indeed deeply changed, and so as well had Dickens. He was now the most famous writer in the world, with – though he did not know it – nearly all of his major fiction already written. In recent years he had extended his fame and fortunes in Britain with his great reading tours and self-dramatizations, to which, according to a highly punishing schedule, he now devoted most of his time. At last, following an important American custom, he was coming to the United States on a lecture tour, to present these dramatized readings to Americans. In Boston on his previous visit, he had already encountered the American taste for Lyceum lectures, and in *Martin Chuzzlewit* Martin hears of a typical schedule: "The Philosophy of Crime" on Mondays, "Government" on Tuesdays, "The Philosophy of the Vegetable" on Fridays. The transcontinental literary lecture tour had in fact now become a familiar phenomenon (as Oscar Wilde's Lord Illingworth was to say, in *A Woman of No Importance*, "All Americans lecture, I believe. I suppose it is something in their climate"), and British lecturers had already proven especially popular. It was as a lecturer that Thackeray came to America in 1852-3, and from the 1860s on – when big lecture agencies were established – many British writers, including Charles Kingsley, Wilkie Collins, Matthew Arnold and the youthful and outrageous Oscar Wilde, made their way round the profitable, and hospitable, circuit. It became a mark of fame, and a significant extra source of literary income, as well as a way of seeing America and gathering material. "I . . . agglomerate dollars with prodigious rapidity," Thackeray noted appreciatively on his own tour; evidently English novelists were not eternally averse to the value of the Almighty Dollar.

Nor was Dickens, who had sent his agent Dolby ahead to test the water, carefully did his financial transactions, and estimated he might earn £10,000 from a four-and-a-half-month tour – a just reward, he seems to have felt, for the fortunes the American custom of book pirating had deprived him of.[12] And in the event, of all the many tours that now flourished in the age of the steamship and easy internal train travel, no tour was more notable nor more successful than Dickens'. Despite his earlier writings, and the fact that, despite his hatred of slavery, he had implicitly supported the South during the Civil War, there was, this time, no acrimony, no bitterness, no political unhappiness. His public message, delivered even before he sailed, was one of effusive transatlantic friendship. The troubled Anglo-American relations of twenty-five years earlier had largely disappeared into the past. If some British writers did still manage sometimes to condescend to their American cousins, it was generally in a spirit of far greater sympathy, and born of a far closer contact. The Americans put themselves out to welcome the man who had become the world's most famous writer; the streets of Boston were swept twice in advance of his arrival. Vast lines queued overnight at the ticket offices to hear his reading performances, so much talked of ahead of time they did not even have to be advertised. Six thousand came in Philadelphia, eight thousand in Brooklyn, and the final performance in Boston collected $3,456 at the box office, a theatrical record. His novels sold in quite extraordinary quantities, and his lecture earnings wildly exceeded his own predictions, amounting to a remarkable $200,000. Everywhere he went he enjoyed a triumphant passage, and the American press was particularly warm in his praise. As was everywhere acknowledged, he performed superbly, "mesmerically" (unlike some of his compatriots, such as the less than audible Matthew Arnold), reading the famous

[12] The experiences of nineteenth-century British writers on the American lecture circuit are entertainingly discussed in Philip Collins, " 'Agglomerating Dollars With Prodigious Rapidity': British Pioneers on the American Lecture Circuit," in J. R. Kincaid and A. J. Kuhn (eds), *Victorian Literature and Society: Essays Presented to Richard D. Altick* (Ohio State University Press, 1984), to which I am indebted.

passages, recreating on-stage his famous characters, holding audiences spellbound everywhere.

At the final dinner given by two hundred of the American Press in New York City, Dickens made a striking speech, warmly acknowledging "the amazing changes I have seen around me on every side, – changes moral, changes physical, changes in the amount of land subdued and peopled, changes in the rise of vast new cities, changes in the growth of older cities almost out of recognition, changes in the graces and amenities of life, changes in the Press, without whose advancement no advancement can take place anywhere." He spoke warmly of the "unsurpassable politeness, delicacy, sweet temper, hospitality, consideration, and . . . unsurpassable respect for privacy" with which he had been received, assured his audience (to their disappointment) that he would never write another American book, and promised, "so long as I live," to reprint this testimony "as an appendix to every copy of those two books of mine in which I have referred to America." The final peace was made, the tour ended with a last triumph. However, as his American friends and admirers noted, Dickens throughout appeared under strain, and was looking prematurely aged. He was still in his middle fifties, but the extended tour, his demanding performances, the American winter and its ailments, had clearly strained him. His health, already enfeebled, grew steadily worse over the course of the visit. It was never to be fully restored; and by the time he came back to Britain, his fictional career was already coming to its close. He never did write another American book; indeed he would start, and never finish, only one more novel, *The Mystery of Edwin Drood*. Two years later, on 8 June 1870, at the age of 58, he died suddenly at his home at Gad's Hill Place. With him, it was generally agreed, there also died the high era of the Victorian novel, a major period of writing. It was later noticed that of the large fortune that he left on his death, one-fifth came from his reading tour in the United States.

At Dickens' valedictory reading in New York City, there sat in the audience a young American writer from the same Mississippi Valley where Martin Chuzzlewit had stumbled upon his stagnant Eden, and where he had learned the lesson of the regeneration of man. Mark Twain had only just begun his own career, and he would come to fame a year later with a book, *The Innocents Abroad, Or the New Pilgrim's Progress*, that reflected the new age of transatlantic tourism that had dawned after the Civil War, a book about a European tour meant to suggest to the reader "how he would be likely to see Europe and the East if he looked at them with his own eyes instead of those who travelled in these countries before him."[13] Twain himself would shortly be taking his place on the same international reading circuit that Dickens had travelled, offering his audiences comic and sentimental performances of no less power and impact. And his novels, those wonderful comic satires looking at the vast distance that had been travelled between the old pastoral Mississippi Valley and the age of the machine and new industrialism, would duly earn him a reputation as the American Dickens. Meanwhile, just as Dickens returned to America, another young American writer, Henry James, was starting out on his own literary adventures on the "lighted stage" of Europe, and, following his chosen "complex fate," was setting out to write of a world that had been cosmopolitanized and internationalized by the transatlantic traffic. He would soon become an inheritor, and a new energizer, of the tradition not just of the American but the British novel. So, as Dickens died, a new age in transatlantic reflections and refractions was just beginning, and for that matter a new age in the fortunes of the novel. But there was no doubt of the importance to it all of Dickens' shadow – or of his ambiguous American glimpse of the regeneration of man. Yet Dickens' sour vision of the wonder of America was never quite forgotten. It took a long time before British fictional treatments of America were thought by Americans as anything other than critical or condescending. British writers, it seemed, were not inclined to cast America in the romantic glow that came from many German nineteenth-century novels, or offer the same sense of wondrous modernity that was often displayed by the French. Blowing up the 'Merrikins became, with *Martin Chuzzlewit*, a kind of British literary custom, almost an act of friendship, and it took nearly a century for this really to change.

[13] The new tourist traffic worked both ways across the Atlantic, unleashing on the British public another large wave of travel books about America in the years after 1865. Regular steamship services and good rail networks made the journey easier, as was clear from Henry Morford's *Morford's Short-Trip Guide to America* (1877), which noted that "steam-transit between the two continents" was now "so rapid and reliable that the ocean passage . . . [was] now little more than that of a ferry." Morford's guide was also highly reassuring on safety, remarking that it was worth remembering that "more than an hundred runs are made without a single accident, and more than five hundred without the total loss of a vessel." I am indebted for this quotation to R. A. Burchill, *British Travellers Report on the White Conquest of the Trans-Mississippi West* (London, The British Library, 1993).

FOUR

The Rogue and the Detectives:
Hawthorne, Melville and the European ruins

I.

In April 1841, amid a sudden snowstorm, Nathaniel Hawthorne, then aged thirty-six, set out from Boston on an exciting adventure. Like Dickens he was going to Utopia – though happily in his case it lay only nine miles away, on the Charles River at West Roxbury, in rural Massachusetts. Here, on an old farm, was forming one of those novel colonies or brotherhoods that had been part of American life from the first Puritan settlements: alternative societies dedicated to this sect or that schism, this or that wise guru, this Pantisocracy (the ideal society Coleridge and others planned on the banks of the Susquehanna) or that new socialistic way of living, nowadays shaped by the reforming socialist-arcadian ideas of Robert Owen or Charles Fourier. "What are the great United States for, sir, if not for the regeneration of man?" General Choke asks Martin Chuzzlewit in Dickens' novel of the following year, pointing the way to Eden. And what indeed? Utopia was a part of the American Dream itself – dedicated as it was to millenarian ideals – of Virgin Land, the City Upon A Hill, the frontier of the New Man, the promise of the New Start. And in New England – that land of mission that gave America so many religions, from Wonder-Working Providence to the Great Awakening, Latter-Day Saints to Christian Science – such Utopian visions were widespread. "We are all a little wild here with numberless projects of social reform," Ralph Waldo Emerson, leader of the Transcendentalist movement, wrote to his British friend Thomas Carlyle in 1840. "Not a reading man but has a draft of a new community in his pocket. I am gently mad myself, and am resolved to live cleanly. George Ripley is taking up a colony of agriculturalists and scholars, with whom he threatens to take the field and the book. One man renounces the use of animal food; and another of coin; and another of domestic hired service; and another of the State; and on the whole we have a commendable share of reason and hope." It was to George Ripley's Transcendentalist community of agriculturalists and scholars, taking shape at Brook Farm, West Roxbury, that Hawthorne, with a band of the best of Boston, set out in a snowstorm just a year later.

Why not? Given his origins, Hawthorne seemed destined for Transcendentalism. Born in 1804, in the witch-haunted port of Salem, Massachusetts, he came of a family that went right back to the Pilgrim Fathers and the Puritan ascendancy. One of his ancestors, William Hathorne – Nathaniel himself added the 'w' to the family name – migrated from near Macclesfield, Cheshire, at the start of Massachusetts Colony in 1630, to become a leading Puritan with a reputation for "pitiless severity." His son, Judge John Hathorne, was a judge at the still-remembered Salem Witch Trial of 1692, though later he regretted his part in it. These two steeple-hatted figures were to bequeath to Hawthorne some of the imaginative stimulation that shaped – and the creative guilt that nearly silenced – his first and most famous novel, *The Scarlet Letter* (1850). Then in the eighteenth century, when millennial dreams began to turn into commercial adventures, Salem grew rich on the East India trade. So did the Hawthornes, who became seafarers. Nathaniel's grandfather won fame for commanding a privateer in the Revolutionary War. His father, captain of the *America*, sailed the Pacific, and died of typhoid in Surinam when Nathaniel was four. Rich but declining, Salem was now becoming a place of history and faded grandeurs, stocked with Puritan traces, genteel but impoverished families, fine seafarers' houses, memories of the past. All this would go into Hawthorne's second novel, *The House of the Seven Gables*. As a result Nathaniel grew up in a household of women, dependent on relatives, and a reclusive environment, rather like that of the Pyncheons in his novel (there were murmurs of incest in the background). By now the old Puritanism had almost faded, softening into a far less doctrinal and more benign religion, Unitarianism (it was said of its devotees that they believed in at the most one God, and prayed To Whom It May Concern). But even Unitarianism was too doctrinal for some, like Emerson. By the time Hawthorne reached adult life, the climate was changing again. Now came the even vaguer and grander faith of Transcendentalism – in which God shook hands with Coleridge and Kant, the Seen with the Unseen, the Soul with the

Oversoul, the Poet with the Universe, and an "optative mood" prevailed.[1]

Like many good writers of his day – they included Dickens and his future friend Herman Melville – Hawthorne hence came from a family that had been up but was now a little down in the world, from a background of Great Expectations dashed. He was also intensely conscious of the historical and religious weight on his family, region and imaginative sensibility, as they followed the New England path from Puritan devotion to the age of modern getting and spending. When in time his very reclusiveness led him to become a writer, the lasting mark of this powerful bloodstained past – its taint, its stain, its guilt – would be imprinted on his work. It meant that if there was writing (and poetry, the imagination, was one of the great instruments of the Transcendentalists, who considered the poet the voice of the universe and the Oversoul) there was also guilt about writing, a remembrance of the Puritan distrust of the realm of idle imagining. There were other guilts, too, not least over the matter of his whole relation to his age and society. Early in life, Hawthorne had acquired what he would call "a cursed habit of solitude," a dependence on the solitary life of the imagination. Through his busy life, he would never really acquire an entirely enthusiastic attitude toward reality – society, the commonplace, the everyday world, where so much is a-doing and so little is done. An early childhood injury to his foot (a disability he oddly shared with his great admirer and literary descendant, Henry James) kept him for a time from school. His family, already reclusive, withdrew for a while to the wilderness of rural Maine, where he "ran quite wild." When, from 1821 to 1825, he attended Bowdoin College in Brunswick, Maine (where classmates included Henry Wadsworth Longfellow and Franklin Pierce, future president of the United States), he was a withdrawn student. He withdrew into writing a novel about withdrawal, *Fanshawe*, which he published in 1828 at his own expense, then withdrew from print. After he went home to Salem in 1825, he withdrew upstairs into his "haunted chamber," a room under the eaves in the house his mother rented from relatives, and sat down to write. "In this dismal and squalid chamber FAME was won," he wrote ironically later.

[1] The main life is Arlin Turner's *Nathaniel Hawthorne: A Biography* (New York and London, Oxford University Press, 1980), but also see Edwin Haviland Miller's *Salem Is My Dwelling Place* (London, Duckworth, 1991).

It was, but not until after he had done a twelve-year apprenticeship as an unknown and unappreciated writer. Like many early American authors in a time dominated by sentimental female album fiction or pirated works from Britain, his works would always seem half-reclusive productions. Nor were they a financial success; the stories he wrote under the eaves were hardly commercial. They came from the conflicts of his own life: of past and present, old Calvinism and new Romanticism, the solitary imagination and the life of society. They examined the conflict of nature and religion, the guilt of authorship, their own nature as text or writing. All through his life he would puritanically continue to associate writing with retreat, avoidance, the dubious standpoint of the watcher on the world. Unsurprisingly, this has provoked modern critics and psychologists (most fascinatingly the French critic Jean Normand, who studied what he calls Hawthorne's complex "interior cinema") into elaborate speculation about the nature of his odd and disturbing creativity.[2] The problem can be exaggerated. A taste for solitude is not uncommon in writers; many authors are very sensibly the reverse of adventurers – inner speculators, shapers of self-created signs, explorers of the distinctive universe of fiction and the imaginary. And, as we shall see, Hawthorne always chose to exaggerate, mythologize, his own solitude and separation from the rush of life, make it part of the very drama of creation. Even so, as solitaries go, Hawthorne, while never as extreme as a fellow New Englander, the reclusive poet Emily Dickinson, can be put fairly high on the list.

But it is important to remember that for Hawthorne – as for Poe and Melville, the other great American explorers of fiction in his generation – obscurity was a real literary fact. Writers' careers were only just starting to exist. His early stories appeared, either anonymously or under pseudonyms, in a variety of ill-paying popular albums and magazines. Many were rejected, and, when rejected, often burned. It took twelve years before the tales he wrote in solitude – they include some of his finest and most famous, like "My Kinsman, Major Molineux," "Roger Malvin's Burial," "The Minister's Black Veil,"

---

[2] Two important studies of Hawthorne's creativity are Jean Normand, *Nathaniel Hawthorne: An Approach to an Analysis of Literary Creation*, trans. Derek Coltman (Cleveland and London, The Press of Case Western Reserve University, 1970), and Frederick Crews's more Freudian *The Sins of the Fathers: Hawthorne's Psychological Themes* (New York and London, Oxford University Press, 1966).

and "Young Goodman Brown," mostly about the power of the Puritan heritage – attracted real attention. He came to see himself as "the obscurest man of letters in America"; as late as 1847 Edgar Allan Poe, himself a specialist in the pains and struggles of literary obscurity, still called him "*the* example, *par excellence*, in this country, of the privately-admired and publicly-unappreciated man of genius." But then, near the close of the 1830s, Hawthorne began emerging into the light. In 1837 the first work to bear his name, *Twice-Told Tales*, a collection of eighteen stories (some among his best), came out. The book represented, he said, his "attempts, and very imperfectly successful ones, to open an intercourse with the world." They sold poorly, but won him critical respect, especially thanks to a laudatory review from his Bowdoin classmate Henry Wadsworth Longfellow. They also came out at a crucial time. 1837 was a year of financial panic, the aftermath of Jacksonian economics, which put American dreams into doubt; but the nation was also seeing its Manifest Destiny extend in the West. It was also a time when a fundamental change, a deepening, a sense of greater complexity, was taking hold in American culture. What F. O. Matthiessen defines as "the American Renaissance" – actually a Naissance, the first real declaration of a significant American literature – now truly began to disclose itself ("the starting point for this book was my realization of how great a number of our great masterpieces were produced in one extraordinary concentrated moment of expression," Matthiessen was to explain in his great study *The American Renaissance*, the book that explores this theme[3]). The year of *Twice-Told Tales* was also the year of Emerson's "The American Scholar," of Edgar Allan Poe's *The Narrative of Arthur Gordon Pym*. Hawthorne's good fortune was that his attempt to open his "intercourse with the world" exactly coincided with Matthiessen's "one extraordinary concentrated moment of expression." And his career as a writer would follow its course, chart its evolution – and eventually register its demise.

The great change coming in American literature had much to do with the dawn of Transcendentalism – the great new thought-wave of mid-century New England, the part of America that had long seen itself as cultural hub and depository of national conscience and consciousness. A place of Great Awakenings, it woke again, stirred by this

[3] F. O. Matthiessen, *American Renaissance: Art and Expression in the Age of Emerson and Whitman* (New York and London, Oxford University Press, 1941).

belated, highly idealist, very optimistic American version of the European revolution, which would do so much to shape distinctive American literary identity. It must be said that what Transcendentalism actually meant was, and still remains, a touch obscure. "Transcendentalism means, says our accomplished Miss B., with a wave of the hand, *a little beyond*," Emerson noted in his journal, recording a meeting of his own and George Ripley's Transcendentalist Club in Boston in 1836, right at the start of it all. Emerson was the crucial figure, the former Unitarian minister from a family of ministers who, in 1832, doubted his faith and resigned his living, then sailed off to Europe to take the full blow of romantic idealist philosophy ("we go to Europe to be Americanized," he later explained). He returned to the historic village of Concord, Massachusetts (where was fired the revolutionary shot heard round the world) to reflect seriously on the American soul and its special relationship with the Universe. In 1837, that same crucial year of panic and change, he gave a famous Harvard oration, "The American Scholar." This is usually taken as a declaration of two things. One is as an opening statement of the spirit of Transcendentalism itself, and its idealist notion that "Life consists of what a man is thinking all day." The other is as an assertion of the need of the American arts to cut the link with the "courtly muses of Europe"; Oliver Wendell Holmes defined the oration as "our intellectual Declaration of Independence." By 1840, Transcendentalism was confident enough to begin its own magazine, *The Dial*, and was coming to seem the heart, soul and Oversoul of New England's reforming energy. Its philanthropic passion, its redemptive zeal, its optative mood, its symbolist imagination, its Romantic desire to read spiritual signs in natural facts, expressed the radicalism of the New England spirit. It questioned the rising industrial order, the life of getting and spending, smoking chimneys and crowded cities. It challenged the relation of the sexes, the mix of classes, the wrongs of slavery, the division of money and spirit, the collapse into mechanism and utility, and soon talked of the making of a new society. Above all it celebrated the poet, the imaginative maker, as the shaper of change. No wonder, then, that Hawthorne thought he too might be a Transcendentalist, and found his way to Brook Farm.

2.

By the early 1840s Transcendentalism was what the chattering classes of New England chattered about. And it was not just every reading man but every thinking woman who had a draft of a new community in his pocket, or her placket. It was George Ripley who planned the Utopian community of Brook Farm, and found the site at West Roxbury. But two leading advocates were Margaret Fuller and Elizabeth Peabody, powerful supporters of the new spirit and founder-editors of *The Dial*. Fuller, that passionate and powerfully intellectual feminist, would shortly reach the peak of her fame with *Women in the Nineteenth Century* (1845). Elizabeth Peabody, from Salem, would become known as "the godmother of Boston" and as the source for "Miss Birdseye" in Henry James's *The Bostonians* (1886). She wrote the prospectus for Brook Farm in *The Dial*, explaining its aim, which was to create "leisure to live in all the faculties of the soul." This was just the kind of accommodation young Transcendentalists were seeking, and the likes of Bronson Alcott, William Henry Channing, and the young Charles A. Dana, all names to conjure with in Brahmin Boston, gave their support and indeed their cash; Brook Farm was a joint stock company. It must be confessed that Hawthorne, with his "cursed habit of solitude," was never a natural member of a bold communitarian experiment. No more was Emerson, who was asked to join, but declined. He believed this was the age of "the first person singular" (it certainly was), and said that to join the scheme would upset his much trumpeted theory that "one man is the counterpoise to a city, – that a man is stronger than a city, that his solitude is more prevalent and beneficent than the concert of crowds." Hawthorne was just as much a believer in solitude, but his talents had been discovered by the energetic Elizabeth Peabody, who determined to bring him into the light. In 1839 she got him the post of weigher and gauger in the Boston Custom House – he resigned from it a year later, finding its excess of life stifled his imagination. Meantime, though, he had become engaged to Miss Peabody's semi-invalid sister Sophia, and was hunting an ideal home, located somewhere between the Actual and the Imaginary, near society but a little apart from it, for his married life. Brook Farm seemed the perfect answer. He invested the substantial sum of $1,000 in the project, and rode off, in the spring snowstorm, to join the great human experiment.

Like Charles Dickens, who would soon be setting off over the

Atlantic for his American Utopia – and like Miles Coverdale, the imperfect narrator-hero of *The Blithedale Romance* (1853), the retrospective novel Hawthorne wrote about this utopian adventure – he went off on his journey with an arcadian mythology, an entire version of the American dream, in his head. Like Dickens and Coverdale, he would not find himself quite at ease in the utopian life he had dreamed of. For he also set out with a burden of doubt and guilt, what he called his "involuntary reserve," a source of inner dismay which nonetheless, he said, had "given the objectivity to my writings." The reserve also took the form of comic irony, a sceptical eye cast over the romantic view of life. This was to be much in evidence in the arcadian experiences to follow. "Here is thy poor husband in a polar Paradise!" he wrote to Sophia. "Alas, what a difference between the ideal and the real!" he wrote in his notebook when May Day proved equally chilly. Utopia was soon granting him many comic or ironic paradoxes, like a snow-filled Eden. Brook Farm was a confident idyll, a very American dream indeed – some of its members used to head their letters home simply "Heaven." But communitarian dreams were constantly upset by hard fact, "leisure to live in all the faculties of the soul" by painful digging of potatoes, the life outside getting and spending with big cash-flow problems. Margaret Fuller's "transcendentalist heifer" would not yield milk: "She is not an amiable cow," he wrote (of the heifer), "but she has a very intelligent face, and seems to be of a reflective cast of character." Most of the problems of utopias and ideal human communities, sexual, ideological, and emotional, surfaced. It seemed Utopia was one reason why privacy was originally invented, just as paradise was a good reason for the invention of sin. There was another ancient problem of Eden. It was difficult to move from literary solitude to agriculture, even though, he claimed, "I feel the original Adam reviving in me." It proved hard to work out the relationship between digging potatoes and imaginative stimulation. Though Ripley praised him as "very athletic and able-bodied in the barnyard and field," Hawthorne complained that Ripley "perceives, or imagines, a more intimate connection between our present farming operations and our ultimate enterprise than is visible to my perceptions." Soon he was jotting in his notebook that "this present life of mine gives me an antipathy to pen and ink, even more than my Custom House experience did," and spending a good deal of time up a white pine tree, looking for the solitude and imaginative insight missing from the communitarian goings-on below.

"The real Me was never an associate of the community," he finally noted; "there has been a spectral appearance there, sounding the horn at daybreak, and milking the cows, and hoeing potatoes, and raking hay, toiling in the sun, and doing me the honor to assume my name. But this spectre was not myself." Meantime, a good Transcendentalist in this at least, he filled his notebooks with many observations on nature, including human, later to prove of considerable use. He noted a passion among the faithful for "magnetic miracles," various neo-scientific mysticisms like mesmerism (they also fascinated Dickens), looked with more secular attention on the arrival of a small seamstress from Boston ("she herself is an expression, well worth studying"). Finally eight months of paradise proved quite enough. He withdrew again, reflecting he could "best attain the higher ends of life by retaining his ordinary relation to society." But his last notebook contains several significant entries that show us his Brook Farm life was not wasted. "To symbolize moral or spiritual disease by disease of the body; – thus, when a person committed any sin, it might cause a sore to appear on the body; – this to be wrought out," he jotted, setting down the germ of what would be his greatest novel, *The Scarlet Letter*. And the notebooks as a whole would provide the germ for his most comic and satirical novel, *The Blithedale Romance* – his *Martin Chuzzlewit*, a book he would call "a faint and not very faithful shadowing of Brook Farm," though friends knew better. But both these works lay nearly a decade ahead in the future. By that time the great communitarian adventure had come to a less than idyllic end. The Phalanstery (the Fourierist name for the main social building) burned down in 1846. The entire community, which now had school and newspaper, closed down the following year, the land was sold. Margaret Fuller –who often visited the Farm to lecture ("I defended nature, as I always do"), and appears in Hawthorne's novel as the vivid character "Zenobia" – had responded to the impact of the great revolutions that swept through Europe in 1848, and gone to Italy to support the fight for liberation, and write a book about Mazzini – but, returning to New York in 1850, she drowned at sea in a shipwreck. But, in darker days, Brook Farm was remembered as a true American romance. As *Harper's Monthly* put it: "there were never such witty potato-patches and such sparkling cornfields before or since. The weeds were scratched out of the ground to the music of Tennyson and Browning, and the nooning was an hour as bright as any brilliant moonlight at Ambrose's." And *The Blithedale Romance* became the story of a past ambiguous Eden, a fascinating American Utopia – and one of the first campus novels.[4]

3·

As for Hawthorne, he did not really retreat all that far. He moved to Concord, renting a house, the Old Manse, from the Emerson family, "at the opposite extremity of [Emerson's] village." Here he began married life with Sophia in the summer of 1842. Concord was in process of changing from a village of "great simplicity" to a commercial town, linked by railroad to Boston in 1844: the industrial change sweeping America in the 1840s had arrived. So had Transcendentalism; many of the Transcendentalist circle – Emerson, Channing, Alcott, Margaret Fuller, and Henry David Thoreau, who set up his small hut at Walden Pond, near to nature and the Boston railroad – were all about, some even commuting to the Farm. As Hawthorne said, Transcendentalist fires burned here too, like "a beacon burning on a hilltop." But the change proved happy, married life pleasant, above all, living on potatoes and no money, he was writing again. Over the three Concord years he produced some twenty fine tales and sketches, including the famous "The Artist of the Beautiful" and "Rappaccini's Daughter." They went into his second book of tales, *Mosses from an Old Manse*, which appeared in 1846, a year after his lease ended and he returned to Salem. His preface whimsically records the Concord years, and shows his view of some of the Transcendentalist faithful; his doubts about the "optative mood" had plainly grown by the day. "Never was poor little country village invested with such a variety of queer, strangely dressed, oddly behaved mortals, most of whom took it on themselves to be important agents of the world's destiny, yet were simply bores of a very intense water," he reflected. What had drawn them was the presence of a "great original thinker" – Emerson, whose thought had, "in the brains of some people, wrought a singular giddiness – new truth being

[4] The best study of American Utopianism is Carl J. Guarneri, *The Utopian Alternative: Fourierism and Nineteenth Century America* (Ithaca, N.Y., Cornell University Press). Henry W. Sams (ed.), *Autobiography of Brook Farm* (Englewood Cliffs, N. J., Prentice Hall, 1958), also tells the story from the participants' point of view. And A. N. Kaul, *The American Vision: Actual and Ideal Society in Nineteenth-Century Fiction* (New Haven, Yale University Press, 1963), shows its literary importance.

as heady as new wine." It was a wine he had supped with caution: "For myself, there have been epochs in my life when I too might have asked of this prophet the master word that would solve me the riddle of the universe, but, now, being happy, I felt there were no questions to be put, and therefore admired Emerson as a poet of deep beauty and austere tenderness, but sought nothing from him as a philosopher." He felt he learned more from Thoreau, "a keen and delicate observer of nature – a genuine observer, which . . . is almost as rare a character as an original poet." Like most thinking people in his New England day, he took many of his bearings in relation to Transcendentalism. But it was an angular, critical, independent-minded pact he had with it. And as the stories he now wrote made clear, at least to a few, he had now come to see the world in darker, more ironic, more complicated shades.

It took another literary observer to see the crucial significance of this. Herman Melville was no New Englander, and had a more critical angle on its thought. Born in New York City in 1819, he grew up there and in Albany, the son of a successful businessman wiped out, driven to insanity and early death, by 1830s financial panics. Another young man with great expectations dashed, he was forced at twenty to go to sea, and led an adventurous life on sea-packets, whalers, navy vessels and steamboats of the Atlantic, the South Seas, and the Mississippi before he turned to writing. In 1846 his first book, *Typee*, about his exotic adventures among the cannibals of the Marquesas Islands, was taken in London by John Murray, and won great acclaim. He followed it with more traveller's tales – *Omoo* (1847), set in the South Seas, then an obscure "philosophical romance," *Mardi and a Voyage Thither* (1849). Hawthorne came across these novels by his younger contemporary, and wrote admiringly about them. The regard was mutual; Melville was reading him, and found a writer quite unlike the sunny Transcendentalist some thought him. In 1850 he produced a belated essay about *Mosses from an Old Manse*, "Hawthorne and His Mosses" (1850), where he noted that a volume containing such tales as "Young Goodman Brown" and "Rappaccini's Daughter" was hardly the work of someone content with the sublime equation of self and divine universe, Soul and Oversoul. He defined Hawthorne as a transatlantic Shakespeare ("Some may start to read of Shakespeare and Hawthorne on the same page"), a great original, his voice as American and distinctive as Niagara's. He was a writer with a "black conceit," explorer of a veiled universe – as a writer, in fact, very much like himself. And what surely marked his work, he said, was his awareness of the taint in Eden, his power of blackness: "Certain it is that this great power of blackness in him derives its force from that Calvinistic sense of Innate Depravity and Original Sin, from whose visitations, in some shape or another, no thinking mind is always and wholly free."

Meantime, thanks to Democrat patronage, Hawthorne was working again. In 1846 he became Surveyor in the Salem Custom House; his imaginative faculty withered again. But in 1849 the change of administration brought his office to an end; the break was the crucial moment in his life. The result (as he tells us elaborately in the book's long preface "The Custom House") was the writing of *The Scarlet Letter*: the book from which we can reasonably date the emergence of the novel in America as a serious literary genre. It came out in 1850, exactly at mid-century, and though the story is set in the Puritan Boston of two hundred years before it is a distilling book of its age. That summer Hawthorne moved to Lenox, in the Massachusetts Berkshires, to find Melville was also living there as a neighbour. The two met at a picnic and became close friends. It was a crucial literary bonding, central to the fate and fortunes of American fiction. Each man found his reflection in the other; from this emerged the most fertile period in the writing lives of each. Melville "answered" *The Scarlet Letter* with the extraordinary *Moby-Dick* (1851), perhaps the greatest American novel ever written, dedicating it to Hawthorne "in token of my admiration for his genius." That year Hawthorne produced his second novel, *The House of the Seven Gables*, a study of the Puritan "curse" on the present, and *The Blithedale Romance*, his tale of the Transcendentalist Utopia, came a year after. Melville replied with his most difficult and obscure novel, *Pierre, Or the Ambiguities*, another challenge to Transcendentalism. Melville was in effect laying claim to Hawthorne, and a noted letter shows how much he identified with him. "There is a grand truth about Nathaniel Hawthorne," he wrote. "He says NO! in thunder, and the Devil himself cannot make him say *yes*. For men who say *yes*, lie; and all men who say *no*, – why, they are in the happy condition of judicious, unincumbered travellers in Europe; they cross frontiers into Eternity with nothing but a carpetbag . . ."

Later, when the relationship grew chillier and more complicated, Melville was to acknowledge that it was not Hawthorne's nature to say anything in thunder. His *no* is always there, but like everything in Hawthorne it is ambiguous, shaded – nothing like Melville's challenge to the universe in *Moby-Dick*, a meditation on those who believe too arrogantly they can break through the pasteboard mask of the universe and find eternal meaning beyond, and a book baptized, he said, in the name of the devil. Still, it is from Melville's view of him that there grew our modern sense of Hawthorne: that there were really *two* Hawthornes, one the prophet of romantic and utopian consecration, and the other the dark imaginer of a world stricken with sin and evil, whose writing links not with Emerson and Thoreau but with Poe and Melville himself.[5] What is clear is that Melville, with his doubts and dark shadows, was a virtual antithesis to Emerson and Transcendentalism. That antithesis also clearly has something to do with the coming of the serious, complex, symbolist novel to America. For Emerson the "orphic hero" was the poet and seer, ever in communication with the unseen; the two writers who transformed the fortunes of American fiction at mid-century shared fiction as their medium – a form suited not to lyric hope but to tension, conflict, polyphony, multiplicity, ambiguity and irony. In this great coming of fictions, Melville's voice is ravelled yet clear, Hawthorne's less urgent and more ambiguous. He had become one of the great American ironists and self-ironists – a writer caught, as he saw himself, in suspension between gloomy Puritan and hopeful Transcendentalist. As R. W. B. Lewis once put it: "The characteristic situation in his fiction is that of the Emersonian figure, the man of hope, who by some frightened mischance has stumbled into the time-burdened world of Jonathan Edwards."[6]

Hawthorne's own version of his ambiguous and divided place in American writing was typically self-effacing. Presenting himself in the preface to his Italianate allegory "Rappaccini's Daughter" as "M. de l'Aubépine" (in other words Mr Hawthorne), he described himself writing between the "great body of pen-and-ink men who address the intellect and the sympathies of the multitude" and the "Transcendentalists who (under one name or another) have a share in all the

---

[5] A famous statement of this "modern" view of Hawthorne is Lionel Trilling's essay "Hawthorne in Our Time," in *Beyond Culture* (New York, Viking, 1965), where he describes Hawthorne as "our dark poet, charged with chthonic knowledge." He adds: "Everyone perceives certain likenesses between Hawthorne and Kafka," though the matter is more complicated: Hawthorne expresses, as he puts it, "the yes and no of the culture," as many great writers have.

[6] R. W. B. Lewis, *The American Adam: Innocence, Tragedy, and Tradition in the Nineteenth Century* (Chicago, University of Chicago Press, 1955).

current literature of the world." Hawthorne wrote from a divided consciousness; he was of no party but his own. And it was Henry James, Sr, the eminent Swedenborgian philosopher, and the man who would become proud parent to both the greatest novelist (Henry) and the greatest philosopher (William) of the next generation, who summed him up best. In 1861 he attended 'a dinner of the Saturday Club, an idealist group, at the Parker House in Boston. Recording his impressions for his friend Emerson, he described Hawthorne: "he had the look all the time, to one who didn't know him, of a rogue who suddenly finds himself in the company of detectives." He was perfectly right. The time of the New England idealists was an age of metaphysical detectives, hoping with such hope to detect the very meaning of eternity and the universe. And Hawthorne was always to be the rogue, displaced, detached and teasing amidst all this philanthropy and visionary utopianism. Indeed he was and remains the most ironic, the most comic, the most elusively unreliable and unnerving, often the most profound, of the remarkable writers of the key literary generation of the middle of the nineteenth century.

4.

The five years on from mid-century were in fact to become some of the most remarkable in all American literature. Through the early 1850s the great books came. In a brief span of years Emerson brought out his *Representative Men* (1850) and *English Traits* (1856), and Harriet Beecher Stowe her abolitionist fiction *Uncle Tom's Cabin* (1852), a book directly dictated to her, she claimed, by none other than God himself. The first great American world bestseller, it had a profound effect on the events that were to come as this uneasy decade closed ("So this is the little lady who made this big war!" Lincoln said to her). Now Thoreau published *Walden* (1854), Longfellow *The Song of Hiawatha* (1855), and an anonymous poet who proved to be Walt Whitman printed the first edition of *Leaves of Grass* (1855). To these "idealist" works, the fiction of Hawthorne and Melville came as a kind of counterpoint. In an extraordinary burst of creativity, and in very quick succession, Hawthorne published his three major novels, *The Scarlet Letter* (1850), *The House of the Seven Gables* (1851) and *The Blithedale Romance* (1852), and then, for a time, fell silent. Melville appeared with *White-Jacket*

(1850), *Moby-Dick* (1851), *Pierre* (1852), the two remarkable novellas "Benito Cereno" and "Bartleby the Scrivener," about the man who "prefers not to" (1853), *Israel Potter* (1855), and the story-collection *The Piazza Tales* (1856), and then fell silent too. Over a few brief years, American literature had moved from having very little to offer to having a great deal. It certainly was an American Renaissance, but one that would prove tragically short-lived; and not least because the decade was already being split and shaken by the big war that was in the making. Over three years America's "obscurest man of letters," whose imagination faded so often, published his major novels and secured his fame as one of the greatest American novelists. And Melville's achievement from 1851 to 1856 is quite as striking – at least one great novel and some of the finest American short stories ever written – and not least because the period coincided with the beginnings of a breakdown, which he attempted to stave off in 1856–7 by taking a long tour to Europe.

The contrast of their works is also striking. Hawthorne's three novels form a kind of New England trilogy, and in England, where his work was well received, he would come to be perceived as a kind of American George Eliot, as her early work came out over the course of the decade. But they all share a common theme, the ambiguous development of the American Utopia from the Pilgrim beginnings to the present age. Set in Puritan Boston, two hundred years earlier, *The Scarlet Letter* deals with the Calvinist Utopia taking shape on the American strand. Hawthorne explains the ambiguity in the second paragraph: "The founders of a new colony, whatever Utopia of human virtue and happiness they might originally project, have inevitably recognized it among their earliest practical necessities to allot a portion of the virgin soil as a cemetery, and another portion as the site of a prison." He depicts the colony in a double character: as a regenerative religious society, and as an iron-bound social system where law is religion and religion law, based on a rigid structure of church, state, prison, scaffold, cemetery. What is lacking in its regenerative hope are the independent sanctions of love and nature, symbolized by the wild rose bush growing outside the prison door. About the search to break free from the Puritan prison, the book's theme is the nineteenth-century one of adultery: unsanctified romantic love, the love of Hester Prynne and Arthur Dimmesdale. Two doors of escape open. One is to the west: the frontier, the forest, the wilderness, where love has an Edenic consecration of its own. The other is the world to the east: Europe, where the Puritan has its opposite in the Cavalier, the scaffold in the maypole. After all, as he notes, even the sombre Puritans were once "native Englishmen, whose fathers had lived in the sunny richness of the Elizabethan epoch; a time when the life of England . . . would appear to have been as stately, magnificent, and joyous as the world has ever witnessed." Beyond Boston there are two outer poles of American culture, though Hawthorne keeps the story within the framework of the Calvinist world. At the last society dominates nature, the lovers make their public confessions on the scaffold, and accept the sacrifice of romantic love to religious law.

The House of the Seven Gables follows the story from past to present, linking "a bygone time with the very present that is flitting away from us," and takes us from the Puritan age to the age of "the visionary and impalpable Now." The story is set in Hawthorne's own town of Salem; the house of the title is a symbol of history as ancestral decay and the power of the Puritan "Maule's curse." The genteel decline of its tenants, the Pyncheons, shows the power of the past, and equally that "in this republican country, amid the fluctuating waves of our social life, somebody is always at drowning point." But history is also a contemporary process, running ahead fast; like Melville, Hawthorne is urgently concerned with the speed of change in contemporary America, where the world of nature is fast being overwhelmed by the age of the machine, the era of religion by the spirit of materialism. History is the train that takes Clifford and Hepzibah Pyncheon, the two "lost owls," out of Salem and into the lonely way-station of the future, where faith and the past have gone, and time lives only for itself. The present age is its own Utopia, and it is typified in one of the central characters, Holgrave, who is that most supreme of modern literalists; he is a daguerrotypist, a forerunner of the modern photographer. He is the modern man as *bricoleur*, made up of a little of everything and an amount of nothing, product of a fast-moving age. Hawthorne sums him up:

> Altogether in his culture and his want of culture, in his crude, wild, and misty philosophy, and the practical experience that counteracted some of its tendencies; in his magnanimous zeal for man's welfare, and his recklessness of whatever the ages had established in man's behalf; in his faith, and his infidelity; in what he had and in what he lacked, – the artist might fitly enough stand forth as the representative of many compeers in his native land.

Holgrave has been a peddler, and a traveller to Europe, been a Fourierist, a Mesmerist, an Emersonian. Hawthorne both supports and distrusts him; the ancestral curse, the taint of ancient sins and values, is lifted by him, yet he also contains the infidelity of the present.

The Blithedale Romance, Hawthorne's most comic novel, completes the sequence, and makes it clear that the new American Utopia, a present with no past, is not easily won. Though Blithedale, the socialistic colony that seeks to be a modern and sinless Arcadia, is, his preface tells us, "a faint and not very faithful shadowing of Brook Farm," the parallels between the short-lived colony and Hawthorne's experiences there are precise. The central character, Miles Coverdale, is a writer of ironic and self-doubting disposition who departs Boston in a snowstorm in search of a modern arcadia, "the better life," "Paradise anew." It can be no accident that the real Myles Coverdale made the first English Protestant translation of the Bible in 1535, for the entire tale is overlaid with Christian and Puritan motifs. The colonists link their adventure with that of the Pilgrim Fathers, who also arrived in a snowstorm, "whose high enterprise, as we sometimes flattered ourselves, we had taken up, and were carrying onward and aloft, to a point which they never dreamed of attaining." But now the aim is the regeneration not of faith but of humankind. "We had left the rusty iron framework of society behind us; we had broken through the many hindrances that are powerful enough to keep most men on the weary tread-mill of the established system, even while they feel its irksomeness almost as intolerable as we did. We had stepped down from the pulpit; we had flung aside the pen; we had shut down the ledger . . ." This is the romantic Utopia, paradise without sin. The arcadians read all the right contemporary works about it: "Being much alone, during my recovery," Coverdale reports after he has fallen strangely ill in paradise, "I read interminably in Mr Emerson's essays, The Dial, Carlyle's works, George Eliot's romances . . . Agreeing in little else, most of these utterances were like the cry of some solitary sentinel, whose station was on the outposts of human progress . . . They were well adapted . . . to pilgrims like ourselves, whose present bivouac was considerably further into the waste of chaos than any mortal army of crusaders had ever marched before." But actuality is soon intruding on what begins as innocent pastoral, and there are (as in Dickens) plentiful indications that Eden has its share of serpents, and that it is simply "a counterfeit Arcadia" soon to suffer the fate of its predecessors, as sin and the real world test the realm of innocence.

Soon "cold, desolate, distrustful phantoms" are haunting Blithedale. There is the Veiled Lady, with her disturbing prophecies. There is Zenobia, who by contrast begins promising to unveil herself: " 'As for the garb of Eden,' added she, shivering playfully, 'I shall not assume it till after May-day!' " Not surprisingly Coverdale is soon thinking of Eve in some of her less innocent meanings, and Zenobia, recognizing implicit sexual harassment when she sees it, is complaining "I have been exposed to a great deal of eye-shot in the few years of my mixing in the world, but never, I think, to precisely such glances as you are in the habit of favouring me with." Beside sex, there are other eternal human problems: class, wealth, labour, competition. The Arcadians cannot leave the economics of the world, and are forced into competitive strife with those they have tried to leave behind, battling "with the outside barbarians in their old field of labour." Innocent present is intruded on by guilty past; Professor Westervelt, with his diabolic laugh and serpent-headed stick, introduces something Satanic into Eden. The colonists may have set out to "dream awake," but the real world they have left behind intrudes constantly on the colony (in fact the colonists regularly return to Boston on weekend pass). Margaret Fuller had claimed mankind could become "more divine – destroying sin in principle, we attain to absolute freedom, we return to God . . . In short, we become gods." The colonists cannot destroy sin, and do not become gods. Hollingsworth, the great philanthropist, disputes Charles Fourier's ideals for a utopian community, challenging not just his notorious conviction that when the world reaches final perfection the seas will turn to lemonade, but his view that selfishness is the motor of human progress and the model community ("I will never believe this fellow! He has committed the unpardonable sin"). It soon becomes apparent, though, that sin lies in Hollingsworth himself and his selfish plotting philanthropy. The book's central figure, he is degenerated by his search for regeneration, corrupted by his own philanthropic will. What starts in comic innocence ends in sin and tragedy. "I am awake, disenchanted, disenthralled," cries Zenobia, as it grows plain that selfishness and hypocrisy are widespread among the Utopians. Finally she draws the same lesson as in *Martin Chuzzlewit*, in just the same telling words: "Self, self, self."

It is self that finally destroys Blithedale, just as it does Dickens'

America. The book ends on Zenobia's suicide by drowning (possibly suggested by the death of Margaret Fuller, on whom the character is plainly modelled). The farm adds a burial ground and becomes the soil of her grave. As in the Puritan Boston of *The Scarlet Letter*, a portion of the virgin ground has to be allotted as a cemetery (and Hollingworth's "selfish" aim is to turn it into a reformist prison). Arcadia becomes again what it almost always was: a momentary idyll, but also a *memento mori* ("*et in arcadia ego*"). The book owes much to Hawthorne's disenchanted experience at Brook Farm, and surely something to Dickens' vision of the serpent in the American Eden. But it would not do to overlook the strange role, in the story, of its narrator, Miles Coverdale, who is well-named indeed. A failed poet, he has helped both to engineer the masquerade and produce its final collapse. For it is he who has seen it throughout as a "masquerade," a world of veils – of veiled ladies, veiled houses, veiled intentions. In turn he has taken up his own oblique and ambiguous viewpoints, his neo-Jamesian angles of vision: up a white pine tree, a prime site for contemplation but also for eavesdropping; or going to Boston and staring into the revealing back windows of its proud-fronted houses (for, as he says, the front of a house is always artificial: "it is meant for the world's eye, and is therefore a veil and a concealment. Realities keep in the rear"). Coverdale is a specialist in the realities that keep in the rear, and feels assigned "to endeavour – by generous sympathies, by delicate intuitions, by taking note of things too slight to record, and by bringing my human spirit into manifold accordance with the companions God assigned me – to learn the secret which was hidden even from themselves." Coverdale is a case of the Modernist "unreliable narrator" – and also, again, the rogue among the detectives.

With these three books, Hawthorne completed what Leo Marx once defined as a "complex pastoral": fictions (like Scott Fitzgerald's *The Great Gatsby*, or the novels of William Faulkner) where the myth of American pastoral innocence is created only to be tested and challenged.[7] They also completed a personal Odyssey, an ambiguous exploration of the passage from sin-laden Calvinism to sinless Transcendentalism. And they seemed to end an entire period of

---

[7] See Leo Marx, *The Machine in the Garden: Technology and the Pastoral Idea in America* (New York, Oxford University Press, 1967). Marx defines "complex pastoral" as a form where the pastoral ideal – so associated with the idea of America itself – is exposed to the force of change and history, frequently the history of modern industrialism.

Hawthorne's writing. Just as Coverdale ends the book a failure, a silenced spy in the green fields of Utopia, looking back on it as a failed past in his own life, so Hawthorne seems to have felt much the same. He was now a critically well-regarded writer, his days of obscurity over. He had earned enough to return to Concord and buy Bronson Alcott's house "Wayside," but he still remained poor. But 1852, the year of *Blithedale*, was productive, and he also produced a *Wonder Book* for children and, for his old friend and Bowdoin classmate Franklin Pierce, a campaign biography – he was running as a Democrat for US President. It was this now unread work that resolved his financial problems and shaped what came next. Pierce was elected to office, to inherit the Presidency at a troubled moment; he would become famous, or if you were an abolitionist notorious, for attempting various political compromises to prevent both Southern Secession and Civil War over the matter of slavery. Hawthorne gained his reward, a plum diplomatic post; he was appointed as US Consul General in Liverpool, the American point of entry to Europe (it was in fact the best-paid office in the foreign service, and he would make over $20,000 from it). He was a very American writer, who had never travelled abroad, except, occasionally, in his imagination, and whose writing, he said himself, had "the pale tint of flowers that blossomed in too retired a shade." But in 1853 he sailed for Liverpool, "the gateway between the Old World and the New," and on the journey that would slowly lead, eight years on, to a very different final novel, written in a different country in a very different mood.

5.

Herman Melville, by contrast, represented almost the opposite aspect of American fiction. "Call me Ishmael," announces the otherwise unnamed narrator of his great novel *Moby-Dick*, explaining that he has never found anything to interest him onshore, and has always preferred to see "the watery part of the world." So too had Melville himself. When his father died and his family struggled in financial difficulty, he had shipped off at twenty as a young and untutored sailor, signing up for a four-month voyage on a ship, the *Saint Lawrence*, that sailed between New York and Liverpool. So the city that Hawthorne was now about to see as a diplomat Melville had seen from the dark underside, as a place of vice and squalor; he never forgot the experience, and it provided the material for his fourth book, *Redburn: His First Voyage* (1849). He then tried the landward frontier, via the Erie Canal which had opened up New York and made it the major national port; a journey on the extraordinary steamboats that had turned the Mississippi River into the national artery provided him with material he would use in his *The Confidence Man: His Masquerade* (1857), a story of those who lived on the river: "Natives of all sorts, and foreigners; men of business and men of pleasure . . . farm-hunters and fame-hunters; heiress-hunters, gold-hunters, buffalo-hunters, bee-hunters, happiness-hunters, truth-hunters, and still keener hunters after all these hunters." His next trip, on the whaler the *Acushnet*, began a voyage that lasted four years, took him to the South Pacific and the Galapagos and the Marquesas islands, and justified Ishmael's famous claim that "A whaling ship was my Yale College and my Harvard." From all this came the material of the novels or romances he now wrote – and they were essentially novels of America's far-ranging sea-frontiers, written from the standpoint of the sailor-traveller, the eternally wandering soul, the American Ishmael who has seen foreign hells and foreign paradises, and for whom the world is vast and wide.[8]

Redburn was not a book Melville was proud of, but it is important, because it tells a myth increasingly important to his times, and to the author himself: the tale of the innocent young man journeying into evil, experience, ambiguity, and encountering the world's strange deceptions, which make it impossible to read life simply or clearly. As one critic of the book puts it: "Every event kills a comfortable myth, every experience destroys an illusion." Wellingborough Redburn's experiences mirror Melville's own; he is the innocent young man of genteel background come down in the world, which does not fit his understanding of it. His dead father had been a great traveller, and his "continual dwelling on foreign associations, bred in me a vague prophetic thought, that I was fated, one day or other, to be a great voyager." Leaving his mother's house in the Hudson Valley for New York, he is soon exploited and misused, forced to learn the lessons of poverty and human corruption, and put on the clothes of experience, which are ragged ones. Like most of Melville's heroes, he signs on as a

[8] The chief biographies of Melville are Leon Howard, *Herman Melville: A Biography* (Berkeley, University of California Press, 1951), and Jay Leyda, *The Melville Log* (2 vols, New York, Harcourt Brace, 1951).

common sailor. On the *Highlander*, a hard ship with a grim captain, he makes his passage to Europe, Liverpool. Among his illusions is a false myth of Europe itself; he carries his father's old guidebook, evidently Irvingesque and describing the castles and fields of a pastoral and ancestral England. It in no way fits what he finds; it is literature, and nothing he sees matches the prefigured descriptions, the familiar images. He has encountered Britain not as tourist but as poor common sailor. Liverpool is no ancient European city, but a modern Babylon, a *fourmillante cité*, filled with noise, disease, poverty, starvation, human despair. He tries to match myth and reality: "Ah me, and ten times alas!" he cries, "am I to visit Old England in vain? In the land of Thomas-à-Becket and stout John of Gaunt, not to catch the least glimpse of priory or castle? Is there nothing in all the British Empire but these smoky ranges of old shops and warehouses? Is Liverpool but a brick-kiln? 'Tis a deceit! – a gull – a sham – a hoax!"

The hoax, of course, is of his own making, but also literature's. The book is about false illusions and the way they create maps of the world; in their making writers have a hand. Redburn travels with an old, deceptive yet familiar map, and the disillusion runs deep. Melville was the first American novelist to disencumber the Irvingesque myth, and portray Europe, England, not as reassuring rural past but as threatening industrial and urban future. Like Dickens, he takes an old myth and subverts it by subjecting it to new realities. Liverpool is a city of grim industrial poverty and beggary; Melville also represents it with apocalyptic exaggeration as the grim city of the future, an exaggerated version of what America itself threatens to be. It is, Redburn notes, "very much such a place as New York," and "I began to think that I had been born in Liverpool." London proves yet more extravagant and apocalyptic; these sections leave grim realism for mystical fantasy. Society is polarized; "that hereditary crowd – gulf stream of humanity" pours across London Bridge, as it will in T. S. Eliot's no less apocalyptic "The Waste Land." But Redburn meets strange figures (Lord Lovely) and goes to strange and surreal locations, like "Aladdin's Palace," and encounters, "gilded and golden . . . the serpent of vice." Division and hierarchy are more obvious than in America, and European nature turns out to consist of enclosed and guarded property. But Old World and New are bound together in one fast-changing, mammonizing world – the world of money, poverty, vice, and the confused, nameless realm of modern urbanization. In fact there are two transatlantic voyages in the book: Redburn's gullible outward voyage, to the dark confusion and strangeness hidden beneath the "romance" of Europe; then his return passage, which hints at a new possibility, but also shows that dark chaos also underlies the American dream. The outward voyage has been associated with death, the returning one with rebirth. The vessel is packed with Irish immigrants, departing European poverty for American hope. Melville summons up the American promise: "We are the heirs to all time, and with all nations we divide our inheritance." But conditions on shipboard are horrific and filled with symbolic warnings, and the images of death return. A corpse has been smuggled aboard; then an epidemic hits the ship, and a number of the immigrants die on the passage. The rest arrive in an America as commercial as the world left behind; Europe's dark lessons have meaning in America too.

Indeed Melville's chief theme is less the difference between Europe and America than the split between the old democratic, libertarian, pastoral world and the new age of dark cities and grim industrialism. He was perhaps the first American writer of fiction to see England and Europe not as America's historic past but as its grim potential future, and not as a pastoral space but as an industrial realm. The Liverpool and London of his novel is more like the *fourmillante cité* of the Impressionists and the Modernists than it is like the cities of Irving or indeed the early Henry James. And what he had seen in Europe also applied to transforming America, as a good deal of the following tales, from "Bartleby the Scrivener" and *The Tartarus of Maids* to *The Confidence Man* showed. In the 1850s his sense of a world fallen into material disorder, engulfing its viewer in illusion and masquerade, a mockery of its old pastoral and democratic myths, was to become his chief subject. This, and the ironic complexity of voice Melville brought to his writing, did not attract the readers, and in fact the period of much of his best work is also the period of his critical decline. *Pierre* began the descent, and a fire at his publishers which destroyed the stock of his books increased his sense of disaster. Hawthorne tried to use his office to get him political patronage, without success. By 1857 he was so beset by the failure of his fiction that he finished with the novel form. In November 1856, ill and in the midst of near-breakdown, he was persuaded to take a European tour. He travelled to Britain, Italy and the Holy Land, a journey of gloom and disappointment. In Liverpool he called on Hawthorne at the consulate; the two men walked together on the Southport sands, discussing metaphysics and the fate of their writing. Perhaps with some personal foreboding, Hawthorne recorded the meeting, the last time the two men met, in his journal, noting that Melville told him he had "pretty much made up his mind to be annihilated." As in effect he was: from then on, till his almost unnoticed death in 1891 at the age of seventy-two, he was a near-forgotten writer, producing the occasional poem. Strangely enough, he ended up, just like the young Hawthorne, working for two decades in a Custom House, in New York City.[9]

On Melville's death, a remarkable unfinished work, *Billy Budd, Sailor*, dating from 1888, was found in his papers – not to see print until 1924, and since published from the confused manuscript in various versions. His last great myth, it tells, in a larger form, a story not unlike *Redburn*. Set in the British navy around the time of the Nore Mutiny, it tells of Billy Budd, a "Handsome Sailor," a faun-like creature from an older, libertarian world, suddenly impressed from his first vessel – aptly called the *Rights of Man* – onto a nineteenth-century warship, *The Bellipotent*, which proves to be an ironclad version of modern life itself. Like "the beautiful woman in one of Hawthorne's stories," we learn, Billy has one fatal human flaw, a stammer. When he encounters John Claggart, the ship's master-at-arms, who possesses "a depravity according to nature," he goads Billy into stammering silence. Billy strikes and kills him, and "innocence and guilt change places." Though Billy's innocence is acknowledged, justice must be seen done, and this is a story of the modern fall of man. He is hanged from the yard-arm, crying, "God bless Captain Vere!" The story is one of tragic irony, of an age of innocence turned into an age of violence and guilt. It has been noted by the critics that the story of Billy Budd, the faun-like innocent thrown into a fallen world, bears a considerable resemblance to the story of Donatello, the central figure of Hawthorne's final novel, *The Marble Faun*.

[9] The record of two of Melville's European visits, the first to ensure publication of his books in Britain and the second the gloomy eight-month tour of 1856–7, are in Eleanor M. Metcalf (ed.), *Journal of a Visit to London and the Continent, 1849–1850* (Cambridge, Harvard University Press, 1948), and Howard C. Horsford (ed.), *Journals of a Visit to Europe and the Levant, October 11, 1856 – May 6, 1857* (Princeton, Princeton University Press, 1955).

6.

Thus the Europe Melville had once seen in youth from the underside Hawthorne was to see late in his life, and from the overside. He arrived in 1853 a diplomatic eminence in a Liverpool that was the major point of American access to Europe and the hub of transatlantic traffic, as it was still when Henry James' Lambert Strether lands there at the start of *The Ambassadors* (1903). For the next four years of Pierce's troubled Presidential term, Hawthorne sat in the old Washington Building, in Brunswick Street, beneath a portrait of Andrew Jackson, "Old Hickory," the former president who had defeated the British at the Battle of New Orleans. He effectively performed his many consular and diplomatic duties: developing political and commercial relationships, assisting the oddly numerous American claimants to British estates, aiding poor unshipped American sailors, such as Melville had been, representing his nation on official occasions, giving speeches at mayoral banquets, one in the City of London. He saw the great contrasts of English life, visiting, he explained, "prisons, police-courts, hospitals, lunatic asylums, coroners' inquests, death-beds, funerals," and met "insane people, criminals, ruined speculators, wild adventurers, diplomatists, brother-consuls, and all manner of simpletons and unfortunates, in greater number and variety than I had ever dreamed of as pertaining to America." But he was a reluctant consul; he had not lost his "involuntary reserve," and always saw something strange about his office. As he put it: "I could scarce believe that it was I, – that figure whom they called a Consul, – but a sort of Double Ganger, who had been permitted to assume my aspect, under which he went through his shadowy duties with a tolerable show of efficiency, while my real self had laid, as regarded my proper mode of being and acting, in a state of suspended animation."

Not surprisingly, this being Nathaniel Hawthorne, his responses to England and the Europe he encountered in actuality were both reserved and ambiguous. He did not travel widely, or spend much time exploring the sites of the past that so fascinated Irving. He rarely kept company with British writers, and, despite his office, showed no great interest in political events or social or industrial development. Still, he filled his notebooks with observations, travelling on the Birkenhead ferry, exploring and recording English cities like Leamington and Litchfield, and the English countryside ("This old church answered to my transatlantic fancies of England, better than anything I have ever yet seen," he soon notes: "Not far from it was the Rectory, behind a deep grove of ancient trees; and there lives the Rector, enjoying a thousand pounds a year and his nothing-to-do, while a curate does real duty on a stipend of eighty pounds"). He observed the constant contrasts of wealth and poverty, the trim neatness of English nature, so different from the wildness in the American landscape. He seemed to prefer the land to its citizens. He is struck by the weight and solidity, the sheer beefiness, of the English, whose women are "made of steaks and sirloins." Sometimes the heaviness, the custom, the social density, seem too much, and he longs for American lightness; often he compares the people, the weather, the institutions, even the vegetables unfavourably with their American variants. The solidity of everything often offends his democratic instinct, his sense of the right relation between past and present. England, he says, is weighed down by "the monotony of sluggish ages," and he begins to long for American republicanism: "Better than this is the lot of our restless countrymen, whose modern instinct has them tend always toward 'fresh woods and pastures new.' " Yet there is also a growing sense of being exiled from America, an increasingly atavistic response to a world that has greater depth than life at home. His reactions oscillate, in familiar Hawthornean style. He calls London "the dream city of my youth"; it creates "a home-feeling like nowhere else in the world." England, he notes, "is our forefathers' land – our land, for I would not give up such a precious inheritance"; he feels "the imprint of a recollection in some ancestral mind." At times he wants to stay forever, sometimes to leave at once. "I am weary, weary of London and of England," he wrote in 1857: "And yet there is still pleasure in being in this dingy, smoky midmost haunt of men." He was also having similar ambiguous feelings about his troubled America. "The United States are fit for many excellent purposes," he wrote home later, "but they are certainly not fit to live in."

Still, another crucial myth was building, which would have great effect on writers later, including Henry James. This was a myth of England as "our old home," a world of ancestral weight and beefy solidity that contrasted with the "fleetingness" of life at home. Perhaps, he reflected, it was no wonder American writers wrote "romances," works of fancy and the imaginary, and the British wrote novels made dense and real with the weight of society and its things. Hawthorne had come to Britain, the famed Old World, brooding another novel, his fourth (or fifth, if you count the aborted *Fanshawe*). Its theme seemed clear; it would be based on the notion of the "ancestral footstep," the actual or metaphoric desire of the American claimant to secure his old English estate, a theme he would pass both to Twain and James. But his duties kept him busy, his imaginative faculty faded again. As preparation he kept voluminous notebooks, running to over 300,000 words, filled with observations and sketches of English life, background for the book that might have been.[10] The notes bear all the marks of his shifting, ironic vision of the ancient mystery of the Old World, a world of social density, history, poetry and art, lacking the vitality of the present but rich in the things time confers. Hawthorne's English romance never was completed. What we have are two draft versions – *Doctor Grimshawe's Secret* (written in 1858, mostly in Rome) and *The Ancestral Footstep* (written 1860–1, back in the United States) – which go in different directions and finally appeared posthumously as fragments.[11] Instead he worked up his notebooks into *Our Old Home*, a collection of essays and travel pieces, which did not appear until 1863, by which time the Civil War he dreaded was well under way. It is, he says, a substitute for the unwritten fiction: its contents were "intended for the side-scenes and backgrounds and exterior adornment of a work of fiction of which the plan had imperfectly developed itself in my mind, and into which I ambitiously proposed to convey more of various modes of truth than I could have grasped by a direct effort." But the planned English romance had to be cast aside: "The Present, the Immediate, the Actual, has proved too potent for me," he explained. "It takes away not only my scanty faculty, but even my desire for imaginative composition, and leaves me sadly content to scatter a thousand peaceful fantasies upon the hurricane that is sweeping us all along with it, possibly, into a Limbo where our nation and its polity

---

[10] The *English Note-Books* were published by Sophia Hawthorne in 1870, after her husband's death. See Randall Stewart (ed.), *The English Notebooks by Nathaniel Hawthorne* (New York and London, 1941). Also see Raymona E. Hull, *Hawthorne: The English Experience, 1853–1864* (Pittsburgh, University of Pittsburgh Press, 1980).

[11] Hawthorne left several unfinished romances. The two about England have related themes, exploring "the deep yearning which a sensitive American – his mind full of English thoughts, his imagination of English poetry, his heart full of English character and sentiment, – cannot fail to be influenced by – the yearning of the blood within his veins for that from which he had been estranged." See E. H. Davidson (ed.), *Hawthorne's 'Doctor Grimshawe's Secret'* (Cambridge, Mass., 1954).

may be as literally the fragments of a shattered dream as my unwritten Romance."

But the actuality that challenged his imagination was not just his consular duties, but the collapsing of the American political order itself, as during the 1850s the great Utopia dissolved into internecine conflict. *Our Old Home* could not have appeared at a worse time. It stirred controversy in Britain, where even the admired Hawthorne received negative reviews. "Your book is thoroughly saturated with what seems ill-nature and spite," complained *Punch*, criticizing his distrust of British institutions and his ungallantry to English women; others saw it as bitter commentary on British attitudes to the Civil War itself. But there was just as much controversy in the United States, above all because of the dedication to Franklin Pierce, who in Lincolnian days many thought discredited. Like Dickens, Hawthorne found it is never easy to write transatlantic tales, even though his book later did a good deal to shape Anglo-American sensibility. However, a European romance did finally come. In 1857 Pierce's presidency ended, and Hawthorne was free to return home. He did not; dismayed by political events, aware of his long literary silence and Melville's fate, and encouraged by Sophia, a keen student of art, he decided to travel to Italy. At the start of 1858 his party set off – Sophia, their three children, and a governess – on a visit to Rome and Florence that would last for seventeen months. It was a final reckoning, and it succeeded. Once away from office, and in a quite new world, his imagination stirred again. Thus there was another novel, a European romance – his final complete work of fiction, *The Marble Faun*.

· 7 ·

The Rome the Hawthornes entered in January 1858 was a considerable contrast both to America and Britain. Italy was not unified, and it was still a Papal City, "the capital of the world." Landing at Civitavecchia, you had to cross a desolate Campagna famous for dangerous *banditi*, and find your way to a city no less famous for its malaria (the *perniciosa*). The streets were crowded, lodgings cold, the noble past challenged by the chaos, fleas, chill and poverty of the uncomfortable present ("cold, nastiness, evil smells," Hawthorne noted in the no less voluminous journals he kept on the Italian stage of his experience; "Of course there are better and truer things to be said; but old Rome does seem to lie here like a dead and mostly decaying corpse, retaining here and there a trace of the noble shape it was"). There was great political upheaval; since 1848 nationalists had been trying to throw off the Austrian and French yoke, Rome was garrisoned with French troops, Cavour was plotting Italian independence, Garibaldi fighting in the South. These were matters that occupied other more political American visitors, such as Margaret Fuller, who had supported the revolutionary republic of 1848, or Henry Adams, visiting at the same time as Hawthorne. But the Hawthornes came for another historic purpose; they were here, as he said, to "sight-see," as had the many Grand Tourists who had come to the city over generations. Most had been from Northern Europe, but now Americans were joining their numbers, and some 1,000 a year came to Rome around this date. Hawthorne had written Gothic tales of Italy, like "Rappaccini's Daughter," and knew it as the great land of art. "Sight-see" they did – intensively, conscientiously, and studiously, visiting the sites, museums, galleries, and the new archaeological excavations of ancient tombs on the Via Latina. Following the custom, they also both kept a careful record of these artistic experiences.[12]

They spent two winters in Rome and a summer in Florence, and not all went well. In the second winter their fifteen-year-old daughter Una contracted the pervasive malaria, and Hawthorne noted that the atmosphere had "a peculiar quality of malignity" (malaria, the "Roman fever," would be a symbolic power both in Henry James' *Daisy Miller* (1878) and Edith Wharton's "Roman Fever" (1936)). The city also brought out his familiar ambivalence, his doubled view of all things. Rome itself became for him a doubled city, elegant and dirty, magnificent and corrupted: "It is a most beautiful place, and the Malaria is its true master and inhabitant." He felt he knew it better than his birth-place, yet "(life being too short for such questionable and troublesome enjoyments) I desire never to set eyes on it again." The visit to Tuscany proved a pleasure, a visit to a new Arcadia where he felt at last he was "really away from America." With its weighty past, "the smell of ruin and decaying generations," its poverty, discomfort, and Catholic corruptions, Italy was no innocent Utopia. But here too

[12] See Nathaniel Hawthorne, *The French and Italian Notebooks* (Columbus, Ohio State University Press (Hawthorne Centenary Edition, vol. 18), 1980). Sophia also recorded her more intense artistic experiences in Sophia Peabody Hawthorne, *Notes on England and Italy* (1871).

had been Arcadia, the classic past of the unfallen world. The great heritage of Classical and Renaissance civilization shaped the architecture, filled the museums and galleries, designed its countryside. The taint of human sin and the ruinous decline of history touched every detail of the present. But, as nowhere else in the world, Rome was the city of art. It was, he would say in *The Marble Faun*, the "central clime . . . whither the eyes and heart of every artist turn, as if pictures could not be made to glow in any other atmosphere, as if statues could not assume grace and expression save in that land of whitest marble." Yet, as it always had, ambiguity extended to this too. He was not, unlike Sophia, a complete enthusiast for the art he saw. His artistic tastes were limited, and inclined toward the conventional; a good New Englander, he had his Puritan reservations, about the artistic duties Rome imposed on the serious visitor, and his suspicions of the nude. His interest often waned (a familiar touristic experience), and he often ironically questioned the value or the prevailing interpretation of the innumerable works of art he saw. But what plainly overwhelmed him was the notion of an artistic city which somehow gathered up together both the wonders and corruptions of art itself.

The idea of Rome and Florence as artistic capitals, centres of art and aesthetic feeling, to which Hawthorne was paying his homage went back, of course, a long way. Many romantic artists – Byron and Shelley, Stendhal and Gogol, Keats and Landor, Browning and George Eliot, who was there round the same time as Hawthorne – had long been coming to "the Eternal City" to experience what Henry James would soon nicely call its "favouring air." Over the years, Americans, seeking professional training and the example of the great masterworks, had been coming from before the Revolution, joining the great pilgrimage to Italy's Neo-Classical dignity, Romantic sublime, and Gothic thrill, setting up their studios and forming their own distinctive colony. In 1759, when the aspiring young painter Benjamin West, the first American come to study art, arrived in Rome, thirty coachloads of church dignitaries accompanied his visit to the Vatican marbles, to study their effect on an American innocent who had never seen great artistic originals or encountered a nude statue. In 1783 West went to London, made a similar impression (people had never seen a painter who could ice-skate so well) and became court painter to George III and president of the Royal Academy. John Singleton Copley took a similar path over the period of the Revolution, first working in Italy, then on to Britain, where he spent the rest of his life. By the 1830s Rome and Florence had largely replaced London as the centre for American painterly expatriation; half a century on, and the centre would move to bohemian Paris. "She gives him cheaply what gold cannot buy for him at home, a Past at once legendary and authentic, and in which he has equal claim with any other foreigner," James Russell Lowell said of the American artist's dependence on Rome. And where the painters led, the writers followed.[13] The young Washington Irving stayed in Rome with his painter friend Washington Allston, and thought of becoming a painter himself. Allston in his turn wrote poetry and an early novel of American artists in Italy, *Monaldi* – written in the 1820s, though it did not appear until 1841. Cooper visited Rome, dined among the artistic community, had his bust done by Horatio Greenough, and wrote a novel, *The Bravo* (1831), set in Venice. A year before Hawthorne's visit, Harriet Beecher Stowe visited, and later wrote an Italian romance called *Agnes of Sorrento* (1862). Melville also came gloomily this same year, observed that marble statues formed the "true and undying population" of Rome, and asked, "Can art, not life, make the ideal?"

It was when Henry James wrote his study of one of these expatriate artists, the influential Boston sculptor William Wetmore Story, that he made his famous statement about the cosmopolitan tradition: "there are occasions when it comes home to us that, so far as we are contentedly cosmopolite today and moving about in a world that has been made for us both larger and more amusing, we owe much of our extension and diversion to those comparative few who, amid difficulties and dangers, set the example and made out the road." It was, he said, these earlier American artists who "made Europe easy" for the expatriates who came after, and he noted how many did.[14] The tradition would continue, providing James with, for instance, the inspiration for his *The Aspern Papers* (1888), and with models for figures like his American expatriate aesthete Gilbert Osmond, in *The Portrait of a Lady* (1881). The descendants of these visitors would produce a number of significant writers (Constance Fenimore Woolson, a relative

[13] On this see Van Wyck Brooks, *The Dream of Arcadia: American Writers and Artists in Italy, 1760–1915* (New York, Dutton, 1958; London, Dent, 1959), and Nathalia Wright, *American Novelists in Italy: The Discoverers: Allston to James* (Philadelphia, University of Pennsylvania Press, 1965), a study of thirteen novelists in whose work the Italian theme plays a key part.
[14] Henry James, *William Wetmore Story and His Friends* (first published 1903) (2 vols, London, Thames and Hudson, 1957).

of Cooper's, and the exotic F. Marion Crawford), and a new generation of aesthetes, like Bernard Berenson, seeking a land devoted purely to art. Hawthorne was thus joining an already existing tradition of artistic visitors, and he and Sophia quickly became part of the colony of American, and English, painters settled, many for life, in Rome and Florence. They included Story himself, Thomas Crawford, Paul Akers, Louisa Lander (who painted Hawthorne), Hiram Powers, Cephas Thompson, Randolph Rogers and Harriet Hosmer. For once he found himself in bohemia – a place where artists gathered together, aesthetic issues counted, classic encountered romantic, American and European styles merged. Here he was, in the land of art, and his creative juices began flowing again. He filled his notebooks with responses, especially to specific works of art. "I went today to the Sculpture Gallery of the Capitol, and looked pretty thoroughly through the busts of Illustrious Men," he jotted. "I likewise took particular note of the Faun of Praxiteles; because the idea keeps recurring to me of writing a little Romance about it, and for that reason I shall endeavour to set down a somewhat minutely itemized detail of the statue and its surroundings." He did, and thus was born the idea for, and the first chapter of, his "Italian romance," *The Marble Faun, or, The Romance of Monte Beni*.

8.

Hawthorne started the book in the summer in Florence, and continued it over the winter in Rome, as his daughter lay ill with near-fatal malaria, and he listened to the splash of the nearby Trevi fountain. The old polarities of his imagination – of past and present, future-looking America and historic Europe, life and art, reality and imagination, the commonplace and the gothic – had taken fire again. He was well aware that his knowledge of Italy was simply that of the touring visitor, and bound to be superficial. The novel, he carefully explains in the preface, contains almost no reflection of the contemporary Italy of the Risorgimento, and very few Italian characters; in fact the book is set in an almost timeless world. He did not intend a portrait of Italian manners, for he had "lived too long abroad, not to be aware that a foreigner seldom acquires that knowledge of a country, at once flexible and profound, which may justify him in endeavouring to idealize its traits." He was writing in a touristic tradition already as familiar to readers as writers, as he indicates in one passage: "The entrance to these grounds (as all my readers know, for everybody now-a-days has been to Rome) is just outside the Porta del Populo." In fact the expatriate community itself became his subject: his book is a *Kunstlerroman*, a book about the making of artists. Hawthorne's Italian romance stands out from his other novels not just because it is his first expatriate fiction, set in Europe, but because the ambiguous utopia it confronts is none other than that of art itself. The Italy it deals with is itself an artefact, an artistic object, shaped around the painterly myths, of arcadia and decline and fall, that belonged with the subject. Out of the five main characters, three are expatriate artists, two of them American, and the two Italian figures are mythic creatures rather than rounded personages. As one of the first critics observed, *The Marble Faun* is "an art-novel," "a form of literature which has yet to become naturalized among us." But there were other examples – Allston's *Monaldi*, and Henry Greenough's *Ernest Carroll, Or The Artist-Life in Italy* (1858) – and in days to come there would be many more.

The book that started out from a statue in a gallery is thus filled with *objets d'art*, and posed against a landscape of touristic and painterly settings: galleries, museums, churches, catacombs, historical sites, archaeological digs, famous statues and arcadian or gothic scenes. Many of the works – Guido Reni's famed Beatrice Cenci, or Praxiteles' Faun – are classic pieces, but Hawthorne also freely appropriated from the studios of his American friends. As the preface explains, the author has laid "felonious hands upon a certain bust of Milton and a statue of a Pearl-Diver, which he found in the studio of Mr. Paul Akers . . . he committed a further robbery upon a magnificent statue of Cleopatra, the production of Mr. William W. Story, an artist whom his country and the world will not long fail to appreciate." (Akers was a Boston sculptor who worked in Rome from 1855 to 1858; Story, who so interested Henry James, was the son of a Supreme Court justice who remained abroad for most of his life.) Similar art-thefts are acknowledged from the studios of Randolph Rogers, an American sculptor who moved to Italy in 1848, and Harriet Hosmer, who came in 1852, and was a friend to the Brownings and other literary notables. There are a great many references to other famous American expatriates – including Horatio Greenough, an early resident who did a famous bust of George Washington for the Rotunda of the American Capitol, Hiram Powers of Florence, whose noted representational statue "The Greek

Slave" toured America and grossed its maker $23,000, and Thomas Crawford, whose work also decorates the American Capitol. Most started their careers by applying classical themes to American public subjects (though Greenough's Washington proved too nude for American tastes), but once in Italy their work grew increasingly romantic in feeling, more deeply responsive to myth.

Much the same could be said of Hawthorne. Like all his other novels, *The Marble Faun* is a "romance," but the term has now somewhat shifted in meaning. In fact it has something to do with the relation of America to Europe itself. As he explains in a famous passage in the preface:

> Italy, as the site of this Romance, was chiefly valuable . . . as affording a sort of poetic or fairy precinct, where actualities would not be so terribly insisted upon as they are, and must needs be, in America. No author, without a trial, can conceive of the difficulty of writing a romance about a country where there is no shadow, no mystery, no picturesque and gloomy wrong, nor anything but a commonplace prosperity, in broad and simple daylight, as is happily the case with my dear native land. It will be very long, I trust, before romance-writers may find congenial and easily handled themes, either in the annals of our stalwart republic, or in any characteristic and probable events of our individual lives. Romance and poetry, ivy, lichens, and wall-flowers need ruin to make them grow.

For Henry James, writing his fine book on Hawthorne in 1879, what he was doing here was adding to that list of the "absence of forms" – the artistic stimuli lacking in America – that James himself would extend ("No Oxford, nor Eton, nor Harrow . . . no Epsom or Ascot," and so on), and was hence explaining why the American artist depended on Europe. In fact, Hawthorne had written three great American romances where the actual and imaginary had entwined without any great difficulty. He was indeed extending the old mythology that starts with Irving, the notion that American plainness needed the supplement of European darkness. But what is stranger – as has often been noticed – is his suggestion that America lacked a shadow or a gloomy wrong. In fact, just at the moment this book appeared, John Brown's raid on Harper's Ferry would bring the nation to crisis; the nation's gloomy wrong, slavery, was about to erupt into Civil War. Hawthorne's attempt to discriminate between America's "commonplace prosperity, in broad and simple daylight," and the Gothic world of dark and gloomy wrong thus depends on an illusion of which he must have been well aware. It is not surprising that some readers have found in *The Marble Faun* an obscure allegory of the Civil War, in its tale of the fall out of arcadian innocence and into an historical doom, and suggested a lesson is to be found in the final implication: that it may be better to escape the world of art, sin, and decaying history, and live in the world of artless but sinless Utopia.

What is clear is that Hawthorne's novel about art is pervaded with a sense of art's ambiguity. This is his most aesthetic, abstract, meditative and stylized fiction – even for a writer who had always used his stories to meditate on the process of creation or the complex illusion of art. But here, by taking Rome, the artistic city, as his theme, and a group of painters and sculptors as his characters, Hawthorne makes the theme dominant. The story opens in the Capitoline gallery. Beyond is a framed, pictorial view of Rome, which is described as a "three-fold antiquity" (Etruscan, Roman and Christian). Its past is so heavy it renders the present "evanescent and visionary alike," but also weighs that present down with past sins and crimes. Three statues are described to us: the famous Dying Gladiator, a work of heroic classicism; a figure of the Human Soul, "with its choice of Innocence or Evil close to hand, in the pretty figure of a child, clasping a dove to her bosom, but assaulted by a snake" (both doves and snakes will recur in the story); finally Praxiteles' Faun, depicting an Arcadian creature part human and part animal, and evoking a pagan age when man's affinity to nature was closer and the moral senses had not developed. It is this figure that, in effect, steps down from its pedestal when he is identified with the character of Donatello, the chief Italian figure in the tale. He is described as "a creature in a state of development less than what mankind has attained, yet more perfect within himself for that very deficiency." By the end of the first chapter two essential themes are defined: the power of art, and the Fall of Man. Both will test American conceptions: of an essential human innocence, and the moral power of art.

Four characters are also assembled: "three were artists, or connected with Art." Two are Americans, the sculptor Kenyon and the chaste copyist Hilda; the third, the painter Miriam, has an obscure cosmopolitan background and is "plucked out of a mystery." Hilda and Miriam are two contrasting versions of Womanhood. Hilda is fair and virginal, "faithful Protestant, and daughter of the Puritans," and a child-like symbol of purity; Miriam is "experienced," sensual, a risk-taking artist hungry to bring "a simple and imperfect Nature to the point of feeling and intelligence." Just as Miriam's careless energy is counterpoint to Hilda's chaste ardour, Donatello's instinctive crime, the heart of the story, is counterfoil to Kenyon's desire to comprehend sin and redemption and express this as art. The story that unfolds is thus a moral quest explored on sites, against statues, or noted works of architecture; meantime a complex mythology summoned out of art is deployed. The Italian setting is variously associated with Classicism (Arcadia, and "fables, lovely, if insubstantial, of a Golden Age") and Gothic Romanticism (crimes, ruin, the Piranesian sensibility of decline). Tuscany provides the Arcadian hope, Rome is the dark stage of art and corruption. Ancient sins and unspecified crimes haunt it, "a contagious element, rising fog-like . . . and brooding over the dead and half-rotten city, as nowhere else on earth." The Arcadian and the fallen world meet, childlike animal innocence encounters the black corruption of man and nature. Like Billy Budd, Donatello is led to commit murder, and leave his simplicity for the state of self-conscious human sin. Miriam, who has led him to this disaster, draws the lesson at once: "The story of the fall of man!" she cries. It is left to Kenyon and Hilda to interpret this, and they do so in different ways. Hilda, trying to keep human sin at a distance, shuts herself in her tower, her innocence tortured by the guilt of others – until, by the end of the tale, she becomes mysteriously involved herself. Kenyon hopes to draw a happier lesson, a hope that guilt leads, through redemption, to moral progress. "Sin has educated Donatello, and elevated him," he suggests to Hilda. "Is Sin, then – which we deem such a dreadful blackness in the Universe – is it, like Sorrow, merely an element of human education, through which we struggle to a higher and purer state than we could otherwise have attained?" It will not do: "Oh, hush!" cries Hilda. "This is terrible . . . You have shocked me beyond words!"

Melville had said all literature is made of guidebooks, and *The Marble Faun* is a guidebook, to Rome and its art – and the cost of both to American Protestant conscience. As the story unfolds, and many works of art, including Reni's Beatrice Cenci, are examined, we can sense that Hawthorne is probing an almost unresolvable conflict within the Puritan imagination. Nature and Art, Past and Present, Innocence and Sin, Protestant and Catholic are in constant opposition (as in George Eliot's *Middlemarch*, 1872, whose Roman scenes surely owe something to Hawthorne). Like Irving, but at a far more complex level, Hawthorne had polarized the two different worlds of Europe and

America. Europe here is ancient, Catholic, freighted with a guilty past, in a state of indigent corruption; it does, however, contain the complex secret of art. America is new, simple, Protestant, advancing into the moral future; but its artists find it hard to confront life's intensity, or the dangerous mysteries of sin. Kenyon even offers to solve Donatello's problem of guilt by taking him to America: "In that fortunate land, each generation has only its own sins and sorrows to bear. Here it seems as if all the weary and dreary Past were piled on the back of the Present." But when everything ends amid the strange disguises, confused identities and moral chaos of a Carnival, only one solution seems left. Leaving Donatello and Miriam behind in Europe to keep the mystery going, Hilda and Kenyon, now engaged to be married, decide to depart artful, sinful Italy for America's innocent shore. Hawthorne says their farewell to Italy, observing:

> . . . now that life had so much human promise in it, they resolved to go back to their own land, because the years, after all, have a kind of emptiness, when we spend too many of them on a foreign shore. We defer the reality of life, in such cases, until a future moment, when we shall again breathe our native air; but, by-and-by, there are no such future moments; or, if we do return, we find that the native air has lost its invigorating quality, and that life has shifted its reality to the spot where we have deemed ourselves only temporary residents. Thus, between two countries, we have none at all . . .

9.

It still seems appropriate that Hawthorne's last novel was finished neither in Italy's degenerate but golden air, nor on America's innocent but artless shore. He drafted the book in Italy, but he completed it in England – which he now came to see as an ancestral middle ground between America and Catholic Italy. The book was concluded, he carefully tells us in the preface, in the land of cold winds and hard realism: "on the broad and dreary sands of Redcar [Yorkshire], with the gray German Ocean tumbling in upon me, and the northern blast always howling in my ears." Like several of his novels, it ends in ambiguity, still in suspension between real and ideal, literal and symbolic, degeneration and regeneration: or, we might say, between America and Europe. It came out in England first, in 1860, under the title *Transformation* (reasonably enough, for it is about art transformed

into life, and life into art, but Hawthorne thought it a pantomime title).
A month later it appeared in the USA under the now accepted title of
The Marble Faun, or, The Romance of Monte Beni. As it came out, he went
home at last, to find his nation on the brink of a war he thought never
should have happened. America itself was, he said, a "shattered
Romance," a fallen Utopia; the great era of New England writing was
about to dissolve into the new arts of battle. Melville had already given
up the novel; Hawthorne himself retired depressed to Concord, and
tried to work on four different versions of the English romance, but "the
Present, the Immediate, the Actual" proved too potent. He visited
soldiers on both sides, observed accurately that, after the War, "One
bullet-headed general will succeed another in the Presidential chair,"
and hoped to return to England. In 1864, the year before the war ended,
and a new era of American history and writing began, he died, at the
age of sixty, on a journey with Franklin Pierce, conscious that his
imaginative powers had once more ebbed away. Emerson, whose own
writing was now fading, commented in his journal on Hawthorne's
unhappy spirit, and his "painful solitude . . . which, I suppose, could
no longer be endured." Sophia moved back to Europe, to Dresden, and
died in London in 1871.

But Hawthorne's novels went on to have a strange afterlife; with
their awareness of the complexities of innocence and sin, utopia and the
power of commonplace reality, they lived on in American fiction,
bequeathing their sense of ambiguity and irony to writers right up to
the present day. As for *The Marble Faun*, distinguished from the other
three romances by its sense of artistic ambiguity and its European
theme, it has always seemed a special case. When the Civil War ended,
and the bullet-headed generals took over the direction of the nation, a
new age of American wealth, industry and travel began. Detached from
their recent past, and aware they too were now stained by history,
Americans increasingly turned to Europe and its "culture." Transatlantic tourism flourished, and the newly wealthy demanded their
share of the history of art. So travel to Italy multiplied, and among the
books the new travellers took with them was not just their Baedeker and
their Murray but Hawthorne's final novel. The next generation of
writers also looked to Italy, and all three of the major writers who
emerged at the end of the same decade that Hawthorne died, and who
became the central figures of the post-Transcendentalist generation,
Mark Twain, William Dean Howells, and Henry James, visited the

country and wrote about it. Mark Twain made his career mocking the culture-religion that Hawthorne's book so ambiguously expressed. Howells, consul in Venice during the War, wrote extensively of his travels there, and introduced them into his novels. Henry James, who visited Italy in 1869 and was overwhelmed by the experience ("At last – for the first time – I live!"), drew the deepest lesson. As he recalls the matter in the rotund style of his late-life autobiography, he sat in Rome and pondered the importance of *The Marble Faun*, the book all Americans now took to Italy. Though Hawthorne was, in essence, a provincial writer, it was charged, he felt, with a cosmopolitan tone no other American novel had ever possessed:

> And the tone had been, in its beauty – for me at least – ever so appreciably American; which proved to what use European matter could be put by an American hand: a consummation involving, it appeared, the happiest moral. For the moral was that an American could be an artist, one of the finest, without "going outside" about it, as I liked to say; quite in fact as if Hawthorne had become one just by being American *enough*, by the felicity of how the artist in him missed nothing, suspected nothing, that the ambient air didn't affect him as containing. Thus he was at once so clear and so entire – clear without thinness, for he might have seemed underfed, that was his danger; and entire without heterogeneity, which might, with less luck and to the discredit of our sufficing manners, have to be in his help.[15]

This reading was crucial. James would in effect tell the same story again, though in a spirit far closer to realism, in his own first mature novel, *Roderick Hudson* (1876) – the fable of an American sculptor who goes to Rome to drink the cup of experience, and is both enlarged and destroyed by it ("If I had not come to Rome I shouldn't have risen and if I hadn't risen I shouldn't have fallen"). Many of James' early stories, with their passionate pilgrims and ancestral claimants, were prompted by the same source. *Daisy Miller* (1878), about the young American girl who falls to the malaria of Rome, is particularly in Hawthorne's debt, and probably alludes to what had happened to his daughter Una. And when in 1879 James wrote (in the "English Men of Letters" series) his delightful study of Hawthorne, he placed himself squarely in the tradition Hawthorne had begun, though he also acknowledged the difference brought to the world by the Civil War, which ended the era of

[15] Henry James, *Notes of a Son and Brother* (1914), reprinted in F. W. Dupee (ed.), *Henry James: Autobiography* (New York, Criterion; London, W. H. Allen, 1956).

simplicity. "The subsidence of that great convulsion has left a different tone from the tone it found," he noted – for the good American "has eaten of the tree of knowledge."[16] Like the painters he followed, and whose work he depicted, Hawthorne too had "set the example and made out the road" – a road James was determined to take to a further destination. The "international theme" so important to his fiction – the careful balancing of American lightness with European weight, American futurism with the European past, American innocence with European experience – clearly starts out from *The Marble Faun*, and then moves toward its later Jamesian complexity.[17] If there was a complex romance of America to examine, there was, James considered, now a no less significant romance of Europe to consider as well. It was an anxious affair, but it now demanded not an ambiguous retreat from art and experience, rather a direct encounter. The Old World could no longer be discarded; it was an essential resort of the imagination. "There's no romance here but what you may have brought with you," says Ralph Touchett to the American Isabel Archer in James' *The Portrait of a Lady* (1881), where the theme is extended into a new complexity. "I've brought a great deal, but it seems to me I've brought it to the right place," Isabel replies – speaking for James, for Hawthorne, and a great many more American writers ever since.

[16] Tony Tanner discusses this connection fruitfully in his introduction to Henry James, *Hawthorne . . . With introduction and notes by Tony Tanner* (London, Macmillan; New York, Saint Martin's Press, 1967).

[17] In his excellent essay on *The Marble Faun*, "Statues from Italy: The Marble Faun," Harry Levin comments on this: "If an innocent New World met a corrupting Old World to frame a beginner's formula for James, he could develop the corollaries and vary the complications: a refined example is the adjustment of the Italian prince in *The Golden Bowl*, who is so propitiously named Amerigo." See Harry Levin, *Refractions: Essays in Comparative Literature* (New York and London, Oxford University Press, 1966).

FIVE

The Lighted Stage:
Twain, James and the European shrine

I.

Right after the American Civil War ended – as the nation began slowly to pull itself back into a union again, the westward motion resumed, and the flavour of national sentiment changed completely – a new and very original American writer announced that he was about to join in a great popular movement:

> Everybody was going to Europe – I, too, was going to Europe. Everybody was going to the famous Paris Exposition – I, too, was going to the Paris Exposition. The steamship lines were carrying Americans out of the various ports of the country at the rate of four or five thousand a week in the aggregate. If I met a dozen individuals during that month who were not going to Europe directly, I have no distinct remembrance of it now.

The writer – the comic note surely tells us this at once – was Samuel Langhorne Clemens, better known as "Mark Twain." He is describing, at the start of his *The Innocents Abroad* (1869), the book that would establish his reputation as modern realist, comic iconoclast, and true western American original, how he came to go on his first European pilgrimage (there would be several more to come). He is also noting the birth of an important new phenomenon that was changing the tone of American culture, the nature of transatlantic relations, the national attitude to the world abroad. In the age of post-war Reconstruction, as the nation boomed again, and the industrial energies the war had released started to bring prosperity to a new generation, Americans were indeed indulging fresh opportunities to go abroad. The ports had reopened, and it was now the great age of the steamship, which by 1867 carried 92 per cent of the travellers to New York. There was a fourteen-day passage, in regular and comfortable ships. Transatlantic travel was easier, quicker, safer, and more popular – for this was the era of Thomas Cunard, Thomas Cook, and the organized tour. As a result, two large migratory tides began passing each other in midatlantic. One was an ever-increasing number of European immigrants, not just from Northern but from Southern or Eastern Europe, shipping west in steerage to the land of the new start, drawn by glowing reports of cheap land on the prairies, or the prospect of jobs in the new industrial cities. The other was the growing number of wealthy Americans who, enriched by just that industry, sailed back in the first-class cabins – toward their origins, the past, and what was increasingly granted the name of "culture."

The age of tourism was here to stay. As Hawthorne left Rome in 1860, something like a thousand American tourists a year visited to inspect its sites, with their Murray, their Baedeker, soon *The Marble Faun*, in hand. Forty years on the numbers would be thirty thousand, and Americans were now replacing the British as Italy's typical tourists. 1867 was the year that set the trend. This was the year of the Paris Exposition, one of the world fairs that displayed the culture, arts and technologies of the industrial, imperial age. They had started with the Great Exhibition in London in 1851, continued at regular intervals through the rest of the century, and told much of its transatlantic story. Americans took particular interest, as they watched their technologies first compete with and then outrun those of the world. In 1876, after a hundred years of nationhood, the Centennial Exhibition was held in Philadelphia. In 1889, after a hundred years of Revolution, the French held another Centennial exhibition, in Paris. In 1893, four hundred years after Columbus, the World's Columbian Exhibition would be held in Chicago. Each used its anniversary reference to celebrate the advance of new technologies, in which America was the rising power. In Paris in 1867, the McCormick reaper and the Singer sewing machine would fascinate the crowds at the fair. Philadelphia nine years on displayed the desktop age of the typewriter, Thomas Alva Edison's telegraph, Andrew Graham Bell's telephone. For the Paris Exposition of 1889 Gustave Eiffel raised his great iron tower – the "first monument of Modernism," it has been called – but the American spirit was here too; the entire fair was lit up by Edison's incandescent bulbs. At Chicago in 1893, the Manufacturing Hall dominated the fair; the historian Henry Adams would reflect that the world had left the old God-granted universe behind, and entered the modern "multiverse."

Technological comparison was one reason why Americans looked to Europe in 1867, but there were others of a more romantic kind. For, precisely because the coming multiverse seemed to be based on industry and technology, generating more wealth than human satisfaction, the travellers of America looked to Europe for something else. The new order transforming the country, linking its coasts together by transcontinental railroad and mastering its mineral resources, brought a growing fear that the new America was losing its heart, becoming a land of business and struggle. What might compensate for the age of "things in the saddle" had been prescribed by Emerson: "The word of ambition at the present day is Culture." Culture drew Americans to Lyceum lectures, on art and history; culture encouraged the educated patriciate of New England to believe it performed an important national office, and tempted them to Europe. Now the *nouveaux riches* of a boom-time began to follow the same path, looking to Europe for education and cultural acquisition, in the spirit of what Thorstein Veblen, in his *Theory of the Leisure Class* (1899), nicely called "pecuniary emulation." In 1867 this new world to the east was just beginning to open. Thanks to the Paris Exposition, and the desire for cultural tourism, demand was so great that all the many new steamship berths were booked up even before the year began. Mark Twain was entirely right. Everyone was going to Europe, and it was a new and highly significant social phenomenon.

2.

As for Mark Twain himself, he certainly did not come from the American classes who were historically associated with culture, the genteel tradition, or dutiful trips to the Europe of Our Old Home. Born in 1835 in Florida, Missouri, in what was still new territory, he was what was called a "Westerner," though he came of Southern, Virginian stock. In 1821 Missouri had been grudgingly admitted to the Union as a slaveholding state under the "Missouri Compromise," and so he grew up in a family with household slaves. When he was four the family moved to Hannibal, Missouri, 120 miles north of Saint Louis on the west bank of the mile-wide Mississippi. This was now a world quite unlike that of Chateaubriand's *Atala*, or even of Charles Dickens' rotting "Eden." By now the American waterway system linked the nation. The world's largest river had become chief artery of the bustling, westward-spreading America of the expanding years before the Civil War, which was itself provoked by the slavery that still survived in Hannibal and threatened to spread through the West. The river, banked with levees, had become the American heartland, an exciting place for a child to grow up. An enormous bustling river traffic, with boats every hour, linked Hannibal to Saint Louis, and on to Memphis and New Orleans; and by branching up the Ohio river you could readily reach Cincinnati and the ports of the East. Out of forty-four tributaries, from up near the Canadian border to the Mexican Gulf, the goods and products poured. Past the rising settlements, towns and cities that lined the leveed banks flatboats swept, loaded with freight, cotton, grain and lumber for the settlements right down to the Gulf and the world beyond. There was quite enough "sivilization" and pious Christianity to ruin boyhood life ("Miss Watson she took me in the closet and prayed, but nothing came of it," Huck Finn would complain). Cats sat lazily on the geraniumed window-sills, and Lyceum lecturers and Shakespearean actors of ambiguous quality came regularly by.

Indeed the river – "flaked with coal-fleets and timber-rafts" – had a distinctive, cosmopolitan culture all its own. Ornate Gothic steamboats, even brightly lit showboats, plied it, stopping at the main landings. Herman Melville's last novel, *The Confidence Man* (1857), written during his unhappy European tour and finished off in Venice, wonderfully records this river world and its mixed cast of characters. A parable of America itself, the book is set on a great river boat, the *Fidèle*, described as if it were a Gothic castle, with "Fine promenades, domed saloons, long galleries, sunny balconies, confidential passages, bridal chambers, staterooms plenty as pigeon-holes, and out-of-the-way retreats like secret drawers in an escritoire." These boats carried, as he tells us, all the strangers and wanderers of the world, as varied as Chaucer's pilgrims: "Natives of all sorts, and foreigners; men of business and men of pleasure; parlor men and backwoodsmen; farm-hunters and fame-hunters; heiress-hunters, gold-hunters, buffalo-hunters, bee-hunters, happiness-hunters, truth-hunters, and still keener hunters after all these hunters. Fine ladies in slippers, and moccasined squaws; Northern speculators and Eastern philosophers; English, Irish, German, Scotch, Danes . . ." For Twain the Mississippi – a cosmopolitan river, where every kind of traveller came, and every kind of performance – was a culture as dense as Europe's. Not only was it the main travel and trade route through the American heartland, where British and French, American and Indian, Northern and Southern, histories met. It was also the point of access to the west and the ever advancing frontier. Along its river bluffs wagon trains assembled to take the Oregon and California trails, immigrants gathered to claim their lots on the prairie, and the gold and silver rushes that fed the Western dream began.

Like Melville, Twain learned much of his America on the Mississippi, where he trained as a riverboat pilot – the best job he ever did, he later said. The river was a great parade, and all human life was here ("When I find a well-drawn character in fiction or biography I generally take a warm personal interest in him, for the reason that I have known him before – met him on the river"). As he explained in his memoir *Life on the Mississippi* (1883), the world's biggest waterway had a long, compelling history, "well worth reading about." "When De Soto took his first glimpse of the river, Ignatius Loyola was an obscure name; the order of Jesuits was not a year old; Michael Angelo's paint was not yet dry on the 'Last Judgement' in the Sistine Chapel; Mary Queen of Scots was not yet born." It had Legends and Scenery, Manufactures and Miscreants, Castles and Culture (both influenced by the romanticism of Walter Scott). But it was a life that largely died when the Civil War shattered the river trade of North and South. Then it declined further in importance as the line of traffic shifted, when the transcontinental railroad opened to the Pacific. Twain lost his river profession, served briefly, obscurely in the Confederate Army for a few weeks, then looked, like many another, to the West. He joined the silver rush, roughed it in Nevada, and went on to California, where he became a newspaper man (it ran in the family). An indefatigable traveller, fascinated by human nature, he reported his adventures on the Coast and in Hawaii for the California newspapers. He was that very southwestern thing, a "humorist," calling himself "Mark Twain," his name taken from one of the sounding calls on the river. In 1866, with the war ended, he felt he had "a 'call' to literature, of a low order – i.e. humorous," and decided to risk his career in the East. His stock in trade was the success of a short story, "The Celebrated Jumping Frog of Calaveras County" (1865), and the reports of an Hawaiian tour for the Sacramento *Union*. Settled in bohemian New York, he looked round for a suitable subject, noted the vogue for European travels – and ensured his literary fame.

3.

Of all the cruises New York had on offer, there was no doubt the finest was on the two-masted side-wheeler the SS *Quaker City*, engagingly titled "The Grand Holy Land Pleasure Excursion." Largely planned by the Plymouth church in Brooklyn, which had Henry Ward Beecher for its pastor, the *Quaker City* pleasure cruise was to last five-and-a-half months. The Paris Exposition was just one on the massive list of destinations it promised – and in the event the Exposition proved to be so far away from the docking port, Marseilles, that some of the tourists missed it entirely. The excursion would go to the Azores, Spain, France, Italy, Greece, Turkey, the Holy Land and Egypt; it was to be both a great travelling pleasure cruise and a pious cultural and religious pilgrimage to the great shrines of Europe. No detail or refinement would be spared. The cruise was to be accompanied, the enormous press publicity explained, by two notable American figures: General William Sherman, who had so recently achieved national fame by burning Georgia, and the Rev. Beecher himself, America's leading preacher, "the high priest of emotional liberalism," who (following the custom of great religious charismatics) would be caught in sexual scandal with one of his parishioners, and also advertise Pears Soap. Travel and excursion had already proved ideal subjects for Twain, so he decided to offer his services too – first, rather improbably, as the Rev. Mark Twain, a Baptist minister in good standing, and then, when this failed, as cruise correspondent for the California *Alta*, a San Francisco newspaper, which agreed to meet his expenses to the tune of $1,250, and pay for the reports he sent home.

In the event, neither of the two advertised celebrities made the trip. General Sherman preferred to go off to the west and kill Indians, and Beecher found he had a sentimental novel about New England life he had to finish. Consequently Twain, still only thirty-two, the same age as Dickens on his first transatlantic trip, found himself the true celebrity on the cruise. Sent on its way by "a battery of guns," the *Quaker City* set sail from New York harbour on 8 July 1867, with sixty-five passengers, mostly on the far side of fifty, then anchored for a night just outside it to let a passing storm through. Along with "three ministers of the gospel, eight doctors, sixteen or eighteen ladies, several military and naval chieftains, and an ample crop of 'professors,' " Twain was off for the next five months on what he later, with bitter humour, recalled as "the Grand Holy Land Funeral Procession." "The whole affair was a huge practical joke," Bret Harte commented later, "of which not the least amusing feature was the fact that 'Mark Twain' had embarked on it." If so, the joke was not exactly visible to the pilgrims who travelled. It was, however, to the readers of the *Alta* when they saw the fifty-eight travel letters Twain sent back recounting the great European adventure – and then, a year later, the entire American reading public, when he worked up the letters to greater length and published the whole serio-comic tale as a book.[1]

What the patrons of the *Quaker City* cruise had done, according to Twain, was to invent the idea of a pleasure cruise that contained absolutely no pleasure; in fact it was, he said, a "funeral excursion without a corpse." As he explained, his venerable travelling companions on the European adventure were hardly "gay and frisky. They played no blind man's buff; they dealt not in whist; they shirked not the the irksome journal for, alas! most of them were even writing books." It was in fact unsurprising that those who enrolled for the famous and highly expensive tour were not only elderly and wealthy but inclined toward piety and pomposity. Some were parishioners of the absent Beecher, others solemn culture-vultures off to worship for the first time at the famed cultural and religious shrines of Europe. Twain was a young unmarried man with no regard for East Coast gentility, or for religion ("Heaven for climate, Hell for company," was his motto), and so it might have been expected that a shipboard life of what he called "solemnity, decorum, dinner, dominoes, devotions, slander" failed to suit him. Then there was that rare thing among seafarers, a temperance captain. Regular prayer-meetings were called and sermons frequently given; the passengers wavered between epidemics of seasickness and epidemics of homesickness. But above all there was Europe itself. "None of us had ever been anywhere before; we hailed from the interior; travel was a wild novelty to us," Twain revealingly reported.

[1] The story of Mark Twain's *Quaker City* voyage is well told both in Justin Kaplan, *Mr Clemens and Mark Twain: A Biography* (London, Cape, 1967), and, in full detail, by Dewey Ganzel, *Mark Twain Abroad: The Cruise of the Quaker City* (Chicago and London, University of Chicago Press, 1968).

"When we found that a good many foreigners had hardly heard of America, and that a good many more knew it only as a barbarous province away off somewhere, that had lately been in a war with somebody, we pitied the ignorance of the Old World, but abated no jot of our importance. Many a simple community in the Eastern hemisphere will remember for years the incursion of the strange horde in the year of our Lord 1867 that called themselves Americans and seem to imagine in some unaccountable way they had a right to be proud of it."

Once the Atlantic had been crossed, the European continent been detected, and the task of foreign tourism begun, there were severe difficulties on hand for all parties. For the Americans there were the perils of tourism in an unfamiliar continent, for the Europeans there were the no less serious perils of encountering unfamiliar American tourists. The travellers found dirt and disease, touts and tricksters, beggars and false guides, everywhere bands of swarthy gesticulating foreigners with fraud in their hearts. Europeans observed a wandering, oddly-dressed white tribe who expected Europe to be more like America, cleaner and simpler and more respectful. Soon there would be regular angry dust-ups with the various foreign port authorities, when it turned out the travellers had to be quarantined, fumigated, searched or just refused the right to land. There were complicated treks overland by train or jolting carriage, trips through the blank desert aboard donkey or camel. Social transactions proved difficult – foreigners, even the supposedly civilized French, did not speak the languages they were expected to or use the words in the phrase-books: "We never did succeed in making those idiots understand their own language," Twain explained. Every homage was paid to local practice: "we took kindly to their manners and customs, and especially to the fashions of the people we visited . . . When we came back from Tangier, in Africa, we were topped with fezzes of the bloodiest hue . . . In France and Spain we attracted some attention in these costumes . . . We made Rome howl. We could have made any place howl when we had all our clothes on." Above all there was the unremitting supply of sites and museums, churches and chapels, tombs and pyramids, monuments and holy places. Europe was full of them. Everywhere were galleries to gallop through, crammed with works of the Old Masters: "We examined modern and ancient statuary with a critical eye in Florence, Rome, or anywhere we found it, and praised it if we saw fit, and if we didn't said we preferred the wooden Indians in front of the cigar stores of

America." What Nathaniel Hawthorne had gazed on nine years earlier with anxious Puritan awe, the new pilgrims gazed on with a baffled mystification or, in Twain's own case, unconcealed comic delight. For the anarchist Western humorist who found himself cast into the solemn Old World, this encounter was, after all, perfect material, the stuff of a lifetime.

Five months later – it was just as Charles Dickens was arriving in New York for his second American visit – Twain regained the soil of New York harbour, not without a sigh of relief. He found his reports back home had been widely read, and earned him much fame. Persuaded by a publisher to rework the fifty-eight travel letters, he expanded them – borrowing notes from some of his more amenable fellow-passengers – into a substantial book. It appeared in 1869 as *The Innocents Abroad, Or the New Pilgrim's Progress*, called on its title page an account of the *Quaker City* pleasure excursion "with descriptions of countries, nations, incidents and adventures as they appeared to the author." In it Twain declared his literary aim: it was, he said, "to suggest to the reader how *he* would be likely to see Europe and the East if he looked at them with his own eyes instead of the eyes of those who travelled in those countries before him." And he added: "I think I have written at least honestly, whether wisely or not." Twain's "honesty" was – as critics have pointed out – a double-edged tool, assaulting both American provincialism and American cosmopolitanism, mocking American manners while burlesquing the antiquities, the manners and the famed sites of venerated Europe. The basic note was the naughty-boy posture that would become essential to his comic imagination, and later permit him his remarkable identification with heroes like Tom Sawyer and Huck Finn. But Twain's Western innocence and naïveté is a rather more sophisticated weapon than he chose to admit. As he says, this was no account of a serious scientific expedition, which might require a certain gravity from its author. It was the account of a failed "picnic," where all the pleasure had somehow gone missing. Clearly it had to be supplied, by the comic elaboration of an impertinent author.

So, in *The Innocents Abroad*, a scandal to some, a delight to others, the comic tone carries all before it. No one and nothing is spared. It tackles both his travelling companions, whom he called "American Vandals" and the "Barbarians," and the object of their veneration, cultural and religious Europe itself. The "Vandals" appear as a band of naïve dotards seeking a false Europe, scurrying through galleries giving their awe to the wrong masterpieces, and preferring copies to originals because the paint is fresher (a thought that probably suggested valuable ideas to Evelyn Waugh, writing his American novel *The Loved One* eighty years later). They were new American types, and he observed them well, teasing their culture-religion, their solemnity, their puritan, protestant piety, their vulgarity. Meanwhile Twain has a vulgarity all his own. He too is an American "vandal," exploiting his own ignorance, often to excess, to display his independent, comic and "natural" vision. Henry James would shortly observe it was the American "complex fate" to struggle with a superstitious valuation of Europe. For Twain there is no contest. He has no superstition, no valuation. From the start he presumes that very little in Europe will match America's natural wonder and democratic splendour. This is the comedy of assumed innocence; everything that is seen and done has to be sifted through the filter of his simple Western vision. In fact the book is a complex literary text, a reversed guidebook. "Guide-books, Wellingborough, are the least reliable books in all literature," the young hero of Melville's *Redburn* had discovered, "and nearly all literature, in one sense, is made of guide-books." The *Quaker City* pilgrims had been advised, as is customary on foreign tours, to take along "a few guide-books, a Bible, and some standard works of travel. A list was appended . . ." Twain knows these books; indeed he borrows from them, both to take his cultural and historical bearings and to burlesque them. His book is an anti-Baedeker, a counter-Murray, reporting the world of European cultural piecework not as it is generally seen, in the light of veneration and solemn monumentaliza-tion, but "as they appeared to the author." Guidebook prose is there for the taking. "Toward nightfall the next evening, we steamed into the great artificial harbour of this noble city of Marseilles, and saw the dying sunlight gild its clustering spires and ramparts, and flood its leagues of environing verdure with a mellow radiance that touched with an added charm the white villas that flecked the landscape far and near," he grandly writes, then adding: "Copyright secured according to law."

Twain is that highly familiar thing, the bored tourist. But he never really steps right out of line, breaks free of the fundamental itinerary, or heads for new places of his own. He follows Baedeker's code to the letter, but is somehow the awkward visitor to every museum, the unwilling acolyte at almost every shrine. Admittedly, Leonardo's

"Last Supper" was a miracle of art once. But that was three hundred years ago, and now it is in a dirty state. Lake Como does not come out well if you know Lake Tahoe. Venice is still waiting for its streets to dry out. Italy suffers from a glut of Old Masters, and, as he put it in a famous phrase, "to me it seemed that once one had seen one of these old martyrs I had seen them all." He felt it was time we had a comic playbill for the old gladiatorial shows at the Colosseum, and that what Palestine really needs is a good coat of paint. The reason there had been no Second Coming is that Jesus had seen the Holy Land once, and once was enough. When no shrine was there to suit the comic purpose, he invented one. There was Adam's Tomb in Jerusalem, for instance; no one had heard of it before, but he described it compellingly, sending later American tourists off on a false quest for many years to come. But all this is heavily modulated; Twain has an instinct for veneration, but on his own terms. Large parts of the book are actually deeply sentimental and historically evocative, given to "fine writing." The comments on dirty Venice and its disappointing gondolas are soon followed by a very romantic recreation of the city ("In the glare of day there is little poetry about Venice, but under the charitable moon her stained palaces are white again"), and he complains bitterly about tourist sacrilege. The famous jokes at the expense of the Old Masters are shaded with guilty thoughts; perhaps he ought not to confess his opinions, "since one has no opportunity in America to acquire a critical judgement in art." He finds it hard to accept the past for not being the present, and culture for not being nature, which is what America is good at; he finds it difficult to accept monarchies for not being democracies, a theme that would last through his writing. Yet his conviction that all the emperors have no clothes shifts to sudden respect when he actually meets one: Napoleon III, or the Russian Czar.

The Innocents Abroad is actually a book of constantly shifting tones. You can read it as an attack on the false idols of Europe, or the innocent vulgarity of American tourists, not excluding himself. You can see it as a burlesque of the old, monumental guidebooks, or as a new, often highly romantic and sentimental guidebook to a dream-like comic Europe. It assaults the past from the virtuous standpoint of the democratic American present; it insults the vulgarities of the present when they are set against the grandeurs of the past. It is a book of rejection, but also a book of personal self-discovery. The shrines that are mocked are often reconstructed, if from a different angle of vision;

Venice becomes magical by night, and an illicit night visit to the Acropolis makes up for what is wrong with it by day. He is awed by the mystery of the Sphinx, infuriated when a vandal – a fellow American tourist – is seen trying to chip away a rock from its nose. It was the young William Dean Howells, reviewing the book in the august *Atlantic Monthly*, who picked up the point: "There is an amount of pure human nature in the book that rarely gets into literature." Twain had found a way to put an innocent Western vision – his own culture – onto a level with the solemnity of European history, and *The Innocents Abroad* is one of those books that (like *Lucky Jim* or *The Catcher in the Rye*) upturns and refreshes a conventional, solemnized view of culture, creating a fresh voice and a new spirit in the writing of prose. And that was how it was marketed; deliberately described by its publishers as a work by "the people's author," and sold through new subscription circuits, its sales and fame were backed by a highly successful lecture tour on which Twain comically recounted his experiences from the platform. Like Dickens, Twain was effectively constructing a new audience for the creation of himself; indeed he was, critics noted, in his way the "American Dickens," who had defined, with a single book, a radical, vernacular new version of the American humorist's role. It was to deflate religious, moral and cultural pretensions, challenge "nobilities and privileges and all kindred swindles," to use comic hyperbole both to summon up his own distinctive and gothic Western culture, and question the flavour of genteel America in what he himself named "the Gilded Age." The book was to outsell all Twain's other titles for his entire career; with it he became America's favourite "vandal," a role he maintained till the very end of his life. But the crucial point was that, just at a time when the American literary imagination, building on several generations of fictional invention, had passed on its vision to the tourist industry, which was now creating its American "Europe," Twain, with gleeful comic energy, was busily deconstructing it.

4.

Because of the pre-bellum Mississippi River setting of some of his very finest books (*Tom Sawyer*, *Huckleberry Finn*, *Pudd'nhead Wilson*), we generally like to think of Mark Twain as a Western writer out of the period before the Civil War. But the fact is that he was very much an author of the Gilded Age America that came after it: the age that committed itself to progress, national expansion, Social Darwinism and the "genteel tradition," the age of what has been called "the Incorporation of America."[2] With the success of *The Innocents Abroad*, the white-suited Western humorist was quite ready to become a literary Easterner. In 1870 he married the coal-owning heiress Olivia Langdon – he met her brother on the *Quaker City* cruise – and the next year settled in Hartford, Connecticut, midway between Boston and New York, and near the literary "Nook Farm" group, where they lived in high and embarrassingly expensive style for the next seventeen years. His books returned to his primal scene – in *Roughing It* (1872) the Nevada mining camps – but they also confronted the fast-changing age of "progress." *The Gilded Age* (1873), written with Charles Dudley Warner, is a satire on the post-war boom, noted for its portrait of the very Dickensian speculator and opportunist Colonel Sellers; with it he became the laureate of his age. But with *The Adventures of Tom Sawyer* (1876), he found his essential subject matter, the pastoral days of the Mississippi Valley before the Civil War, the homeland of American energy and innocent childhood simplicity. It was well-remembered country; he returned to it often. He recreated and celebrated the bustling flavour and history of the river in *Life on the Mississippi* (1883), and began but blocked on the greatest book of all, the story, told in the vernacular, of two people on a Mississippi raft trying to find the way toward freedom, *The Adventures of Huckleberry Finn* – which he finally completed and published in 1885.

Meantime Twain, always something of a Colonel Sellers himself, was investing energetically in many of the opportunities of the entrepreneurial era. The first American novelist to use a typewriter, he thought himself another of the great American inventors. He became a partner in the publishing house that printed General U. S. Grant's *Memoirs*, regarded his copyrights as, in effect, patents, and even organized literary mass-production, once planning to send another humorist to the South African diamond fields to scout a text he could rework as a second *Roughing It*. He invested in something called the

---

[2] See Alan Trachtenberg, *The Incorporation of America: Culture and Society in the Gilded Age* (New York, Hill and Wang, 1982). Trachtenberg's excellent study is concerned with the expansion of the industrialist capitalist system right across the continent, the binding together of transport and communications, the drawing together of all regions into a market economy, and the change in American cultural vision this produced.

Paige Typesetting Machine, which unfortunately didn't. Yet at the same time he remained a satirist, as the years went by an increasingly bitter one. Something else told him that money-lust could be a corruption ("The Man That Corrupted Hadleyburg"), technological materialism a disaster. His books may seem buoyant descriptions of childish delight in American wonders; some are. But the world of childhood arcadia was far distant, and Twain wrote often of the problems of the contemporary world. *Tom Sawyer* is a tale of childlike play, but *Huckleberry Finn* – "the best book we've had," said Ernest Hemingway – intrudes profound adult anxieties onto the world of the raft. By *Pudd'nhead Wilson* (1893) – a book that, as Twain said, turned from comedy to tragedy as it went along – his vision had grown bleak. There were strong personal reasons for this – the death of a daughter, then in 1894 the experience of bankruptcy as a result of his speculative investments. But even before misfortune fell, the sense of growing moral ambiguity is clear from his books. His writing alternated between fables of a world redeemed by science, technology and commerce, the world of the America of his day, and a world lost because of these things, as men became victims or machines, powerless in personality and moral action. Prompted alike by money worries, and the demands of his humour, which often seemed to him a demonic possession not under his control, he ran into a mental confusion that was, to a large degree, the confusion of his age itself. What began to concern him were not simply the promptings of the voice of conscience, the inner voice that makes Huck Finn decide he will go to hell and save Jim, but the feeling that in this world of vast new forces it was impossible to have any conscience at all.

The Gilded Age became an age both of national redemption and greatness, and of moral flux and bewilderment. He turned to the past, he feared, because of distrust of the present – but wasn't it "mental and moral masturbation"? Like many contemporaries, he reacted against positivism, seeing the world as a machine out of control, and needing the spirit of fantasy and dream to save it. And now he looked once again to Europe. It had never really been all that far from his imagination, at the opposite pole of his fascination with the old West and the river. Indeed, Europe had always been right there on the river, as he had shown in the "Castles and Culture" section of *Life on the Mississippi*, or in the influence of those counterfeit aristocrats (and precursors of some of the great black musicians of jazz), the "Duke" and the "King," in

Huckleberry Finn. Perhaps it was the baleful romanticism of Walter Scott that led the South into the Civil War; the fact remains that European myths, manners and aristocratic romanticism figured very regularly in his own fictional play, and in one late novel he actually sent Tom Sawyer and Huck Finn off to Europe to have their turn at adventures there. He greatly enjoyed reading European historical romances, and quite a number of his works are actually avaricious, delighted burlesques of them. *The Prince and the Pauper* (1881) tells the story of two English children, a royal son and a beggar's child, who are exchanged in the cradle (cradle exchanges never ceased to fascinate him, the true mark of the romantic). And if the book shows his burlesque delight and his republican dislike of monarchs and courts, it also displays his innocent, unrelieved fascination with aristocratic things; Twain always had a way of associating Europe with courts and kings. In a later work, *The American Claimant* (1892), Twain picks up and burlesques an old Hawthorne plot, and actually has the wealth-hungry Colonel Sellers from *The Gilded Age* aspiring to an English earldom – but then Twain himself was always the mischievous American claimant, with no time for the culture-religion, but quite a bit for the social presige Europe could represent.

The supreme example is *A Connecticut Yankee in King Arthur's Court* (1889) – his burlesquing satire on the Arthurian wonderland, the cult of medievalism, feudalism, chivalry and other fabulous flummery he had observed in Scott, Tennyson, Morris and the Pre-Raphaelites, and also found in the Old South, and no doubt somewhere in his own soul. With a blow to the head, Twain takes Hank Morgan, an ingenious republican machine-shop superintendent from the Colt gun factory in Hartford, Connecticut, back to sixth-century Camelot. He survives the time-shift with his Yankee ingenuity intact. He affects the Western style, impresses the Arthurians with his technical know-how and knowledge of the future, and becomes "Sir Boss." So far so good; Twain now seizes all the opportunities for burlesquing the medieval Victorian dream-world from the plain, practical American standpoint. Hank soon has Arthur's knights riding modern bicycles, and wearing advertising slogans ("Peterson's Prophylactic Toothbrushes"). He marries and has a daughter he calls "Hello-Central." Meanwhile, using his shrewd Yankee common sense and blatant commercialism, he drags the Arthurians out of their slough of monarchic and religious ignorance. He challenges feudalism, abolishes slavery, disproves magic (using new magic), undermines court and church, introduces electricity, newspapers, telephones, schools (called "Man-Factories"), and a stock exchange, and advances the twin principles of mechanism and democracy. He is also celebrating a Western dream in a European setting; sixshooters and "the cowboy business" obsess him, and Arthur's court becomes his new frontier. No wonder Howells called the book a "glorious gospel of equality," though its meaning is surely quite different. For, whether by clear intention or not, the plot suddenly turns, and technology and democracy reverse their meaning. Hank, the democratic technological redeemer, becomes the destroyer, and the machine becomes a weapon, not a reforming principle. Hank ends by frenziedly eloctrocuting the knights and destroying everyone in the fabulous world around him in an all-too-modern technological holocaust. Whether Twain meant it or no, the story had opened the doors of his own unease; this was another book that turned from comedy to tragedy as he wrote it.

In all this Twain was again reflecting many of the anxieties of his own time. As Larzer Ziff notes in his fine study of the 1890s,[3] the nineteenth century in America was closing in turbulence: the unorganized rise of the city and technology, the growth of trusts and corporations, the use of immigrants as cheap labour, unprecedented social problems, increasing unrest and public violence, the rise of progressivism and early unionism – all this had begun to diminish confidence in the national spirit of progress that had guided the country since the Civil War. Many more than Twain were conscious of living in an age of national unease and bewilderment. His vision grew ever grimmer, his satire more bitter and bleak, as he watched the century close. For nearly ten years, in the period of his bankruptcy, he lived in Europe. In the course of his life he crossed the Atlantic thirty-nine times; by his death he had spent something like fourteen years in Europe. In 1873, reversing the role of Dickens, he made a triumphal lecture tour in Britain. "I would rather live in England than America – which is treason," he noted. Five years later, when his extravagance was already leading him into financial problems, he went on a walking tour in Germany, to "go and breathe the free air of Europe." The sixteen-month tour led to a no less comic and burlesque but much more sympathetic book about his European travels and adventures, *A Tramp*

3 Larzer Ziff, *The American 1890s: The Life and Times of a Lost Generation* (London, Chatto and Windus, 1967).

Abroad (1880). As his fame grew, and the gilded age he stood for expanded and grew corporate, Europe became his place of relief. Here he could live more cheaply, delight not just in its comic absurdities but its social pleasures, and take a fresh look at his own America. Ahead of his bankruptcy, in 1891 he became in effect an expatriate, living happily in Austria and Italy, enjoying the rewards of his European fame even as he tried to write his way back into profit. As the new century dawned, his financial situation was restored, and he returned in acclaim to the United States. In 1907 he came back to Britain to accept the honorary degree of doctor of letters at Oxford University, "a loftier distinction than is conferrable by any other university" (William Dean Howells had had the same honour three years before); he told the reporters he had come to show Oxford "what a real American college boy looks like." The dockers cheered at Tilbury; at Saint Pancras Station George Bernard Shaw waited to proclaim him as "by far the greatest American writer," and the democratic American claimant now got his reward – he was received by King Edward VII at Windsor.[4]

Like Cooper's *The Prairie*, Twain's *Pudd'nhead Wilson* – not his best but in several ways his most complex and interesting work – is an expatriate novel, a long-distance view of the Mississippi Valley world of the 1830s from which he started. Again two children are exchanged in the cradle, one black and one white. The book suggests not only that slavery was the American stain, but that it is the universal human condition; the detective-story plot, perhaps borrowed a little from Sherlock Holmes, turns on fingerprinting and the whole question of genetic as well as social determinism. The long perspective of Italy is laid over the book, while its preface comically but also seriously explains his right to a European literary ancestry. The book was written, he gleefully explains, in Settignano, "three miles back of Florence, on the hills," with "the busts of Cerretani senators and other grandees of the line looking approvingly down on me as they used to look down on Dante, and mutely asking me to adopt them into my family, which I do with pleasure, for my remotest ancestors are but spring chickens compared with these robed and stately antiques, and it

---

[4] D. S. R. Welland, *Mark Twain in England* (London, Chatto, 1978), gives us a useful account of Twain's English visits and his British reputation. Also see Marcus Cunliffe, "Mark Twain and his 'English' Novels," in *In Search of America: Transatlantic Essays, 1951–1990* (New York, Westport; London, Greenwood Press, 1991).

will be a great and satisfying lift for me, that six hundred years will." Other important work came out of this late-life expatriation. The pessimistic and tragic story *The Mysterious Stranger* (which he left incomplete; it was published posthumously in 1916), one of his most revealing late works, was started in Vienna, and set in medieval Austria; he also completed his despairing commentary *What Is Man?*, about man as machine. In his strengths and indeed his weaknesses, Twain always remained a deeply American writer; but over the years Europe had become an ever more important part of his literary map and background, a contrast to the delights and the despairs of his America. Perhaps the clue was always there, back at the beginning, in *The Innocents Abroad*, where even in his Western iconoclasm there resides a clear element of superstitious valuation.

5.

In 1868, a year before Twain set sail on the Great Holy Land Funeral Procession, John William De Forest, author of one of the few contemporary novels of the Civil War, *Miss Ravenel's Conversion from Secession to Loyalty* (1867), published a famous article whose title stuck in American literary consciousness right up to the days of Tom Wolfe. The essay was called "The Great American Novel," and was a rallying call for a new post-war spirit in fiction, one which drew a truthful "picture of the ordinary emotions and manners of American existence." American fiction could never be the same again, he said. It was in change, just like the society itself, hastening away from its troubled past through the mechanisms of progress. This was true enough: with the end of the War not only had America totally changed, but the previous generation of novelists had almost entirely disappeared. Cooper and Hawthorne were dead, and Melville was silent except for poetry. And no less dead, after all the bitterness and grimness of recent years, was the high, innocent tradition of the American "romance." De Forest's essay firmly dismisses Hawthorne's playful fiction ("only a vague consciousness of life"); he equally dismisses the familiar kind of American writer who "neglected the trials of sketching American life and fled abroad for his subject." But regionalism and local colour were not the answer either. The "great American novel," claimed De Forest, would have to be a novel of the national realities, written in the spirit of contemporary realism. Manifestos are generally cries into empty air; in De Forest's case no sooner were his demands uttered than they appeared answered. For in the wake of war a new, remarkable generation of American novelists promptly emerged; they would dominate American fiction for the next several decades. The three most significant figures were Twain himself, William Dean Howells, and Henry James; all much of an age, they sprang into writing within a few years of each other (and would get their honorary degrees from Oxford University within a few years of each other, but nearly fifty years on). All of them sought to redefine the task of the Great American Novel; all professed some version of fictional realism. "I think I have written at least honestly, whether wisely or not," said Twain of his first book. "I may therefore venture to say that the air of reality (solidity of specification) seems to me the supreme virtue of a novel," James would pronounce, from Europe, when people began to listen to the lesson of the master. "Is it true? – true to the motives, the impulses, the principles that shape the life of actual men and women?" demanded William Dean Howells – the "Dean" of American literature, they said, when, as novelist, critic, and editor both of the *Atlantic Monthly* and *Harper's*, he dominated the direction of American fiction for the next forty years. And the great cause he always favoured was realism – "the only movement of our times that seems to me to have any vitality in it," he said.

It is not too much to say that between them these writers mapped the guiding geography of modern American fiction. Caught up in this was another question, of where literature actually came from – regionality, nationality, internationality? All had their different views; you could say that Twain chose the first, Howells the second, James the third. Yet they were friends, Howells in the centre, and their work and views affected each other. Howells started as a midwestern writer; born in Martin's Ferry, Ohio, he had his first success when – very like Hawthorne – he wrote a campaign biography for a future president. The president was another midwesterner, Abraham Lincoln, and when Lincoln took office in America's most difficult time, Howells got the familiar reward, a foreign diplomatic post. So, while America's bitter drama unfolded at home, the twenty-four-year-old Howells went to Venice as American consul over the crucial years of 1861–5 (he had asked for Munich, being interested in German literature, but the salary was too low). America had few interests here in wartime; tourism ceased, and only four American ships appeared in his term of office. Guilty about being away, he still fell in love with the "wonder city," a place, he said, of "peerless strangeness," and took full advantage of his undemanding duties. He learned Italian, studied European literature, explored the contemporary movement of realism, refined himself as a critic, and devoted himself to becoming a novelist. In very different vein from Twain, he sent European travel letters back to the Boston papers. In 1866 these vivid impressions were collected as *Venetian Life*; "Venice has been the university in which he has fairly earned the degree of Master," observed James Russell Lowell, one of his warm supporters in Boston. A second volume, *Italian Journeys*, describing other Italian cities, appeared in 1867, to equal acclaim, and encouraged many American tourists on the European quest. Meanwhile Howells himself was struggling with a question that would worry him throughout life, the problem of what he called "literary absenteeism." For an American, he had to admit, Europe was dangerously tempting. "I find myself almost expatriated," he wrote to Lowell, a keen Europhile who became American ambassador to Britain, "and I have seen enough of uncountryed Americans in Europe to disgust me with voluntary exile . . . but with what unspeakable regret I shall leave Italy! . . . in a year or two more of lotus-eating, I shouldn't want to go home at all."

But Howells did go home, to Boston, and was warmly received in the cultural citadel as the voice of the new generation. By 1871 he was editing *The Atlantic Monthly*, waging his campaign to bring the great spirit of European realism – the new kind of novel shaped by Tolstoy and Turgenev and George Eliot, the novel of common life and the "day of small things" – onto American soil, telling American writers they should concern themselves with "the more smiling aspects of life, which are the most American, and seek the universal in the individual rather than in the social interests." In some thirty-five novels, often written at the rate of one a year, he became himself one of the nation's great fictional "photographers" (Henry Adams attached the word to him in a review of his first novel), telling vivid and commonplace stories about men of business, journalists, the crowding American cities, honeymooners at Niagara, modern marriage and the new custom of divorce, the world of immigrant poverty, or the lives of New York bohemians. He felt himself destined to redress what he called the "idealizing" tendency in New England life; true romance was in the ordinariness. "Ah! Poor Real Life, which I love, can't I make others share the delight

I find in thy foolish and inspid face?" he asked in his first, delightfully plain novel *The Wedding Journey* (1872), about honeymooning at Niagara. It wasn't just the vividness but the fullness of the record that mattered; besides the novels, there were as many plays, and poetry, criticism, travel writing, social commentary. Some of the books were remarkable works of social truth (*A Modern Instance* (1882), *The Rise of Silas Lapham* (1885), the story of a solid "Man of Boston," a paint-manufacturer, for instance), others not much more than fictionalized journalism. If the socio-moral novel began to acquire a footing in America, this was largely due to Howells, the great delineator of the moral pains and pleasures of the socially mobile, increasingly material world of the post-Civil War decades. His characteristic heroes are in upward social momentum, provincial spirits seeking success, challenging the old social guardians; his theme is often the risk of moral imbalance. His critical influence grew formidable; he read even more than he wrote, including much of the work by the younger writers who followed him along the path of realism, journalism and local colour over the next thirty years, and whom he supported. Friend both of Twain and James, he somehow stood between them: never as vernacular or sentimental as the one, he never became a distanced self-conscious artist like the other. When America felt change, he felt it too, responding furiously to the hanging of the anarchists after the Chicago Haymarket Riots of the 1880s, or warmly supporting the new muckraking Naturalism that swept the 1890s. In a different way from Twain, but with the same potency, he *was* the spirit of American fiction.

When James wrote in his study of Hawthorne (1879) of the absence of "forms" in America (no castles, no manors, no parsonages, no Oxford, no Eton, no Ascot, and so on), Howells crisply observed that there was just all of human life remaining. But he was also a crypto-European, frequently returning to Europe and acknowledging its claim on the American writer. He made many European trips (eight in the last ten years of his life) and published five more European travel-books. And, at very different stages of his life and writing, memories of his unforgettable Italy lit up his fiction. Several of his novels – *A Foregone Conclusion* (1875), *The Lady of the Aroostook* (1879), *Indian Summer* (1885), and more – draw, in his distinctively realistic vein, on his European travels and experiences, and the world his own travel writings had celebrated.[5] They are – and he developed the term himself

[5] There is a good brief account of them in Nathalia Wright, *American Novelists in Italy*, cited above.

– "international novels," a form in which he was to be acknowledged a pioneer. (After all, his *A Foregone Conclusion* came out at just the same time Henry James opened his career in the genre with *Roderick Hudson*). These books generally have Venetian or Italian settings, and deal with encounters between Americans and European values, the identifying feature of the genre. Young American girls are lured by European complexity, or American artists expatriate to the Italian scene, which is dense, strange and romantic. But, as in Hawthorne's *Marble Faun*, a book Howells constantly harks back to, Europe, mostly Italy, is eternally threatening to American simplicity and modern morality. In the pages of the best of them, *Indian Summer*, Howells' own favourite, a group of American expatriates in romantic Florence live "simple and innocent lives in the world of the ideal." The central figure, Theodore Colville, a middle-aged and midwestern newspaperman returning to Europe to realize "he has not yet lived his life," is a prefiguration of many of James' heroes, above all Lambert Strether in *The Ambassadors*, who, as we shall see, owes a lot to Howells. But Howells somehow feels the need to check the impulse, and give the American real and the spirit of the modern the final advantage. So most of his characters (not all) are finally returned home to the great American commonplace, the course Howells took himself. The danger was that Europe could destabilize the American imagination, become a danger to the honest American truths, represent the falsehood of romance. After all, he said, expressing a common faith, it was "better to have too little past, as we have, than too much, as they have."

The young Henry James, who was in the process of reaching just the opposite conclusions, saw the point clearly when he reviewed *A Foregone Conclusion* in the *North American Review*: "The story passes into another tone . . . out of Venice and the exquisite Venetian suggestiveness, over to Providence, to New York," he wrote. "We ourselves regret the transition, though the motive of our regrets is hard to define. It is a transition from the ideal to the real, to the vulgar, from soft to hard, from colour to something which is not colour." Howells disagreed, of course; and all was fine as long as he could accept his own principle that it was "the smiling aspects of life that are the most American." But, like Twain, Howells found his views darkened with the years, and with the growing crisis of values that came with the great American change. Perhaps not everything, after all, was well with the American present. "After fifty years of optimistic content with [American] 'civilization' and its ability to come out all right in the end, I now abhor it, and feel it is coming out all wrong in the end," he confessed in a letter to James in 1888, after the Haymarket Riots. And, writing on "literary absentee-ism" in the essays of *Literature and Life* (1902), he acknowledged that, in cosmopolitan times, nationality might not be everything, inter-nationality might be a virtue after all. But he had publicly made his choice, the opposite to James'. And those two contrasting choices would go on resounding throughout late nineteenth-century American fiction.[6]

6.

Twain said he wrote *The Innocents Abroad* to discourage the atavistic American desire that took Americans back to Europe. If so, it clearly didn't work, not even in his own case. The years of his career were years of new American cosmopolitanism, and the transatlantic contacts multiplied, decade by decade, year by year. As immigration from Europe surged (ten million immigrants crossed the Atlantic between 1860 and 1890), so did American trips in the other direction (ninety thousand American tourists returned from Europe through the New York customs by 1891). Wealth, better political relations, improving facilities for travel were one reason for this, but another was an increasing sense of a common Americo-European, even an Anglo-Saxon, destiny. There was also a growing disquiet, among American artists and writers, with the blatantly commercial spirit of post-Civil War America. The whole mood seemed different from earlier times, when, Emerson said, Americans went to Europe to be Americanized. According to Van Wyck Brooks, the pre-war literary travellers – Irving, Cooper, Longfellow, Hawthorne and many more – made their transatlantic voyages with "the unquestioning instinct of homing pigeons, which brought them back from every foreign journey." The post-war literary travellers, he said, went in a very different spirit: ". . . as the old causes grew dimmer and dimmer, as the European peasants arrived in thousands, as wealth advanced and tourists multiplied, as the human imagination felt cramped and thwarted in the vast industrial beehive, . . . this yearning for an older homeland rose in

[6] The story is told in detail in James L. Woodress, Jr, *Howells and Italy* (Durham, N.C., Duke University Press, 1952).

people's minds and men of sensibility flocked to Europe, not to study, as in former days, and carry their spoils back, like travelling Romans, but as if they could reascend the river of time."[7] The truth was more complicated. These were times of regionalism and local colour in American writing, and each small town across the continent now seemed to acquire its own literary laureate. "Write of what you know! Write of your very own!" cried one of them, Edward Eggleston. Locality counted, and Howells' suspicion of "literary absenteeism" was common enough; in the time of Teddy Roosevelt it even became a political issue. The fact remains that, for many reasons, the trans-atlantic contact intensified now as never before; many American writers headed for Europe, some for visits, and some for good.

The travellers were of several kinds. Some of them were genteel "paleface" American writers from the East Coast, especially Boston Brahmins who had always kept the European link. (When the young Henry Adams went to London as private secretary to his own father, when he was American Minister in Britain during the Civil War, he described his seven London years as "the biggest piece of luck I ever had," but also observed the extent to which educated Americans were always on their literary knees before the European.) Now growing ever more conscious they were being displaced from their cultural role by an age of industrialism and immigration, robber barons and political jobbery, they improved on the transatlantic connection. British and New England writers now stood together as the standard English-language authors of the day; wasn't Longfellow's bust in Westminster Abbey? As the great Bostonian, Oliver Wendell Holmes, explained in *One Hundred Days in Europe* (1888), Europe had not chosen to sacrifice culture to stark energy, which was why artistic Americans wanted to go there – especially Britain, "that old home of his fathers, so delightful in itself, so infinitely desirable on account of its nearness to Paris, to Geneva, to Rome, to all that is most interesting in Europe. The less wealthy, the less cultivated, the less fastidious class of Americans are not so much haunted by these longings." Part of the temptation was artistic, a traditional response to the cultural past and present of a still world-dominant Europe. Another part was undoubtedly social. As Adams said, *belle-époque* Europe, in an age of grim American

[7] See Van Wyck Brooks, *The Flowering of New England, 1815-1865* (London, Dent, 1936).

mechanism, was a remarkably pleasant place for those with wealth to live in, and offered social pleasures just not available at home.[8] Contacts were reciprocated. European titles were glad to trade with new American dollars. In 1890 the great New York socialite William Astor moved to Britain, bought and restored Hever Castle, and died Viscount Astor of Hever. Paris became such an important stop on the social trail that the *New York Herald* established an edition there, filled with society news. Meantime New York had become such an important matrimonial marketplace for Europeans of rank that American papers published details of marriageable heiresses, with lists of fortunes descending from ten million to one million dollars. In 1895, when the Duke of Marlborough married Consuelo Vanderbilt, the transatlantic marital traffic reached its peak, leading the London *Times* to notice that the House of Lords was "getting a good many American mothers."[9]

All this revealed an age of *belle-époque* alliances based on mingling European style and American wealth. American capitalists built their mansions in *beaux arts* style, or transformed Newport, R.I., Virginia or California with *châteaux* from the Loire, baronial keeps from Scotland, castles from Spain, statues from Italy. Tennessee Williams later called it "the great European fire sale." The dealers of Europe, such as the famous Duveen, sold and shipped all the paintings, the *objets d'art*, the entire transplanted castles and portable ruins Europe could spare, and American wealth was glad to have.[10] A new generation of American cultural specialists emerged: Harvard aesthetes like Bernard Berenson,

---

[8] "I can understand how an American catches English manners; and how they do catch English minds!" complained the American historian Henry Adams, who himself spent a good time in Europe and felt displaced in the new America. "Especially how they do keep such in these days when the English mind is no longer good form even in England." (See Newton Arvin (ed.), *The Selected Letters of Henry Adams* (New York, Farrar Strauss, 1951).)

[9] There is a good account of this in R. H. Heindel, *The American Impact on Great Britain, 1898–1914: A Study of the United States in World History* (Philadelphia, University of Pennsylvania Press, 1940). Also see Dixon Wecter, *The Saga of American Society: A Record of Social Aspirations, 1607–1937* (New York, Scribner, 1937).

[10] Wonderful records of all this are to be found in Matthew Josephson, *The Robber Barons: The Great American Capitalists, 1861–1901* (New York, Harcourt Brace, 1934); Dixon Wecter, cited above; Russell Lynes, *The Tastemakers* (London, Hamish Hamilton, 1954); and Stewart H. Holbrook, *The Age of the Moguls* (London, Gollancz, 1954). Also see Ward McAllister, *Society as I Have Found It* (New York, Cassell, 1890). On the new era of connoisseurship and art dealing, see S. N. Behrman, *Duveen* (London, Hamish Hamilton, 1952).

who departed Boston for Florence and spent the rest of his life there, studying Renaissance art and making his income from authenticating Renaissance pieces on behalf of the art-collecting mania of the new American rich ("nobody before us had dedicated his entire activity, his entire life, to connoisseurship," Berenson explained in *Sketch for a Self-Portrait*, 1949). Berenson saw himself a natural "gentleman" who needed Europe. So did many other Americans, often of wealthy background and cosmopolitan parentage, who settled in Britain, France or Italy: Logan Pearsall Smith (Berenson's brother-in-law) and Howard O. Sturgis in England, Edith Wharton in Paris, Leo Stein and George Santayana in Florence and Rome. And it was no great step from the new aestheticism to the new bohemianism, that stylish aesthetic dissent from our all too material world. In the last quarter of the nineteenth century a great many would-be artists in prose, poetry or paint made their way to Europe, generally following in the wake of Henri Murger's *Scènes de la vie de Bohème* (1848), with its tempting picture of riotous poverty and free-spirited love among the easels and ateliers of Paris (or wherever). Ever since the Paris Exposition of 1867, the city of Montmartre and the painter's garret had become the great lure for young American artists able to depend, in a time of increased wealth, on drafts from home. James McNeill Whistler and Henry Harland, John Singer Sargent, Richard Hovey and James Gibbons Huneker were part of an ever-growing band, who, while looking to live in Paris or its surrounding countryside the life of a Courbet or a Verlaine, also began building an important bridge between the new movements of European art like Impressionism and Naturalism and what was going on at home. In the last quarter of the century significant colonies of American writers – traditional and *avant-garde* – gathered in the European capitals and centres, with fundamental consequences for the Modern movement and America's relation to it. Some became tellers of transatlantic tales, recorders of the whole experience; these travellers themselves became both source and subject matter for a new cosmopolitan note in fiction.

If the palefaces and the aesthetes came, so too did the redskins. Twain was not the only Western writer to take the eastward path. Britain became a regular place of resort for a new breed of Western humorists, whose open ways and comic note appealed to English tastes (even if the humour often turned out at British expense). As Whitman said, there was something in the English breast that "vibrated to the wild horse business." Artemus Ward was invited over to Britain to edit that great national institution, *Punch*. Ambrose Bierce turned up in London a California roughneck, spent three years, and went back, they said, a wit. Joaquin Miller came to London, turned up at social gatherings in a sombrero and cowboy boots, and became the toast of English society hostesses – though even Mark Twain, visiting London, described him as "a discordant note, a disturber and degrader of the solemnities." Also to Twain's fury, his once friend and present enemy Bret Harte was made American consul in Krefeld, Germany, and then got the equivalent posting in Glasgow. In 1885, when his post ended, he moved to London, and remained until his death in 1902. Decked out in monocle and yellow gloves, the once Western Harte looked – reported startled American visitors – a perfect English dandy, and became not just a British literary light but an important pillar of the Royal Thames Yacht Club. When the young Stephen Crane came to Britain in the Nineties and settled as a squire with a sixgun at Brede Place in Sussex, he was in an established tradition. So, later, was Ezra Pound when he brought American populism to European Modernism, or Ernest Hemingway when he appeared in Twenties Paris acting like a hunter from the Michigan woods. Twain's honorary degree at Oxford was an increasingly familiar mark of European respect for those who followed the brave, brazen path of the informal and the vernacular – so long as they came from the United States.

And all of them found their most elaborate and cunning chronicler in Henry James. In our day it is sometimes easy to forget that James – the most important and central figure in this traffic, the third crucial novelist of the post-Civil War generation, and for forty years an expatriate in Europe – was writing his "international theme" out of the stuff of a dense real life. His complex novels of American innocence encountering European experience, or *vice versa*, his portraits of rich American businessmen hungering for some absent culture, of passionate pilgrims and Italianized American aesthetes, of Little Bilhams painting and seeking life in Paris, of artists living wild in the castles of Europe or haunting the ruins of Rome, of wandering American journalists collecting European society stories, of Milly Theale wandering the poorer parts of London, were founded on the doings and the movings of the day. James kept a close and observant account, noting the nature and the danger of their various temptations, the different shadings of what he called, writing of Henry Harland, "the feeling of the American for his famous Europe." When Mrs Margaret Chanler – one of the New York "Four Hundred," also with a home in Italy, where she was born – explained to him she could not possibly tell whether she was American or European, he expressed surprise. "Dear Henry," a friend explained to her, "he forgets how easy it has become to cross the ocean; the issue that so worries him does not exist." But it did, of course, and no writer ever kept a finer account of "the complex fate" of those who felt the transatlantic state of mind, populated the international scene, or suffered the superstitious valuation of Europe. And no writer better explored what these social, cultural and aesthetic transactions actually demanded from writers of fiction. Without his record we would be immensely the poorer; for what came out of the transatlantic traffic was the "international" or the transatlantic novel, which was to prove a major modern form.

7.

In 1904 James, now in his final decade, and having by this date spent thirty years in Europe, recrossed the Atlantic to inspect his native land. He wrote the record of his complex impressions on his eleven-month visit in his troubled late book *The American Scene* (1907). He saw, as he had to confess, many wonders; America was now a new world, and the skyscrapered New York skyline looked like "a broken haircomb turned up." He was far from delighted by much he observed: a high-rise "hotel civilization," an immigrant babble, an American society given to a "passionate pecuniary purpose which plays with all forms, which derides and devours them," a spectacle of "the new, the simple, the cheap, the common, the commercial, the immediate, and, too often the ugly," which forced one to "tighten one's aesthetic waistband." Something had disappeared from American meanings: it was, he said, "the huge democratic broom that has made the clearance and that one seems to see brandished in the empty sky." But a key passage in the book gives a sense of a different America. It describes his return to Newport (where he studied as an art student), his memories of those who wintered there in the days before it became a *belle-époque* social paradise. He recalls the people he knew:

> . . . a collection of the detached, the slightly disenchanted and casually disqualified, and yet of the resigned and contented, of the socially

orthodox: a handful of mild, oh delightfully mild, cosmopolites, united by three common circumstances, that of having for the most part more or less lived in Europe, that of their sacrificing openly to the ivory idol whose name is leisure, and that, not least, of formed critical habit. These things had been felt as making them excrescences on the American surface, where nobody ever criticised, especially after the grand tour, and where the great black ebony god of business was the only one recognized . . . I find myself in fact tenderly evoking them as special interests of the great – or perhaps I have a right only to say of the small – American complication; the state of one's having been so pierced, betimes, by the sharp outland dart as to be able ever afterwards but to move about, vaguely and helplessly, with the shaft in one's side.

It was such figures who represented, as he put it in his study of William Wetmore Story, the pains of the great American drama, "the state of being of the American who has bitten deep into the apple, as we may figure it, of 'Europe,' and then has been obliged to take his lips from the fruit."[11] Portraits of consciousness displaced by the double claims of the transatlantic dreams and new American social reality, they were part of a primary subject to which he devoted his life, and from which he made much of his art. The result was not simply the creation of what we have learned, thanks to Howells and James himself, to call "the international novel," the novel that deals, with a sense of equivalence, with characters and cultural forces from more than one country. It was the making of a form, and of a sense of form, that was born out of that cosmopolitan process: that modern art that came, in the end, from the power of the sharp outland dart.

Of all our writers, James was to take furthest the many dramas, moral and social and artistic, that came out of the now complex transatlantic reflection: the angular relations of innocence and experience, past and present, nationality and cosmopolitanism, historical stasis and historical change, social reality and social unreality, realism and romance, life felt and life seen as impression, the social self and the flowing inner drama of consciousness, pride and guilt, travel and withdrawal. Apples remind us of temptation, and temptation of knowledge, and knowledge of innocence, and innocence of paradise;

[11] Henry James, in *William Wetmore Story and His Friends* (2 vols, 1903; reprinted London, Thames and Hudson, 1957). Reflecting on Story, famously discontented on both sides of the Atlantic, James considers the problem of two apples: "The apple of 'America' is a totally different apple, which, however firm and ruddy, is not to be (and above all half a century ago was not to have been) negotiated, as the newspapers say, by the same set of teeth."

James is the great teaser of transatlantic vocabulary, the great explorer of all the mythic underpinnings that the western traffic had developed. His own drama with the tempting apple of Europe began early and finished late, when his nationality changed almost on his deathbed. It was inherited from his father, Henry James, Sr, Albany citizen, New York millionaire, scholar, Swedenborgian philosopher, a devout American who could not stay away from Europe even though he was an impassioned republican who said he preferred to be with the Indians. "Looking on our four stout boys," he wrote to his Transcendentalist friend Emerson in the summer of 1849, when Henry was six, "who have no playroom within doors, and import shocking bad manners from the street, with much pity, we gravely ponder whether it would not be better to go abroad for a few years with them, allowing them to absorb French and German and get a better sensuous education than they are likely to get here. To be sure, this is but a glimpse of our ground of proceeding – but perhaps you know some decisive word which shall dispense us from any further consideration of the subject."[12] Henry James, Sr was always looking for a reason not to go to Europe, but Emerson cannot have found the decisive word. He went, as he had gone before and would continue to go. Henry spent his childhood shuttling between the land of "the busy, the tipsy, and Daniel Webster" – in fact in the smart Washington Square district of pre-war New York City, to which he returned in the novel *Washington Square* (1881) – and his European "sensuous education," with foreign governesses, schools, and endless exposure to the European arts and landscape. All his first memories, he claimed, were of Europe. He was taken first at the age of six months, which left him with a first recollection of the Napoleonic column in Paris's Place Vendôme: "the poison had entered my veins." Another three-year European visit, which took in Geneva, London and pre-Haussmann Paris during 1855–8, left him with "a general sense of *glory*" and an indelible memory of the artistic splendours of "the bridge to Style" in the Louvre's Galerie d'Apollon.[13]

James had seen his family, as it seemed to him, constantly drawn back through some essential need toward the "vaunted scene" of Europe, and learned the lesson. He had always known, he said, that

[12] Quoted in F. O. Matthiessen (ed.), *The James Family* (New York, Knopf, 1947).
[13] The detailed story of James' life is excellently given in Leon Edel, *The Life of Henry James* (London, 5 vols, Rupert Hart-Davis, 1953–72; revised edition, 2 vols, Penguin, 1977).

there was art in Europe – just as one knew "there were practically no hot rolls and no iced water." So began what he was to call "an enlarged and uplifted gape" that would eventually turn into "a banquet of initiation which was in the event to prolong itself through years and years." James' vocabulary of European veneration – filled with its "gapes" and "awes," its "hallucinations" and "visitations" – was to become an obsessive part of his literary style, that distinctive object, which he would cast over all he saw and all he experienced, refining it almost to the point of total obscurity. The great approach to the shrine of ultimate revelation – "the great good thing," which we may be sure lay somewhere in Europe – grew ever more indirect, more labyrinthine, chased through longer corridors, over changing seas and in ever-shifting cities. It was joy and despair, experience and solitude. It excited and dismayed, demanded ever new adventures in form, style, mythic exploration. Europe was the "vaunted scene," the "gate of the admirations," the "threshold of expectation," the "scene for the reverential spirit," the "world in fine raised to the richest and noblest expression." It was the shaft in one's side, the apple never quite destined to be eaten, but never quite the same as the American apple. The apple's look changed constantly, the adventure turned this way and that, and in the two unfinished novels James left behind at his death in 1916 (the other "great good thing") – *The Sense of the Past* and *The Ivory Tower* – the battle, of past and present, Europe and America, home and homelessness, still goes on, almost to the point of annihilation.[14]

No doubt it indeed started in Newport – where, just before the Civil War, Henry went to train as an artist, saw the power of the "outland dart," and became aware of the American painter expatriates who had

[14] James' vocabulary, eternally somewhere between the literal and the metaphoric, regularly depends on position-taking, on the standpoint and angle of the watcher, the nature of the impression, the weight of its visitation. The tourist, travel writer or sketch painter is one user of these angles and impressions; the photographer or the film cameraman is another – one reason why James' writing strikes us not just as impressionistic but as technical. (So "angle of vision" quickly turns into literary "point-of-view.") Thus he writes of Paris: "I hung over the balcony, and doubtless with my brothers and my sister, though I recover what I felt as so much relation and response to the larger, the largest appeal only, that of the whole perfect Parisianism I seem to myself always to have possessed mentally – even if I had but just turned twelve! – and that now filled out its frame or case for me from every lighted window, up and down, as if each of these had been, for strength of sense, a word in some immortal quotation, the very breath of civilized lips."

"set the example and made out the road" to Europe. Unable to serve in the War because of a "horrid . . . obscure hurt" (which, like so many other things in James, remains obscure to this day) he went for a year to the Harvard Law School, but turned his attention to literature. He began writing for the New England reviews; his first short story appeared in 1865, just as the Civil War ended. Like Howells, just back from Venice, he became a admired youthful member of the Boston literary scene, but he drew different deductions from his situation. The war had darkened American experience forever, but also cosmopolitanized it, opened it out to Europe. And American writers now had the great advantage over Europeans, for they had become "heirs of all the ages": "we can deal freely with forms of civilization not our own, can pick and choose and assimilate and in short (aesthetically &c) claim our property wherever we find it," he explained to a friend. Little wonder that, as the doors to Europe opened wider with the new age of travel, he was soon off again. In 1869–70, aged twenty-six, he went on a fifteen-month visit, hoping to write travel-pieces, which (as Twain and Howells had shown) were now nearly as popular as travel itself; and throughout his lifetime he would remain a major travel writer. He took in England ("a good married matron"), Switzerland ("a magnificent man"), and Italy ("a beautiful dishevelled nymph"). As he realized and noted, the most striking differences were not so much between America and England, but between Americo-England and the other European countries, which each offered to the grasping imagination their own international drama.

The crucial moment was his arrival in Rome, then in its last days as a papal state. Unlike Twain he had no problem with awe; its effect was overwhelming. He toured the city for a delirious five hours without taking breakfast. "Here I am then in the Eternal City . . . At last – for the first time – I live!" he wrote home. "It beats everything: it leaves the Rome of your fancy – your education – nowhere. It makes Venice-Florence-Oxford-London seem like little cities of pasteboard. I went reeling and moaning thro' the streets, in a fever of enjoyment." It was not surprising his father felt it necessary to issue a stern warning about the hazardous effects of the historical picturesque: "The historical consciousness rules to such a distorted excess in Europe that I have always been restless there, and ended by pining for the land of the future exclusively," he replied, not quite accurately: "Condemned to *remain* there I should stifle in a jiffy." James didn't remain there, but promised himself to return. A second visit to Europe of twenty-eight months, in 1872–4, saw him spend half his time in Italy. By now Rome had become capital of the newly unified nation, but to James it was a city "in which your sensation rarely begins and ends with itself; it reverberates – recalls, commemorates, resuscitates something else." He went to Florence, and began work on his first strong novel, *Roderick Hudson* (1876), a latter-day rewriting of Hawthorne's *The Marble Faun*. Roderick is an American sculptor (probably based on William Wetmore Story) who seeks "the real taste of life in Italy," then comes to drink too deep from its cup of experience. The book is filled with James' own exalted enthusiasm for Europe, Italy, and all that goes with it – "knowledge, pleasure, experience." He is also aware of the ambiguity of this Arcadian enterprise; James has Hawthorne's, and Howells', doubt about the moral danger of aesthetic experience, but his deduction is different. This is a novel about the value of the great human quest for experience, emblemized in Roderick's statue of the boy drinking deep from the cup of life, a cup many of his characters would drink. Later James would have doubts about Italy and its "favouring air," saying that the picturesque does not always work best in the land of the picturesque. But he revisited often, and many of his stories are set there, from *The Aspern Papers* to the crisis of *The Portrait of a Lady*.

James himself now returned home, in 1874, to "try New York" – "thinking it my duty to attempt to live at home before I should grow older." But the real direction of his interests, the pull of his material, was quite clear from the writing he published. In 1875 his European travel-pieces appeared as a book, *Transatlantic Sketches*; so did six of his recent tales, published under the apt title of *The Passionate Pilgrim and Other Tales* (his first "sop to the international Cerebus," he called it). They would map many of the key themes of his mature work as a novelist. In the title story, yet another American sees himself as heir to an English estate ("certain London characteristics – monuments, relics, hints of history, local moods and memories – are more deeply suggestive to an American soul than anything else in Europe"), though the story is notable for its careful imagery of English society and landscape. Two Italian tales, "The Last of the Valerii" and "The Madonna of the Future," reflect on the powerful, sometimes deceptive impact of an Italy almost too much impregnated with art on Americans who think themselves to be "the disinherited of Art" ("We're the disinherited of Art! We're condemned to be superficial! . . . The soil of American perception is a poor little barren artificial deposit!"[15]). "Madame de Mauves," set in France, is about titles and endowment, the swopping of European title for American fortune. Together the tales sketch out a basic artistic, moral and social geography – of a material England, a social France, an aesthetic Italy – that he would repeat, reconstruct and rewrite in his later fiction, not least *The Portrait of a Lady.* But by the November of the same year, just as Americans prepared to gaze on the electrical and telephonic wonders of the Philadelphia Centennial Exhibition, which pointed the way to the future, James was off again. "Harry James has gone abroad again, not to return, I fancy, even for visits," reported his friend Howells. He had made his "choice," was back in Europe – and this time it was decisive.

8.

"My choice is the Old World – my choice, my need, my life," he would reflect in a remarkable self-examining passage in his notebook, written in a Boston hotel room on a return visit five years afterwards: "There is no need for me for me today to argue about this; it is an inestimable blessing to me, and a rare good fortune, that the problem was settled long ago, and I have now nothing to do but to act upon the settlement." His choice was not aesthetic Rome, not solid London, but Paris. "This was not what I wanted; what I wanted was London," he noted. "But London appeared to me then impossible." He spent a few days there, but then took a "snug little *troisième*" at 29 Rue de Luxembourg, later the Rue Cambon, near the Place Vendôme. Here he lived for a year, writing – there was no time to waste – his new novel *The American* (which opens, appropriately enough, in the Louvre) and the travel letters he was sending back to the New York *Tribune.*[16] He went often to the *Comédie-Française*, saw (and at this stage did not much admire) the work of the brand-new French "Impressionists," wrote on the contemporary French writers – reacting warmly to their artistic sense, but against the

[15] This, it should be said, does not go unanswered. " 'You seem fairly at home in exile,' I made answer, 'and Florence seems to me a very easy Siberia . . . Nothing is so easy as to talk about our want of nursing air, of a kindly soil, of opportunity, of inspiration, of things that help. The only thing that helps is to do something fine . . .' "
[16] Collected by Leon Edel and Ilse Lind in *Parisian Sketches* (London, 1958).

brute spirit of their realism. He met, crucially, Turgenev, a fellow exile, and through him encountered Flaubert, Maupassant, the Goncourt Brothers, Daudet, Zola, the major French realists of the day. They struck him as impressive, but introverted, parochial, indifferent to the morality of art, while their concern with schools and movements seemed "an excellent engine for the production of limited perfection." "I don't like their wares, and they don't like ours," he complained to Howells, back at home; but some of this was over-stated. James was delighted as well as shocked, and in the following years his indebtedness to their sense of the art of fiction and of the task of the modern novel would grow greatly, his critical respect (as the many marvellous essays he wrote on French fiction show) increase.[17] In any case his horizons were plainly widening in Paris, as he indicated to Howells: "The great merit of the place is that one can arrange one's life here exactly as one pleases – that there are facilities for every kind of habit and taste, and that everything is accepted and understood." However, the American community in Paris was notably oppressive, and the French literary community far too mandarin ("I saw, morever, that I should be an eternal outsider"). "I have done with 'em forever, and I am turning English all over," he wrote to his brother William, "I desire only to feed on English life and the contact of English minds – I only wish I knew some."

He quickly did. In November 1876 he moved to London, taking a lodging at 3 Bolton Street, Piccadilly (in 1886 he moved on to a flat at 34 De Vere Gardens West, Kensington), and noting: "for one who takes it as I take it, London is on the whole the most possible form of life. I take it as an artist and as a bachelor; as one who has the passion of observation and whose business is the study of human life. It is the biggest aggregation of human life – the most complete compendium of the world." It was, he wrote, his "anchorage for life."[18] It was also the safe base for the regular journeys he now took all round Europe – back to Paris (he had not "done with 'em forever"), back to Venice, back to

---

17 By 1884 he was writing: "I have been seeing something of Daudet, Goncourt and Zola; and there is nothing more interesting to me now than the effort and experiment of this little group, with its truly infernal intelligence of art, form, manner."

18 F. O. Matthiessen and Kenneth B. Murdock (eds), *The Notebooks of Henry James* (New York and London, Oxford University Press, 1947; reissued 1961). James wrote these self-conscious notes in Boston, on a return visit in 1881, when, he told himself: "I am 37 years old, I have made my choice, and God knows that I have now no time to waste."

Rome. He also met a good many English minds: "I can hardly say how it was, but little by little I came to know people, to dine out, etc. I did, I was able to do, nothing at all to bring this state of affairs about; it came rather of itself," he wrote in his notebook. He was soon meeting Tennyson, Hardy, Browning, George Eliot, Mr Gladstone, Lord Rosebery of Mentmore, weekending at innumerable great "glittering" country homes, engaging in his "siege" of English society, and dining out 107 times in the winter of 1879. (Evidently once in Britain the writers' life was a social affair.) He was convinced that the English were a more complete race, more largely nourished, "denser, stronger," and he also recognized his connection with the English tradition of fiction, and the work of English moral realists like George Eliot. London, that "most complete compendium," was stimulating his sense of realism, his feel for human density, his sense of the novel's intrinsic solidity ("it takes a great deal of history to produce a little literature . . . it needs a complex social machinery to set a writer into motion"). Not all was joy; he frequently acknowledged London solitude and foggy gloom. As he wrote home: "To tell the truth, I find myself a good deal more of a cosmopolitan (thanks to the combination of the continent and the USA which has formed my lot) than the average Briton of culture; and to be – to have become by force of circumstances – a cosmopolitan is by necessity to be a good deal alone."

His production increased, his art became surer, so did the complexity of his never-to-be-still engagement with Europe. In this founding stage of his work, his subject was, irreducibly, the "international theme." As he explained it himself much later, in his New York Edition preface to the volume containing *Daisy Miller*, Europe was "constantly in requisition as the more salient American stage or more effective *repoussoir*, and yet with any particular *action* on this great lighted and decorated scene depending for more than half its sense on one of my outland importations." And at first it was American travellers who took central place on the lighted and decorated scene. In *Roderick Hudson* it is the American artist in Italy; in *Daisy Miller* (1878), the novella with which he won his early fame in Britain, the passionate artist is replaced by that scandalous vessel of promise, the young American girl, while Rome is not simply the city of art but the home of malaria. In *The American* (1877), the scene switches to France, and the dominant figure is the symbolically named Christopher Newman, the millionaire American businessman, "the great Western Barbarian, stepping forth in his innocence and might, gazing a while at this poor corrupt old world and then swooping down on it." Newman – who "scarcely knew a hard chair from a soft one," "possessed a talent for stretching his legs which quite dispensed with adventitious facilities," and for whom "Raphael and Titian and Reubens were a new kind of arithmetic" – is Columbus in reverse, and surely owes a little to Mark Twain (this is, after all, James' funniest novel, an artful comedy). What he seeks is less art, culture or experience than an aristocratic wife to match his dollars; but as he takes the measure of Europe, it takes the measure of him. James later claimed to distrust the book, feeling it was an arch-romance, where "the way things don't happen may be artfully made to pass for the way things do." That probably reflected his response to London, the "most complete compendium," where even in the curtains of London hotels there was "too much of the superfluous and not enough of the necessary." He was also taken by the solid social realism of the European fictional tradition, the human and moral weightiness of Dickens, George Eliot, Balzac. Perhaps Newman was too much the innocent, the real drama of initiation a good deal more complex; at any rate, James no longer found the romance of Europe a simple subject.

By the turn of the '80s, his writing became an ever more refined, ever more elaborately refracted commentary on the decorated international scene. In *The Europeans* (1879) he reversed direction, and took a group of European characters to puritan New England; by *Washington Square* (1880) America, old New York, is itself subject to the complex distances of a Europeanized irony. But the triumphant treatment comes in *The Portrait of a Lady* (1881), James' most important early novel, started in Florence and Venice, and still one of his most admired (the book to read if the late ones are too labyrinthine). Isabel Archer – with "her meagre knowledge, her inflated ideals, her confidence at once innocent and dogmatic," and her "determination to see, to try, to know" – is his most ambitious heroine, set free not just by Ralph Touchett but by her author himself to see, try and know the European world. She is put in motion through three very different European countries, a green and aristocratic England, a socialite France, an aesthetic, museumized Italy, and provided with suitors from each, three different flavours of European apple. She is given an intense inner psychology, a consciousness whose various shifts and discoveries we follow with care; indeed her consciousness becomes the form of awareness through which the form of the novel discovers itself. She has an anxiety of selfhood that is confronted by the rounder social self of Europe, made of customs and traditions. She is granted her sense of romance – "a swift carriage, on the dark night" – and told that in bringing it to Europe she has brought it to the right place. Finally her motion becomes trapped in the sterile aestheticism of Gilbert Osmond, a Europeanized American expatriate ("He's the incarnation of taste"). Through marriage she enters the enclosed space of his confined Europe, and "she suddenly found the infinite vista of a multiplied life to be a dark, narrow alley with a dead wall at the end." There is sin in the European paradise; romance turns to realism, the trap is sprung, and Isabel is ground in the "mill of the conventional." Even so, she does not entirely renounce her romantic expectations: "Deep in her soul – deeper than any appetite for renunciation – was the sense that life would be her business for a long time to come."

James had started off his fiction with an essential contrast in mind. It was the familiar refraction already explored by Cooper and Hawthorne, the world we see when "we turn back and forth between the distinctively American and the distinctively European outlook." Now he had come to refine it, creating not simply a wider and more detailed map, a more complex moral universe, but seeing everything through those complex angles of vision and difficult transactions of consciousness that were to become his way of exploring the ambiguous face of life and experience, European or otherwise. The longer he was out of America, the deeper he went into Europe, the more the old contrast came to shatter ("If you have lived about you have lost that sense of the absoluteness and sanctity of the habits of your fellow-patriots which once made you so happy in the midst of them," he remarked: "You have seen that there are many *patriae* in the world . . ."). By the later 1880s he was declaring himself "deadly weary of the whole international state of mind," expressing to his brother William an intention "to write in such a way that it would be impossible to say whether I am at any moment an American writing about England or an Englishman writing about America, dealing as I do with both countries, and far from being ashamed of such an ambiguity I should be exceedingly proud of it, for it would be highly civilized." Meantime he had re-parcelled the elements of his inter-national world. He wished, he said, to "prove that I *can* write an American novel," and published *The Bostonians* in 1885. He equally wanted to write a novel steeped in the "great grey Babylon" of London, and in the same year published *The Princess Casamassima*, dealing, as he had never dealt before, with the great social contrasts of the city. Readers, no doubt sensing the sudden change of style, liked neither book. By the turn of the decade James had foresaken the novel and turned, disastrously, to writing for the theatre. When he did, finally, return to his international theme, the world had changed, so had he; and the whole matter, the whole map of geography and feeling, would be very different.[19]

9.

In September 1897 James signed a lease on (and later bought) Lamb House, a charming old house with a walled garden, at still delightful Rye in East Sussex, near to the Romney marshes. "My love of travel grows smaller and smaller," he wrote to William, "I find it perfectly simple and easy to stick to British soil." He was now fifty-five years old, and feeling it. He told A. C. Benson that this was a place where he could retire to "with a certain shrunken decency and wither away in – in a fairly cleanly and pleasantly melancholy manner – towards the tomb" (though he always did keep a base in London). He had a contract for a new novel, *The Awkward Age*, another for a "psychological" ghost story, *The Turn of the Screw*. That year, 1897, had already seen a remarkable event in his writer's development: his triumphant return to the novel. In it he published two strikingly original works, *The Spoils of Poynton* and the complex *What Maisie Knew*, which one critic hailed as "adding a whole new conception of reality to the art of fiction" (though to this day some readers do not know what it is that Maisie knew, or didn't). What James called "the third manner" of his writing had begun; the Jamesian novel had ceased to be a representation and become a difficult "affair." Younger writers, including Joseph Conrad, Ford Madox Hueffer, Rudyard Kipling, H. G. Wells, Stephen Crane and

[19] The various shadings of James' attitude toward his "international theme" are fairly comprehensively examined in Christof Wegelin, *The Image of Europe in Henry James* (Dallas, Texas, Southern Methodist University Press, 1958); and also in Marius Bewley's two books, *The Complex Fate: Hawthorne, Henry James and Some Other American Writers* (London, Chatto, 1952) and *The Eccentric Design: Form in the Classic American Novel* (London, Chatto, 1959).

Edith Wharton, who were concerned with the art of fiction and the modern spirit of the novel now honoured, imitated, surrounded him; he had become "the Master." Dictating directly to a typist, in a sudden burst of creativity, he now produced some of his greatest novels: *The Sacred Fount* (1901), *The Wings of the Dove* (194 days of dictation, 1902), *The Ambassadors* (1903), and *The Golden Bowl* (thirteen months of dictation, 1904). It was not just the discursive method encouraged by speaking his novels out loud, but a growing sense of experiment and of the "beautiful difficulties of fiction," that made these books remarkable. James had reparcelled out his landscape, deepened and complicated his sense of transatlantic experience. These books express a darkening sense of the disordered ripeness of contemporary *belle-époque* society, which is seen as material only, suspect, an object of dangerous knowledge. The literary qualities James had previously associated with his "European" standpoint – "solidity of specification," "accumulated characters," "thickness of motive" – now begin to dissolve. The experience in theatre had led to a preoccupation with the "scenic" or "dramatic" method of fictional presentation, so that James' former moral emphases are far less visible, making his books into masterpieces of presentational technique. Under the influence of "impressionism," there is a great intensification of concern with perception, patterning and symbolic reverberation, and with the entire relation of consciousness to the all too material world. The result is a new abstraction of method which could be called both American and modern, a response to a world of material energy and force which dislocates all significant social forms.[20]

In this new phase of his fiction, the "international theme" was back, but in very different guise. Now, as the century turned, James had lost much of his love of public "society," and distrusted the way "civilization" was going. He increasingly wondered how much he had "given up" by his choice of Europe; and all this is reflected in the marvellous

[20] As F. W. Dupee puts it in his excellent study *Henry James* (New York, Doubleday, 1956), "In his last novels . . . James revived the international subject and made it illustrate the present balance of power as well as his own accumulated experience as an American in Europe. Europe is still, in these novels, the school of worldly experience, and America is still representative of the process by which that experience may be transmuted into moral significance. But there are unmistakable developments over the earlier cycle. Americans now mate directly with Europeans rather than . . . Europeanized types of their own race . . . Out of the stress of national differences, then, come great ultimate images of identity . . ."

late novels. So is much else: the growth of a society based purely on wealth and materiality, on what he called in *The Spoils of Poynton* "things – always the splendid things," the massive rise of American power and the new equivalence of transatlantic relations in the era of Anglo-Saxon imperial and technological dominance, which had made the material process common to both sides of the Atlantic, the increase in transatlantic marriages, the significance of the American heiress and the American "robber baron" art collector. The kindest and warmest of the late books, *The Ambassadors*, took its source from a tale he had heard about his friend Howells, coming to Paris in the 1890s and recognizing, like his own Theodore Colville, how little he had lived. ("The moral is that you are responsible for the whole business," James explained to Howells.) But the "life" the middle-aged American visitor, Lambert Strether from Woollett, discovers in the book is hardly the obvious one of sensual temptation. "There was the dreadful little old tradition, one of the platitudes of the human comedy, that people's moral scheme *does* break down in Paris," James says in the Preface. But, knowing the "dreadful little old tradition" all too well, James then studiously avoids it. What Strether experiences in Paris is a much more difficult and obscure drama, a "drama of discrimination" as he weighs the lives of others. As James puts it: "he was to be thrown forward . . . upon his lifelong trick of intense reflection: which friendly test was to bring him out, through winding passages, through alternations of darkness and light, very much *in* Paris . . ." He learns not to live life, that vulgarest of all human options, but to *see* it – to bring it, with his "wonderful impressions," to consciousness. Strether learns other lessons too, above all that of the inevitable homelessness of the man of "wonderful impressions": "Where *is* your home moreover now – what has become of it?" Madame de Vionnet asks at last. Against the comedy of confusions that is *The Ambassadors*, James then set to work on the tragedy of international manipulations that is *The Wings of the Dove*. Here the young American girl Millie Theale – heiress not just to all the ages, but also to a dangerously attractive fortune – unleashes the brute materiality of the European world, which corrupts love, releases evil, and finally ends with a death in Venice. But as *The Golden Bowl* makes clear, innocence and experience are no longer to be clearly designated as national entities: innocent America, experienced or corrupted Europe. Prince Amerigo, with his doubly allusive name, and Adam Verver, the American materialist and "consummate collector," show that moral shades have now become strangely oblique and obscure, and both Europe and America are ambiguous entities.

This extraordinary episode of James' writing, which coincided with his move to Lamb House, his acquisition of a secretary, and a period of enlivening contacts with a new generation of writers who had settled, a nest of singing birds, in the area, began to close in 1904. This was the year when – a "returning pilgrim," a "restless analyst" – he returned to the United States on his ten-month visit. The impact of the visit on his mind was enormous, the record of the event *The American Scene*. The American scene has indeed fundamentally changed, provoking the novelist, the ultimate restless analyst, into a sense of new enormity and crisis. The lecture James delivered on his travels was his powerful statement about fiction, "The Lesson of Balzac"; the lesson of America was the scale of the business a modern Balzac had to confront. This America, of the skyscraper, of "pecuniary emulation," of cities that seemed to lie on a new planet, of masses and crowds and migrants and tenements, demanded a changed imagination, a new structure of prose. Henry Adams, revisiting New York City in the very next year, had almost the same response: "The outline of the city became frantic in its effort to explain something that defied meaning . . . The cylinder had exploded." James too found himself looking at an urban America of exploded cylinders, unprecedented newness, unorganized power, rising up amid the traces of an older simplicity and civility, and the book he wrote about it is itself a studied mediation between an old, well-loved and well-remembered America and a new one that ravages sensibility and prose. His reaction is perhaps best captured in a passage about the sight of New York harbour: "The aspect the power wears then is indescribable," he writes; "it is the power of the most extravagant of cities, rejoicing, as with the voice of the morning, in its might, its fortune, its unsurpassable conditions, and imparting to every object and element, to the motion and expression of every floating, hurrying, panting thing, to the throb of ferries and tugs, to the plash of waves and the play of winds and the glint of lights and the shrill of whistles and the quality and authority of breeze-born cries . . . something of its sharp free accent . . ." and so on. Even his return to Newport, former home of those pining for the European "apple," was a challenging shock; it was now a place of great Europeanate mansions, the "multiplied excrescences," of the new rich. But it did its work, and provoked the subject-matter of his last powerful book, *The Ivory Tower* –

abandoned, alas, because the Great War came, so that it appeared, unfinished, only after his death, a last trace of the great American theme.

But, for all the pleasures and terrors of revisiting the "long neglected and long unseen land of one's birth – especially when that land affects one as such a living and breathing and feeling and moving great monster," the visit left James "transcendently homesick" for Lamb House and his burrow in the ancient world. Still, he returned there, as he said, a "saturated sponge," to begin making his final reckoning with the modern. The visit had one happy product: a project for a collected "New York Edition" of his works, each with "a preface of a rather intimate character by their author." The result was an important late-life task, one of his great achievements; for the prefaces he now wrote, each one telling "the story of a story," are a bible for the writing of modern fiction. "I sat for a long while with the closed volume in my hand going over the preface in my mind and thinking – that's how it began, that's how it was done," his friend Joseph Conrad noted; here indeed was the lesson of the master. The trip also helped provoke the idea of an autobiography; it had wakened his reflections on the whole long story, not only of himself but of the complex changing culture of the entire international era. *A Small Boy and Others* appeared in 1913, *Notes of a Son and Brother* in 1914, *The Middle Years*, unfinished, in 1917; they brought the record up to the early London days, and the opening courses of the "banquet of initiation which was in the event to prolong itself through years and years." He was on the final round now, as the international culture around him moved closer toward both modernity and crisis. In 1910 Oxford University awarded him an honorary degree, the last of the great American writers of his era to be so honoured. Then in 1914, from Lamb House, he watched the civilization of that era plunge into "this abyss of blood and darkness," as the Great War began. It was, he said, the "great Niagara," a flooding of disaster, and the war had used up words.

In the autumn he moved back to London, to Cheyne Walk; the next year, to display his support for the British cause, he was naturalized a British citizen. "The odd thing is that nothing seems to have happened and that I don't feel a bit different," he wrote Edmund Gosse, "so that I see not at all how associated I have become, but that I was really too associated before for any nominal change to matter." On 28 February 1916, just after receiving the British Order of Merit, he died, at Cheyne

Walk, at the age of seventy-two. Like the death of Dickens in 1870, this marked the clear end of an era – a period of fictional experiment and also of transatlantic literary internationalism such as had never been seen before. He was cremated in Britain, but, appropriately enough, his ashes were taken to the family tomb in Cambridge, Massachusetts, and a good many of his papers crossed the Atlantic. (Ironically, in 1940, part of Lamb House, which had been let to the English writer E. F. Benson, took a direct hit from a German bomb, and his pictures and some two hundred of his books were destroyed, though much has now been replaced.) Meantime, though, a whole new generation of American expatriates had come across the ocean, following the path of Modernism, a journey of which he had been a fundamental pioneer, and a new wave would come to Europe as participants or active spectators when America entered the war in 1917. In 1918 Margaret Anderson's Chicago magazine, the *Little Review*, ran a Henry James number, organized by Ezra Pound, from the next generation of American artistic expatriates, all making their tributes. Pound, himself an expatriate in London, wrote of James' "whole great assaying and weighing, the research for the significance of nationality, French, English, American," and the importance of that internationalist quest for the spirit of the modern arts. T. S. Eliot, also now expatriate to London, wrote that James represented the value of being "everywhere a foreigner," adding: "It is the final perfection, the consummation of an American to become, not an Englishman, but a European – something which no born European, no person of European nationality, can become." The view that by perfecting his Americanness James had turned into an ideal European, a figure of culture larger than that bred by any single nationality, was in turn to shape Eliot's own lifelong quest for the "European mind," a quest that was to pass through yet further eras of disaster. By now the importance of James' work had become clear; a new phase of writing, a "modern tradition," international in spirit, had begun. Many of its writers were wanderers or exiles, also in search of modern form; many of its works asked Madame de Vionnet's question to the modern artist: "Where *is* your home moreover now – what has become of it?" As he foresaw, it still remains hard, but perhaps unnecessary, to say whether James was an American, a British or a European writer. His work had helped construct a new international geography of the arts, a great fiction of imaginative interrelations. The lesson of the master fundamentally influenced every one of these traditions, and also something larger still, the "modern tradition," so much more than national, itself. It was not just the art of fiction but the entire mythic geography of modern writing that had been altered by his banquet of initiation; it still is.

SIX

Christmas at Brede:
American realities, European romance

Back in 1882, the baffled customs officials of New York – more used to
dealing with swarms of huddled immigrants (half a million came in the
decade, more than the United States had ever seen before) who sailed in
past the harbour site which still awaited the French-built Statue of Liberty
– were faced by the arrival of a strange figure, kitted in a green overcoat of
otter fur and a sealskin hat, and speaking English if anything too well by
half. "I have nothing to declare, except my genius," he proclaimed. The
young Oscar Wilde had swanned into town. Still only twenty-seven, and
known in Britain as much for walking through Oxford carrying a green
carnation as for producing his one slim volume of poems, he had sailed to
the United States to perform one of those now familiar lecture-tours,
whereon the best of British writers offered their wisdom to the transcontinental audiences of America. He was thus to mount the lecterns in the
footsteps of such famous antecedents as Dickens and Thackeray, though
also Annie Besant and Martin Tupper. His planned one-year tour did,
though, have one unusual feature. Most of these other writers had come
under the auspices of the well-known lecture agencies, set up for just such
a purpose. Wilde's was sponsored by the British theatrical impresario
D'Oyly Carte, who was mounting his version of Gilbert and Sullivan's
musical comedy *Patience* in New York. This delightful work was supposed
to depict Wilde himself in the figure of the Fleshly Poet and Aesthete
"Reginald Bunthorne," though it is more likely Dante Gabriel Rossetti
was the intended original. The truth is that, as one commentator puts it,
Wilde really went to the States as a poster for the operetta.[1]

[1] Peter Conrad, *Imagining America* (London, Routledge, 1980). There are fuller details
of Wilde's American visit in Richard Ellmann, *Oscar Wilde* (London, Hamish
Hamilton, 1987), and a splendid account of the "Wilde era" in Holbrook Jackson, *The
1890s* (London, 1913; reissued by Cresset Library, 1988).

Still, he anticipated doing very well out of the proceedings, and gathering up, as he put it, "the golden fruits of America." Thackeray had said it actually rained dollars in New York; Wilde hoped to make at least a thousand of them from his tour, then spend them on something more beautiful, like Italy. But, being Oscar Wilde, he also hoped to make, of course, an impact. As he explained, "the Americans are certainly great hero-worshippers, and always take their heroes from the criminal classes," so he expected to do well. He did. His visit was timely; he caught America just as it was starting to think about the beautiful. The late nineteenth-century taste for arts-and-crafts and high aestheticism was just beginning to flourish. Wilde kindly explained he had come to America with no other aim than to civilize it. It would be disappointing, he announced, to depart the country without making "one person love beautiful things a little more." He himself was one of the beautiful things he put on offer, along with other such delights as the Italian Renaissance and Pre-Raphaelite poetry and design. Plain-speaking America was not used to such figures, though they had had Edgar Allan Poe and were still having slouch-hatted Walt Whitman. The press responded, with glee and column inches, to his dandy's style, his mannerisms, wit, endless wardrobe, his narcissistic consumption of his own self, his great love of publicity. It was so different from the reclusive Charles Dickens. And if the American public had seen nothing at all like Wilde, Wilde had seen nothing at all like the American public. "I am torn to bits by Society. Immense receptions, wonderful dinners, crowds wait for my carriage," he soon reported in delight, "I have a sort of triumphal progress, live like a young sybarite, travel like a young god." Who could have wished for better? In New York he claimed he had to employ three secretaries: "One writes my autographs all day for my admirers, the other receives the flowers that are really left every ten minutes. A third whose hair resembles mine is obliged to send off locks of his own hair to the myriad maidens of the city, and so is rapidly becoming bald."

His triumphal progress continued right through middle America, now easily accessible in these days of universal railroad travel. He delivered his witticisms, telling Americans, apparently by way of a compliment, that their nation had progressed from barbarism to decadence without going through the statutory stage of civilization between, and paraded his dandyish tastes. He gave mannered lectures on such topics as "The Decorative Arts in America" and "The English

Renaissance of Art," and urged his audiences toward the beautiful. For instance, he advised the silver miners of Leadsville, Colorado, "let there be no flower in your meadows that does not wreathe its tendrils around your pillows, no little leaf in your Titan forests that does not lend its form to design." Even when talking of Tintoretto, he managed to weave in references to Gilbert and Sullivan's *Patience*, and the reporters regularly mistook his mentions of Beethoven for mentions of Bunthorne. He took great care to explain his lectures were less important than what he wore to them. He loved, he said, seeing his name plastered all over the posters –"printed it is true in those primary colours against which I pass my life protesting, but still it is fame." Even the Leadsville miners, famed for shooting the pianist when they thought he wasn't doing his best, were won over. No doubt wearing a lily in his buttonhole, he told them of Shakespeare, and they said he sounded so good he should have come along too. It was topped or rather bottomed off by a banquet down a silver mine. "The amazement of the miners when they saw that art and appetite could go hand in hand knew no bounds; and when I lit a long cigar they cheered till the silver fell in dust from the roof onto our plates; and when I quaffed a cocktail without flinching, they unanimously pronounced me in their grand simple way 'a bully boy with no glass eye'," he reported, maybe with a mite of exaggeration. Though the plains bored him, he enjoyed the air of criminal depravity displayed by American cities. Nature, of which America had a lot, he generally found disappointing (but then he never approved of it). Except for the fun of dressing in waterproofs, he considered Niagara Falls very dull. "Every American bride is taken there," he famously observed, "and the sight of the stupendous waterfall must be one of the earliest if not the keenest disappointments in American married life."

Like many British literary visitors, Wilde did not take his profit simply by taking his lectures across the Atlantic (this was another disappointment: "I am not exactly pleased with the Atlantic," he complained). He also earned it a second time, by lecturing on his experiences when he returned home.[2] Unlike many British visitors (Lord Bryce, for instance, whose thoughtful and respectful account of American institutions appeared in the 1880s), he showed no interest in American politics or geography; that was reality, the hobgoblin of little

2 Wilde's lectures were collected in the posthumous *Essays and Lectures* (1908).

minds. What he observed was a very large land without an evident past and a great excess of nature, a place so proud of being a young country it had a tradition of it going back at least three hundred years. It was a nation where "the horrors of domesticity are almost entirely unknown," the men were women and the women men, the children "always ready to give to those who are older than themselves the full benefits of their inexperience." Still, he was grateful; America had granted the more or less unknown Wilde a chance of fame and stardom, and he never forgot the experience. When, at the end of the decade, his reputation in Britain surged, and the aesthetic adventure began to flourish everywhere, the tour was still in his mind. The "Wilde era" began, it is generally agreed, in 1889, the year he published "The Decay of Lying" ("Art is our spirited protest, our attempt to teach Nature her proper place"), surviving till the scandal of his trial in 1895. His novel about an artistic and artificial life, *The Picture of Dorian Gray* (1891), became a bible of the "new hedonism"; his witty plays, expressing the fragile spirit of the *fin de siècle*, earned him theatrical fame. America is a recurrent reference point; though it attracts the high disdain of his aristocratic characters, it also blows a youthful wind of change through the stuffy social conventions. The young American girl, that reforming figure, appears in *A Woman of No Importance* (1893) ("They say you have no ruins, and no curiosities." "What nonsense! They have their mothers, and their manners").

Back in the States too, Wilde left his influence behind. People talked of his visit for years; some hoped it would never be repeated (not everyone liked to hear their progress called decadence), others saw it as a great aesthetic ray of hope. Wilde told Max Beerbohm he had civilized America. Hardly; but he certainly helped aestheticize it. He raised the flag of dandyism, encouraged thoughts of art and bohemia. For now, as doubt grew about purely material progress, and European styles came in with each new wave of immigration, the bohemian way was beginning to reach American cities. Over the Eighties Anglo-Saxon dominance and the Puritan spirit began to fade. Urban population quadrupled in the four last decades of the century; by 1900 the foreign-born made up three-quarters of the population of New York and the other key cities of the East and Midwest. Chicago, for instance, a village of 250 in 1833, laid waste by fire in 1871, saw a five-fold growth between 1870 and 1900, and suddenly became the nation's Second City – with more Poles than Warsaw, more Jews than Lithuania. As people fled not just European woes and pogroms but the American land (it was a time of deep agricultural depression), American cities saw a spectacular rise in every sense, including upward. Americans were now becoming an urban people with urban values, and they acquired their ethnic bohemias – a German bohemia, a Yiddish bohemia, a French bohemia, a Russian bohemia, even a Bohemian bohemia – which became centres of the arts.

The urbanizing process, the great transformation of cities, was taking place all over Europe too; Paris and Vienna and Berlin went through great civic reconstruction at this time. But American cities were distinctive. They had their own new-minted polyglot character, were places of confusion and huge contrast – between rich and poor, native and immigrant, business and leisure, high-rise office block and dumb-bell tenement, opulent mansion and sweatshop. From the 1870s, soon aided by steel construction and the invention of the elevator and the revolving door, skyscrapers rose in Chicago and New York. Distinctively American, they displayed not just great technological skill but the dominance of commerce over all. Other notable urban inventions – the streetcar, street railway, the "metropolitan" underground – passed in between. While the homes of the rich copied the best of European *beaux arts* splendours, cramped high apartment blocks housed grim immigrant overcrowding and poverty. Many foreign-language newspapers testified to the way American culture was changing and growing less Anglo-Saxon. By the 1890s the rise of distinct foreign-language districts, like New York's Jewish Lower East Side, made its cities seem a human "melting-pot." Urban grimness and contrast at once discouraged art and stimulated a need of it. In places like Greenwich Village – that oddly European district of winding streets and old houses, lofts and stables in lower Manhattan, spared much industrial development because it had escaped the grid-plan of uptown – signs of bohemia had already emerged by the time of Wilde's visit, as young people seeking what he would have hated to hear called a "new life-style" took these properties and turned them into cold-water apartments and studios, became radical thinkers, or artist's models, and set out to challenge urban misery or *épater* the bourgeois. Like the new sociologists or the "muckracking" journalists, they observed the infinite contrasts and shaded impressions of the city, caught the mix of peoples, tongues and castes, the double spectacle of wealth and poverty, the daily witness to social change, urban problems, and the way the other half lived.

In writing, as in painting, two distinct movements began developing side by side. One was toward a greater, more scientific realism, named "Naturalism" or sometimes "Veritism." This was the movement promoted by Howells, developed by Frank Norris, Hamlin Garland, Theodore Dreiser, and the "muckraking" journalists and social reporters. They went into the streets, looked at the political problems and corruptions of the city, examined the powers of social determinism and the prospects for change. The other, the movement represented, in effect, by Wilde's presence, was concerned with the flowering of art, with style and manner, impression and effect, consciousness and the trembling of the veil as a new age and century came. Often the movements met, merged, crossed over: here in bohemia, or in the further bohemias to be found on the far side of the not so disappointing Atlantic. Presaged no doubt by his American visit, the "Wilde era" was coming to America too; Wilde even had his own strange counterpart in Walt Whitman, with his new "barbaric yawp" and his taste for the open road. Bohemian manners and styles started to flourish. "I had a sweet fluffy beard," noted James Gibbons Huneker, describing his youthful self around this time. "Was I not a bohemian in Paris? Velveteen coat, Scotch cap, open shirt. Oh! What a guy I must have been." Huneker was one of many who went to Paris to train as a painter, though then it was back to commonplace America – the land, he noted, of "bathtubs, not Bohemia."[3] Henry Harland (of him more later) started as a novelist writing in New York's Jewish ghetto, headed for Paris, inviting all his friends to join him (it was the most enchanting spot in the universe, he said), and ended in Wildean London editing that aesthete's bible, the *Yellow Book*. Richard Hovey hastened to bohemian Europe; Chicago-born Frank Norris, eventually to become one of the leading Naturalists, writing of trusts and freight-rates, started in Paris as a painter. Others like Stuart Merrill and Francis Vielé-Griffin (real name Egbert Ludovicus Griffin) went the whole

---

[3] See James Gibbons Huneker, *Promenades of an Impressionist* (New York, Scribner; London, Laurie, 1910), in which he points out Paris's role as the universal culture capital: "there is no thought-wave in modern art that does not emanate from Paris or finally reach Paris." On the other hand, one could tire even of bohemia. "Yes, you are right, bathtubs, not Bohemia, now-a-days for me," he wrote to a friend in 1907, "I loathe Paris to live in – unless one has steam heat and running water. I am becoming materialistic. I wouldn't live in the Latin Quarter with its dirt, genius, squalor and gaiety for the price of a house. Once when you are very young – then is Paris a fairy dream in its settings. But don't peep behind the scenes . . ." In Josephine Huneker (ed.), *Letters of James Gibbons Huneker* (New York and London, Scribner, 1922).

hog, staying on in Montmartre to become symbolist poets, writing in French. Bernard Berenson and George Santayana ("the last Puritan") settled in Italy, where Berenson became the great authenticator of those Renaissance painters Wilde had talked of on his tour. Back in Europe, Wilde kept company with, and quarrelled with, new American expatriate painters who flitted freely between London and Paris – John Singer Sargent, born in Italy, above all the great urban Impressionist and public wit James McNeill Whistler ("I wish I had said that." "You will, Oscar, you will").

Within a decade of Wilde's flamboyant visit, Bohemia was as much the vogue in the United States as it was in Europe, from whose poverty and artistic alienations it had first been born. In 1894, George du Maurier, the Anglo-French writer-painter who once shared a studio with Whistler, decided to write a tale of Paris bohemia, encouraged in his task by none other than Henry James. When *Trilby* – with its portrait of the Parisian *vie de bohème*, haunted by the strange and mesmeric figure of Svengali – came out, it was first serialized in an American magazine. Trilby fever swept through the nation like a frenzy; a hat, a cigarette, even a Florida town were named after the book, or its author. Everyone wanted to smoke, be an artist or at least a model. Everyone wondered how you could keep them down on the farm when they could see Paree, and many went there to look for the rather elusive Latin Quarter.[4] Everyone started writing bohemian novels: Howells his *The Coast of Bohemia* (1893), about rather staid bohemians in New York; Stephen Crane, similarly, in *The Third Violet* (1895); Gertrude Christian Fosdick with her *Out of Bohemia: A Story of Paris Student Life* (1894), a daring tale of American bohemian girls in the Latin Quarter. Two decades after Wilde's American tour, in 1908, the young American poet Ezra Pound – from Hailey, Idaho, by way of Philadelphia and Venice – arrived in London, following the lure of Arthur Symons' book on the aesthetic Nineties, *The Symbolist Movement in Literature* (1899). He was looking for the English *avant-garde*, not

[4] "The immense foregathering, as if drawn by some irresistible magnet, of aesthetic Americans in Paris was remarkable as a mass phenomenon," reported one of these American seekers after the aesthetic, Logan Pearsall Smith. "They had come to Paris from almost every region of my native country at who knows what sacrifice to themselves and to their parents, to study art, but in art itself they seemed to take hardly any interest . . . Their talk was all of their own or each other's pictures." Smith records his own expatriation, which kept him in Britain as an aesthete and scholar, in *Unforgotten Years* (London, Constable, 1938).

always that easy to find, and for "mouvemongs" on the French model. Like Wilde, he was also determined to be, and look like, a genius. "He would wear trousers made of green billiard cloth, a pink coat, a blue shirt, a tie hand-painted by a Japanese friend, an immense sombrero, a flaming beard cut to a point and a single, large blue ear-ring," reported Ford Madox Hueffer, who adopted this mixture of Wilde and Whitman as a protégé in advancing the cause of literary modernity in crass commercial Britain. The Wilde trial of 1895 had certainly changed things ("The aesthetic cult, in his nasty form, is over," said the London *News of the World*); jingoism and virile adventure came back with the Boer War. Wilde himself died in neglect, as "Sebastian Melmoth," in Paris in 1900; it was no longer the *fin* but the *aube de siècle*. But, as Pound showed, the day of the dandy wasn't done, the Wilde era not over yet.[5]

2.

In 1893, four hundred years give or take after Columbus' first voyage, Americans decided to celebrate it and their national progress by mounting yet another great exhibition: the World's Columbian Exposition. They chose, suitably enough, to stage it in the shock city of Chicago, which over six decades had transformed from small Indian village to the nation's Second City. As one of its poets, Carl Sandburg, would declaim, it was now hog butcher for the world, tool maker, stacker of wheat, player with railroads and the nation's freight handler. Its huge railhead was one of the American wonders, its stockyards, where immigrants slaved in bleak conditions, the vastest in the world. On 700 acres of former swampland near Lake Michigan, another sudden city rose, to a ground plan by the urban planner Olmsted, and under the supervision of the Chicago architect David Burnham. The second second city was not like the first. Venetian canals, lagoons and piers appeared at speed on the waterfilled site. Palaces in Renaissance style (many Renaissance styles), temples and domes, obelisks and great cathedrals for new kinds of worship rose on the canal banks, lined the great public piazza. The 400 steel-frame temporary buildings were

[5] The story of American bohemianism is wonderfully (though not always accurately) told in Albert Parry, *Garrets and Pretenders: A History of Bohemianism in America* (New York, Covici-Friede, 1933; revised and extended edition, New York and London, Dover and Constable, 1960).

mostly clad in white plaster of paris, and designed in a mixture of *beaux arts* styles laid atop American technological modernity. It was a "White City," comparable to the remodelled *belle-époque* cities of Europe and South America that flowered in the late nineteenth century (Vienna, Budapest, Buenos Aires) though also to what would soon be called a "film-set." It was, all the reports said, a "Fairy Land," but it was also, as it was meant to be, a decorated display of something else: American technological ingenuity, the novelty of the nation.

So the Manufacturers and Liberal Arts Building, a great neo-classical hall 1,280 feet long, was described as the biggest building in the world. The Machinery Hall – also the biggest building in the world, thoughtfully built so that it could be taken down and used for train sheds – housed a two-thousand-horsepower dynamo which enabled the whole Fair to be lit by Edison's electric light: the first time the many visitors – thirty million came – had seen it. California created an Egyptian obelisk made entirely of oranges; there was a Temple of Womanhood; a rococo Columbian fountain, costing $48,000, allegorically depicted, the guidebook explained, not Columbus but Columbia, "sitting aloft on the Barge of State, heralded by Fame at the prow, oared by the Arts and Industries, guided by Time at the helm, and drawn by the sea-horses of Commerce," though Columbus got a statue too. "Happy must be the birds that fly over the White City of the Columbian Exposition," said the guidebook. "They can certainly rejoice in views as are not given to mortals." The normally sighted were just as impressed; one of the many British reporters who came over called the Fair "the grandest sight the human eye has ever encountered." The Exposition had a strange effect on public prose, but the prose, like the buildings, decorated a deeper significance. As the century came to its troubled close (a major depression was taking place in 1893, causing great social unrest) Americans wanted to celebrate, in the highest and grandest style, both their culture itself and their claims to commercial and technological dominance. As Andrew Carnegie had said a few years before: "the old nations of the world creep on at a snail's pace; the Republic thunders past with the rush of an express." It was becoming a common thought that American power and progress were now outrunning the European; this was one point the Fair was meant to prove.[6]

[6] Alan Trachtenberg's *The Incorporation of America: Culture and Society in the Gilded Age* (cited above, p. 170), has a brilliant last chapter devoted to the Columbian World Exposition. Also see Larzer Ziff, *The American 1890s: The Life and Times of a Lost Generation* (cited above, p. 173).

The thirty million visitors who saw the Fair ranged from the poor and the huddled – but not the black – to the most notable, and from Charles Eliot Norton to Buffalo Bill. The American Pragmatist philosophers held a meeting at the Fair, perhaps to decide whether it was there or not. The American Historical Association foregathered, and heard a famous statement: Frederick Jackson Turner delivered his lecture on "The Significance of the Frontier in American History," explaining the importance of the frontier West, the place where the course of the American empire had unfolded, in the formation of the unique American character, distinct from the European. Unfortunately the frontier had officially closed three years before, when its line disappeared, and the new frontier was surely the city. Wanting to test the widespread notion that America was now on the cusp of leadership in world development, another very notable historian, Henry Adams – that eminent, disgruntled figure who had spent most of his days between Boston, Washington and Europe – crossed the Atlantic to take a look. He had come from the staid world of London, crossing the Atlantic in modern grand comfort on a "steamer of the new type," the *Teutonic*. It reminded him that "Europe seemed to have been stationary for twenty years"; so, he came to feel, had he. On the voyage fate – he reports in his wonderfully ironic, third-person autobiography *The Education of Henry Adams* (1907) – was kind. He found an interesting fellow passenger in the young Rudyard Kipling (the "infant monster," Henry James called him), lately shot to fame with his *Plain Tales from the Hills* (1889) and *The Light That Failed* (1891). According to Adams, it was James who had advised him to take this, his wedding trip, to America (we now know economic reasons, the collapse of a bank, had curtailed an intended honeymoon in Japan, and the Kiplings were now seeking the economies of a four-year, often unhappy residence in Brattleboro, Vermont, where, until a bitter feud developed with his brother-in-law, Kipling thought of settling for good). Adams had always been conscious of Bostonian homage to European literary culture; could it be that even that was changing? "All through life, one had seen the American on his literary knees to the European, and all through many lives back for some two centuries, one had seen the European snub or patronize the American; not always intentionally, but effectually," he noted, with his usual complicated irony. "Kipling neither snubbed nor patronized; he was all gaiety and good-nature; but he was the first to feel what was meant. Genius has to pay itself that unwilling self-respect."[7]

But, for Adams – the historian trying to understand the mechanism of the future – the way pointed inevitably west, to Chicago. His look lasted a whole fortnight, and by the time he had done he decided that his entire nineteenth-century education was now useless. "He found matter of study to fill a hundred years, and his education spread over into chaos . . . no such Babel of loose and ill-joined, such vague and ill-defined and unrelated thoughts and half-thoughts and experimental outcries as the Exposition, had ever ruffled the surface of the Lakes." What he observed – "a sort of industrial, speculative growth and product of the Beaux Arts artistically induced to pass the summer on the shore of Lake Michigan" – made him sit down in "helpless reflection" to consider the processes driving American culture and the modernizing future, now very probably the same thing. The plaster buildings were one thing, but in them he felt he had seen the point of fundamental transition: the Age of the Virgin had ended and the Age of the Dynamo had dawned, giving "to history a new phase." Machines now made machines, and the nation was now committed to energy, capitalism and exponential growth. "Chicago," he recorded, "asked in 1893 for the first time the question of whether the American people knew where they were driving . . . Chicago was the first expression of American thought as a unity."

Writers in quantity also came to the Fair to interpret, or eulogize, its importance; the Fair's motto was, after all, "Make Culture Hum!" It even had its own poet laureate in the person of Harriet Monroe, who composed for the dedication in 1892 a patriotic "Columbian Ode" to be declaimed above a white-gowned chorus of five thousand voices. (Twenty years later she would make her amends by founding the admirable magazine *Poetry (Chicago)*, which, steered along by Ezra Pound as foreign correspondent, published not only such notable Chicago poets as Carl Sandburg, Edgar Lee Masters and Vachel

---

[7] Kipling had in fact previously visited America in 1889, on his journey from India to Britain, and written up his experience in the travel sketches of *From Sea to Sea* (1899). On the visit in 1892 when he met Adams, he had just married the sister of his former American collaborator Woolcott Balestier, and they were headed for Brattleboro, Vermont, where the Balestier family had land. They bought some, and remained there from 1892 to 1896, when the lawsuit occurred. Here Kipling wrote *The Jungle Books* (1894–5). He wrote one American novel, *Captains Courageous: A Story of the Grand Banks* (1897), about a robber baron's son who falls from an Atlantic liner and, rescued by a fishing boat, learns the ways of the sea – a Kiplingesque tale of work, skill and initiation.

Lindsay, but T. S. Eliot's "Prufrock" and much of early Wallace Stevens.) A great Congress of Literature was held. Howells came, wrote about the Exposition in his utopian novel *A Traveler from Alturia* (1894), and called it "a foretaste of heaven." His fellow utopian novelist Edward Bellamy took a different view: "The underlying motive of the whole exhibition, under a sham pretence of patriotism, is business, advertised with a view to individual money-making." The twenty-two-year-old Theodore Dreiser, reporting for a Saint Louis paper, felt "as though some brooding spirit of beauty, inherent possibly in some directing oversoul, had waved a magic wand" – but his prose would improve somewhat later. Hamlin Garland, the "veritist," much influenced by scientific and Darwinian theory, gave a famous lecture on "Local Color in Fiction," which not only urged on fellow writers the need to write of the Midwest and West, and rejected Boston as "too near London," but advanced the need for harsh scientific realism, causing much controversy amid the romantic white buildings. "Here flames the spirit of youth," he proclaimed. "Here throbs the heart of America." True to his convictions ("From being a huge, muddy windy market-place [Chicago] seemed about to take its place among the literary capitals of the world," he would comment), he took up residence and became a Chicago writer; he was to have the satisfaction of seeing at least some of his prophecies realized. For whether because of the Fair or despite it Chicago and the Midwest were in process of becoming important literary subject-matter; and the "Chicago Renaissance" that would follow – bringing forth the fiction of writers like Dreiser, Frank Norris, Upton Sinclair and eventually Sherwood Anderson – could indeed have been born from the new cultural self-consciousness encouraged by Garland and the White City Fair.

Or perhaps by the hard facts of Chicago itself. For "the fairy tale" Exposition was only one part of what was happening in Chicago in 1893. It was a fast-moving politically troubled city; there had been the Haymarket Riots of 1886, there was financial panic in 1893, there would be the Pullman strike of 1894. Jane Addams started her settlement centre Hull House; the "Chicago School" of urban sociologists was born in response to the troubling conditions of the sweatshops and the ghettos; the English journalist W. T. Stead would soon be chronicling its social inequities (much as the American journalist Jack London would in turn do in East-End London). It was, indeed, the modern shock city; Rudyard Kipling, passing through on an earlier visit, had observed flatly: "Having seen it, I urgently desire never to see it again. It is inhabited by savages." Downtown in 1893, as visitors also noted, a very unfairy-like America was building at speed. In the Loop, great skyscrapers, flat-topped blocks of ten storeys and more in what was already known as the "Chicago style," had been made possible by the destruction of the Chicago fire of 1871, the invention of the elevator, rockhard land. "A proud and soaring thing," "a unit without a single dissenting line," was how Louis Sullivan, one of the chief architects of these novelties, creator of the Auditorium Building, described the modern office blocks for which the city grew famous. The real Chicago was business: large department stores (Marshall Field), big merchandizing operations (Sears Roebuck, Montgomery Ward), elevated railways, stockyards where the cattle moved on overhead tracks and were slaughtered and quartered at the rate of five a minute ("It was pork-making by machinery, pork-making by applied mathematics," reported Upton Sinclair in *The Jungle*, 1906). It was the material city, proud of its growth, its mass, its wealth, its agglomeration: "tall bold slugger set vivid against the little soft cities," said Carl Sandburg.

It was, by way of supplement, also proud of its culture. Its Art Institute was founded in 1879, and, thanks to the wealthy patrons and collectors of the city, who went often to Europe, it would duly house some of the great works of European Impressionism and Modernism. There was the Newberry Library, the Fine Arts Building; in the key year of 1893 John D. Rockefeller gave two and a half million dollars to found the great University of Chicago. Though part of the Fair burned down shortly after it closed, some of the cheap urban housing put up for it began attracting young regional writers into the city. Bohemia started to flourish in Chicago. There was a Bohemian Club, a Cipher Club ("where Mrs Grundy has no sway"), a bohemian magazine, the *Chap-Book*, founded in 1894, printing the works of Verlaine and Wilde alongside local talents. Even the British Naturalist George Gissing had spent a period in Chicago in the 1870s, coming on an emigrant ticket and arriving with five dollars in his pocket. Powerful newspapers like the Chicago *Tribune*, *Post* and *Globe* attracted promising journalists, including George Ade, F. P. A. Addams, and Finlay Peter Dunne, inventor of the opinionated "Mr Dooley," Dreiser and, later, Ben Hecht. Chicago now found writers who could tell its story – usually a material story – after the stimulus of 1893. And so it did. By 1912, when the idea of the "new arts" spread across America, it was indeed possible to talk of a "Chicago Renaissance," and claim the Windy City as the second literary city to New York.

3.

And it was, appropriately, in 1893 that Henry Blake Fuller, eminent Chicago banker and novelist, published his striking novel *The Cliff-Dwellers*, set in the world of commercial life around a new Chicago skyscraper. It portrayed a city of canyons and traffic, a "seething flood of carts, carriages, omnibuses, messengers, shoppers, clerks and capitalists, which surges with increasing violence for every passing day," where "the bare scaffoldings of materialism felt themselves quite independent of the graces and draperies of culture." Fuller produced a second Chicago novel, *With the Procession* (1895), which followed the fortunes of an established and old-fashioned Chicago banker (like himself) as his family juggles the claims of commerce and culture in a city which "labours under one peculiar disadvantage: it is the only great city in the world to which all its citizens have come for the one common, avowed object of making money." Fuller himself was a curious, though maybe typical, Chicago figure. Born in the city back in 1857, to a New England family which went back to Dr Samuel Fuller of the *Mayflower*, and was linked to the formidable Margaret Fuller, he inherited the family interests in banking and real estate. But in 1879, a young man with a passion for architecture, he had made a European *Wanderjahr*, and come back with his notebooks full of Italian impressions, noting that his contacts with the Old World had left him "panting for the old, the fair." Then a second visit in 1883 reinforced his European preoccupations; he celebrated them in some verse equally remarkable for content and infelicity ("I'd write, or build, or souls with music thrill; / And I would know the Old World through and through").

A distinguished resident of material and booming Chicago, Fuller continued his regular visits to Italy. He also worked quietly on two elegant, highly mannerist novels with fantastical Italian settings, *The Chevalier of Pensieri-Vani* (privately printed, 1886; reissued 1890) and The *Châtelaine of La Trinité* (1892), which had a vogue with a coterie audience, especially in Boston. Both evoke an exotic Italian world, and both display the troubled drama of the guilty midwestern soul. *The Chevalier*, set in several Italian towns, is mainly concerned with mannered Italian aristocratic characters. But it also features a debate between a high-souled Italian and an American called (perhaps too inevitably) George Occident, who "felt his position one of peculiar hardship. Birth and habit drew him in one direction; culture and aspiration, in another; but he had never been a good American, and he feared he should never be a good European." Occident oscillates, and so did Fuller, filling the book with the drama of affiliation and disaffiliation. In *The Châtelaine*, written in equally mannered prose, the American is a woman called "Aurelia West" who attempts to advance the causes of progress and feminism to the Châtelaine Bertha, who is hardly convinced by the charms of this Americanization. Fuller then turned to his novels of contemporary Chicago life, written in the highly realistic manner of Howells, by whom they were plainly influenced. But, for all their success, Fuller soon returned to his Old World preoccupations. In 1897 he returned for another five-month trip to Italy, became influenced by James and Maeterlinck, writers who were the very antithesis of Howells, and produced *From the Other Side*, a collection of "transatlantic sketches." Then came *The New Flag* (1898) and a Sicilian romance, *The Last Refuge*, in 1900; inevitably enough it was a story of missed American opportunities. In the short stories of *Under the Skylights* (1901), he revisited Chicago themes with several satirical portraits of the city's bohemia. One story, about the eternal conflict between realism and romance, is plainly about his friend Garland, who had gone from realism to writing frontier romances; another concerns the endless conflict of art and capital. In 1908 he published *Waldo Trench and Others*, troubled stories about artistic Americans in Italy. His style grew ever more mannerist and heavy, as seemed to be the way with those who dealt with Italian themes or grew too fascinated by James. Fuller's concern with the problem of balancing two styles and two worlds lasted to his death in 1929. In some verses in the volume *Lines Long and Short* (1917) he wrote what is in effect his own mock obituary: 'When Albert C. McComb / Died in his native Dodgetown/At the age of sixty-odd, / People said – the few who said anything at all – / That he had lived a futile life, / And that Europe was to blame:/His continual hankering after the Old World/Had made him a failure in the New."

There were two Henry Blake Fullers, two distinct literary careers.

Perhaps Adams was wrong after all, and Chicago was not the expression of American thought as a unity but as a diversity. For there was Fuller the Chicago realist, whose books dealt vividly with the city's canyon-streets, with systems, methods of work, material preoccupations. "If one wanted to put finger on the man who . . . strove to work true to his ideas and pioneered the way for a real expression of American life, I should say put it on the name of Henry B. Fuller," wrote Theodore Dreiser, claiming him as the first true novelist of the American city. And there was Fuller the author of exotic Italian romances, dense with atmosphere, art and fancy. These are two contrary versions of fiction, two different writers might have written them; though maybe they did no more than express the Chicago condition, and parallel the real and the fairyland cities of Chicago in the year of the Fair. In 1884 after a visit to Boston Fuller wrote a (still unpublished) essay, "Howells or James?" He wrote admiringly of *The Portrait of a Lady*, but expressed his unease about James' attitude both to realism and his country ("That James deals, ultimately, in realities, is true enough, but a realism made up of select actualities is pretty apt to come out idealistically in the end"). He asks himself who best serves the process of American culture, "he who deals with the normal earning of money at home, or he who prefers to deal with the exceptional and privileged spending of money abroad?" The theoretical sympathies all lie very plainly with Howells (who, after all, had written his own Italian romances, but chosen to stay at home); but the aesthetic and personal identification all lies with James. "Howells or James" seemed to be the problem of a generation of writers – especially if they lived in muscular, difficult Chicago.

Yet with his praise for Fuller's Chicago fiction, Dreiser was right enough. For all his contradictions of style and his sense of aesthetic failure, Fuller had set down the essential mythic theme of Chicago fiction, opening the way for many another Chicago novelist. Dreiser himself took the plunge with his *Sister Carrie* (1900), a Chicago tale found so scandalous it was virtually suppressed. It opens when Carrie Meeber, "a waif amid forces," is drawn from her small midwestern town by the seductive "magnet" of Chicago, which resembles both a machine and a lover. It is a place of numbers and systems, which Dreiser naturalistically details: "Before following her in her round of seeking, let us look at the sphere in which her future was to lie. In 1889 Chicago had the peculiar qualifications of growth which made it such an adventurous pilgrimage ... Its many and growing commercial opportunities gave it widespread fame which made of it a giant magnet, drawing to itself from all quarters the hopeful and the hopeless ... It was a city of over 500,000, with the ambition, the daring, the activity of a metropolis of a million. Its streets and houses were already scattered over an area of seventy-five square miles." But Carrie (like Chicago and Dreiser himself) longs for culture. Once she has made her body a marketable commodity, and become a successful actress, indeed a modern star, it is art and education she longs for in the end. In Chicago-born Frank Norris' *The Pit* (1903), a novel set in the business community and around the world's largest grain-trading exchange, the "pit" at the Chicago Board of Trade, he too notes the gap between numbers and culture. Upton Sinclair's "muckraking" *The Jungle* (1906) deals with the poverty and social ignorance of the Lithuanian ghetto and the slaughter-work of the stockyards. There are many more numbers: "There is half a square mile of space in the yards, and more than half of it is occupied by cattle pens ... There are two hundred and fifty miles of track within the yards ... One [man] scraped the outside of a leg; another scraped the inside of the same leg. One with a swift stroke cut the throat; another with two swift strokes severed the head ..." Sinclair too asks how Chicago is to be saved; his answer is Socialism. Naturalism and Chicago somehow continued to go together, on to James T. Farrell's *Studs Lonigan* trilogy (1932–6) about growing up poor on the immigrant South Side, Richard Wright and Nelson Algren. And the theme has lasted, right to Saul Bellow's delightful *Humboldt's Gift* (1975) – a modern if not postmodern story of contemporary Chicago, a "cultureless city pervaded nonetheless by Mind."[8]

4.

Howells or James? Fuller's difficult, never-resolved choice was to trouble many American writers of the new Nineties generation as the

[8] I have drawn heavily here and in what follows on David Cheshire and Malcolm Bradbury, "American Realism and the Romance of Europe," in *Perspectives in American History*, Vol. 4 (1970), in turn indebted to Bernard Bowron, "Henry B. Fuller: A Critical Study" (unpublished PhD thesis, Harvard, 1948). Larzer Ziff also has some admirable comments on Fuller and Chicago in *The American 1890s*, cited above, p. 173.

century moved uneasily toward its close. On the face of it the answer was easy. James had left, and Howells stayed. James wrote of distant Europe, Howells of commonplace America. James created art, Howells reported life. And Howells had done his work well; in one form or other the realism he promoted had become the voice of most American fiction, shaping local-colour writing, urban report, journalism, "muck-raking." The America of industrialism, progress, trusts and corporations was an age of realism, and, though Howells summoned it from the European writing of Tolstoy, George Eliot, Flaubert, Zola, it seemed the American way. It was not a literary movement but a direct representation. It was born, Alfred Kazin has argued, "on native grounds," from a critical response to the problems of American life as economic problems mounted, the frontier closed, immigration grew, cities reached crisis; it grew out of "the bewilderment, and thrived on the simple grimness, of a generation suddenly brought face to face with the pervasive materialism of industrial capitalism." It "poured sullenly out of agrarian bitterness, the class hatreds of the eighties and nineties, the bleakness of small-town life, the mockery of the nouveaux riches, and the bitterness of the great new proletarian cities," had "no centre, no unifying principle, no philosophy, no joy in its coming, no climate of experiment." James wrote of culture, the American realists wrote of "life." Said Hamlin Garland: "We are forming a literature from direct contact with life, and such a literature can be estimated only by unbiased minds and by comparison with nature and the life we live." "The muse of American fiction is . . . a robust red-armed *bonne femme*, who rough-shoulders her way among men and among affairs, who finds healthy pleasure in the honest, rough-and-tumble, Anglo-Saxon give-and-take knockabout that for us means life," claimed Frank Norris. "She will lead you far from the studios and the aesthetes, the velvet jackets and the uncut hair, far from the sexless creatures who cultivate their little art of writing as the fancier cultivates his orchids . . . into a world of Working Men, crude of speech, swift of action . . ."[9]

None of this was quite true. Realism in America *was* an aesthetic movement, developing in parallel with similar Naturalist tendencies in Europe. Howells remained close to Europe, and felt he had missed another "life" in Paris. Norris may have ended up, like his novelist

[9] See Alfred Kazin, *On Native Grounds: An Interpretation of Modern American Prose Literature* (New York, 1942; rev. ed., New York, Harcourt Brace, 1956).

Presley in *The Octopus* (1901), who goes to California to write a Spanish romance and finds himself fighting with the ranchers against unjust grain-rates and freight-tariffs; but he started in Paris amid the studios and the aesthetes, and came back carrying a yellow novel of Zola's in his hand. Howells, Norris and Garland all published works of literary theory in the Nineties – from which these remarks against theory are taken. Nor did any of them consider realism the only mode of fiction, and all produced their fair share of "romance," the kind of writing Robert Louis Stevenson (another visitor to the United States) had argued for in Britain. But one very striking thing was that, when such writers looked for the proper "romance" subject, they constantly turned (like the designers of the White City) to Europe. On the one hand they wrote American novels, about the ghetto, the trust, the bankrupt farmstead; on the other they produced European tales about society, great cities, Italian *duchessas*. "What has art to do with truth? Is not truth the imagination's deadly enemy?" asked one of the most successful producers of these, F. Marion Crawford, scion of American painters in Italy. Crawford wrote move than forty of these romances, appealing to an old European world of honour and chivalry. Then there were Fuller's impressionistic romances, Edith Wharton's dense social fictions, Henry Harland's Italianate exotica, Constance Fenimore Woolson's Italian tales, the rich, suspenseful European romances of Richard Harding Davis, and many more. Often they came from exactly the same writers who wrote American "realism" (Wharton, for example, produced a realist tale in *Ethan Frome*, 1911), as if Europe somehow opened out not only social dreams but artistic possibilities America denied to its writers. It was as if America was, quite simply, more "real" than Europe: more exposed to sociological, economic and material forces, less shaded by the mitigating influence of tradition, culture, romance, even femininity. Dreiser called Chicago a city of "power and fact," and felt compelled to write of it as such, cutting his world down to one of hard materialism; Chicago's inherent materiality struck Henry James in 1904 ("What monstrous ugliness!" he said of the South Side), and he recorded the impression in *The American Scene*; Waldo Frank spoke of American writers submerged in "a blind cult of the American Fact." According to George Santayana's famous lecture of 1911, "The Genteel Tradition in American Philosophy," this was in effect the philosophical problem of the nation itself: "The American will inhabits the skyscraper; the American intellect inhabits the colonial mansion. The one is the sphere of the American man; the other, at least predominantly, of the American woman. The one is all aggressive enterprise; the other is all genteel tradition." In his divided consciousness, Henry Blake Fuller was far from alone.

There was, for example, the case of Harold Frederic. Born in 1856 in Utica, New York, he became an influential regional newspaperman, editor of the Albany *Evening Journal*. He also became, with a series of striking novels set in the Mohawk Valley, a major chronicler and recorder of his region, in works like *Seth's Brother's Wife* (1887), *The Lawton Girl* (1890), *In the Valley*, (1890), and *The Copperhead* (1893). Some were historical, some contemporary; all were written with a sense of journalistic realism. The finest and best-known is *The Damnation of Theron Ware* (1896), the story of a small-town fundamentalist Methodist minister who loses his faith when he is sensually awakened by sexual need, decadent artistic possibilities, German poetry, French claret, Italian Catholic ritual, Pre-Raphaelite sensibility and the temptations of Darwinian doctrine. This is one of those novels of sensory "awakening" common in the transitional end-of-century mood (another is Kate Chopin's *The Awakening*); but all the temptations are associated with Europe, to which the central female character, Celia Madden, returns. One notable feature about all of these "Mohawk Valley" novels is that they were actually written in Britain. For in March 1884, when his Albany newspaper was sold, Frederic was appointed the London correspondent of the *New York Times*. In Britain as bureau chief for the next fourteen years, he distinguished himself for his aggressive reporting of, among other things, the Toulon cholera epidemic and Jewish pogroms in Russia. His domestic life grew complicated; he set up two households, one in London for his wife Grace, another in Surrey for his mistress, Kate Lyon. He remained a very aggressively American figure, out of tune with such aesthetic or socially ambitious fellow American expatriates as Bret Harte, Logan Pearsall Smith or Howard O. Sturgis – author of the English society romance *Belchamber* (1904), who went to Eton and lived near it ever after in his fine house Qu'Acre, a great mannerist whom even his friend Henry James called "a richly sugared cake." It was Harold Frederic who famously dismissed James himself as "an effeminate old donkey who lives with a herd of other donkeys around him and insists on being treated as if he were the Pope," and who had "licked the dust from the floor of every third rate hostess in England." Asked his profession on some form, Frederic wrote, in very un-Jamesian fashion, "paper-stainer," and he always preferred the clubbable company of writers who hung firmly onto virile American egos – Ambrose Bierce, the young Stephen Crane – and were in Britain less to satisfy social needs than for journalistic or even sexual motives.

Frederic announced himself "a Howells man to the end"; but his fiction too oscillated between something near to American Naturalism and something very like European romance. After the publication of *The Damnation of Theron Ware*, nearly all the novels he produced were set in England, or in one case, *The Return of the O'Mahony* (1892), Ireland. "It is natural that since Frederic has lived so long in England, his pen should turn toward English life," Stephen Crane – with whom, since Crane's arrival in Britain in 1897, Frederic had struck up a close friendship – wrote in the Chicago *Chap-Book* in 1898. "One does not look upon this fact with unmixed joy. It is mournful to lose his work even for a time. It is for this reason that I have made myself disagreeable on several occasions by my expressed views of *March Hares*. It is a worthy book, but one has a sense of desertion." Even while Frederic advised Crane himself to stick to familiar American subjects, he maintained his desertion over his next three novels: *March Hares* (1896), *Gloria Mundi* (1898) and *The Market Place* (post., 1899). These are marked not just by shift in subject-matter but in literary style. *March Hares* owes a lot to Oscar Wilde, and is a social romp coming near to comic opera. The other two works are tighter mixtures of romance and critical analysis, but lack the reality and nuance of Frederic's American fiction. *Gloria Mundi* is a satire on the English upper classes, and suggests a solution to political problems based on profit-sharing, but draws on fashionable social novelettes for its plot. *The Market Place* (which brings back Celia Madden from *Theron Ware*, now in Britain) is set round the London stock exchange, and deals with social reform in the age of technocracy. Frederic was having serious emotional and financial problems, and may have helped to solve them with English society romances, but he was losing touch with his finest and most truthful material. In October 1898, at the age of forty-two, he died suddenly of a stroke, after his mistress, a Christian Scientist, failed to call a doctor. Among the manuscript notes he left behind, there were plans only for yet more English books.[10]

---

[10] For accounts of Frederic, see Thomas F. O. O'Donnell and Hoyt G. Franchere, *Harold Frederic* (New York, Twayne, 1961), and Austin Briggs, *The Novels of Harold Frederic* (New York, Cornell University Press, 1969).

5.

Then again there was Henry Harland, a writer who obscured his origins so well the handbooks are still having trouble with his life. He claimed to have been born in Saint Petersburg (so did James McNeill Whistler); in truth his birthplace was nowhere more exotic than New York City. Among many other jugglings of identity were a claim to be descended from the Harlands of Sprague Hall, Suffolk, the assertion that he was Jewish, had been educated in Paris, had trained for the priesthood in Rome, was an illegitimate child of the Habsburg emperor Franz Joseph, and so on. "A man should never live in the land of his birth; a theory that certainly [leaves me] few lands to live in," he joked. This endless play of identity had him working, during the Eighties, in the New York Jewish literary community, using the Jewish pen-name of "Sidney Luska," and writing novels about New York Jewish life. In a whole exotic row of books – *As It Was Written* (1885), *Mrs Peixada* (1886), *The Yoke of the Thorah* (1887), *My Uncle Florimund* (1888), *Mr Sonnenschein's Inheritance* (1888) – he left a strong, vivid, even convincing fictional record of ghetto life. "I praised what seemed a tendency to realism in them," said (of course) the ubiquitous Howells, but he had to admit that Harland "was naturally and incurably romantic." For these novels also contain their share of sensationalism, fantasy and Gothic romance, include the odd murder, various lost inheritances, and a celebration of "warmer blood," and display – as in *My Uncle Florimund* – their author's aristocratic dreams ("I was rich! I could take my proper station now, and cut my proper figure in the world"). Harland's imperfect credentials were finally unmasked when one of the books advocated marriage between Jews and Gentiles. The truth was that he was a self-creating figure from the dandyish spirit of New York bohemia; and he now went on to follow his appropriately bohemian destiny.

He moved on with his wife to Paris, now filled with young Americans questing for the life of the Latin Quarter. Here, in a city whose Americanization had already well begun, he displayed his usual chameleon gifts of impersonation. "Harland was one of those Americans in love with Paris who seem more French than the French themselves, a slim, gesticulating, goateed, snub-nosed, lovable figure, smoking innumerable cigarettes as he galvanically pranced round the room, excitingly pronouncing the *dernier mot* on the build of the short story or the art of prose," noted Richard Le Gallienne in *The Romantic Nineties*.

"Ah, you're not mad about style, but I am," he wrote. "Why doesn't everyone live in Paris?"[11] But Harland himself didn't do so for long; in 1889 he moved to London, changing character again, and assuring everyone he was of English aristocratic descent. The year was well chosen; it was the year when "the Wilde spirit" began to flourish, and the aesthetic mood of the Nineties began. Harland carried letters of introduction from his writer-godfather Edmund Clarence Stedman to Henry James, "the only master of considered prose style we've got." James was to prove remarkably helpful, even if he was not entirely convinced, as he revealed to Edmund Gosse after meeting his *protégé* in Paris: "Poor Harland came and spent two or three hours with me the other afternoon . . . He looked better than the time previous, but not well, and I am afraid things are not well *with* him. One would like to help him – and I try to – in talk; but he is not too helpable, for there is a chasm too deep to bridge, I fear, in the pitfall of his literary longings unaccompanied by the faculty."

Even so, "poor Harland" flourished in London. He perfectly caught the changing mood, converted – inevitably enough – to Catholicism, and in his writing switched from New York urban realism to Nineties aesthetic camp. Now he wrote mannered novels and stories set in the dense world of Europe, in Italy or the exotic Parisian Latin Quarter, including *Mademoiselle Miss* and *Comedies and Errors* (both 1898), with their tales of American girls on the Left Bank. Two of them, *The Cardinal's Snuff Box* (1890) and *My Friend Prospero* (1904), are especially interesting, and well worth the reading still. *The Cardinal's Snuff Box*, set in Italy, is told in high-styled prose, and filled with false identities, crafty cardinals and *duchessas*. The book proved so successful the critics compared it with the work of the Master himself, whom Harland had plainly sought to emulate. It sold 100,000 copies by 1902, which is more than any work by James, who really did have the faculty, ever had.[12]

11 For details see Albert Parry, *Garrets and Pretenders* (cited above), especially the two chapters called "Our Sinful Abroad" and "*The Yellow Book*, and More About Expatriates." Also Richard Le Gallienne, *The Romantic Nineties* (New York, 1925), and Katharine Lyon Mix, *A Study in Yellow: The "Yellow Book" and Its Contributors* (Lawrence, Kansas, 1960).

12 A quotation suggests its late Jamesian flavour: " 'And meanwhile they get their breadcrumbs,' she said. 'They certainly get their breadcrumbs,' he admitted. 'I'm afraid' – she smiled, as one who has conducted a syllogism safely to its conclusion – 'I'm afraid I do not think your compensation compensates.' 'To be quite honest, I dare say it doesn't,' he confessed. 'And anyhow' – she followed her victory up – 'I shouldn't wish any garden to represent the universal war . . . I should wish it to be a retreat from the battle – an abode of peace – a happy valley – a sanctuary for the snatched-from.' " (The topic is feeding sparrows.)

Then in 1894 Harland met the twenty-two-year-old Aubrey Beardsley, and they planned the famous Nineties quarterly *The Yellow Book*, "perhaps his most beguiling dream and most rewarding hours," said James. Beautifully produced, published by John Lane from 1894 to 1897, it became the aesthete's bible of the Wilde era – even though Wilde himself was never in it (though James, much to his own unease, was). It both expressed and stylishly teased the decadence, and displayed all Harland's nostalgia for the life of the Latin Quarter. He contributed to every one of the thirteen issues, generally using the pseudonym of "The Yellow Dwarf," a mischievous, impish figure Max Beerbohm illustrated for the readers. The "decadent" style of the volume was imitated throughout the United States; in most major cities versions of the *Yellow Book* appeared, bringing the aesthetic spirit to the politically troubled American Nineties. Wilde's visit had certainly not been wasted. As for Harland, he had been suffering since 1890 from tuberculosis, that recurrent literary disease of the decade. After a final brief return to New York in 1903, he died in Italy, at San Remo, on 20 December 1905, at the age of forty-four – yet another victim of the ever-fragile Nineties.

It was left to James best to sum up "poor Harland," which he did in a famous review of *Comedies and Errors* in 1898. Perhaps because their work had been often compared (sometimes to Harland's advantage), James devotes the essay to some of his most elaborate discriminations on the topic he was now the great expert in – the question of what he called "the feeling of the American for his famous Europe." He notes the decline of regional loyalties in literature, the growth of an art of cosmopolitanism. Where Harland's interest lies, he says, is in his peculiarly American sense of Europe. He writes without a single direct glance at American life, so his book presents a "disencumbered, sensitive surface for the wonderful Europe to play on." Yet it remains a surface; he does not dig deep. As for Europe, it has become not only a subject but a style, a form, a feeling, and "the feeling of things – in especial of the particular place, of the last and regretted period and chance, always, to fond fancy, supremely charming and queer and exquisite – is Mr Harland's general subject and most frequent inspiration." A writer from an age when the world is, he says, "fast shrinking, for the imagination, to the size of an orange that can be played with," Harland's vision is not that of the writer who is (like James himself) expatriated, but "dispatriated":

He is lost in the vision, all whimsical and picturesque, of palace secrets, rulers and pretenders and ministers of bewilderingly light comedy, in indiscoverable Balkan states, Bohemias of the seaboard . . . ; in the heavy, many-voiced air of the old Roman streets and of the high Roman saloons where cardinals are a part of the furniture; in the hum of prodigious Paris, heard in the corners of old cafés; in the sense of the deep English background as much as that of any of these; in a general facility of reference, in short, to the composite spectacle and the polyglot doom.[13]

In a cosmopolitan age, Harland, James explained, had acquired an over-acute "sense of the 'Europe' – synthetic symbol! – of the American mind." In short, he had sacrificed himself to a European fiction, lost himself, as far as literature's truth was concerned, in its infinite romance. It was a weighty judgement, not just on Harland but on a whole direction in American writing. For who knew more about the subtle shades of the "polyglot doom" than Henry James?

6.

Perhaps it was because of the impact on American confidence of the Columbian World Fair, perhaps because the American Nineties were starting, but 1893 was a strangely important year for the emergence of new American writers and their books. One of these, published at the author's (or rather his brother's) expense, in a yellow cover and under the pseudonym of "Johnston Smith," was *Maggie: A Girl of the Streets: A Story of New York*. Its twenty-two-year-old author was Stephen Townley Crane, rebel son from a pious home. His father was a New Jersey Methodist minister, his mother became noted for her religious journalism. Crane had not proved a good student: at Claverack College he was more interested in baseball and journalism, at Syracuse University he lasted only one semester. He decided to "recover from college" by moving to New York – to the "Tenderloin" district, living in an old building, once the Art Students League, shared by a group of artists on East 23rd Street, where he intended to live by writing. The setting was doubly appropriate. Here he was, living in fashionable if necessary poverty, among artists in Manhattan "Bohemia," and

13 James' comments are in the essay "The Story-Teller at Large: Mr Henry Harland," originally published in *The Fortnightly Review*, April 1898. It is reprinted in Leon Edel (ed.), *Henry James: The American Essays* (New York, Vintage, 1956), along with other essays reflecting on similar expatriated authors.

enjoying himself. But he was also close to the Bowery, ideal subject-matter at a time when – in painting, photography and journalism – urban subjects were growing popular. In 1890 Jacob Riis published *How The Other Half Lives*, his study of tenement life on the Lower East Side, with powerful photographs, and caused national consternation; and Alfred Stieglitz's experimental photographs with hand-held camera in *Picturesque Bits of New York* (1897) would soon attract attention. Crane determined to write "Bowery Tales," "experiments in misery," studies of poor life and the great contrasts of the city. Working as a journalist, mostly for the New York *Tribune*, he set out, mixing fiction and documentary, to capture his "impressions," of street-corner glimpses, fragments of inequality, details of poor urban life.

Crane probably began *Maggie* (later to be reprinted with a companion piece, *George's Mother*) at college, when he was much under the influence of Rudyard Kipling's *The Light That Failed* (1891), about an artist tugged between the claims of pure art and action. A "slum novel" with a conventional enough Victorian theme, it tells the story of a good poor girl abused, exploited, and driven into prostitution, who finally kills herself in neglect and shame. It plainly professes the spirit of realism, naturalism: "it tries to show that environment is a tremendous thing and frequently shapes lives regardless," Crane wrote in his presentation copies. "If one proves that theory one makes room in Heaven for all sorts of souls (notably an occasional street girl) who are not confidently expected to be there by many excellent people." But it is also an aesthetic book, and what made it really notable was its method: its vignette-like style of presentation, its strange irony, its angular prose, its distinctive neo-naturalist technique. Set in the New York tenements of "Rum Alley," and the dray-filled, crowded Darwinian streets, the bars and the theatres, it captured the urban struggle for existence, control and domination in stylized moments of vivid sensation. Crane aimed, he later explained, to press "toward the goal described by that misunderstood and abused word, 'realism' " – though his aim was not so much to create a vivid report on city life as to form a stylized portrait of it. He meant to renounce "the clever school in literature," and follow the credo of "nature and truth": "Later I discovered that my creed was identical with that of Howells and Garland."

In fact one of those signed presentation copies went to Hamlin Garland, who passed it to Howells. Both recognized a successor, and offered support and advice. Happily Garland was to hand to salvage another longer work Crane had been writing: a story of the American Civil War. Crane had already completed, by 1893, a draft of the work he then called a "potboiler," though later he called it "an effort born of pain." He was broke, having trouble getting journalistic commissions, and Garland had to lend him money to reclaim the manuscript from an unpaid typist. In fact Crane offered to sell him his writing prospects for $23 cash – which could have been a bargain, had Crane ever in his life found out how to keep his income above his expenditure. He showed the book, really a novella, to publishers, who showed little interest; he nearly discarded it, but finally managed to print a short version in a newspaper, the *Philadelphia Press*, in 1894. In September of the next year, when he was still just twenty-four, the firm of D. Appleton published the work, *The Red Badge of Courage: An Episode of the American Civil War.* American reviews were warm, but it was seen either as another piece of Naturalism, of what Howells and Garland said was making writing more precise, scientific, closer to life, or as part of the revived vogue for fiction and memoirs about the Civil War, which returned to public interest thanks to writers like Ambrose Bierce and, no doubt, the atmosphere of a decade that seemed destined for imperial wars. Some American reviewers saw him as an American Kipling (Kipling's war writing and concern with the life of action doubtless had its effect on the novel). But the tide turned for Crane in November, when the book appeared in Britain from Heinemann in their Pioneer Series of Modern Fiction. It at once caught the imagination of British reviewers, many of whom were wildly enthusiastic. "In the whole range of literature we can call to mind nothing so searching in its analysis," said the *Daily Chronicle*. "A remarkable book," wrote George Wyndham, former soldier as well as critic, in the *New Review* in January 1896, going on to say that Crane "achieves by his singleness of purpose a truer and completer picture of war than either Tolstoi [in *War and Peace*], bent also upon proving the insignificance of his heroes, or Zola [in *Le Débâcle*], bent also on prophesying the regeneration of France." He then added, with a very *fin-de-siècle* sense of gloomy prophecy, "It is but a further step to recognize all life for a battle and this earth for a vessel lost in space."

The reception was striking, not least for the very different way the book was seen in the two countries. For American readers *The Red Badge* . . . was a somewhat strange example of the Naturalism it seemed to profess. Crane trained as a journalist, and his previous work had been mostly urban sketches done in the manner of documentary realism. It was a cardinal law of the naturalist's and journalist's rule-book that the writer had been there, known the event, experienced the reality. Crane certainly had not, though he would more than make up later. In 1863, when the Battle of Chancellorsville (on which it is generally agreed the tale is based) took place, he wasn't born; indeed he would delay his coming for eight more years. "Of course I have never been in a battle, but I believe I got my sense of the rage of conflict on the football field, or else fighting is an hereditary instinct, and I wrote it intuitively," Crane explained to a friendly critic, James Northern Hilliard, when the American public demanded to know whether he was a veteran of the battle. "He knows nothing of war, yet he is drenched in blood," wrote Ambrose Bierce, who really had been in battle and had written vividly of it in his own Civil War stories, *Tales of Soldiers and Civilians* (1891). But Crane was perfectly right. What he did understand were the claims of action and the "rage of conflict," and he had the naturalist's sense of the struggle for life conducted in a world of aggressive, death-dealing reality where a man is ironized by violence, insignificance, the blank indifference of nature, the anonymous weight of the collective military mass. And in the end no book more vividly gives the sensation of "being there," seeing and experiencing the details, the sensations, the impressions, the psychological responses of battle right at the side of the only once-named hero, Henry Fleming, "the Youth," as over two days of shifting conflict he suffers its stifling fear, danger and chaos, its pain and its final moment of initiation, its special red badge, the wound – which may or may not be the red badge of courage.

What was remarkable about *The Red Badge* . . . , in short, was more than its subject; it was its powerful literary method. The book does not see war as the product of a just cause, nor root it in history; only incidentally is it clear it is about the American Civil War at all, rather it is set on some universal battlefield of modern life. The minimalization of everything extraneous to the battle scene goes even further, reducing and fragmenting the detail of the fighting itself. We see essentially through Henry's eyes or his consciousness. That itself grows ever narrower, as it reduces from his first heroic and romantic "thought-images" to the scenic concentration of the instants of war. The story begins by removing him from all his previous, inherited notions of war as chivalry, all faith in religion as a guide, or in nature as a benignly reassuring force. He becomes a figure in a test, an "experiment," and sees himself that he must have "blaze, blood, and danger, even as a chemist requires this, that, or the other." So he conducts a naturalist experiment on himself by going into battle ("He finally concluded that the only way to prove himself was to go into the blaze, and then figuratively to watch his legs to discover their merits and faults"). Battle then becomes a terrible embroilment in flux, movement, sensation, colour, herd instinct, individual isolation, danger, boredom, sudden action. The mind becomes a machine for perception rather than a source of judgement or comprehension, turns scenic and experiential: "His accumulated thought upon such subjects was used to form scenes." Sensations point to actions, and consciousness is rendered as a strangely self-knowing yet unreliable mechanism, a psychology taking into itself and ordering the sensationalism and surprise of an exposed naked world. Henry is a kind of impressionist ("His mind took a mechanical but firm impression, so that afterward everything was pictured and explained to him, save why he himself was there") in the hands of a larger impressionist, the author – always conscious of the impression of the moment on Henry, but also of the impression on the reader the text itself must convey.

It was to this that the British readers, above all the fellow writers of his own generation, responded. And if American writers in the 1890s were highly preoccupied with Naturalism and its variants, British ones were now growing preoccupied by something else. In Europe, Naturalism was dying; indeed its obituary was pronounced in the Paris press in that same year of 1893. A new generation of novelists, with a new view of the powers of the novel, was just starting to form. They were breaking up the solid mass, the social and moral weight, the authorial certainty, of Victorian fiction, and growing interested in new theories of consciousness and psychology, and the more illusory techniques of literary impressionism. The signs were there in the work of Henry James, who, as we know, had left fiction for the theatre for a time, but was drawn back to the novel by, precisely, these new tendencies. And another key figure was Joseph Conrad, whose first novel, *Almayer's Folly*, appeared in 1895, the same year as *The Red Badge* . . . . He would approvingly explain to Crane, when the two men finally met: "Your method is fascinating. You are the complete impressionist. The illusions of life come out of your hand without a flaw. It is not life – which nobody wants – it is art." Conrad's friend

Edward Garnett, publisher and friend to many new writers, similarly hailed Crane as "the chief impressionist of our day." But perhaps it was H. G. Wells, who had also just published his first novel, *The Time Machine*, in 1895, who captured him best. *The Red Badge* . . . was, he said, "a new thing, in a new school," from a newly independent American generation with a fresh American directness and vigour, comparable in effect to Whistler. "In style, in method, in all that is distinctively *not* found in his books, he is sharply defined, the expression in art of certain enormous repudiations." The fact was that Crane was now being welcomed into various branches of what would prove to be the beginnings of the modern movement. There were two Stephen Cranes, two *Red Badges* . . . – one a work of American naturalism, the other a work of new European impressionism.

7.

Soon American journalists in London – not least of them Harold Frederic, who wrote a laudatory, understanding article about the book in the *New York Times* – began reporting the British reviews to the press back home. Crane's British fame crossed back over the Atlantic, his American sales and reputation surged, and the short novel became a national bestseller. Crane's other work, old and new, started to pour from the presses, and English publishers chased him. In the United States the big press syndicates sought his services. When he wrote *The Red Badge* . . . Crane had never seen a battlefield; soon he was attending many; he now became that much admired figure, the acme of the modern journalist, the war correspondent. Sent by the New York *Journal* to cover Cuban war news, he joined up with a filibustering expedition to take arms by sea to the insurgents. Shipwrecked on the voyage, he survived thirty hours adrift in an open boat, and was reported dead; the experience led to his finest short story, "The Open Boat" (1898) ("None of them knew the colour of the sky . . ."). On this trip he encountered the twice-married Cora Taylor, owner of a high-class brothel in Jacksonville, Florida, charmingly named the Hotel de Dream, and improbably described by her biographer as "primarily a place for the enjoyment of superior food and entertainment." The two fell in love, and Cora, taking the literary pseudonym of "Imogen Carter," joined Crane when the *Journal* sent him off to Greece to cover the Greco-Turkish War. En route they stopped in London, where Cora had lived (and married) before. Here he met Harold Frederic, and renewed acquaintance with Richard Harding Davis, noted American war reporter and patriotic novelist, also en route for the conflict. The fighting lasted only a month, and would provide Crane with the material for a later, weaker war novel, *Active Service* (1899). At the end, Crane and Cora returned, in June 1897, not to the States but to London.[14]

It was Crane's twenty-sixth year – the year he published a collection of Civil War stories, *The Little Regiment*, and *The Third Violet*, a story "of life among the poorer and poorer artists in New York," based on his life in Manhattan's bohemia. For the next three years, which meant the remainder of his life, Crane would remain mostly in Britain, where a very considerable portion of his writing was done. It must be said that, in coming to Britain, he and Cora were certainly no Jamesian passionate pilgrims, and belonged to the redskin rather than the paleface tradition of visiting expatriates. Crane was a somewhat scandalous young bohemian who, especially after various adventures in the West and Mexico, affected the Western style; Cora, several years older, had the ways of a *grande dame* madame. There were several sound reasons for a change of scene. Crane was in trouble with the New York police for his protection of a streetwalker, Cora's divorce had not come through, and the two may or may not have gone through a marriage ceremony. At home there were religious relatives to consider; among the literary figures of Britain such unconventional *ménages* seemed entirely *à la mode*, as Frederic's own arrangements showed. Crane told an American reporter: "the English aren't as shocked as we are." He also said: "You can have an idea in England without being sent to court for it." Neither opinion would have satisfied Oscar Wilde, who was already languishing in Reading Gaol, nor Crane's new friend Ford Madox Hueffer, who a couple of decades later would be hounded from the country for a similarly unconventional *ménage*. But then Crane also said of the English: "They will believe anything wild or impossible you tell them." And London offered the couple social freedom, warm hospitality and pleasant friendships, not least with Frederic and his

[14] A key source for details of Crane's life and relationships is R. W. Stallman and Lillian Gilkes (eds), *Stephen Crane: Letters* (London, Peter Owen, 1960); and also see Stanley Wertheim and Paul Sorrentino (eds), *The Correspondence of Stephen Crane* (New York, Columbia University Press, 1988).

mistress Kate Lyon. There were now 50,000 Americans settled in the city, as well as many American war correspondents ("It was a fat time for American correspondents and they all went to the Savage Club," reported Ford Madox Hueffer, later Ford). Cora had social ambitions and, surprisingly given her *curriculum vitae*, even held hopes of being presented to Queen Victoria. But society hostesses proved delighted to welcome the unconventional, often shy young American writer every-one said was a genius: "He seems to have been received by half the Cabinet and a perfect galaxy of Irish peeresses," Hueffer observed.

Literary reasons were important too. Crane had planned to visit Britain as a result of his critical reception, and the fact that here he had been acknowledged as a serious artist: "I have only one pride, and that is that the English edition of *The Red Badge of Courage* has been received with great praise," he wrote in a letter. So "Mr Stephen Crane has settled down in this country for an indefinite period," the London *Bookman* noted that summer. They rented a "hideous villa," Ravens-brook, near Oxted, Surrey, in a part of Britain much favoured by writers. Frederic had a place nearby, "Homefield" at Kenley; Edward Garnett lived close at Limpsfield, where he entertained the Conrads. London was near, and offered its literary rewards: lunch with J. M. Barrie, tea with Algernon Charles Swinburne, lunch again with Edmund Gosse, a meeting with "poor Harland" (they had a quarrel about Wilde, whose work Crane disliked). With Frederic and Robert Barr he formed a happy journalistic triumvirate, "the three musketeers"; other journalists joined the ranks. He met Henry James, reputedly at a London party where a Madame Zipango poured champagne into his top hat, and Crane courteously rescued it. There was the crucial, much-sought meeting with Joseph Conrad at a lunch arranged by their joint publisher. They had what Conrad called "a good pow-wow," talking long into the afternoon about literature, action, and war ("My picture of war was all right!" he told Conrad, "I found it just as I imagined it"). Each admired the work of the other, and they found they shared a common interest in "the psychology of the mass" under pressure. Conrad observed on this first meeting that "Crane had not the face of a lucky man"; but the two became good friends, and talked of writing a play, and buying a boat, together. Crane, in debt as usual, was writing furiously, fiction and travel reports, but entertaining heavily, encouraged by the social Cora. As Hueffer, himself one of the visitors, put it: "no sooner did the word go round that there was at Oxted, and afterwards at Brede, a shining young American of genius . . . ready to sit up all night dispensing endless hampers of caviare, *foie gras*, champagne and oysters in season . . . ah, then, there was tumult indeed . . ." Notable was the group Crane, borrowing the name he had given his fellow-bohemians on the Bowery, called "the Indians," centred around Frederic. An American visitor described one of their weekend incursions: "Mr Frederic is not at all agreeable. He is funny in a sarcastic way about politics and people but he kept interrupting everybody else and was downright rude to Mr Crane several times. They made Mr Crane shoot with his revolver after lunch and he is a fine shot."

In fact Crane – who liked to cultivate his Western image, down to writing some wonderful Western stories ("The Bride Comes to Yellow Sky" (1897), "The Blue Hotel" (1898)) – made much of his skill with a sixgun, even killing flies with it, according to Hueffer: "Crane in those days, and for my benefit, was in the habit of posing as an almost fabulous Billy the Kid, just as later, to *épater* Henry James, he insisted on posing as, and exaggerating the characteristics of, a Bowery boy of the most hideous type . . . we wore breeches, riding leggings, spurs, a cowboy's shirt, and there was always a gun near him . . ." But his expenses were fast outrunning his literary income, and, like Scott Fitzgerald later, he was having to pour out writing in quantity to keep the creditors off. As a result, though some of his best short stories – "The Open Boat," "The Monster," "The Bride Comes to Yellow Sky," "The Blue Hotel" – come from the English years, so did a rush of journalism and potboiling, designed to fill print, bring in quick cheques, and keep off the bailiffs. It must have been almost a relief when the US battleship *Maine* mysteriously blew up in Havana harbour, initiating the Spanish-American War in April 1898. Scenting action again, Crane, borrowing money from the impoverished Conrad to pay the passage, hurried back to New York, meaning to join the US navy. He was rejected for ill-health; in fact the tuberculosis that was soon to threaten his life was diagnosed. Instead, then, along with Frank Norris and Richard Harding Davis, he got himself commissioned to go to Cuba as a war correspondent. The War – America's great end-of-century imperial adventure, which brought Spanish control on the continent to a close – lasted only 115 days. Crane showed himself courageous at the scene, covered the Battle of San Juan Hill, exulted in the action, and wrote some of his finest journalism. He also disappeared for a while, and showed evident doubts about resuming his complicated marital and social life in Britain. He found, though, that his reputation in the States was far from high ("It seems that in New York, outside the immediate circle of men who know me well, I am some kind of Simon Legree who goes around knocking women into the gutter . . ."). Meantime Cora, grand as ever, was renting an opulent property, the distinguished though dilapidated country manor of Brede, an ancient house with a hundred acres, seven miles from Winchelsea in East Sussex. In January 1899 he shipped back to England, and once more the Cranes moved on, the rent at Ravensbrook still owing, to the manorship of Brede.

8.

Brede Place, which Cora rented from the notable Frewen family, patrons of the arts, was a fourteenth-century house remodelled in the Elizabethan period. Once linked with smuggling, it was said to be haunted by "the bloody shade of Sir Goddard Oxenbridge," a giant figure who attended Henry VIII at the Field of the Cloth of Gold, and was reputedly slaughtered by the locals. Cora delighted in the house, in the Sussex hills just over the sea: "Cora believes that Sir Walter Scott designed it for her," Crane said, while, according to Edward Garnett, who found the house for them, Crane himself was attracted by its unlucky chequered history. For all its charm and distinction, the house at the time was rambling, dank and decaying, and, though Cora called in an architect, the Cranes took up a somewhat marginal residence there, with cheap or borrowed furniture.[15] Young, gaunt, the famous "genius," Crane became "Baron Brede," a kind of roughneck Western squire, with Cora, dressed in long medieval sleeves, as his chatelaine. To some of the many Americans who visited him there, he had now become that familiar expatriate figure, the bohemian turned snob, and he was indeed trying to live like a lord on an insufficient income (*just* like a lord, in fact). However, Cora explained her intentions: "I hope the perfect quiet of Brede Place and the freedom from a lot of dear good

[15] Brede Place continued to have a notable history (Clare Sheridan, who sculpted Trotsky and travelled widely as an artist, lived there). It suffered a fire in the 1970s, and has since been modernly restored. I am indebted for details to Mrs Mary Frewen of Rye.

people who take his mind from his work, will let him show the world a book that will live." Alas, it did not work out. Their expenses rose, their entertaining became more lavish, their hospitality more exploited, their dependents grew (they included the illegitimate children of Harold Frederic, who died just before the move to Brede). As a result, according to Hueffer, an occasional visitor, you found behind the house's ancient façade "a rabbit warren of passages with beer barrels set up at odd corners, and barons of beef for real tramps at the kitchen door, and troops of dogs and maids and butlers and sham tramps of the New York newspaper world and women who couldn't sell their manuscripts." Dogs fought for scraps in the rushes under the table, Crane killed flies with his sixgun, the creditors gathered. As grew clear over the next months, Crane, struggling against growing ill-health, and pushing his writing, was running up expenses that – however fast he wrote, however high his price, and however much Cora aggressively dunned his publishers, editors and his agent, J. B. Pinker – he could never possibly meet.[16]

Brede brought many problems for Crane, and its expenses and perhaps its dampness may well have hastened his death. On the other hand it also turned out to be an ideal literary choice. It so happened that most of what was interesting, discovering and experimental in the British fictional scene of the day was somehow becoming concentrated in this small part of southern England, close to the remote Romney Marshes. Henry James had just become resident at Lamb House in Rye, only a bicycle ride away. Conrad was not so very far away at Pent Farm near Aldington in Kent, Ford Madox Hueffer was first at Aldington, then moved even nearer, to Winchelsea. Edward Garnett's house was at no great distance. H. G. Wells lived in a cottage, then in a big house he built from his suddenly surging literary earnings, in nearby Sandgate; Rudyard Kipling at Bathgate was not far off, John Galsworthy weekended regularly in the district. It was a remarkable and to some degree chance grouping of major talents – for this international band of writers, British, American, Polish, was, each one in his own way, changing the whole climate of modern fiction. Wells was said to have written a wry letter to the papers to say that a ring of foreign conspirators plotting against English letters was working at no

16 There is an excellent record of all this in Iain Finlayson, *Writers in Romney Marsh* (London, Severn House, 1986), a lively account of James, Conrad, Hueffer, Wells, Crane, and their literary successors, to which I am indebted.

distance from his house.[17] Not all of the parties agreed well with each other, but all agreed in their regard and friendship for the friendly young Crane. He became an important part – a youthful figurehead – of the new trend or movement that was developing, if in several different directions. James, who bicycled over several times, regarded him highly, and thought him a young genius. He also generously showed Crane his recent work; Crane seems to have read it with some bafflement, though there are critics who think he was greatly influenced by it. Conrad warmly acknowledged Crane's worth and his influence: "Here we had an artist, a man not of experience but a man inspired, a seer with a gift for rendering the significant on the surface of things and with an incomparable insight into primitive emotions . . ." Hueffer held Crane the inventor of the modern technique he called (in French of course) *progression d'effet*, and described him as "Poor, frail Stevie . . . writing incessantly – like a spider that gave its entrails to nourish a wilderness of parasites." Wells, still at the aesthetic stage in his writing (when he thought fiction a refined and experimental art rather than, as later, a bludgeon), admiringly described him as a "lean, blond, slow-speaking, perceptive, tuberculous being, too adventurous to be temperate with anything."[18]

In truth, a bitter tug-of-war, very emblematic of the artistic divisions of the period, was developing for possession of Crane's artistic soul. On one side gathered the "Indians," the hardnosed journalists or travelling American adventurers, who included Robert Barr, H. B. Marriott-Watson and Edwin Pugh. Until his death, Frederic had been the dominant figure in their number, a close friend of Crane and a dispenser of influential literary advice. He told Crane that his most important task was to stay as American as possible and tempt English writing westward. He even recommended he tear up his fine literary story "The Monster," and concentrate on writing taken directly from journalistic experience, like the much inferior *Active Service*. On the other side were Crane's new literary friends, who were all profoundly serious about writing, technique, the art of the novel. They thought

[17] See Miranda Seymour, *The Ring of Conspirators* (London, Hodder, 1988).
[18] Eric Solomon gives a fine account of this, and Crane's British experience in general, in *Stephen Crane in England: A Portrait of the Artist* (Columbus, Ohio, Ohio State UP, 1964), to which I am generally indebted. John Berryman, *Stephen Crane* (London, Methuen, 1950), is another important source. Also see James B. Colvert, *Stephen Crane* (New York, Harcourt Brace, 1984), and Christopher Benfey, *The Double Life of Stephen Crane* (New York, Knopf, 1992).

little of what they called the "parasites" and believed they were leading Crane out of art and into bad work as well as financial difficulties (Conrad grimly called Frederic "a gross man who lived grossly and died abominably"). Plainly no love was lost, and the disagreements even reached public print. In a warm newspaper appreciation late in 1898 (much appreciated by Crane), Edward Garnett wrote warningly: "What Mr Crane has to do is very simple; he must not mix his reporting with his writing . . . he is thrown away as a picturesque reporter." Crane's problem, he would later explain, was that, having come from journalism, he was haunted "well! by a crew of journalists," while his real gift was for those "two forces of passion and irony" which raised his work to "the higher zone of man's tragic conflict with the universe." Conrad would also tell Garnett that Crane never knew how good his best work was – though he still thought him a master of consummate technique, "one of us." But it was the technique of the intuitive young writer who still had to take the measure of his talent – a writer who, Wells put it approvingly, seemed to come into writing "without a predecessor."

This battle of influences was to have great consequences, not least for Crane's own sense of himself as a writer. To this day it affects the different ways in which his work is seen. Crane was not – it was generally agreed, not least by Crane himself – particularly well-read. He certainly never opened many of the works the critics would have him be influenced by. He was consciously writing in a fresh, radical but not especially theoretical way; and, unlike most of his fellow American naturalists, he was rarely given to making large aesthetic statements. He had come to Britain keenly wanting to be taken seriously as an artist; he was equally aware that his journalistic background, his interest in action, his American material were the chief resources of his writing. The work he did now was mostly short fiction set in the United States (the "Whilomville" stories, war tales, tales of the American West), as well as the novel *Active Service*; he also poured out tales for the cheap magazines. But he had chosen to become part of a community of writers remarkably concerned with complex matters of modern form and technique, who regarded him as central to the direction they were taking. He responded, began reading far more extensively, exchanging theoretical talk, developing his sense of writing as a considered art – just as a serious young writer must. But he was also working under impossible pressure, writing furiously, drawing desperately on his

American and wartime experiences. So the work he produced in the difficult Ravensbrook and Brede years was almost entirely set outside Britain (though there was the unfinished Irish novel *The O'Ruddy* (1903)). And he was never again to reach the artistic complexity he had achieved in *The Red Badge of Courage*.

Moreover, for Crane there was always that crucial pull beyond literature, to life. It had culminated in the excitement of the Battle of San Juan Hill – when, as he said, expression was thrown to the winds, and he could be satisfied "to wholly feel." Yet there remained the aesthete's desire to shape a vision of experience, refine his distinctive fictional style, find artistic form and revelation. As he put it: "I try to give to readers a slice out of life; and if there is any moral or lesson in it, I do not try to point it out. I let the reader find it for himself . . . As Emerson said, 'There should be a long logic beneath the story, but it should be kept carefully out of sight.' " Yet the idea of a "long logic" pointed to a selective, aesthetic art, of exactly the kind James and Conrad now began to emphasize. Uncertainty over this matter – life or art – produced a strange, evasive humility that would haunt nearly all Crane's comments on writing. "The one thing that deeply pleases me in my literary life . . . is the fact that men of sense believe me to be sincere," he writes in a letter, adding oddly, "Personally I am aware that my work does not amount to a string of dried beans." "I go ahead, for I understand that a man is born into the world with his own pair of eyes, and he is not responsible for his visions – he is merely responsible for the quality of personal honesty," he wrote likewise. "I, however, do not say I am honest. I merely say that I am as nearly honest as a weak mental machinery will allow." We can feel these uncertainties right down in the deep texture of his work. Was what he, or his characters, saw or felt a visionary revelation or impression of "life" (like Strether's in Paris), or was the mind the flat recorder of how things were? Was the account a statement of life's truth, or did it obscure its meanings? Wasn't the key to experience the experience itself – so that there was, literally, nothing to say about it? The result is frequently a distinctive Cranean ambiguity. He withdraws from expressing a specific philosophy or aesthetic vision, yet he often hints at some ultimate symbolic revelation – as he does, to the distrust of many critics, at the close of *The Red Badge of Courage*. Crane's writing came out of a double conflict of the times: a symbolist crisis (the belief that even if there is disorder and fragmentation in life there is wholeness in the image or word) and an existential crisis (an exposure to existence without essence). The result is a fiction of symbolist intuitions and ironic juxtapositions open to a variety of meanings, and a vividly distinctive style that has struck some critics as lying between realism and parody. But this, in a way, is precisely what it means to be what Conrad called him, "a complete impressionist." To the end, there were two Stephen Cranes.

9.

In December 1899, as thè old century waned, Crane planned a special Christmas party at baronial Brede. Despite his wild writing schedule, he had written a play – suitably for Brede, it was a ghost story, and "awful rubbish" – to be presented to the villagers: "But to make the thing historic, I have hit upon a plan of making the programmes choice by printing thereon a terrible list of the authors of the comedy and to that end I have asked Henry James, Robert Barr, Joseph Conrad, A. E. W. Mason, H. G. Wells, Edwin Pugh, George Gissing, Rider Haggard and yourself [H. B. Marriott-Watson] to write a mere word – any word 'it,' 'they,' 'you,' – any word and thus identify with the crime." Crane was gathering his literary friends, "Indians" and palefaces, American and British, journalists and high symbolists, around him. Ten noted collaborators were identified with the drama, the programme of which survives, though not all of them attended.[19] James (who had been famously photographed at the Brede summer fête, eating what is unmistakably a doughnut), Conrad, Rider Haggard and George Gissing were all, for various reasons, unable to come, but others did gather for what remains a very remarkable literary occasion. H. G. Wells arrived early, and so was fortunate enough to get a room: "Nobody else did – because although some thirty or forty invitations had been issued, there were not as a matter of fact more than three or four bedrooms available," he reported. The house's sanitary equipment still dated from the seventeenth century, filling the grounds with disconsolate, exploding male guests hunting the fifteenth-century outside privies, for they were unable to reach the inadequate interior facilities on the far side of the womens' dormitory. On Boxing Day the

---

[19] For details see Stallman and Gilkes (eds), *Stephen Crane: Letters*, cited above.

play, "The Ghost," was rehearsed, and then performed in the village on 28 December, with Mason playing the ghost, and H. G. Wells on piano. Then there followed an elaborate tense party, a troubled and memorable occasion. Wells described it as "an extraordinary lark – but shot, at the close, with red intimations of a coming tragedy." American food – corn on the cob and sweet potatoes – was served. Crane mostly watched and played poker, but appeared worried, sulky, and ill. On the following night, as he was playing a guitar, he collapsed against a friend, haemorrhaging from the lungs.

He recovered, as his friends worried; the familiar desperate struggle for money and publication resumed. Cora became yet more an ogre to agents and publishers. Crane now considered moving to Texas, but his problems were too great. On 31 March 1900, when Cora was in Paris, he bent to pat a dog and haemorrhaged again. This time matters were more serious; his "Cuban fever," malaria, also returned. Cora, rushing back, summoned specialists, and desperately planned an elaborate operation to move him for treatment to a famous clinic in the German Black Forest. The expenses were great, and she dunned everyone for help; James gave her £50 as "my tender benediction to him." Crane was taken on a stretcher to Dover, where Conrad, Wells and Robert Barr anxiously saw him off. He was carried across Europe, a difficult and expensive journey, to the Bavarian sanatorium, the Villa Eberhardt in Badenweiler, where he struggled to write on, as Cora corrected proofs at his bedside. In the night of 5 June 1900, he died, five months before his twenty-ninth birthday. It was, said James, "an unmitigated, unredeemed catastrophe." His body was, ever expensively, brought back to London, then interred in New Jersey. Burdened with debts, Cora tried living in London for a time, hoping to start a boarding house. For a while she attempted to produce a biography of Crane, and live by writing pulp fiction. Finally she went back to Jacksonville, Florida, and opened up a new brothel called The Court, which she ran till her death in 1910.

Crane's death was part of a whole row of artistic catastrophes that marked British, European and American writing at the turn of the century, and brought a great change in the literary atmosphere. For the moment, a whole transatlantic era seemed over. Frederic had collapsed eighteen months earlier. Wilde died in social disgrace and neglect in a hotel in the Rue des Beaux Arts in Paris in the same year as Crane (he had once observed that the artistic life is "a long and lovely suicide," but no less remarked that a desire to be buried in Paris "hardly points to any very serious state of mind at the last".) That same year Ernest Dowson died, also in France. In 1902 Zola died suddenly in a room filled with charcoal fumes. In 1903 Frank Norris would die of peritonitis, and Henry Harland of tuberculosis in Italy in 1905. Then there were the famous literary suicides, most notably that of Hubert Crackanthorpe in 1896. In many respects the "Wilde" era – which perhaps started when the good Oscar landed in his finery in New York near the start of the Eighties – had come to its mortal end; for few of the writers who had represented the "aesthetic" and the "naturalistic" spirit that peaked in the 1890s long outlasted the decade. Crane was essentially a part of this same "bohemian" era, and in the event all his work would be concentrated within the short frame of the Nineties. Nonetheless, so busy was his production that his collected writings would eventually run to a long shelf of twelve volumes. Most of this publication was posthumous, the product of the publication frenzy of his English years, when he sat at Ravensbrook and Brede writing furiously – aware, as it now seems, not only of the pressure of his creditors but of the likely brevity of his life. A large group of writings – *Bowery Tales*; *The Whilomville Stories*, tales of his New Jersey childhood; *Wounds in the Rain*, his stories and accounts of the Spanish-American War – came out just after his death in 1900, not least to help Cora clear her debts. The compilation *Great Battles of the World* came out in 1901, and a notable story collection, *Last Words*, in 1902. *The O'Ruddy*, the Irish romance that had been prompted by Frederic, which Crane left unfinished on his death, was completed by Robert Barr, and published in 1903, and the scholars have found a good deal more since. But "Who's Crane? Who cares for Crane?" Conrad asked bitterly in 1912: "Nowadays when one is dead one is dead for good. Mere literary excellence won't save a man's memory."

Fortunately Conrad was wrong, and Crane was to take his key place in the story of transatlantic fiction. But his reputation essentially stood, and still does, on one short novel, *The Red Badge of Courage*, two novellas (*Maggie* and its later companion *George's Mother*, 1896), a body of brilliant short stories and some important, ironic poetry. But this fact, his short writing life, and his confused transatlantic reputation, left and still leaves the critics in a quandary. What kind of writer was Crane, at his best – a brilliant amateur or a great experimenter, a reporter of life or the inventor of a new literary vision and language, an American

243

Naturalist or a cosmopolitan Aesthete? The double image would continue for a long time. Conrad, Hueffer, Wells and Garnett all wrote very powerful memoirs of Crane, establishing at least one part of his importance by binding his fate to that of modern experiment itself. Conrad named him the "foremost impressionist of his time," Wells called him "the opening mind of a new period, or, at least, the early emphatic phase of a new initiative."[20] It now came to seem that Crane had taken up a central, a mythic place in the development of modern fiction as it emerged over a few short years in Britain. In the brief span of Crane's British residence, an extraordinary transformation had indeed taken place. Henry James had returned to the novel, and entered his "late phase." Conrad and Hueffer, encouraged by this and Crane's work, began collaborating together, and agreed to call themselves "impressionists": "We accepted the name of impressionists because we saw that life did not narrate but made impressions on our brains," Hueffer explained in *Joseph Conrad: A Reminiscence* (1924). "We in turn, if we wished to produce an effect of life, must not narrate but render impressions." In 1898 Conrad published *The Nigger of the "Narcissus,"* which Crane admired. With its famous preface – "My task which I am trying to achieve is, by the power of the written word to make you feel – it is, before all, to make you see. That – and no more, and it is everything" – it is often seen as the first British expression of Modernism. It seems unlikely that Conrad would have written his words without some consciousness of the impact of Stephen Crane.

For Crane's best work – with its instinct for compression and vivid rendering, its concern to convey sensation and emotional and pictorial effect – made him, as Wells rightly said, "more than himself . . . the first expression of the opening mind of a new period." What sustained *The Red Badge* . . . was not so much its account of the objective world, but its power to inhabit and dramatize the shifting tense consciousness of the key witness. Crane's fiction carried weight not just because it pulled strangely together two different notions of fiction – one Naturalist, the other Impressionist – but because his way of doing it suggested a

---

[20] See Joseph Conrad, *Last Essays* (London and New York, 1926); Edward Garnett, *Friday Nights* (London, 1922); H. G. Wells, "Stephen Crane from an English Standpoint," *North American Review* (August 1900); Ford Madox Ford (Hueffer), *Mightier Than the Sword: Memories and Criticisms* (London, Allen and Unwin, 1938), publ. in the USA as *Portraits from Life* (Boston, Houghton Mifflin, 1937). Also see Henry James, *Autobiography*, cited above, p. 156.

path to a new mode in the novel. Now it seems clear enough that the spirit of modern fiction owes much to such stylistic mixtures, as they boiled in the crucible of the Nineties. Edmund Wilson put the point brilliantly in his study of Modernism, *Axel's Castle* (1931), when he notes that "The literary history of our time is to a great extent that of the development of symbolism and of its fusion or conflict with Naturalism." In his mixture of naturalism and impressionism, his movement away from objectivity toward consciousness, his anxious use of symbol and his sense of the ironic status of the human figure in an animalist world, Crane had somehow youthfully, perhaps innocently, searched his way through many of the artistic complications that would concern those trying to grasp "the spirit of the new." Because of this, and his British friendships, he slowly took his place as forerunner among the new novelists who, over the next two decades, would establish the novel as an "affair," its telling a "treatment," its method a display of what James – writing about Conrad – calls "the baffled relationship between the subject-matter and its emergence." When one literary generation later the newer writers gathered, this time further west in Sussex, around Charleston, the resort of the Bloomsbury group, Crane cast the same spell that James himself did, as an exemplary figure of American experimental writing.

To American eyes, his works continued to look rather different. Naturalism in America well outlasted its fortunes in Europe, while the idea of experiment passed on to yet more extraordinary expatriate figures like Gertrude Stein. Many American novelists were also journalists, who made much of the cult of action and the social fact. To his American successors Crane was more recognizably a case of that familiar thing, the writer as man of action – the writer who got up and did, going to war, encountering nature, joining the social struggle. Jack London and Upton Sinclair, John Steinbeck and Ernest Hemingway were the real successors: writers who went into the thick of experience, the urban jungle, the war, the mountains, life as test, writers who quite frequently ended up with their own red badge. Crane's influence was to pass on above all to what became the most central, but tragic, form to deal with the condition of modernity – the war novel. The great successor was Ernest Hemingway, who praised *The Red Badge of Courage* as "one of the finest books in our literature," and who was a crucial expatriate figure of a later American generation. In Hemingway's work too, nature indifferently watches the human struggle, the landscape is an assailant, the language of romanticism has to be controlled and minimized, so that a direct and existential sense of experience always shows through. But the real importance of Crane was to build the bridge between both lines of writing. Just like James, if in another realm, Crane was to leave his influence on two constantly refracting traditions, as his work took its place in modern fiction: in one way in Britain, in another in the United States.

SEVEN

Dentists at Home:
Gertrude Stein, D. H. Lawrence and the modern century

I.

"So the twentieth century had come it began with 1901," wrote Gertrude Stein, with her usual simple sagacity, in her late book *Paris France* (1940). And, give or take a year or so, she was right. But the twentieth century was not, she pointed out, some mere fact of the calendar. It also meant a whole new attitude to the universe, which in turn meant a whole new view of art. Indeed if you really wanted to know where the twentieth century was most fully embodied, you only need look to Miss Stein herself. She had long possessed a peculiar intimacy with history; this was one reason why, as she kept telling everyone, she was – along with Picasso and Alfred Whitehead (and she sometimes added Einstein) – a genius.[1] Miss Stein, who was never much troubled by modesty, knew she had been created to fulfill an historical destiny: "I was there to kill what was not dead, the nineteenth century which was so sure of evolution and prayers." Thus the twentieth century did not come just anywhere, or to just anyone. It happened in France (Miss Stein wisely chose to move to Paris in 1903), it happened to Americans (she had the tactical advantage there too), and it came to those who knew how to be modern (again that especially meant Americans, who had, she said, been modern for so much longer than anyone else). When the modern came along, the French simply took it in their stride, for "what is was and what was is, was their point of view of which they were not very conscious," while

---

[1] "I may say that only three times in my life have I met a genius and each time a bell within me rang and I was not mistaken . . . The three geniuses of whom I wish to speak are Gertrude Stein, Pablo Picasso and Alfred Whitehead." *The Autobiography of Alice B. Toklas* (New York, Harcourt Brace, 1933). The *Autobiography* was written, of course, by Miss Stein herself.

the British consciously refused the whole enterprise, "knowing full well that they had gloriously created the nineteenth century and perhaps the twentieth was going to be too many for them." But the Americans seized it, and they seized it in Paris.

For sound membership of the new century, then, the ideal combination was to be a modern American in France, which had all the best of the new age – scientific method, machines, electricity – but knew too that life was "tradition and human nature." This was why, when the great discoverers of the new arts appeared, they absolutely had to turn to France, "where tradition was so firm that they could look modern without being different, and where their acceptance of reality is so great they could let anyone have the emotion of unreality . . . And so in the beginning of the twentieth century when a new way had to be found naturally they needed France."[2] In saying all this, Stein – who may have been an expatriate but was also a staunch patriot (when reporters called her an expatriate, she said, "I get so mad, all of a sudden"[3]) – was stating an old, much honoured American conviction: that her country was a nation granted a special disposition toward progress, and had a distinctive relation to the future. The twentieth century was to be the American century. Now, with her technological innovation, instinctive response to history, and her experimental view of life, America was ready to lead the way into the modern world. In the sphere of power and technology, this truth was becoming self-evident. The British Prime Minister, Mr Gladstone, acknowledged it back in 1878, drawing a highly Victorian analogy: "While we have been advancing with portentous rapidity, America is passing us by as if in a canter . . . She will probably become what we are now – head servant in the great household of the world, the employer of all employed, because her service will be the most and ablest." And by the century's turn America was clearly in the vanguard of industrial progress – not just competing with the other two great industrial powers, Britain and Germany, but outstripping their industrial production combined. Ahead in invention and investment, it was also forging amazing

[2] Quotations here and latter come from Gertrude Stein's late book *Paris France* (New York and London, Scribner and Batsford, 1940), written in 1939 as the Second World War (which Stein did not think would happen) loomed, and most of the American artists left in Europe were going home.

[3] Eleanor Wakefield, "Stormy Petrel of Modernism is Patriotic," *New York World*, 18 May 1930.

technologies and systems (mass production), discovering new scientific applications, raising up novel, formidable cities that somehow mythically represented the skyline of the modern world. With the end of the Spanish-American War, its control on the continent was almost secure. As the "modern" century turned, the distinguished Senator Albert J. Beveridge made a famous pronouncement that, three decades later, John Dos Passos would set ironically at the start of his huge trilogy *USA* (1937): "The twentieth century will be American . . . The regeneration of the world, physical as well as moral, has begun . . ." Gertrude Stein had, in Cubist form, much the same view.

But her claim went further. Americans were in the business not just of physical and moral regeneration, but artistic regeneration as well. This too was no new thought. Herman Melville had seen not just the American artist but the entire nation as an *avant-garde*, moving through the wilderness of untried things. Walt Whitman, who could always incorporate everything into his democratic American self, declared his own new free-line verse was no more than poetic expression of America's experimental destiny: "For these new and evolutionary facts, meanings, purposes, new poetic messages, new forms and expressions, are inevitable."[4] However, as the nineteenth century closed, the spirit of radical artistic innovation for which Whitman spoke, sang, yawped, was far from apparent. America might have energy, power and progress on its side, but there was little sign of its dominance in the modern arts. Edith Wharton's Ned Winsett, in *The Age of Innocence* (1920), set forty years earlier, is an aesthetic outcast in America, "man of letters untimely born into a world that had no need of letters." America, explained James Gibbon Huneker, was meant to be the land of "bathtubs, not bohemia." Henry James, revisiting America after his long and anxious absence just around the same time Stein was leaving it, found a formless energy not yet capable of expressing itself as art. When Ezra Pound left America in 1905 to become a twentieth-century European troubadour – moving to London in 1908, he would perform much the same office, the modernization of the arts, Stein was then assuming in Paris – he noted "Am I American?"

[4] Or as Whitman put it in his poem "Thou Mother with thy Equal Brood":
   "Brain of the New World, what a task is thine,
   To formulate the Modern – out of the peerless grandeur of the modern,
   Out of thyself, comprising science, to recast poems, churches, art
   (Recast, maybe discard them, end them – maybe their work is done, who knows?)"

Yes, and bugger the present state of the country." America was, he said, "a savage country, out-of-date." The American artist required a new tradition and a new stimulus, and the only place to find them was in Europe, in the great "double city" of London and Paris – for, he said, "if you have any vital interest in art and letters and happen to like talking about them, you sooner or later have to leave the country." As late as 1915, when the mood had changed, the experimental spirit had reached New York, and there were real signs artistic America was "coming of age," Van Wyck Brooks was still commenting: "Human nature in America exists on two irreconcilable planes, the plane of stark intellectuality and the plane of stark business; and in the back of its mind lies heaven knows what world of poetry, hidden away, too inaccessible, too intangible, too unreal in fact ever to be brought into the open . . ."[5] All this was the famous "poet's quarrel" American artists were supposed to have with their country, and it certainly continued to the end of the Twenties. But Stein would have none of it. She lived most of her life in Paris, she said, because she enjoyed "being alone with English and myself." "America is my country and Paris is my home town and it is as it has come to be," she explained. Or, as she jotted in her notebook, now among her voluminous papers at Yale: "*L'Amérique est mon pays mais la France est mon chez moi. Essayer c'est adopter. Oui. Avec la France . . . On peut dire ou doit dire que l'Amérique est aujourd'hui, de beaucoup le plus aimée des pays du monde.*" In short, she was an American who had come to Europe only to claim her historical inheritance; and then, through her modern "genius," restore it back to the United States.

Yet, as Henry Adams argued – still following the quest for the meaning of modern history and an appropriate modern education that had started out at Chicago's White City in 1893 – the problem of modernity and America was a profound one. In 1900 he too came to Paris, to devote another summer to another exposition. This time it was the Paris Universal Exposition – even bigger than the Centennial Exposition of 1889, for which Eiffel built his great, temporary iron tower. But, despite many attempts to have it pulled down, by affronted romantic poets and shopkeepers frightened it would topple onto them, the tower remained to dominate the stylish *art nouveau* exhibition, whose façades ran for over a mile on each bank of the Seine, and it would soon

[5] Van Wyck Brooks, *America's Coming of Age* (New York, Dutton, 1915).

become a mast for the new age of wireless communication. Adams, looking round the exhibits in millennial fascination, concluded that Paris had completed what Chicago had begun. In those intervening seven years, the world had, he reckoned, changed fundamentally. The era of nineteenth-century liberal positivism had died: in Paris the Curies had isolated radium, "that metaphysical bomb"; in Würzburg Roentgen had discovered X-rays; and the German Daimler's automobile was already "a nightmare at a hundred kilometers an hour." Adams could easily have extended his striking list. Over this same interval Marconi had invented wireless telegraphy, the Lumière brothers the cinematograph, S. P. Langley a flying machine, Count Zeppelin an airship, Max Planck had defined quantum theory, and Freud in Vienna had begun a "talking cure" and spoken of the "unconscious." Paris had opened its new three-car Métro, and motor buses ran in London streets. All the great cities of the West were changing, rebuilding, electrifying, "modernizing," adopting new civic styles of architecture and taste, showing the spirit of the *belle époque*, *art nouveau* and *Jugendstil*. 1900, said Adams, showed itself as the key year, when "the continuity snapped." The world had ceased to be a unity and become a multiple, the human mind had taken on a new relationship to power and force. So in Paris – as he recorded in his *Education . . .* (1907) – he found himself lying in the Exposition's Gallery of Machines, "his historical neck broken by the sudden irruption of forces totally new." Now "an avalanche of forces had fallen on [the mind] which needed new mental powers to control . . . It must merge with the supersensual universe, or succumb to it." Clearly the laurels would now go to the society that produced the most energy, and that above all meant the "twenty-million horse-power society," the United States. Americans would now have to choose between being "the child of new forces or the chance sport of nature" – in other words between energy without intellect or some new form of control.

By instinct, observation, or as she would say "genius," it was to a similar vision Gertrude Stein responded. She well knew the world had ceased to be a unity and become a multiple, the present not a continuation of the past but its own novel self (as she said, in the twentieth century daily living was no longer being lived every day). What's more, she did not intend to be any chance sport of nature – another reason why she chose Paris, art and modernity, and why in the next twenty-five years many Americans followed the same lead. "Of course they came to Paris a great many of them to paint pictures and naturally they could not do that at home, or write they could not do that at home either, they could be dentists at home." As she explained, the writer always had to have "two countries, the one where they belong and the one in which they live really. The second one is romantic, it is separate from themselves, it is not real but it is really there." So, settling in Montparnasse in 1903 and remaining for the next forty-odd years, her patriotism intact, she became a kind of artistic ambassador to the court of Cézanne, Matisse, Picasso and Braque, a free-spirited emissary from the West come to the land of art's modernization. Here, the "great stoneface," she brooded on space, time and words, funded artistic terrorism, provoked originality, sponsored and provided patronage, attracted many foreign visitors, served tea, and always reported home. She wrote herself, in the newest, most modern way – sometimes very importantly and originally, in *Three Lives* (1907) and *Tender Buttons* (1913), sometimes with monumental vanity (*The Autobiography of Alice B. Toklas*, 1935), sometimes with a wild overload of the random free association her method sanctioned. She dispensed with the daily past to attend to the moving present ("The business of Art is to live in the actual present, that is the complete actual present, and to express that complete actual present," she would explain in her *Lectures in America*, 1935), and always tried to render the modern composition, the spirit of the new age that had left its old daily living behind.

But her writing itself – and there is a very great deal of it (eight volumes in the Yale Edition of her unpublished writings, and something like forty titles in all) – was never the only measure of her significance, even though some of it is of real importance. She belonged to a time in revolt against the heavy weight of the previous "Victorian" age, when the makers and shakers of art emerged from this country or that to gather in artistic centres and forge the spirit of the new. They gathered in Paris, in schools and movements, studios and garrets, cafés and cabarets, or in the salons of various powerful brokers, the hostesses and patronesses who attached themselves firmly to the modern spirit. A good many of these were wealthy American women – Mabel Dodge and Harriet Monroe, Amy Lowell and Harriet Shaw Weaver, the Cone Sisters and Nathalie Barney – who drew on the funds of American commercial enterprise to fund or invest in the new frontiers of the arts. Stein was a Radcliffe bluestocking, a *rentier* from a successful Jewish-American commercial family, not especially wealthy and not given to high social display. The fact was that she was to become Modernism's greatest hostess. Over three decades her quiet courtyard apartment at 27 Rue de Fleurus, a stone's throw away from the chattering, artist-filled cafés of the Boulevard Montparnasse, became the great hub of cosmopolitan aesthetic activity. She was not the only new American fascinated by the modern; indeed her role depended in part on being an intermediary. For American buyers and other free spirits were coming into Paris from New York, Chicago, Philadelphia or her own Baltimore, doing the artistic rounds, grasping at the aesthetic excite-ments they missed at home, and buying, out of curiosity and for very modest prices, the work of the most radical, most *avant-garde*, interest-ing and indigent of the new artists to take back home. As it turned out, they filled first their own houses and then the great metropolitan American museums with what became, thanks to their skilful invest-ment, some of the most significant art works of the century. The reputations they created became crucial, the fruits of their enterprise are there for us to inspect with delight today.[6] But they needed assistance, a bridge to the modern, and no one could provide it better than Miss Stein.

So 27 Rue de Fleurus became the place where new Paris artists (who might come from anywhere, Spain or Russia or Romania), horse-bussing over from the studios of Montmartre, met, beneath walls covered to the ceilings with the formidable array of modern painters Gertrude and her brother Leo had amassed, these new American patrons, ready to thrill to the modern note, the spirit of the twentieth-century *avant-garde*. The traffic was not one way; each group was aware they confronted a fresh breed. As Pablo Picasso, who became a regular visitor, said of those he found at the Stein Saturday nights: "*Il sont pas des hommes, ils sont pas des femmes, ils sont des Américains.*" This referred not just to the sexual ambiguity in the household – increased when, to Leo's disquiet, Stein took in Alice B. Toklas as lifetime companion – but to the encounter of two different modernities: European experimenters in art, American experimenters with life. With her refusal to have a past, even in grammar, her obsessive preoccupation with the continuous present, her determination to possess not so much an identity as an

6 There are useful accounts of this highly important activity in Aline Saarinen, *The Proud Possessors: The Lives, Times, and Tastes of Some Adventurous American Art Collectors* (New York, Random House, 1958), and in Barbara Pollack, *The Collectors: Dr Claribel and Miss Etta Cone* (New York, Bobbs-Merrill, 1962).

egotism ("I am I because my little dog knows me," which turned in time into "I am I because America knows me"), Stein, and her band of fellow Americans, became a kind of living embodiment of futurism. Picasso effectively acknowledged this when, against the odds, he struggled to paint Gertrude's portrait; it took some ninety sittings to gain the right effect. For she, it seemed, gave to the very idea of abstraction itself a body, an appearance and a home. She was Cubist America itself, which is what she chose to be. It was, as it turned out, a brilliant choice. For, as the hopeful modern world went on its angst-ridden and ever more Americanizing way, as the older structures of Europe disentangled and collapsed, the great transition she prophesied and embodied had largely come about. It took two world wars and the rise of Fascism to complete the process, but by the time of Stein's death in 1945 ("What is the answer?" she asked at the end, and then "What is the question?") it had almost been achieved. Modernism had moved to the site of maximum modernity, the United States. Bauhaus had become Our House, the futuristic workers' city had become the Seagram Building, Pablo Picasso had turned into Paloma Picasso, Proust into Pynchon and Rimbaud into Rambo. Westward the course of modernist empire had once again made its way, and the *entente cordiale* that Stein created had become her largest monument. Stein may have created some of the century's most obscure and some would say unreadable books, and grown submerged in her own massive vanity ("Twentieth-century literature is Gertrude Stein," she once said). But in facilitating one of the great cultural transactions of the century, the transatlantic passage of the modern, she was, as she said, a power, a legend and, well, a genius.

2.

"I have generations of Americans behind me. Americanism is born in me," Gertrude Stein once claimed.[7] But this, like much else, was a considerable exaggeration. She was born in 1874 in Allegheny, next to Pittsburgh, Pennsylvania, the seventh and last child of a family of wealthy immigrant Bavarian Jews, and her father came to America at the age of eight at the start of the 1840s, to enter the family's clothing business, Stein Bros. Throughout his life his fortunes, like his temper,

[7] In the interview with Eleanor Wakefield cited above.

fluctuated, but in good times and ill the Steins stayed a well-off, cultivated family from the European bourgeoisie. And like Henry James (whom Stein admired greatly: "Henry James never came amiss. He did not come slowly nor did he come to kiss," she said approvingly), Gertrude acquired most of her sensuous education in Europe. In 1874, when she was eight months old, her father, hoping to widen his children's education and scenting an opportunity in wool, took the family back to the bourgeois comforts of imperial Vienna, where they stayed for three years. "And so we were in Vienna," Stein reported in *Wars I Have Seen* (1945). "And there was my mother and my brothers on horse-back and there was a Czech tutor, one did not realize how important all these nationalities were going to be to everyone then." The father returned home, but the rest of the family moved to Paris in 1878: "I was only four years old when I was first in Paris and talked French there . . . So I was in Paris a year when I was four to five and then I was back in America," she explained, adding that then her emotions "began to feel themselves in French." In fact there was always to be something polyglot about her way of writing and thinking, and it has been fairly argued that her distinctive way with grammar and tense owed something to an imperfect training in English, still evident in her Harvard essays. If so, she was able to capitalize on this later with an elaborate grammatical cunning. The family returned to the USA and stayed for a while with Baltimore relatives, before moving to Oakland, California, where her father had become vice-president of a San Francisco cable-car company. It was the old westering motion that had always made Americans, and would become a basic trope of Stein's *The Making of Americans* (1925), itself an eternal immigrants' tale.

Here Stein began to read, and eat, extensively ("books and food, food and books, both excellent things"), and grew close to her slightly older brother Leo, a kinship that increased when both her parents died during her adolescence. An older brother Michael rescued and managed the family fortunes, which still stretched to giving both Leo and Gertrude a good academic education. Leo went to Harvard, Gertrude returned for a while to Baltimore before following Leo to Cambridge, Mass., to enrol at the Harvard Annex, which in 1894 became Radcliffe College, to study philosophy, botany, and English.[8]

[8] Stein tells her own autobiographical story, not always with great reliability, in several places: notably in *The Autobiography of Alice B. Toklas* (London, Bodley Head, 1933); *Everybody's Autobiography* (New York, Random House, 1937; London, Heinemann, 1938); and *Wars I Have Seen* (New York, Random House, 1945; London, Batsford, 1945).

Even then she was no conventional scholar. She adopted a mannish style ("I always did thank God I wasn't born a woman," she once said) and was at first reported an indifferent student, though she managed, she said, to get high grades from William James for *not* doing the examinations because the weather was too hot (she similarly objected later, when she was a medical student, that many of the people she met were ill). Happily the university was in a fertile transitional period. For one thing, this was the heyday of Harvard Aestheticism, personified by Bernard Berenson – the aristocratic young Jew from the Lithuanian Pale who came to the States as a child and determined to devote his life to connoisseurship. By the time of his graduation from Harvard in 1887, several admiring friends and sponsors, including the Boston patroness Isabella Stewart Gardner, had raised $1,500 to send him for further artistic study in Europe, and before long he was settled in Florence. In 1900 he became master of the forty-roomed aesthetic stronghold of I Tatti, on the doorstep of which Leo – who thought himself just such another connoisseur-aesthete – would appear that year.[9] Now Harvard Aestheticism was already becoming, under the influence of Wilde, Swinburne, the *Yellow Book* and its American imitators, the new *japonaiserie* and the cult of the Dandy, the Harvard Decadence, and by the turn of the century Wallace Stevens, class of 1900, was already writing Frenchified symbolist verse in the new way, under the name of "Peter Parasol." The end-of-century veil was trembling, even in Harvard Yard.

And other great changes were shaking the intellectual and artistic climate. Stein managed to study with William James, Henry's brother, who was at the peak of his influence in American philosophy. In 1890 he published his *Principles of Psychology*, a key study in that new and coming science, and in one chapter, "The Stream of Thought," he employed a decisive and guiding phrase, "the stream-of-consciousness," that would be well-remembered by writers. With his philosopher-colleague Josiah Royce he was also becoming a central figure of the very American movement of Pragmatism – an attempt to resolve

[9] According to his autobiography, *Sketch for a Self-Portrait* (New York, Pantheon Books, 1949), this choice was not entirely a satisfying one: "I cannot rid myself of the insistent inner voice that keeps whispering and at times hissing, 'You should not have competed with the learned nor let yourself become that equivocal thing, an expert . . . Remember, you mapped out one book on ideated sensations, and another on life-enhancement, and a third on the portrait.' "

the crisis in thought that saw intellect as divorced from action (Richard Rorty defines it as a refusal "to contrast the world with what the world is known as," a highly Steinian remark). Stein took courses with both of them, and did experimental laboratory work in motor reactions and automatic writing. "I was interested in biology and I was interested in psychology and philosophy and history, that was all natural enough. I came out of the nineteenth century and you had to be interested in evolution and biology," she explained. Still, if she came out of the nineteenth century, she had no intention of staying there. Her key conviction that something was dissolving – solidity, identity, daily life – dates from this time, and her exposure to psychology, automatic writing and medicine. She developed distinctive if not idiosyncratic notions of consciousness that led away from determinism toward theories of anti-realism, and grew concerned, she said, not with what had happened but with what is beginning happening.[10] Meantime Leo was cutting class a good deal and travelling extensively in Europe, to develop his aesthetic interests; in 1896 Gertrude joined him for the summer in Italy, a practice she followed most summers thereafter. Later in 1896 Leo went to Japan and started collecting Japanese prints, a taste which was spreading among the new aesthetes and writers, and which had a good deal to do with the Impressionist and Post-Impressionist revolution in which he was now interested.[11]

Then, after graduating from Harvard, Leo went back to Johns Hopkins University in Baltimore, and Gertrude followed again. They set up house together, and she enrolled in the graduate medical school. She was now on her way to becoming a new career woman of the Nineties, just at a time when opportunities were widening for young middle-class Americans of either sex to lead more freely professional, intellectual or artistic lives. This was, in fact, the generation which would have so much cultural impact on ideas and the arts in the period just before the Great War, and Gertrude was not alone. A little later, at the University of Pennsylvania, *circa* 1901–5, three young people who

10 Useful biographies of Gertrude Stein are Elizabeth Sprigge, *Gertrude Stein: Her Life and Work* (London, Hamish Hamilton, 1957); the substantial John Malcolm Brinnin, *The Third Rose: Gertrude Stein and Her World* (Boston, Little, Brown, 1959; London, Weidenfeld and Nicolson, 1960); and Janet Hobhouse, *Everybody Who Was Anybody: A Biography of Gertrude Stein* (London, Weidenfeld and Nicolson, 1975). Also see Edmund Fuller (ed.), *Journey Into the Self: Being the Letters, Papers and Journals of Leo Stein* (New York, Crown, 1950).
11 Earl Miner's *The Japanese Tradition in British and American Literature* (Princeton, Princeton University Press, rev. ed., 1966), is a good study of this.

would be among the most important poets of the next age, Ezra Pound, Hilda Doolittle ("H.D.") and William Carlos Williams, were reading in symbolist and Oriental literature, and seeking a new definition of art and culture. At Harvard as the new century came, Wallace Stevens, T. S. Eliot, Conrad Aiken and others would pick up the Nineties cult of symbolism, and acquaint themselves with the gnomic lure of the Japanese *haiku*. In Baltimore, where Stein worked on the brain, she found herself in a similarly aesthetic community, and embarked on a none too happy lesbian affair. Then Leo broke with America, dropping his studies, and in 1900 he went to Europe, taking up the aesthete's almost statutory residence in Florence, where, living at 20 Lungarno Acciaioli, he became a rabbinical disciple of Berenson. Gertrude joined him for another European tour, and grew bored with her work, failing her medical examinations the following year. In 1902 she spent most of the year with Leo in England, for his patron Berenson had an English home near Haslemere. They then rented rooms in Bloomsbury Square, and who knows how the whole Bloomsbury adventure might have worked out had Gertrude chosen to remain? But though they met a number of people of interest –Israel Zangwill and Bertrand Russell among them– "Gertrude Stein was not very much amused," she noted. She enjoyed reading in the British Museum, but found the streets "infinitely depressing and dismal": "the dismalness of London and the drunken women and children and the gloom and the lonesomeness brought back all the melancholy of her adolescence and one day she said she was leaving for America and she left."[12] Staying with friends in New York City, she began a novel, *Q.E.D.*, opening on a boat to Europe, and based on her lesbian affair. The book used a method she called "disembodiment," which drew on the ideas of William (and Henry) James. It was not a book she was proud of; after she finished it in Paris, she put it away and it remained unpublished until after her death, coming out in 1950 in an edition of 516 copies as *Things As They Are*.[13] By then she was universally famous, the very spirit of the

[12] Gertrude Stein, *The Autobiography of Alice B. Toklas*, cited above.

[13] Reviewing it in *The New Yorker* Edmund Wilson commented: "It is a production of some literary merit and much psychological interest. The reviewer had occasion to go through Miss Stein's work chronologically, and he came to the conclusion that the vagueness which began to blur it from about 1910 on and the masking by unexplained metaphors that later made it seem opaque, though partly the result of the effort to emulate modern painting, were partly also due to a need exposed by the problem of writing about relationships between women of a kind that the standards of the era would not have allowed her to describe more explicitly." Edmund Wilson, "Books," *The New Yorker*, 15 September 1951.

Modern, which she became as a result of what happened next.

3.

It was in the summer of 1903 that the great moment of choice came. Leo had now decided to be a painter (the inspiration was apparently so powerful he stripped to the nude to begin), and he moved from Florence to Paris. He found a pleasant if unfashionable ground-floor apartment and studio near the Luxembourg Gardens in Montparnasse, at 27 Rue de Fleurus, and Gertrude, then aged twenty-nine, joined him for the summer. Again they decided to set up house together, and here she would remain (apart from wartime interruptions, the odd visit home, and a final late change of address) up to her death. Montparnasse had yet to acquire its bohemian character; it was "a dingy suburb enlivened by English and American painters," according to Clive Bell, and "There was no *Rotonde*, no *Select*, no *Bal Nègre*, no *Boule Blanche*, though the scrubby little café on which I looked from my bedroom window was called *Le Dôme*."[14] The artists' quarter was still Montmartre, where the great bulk of Sacré Coeur had just risen, though the change began later in the decade, when Guillaume Apollinaire – poet, critic, *le prince de l'esprit moderne*, friend of Picasso and the Steins – moved to Montparnasse and celebrated it in newspaper articles. In fact the Paris of 1903 was generally low on *avant-garde* excitements. The *belle époque* flourished, decadence was decaying; the twin movements of Naturalism and Symbolism, which dominated the 1880s and 1890s, had lost much of their fervour; the death of Zola, suffocated by his own charcoal stove in 1902, marked the end of a charged, bitter era, dominated by anarchism, experiment, *l'affaire Dreyfus*. *Les Stein*, as they came to be called, lived a typical, quiet *rentier* existence in what was, away from its studios, cafés and clubs, a notably conservative city. Michael Stein, whose business skill funded the whole enterprise, soon also moved to Paris with his wife Sarah. The Steins strolled in the Luxembourg Gardens, attended art exhibitions, and, on a budget (from Michael) of around $150 a month, bought a few pictures – not, like the great Fricks and Huntingdons, for prestige or investment, but out of curiosity and to satisfy their changing aesthetic tastes.

14 Clive Bell, *Old Friends: Personal Recollections* (London, Chatto and Windus, 1956).

In fact the Paris of the *belle époque* was attracting many American residents. The doings of a lively colony of social Americans – Muriel Draper, Mildred Aldrich, Sarah King, Cole Porter, Elsa Maxwell – filled the pages of the English-language press. In 1907 the novelist Edith Wharton – formerly Edith Jones of Newport and the New York "Four Hundred" (she was once described as being herself "a novel of [Henry] James, no doubt in his earlier manner") – moved, with six servants, to 58, later 53, Rue de Varenne in the Faubourg Saint-Germain. She was looking, she said, for "aristocratic seclusion" and a literary life ("In Paris no one could live without literature, and the fact that I was a professional writer, instead of frightening away my fashionable friends, interested them . . . Culture in France is an eminently social quality, while in Anglo-Saxon countries it might also be called anti-social"). It was a perfect time, she said, of *la douceur de vivre*: the time of Isadora Duncan's dance, the Russian ballet, the arrival of Proust as a novelist.[15] And there were other attractions; the unhappily married Wharton had an affair with the rakish American newspaperman Morton Fullerton (a *protégé* of Henry James) and discovered, in life and fiction, a social and erotic freedom her strict social life in Newport and New York never allowed her. She wrote her American novel *Ethan Frome* (1911), *The Reef* (1912), set in France, and the biting, brilliant *The Custom of the Country* (1912), an international satire on the times, in which an American woman following the custom of her country – regular divorce – attempts to win European social recognition. What appealed to her in Paris is clear enough from her novels. At the end of *The Age of Innocence* (1920), Newland Archer, his cultural needs and emotional desires totally ungratified in America, comes to Paris after his lost love, the Europeanized Countess Olenska. He reflects disappointedly on the kind of life she must have lived here: "He thought of the theatres she must have been to, the pictures she must have looked at, the sober and splendid old houses she must have frequented, the people she must have talked with, the incessant stir of ideas, curiosities, images and associations thrown out by an intensely social race in a setting of immemorial manners . . ." But

[15] "*La douceur de vivre*: which of us does not apply Talleyrand's saying to those last pre-war years? – and I for one, with a difference, am persuaded that the end of the *ancien régime* offered no treasures comparable to the Isadora Duncan of 1909–10, to the Russian ballet, to the first reading of Proust's *Du côté de chez Swann*." Quoted in Percy Lubbock, *Portrait of Edith Wharton*, see below, p. 261.

Wharton's Paris was as different from Stein's as her fiction, the story of what has happened, differed from her fiction of what is beginning happening. Though they both represented the spirit of the American arts, their two worlds scarcely overlapped. Wharton wrote, with fine satire, of a dense, material, richly cosmopolitan world that would, in effect, fade with the Great War; she is a brilliant writer of the *belle époque*. Stein wrote in and would become part of the radical order that came, over the next decades, to replace it; she is, unmistakably, a writer of modernism.[16]

Chance played its part in this; it was the great good fortune of *Les Stein* first to coincide with, then become a key part of, an extraordinary new wave of *avant-garde* excitement that surged through Paris and the other Western capitals in the years soon after their arrival, right through to the Great War and beyond. Starting around 1905, peaking around 1913, the haunting idea of the "modern" which had decadently fascinated the previous decade now took on the character of a radical and urgent campaign. "Europe was full of titanic stirrings and snortings – a new art coming into flower to celebrate or announce a 'new age,'" Wyndham Lewis said of these famous years: though, he added, "down came the lid – the day was lost, for art, at Sarajevo."[17] It was these stirrings and snortings, as they appeared on canvas, that came the way of *Les Stein* as they made their way round the autumn exhibitions. Leo had little inclination at first for the Post-Impressionists, but followed Berenson's advice to buy Cézanne, then Manet, Toulouse-Lautrec, Gauguin and Renoir. Then in 1905 came the controversial "Fauviste" autumn exhibition, which attracted hostile comment from most critics, apart from Apollinaire. Matisse's "Femme au chapeau" was particularly attacked, and Leo promptly bought it for five hundred francs. Soon, for something like £10, he purchased "Girl With a Basket of Flowers" by Pablo Picasso, the Catalan friend of Apollinaire who had come back the year before to Paris. He soon met its painter, who had set up his easel in the Bateau Lavoir, a studio complex at 13 Rue de Ravignan in Montmartre, so

---

16 See Edith Wharton, *A Backward Glance* (New York and London, Appleton Century, 1934). There are interesting biographies by Percy Lubbock, *Portrait of Edith Wharton* (London, Cape, 1947); R. W. B. Lewis, *Edith Wharton: A Biography* (New York, Harper and Row, and London, Constable, 1975); and Cynthia Griffin Wolff, *A Feast of Words: The Triumph of Edith Wharton* (New York, Oxford University Press, 1977).
17 Wyndham Lewis, *Blasting and Bombardiering* (London, Eyre and Spottiswoode, 1937).

named because it resembled the laundry boats still moored on the Seine. The Steins were now holding Saturday night *salons* to display their collection as it climbed the walls, and began collecting painters as they collected paintings (in fact the painters rather than the paintings most interested Gertrude). Here the new Paris artists – Matisse, Picasso, Juan Gris, Apollinaire, Marie Laurencin, Max Jacob – began meeting visiting Americans, some to be notable artists themselves, including Joseph Stella, Alfred Stieglitz, Marsden Hartley, Mary Cassatt, Charles Sheeler and Charles Demuth, as well as Isadora and Raymond Duncan, old Stein friends from California. Leo offered serious little lectures on *l'art moderne*, and encouraged visitors to purchase; Gertrude offered tea. In 1906 Picasso began Gertrude's portrait at the Bateau Lavoir; she later claimed it was his "long struggle with the portrait of Gertrude Stein" that led him from Harlequinism to Cubism. (Friends told Picasso Gertrude looked nothing like the painting: "She will," he said, and she would.) The common search for the "modern" was on.

Meantime, back at 27, under the Cézanne, another artistic struggle was taking place. Gertrude had started a translation of Flaubert's late-realist volume of stories, *Trois Contes*. She shifted the tales to an American setting, and it turned into three linked stories, "The Good Anna," "Melanctha," and "The Gentle Lena," about servant girls in Bridgepoint (Baltimore). The book, which she called "a noble combination of Swift and Matisse," finally appeared as *Three Lives* in 1909 from a vanity press in New York. As the publisher said, it was a "very peculiar book," and the middle story particularly showed a distinctive style: repetition, synchronicity, the present tense and present participle dominate. Stein later explained in her lecture-essay "Composition as Explanation," given in England in 1926, that this represented the method of the "synchronic present" ("there was a continuous recurring and beginning there was a marked direction in the direction of being in the present although naturally I had been accustomed to the past present and future and why, because the composition around me was a prolonged present"), and that it marked the "first definite step away from the nineteenth century and into the twentieth century in literature." She also began applying similar methods to a full-length (some would say a more than full-length) novel, *The Making of Americans: The Hersland Family*. This massive text of some 1,000 pages was mostly written around 1906–8, as Cubism took shape. It did not appear however until 1925, from a small expatriate press, by which date the experimental fictional text was a Parisian speciality, the Modern movement more or less secure.[18] It was based in effect on her developing proposition that Americans themselves were cubists – products of the new composition, coming from "the space of a time that is filled with moving." In terms of technique, this required the defeat of the realist noun, the principle of composition by paragraph, the elimination of remembering as a basis for causality, and abstraction through collectivity –the history of one being the history of all. Stein's devices, as devices, remain interesting, as do her explanations of them.[19] But the novel also has the anecdotal spirit of the traditional freely associating oral storyteller: "The old people in a new world, the new people made out of the old, that is the story that I mean to tell, for that is what really is and what I really know." For all her vital sense of the present, Stein lacked the narrative sense, and also, despite her concern with "consciousness," any inward identification with character. The book is conceptually a work of innovation, but it also remains an anecdotal family biography. Despite her claim that it was the American equivalent of Proust's *A la recherche du temps perdu* or Joyce's *Ulysses*, it lacks their glorious complexity or wholeness of vision. Stein's interest was in producing a spatial or synchronic object, more like a picture. It was not surprising that most of the work that came next was briefer, more fragmentary, not an attempt at narrative but at a form of prose painting, analogous to what was happening among the painters among whom she worked.

4.

So, roughly paralleling the thematic and technical development of Cubism itself, Stein over the next years turned in her work to verbal still lifes, collages, free-association prose-poems, and discontinuous accounts of the sense-impressions conveyed by natural objects, all based on the principle of illumination by repetition. There was *A Long*

[18] First published by Robert McAlmon's Contact Editions in Paris in 1925, the novel was reissued in shorter form in New York in 1934, with a preface by Bernard Fay, and reprinted in 1962.
[19] See Patricia Meyerowitz (ed.), *Gertrude Stein: Look At Me Now and Here I Am: Writings and Lectures, 1901-45* (London, Peter Owen, 1967; reprinted Penguin, 1971).

Gay Book, about couples, and there were her abstract portraits – "portraits of anybody and anything . . . They started me composing anything into one thing" – some of fellow artists like Apollinaire, Satie, Matisse and Picasso ("One whom some were certainly following was one who was completely charming"), some of friends like her companion Alice B. Toklas ("Ada"), Constance Fletcher ("George Fleming") or, and most importantly, Mabel Dodge, the wealthy mistress of the Villa Curonia near Florence. Mabel Dodge, for the moment married to a noted Boston architect, was a flamboyant representative of the new social Americans who were taking house in Europe. By 1910 their villas spread on the Tuscan slopes, their apartments employed the services of the Paris interior designers, their wardrobes established the city as capital of *couture*. Their hospitality grew famous among American artistic visitors, like Carl Van Vechten, John Reed, Hutchins Hapgood, Robert Edmond Jones, Henry McBride, who found Greenwich Village could be yet more comfortable abroad. "We Americans, for whom the world is in its infancy, lay claim to the past of your continent – it is ours," Dodge proclaimed, much to the delight of Italian craftsmen, for she proceeded to spend 50,000 dollars on the Villa Curonia. She then kept it peopled with artistic Anglo-American guests, including Gertrude and Leo Stein. So, while in the next bedroom Dodge pursued an affair with the children's tutor, Gertrude produced by night, in a red exercise book, her obscure, lyrical *Portrait of Mabel Dodge at the Villa Curonia* (1912): "The days are wonderful and the nights are wonderful and the life is pleasant," it began. Elegantly printed up by its subject – who in 1913 decided to plant her ostentatious, influential *avant-garde* salon back at 23 Fifth Avenue in New York – this little work was used by Dodge for her own experimental self-promotion.

And on each side of the Atlantic 1913 proved the key year. Back in Paris, *Les Stein* fell out over the modern: Michael and Sarah voted for Matisse, Gertrude for Picasso, and Leo reverted to Renoir. Probably dismayed by the presence of Alice Toklas, he also took up with a model he later married, and left for Florence, later to reappear in Freudian analysis in New York. Meantime the Paris *avant-garde* was moving toward the peak of outrage. Apollinaire published three key works on and of experiment: *Les Peintres cubistes*, celebrating the movement as far as Duchamp, *L'Anti-tradition futuriste*, exploring Italian Futurism, and his famous volume of "calligrammic" free verse *Alcools*. Meantime,

Diaghilev's Ballets Russes, which had fascinated Paris for several years, staged their most famous event, Stravinsky's cacophonic *Sacre du printemps* (*The Rites of Spring*), the "moment of modern music," it was soon called. Marcel Proust brought out the two-volume *Du côté de chez Swann* (*Swann's Way*), and so began the long open-ended adventure of *A la recherche du temps perdu;* Alain-Fournier published *Le Grand Meaulnes*, and André Gide his novel of *l'acte gratuit, Les Caves du Vatican* (*The Vatican Cellars*). Even across the Channel in London, the energy of modernist revolt was plain. Ezra Pound had announced his poetic movement of Imagism in 1912, but, after various quarrels, joined Wyndham Lewis to invent "Vorticism," which would soon produce the manifesto magazine *Blast*, which blasted the past, blessed the radical present, and inadvertently prefigured the war. Ford Madox Hueffer began *The Good Soldier*, the best French novel in the English language, the story of an innocent American at the German spa of Nauheim (where, it so happened, William James had gone for treatment). D. H. Lawrence, now wandering Europe with his new companion Frieda von Richthofen Weekley, published his Freudianized novel of a young man's birth into art, *Sons and Lovers*. In Trieste James Joyce finally finished his *A Portrait of the Artist as a Young Man*, and offered it to *The Egoist* of Harriet Shaw Weaver, another key patroness. He thus came into contact with Pound, who was its "literary editor," and also the "foreign editor" of Harriet Monroe's new *Poetry (Chicago)*. Pound was thus placed to publish European writers in America, American ones in Britain, and expatriate ones on both sides of the Atlantic. Like Stein, he was an emblematic figure of the new American cosmopolitanism, and another advocate of what he had, he said, so long desired, "the American Risorgimento," which was clearly a very international affair.

It was this "Risorgimento," in all its internationalism, that hit New York in 1913. At the 69th Regiment Armory on Lexington Avenue, an eclectic exhibition of the new American and European paintings was staged under the sponsorship of the Association of American Painters and Sculptors, and exhibited 1,300 works under the title "International Exhibition of Modern Art." The "Armory Show" was highly varied, but notable in two respects. It brought the American public face to face for the first time with the experimental movements that had been developing in Europe in the century's first decade: Impressionism, Post-Impressionism, Fauvism, and the "Cubist Room," with seven Picassos, works by Brancusi, and Marcel Duchamp's *Nude Descending a*

Staircase. It came to an America which had just elected Woodrow Wilson as president, and had just given the socialist candidate Eugene Debs a million votes. It was an America excited by progressivism and radicalism, an America suddenly awash with artists, writers, movements and little magazines. Chicago had just seen the birth of the magazine *Poetry*, soon followed by Margaret Anderson's *Little Review*, which displayed a whole new generation of experimental poets. There had been a similar exhibition arranged by Roger Fry at London's Grafton Galleries in 1910; this was, said Virginia Woolf, the moment when "human character changed" and the modern struck. And it now struck New York too, provoking outrage, laughter, and, for that matter, 30,000 visitors as the show toured from Manhattan to Chicago and Boston. The name of Stein was constantly and understandably mentioned, for many of these painters had enjoyed her support. Copies of her Mabel Dodge portrait were made available, by Mabel Dodge, who assumed the role of hostess to the show.[20] Hence, when Stein's gnomic, poetic volume of still lifes, *Tender Buttons: Objects, Food, Rooms*, appeared next year, it was seen as an extension of the same event. In Chicago Sherwood Anderson read it, and found in it a bareness of composition which was, he recognized, vital "for the artist who happens to work with words as his material"; so its literary influence began to grow. As Mabel Dodge proudly put it, "Gertrude Stein was born at the Amory Show." And not Stein alone. As she frankly admitted, "so was 'Mabel Dodge.' "[21] It was indeed the moment of Stein's acceptance, as of that whole modernizing tide that had been sweeping over art and taste from the 1890s on. "Looking back on it now," Dodge said in her autobiography, aptly called *Movers and Shakers*, "it seems as though everywhere, in that year of 1913, barriers went down and people reached each other who had never been in touch before; there were all sorts of new ways to communicate as well as new communications. The new spirit was abroad and swept us all together."

[20] Mabel Dodge then moved to Taos, New Mexico, married a Tiwa Indian named Antonio Luhan, and, as Mabel Dodge Luhan, recorded her life in *Intimate Memories* (New York, 4 vols, Harcourt Brace, 1933–7). The four volumes are *Background* (1933), *European Experiences* (1935), *Movers and Shakers* (1936), and *The Edge of the Desert: An Escape to Reality* (1937).
[21] There is a splendid account of all this in Steven Watson's admirable compendium *Strange Bedfellows: The First American Avant-Garde* (New York/ London/ Paris, Abbeville Press, 1991).

The Armory show was a vast, contentious, very public, noisily debated signal of the coming of the modern to the American shore. Like the London show, it had its bitter and mocking adversaries, and the consequences would hang over the coming war and the fears about cultural and social degeneration it provoked. But, like the London show, it had long-lasting effects. It was a Euro- or rather a Franco-American display, like the Statue of Liberty, and it revealed a whole new web of international and transatlantic relations in culture. For the moment the French, or those who worked in France, were cast in the role of creators, and Americans in the role of consumers or patrons, though that would slowly change. But the show converted influential taste, especially that of art patrons, the well-endowed beneficiaries of American industrialism and corporatism, whose sponsorship was so necessary for the whole *avant-garde* transaction. It also fundamentally challenged and changed the perceptions of American artists and writers, stimulating experimental confidence among the new native *avant-garde*, Williams and Stevens and Demuth and Scheeler and O'Keeffe, who emerged in large numbers in the wake of the Armory excitements, to dominate American painting in the Twenties. "France is almost outplayed," the Cuban-born painter Francis Picabia, over from France, reassuringly told the *New York Times*. "It is in America that I believe the theories of the New Art will hold most tenaciously. I have come here to appeal to the American people to accept the New Movement in Art." So they did – or rather, for the moment, many of the new artists and the most powerful patrons did – through the exciting, radical period between the Armory exhibition and the entry of the United States into European war on 6 April 1917.

5.

So, on the very brink of European war, Stein at last gained the "glory" she had long been seeking, and she would live in its glow and with its consequences for the next thirty years. She was American Modernism's best-known literary monument, and in the very different Paris of the experimental and crisis-ridden Twenties the first port of call for the visiting expatriate was the studio at 27 Rue de Fleurus, and the feet of Gertrude Stein. But the change that came now was a complicated phenomenon, above all because of what happened on 6 August 1914, when Europe went to war. In the United States the euphoria of the Modern continued. In a brief space of time a whole wave of new and experimental writers, mostly poets and dramatists – Carl Sandburg, Vachel Lindsay, Williams, Stevens, "H.D.," Marianne Moore, e.e. cummings, Eugene O'Neill, Susan Glaspell – wonderfully emerged, mostly out of the spirit of Greenwich Village bohemia and its offshoots. (The achievement in fiction would have to wait a few more years.) By 1915 Henry McBride, the art critic and a keen Stein supporter, was writing to her to announce: "We have become the capital of the arts!" Matters were more complicated, but there is no doubt that there was indeed a deep change in the cultural temper of a United States that was now suddenly casting off much of its earlier cultural, political and indeed sexual simplicity (this was the era when the taste for Sigmund Freud's new wisdoms raged), and when that much touted event, "the end of American innocence," actually seemed to be happening.[22] As Hugh Kenner has rightly said, it was ironic that just as Henry James died, convinced that his work would in future be neglected, there was a great new market for the "outlandish arts." In a great culture-shift, the American arts went "modern." What had happened in poetry – *vers libre*, fragmentation – duly transformed the novel too, and there was a new American literature, written in the modern manner. By the Twenties then, when the world had fundamentally changed, the United States could thus claim its own distinctive spirit of modernism, the experimental art of what Hugh Kenner calls the "homemade world."[23]

Meantime Europe had gone to the battlefields. "The golden era was at an end," reported the American patroness Muriel Draper in her memoir *Music at Midnight* (1929), describing the collapse of the *belle-époque* culture in France in the period after 1914. The climate changed suddenly, and at once. T. S. Eliot, undertaking philosophical studies in Marburg, Germany, hurried to London and became part of the Poundian *avant-garde* there. Amy Lowell, attempting to capture Imagism from Pound's influence, went quickly back to the States, carrying a part of it with her. Henry James, deploring the "great

[22] Henry F. May provides an important account of the change in the American climate in *The End of American Innocence: A Study of the First Years of Our Own Time, 1912–1917* (London, Cape, 1960).
[23] See Hugh Kenner's vivid and evocative study *A Homemade World: The American Modernist Writers* (New York, Morrow, 1975).

Niagara" that was overwhelming his world, became a British citizen. James Joyce fled Trieste, still a Habsburg port, for Zürich, to continue work on the vast novel he had just started to undertake, *Ulysses*. Leo Stein and Mabel Dodge both happened to be in Florence at the time, and each packed up and headed for America. Edith Wharton in Paris tended the wounded troops, and was duly to be awarded the Légion d'Honneur; her experiences are recorded in two novels, *The Marne* (1918) and *A Son at the Front* (1923), now little read. Mildred Aldrich found herself in the middle of a battlefield, and aided the wounded soldiers and refugees all around her, recording her experiences in *A Hilltop on the Marne* (1915). When it all happened, Stein was visiting London with Alice Toklas, exploring with the publisher Jonathan Cape the possibility of an English edition of *Three Lives*, and hoping to meet Henry James (alas, the Master neglected to come, civilly pleading illness as his excuse). Neither had noticed the unfolding events; living in the continuous present meant a certain indifference to the activities of history.[24] Since the first German offensive against Paris was threatened, they delayed their return until October; when they went back, it was to find Paris a different, emptied city, threatened by Zeppelins. Artists had been conscripted and many friends had gone to the front; writers were now subject to wartime control and censorship. America became the Great Good Place, and some, notably Francis Picabia and Marcel Duchamp, neither too keen to be called for service, made the passage. Here they allied themselves with American experimentalists like Man Ray and Alfred Stieglitz, and began, in Greenwich Village, their own early and influential version of the newest wartime art-movement, Dada, which was also beginning to flourish in neutral Zürich. For the moment at least, New York seemed the essential stronghold of experiment. And so it remained until 6 April 1917, when the United States declared war on Germany, and the climate immediately changed. It was four days later that the Society of Independent Artists held an exhibition devoted to "free expression" in New York's Grand Central Palace, which was to become more famous not for what it put in but for what it left out. The rejected item was called

---

[24] Stein's grand indifference to history was always striking. When she returned to America on her triumphant progress of 1934, when she referred to herself as the modernist Shakespeare, she appeared to think that Theodore Roosevelt was the American president. When told he was dead, she replied, with her usual cunning, "He may not be as dead as you think."

"Fountain," consisted of an upturned male urinal, and was signed "R. Mutt." The creator, or rather finder, of this Dadaist *objet trouvé* was Duchamp, who explained his reasoning in the New York Dada magazine *Blind Man*: "The only works of art America has given are her plumbing and her bridges." As it happened, the exhibition was the last gasp of the pre-war experiment; soon war censorship had come to America too, left-wing movements were suppressed, and the progressive impulse began to fade under the pressure of new claims of patriotism, as young Americans, like their fellow Europeans, made their way to the front.

There was no doubt that, with France trapped in war, and European civilization destroying itself in what to many seemed the final European conflict of powers, something in the balance of transatlantic cultural relations had now changed for good. For a while Stein retired to the neutrality of Palma de Mallorca, but returned in 1916 to Paris, and offered her services to the American Fund for French Wounded. She had a Ford car-ambulance shipped over from America, called it "Auntie," and, rather dangerously, since she did not understand the principle of reverse, drove it to aid the wounded troops. In 1917, when the New World came to the rescue of the Old, she helped and entertained the incoming American troops, and this would in fact become the foundation for the new and different alliances of her post-war salon. She remained, throughout, a fundamental figure in the complicated transition. In the pre-war years her Montparnasse studio became, as James R. Mellow has rightly put it, "a cultural halfway house between the European vanguard and the merest beginnings of the avant-garde in the United States."[25] And she herself became a fascinating point of crossover – between Cubist painting (then still essentially a European phenomenon) and her Cubist experimental prose, which she made to seem quintessentially American. As she insisted herself, pointing, for instance, to her debt to William and Henry James: "Henry James just went on doing what American literature had always done, the form was always the form of the contemporary English one, but the disembodied way of disconnecting something from anything and anything from something was the American one. The way it had of often all never having any daily living

25 James Mellow, *Charmed Circle: Gertrude Stein and Company* (New York, Holt, Rinehart, 1974).

was an American one," she said in "What Is English Literature" (1934). But where Edith Wharton showed the Jamesian influence by writing "international fiction," Stein did not; the agonies and contradictions of the outland dart were never for her, and if her fiction could be thought to be set in a real, nominal place at all, then most of it was set in the USA. The issue was the "disembodied way," and the spirit of Modernity, the American speciality; she always lived and wrote, she said, in the American space-time continuum, which made everything so different and strange. Still, her writing was international, transatlantic; as one American publisher who rejected *Three Lives* put it, she applied "French methods to American low life." Her work would never have taken the form it did, assumed the style it did, had her aesthetic notions not come into contact with the arts of Cubism. Nor, in experimental Paris, would it have won the interest it did, made the connections it did, had it not been part of the fascination among European experimentalists with things American – whether it was the "new dance" of the Americans Loie Fuller, Isadora Duncan and Maude Allen, which drew the *avant-garde* from the early 1890s onward, the "new music" increasingly represented by black American jazz, the attractions of American "comics," so loved by Picasso, or the growing allure of the futuristic speed of American cities and life.[26]

Stein was close to the heart of a new transatlantic artistic equation that formed as two great changes happened simultaneously. One was the birth of Modernism in Europe, as deep cultural and social upheaval altered consciousness and expression in all the main artistic centres of the continent. The other was the appearance in those centres of a growing number of artistic figures from an ever more powerful and world-historical America, come to Europe to find not its past culture but its experimental "new arts," and draw them into Pound's "American Risorgimento." The phenomenon was striking, and it shaped the entire cultural direction of the twentieth century. In the pre-war period, the centre of the change was what Ezra Pound called "the twin cities of London and Paris." Paris particularly attracted painters (and you could call Stein a painter in prose), and London, perhaps because of the common language, writers. In both cities the

26 On the fascination of the new American dance, above all that of Loie Fuller, in Paris from 1893 on, and her magical displays of light-based radiation, see Frank Kermode's essay "Poet and Dancer Before Diaghilev," in *Modern Essays* (London, Fontana, rev. ed., 1990).

result was an episode of high experimentalism and cosmopolitanism. From 1908, when Pound reached London, to 1914, when Eliot came, the London *avant-garde* was heavily populated by American writers: Hilda Doolittle and Marianne Moore, Robert Frost and John Gould Fletcher, Conrad Aiken, William Carlos Williams and Amy Lowell. Pound would later boast "All the developments in English verse since 1910 are due almost wholly to Americans." If this was exaggerated (there was, after all, the age of Bloomsbury to come), the expatriates played a fundamental part, to the degree that it is no longer possible to say whether Eliot is an American or British poet (or Auden a British or American one). The point is that if Modernism was indeed chiefly a European movement, sprung from the cultures and contradictions of European life, it became, largely thanks to Americans, an international school with a deeply transatlantic flavour. And in the end the war did not halt the process; indeed it accelerated it. Politically and historically, Americans in wartime encountered the complex and often destructive realities of Europe, and risked their lives among them. The war brought a great disintegration to Europe, and also a new confidence to America, which in more than one sense entered the war a debtor nation, and left it a creditor one.

But the question of the Modern, its nature, its sources and its future, was not over and settled, for reasons that we will see. The war over in 1918, the international school reshaped, and a new Modernist episode began, once again largely stimulated by a large number of Americans eager to return to the seedbed of the modern arts, bringing their modern expectations. But they came in far greater confidence, and to a Europe that was now politically collapsed and economically shattered. And now the artists and writers alike came not to London, which had lost a good deal of its artistic energy, but to Paris. When they did, at 27 Rue de Fleurus, Gertrude Stein was still there and waiting: "the great stoneface," as F. Scott Fitzgerald called her, was as ready for the new movements as she had been for the older ones, and was also a monument of what had already been. "Heaven forbid Gertrude Stein should become a fashion," Katherine Mansfield murmured plaintively in 1920. But it was all too late; she already had, and post-war Paris would not have been the same without her. Under the Cézannes, still serving tea, she outlasted several more generations, two more decades of movements, an infinity of artistic visitors, a revolt against her influence (*transition* magazine's "testimony against Gertrude Stein"), a time of return when most of the American expatriates went home. She saw another war and yet another tragic historical transition. It was in 1939, as war resumed and the German occupation began, as a gesture of solidarity and of her decision to remain in the country, that she published her *Paris France* as an act of gratitude and a gesture of solidarity. "Paris was the place that suited those of us that were to create the twentieth century art and literature, naturally enough," she said, "England had the disadvantage of believing in progress." Paris and Stein were modernity as she understood it, and who is to say she wasn't right?

6.

To this day it stays interesting to ask how two fundamental modern processes interacted with each other. One of these processes is Modernism, the modern experimental tradition in the arts, which over time came to seem the essential new heritage of writing, painting, and music, and which to begin with had distinctly European origins. The other is the far vaster and more encompassing process of modernization, a fundamental reconstruction of the conditions of life and the workings of society, a process which also had European origins but in which the United States came to possess a dominant role. It is quite clear that the two were certainly not always mutually sympathetic; one important aspect of at least one wing of the Modern movement is indeed its revolt against the modernization of life. Modernism was a highly self-conscious, radical apocalyptic movement in art, culture and consciousness; Modernity was a massive and, it often seemed, ungovernable process of human change, a vast transformation that was taking place in the momentum of progress, the advancement of science and technology, a system of production, invention and development which swept away all that was in its path. Yet it was roughly the same band of years – the two decades just before the Great War – that saw the great massing of the social, scientific and technological changes we name modern, and the birth of the *avant-garde* arts. These arts were *avant-garde*, ahead of things, because they claimed to be (as in Stein's work) a probe into the future, an adventure beyond familiar "daily life" into the new "supersensual chaos" dissolving the structures of the known world. They proclaimed the great break with the past, a crisis of the present, an ambiguous relation to the future. Modernism was a fundamental revolt against artistic habit, conventional portraiture, familiar representation in which, as one judge, Herbert Read, put it, the aims of five centuries of art were openly abandoned. It marked an upturning of image and discourse, perception and consciousness. It was a Revolution of the Word, though it implied or revealed a Revolution of the World. But the Modern arts no longer claimed directly to record the life of the modern, indeed they generally rejected the familiar, direct representation, "mimesis." They expressed the new fragmentation of representation, the fracturing of cultural types and icons, genres and structures. What Stein called "seeing something without turning it into identity" became one of the essential projects of their adventure. In the pre-war years Modernism was an experiment, and had not become a crisis. It was an art of visionary reconstruction, not an art of political extremity. As science, technology, philosophy, architecture probed the orders of the future, as the processes of urbanization, mechanization and secularization advanced, so artistic Moderns dissolved the forms and consciousness of the past, and probed those of the future, trying, as Ezra Pound said, to Make It New.

The New was a changed condition of being, but also a new, modern landscape and cityscape. And – here Stein was right – America, its forms and structures, its "new space-time continuum," had a key part to play, for America had become ever more a physical emblem of the shape of things to come. Hegel, in his philosophy of history, had called it "the land of the future, where, in the ages to come, the burden of the world's history will reveal itself." It was a world beyond the tired historical dialectic of Europe, a world without a past – "the land of desire for those who are weary of the historical lumber-room of old Europe." But over the course of the nineteenth century the image of the American future changed fundamentally, as did America itself. To Charles Dickens, the idealized image of America was the New Eden, the reality was the rattling machine of the railway train, steaming over the prairie and laying waste all in its path. Many European writers, like the German Charles Sealsfield, wrote of mythic America in what came to be called "the immigrant novel," the tale of the American Dream, which, as many critics have pointed out, was itself largely an import of the European imagination. But the American Dream was changing too, and the immigrant novels of around the turn of the century – from, say, Abraham Cahan's *Yekl: A Tale of the New York Ghetto* (1896) to his

The Rise of David Levinsky (1917), the exemplary story of a Jewish immigrant who arrives in New York with four cents in his pocket, and becomes a disappointed millionaire – depicted less and less the land of the self-reliant pioneer, more usually the poor Eastern European cast into the urban commercial and industrial jungle and struggling to survive and succeed. America was not just the land of the future, but the land of modernity, with all that implied: the elimination of the past, the growth of vast new cities, the dominance of machines and invention, the rise of science, the forming of corporations, the material exploitation of nature, goods and people, of crowded masses, mingled races, new political organizations, new types of industrial production – Adams' "twenty-million horse-power society" indeed. Increasingly, when Europeans imagined the future, they imagined it like America, and the future they imagined was shaped by images of steam and electric power, applied science, fantastic invention, technological discovery. What is more, these processes were developing in Europe too. By the 1860s the Goncourt Brothers were already complaining of *"l'américanisation de la France,"* and many others issued ominous warnings, in a debate that lasts to this day. Meantime the various great late nineteenth-century exhibitions in Paris and London, with their displays of American products, techniques and inventions, encouraged notions of a great new age of machines in which the most fundamental tasks, from heating and lighting to fighting wars, would be done by mechanical device. European architects, designers and manufacturers increasingly looked to America, and almost every new stylistic movement, and above all the Art Nouveau of the 1890s, drew on American influence.

From the 1860s onward, dreams or nightmares of the American future haunted the minds of Europeans as they tried to see the shape of things to come. It was in the 1860s that readers, first in France, then worldwide, started to anticipate the annual thrill of yet another of the *Voyages extraordinaires*: the fantastic tales of Jules Verne, which had titles like *Journey to the Centre of the Earth* (1864), *From the Earth to the Moon* (1866), *Twenty Thousand Leagues Under the Sea* (1870) and *Around the World in Eighty Days* (1873). These highly popular stories, filled with submarines, bathyscopes, balloons, flying machines, technologies, strange cities, amazing inventions, continued to appear regularly until his death in 1905. They were works of "anticipations," summoning the European imagination to fantastic thoughts of "the world of things to come" – a world that, as change came faster and faster, decade by decade, seemed increasingly real and imminent. Unsurprisingly, they frequently involved America or Americans, so intimately associated with the idea of *la vie future*. Verne was not alone; though many warned of the American danger, the French imagination, delighted by the transatlantic wonders on display at the various Paris exhibitions, and hungry to keep pace with modernity of style, revelled in the spirit of *la vie future* and *art nouveau*. So engaging was the motif that one of the most aesthetic and symbolist of French writers, Villiers de l'Isle Adam (inventor of the famous phrase "Live! Our servants can do that for us," and an influence on Wilde), published in 1886 a novel, *L'Eve future* (*The Eve of the Future*), where he has Thomas Alva Edison invent a female android or feminist robot intended to afford the book's hero, a British nobleman, the sexual solace he cannot find in human form. In the book's preface Adam extols Edison: "In America and in Europe a legend has thus grown up in the popular imagination about this great citizen of the United States. He goes by such fantastic titles as 'the Magician of the Century, the Wizard of Menlo Park, and the Father of the Photograph.' The most understandable enthusiasm in his own country and abroad has given him a kind of mysterious quality rather like that of many spirits." It was this "mysterious quality" Adam set out, in his decadent decorative way, to summon. The Edison legend reached its height at the Paris Centennial Exposition of 1889, when the whole fair was illuminated not just by Edison's amazing incandescent bulbs but by a visit from the great magician himself. When in 1892 the American dancer Loie Fuller appeared at the Folies Bergères, "playing strangely with her veils and electric light," she too became a symbolist icon, admired and represented by the major French artists, including Toulouse-Lautrec; she similarly conquered London the following year, and became a mythic object of modern unity for W. B. Yeats.

The notion that the world's entire future was being shaped by American invention and ingenuity dominated the whole *fin de siècle*, a time when new utopias and dystopias became the stuff of the general imagination. One crucial book was a utopian fable by the American socialist reformer and Fourierist Edward Bellamy, who brought out *Looking Backward: 2000–1887* (1888). It soon sold a million copies worldwide, to become America's second great international bestseller (the first was Stowe's *Uncle Tom's Cabin*). In it a sleeper awakes to find himself in the city of Boston in the year 2000. Poverty has been abolished, collectivism rules, everyone is enlisted in the massive workforce, strange technologies benignly work for the common good of all. William Morris wrote his *News from Nowhere* (1890) to answer this technological Utopia; he offered a different socialist arcadia, where factories are abolished, work is not technological but craftlike, creative, and futurist London peculiarly resembles the Oxfordshire countryside. The *fin de siècle* may have been preoccupied with endings, but from the start of the 1890s, a time of great stylistic change, concern with the "modern world," the "machine age," the "art of the new," the "shape of the future," was intense right across the West. After all, it was, of course, not just American but European cities, factories, buildings, hospitals, streets and homes that were changing under the powers of constant technological innovation. In the big European centres, streetcars, underground railways, electric light, the bicycle, the steam train, the motor car were changing the look and structure of the metropolis and altering the fundamental rules and conditions of life. Life happened in cities, departing the countryside, and the confusions, fragmentations and strange impressions of urban existence became the essential stuff of art. A new urban mass age was dawning, and books and articles about future utopias or dystopias – stories of a coming world that would be made or lost by the new technologies – became the stuff of the popular arts.

   In Britain the writer who captured the mood most powerfully was H. G. Wells, who burst on popular attention in the middle of the decade. In 1895, the year his good friend Stephen Crane published *The Red Badge of Courage*, he suddenly came to notice with *The Time Machine* – his still remarkable tale of a "time traveller" who journeys forward through the millennia not just to Bellamy's year 2000 but to the year 802701. Here he finds the world divided between a dominant intellectual élite and an underclass; in short, the future is an eternal extension of the social difficulties and transformations of the present. Wells, who had been born of servant origins, and acquired a new kind of scientific education at the (later Royal) College of Science, had good reasons, political as much as scientific, for probing the way into the technical, socialist, world-historical future. He liked to call his kind of fiction "scientific romance" – we prefer "science fiction" – and based it not, like Verne, solely on technological and scientific speculation, but on the social hopes and disappointments the new systems raised. G. K.

Chesterton rightly said that his "first importance was that he wrote great adventure stories in the new world the men of science had discovered," and for all his later fame as a world thinker these early scientific romances from the 1890s remain his best, most visionary work. As Bernard Bergonzi has pointed out, they are true expressions of the *fin de siècle*, ever alternating between excited delight in future marvels and grim visions of war and Doomsday.[27] His futures were paradoxical; he alike explored the dreams of advanced scientific utopias and the nightmares of future global and intergalactic conflict. The writer who could conceive blissful scientific prospects and benign new societies could equally write in *The War of the Worlds* (1898) of killer rays and technological destruction, in *The First Men on the Moon* (1901) of the complexities of space travel, in *The World Set Free* (1914) of the "atomic bomb," elsewhere of great racial conflict or the coming totalitarian state. His fantasies were not just amazing romances but analytical myths; his work was so well regarded that Henry James once talked of "doing Mars" with him (it remains one of history's great unwritten books).

Wells may have been one of the new British socialists, but what cannot be missed is that his "anticipations" – which peaked around the turn of the century – took for their models of technologies, cityscapes and social problems the life of the United States. That grew yet clearer when in 1898 an American newspaper, the New York *Journal* (for which Crane had worked) republished what was surely his most powerful fable, *The War of the Worlds*. Wells set the story in Surrey and London, but (ignoring the small matter of author's permission) the paper shifted the scene to Manhattan, having Brooklyn Bridge and Columbia University zapped by the Martian invaders. It then added an unauthorized sequel, *Edison's Conquest of Mars*, where the planet is avenged by none other than the Wizard of Menlo Park. It was clear Wells' story had founded a new transatlantic archetype, and many more American borrowings and rewritings of the famous tale were to come. The classic case came forty years on from first publication, on Hallowe'en 1938, at a time when the American Depression still created despair and war fever was rising across Europe and the world at large. The aspiring movie-maker Orson Welles terrified the American radio

[27] Bernard Bergonzi, *The Early H. G. Wells: A Study of the Scientific Romances* (Manchester, Manchester University Press, 1961).

audience with a contemporary adaptation of the universal story, reporting through "live" newsflashes a Martian invasion of America. Thousands fled their homes or hid in cellars; "Tidal Wave of Panic Sweeps the Nation," said the newspaper headlines next day. By now Wells was, in many eyes, virtually an American author, just as the form of "science fiction" he invented had become virtually an American form. The connection had been pursued by Wells himself. In 1905 he published his largest vision of the scientific and political future, *A Modern Utopia*; a year later he made his first visit to the USA, to test it against his own imaginings. He was going, he said, like Tocqueville, to see not what America was but what it might become; he published his report as *The Future in America: A Search after Realities*, declaring he had indeed seen the land of the future, a nation of bursting technological energies that simply required the application of statism, a new political system that went with the futuristic processes he observed. And one of his concerns, he made clear, was with the technologization of the arts themselves. When the great new technological art, film, came along, he hailed it; it was here, he said, that the "mystery of modern mechanics" unfolded. Film, he suggested, was the key form for constructing the dreams and nightmares of the future, and he recognized as a great moment the making of Fritz Lang's German Expressionist film *Metropolis* (1926), a future fantasy which transformed nightmarish Berlin into the likeness of New York. Though he disliked the film's argument, he perceived its importance, and was soon turning to the medium to advance his own ideas. He produced a futuristic script for Hollywood, *The King Who Was a King* (1929), which was never made, and one for Alexander Korda, *Things to Come* (1936), based on his novel about Nazi totalitarianism, *The Shape of Things to Come*, which was. Both depend on a futuristic cityscape based on the model of New York, now in process of becoming the great experimental film-set of the age. It had become clear the forms Wells invented were completely at home with the American cityscape, and he was a maker of its myths. To this day the vast content of future fantasy that has fed the American movie industry and its extensions in the video-game world owes more than a little to the fertile, futuristic, space-oriented, ever-speculating mind of Wells.[28]

[28] I am much indebted in this section to two fascinating books on utopianism and future prediction in literature by I. F. Clarke, *The Pattern of Expectation, 1644–2001* (London, Cape, 1979), and *Voices Prophesying War: Future Wars 1963–3749* (Oxford and New York, Oxford University Press, new edition, 1992).

7.

In fact Wells was nothing other than a modern, popular Futurist. And Futurism, in various forms, was already becoming the preoccupation of many of the European artists, writers, architects and musicians who followed up the idea of the New as the twentieth century dawned. Cubism may have had as an essential aesthetic concept what Worringer and others called "abstraction," but if you inspected what lay behind the shattered forms of Picasso, Braque, Delaunay, Picabia, you found a glimpse of the styles and shapes, the machines and skyscrapers, that signalled the future, and in one case, as we have seen, Gertrude Stein. "I have been profoundly impressed by the vast mechanical development of America," Picabia explained, "I have enlisted the machinery of the modern world and introduced it into my studio." First the architects of Art Nouveau and *Jugendstil*, then the technological futurists of Bauhaus, like Mies van der Rohe and Walter Gropius, aimed to remodel European cities with designs drawing on American architectural invention (and both of them eventually ended up in the USA). In Italy, the movement that named itself Futurism likewise owed almost everything to American images: when the founder, F. T. Marinetti, went to Paris in 1909 to proclaim *The Futurist Manifesto*, he explained it as a break with the museum spirit of the past, a mechanical, violent art of the airplane, the automobile, speed, war, the city as machine: "We shall sing of great crowds in the excitement of Labour, Pleasure or Rebellion; of the nocturnal vibration of arsenals and workshops beneath their electric moons; of greedy stations swallowing smoking snakes; of adventurous liners seeking the horizon; of broadchested locomotives galloping on wheels," the manifesto declared. It sounded like modern America, just as Futurist drawing and architecture borrowed from the same source – until, after the Great War, it forged an alliance with Fascism, which, in its own obsession with the modern mass, the new city, the great machine, also had its share of American myths. Russian Futurism (later Constructivism), a distinctive brand of a similar tendency, had similar imaginings; when its leading poet, Vladimir Mayakovsky, finally visited the USA in the Twenties, he recognized skyscraper Manhattan as the place to which his fantasies pointed, and when that movement too made its alliance with the Bolshevik Revolution, it, once again, had a debt to the USA. The same was true in Germany, where the dominant new movement was Expressionism. It, too, had a cult of the great modern city, where, as the Expressionist poet Julius Hart put it, one is "born violently into the wild life." In 1913 there appeared a science-fiction novel, Bernhard Kellerman's *The Tunnel*, which imagined Europe and America linked technologically and scientifically by a transatlantic tunnel. And similar motifs were to extend into the Expressionist film of the Twenties, above all Lang's *Metropolis*.

In France, too, the image of futuristic America became a pre-dominant theme – not always affirmatively. In fiction, Anatole France published his apocalyptic American satire *L'Ile des Pingouins* (*Penguin Island*) (1908) and Paul Adam satirized American corporatism in *Le Trust* (1910), and this world of monstrous skyscrapers and deadening cities continued into such studies as George Duhamel's *Scènes de la vie future* in 1930. Others embraced the identification of America and the new with a greater pleasure. Picasso's delight in Gertrude Stein was part of a Cubist fascination with contemporary America which encompassed its comics, its jazz, and folk-heroes like Buffalo Bill. The experimentalists' love affair with America was to have enormous consequences, not least in the gradually growing process of migration of artists and musicians across the Atlantic from Europe to the USA over the next quarter-century. A classic example came in wartime Paris in 1917 (the year America entered the war), when Picasso, Jean Cocteau, Leonide Massine, Erik Satie, and Sergei Diaghilev put their talents together to produce the "futuristic" ballet *Parade* for the Ballets Russes. It was a carnivalesque event drawing together a wild mixture of contemporary motifs, many of them American: the skyscraper and the cakewalk, the Little American Girl (based on Mary Pickford) and the American Manager (complete with cowboy chaps), Charlie Chaplin and ragtime, many of them drawn from Cocteau's fascination with a country he had never actually seen. But, as he would explain later: "On October 12, 1492, Columbus discovered America. The foundling has come a long way. In recent years, our own artists have worked under its influence. Composers use its ragtime, painters its landscapes of iron and concrete, poets its advertising and its films. Its machines, skyscrapers, ocean liners and Negroes were certainly the source of a new and excellent direction."[29] Cocteau was later to withdraw from his fascination with

[29] Quoted in Robert Phelps (ed.), *Professional Secrets: An Autobiography of Jean Cocteau* (New York, Farrer, Strauss & Giroux, 1970).

the futuristic land of the skyscraper, but the inheritance lasted into the warm acceptance given to the American expatriates of the Twenties, who, following in the footsteps of Stein and Fuller and Isadora Duncan and many more, were seen as modern style-bringers: not men, not women, but Americans.

But probably the most striking example of futuristic American myth came from the most improbable of sources. In Prague in 1912–13, the young Franz Kafka was writing "Metamorphosis," and miserably wooing Felice Bauer. But he was also starting work on a novel he would never complete, provisionally entitled *The Man Who Disappeared*. The book is set in America – a place Kafka had never visited, never expected to visit, never would visit. But he knew very well all the powerful myths that had shaped the massive human traffic that had passed from mid-Europe to America. He had read Benjamin Franklin's *Autobiography*, the first great tale about the industrious young man making his new American start, and probably Horatio Alger too. He was also steeped in the many immigrant fictions that had appeared from German and other European authors, like Charles Sealsfield, over the previous century – stories of the American Dream, the American rebirth, the beginning of a new life, of prospects of self-creation on the great American prairie or in the tumultuous American city. This is the prototype he follows, following the familiar conventions almost exactly: "As Karl Rossmann, a poor boy of sixteen who had been packed off to America by his parents because a servant girl had seduced him and got herself with child by him, stood on the liner slowly entering the harbour of New York, a sudden burst of sunshine seem to illumine the Statue of Liberty, so that he saw it in a new light, although he had sighted it long before" – so the strangest of Kafka's always strange novels begins. But it is not just young Karl Rossmann who sees the Land of Liberty in a new light. So does Kafka, as he adds to the familiar immigrant myths his own distinctive sense of estrangement, his struggling hunger for identity, role, acceptance, artistic recognition. Karl at first appears the classic immigrant hero, the innocent young man going through the great transatlantic rite of passage and experiencing the classic sense of self-renewal ("The first days in America might be likened to a re-birth"). On arrival, he undergoes all the traditional immigrant rituals: there are relatives to find, a language to learn, pretty girls to look at, and there is the eternal question of what place one will take in the new society. And there are great and mysterious machines, strange inventions (an extraordinary writing-desk, for instance), while New York, a city of unending traffic, is "an inextricable confusion, for ever newly emphasized." There is grinding poverty, coarse and open manners, and a constant blurring of identity.

But this is Kafka, and the new start soon turns into deeper mystery. There are also odd journeys, strange tasks, and mysterious systems and organizations to encounter. Working as a lift-boy in a huge surreal hotel, Karl finds himself in a world of Babelian confusion and obscure deference; he may be in America, but he is certainly also in the world of Kafka. The urban myth gives way to the prairie myth. At last he falls in with the welcoming "Nature Theatre of Oklahoma" ("If you want to be an artist, join our company! Our Theatre can find employment for everyone, a place for everyone!"). He is greeted by a band of women dressed as angels, and given an armband that describes him as a "technical worker." We leave him in a company of expectant people, headed, as America always insists, for the West ("Only now did Karl understand how huge America was"), and all of them looking for a place and destination in the world. Like all Kafka's novels, this can be read as expressionist allegory, the story of a passive dreamer who longs somehow to be an artist but seems fated only to be a servant, or a "technical worker" in someone else's obscure system – though Kafka did indicate to friends that he meant the book to end with Karl being rewarded at last with a job and an identity. The result is Kafka's longest, most frankly comic and even buoyant novel. But, like most of his extended work, it was left incomplete. Recovered on his death, it was edited and published in 1927 by his friend Max Brod: who gave it the title *Amerika*.

8.

"Listen to the States asserting: 'The hour has struck! Americans shall be American. The USA has now grown up artistically . . .' All right, Americans, let's see how you set about it. Go on then, let the precious cat out of the bag." These provocative words are the opening of D. H. Lawrence's *Studies in Classic American Literature*, a collection of essays published in the United States in 1923, and still one of the most remarkable studies of American writing to appear this century. No less striking than their challenging and vigorous argument – the book goes on in the same note – is the fact that it should have been Lawrence, the Nottinghamshire miner's son whose pre-war novels seemed set to extend the tradition of the English regional novel beyond Hardy and into the new century, who turned his mind and passions to the rewriting of the American tradition. It began in 1913, soon after he had published *Sons and Lovers*, and while he was travelling through Europe with his new companion Frieda von Richthofen. Now he started on a vast new project, a work – originally titled *The Sisters* – that was to link his own regional past to the age of modern mechanism and futurism. It was, as he passionately explained to his editor Edward Garnett, a work with a quite new conception, "like a novel in a foreign language." He made the comparison with Marinetti's Futurism, saying the book dispensed with "the old-fashioned human element," and followed a Futurist "inhuman will" – a surprising statement, for it was always to be apparent that Lawrence, for all his instinct for modernity, was no lover of the machine age. As war approached, he worked on the book over four draftings, and it became so vast that it split into two parts (various rejections of his manuscript also affected it). The first told a story of the Nottinghamshire countryside from the Victorian age to the mechanistic present, and, as its title, *The Rainbow*, proclaimed, it was an "apocalyptic" book – the more so since, by the time it was finished, war had begun, and the final draft reflected, especially in the ending, the war's grim harvest of death and extinction, though also a prospect of a resurrection through sexual energy and recovered vitalism.

When the war broke out, Lawrence and Frieda happened to be back in Britain; Frieda's divorce had just come through, and they returned to marry. Caught in the country, both became objects of official suspicion; Lawrence resented the war, Frieda, with her German background, frankly expressed pro-German sentiments, and he was increasingly harassed by the British authorities, who suspected him of spying. To make their difficulties worse, when *The Rainbow* appeared in 1915, its frank sexual theme attracted police attention. It was prosecuted for obscenity at Bow Street Magistrate's Court, and with the publishers' consent all stock copies were destroyed. In this crisis, Lawrence found few defenders; in the climate of wartime censorship, experimental fiction no longer seemed so important, and he had been busy falling out with his Bloomsbury friends. All this went to convince him that the apocalyptic prophecy of the novel – the age was destroying itself by its own violent mechanical deathliness – was justified. 1915 became the year of modern crisis: "In the winter of 1915–16, the spirit of old London collapsed," he later wrote in *Kangaroo*. "The city, in some way, perished, perished from being the heart of the world, and became a vortex of broken passions, lusts, hopes, fears, and horrors." England was finished, Europe was destroying itself, and, like many others at the time, he looked to America to escape the horrors that were happening. But the America he had in mind was not that of the other Futurists: indeed the machine-age America they celebrated revolted him. The dream was simpler and more primitive; what he was looking for was a land that had reached "the extremity," a land that beyond its mechanical present had deep prehistoric roots, leading back beyond Anglo-Saxon consciousness to mystery and primal simplicity. America, too, was the land of the utopian spirit, and one aim was to found a utopian colony of like-minded friends, Rananim, in Florida. "America is bad, but at least it has a future," he noted, and applied for a passport. But despite his weak health he was a potential conscript, and it was refused. Trapped for the moment in wartime Britain, he angrily sat down to rework the second part of *The Sisters*, which he first titled *Dies Irae*, and which appeared in 1920 in the USA as *Women in Love* – a work of modern historical despair, about the deathly power of the modern machine. And it was now, feeling "unable to write of England any more," that he turned his thoughts onto the classic American writers, and in 1917, as America entered the war, he produced thirteen vivid critical essays on the classic figures, Cooper, Whitman, Melville and others, publishing eight of them in the *English Review*. As soon as the Armistice was signed the following year, he left what he called "the coffin of England" for an angry exile that would last the rest of his days. He was not an expatriate, but a driven exile, and his journey was, he felt, emblematic. He was fleeing a dead land in search of a resurrection, a new aboriginality, looking for the primitive, the uncreated flux, the new skin, the pure self, the "savage god." From this point onward, everything he wrote had as its central term "crisis." The long quest that followed – his "savage pilgrimage" – had no certain destination, though it was certainly away from the modern machine age. But it was, it seemed, obscurely drawn toward America.

The Lawrences went first to Italy, where he revised his American essays again in the light of his changing vision. They would be revised a third time before they at last appeared, in the United States in 1922, by which time his own journey had brought him to the continent. To this day, Lawrence's *Studies in Classic American Literature* remains a remarkable book, for several different reasons. For one thing, it could be seen as an unusual opening foray in the new remythification of American literature. For, during the Twenties, as American writing grew in experimental and artistic confidence, its writers and critics began hunting a new usable past. This meant looking beyond the old "genteel tradition" of Irving, Bryant, Lowell and Longfellow, to writers of greater obscurity, and outside the Anglo-Saxon tradition too. And these were much the writers Lawrence looked to to shape his own tradition, Crèvecoeur and Franklin, Poe and Hawthorne, Dana, Melville and Whitman, writers for whom the making of American meaning out of white European roots had been a violent struggle, a battle of consciousness, just like Lawrence's own. Like him, they fought not to master the Anglo-Saxon tradition but to break free, writers of a "masterless race," reaching beyond culture to nature, reason to instinct, white experience to a great decomposition. This struggle constituted their modernity and their "extremity": "Two bodies of modern literature seem to me to have come to a real verge: the Russian and the American," he noted. "The furthest frenzies of French modernism or futurism have not yet reached the pitch of extreme consciousness that Poe, Melville, Hawthorne, Whitman reached. The European modernists are all *trying* to be extreme. The great Americans I mention just were it. Which is why the world has funked them, and funks them today." Lawrence's "classic American literature" is thus, at the least, powerful and original, and what he had to say would soon be echoed by American critics who also saw the task of the modern writer as a great breaking free. But Lawrence's essays were also in the deepest sense prophetic: the usable past he was seeking was a past for himself and his own revolution of consciousness. The path down which they pointed was toward the ancient dream of an innocent, savage, pre-historical America, a world that lay beyond reason and before Western consciousness. "Doom! Doom! Doom!" he cries in the later, most apocalyptic pages of his study of the writers of the masterless race. "Doom of our white day . . . And the doom is in America."[30] White American experience, Lawrence felt, had already sunk with the *Pequod*,

[30] D. H. Lawrence, *Studies in Classic American Literature* (New York, 1923; London, 1924). The early versions of the essays are mostly to be found in Armin Arnold (ed.), *The Symbolic Meaning: The Uncollected Versions of 'Studies in Classic American Literature'* (New York, Centaur Press, 1962).

something in the American mind ever moved back toward its founding aboriginality in the pure Indian, who represented true America. In modern form, he reverted to an old European myth – the dream of America as the primitive alternative to European civilization, an idea that, as he says, had been in the European mind from the sixteenth century on.

But Lawrence's aboriginal dream would not have reached the strange fulfilment it did had it not been for intervention from a most unexpected source. In 1917, Mabel Dodge, Modernism's representative in Manhattan, had also begun to grow weary of the Western soul. Assisted by the fashionable science of psychoanalysis (she reported hers voluminously in the American press), she also was hungry for the vitalism that would restore the primitive soul to a mechanical age. Armed with some books on the Aztecs that were given her by a fellow analysand (none other than Leo Stein), and assured by an occultist it was her unique destiny to bring white and Indian races together, she set out for New Mexico. Purchasing twelve acres of meadowland round the beautiful adobe town of Taos, she built a great hacienda (Los Gallos), acquired a Tiwa Indian lover, Antonio Luhan, and began to tempt out a fair number of former residents from Greenwich Village. Her instincts were not amiss; all this had very considerable consequences for the spirit of modernist American culture, which acquired an important Western dimension (thus one of those drawn to Taos was Georgia O'Keeffe).[31] But what Taos seemed to lack was the vitalistic writer to explore its deeper Indian spirit. When, though, Dodge read in 1921 Lawrence's remarkable, vivid study *Sea and Sardinia*, the answer seemed obvious. She wrote straightway to Lawrence in Sicily, inviting him to take an adobe house on the property. At first he was far from tempted. He disliked the thought of joining what he called an "arty" colony; in any case for the moment the quest for aboriginality pointed not westward but eastward. Lawrence was always careful about his spiritual geography, scrupulously hunting his own frontiers of culture and consciousness. "You've got to go all round the world, and then halfway round again, until you get back," he wrote in *Kangaroo* (1923), the book that came from the next phase of his pilgrimage, which took him onward to Ceylon and then Australia.

[31] The "Mabel Dodge Luhan House" is now a national and state landmark and a hotel. Smoking is not permitted in the bedrooms.

However Mrs Dodge was a woman not used to being denied. In any case the Lawrences were poor and increasingly dependent on the kindness of strangers. When he expressed his doubts, Mrs Dodge set to work, she tells us, to "will" him to Taos – sinking into the core of her being and trying to merge with the core of Lawrence (she got Luhan to use Indian powers to do the same). It was all, she said, an impulse of the evolutionary will, "apart from me, using me for its own purpose." Despite the chthonic energies put to work, the coming was a slow process. As Mrs Dodge tried to tug him west, Lawrence went ever east. But, as he began to suspect, he was approaching America by indirection, choosing to come circuitously – "from the West, over the Pacific," as he put it – and so avoiding the eastern urban states of "future America," which he condemned. Finally, though, on 11 September 1922, his thirty-seventh birthday, Lawrence and Frieda landed in San Francisco, critically inspected California, and then took the train to New Mexico. Mabel was all ready and waiting: "The womb in me roused to reach out and take him," she frankly explained. So Lawrence arrived in Taos, or as he called it "Mabeltown," and the turbulences, passional struggles of will, confusions and absurdities that now followed would outlast his life, and consume many acres of print. No doubt partly because of the bodily presence of sturdy Frieda, the precious blood intimacy Mabel foresaw did not transpire. Nor did she gratify her ambition that Lawrence – "Lorenzo," she named him – should immortalize her in a book. The great tale soon reached Paris (these days *avant-garde* news travelled fast): "Is she completely mired in D. Lawrence who it seems does *not* want to put her in a book?" Gertrude Stein, no longer a Dodge admirer, enquired of a friend. But, despite, perhaps even because of, the enormous soul struggles that ensued, the Lawrences remained in or around Taos – mostly at a safe distance, up at ranches in the mountains – on and off for the next three years. In fact they would acquire a property there; Frieda eventually exchanged the manuscript of *Sons and Lovers* for Mabel's Kiowa Ranch, up in the mountains fifteen miles north of Taos, which became a central place in both their lives. "Taos, in its way, is rather thrilling," Lawrence was soon reporting back to Britain in his letters. "We have got a very pretty adobe house, with furniture made in the village . . . It stands on the edge of the Indian reservation . . . I have already learned to ride one of these Indian ponies . . ." In the story *Saint Mawr* he notes: "Ah: it was beauty, beauty absolute, at any hour of the day," and elsewhere he calls it "the greatest experience from the outside world I have ever had."

In fact from the moment of arrival Lawrence's mythic America began: "The moment I saw the brilliant, proud morning sun shine high over the deserts of Santa Fé, something stood still in my soul, and I started to attend."[32] What drew him, he said, was not tourist New Mexico, "the picturesque reservation and playground of the eastern states, very romantic, old Spanish, Red Indian," rather "the fierce, proud silence of the Rockies" and "the roots of the old human consciousness" he sensed round him. Here in the desert and the Indian lands he began to find the savage god somehow even the Orient had failed to yield him. "I had no permanent feeling of religion till I came to New Mexico and penetrated into the old human race-experience there," he wrote in the essay "New Mexico" (1928; reprinted in *Phoenix*, 1936). He came to think – he revised his essays on American writers to fit – he was somehow re-experiencing the great Columbian encounter, which brought white and Indian together on the deep continent in a common mystery of self-cancellation. He even started to acknowledge a metaphoric Indian ancestry ("these old men telling the tribal tale were my fathers. I have a dark-faced, bronze-voiced father far back in the resinous ages. My mother was no virgin. She lay in her hour with this dusky-lipped tribe-father," he wrote in "Indians and an Englishman," 1922). But it was not enough; the trail of the dark gods pointed deeper and further on. In 1923 he moved for a time to Mexico, touring with Witter Bynner, then renting a house in Chapala. Mexico was a far more ambiguous land, corrupted by its Cortezian history, the arrogance of the Spanish settlers, peasant socialism, increasing American intervention. Yet beyond the chaotic, destructive, revolutionary politics of the time, which Malcolm Lowry would revisit in *Under the Volcano* (1947), Lawrence sensed deeper, more compelling myths. He was fascinated by the mysterious fate of the Aztecs and Toltecs, the primal encounter of Spaniard and Indian, the idea of a

---

[32] Mabel Dodge Luhan's account of this whole complicated and much disputed episode is given in her *Lorenzo in Taos* (New York, 1932; London, 1953; New York, 1957). Also see her autobiography, cited above. Witter Bynner, *Journey With Genius: Recollections and Reflections Concerning the D. H. Lawrences* (New York, 1951), also deals with the Lawrences in New Mexico and Mexico.

deeper politics of consciousness, and a resurrected religion that dealt with sex, disintegration and death as well as regeneration.

It all went into two of his most remarkable books: the essays of *Mornings in Mexico* (1927), above all his Mexican novel, originally titled *Quetzalcoatl*, published as *The Plumed Serpent* (1926). It remains one of his strangest, least studied novels, the one of which he was proudest, the book where, like some American writers before him, he explored the paradox of the great American encounter of races: "Was it really the great melting pot, where men from the creative continents were smelted back again, not to a new creation, but down to the homogeneity of death?" From its striking opening at a barbaric bullfight, in a time of political disorder, it sees Mexico as a dark, death-heavy and destructive land, divided between an embittered revolutionary socialism, American capitalism and exploitation, and "black Mexican fatality." The whites have had a soul but have lost it; the Indians are empty, "centreless." It's a land of mixed bloods, tired history, failed racial mergings, as America as a whole is the great continent of undoings, its vital energies corrupted, its instincts deathly. So the central characters of the book must face "the dark negation of the continent," and generate a new religion and philosophy. The quest goes into deep dark places beneath modern civilization, and the brilliant opening sections, recording Kate Leslie's journey toward the lake of Quetzalcoatl, are filled with Lawrence's profound, tense awareness of place and of the power, expressive strangeness, and random danger of the landscape. Here is some of Lawrence's finest writing. What follows, the ritualistic, operatic passages about the making of a new religion (Lawrence invented it himself), founded by the old Indian gods, set aside by Christianity, and now reborn in its death, is heavy, but a key part of his larger quest to define, in a new age of apocalypse and a new spirit of religiosity, a revived manhood and womanhood. As in the two previous novels, *Aaron's Rod* and *Kangaroo*, there is an age of disorder and foolish revolutions from which a new psycho-politics of salvation must be sought, meaning a new cult of the leader. In the novel, Lawrence grants Mexico its new Quetzalcoatl religion, and leaves Kate struggling between her Europe-facing individuality and her search for the spiritual, sexual, dangerous Morning Star.

Kate's struggle at the close of the book – between Europe or Mexico, familiarity or danger, the white self and the Indian self – was being enacted in the lives of the Lawrences themselves. As he finished the first draft of the book, in August 1923, they went off to New York, intending to sail home to England. But at the last moment they quarrelled and Lawrence refused the journey, unwisely leaving Frieda to sail home alone. While she grew involved, sexually and otherwise, with old friends, he returned to California and Mexico, until, responding to her warning summons, he went to London at the end of the year. Hating it as much as ever, he tried to rally his friends in founding "Rananim," now located in Taos. In the event only one friend, Dorothy Brett, joined them on the *Aquitania* when they returned in 1924. This was when they acquired their property, the 160-acre Kiowa Ranch, up at 8,600 feet on the Lobo Mountain, and set to work rebuilding it. But Lawrence was pining to return to Mexico to undertake a major revision of his novel and some new stories. First in Mexico City, then in Oaxaca, he set to work. In the novel he had left his heroine, the widow Kate Leslie, in Mexico, facing the savage god and her ultimate choice of identity and place. Similar themes, relating sensual self-discovery, death and regeneration, guide other remarkable stories from this time – *Saint Mawr*, "The Princess," "The Woman Who Rode Away" (all 1925), the uncompleted novel *The Flying Fish* (published in *Phoenix*) – where encounter with Indian or Mexican origins offers a dangerous, dark renewal through destruction. As he finished the last pages of his revised novel, a major crisis developed. He fell seriously ill with malarial fever and dysentery; his tuberculosis also revived. Like Cora Crane before her, Frieda now had a terrible struggle to take a sick man to safety, back to the Lawrence ranch. Lawrence himself was to acknowledge that Mexico had "done him in," just as his Don Ramón in *The Plumed Serpent* finally recognizes that his goal of leadership and immortality is itself an illusion in the face of death. His adventure with aboriginal, prehistoric America was over. As he said himself: "I feel I never want to see an Indian or an 'aboriginee' or anything in the savage line again."

In September 1925, he was well enough to sail angrily back to Britain ("I don't know what I'm doing on board this ship"). Happily, he had five more years of life to live, mostly spent in further exile, in Germany, Italy, Switzerland and France. The American experience was over, and he began rewriting his new apocalyptic cosmology in European terms – most powerfully in the impassioned text of *Lady Chatterley's Lover* (1928), set back in his native Nottinghamshire, the place from which his journey toward a higher consciousness in a dying historical landscape had begun. Though he sometimes talked of returning, he would never again see Taos in life. On 2 March 1930, he died of tuberculosis at Vence in the South of France. Soon after his death, Frieda married Angelo Ravagli, an Italian army officer who once rented them a house, and the couple moved to the Taos ranch. In 1935 Ravagli went to Vence, arranged for Lawrence's remains to be disinterred and cremated, and brought them (with a small mishap at the railroad station at Lamy, where they were briefly forgotten) to the Kiowa Ranch, where they were to be placed in a small chapel built for the purpose. But an old battle of wills continued. In 1932 Mabel Dodge Luhan (she had now married her Indian) had published her memoir *Lorenzo in Taos*, a vivid appropriation of Lawrence into her life and spiritual and sexual mythologizing. Sure Lawrence had always belonged not to Frieda but to her, she tried to remove the ashes; Frieda reacted by cementing them into the altar, the "Lawrence shrine," with its famous symbol of the phoenix (which also resembled a plumed serpent). They are there still, with Frieda's own tomb in front, on what is now the "Lawrence Ranch," used by the University of New Mexico as a writers' retreat. So are some of Lawrence's "phallic paintings" from his late years, which can be seen for a dollar in the office of the Hotel La Fonda in the square of this pleasant, still artist-heavy adobe town, with its nearby Indian reservation. The gossip about Frieda and Angelo, Brett and Mabel, continues. Strangely, it was and is in Taos, where he met and was perhaps defeated by his dark gods, that the complex legend of Lawrence lasts most vividly – and not, at least until lately, in Eastwood, in the Nottinghamshire mining countryside where, back in 1885, the great pilgrimage toward the transatlantic savage god first started.

9.

Meantime, as Lawrence made his difficult, symbolic journey westward through the East, to escape from the coffin of old Europe and find the resurrectional grave of the dark Indian gods, a whole new generation of young American writers, no less anxious about the mechanical age of the modern, were making their way eastward, where Stein was still working and presiding over the spirit of the new. Writing in the wake of a war that, for them too, had turned the idea of modernity from hope to crisis, and a time when the progressive and *avant-garde* excitements of the pre-war years felt threatened by the commercial age of Harding and Coolidge, they too had their doubts about the "future America" that excited so many in the world. For some of them, modern America was indeed the wild, expressionist excitement of high-rise buildings, gleaming Ford cars on new asphalt highways, bobbed hair, telephones, ice-boxes, and the thrill of a jazz age when nearly every aspect of American life-style seemed in change. But others, like Sherwood Anderson, Hemingway, Faulkner, were writing of an America where the age of city and machine was shattering an older American pastoral and corrupting an earlier dream. Anderson, reacting against the age of "mechanical men," picked up on Stein's "new method of composition," but also on Lawrence's impassioned vitalism; Fitzgerald, in *The Great Gatsby* (1925), depicted the vivid excitements of a Twenties urban America of rushing cars, speeding highways, the World Series, but saw it all under the surveillance of the dulled and sightless eyes of Dr T. J. Eckleburg, whose advertising image gazes blankly over the ash-heaps of modern life. Anderson looked at the "dark laughter" of a deeper presence that mocked the mechanization of contemporary American life, Hemingway turned his exiled attention to the vital primitivism of the bullfight and the lion-hunt; Faulkner explored the curse of possession, time, slaughter and mechanization that had blighted his South, the wonderful green wilderness that had once been an Indian myth. America took care of the future of the machine and business world; but the world of the conscience, of consciousness and the unconscious, had to be sought elsewhere.

Today it seems plain that Stein, with her "new composition," and Lawrence, with his resentment of "future America" and desire to penetrate down to a dark pre-Columbian consciousness, represent two versions – the Eastern and the Western, the cubist and the vitalistic, we might say – of the great quest for the Modern. And, for the writers who followed them a generation on, both traditions had relevance. This generation belonged to the second life of the modern movement, a time when the old maps of power and culture had gone, the world had been modernized, America become dominant. The entire spirit of transatlantic consciousness was shifting. As European writers like Cocteau and Gide, Lowry, Huxley and Waugh wrote of an age of European collapse, and looked anxiously and curiously toward America, the land of mechanism which just might carry in its soul and spirit some useful heritage, American writers looked about them too. From the land of the

Red Scare and the Volstead Act, booming commercial enterprise and fading experimental hopes, they hunted their own alternatives, some, like Dodge or Willa Cather, in the primitive simplicity and pre-Columbian heritage of the old Southwest, or, like Faulkner and the Southern Agrarians, the Old South, while others turned again to Europe. What they found was a war-battered place of political disaster and economic crisis, but one where the new day of the modern was felt. In Paris, especially, the franc was low, the drinks were cheap and alcoholic, and there was Stein's cubist prose, Proust's flowing consciousness, Tzara's Dada, Breton's Surrealism, Joyce's revolution of the word. America was modern, Paris was Modernism. America was the Bon Ton store and Main Street, the assembly line and the Manhattan skyline; Europe was the foggy rain of London or the cafés of Montparnasse, where, in a different world, the artistic spirit survived. These writers lacked Stein's high self-confidence, her optimistic belief in great American prospects, and felt a pervasive sense of historical despair, a distrust of the land of business, boosters and Babbittry. But, under the Cézannes and Picassos, Stein was waiting. Modern writers, she explained to them, needed two countries, their own and a country of art; for the moment at least, Modernism meant nothing less than artistic exile. Or, as she put it later, when the whole self-exiling tradition became so famous it *was* modern art: "Of course they came to France a great many to paint pictures and naturally they could not do that at home, or write they could not do that at home either, they could be dentists at home . . ."

EIGHT

A Generation Lost and Found:
Hemingway, Fitzgerald and the Paris of the Twenties

I.

The great crisis of Ernest Hemingway's young life came suddenly, around midnight on 8 July 1918, three weeks before his nineteenth birthday. A non-combatant ambulance driver serving under the command of the Italian army, he was stationed at Schio in the Dolomites, supporting troops and bringing in the wounded. But, impatient to see more action, he asked for a more dangerous assignment, and got himself moved to Fossalta, on the River Piave, not too far from Venice, closer to the front. "I was an awful dope when we went to the last war," he observed later, when the Second World War of the century was under way, "I can remember just thinking that we were the home team and the Austrians were the visiting team." On the night of 8 July, probably against orders, he went out to distribute cigarettes and chocolates to troops dug in ahead of the front line. An Austrian mortar shell landed in the trench, killing and wounding the Italian soldiers around him, and injuring him seriously with fragments. Attempting to carry an Italian soldier to safety, he was hit yet again, by machine-gun fire which caught him in the legs. "There was one of those big noises you sometimes hear at the front," he was to explain, "I died then. I felt my soul or something coming right out of my body, like you'd pull a silk handkerchief out of the pocket by one corner. It flew all around and then came back and went in again and I wasn't dead any more." Badly injured in the legs and lower body, he was treated first in a field hospital, then moved for surgery back to the brand-new American Red Cross Hospital in Milan. There were eighteen nurses for four patients, and as he slowly recovered he fell in love with one of them, a twenty-six-year-old American girl called Agnes von Kurowsky. Meantime the fame of his actions spread. He was, as it happened, the first American to be wounded in Italy. So he was hailed as a hero, and awarded an Italian Silver Cross for his courage. The American press made much of the story, especially in his home city of Chicago. Hemingway laid claim to 227 scars, and much enjoyed his celebrity. He had excellent reason; he had been tested, shown courage, survived, and somehow become himself.

On war and wounds Hemingway would become the great expert, while the moment of wounding remained perhaps the most important one event of his life. He felt it was his real initiation into life and death; and throughout his career he would always be the novelist of great initiations, the person who got there first. As time went by and his "true sentences" flowed, his wound became the most famous since Philoctetes', his red badge the reddest since Henry Fleming's. It was an emblem of solitary heroism, existential crisis, the brutal violating energy of the modern. It proclaimed the danger he had faced, the risks he had taken, the courage he had shown, the sense of disaster he'd felt. It dislocated him from his past values, robbed him of naïve American innocence, introduced him to death and then, right after, love, in other words made him Hemingway. And it also turned him into a writer of modern, very modern, fiction – a writer with a distinctive hard style, for whom war and battle, or something closely resembling them (the bullfight, the game hunt, the boxing match, the fishing contest) became the stark settings of life and literature, testing places of courage and cowardice, being and nothingness, survival and despair. His novels and stories constantly returned to these themes: wound, hospital, death, endurance, loneliness, *nada*, and the need for man to find in life the few things you cannot lose. All this shaped the distinctive spirit of his most famous novel, *A Farewell to Arms* (1929), which, ten years afterward, tells much this same story: of a young man wounded on the Italian front, a tragic love affair, a disastrous military retreat, and the Wilsonian "separate peace" the hero finally makes with the world, war, love and loneliness. To the end this remained the essence of his sensibility, a key reason for his highly distinctive vision, his choice of subject, even his famous style. In the late novel *Across the River and Into the Trees* (1950), based on a later return to Italy, the battered hero Colonel Robert Cantwell can still only love "people . . . who had fought or been mutilated."

This central part of his life began only two months earlier, in May 1918, just over a year from the day President Wilson committed

American troops to the European conflict to "make the world safe for democracy." Born in Oak Park, Illinois, a Chicago suburb, on 21 July 1899, son of a doctor father and a religious mother, Hemingway had had a comfortable bourgeois existence, and scarcely left the Midwest. Now eighteen, he was a cub reporter learning the journalist's trade on the *Kansas City Star*, one of the best American newspapers. But, like many of the young generation of promising writers, he wanted to get over to Europe and see military action, and he took the train to New York to enlist. The army rejected him because of an eye-defect, but he knew there were other ways to war. An item on his news-desk explained the demand for American Red Cross volunteers to work with the Allied armies. Various ambulance service brigades had formed, some – like the Norton-Harjes Ambulance Corps, which had Harvard/Cambridge connections, and Henry James as patron – with a strong literary or university spirit. A generation of Harvard Aesthetes, including John Dos Passos, E. E. Cummings (later e.e. cummings), Robert Hillyer and William Slater Brown, some newly in print in *Eight Harvard Poets* (1917), had already gone off to see the action. Some were pacifists, others progressives opposed to American intervention in a far-off European war. No matter; the claims of Europe beckoned. Cummings – who landed in a French army prison when he incautiously reported in letters on the French mutinies, the tale he vividly recorded in his experimental novel *The Enormous Room* (1922) – said he wanted "to do something useful and see France at the same time." Dos Passos, a pacifist who ended up serving in the army medical corps, explained: "It was my university, World War I." Others like Malcolm Cowley, Edmund Wilson, Robert Hillyer, Harry Crosby and Dashiell Hammett, who also went to the European battlefields to do ambulance work, came to see this as the formative experience of their lives. As Cummings put it: "World War I was the experience of my generation."

Of all the modern wars, the Great War was a remarkably literary battlefield. From the outbreak of European hostilities in August 1914, youthful poets and writers on both sides had gone to the front with their odes or notebooks, hoping at first to celebrate patriotism, courage, sacrifice, cleansing violence. Many died in its muddy trenches, or came back gassed, wounded or shell-shocked, now often less at war with the enemy than the follies of the old men of their own side who had created the crisis that was killing the young people of Europe and destroying their own dynasties. Their poetry, memoirs and fiction recorded the crisis, the disillusion, the accumulation of horror, the fragmentation of vision. By the time America entered in 1917, the note of disillusion was struck – in the poems of Wilfred Owen, or the fiction of Henri Barbusse, author of *Le Feu* (1916), a tale of the grim experiences of ordinary French soldiery in the trenches, perhaps the most influential novel of wartime. Dos Passos read the English translation (*Under Fire: The Story of a Squad*, 1917) before going to France, Hemingway's Lieutenant Henry in *A Farewell to Arms* reads it when convalescing (like his author) in Milan. Yet Americans still went with some of the same expectations as their predecessors, indeed often with an added note of American high idealism.

For this reason or that, most of the major American writers of the mid-nineteenth century – Hawthorne, Melville, James, Twain, Howells – had missed the Civil War, and hence the literary accountancy of the war's sensations and its psychic and social impact was strikingly thin. This time it was different. A significant number of the young writers of the day attended it, the crisis was directly felt, most of the best writing they produced in the next years was deeply haunted by it. Many reached the battlefields, as combatants or ambulance drivers. Even Gertrude Stein had her own wayward ambulance, "Auntie," while Mildred Aldrich tended the soldiers on the Marne. Others came very close. Scott Fitzgerald trained as an army officer, and was about to ship to France when the Armistice was signed: "I was certain that all the young people were going to be killed in the war, and I wanted to put on paper a record of the strange life they had lived in their time" – so he explained the spirit of his first novel, *This Side of Paradise* (1920), which made him spokesman of his times. Though he trained as an airman with the Royal Canadian Air Force, William Faulkner too did not cross the Atlantic. But he would long pretend he served in France, and his early novels were filled with returning wounded veterans, battered, like their Confederate predecessors, by a historical knowledge not shared by their innocent contemporaries. In one way or another, many of the writers soon to dominate the Twenties first encountered Europe, experience, death and the crisis of modern history over the two-year American involvement, or the disillusioning sequence of events to follow: the contested Versailles Treaty, the failure of the dream of a new peaceable "League of Nations," the withdrawal of the USA into isolationism and "normalcy." Unlike many of them, Hemingway had not been to college, was certainly no pacifist, and was not outraged by the war (though later he covered as a journalist the Lausanne Peace Settlement and was a critical witness to the rise of Italian fascism and militarism, and *A Farewell to Arms* does end in a critical, disillusioned "separate peace"). Like Stephen Crane, or for that matter Teddy Roosevelt, he longed to join the action, face the danger, experience the "real thing," and discover his own bravery or cowardice.

Rejected by the army, he now enlisted as a Second Lieutenant in the American Red Cross Ambulance Service, and was at once shipped with his contingent to France. When he arrived in Paris in June 1918 (later than most) the war was entering its final uncertain phase. Ludendorff's great March offensive had driven a wedge between British and French forces, and brought the German armies close to Paris, threatening Allied defeat. The city was under shelling from the German guns ("Big Berthas") at Château-Thierry; staying at a hotel near the Madeleine with his contingent, Hemingway excitedly hired taxis to go and survey the damage. The city was nervous and nearly empty, though, in his cork-lined room on the Boulevard Haussmann, Marcel Proust continued to write of the *belle-époque* world now in collapse. Other American servicemen and ambulance men were able to see France as a double experience: a place of mud, trenches, defeated soldiers and the grotesque horrors of war, but also art galleries, cathedrals, the Ballets Nègres, the Ballets Russes. Hemingway's first visit to Paris lasted only a few days. In early June, as Pershing's armies counter-attacked and the war turned, his unit was relieved from London and shipped to Milan and the Italian front (here he briefly met up with Dos Passos). On this front too the outcome was still uncertain, and the Austrians engaged in a strong summer counter-offensive. Though not a combatant, Hemingway behaved like one; it was to be entirely appropriate that in *A Farewell to Arms* he made his hero-surrogate Lieutenant Henry an American obscurely and bravely serving with the Italian army over the previous grim summer, when the Italians retreated from Caporetto. Stationed at Fossalta, he drove ambulances, messed with Italian officers, and identified with the fighting troops, growing fascinated by the lie of the terrain, the daily action, the names of weapons and regiments, the ironic contrast between life at the front and the ordinary existence that continued just a little way behind the lines.

It was this contrast that struck him when, seriously wounded, he went through surgery and convalescence in a Milan that was a city of women, parties, society, cafés, pleasures. But the war was never far off, and men constantly left to go to it. Milan and Turin both saw protest riots; there was a general feeling the war was becoming a stalemate, the army demoralized, the prospects of victory evaporating by the day. His wounds healed, Hemingway hurried back to the front, only to be immediately hospitalized again, this time with the more commonplace affliction of jaundice. By the time he had recovered the armistice between Austria and Italy had been signed. With the hostilities over, he lingered in Italy for a while longer, to be near Agnes, who was now nursing the victims of the post-war influenza epidemic. But by January 1919 he was back in Oak Park, still limping badly, convalescent from his wounds, and needing more surgery. He had seen action only for the briefest time, always as a non-combatant, and been away for no more than six months. The war was now a world away, and life back home had scarcely changed. But he had. Like his hero Krebs in the story "A Soldier's Home," he felt an alien in his homeland, someone who could no longer see America in the old way; he contrasted its innocence with his experience. He continued to write to Agnes, until she told him she was in love with an Italian lieutenant. He reacted bitterly; the affair was over, "long ago and far away," he now declared, and "in another country."

Even so, in Oak Park and Chicago, the drama of the war improved in the telling. Hemingway went about in an Italian military cape, the wounded veteran and local hero, recounting his story. Always a man of instant legends, he began to claim he had served in the Italian infantry, or even with the unofficial troops of the Arditti. As he admitted later, when his score of adventures, injuries and accidents had mounted, and there was no need to make false claims to toughness, many men were tempted to exaggerate (as Faulkner had too) their wartime role to those at home who did not understand things. But he never forgot the experience; nor do we. He had been seriously wounded, his life had transformed; he was sure he had come to know a world that cut him off from the generations before him. He needed to claim identity with those who confronted ultimate experience – had been to war, been wounded, known love and death in another country, challenged their own existence. Home in middle America, he was restless and at odds with his family, and his mother ominously warned him "there is nothing before you but bankruptcy – you have overdrawn." He wrote short stories, some of them highly exoticized versions of his Italian experience, and began a novel. Back to journalism, he took a great interest in the tough world of gangsters and prizefighting he found in Chicago. Moving impatiently to Canada, he became a correspondent for the *Toronto Star Weekly*. He had met Hadley Richardson, whom he married in September 1921; she had an inheritance, and he now attempted to get himself sent back as a correspondent to Italy.

A meeting with the now distinguished Chicago writer Sherwood Anderson, author of *Winesburg, Ohio* (1919), an experimental volume about small-town midwestern life that owed a plain debt to Stein and Joyce, changed his mind. Anderson, whom he would unmercifully parody (Hemingway was never generous to benefactors) in his book *The Torrents of Spring* (1926), had just taken an exciting trip to Paris with his wife and a fellow writer, Paul Rosenfeld. Through the good offices of the bookseller Sylvia Beach, he had even met and worshipped at the feet of Gertrude Stein. Anderson said Italy was fine for tourists, but, if you wished to establish yourself as a writer, Paris was the place. He spoke of the creative and economic rewards of life in Montparnasse, where art mattered, midwestern limitations were wonderfully lifted, the dollar stood strong, a new mood of experiment was building. He even passed on the address of a hotel (the Hôtel Jacob et de l'Angleterre at 44 Rue Jacob in the Latin Quarter) and gave letters of introduction. One read: "Dear Miss Stein: I am writing this note to make you acquainted with my friend Ernest Hemingway, who with Mrs Hemingway is going to Paris to live, and will ask him to drop it in the mails when he arrives there. Mr Hemingway is an American writer instinctively in touch with anything worthwhile going on here, and I know you will find Mr and Mrs Hemingway delightful people to know." The *Star* gave him an assignment as roving European correspondent. On 8 December 1921 the delightful people sailed from New York for Paris on the *Leopoldina*, by way of a stopover in Vigo, Spain. For a second time, and now in peacetime, the twenty-two-year-old Hemingway arrived in Europe and France – to discover a very different experience from the one he had seen and suffered earlier.[1]

[1] For details of Hemingway's life, see Charles A. Fenton, *The Apprenticeship of Ernest Hemingway* (New York, Mentor; London, Vision Press, 1954); Carlos Baker, *Ernest Hemingway: A Life Story* (New York, Scribner; London, Collins, 1969); and Jeffrey Meyers, *Hemingway: A Biography* (New York and London, Harper and Row, 1985), as well as Carlos Baker (ed.), *Ernest Hemingway: Selected Letters, 1917–1961* (London and New York, Granada, 1981), and William White (ed.), *Ernest Hemingway, By-Line; Selected Articles and Dispatches of Four Decades* (New York, Scribner, 1967).

2.

The Paris the newly-married Hemingways reached over the cold Christmastide of 1921 was a city much changed from the one Stein found in 1903, Wharton in 1907, or Hemingway himself quickly glimpsed in 1918. The wealth that had shored it was weakened, the age of manners that Proust had captured so exactly, was still capturing, had started to fade. The time of the *belle époque*, the banquet years of upper-class leisure and social power, had not died completely (it hasn't to this day), the city held its charm and elegance. But the old style was fading, as Paris underwent a speedy process of internationalization, indeed Americanization. The reason was the destruction of the European dynasties and the European economies by the war, which had completely changed the balance of economic and cultural power. Where their countries, currencies and leaderships were enfeebled, the USA, which had entered the war a debtor nation, emerged as a creditor one, an undamaged great power confident in its modern future. The franc was steadily falling against the apparently ever more almighty dollar; there were eight francs to the dollar in 1919, thirteen and rising by 1922, thirty-five by 1926, and even the British pound was favoured, at around a hundred francs. Things were even cheaper for Americans in Germany and elsewhere, but life grimmer; Paris retained all its cosmopolitan glow and novel cultural excitement. This, though, had much to do with the growing numbers of literary arrivals, the enlarging bands of international artistic wanderers who took Paris, for a time at least, as their natural home, the place where exiles and avant-gardists gathered. The wartime and post-war disorders in Europe and Russia added to their numbers, and enriched and cosmopolitanized the cultural climate. Red revolutionaries were replaced by White Russian *émigrés* from the Bolshevik Revolution; they included a fair number of painters and writers, and most of the company of the Ballets Russes, which became a very French institution (later it moved to America, when Europe's troubles multiplied). Many disaffiliated Britons and Americans, bored by Anglo-Saxon convention, and rightly regarding Paris as a city of freedom and open display of style and sexual tastes, swelled the ranks, adding to the excitement. Paris had certainly not lost its social and cultural appeal, and displaced aristocrats from many lands and strangers with titles of uncertain provenance gave it a stylish and raffish charm, an air of faded glories mingled with radical chic.

And Paris was still the home of artistic experiment and discovery, the "laboratory of ideas," as Ezra Pound, who shifted allegiance from London to Paris in 1920, put it. But the spirit of experiment was now far more international. Cubism and Futurism were almost fading movements, traditions whose methods were taught in the art schools. New writers and painters went further, looking for forms that expressed the harder, sharper, disoriented, psychologically anxious climate of the Twenties. The clearest successor, Dada, was already a cosmopolitan movement. Started in wartime Zürich, and spread onward to Berlin, it had also had an important New York phase, thanks to the wanderings of Picabia and Duchamp and the work of Man Ray. When the peripatetic Cuban-born Francis Picabia ("Art is a pharmaceutical product for morons") returned to France, he encouraged the two transatlantic wings to move to Paris, drawing the Romanian-born Tristan Tzara in from Zürich, and Man Ray from New York. In 1920 Tzara organized the first tumultuous festival of Dada, which upset and excited the entire city. From then on the movement took on a Parisian existence, capturing both the wartime spirit and the anarchic, disillusioned, carnival mood of the post-war years, the spirit of art as anti-art.[2] Dada proved one of several important bridges between the European and the American experimentalists – especially when the sociable Man Ray arrived in Montparnasse in July 1921, expecting to win fame as a Dadaist artist, though in the end to develop a greater career as a modern photographer.[3] Meantime, advancing the spirit of the recently dead Apollinaire, André Breton, Philippe Soupault and Louis Aragon founded their magazine *Littérature*, and Surrealism was born. Dada and Surrealism were sometimes kin to each other, sometimes enemies. By 1924, when the first manifesto of Surrealism, organized by Breton, formalized many of the "unconscious" principles

[2] There are many accounts of Dada's history, but the usual view is that it was born at the Café Voltaire in Zürich in 1916, when the twenty-year-old poet Tristan Tzara christened it as follows: "Dada is not a literary school. An Anonymous Society for the Exploitation of Ideas, Dada has 391 different attitudes and colours according to the sex of the president. It transforms itself – affirms – at the same time contradicts – without any importance – cries – goes fishing. Dada is the chameleon of rapid and interested change, Dada is opposed to the future, Dada is dead." Picabia was, though, associated with the tendency, and the term gradually became used to explain the activities of his and Duchamp's circle in New York. Picabia returned to Paris and in 1920 encouraged Tzara to come there. Thereafter, argumentatively fought over by André Breton and Jean Cocteau, it became a Parisian movement.

[3] See Man Ray, *Self-Portrait* (London, André Deutsch, 1963).

of the whole tendency, it was clear post-war France could lay claim to a powerful new movement that expressed the sense of crisis, the hunger for inwardness, the fascination of the unconscious, the feeling of displacement, the need for new psychic transaction, that drove the arts – painting, writing, photography, film – onward.

Soon, as one dramatic event followed another, in endless artistic spectacle, the post-war years in Paris acquired a distinctive atmosphere of high and volatile excitement. Major French (and non-French) writers and painters – Breton, Aragon, Paul Claudel, Paul Valéry, André Gide, Jean Cocteau, Miró, Léger, Giacometti - were experimenting with new forms, genres, public manifestations. Each day saw a new happening, as Paris again became a crucible of experiment – a place of manifestos, wild exhibitions, Surrealist public outrages which halted traffic with parades asking, "Do you want to slap a corpse?" As the ever-flamboyant Cocteau, controversially placed between the two often hostile campaigns of Dada and Surrealism, later reflected: "France between 1914 and 1924 presents the spectacle of an incredible literary revolution." Cocteau himself had been the inventor, along with Diaghilev, Satie and Picasso, of the ballet *Parade*; now with Darius Milhaud he developed the masked spectacle-concert *Le Boeuf Sur Le Toit* (1920) and its successor *Les Mariés de la Tour Eiffel* (1921), which both showed new evidence of the animating fascination with things American that now flavoured much of the *avant-garde* activity. Hence the pantomime fantasy *Le Boeuf Sur Le Toit* (which quickly gave its name to a fashionable new café-bar ever popular with American visitors) was fashionably set in the United States under its new *régime sec*, Prohibition. Milhaud went on to write a jazz opera, *The Creation of the World* (1923), using a black Adam and Eve. It was no surprise that visiting American critics like Edmund Wilson and Ezra Pound became warm admirers of the jazz-based modern music of "Les Six" or the "skyscraper" fantasies of the multi-talented, ever unreliable Cocteau. Indeed in February 1922 Wilson, just back from Paris, wrote a *Vanity Fair* article, "The Aesthetic Upheaval in France: The Influence of Jazz in Paris and the Americanization of French Literature and Art," which saw Cocteau's work as one of many signs that American feeling and influence was now imbuing French experiment.[4] Meantime Picasso's

---

[4] This climate was reported on by Margaret Anderson, editor of the Chicago *Little Review*, which published Joyce and duly moved to Paris, in her *My Thirty Years' War: An Autobiography* (New York and London, Knopf, 1930): "The Swedish Ballet gave nightly

paintings were showing ever-stronger American effects; so were Picabia's, Miró's, Braque's, Léger's. Skyscrapers *à l'américaine* peeked out from the backdrop of Cubist and Art Deco paintings. There was a vogue for American jazz and ragtime, American film (and film-stars), American entertainers, American books (one reason why Sylvia Beach started her bookstore Shakespeare and Company in the city), American aviators, culminating in the high excitement of Lindbergh's transatlantic flight to Paris in 1927.

So, as the wealthy American patrons increasingly came to Paris for the style and the chic, as American *Vogue* spawned Parisian *Vogue* and tastes began to merge, it grew plain American styles were becoming more and more acceptable to the French, who in turn gave them their own invaluable stylistic imprimatur. Miss Stein, it seemed, had been right all along: the two countries that instinctively shared in common a love of the modern and a gift for creating it were America and France. There were many different reasons for the Americanization that changed the feel and the very look of Paris over the fast-moving years of the Twenties (and, not without resentment on the part of many French intellectuals and traditionalists, does to this day). The presence of many American troops in wartime had intensified interest in things transatlantic: from *bals nègres* to ragtime, the skyscraper to the automobile, Chaplin movies to the smart culture of the "cocktail." Then the Versailles conference of 1919, where Woodrow Wilson unveiled his Fourteen Points, proposing a great new federation or league of nations, made clear the decisive facts of new American power and hegemony – though Clemenceau had his doubts ("God gave us the Ten Commandments, and we broke them. Wilson gives us the Fourteen Points. We will see," he remarked). The conference itself

galas in the Théâtre des Champs Elysées. Jean Cocteau's *Les Mariés de la Tour Eiffel* was given for the first time, with costumes by Jean Victor Hugo. Groups of insurgent artists prayed for scandal, hissing, booing, blowing on keys . . . Stravinsky gave his *Noces* with the Ballets Russes, Milhaud, Auric, Poulenc and Marcelle Meyer played the four pianos . . . The Ballets Russes had a new curtain by Picasso . . . James Joyce was discovered at all the symphony concerts, no matter how bad. Juan Gris was making beautiful dolls. Gertrude Stein was buying André Masson. Man Ray was photographing pins and combs, sieves and shoe-trees. Fernand Léger was beginning his cubist cinema, Ballet Mécanique, with music by George Antheil. The Boeuf Sur le Toit had a negro saxophonist, and Milhaud and Jean Wiener were beginning their worship of American jazz . . . The Dadaists gave performances at the Théâtre Michel where the rioting was so successful that André Breton broke Tzara's arm. Ezra Pound made an opera of Villon's poetry and had it sung at the old Salle Pleyel . . ."

brought a good many American writers, some of them reporters like Lincoln Steffens, into the city. These were to prove the early ripples of a new American wave that would swell vastly over the coming years. If Americans needed the artistic relief of Europe – and how *were* you going to keep them down on the farm now that they'd seen Paris? – the French saw the stylistic interest as well as the inevitability of the Americanization of European life and culture. One of those who returned in 1919 was John Dos Passos, who sensed a great historical hope in the air – only to be dashed before the work of the conference was done. In his vast modernist trilogy *USA* (1930–6), 1919 and the events of the Paris settlement become the cusp of modern history: a moment of crisis, disappointment, the collapse of American idealism and revolutionary hope. But for now, as he noted, Paris offered the high point of millennial excitement: "Any spring is a time of overrun, but then Lenin was alive, the Seattle general strike seemed the beginning of the flood instead of the beginning of the ebb, Americans in Paris were groggy with theatre and painting and music; Picasso was to rebuild the eye, Stravinsky was cramming the Russian steppes into our ears, currents of energy seemed to be breaking out everywhere as young guys climbed out of their uniforms, imperial America was all shiny with the new idea of the Ritz, in every direction the countries of the world stretched out starving and angry, ready for anything turbulent and new . . ."

Even the mood of disillusioned radicalism he expresses was another, more ironic cause of the Americanization of Twenties Paris. The truth was that by 1919 America was already moving in a different direction – away from internationalism, progressivism, Wilsonian idealism, toward what Wilson's presidental successor of 1920, Warren Harding, dubbed "normalcy" (the times called "not for heroics but healing; not nostrums but normalcy; not revolution but restoration," he said). 1919, in America a year of slump, saw the Red Scare, the passage of the Volstead Act ("Prohibition"), and new immigration restriction, which some called "Anglo-conformity." As Paris grew more radical, America appeared to turn more conservative. Experimental, revolutionary, progressive times seemed over, and, as President Calvin Coolidge, who succeeded Harding as President in 1924, was to say, the business of America was business. If you were an artist, a would-be artist, a sexual or political radical, or any kind of youthful free spirit, then the wonderful pre-war surge of excitement that had grown in ideas, style and the arts was now under challenge in "puritan" America – which, once its post-war depression was over, was fast becoming a modernizing nation most notable for its commercial and consumer invention. The age was dominated by devices and machines that fascinated wondering Europeans, for whom all this – the automobile and the airplane, the radio set and the movie-theatre, the telephone, the icebox, the electric cooker, the well-advertised, time-saving, life-freeing consumer durables of an age that had transformed the nation from producer to consumer economy – was the very stuff of the modern. American *mores* too were changing; this was the era of the flapper and the "It" girl, petting and dating, jazz and popular sports, bobbed hair, boom and surging share prices. There was really no doubt that America was in speedy alteration, indeed that many of its historic ideas and cultural attitudes were quickly slipping into the past. The politics of Harding and Coolidge might have created, among disappointed radicals, the illusion that little had changed; but their economic and industrial policies accelerated the great transformation, the distinctive Jazz Age boom and boost mood that came to seem the very spirit of the nation – until it all tumbled into international disaster in the Great Crash of 1929.[5]

There was certainly energy and invention aplenty in the United States of the Twenties, as the rest of the world quickly came to realize. But, asked its writers and radicals, was there also "civilization"? If you read the influential volume *Civilization in the United States: An Enquiry by Thirty Americans* (1922), edited by Harold E. Stearns, which posed the question, the answer was plain: none at all. Here a band of noted commentators, including Lewis Mumford, H. L. Mencken, Conrad Aiken, Van Wyck Brooks and Ring Lardner, gave a grim negative verdict on American culture and political life, extending into the age of boom and the booboisie the critique that had been growing since the excitements of the pre-war Progressive years. Stearns' preface summarized their views: one, "that in almost every branch of American life there is a sharp dichotomy between preaching and practice"; two, "that whatever else American civilization is, it is not Anglo-Saxon, and that we shall never achieve any genuine nationalistic self-consciousness

[5] An invaluable short general history of the period is William E. Leuchtenburg, *The Perils of Prosperity: 1914–1932* (Chicago and London, Chicago University Press (Chicago History of American Civilization), 1958). Also see Malcolm Bradbury and David Palmer (eds), *The American Novel and the Nineteen Twenties* (London, Edward Arnold, 1971).

as long as we allow certain financial and social minorities to persuade us that we are still an English Colony"; three, "that the most moving and pathetic fact in the social life of America today is emotional and aesthetic starvation . . . We have no heritages or traditions to which to cling except those that have already withered in our hands and turned to dust." No matter: Stearns had his solution ready. In an earlier book, *Liberalism in America* (1919), he argued that the overwhelming, grim spirit of American Puritanism would "tend to drive away our imaginative and intelligent young men to countries like France where they have not yet forgot what living means." In *America and the Young Intellectual* (1921) he held that, while the States rejected its intelligentsia, "one of the most amazing results of Europe's years of misery has been the quickening of all kinds of cultural and intellectual life, in spite of starvation, disease, political chaos, the breakdown of all the old standards of life – indeed, perhaps, because of them . . ." He closed on a famous peroration: "Who can wonder that the young men we should do our best to keep are leaving on every boat . . . They are heartily tired of the fake. They want the real thing, and their sure instinct tells them that in Europe (not in England of course), even in the Europe that is dying from the follies and crimes of its old men, life can still be lived." The book closed with two key words of advice – "Get out!" And, in a huge blaze of publicity, Stearns got out himself, sailing, in July 1921, for France, where, following the "real thing," he duly became well known as a hard-drinking member of the expatriate community, above all as "Peter Pickem," the racing tipster of the Paris edition of the *Chicago Tribune*.[6] There were powerful cultural forces on both sides of the Atlantic that created the distinctive, stylish, experimental, international climate of Twenties Paris.

3.

So, like it or not (and sometimes he did, and sometimes he didn't), by

[6] Stearns' chief books are *Liberalism in America: Its Origin, Its Temporary Collapse, Its Future* (New York, Boni and Liveright, 1919); *America and the Young Intellectual* (New York, Doran and Co., 1921); *Civilization in the United States: An Enquiry by Thirty Americans* (New York, Harcourt Brace; London, Jonathan Cape, 1922); *Rediscovering America* (New York, Boni and Liveright, 1934); and *The Street I Know* (New York, Lee Furman Inc., 1935).

the time Hemingway reached Paris and began work at the start of 1922 – renting a cold workroom because the small, two-room, fourth-floor flat they had taken at 74 Rue du Cardinal-Lemoine, close to the Pantheon and over a *bal musette*, was too small – he was already part of a fast-developing artistic and generational trend. A hard-working, far-travelling, newly-married journalist, Hemingway would never really be the conventional expatriate, and he generally avoided the extremes of bohemian life. "He is not like Stearns, and his wife is charming," Anderson thoughtfully told his Paris friends in advance. The fact remained that in going to Paris he was hardly making his journey alone. In the early years of the Twenties, the transatlantic liners sailing between Manhattan and Cherbourg carried an ever-increasing quantity of young American writers, critics, painters, musicians or cultural tourists making for the various *arrondissements* of Paris, or the countryside outside, or later for the Riviera, Spain, Florence, Rome, Vienna, Munich, Berlin or even more distant parts of Europe. Some had reputations already, some were new aspirants, often just out of college. Some were on an extended travelling vacation, others were determined to commit themselves to the artists' life in the place where, it seemed for the moment, that life was lived. Some were from East Coast families who regularly crossed the Atlantic, others were from the rural midwest and felt they were on a lifetime adventure. In short, Hemingway's arrival coincided almost exactly with the start of a great tidal process that would enormously transform modern transatlantic culture and literature, and include a large wave of new fictional experiment in which American writers like himself would be central.[7]

When later on in life, when he was now "Papa" Hemingway, world-famous author and Nobel Prize winner, and he chose to recall this time in his posthumously published memoir *A Moveable Feast* (1964), he gave a richly sentimental gloss to what had now become a well-told tale. The book settled many old scores with former friends like Gertrude Stein, Scott Fitzgerald, Ford Madox Ford and others in the process, and emphasized his own creative independence and originality; Hemingway was never to be generous in acknowledging his literary debts or his

[7] An excellent recent study of all of this is Humphrey Carpenter's atmospheric *Geniuses Together: American Writers in Paris in the 1920s* (London, Unwin Hyman, 1987). Karen Lane Rood (ed.), *Dictionary of Literary Biography, Vol. 4: American Writers in Paris, 1920–1939* (Chicago, Gale, 1980), records around 100 writers who were in Paris over this time.

intellectual and artistic background. But the truth always was that he was part of a much bigger movement, and arrived in Paris as one piece of a large cultural process, as well as of an ever-expanding community, on whose institutions he came quickly to depend. Here were the bars to write in, the bookshops to read in, the museums and galleries to visit. Above all there was an *avant-garde* salon life which linked American visitors into Parisian culture. The powerful salon hostesses who had much to do with the formation of this environment already included several influential Americans: Gertrude Stein in the Rue de Fleurus, of course; the famous and wealthy "Amazon," Natalie Barney, with salon at 20 Rue de Jacob, her "Temple of Love" and her formidable lesbian culture; and, from the new generation, Sylvia Beach, founder of the bookshop Shakespeare and Company, which over the Twenties became the chief clearing-house for the many new arrivals.

Beach – who played a big part in Hemingway's access to Paris – had lived in the city as a child (her father was a Presbyterian minister in charge of a student atelier), and then returned in 1917 to study literature and take part in the aid effort (she worked for a while in the American Red Cross in Belgrade). Then, back in Paris in 1919, she made a friend of the French bookseller Adrienne Monnier, whose bookshop La Maison des Amis de Livres distributed the work of Zürich Dada in Paris and also promoted new American writing. Beach had originally considered opening up a French bookshop in London, but was convinced it was better to open an Anglo-American bookshop in Montparnasse, both to sell English-language literature and serve as a lending library. Monnier gave her every assistance, and in November 1919 Shakespeare and Company opened, initially as a very small shop at 8 Rue Dupuytren, near the Luxembourg Gardens. "I didn't then foresee, when I opened my bookshop in 1919, that it was going to profit by the suppressions across the sea," Beach later reported. "I think it was partly owing to these suppressions, and the atmosphere they created, that I owed many of my customers – all those pilgrims of the 'twenties who crossed the Ocean and settled in Paris and colonized the Left Bank of the Seine." And within months these new colonists began arriving; the physical Americanization of Montparnasse was soon developing apace. As before, the writers were following the artists to the great good place. In 1920 American literary arrivals in Paris included Stephen Vincent Benét, on a travelling fellowship ("You would like this town," he wrote home, "It is full of liquor, amusing people &

incredibly beautiful works of art"), and Edmund Wilson, alert to the new French experiments. But, above all, this was the year that Ezra Pound, having decisively penned his own farewell to London in the poem "Hugh Selwyn Mauberley," met James Joyce (whose work he had been advancing since 1913) in Italy, and advised him to move from Trieste to Paris, because it was hospitable to the new arts and "the cheapest place last year." Not much later Pound himself made the move and settled, for the next four years, in a "pavillon" at 70 bis Rue Nôtre-Dame-des-Champs, handy for the Dôme. Changing from address to address, Joyce quickly became a key figure in the newly forming international *avant-garde* community. In October 1921, at 5 Boulevard Raspail, he finished surely the greatest novel of the century, *Ulysses*, and one of the essential and monument pieces of the new literature was put in place.[8]

In 1921 the pace quickened further. That summer Shakespeare and Company moved to its more familiar location of 12 Rue de l'Odéon (Joyce's "Stratford-on-Odeon"). Montparnasse still seemed quiet and peaceful, but the new arrivals were increasing in number. Sherwood Anderson came early in the year, and was introduced by Beach to one of her most interesting and demanding customers, Gertrude Stein, so starting off a key Twenties tradition.[9] Stearns arrived in his great glare of publicity, and was soon seen regularly in all the bars and cafés, surrounded by the gathering clan of newspapermen. The young Malcolm Cowley came over on an American Field Service Fellowship to study at a French university, discovered "most of our friends had sailed already," and wrote an article for the American press, "The Youngest Generation," which explained a new experimental generation was emerging in American letters, and chiefly characterized by intellectual, technical and physical progress from London to Paris. The arguments of Stearns and Cowley that the new arts had settled in Paris

---

[8] For the story of Sylvia Beach and the central role of the Shakespeare bookshop, see her own memoir, *Shakespeare and Company* (New York, Harcourt Brace, 1959; London, Faber, 1960), and Noel Riley Fitch, *Sylvia Beach and the Lost Generation: A History of Literary Paris in the Twenties and Thirties* (New York, Norton, 1983; London, Condor Press, 1984).

[9] Anderson records his excitement in *A Story Teller's Story* (Garden City, N.Y., Garden City Publishing Co., 1924): "Out in my own country, when I was a boy, going to Europe meant something tremendous, like going to war for example. It was of infinitely more importance than, let us say, getting married . . . Men and women of the Middle West became famous by way of European trips."

convinced many. Gorham B. Munson arrived with a thousand dollars, determined to start a new experimental literary review, *Secession*. Alfred Kreymborg (former editor of the Greenwich Village *Others*) and Harold Loeb arrived to begin their no less experimental journal *Broom*. Man Ray came in July; Djuna Barnes and Edna St Vincent Millay appeared, and the young Robert M. Coates and Glenway Wescott. So did Robert McAlmon, who was newly and ambiguously married in London to "Bryher" (Winifred Ellerman), and so had access to the great Ellerman shopping fortune, which meant he could finance his literary and publishing ambitions. He soon collected together a volume of his stories, for which Joyce suggested the title *A Hasty Bunch*. It appeared early in 1922, the first imprint of McAlmon's Contact Publishing Company, which, distributed through Beach's bookshop, would duly print Hemingway, and form another important unit in the proliferation of small presses and magazines that would allow the expatriate culture to function.

Now Edmund Wilson, who had served in the Ambulance Corps, returned to Paris, delighted in its experimental atmosphere, and sang its praises. "Paris seems to me an ideal place to live: it combines all the attractions and conveniences of a large city with all the freedom, beauty and regard for the arts and pleasures of a place like Princeton," he wrote his friend Scott Fitzgerald. In May Fitzgerald himself, newly rich and famous for his first, bestselling novel, *This Side of Paradise* (1920), sailed with his wife Zelda on the *Aquitania* on a European tour to coincide with British publication. The visit was not a success. He visited London, Rome and Paris, where he searched for but failed to find Wilson, and went home disappointed: "What an over-estimated place Europe is!" he noted. "God damn the continent of Europe," he also wrote Wilson in a bitter (and racist) letter. "It is of merely antiquarian interest . . . France makes me sick. Its silly pose as the thing the world has to save . . . They're thru and done . . . Culture follows money and all the refinements of aestheticism can't stave off its change of seat . . . We will be the Romans in the next generation as the English are now." Wilson wisely realized that Fitzgerald was piqued by his novel's British reception, and wrote: "Settle down and learn French and apply a little French leisure and measure to that restless and jumpy nervous style. It would be a service to American letters; your novels will never be the same afterwards." Fitzgerald took time to accept the advice; but he famously did, acknowledged the "speciousness" of his first novel, and returned to France three years later to write what would prove his finest, *The Great Gatsby*. Some crucial members of his influential future circle had already arrived in France. Also in 1921 Gerald and Sara Murphy, two key figures of the artistic-socialite community, came to Paris, he so that he could leave behind his business (the Mark Cross leather goods company) and train as a neo-cubist painter and pursue the arts (he worked out a striking ballet with Cole Porter for the Ballets Suèdois). It was the Murphys who went on to "invent" the summer season at Antibes, the magical environment Scott would recreate in his great novel of Twenties retrospection, *Tender Is the Night* (1936).[10] In 1921, too, Fitzgerald's fellow and rival Minnesotan, Sinclair Lewis, already well known as the author of *Main Street* (1920), and about to publish *Babbitt* (1922), visited, drank heartily with Harold Stearns, and commented: "it must be great to be one of that real Parisian bunch." The Parisian bunch did not share the same view of him (he was already too successful, and claimed to speak for American letters); he never forgot his exclusion, and returned later to attack the expatriates.[11]

4.

So it happened that, for the new spirit in the international arts, 1922 – the year Hemingway began work in Paris – was the crucial year. Much that was needed for a great artistic adventure was already there, and 1922 has rightly been called the *annus mirabilis* of literary modernism. Near the start of it, on 2 February, James Joyce's birthday, Beach published *Ulysses* from Shakespeare and Company, after it had become clear the book could not be published in America or Britain. At least she presented Joyce with his author's copy, and put another in her shop window; the rest of the first edition of 1,000 copies (100 signed by the author) came along from the printer in Dijon as the subscription list

---

[10] Calvin Tomkins, *Living Well Is the Best Revenge* (New York, Viking, 1971), vividly tells their story.
[11] On Fitzgerald, see Arthur Mizener, *The Far Side of Paradise* (Boston, Houghton Mifflin, 1951), Andrew Turnbull, *Scott Fitzgerald* (New York, Scribners, 1962), André Le Vot's vivid *F. Scott Fitzgerald: A Biography* (New York, Doubleday, 1983; London, Allen Lane, 1984), and Andrew Turnbull (ed.), *The Letters of Scott Fitzgerald* (New York, Scribners, 1963). On Lewis see R. W. B. Lewis, *Sinclair Lewis: An American Life* (London, Heinemann, 1963).

grew, the fame of the banned book spread, and edition bred edition. Hemingway by now had already become a regular at the bookshop, using it as his mailing address; he assisted the great campaign by sending copies back to a Canadian friend who ferried them over the border. *Ulysses* was not alone; this was a year of remarkable publications. T. S. Eliot's "The Waste Land," heavily edited by Pound in Paris, appeared in London, the great modern poem to match the great modern novel. Paul Valéry's *Charmes*, W. B. Yeats' *Michael Robartes and the Dancer*, Rilke's *Sonnets to Orpheus*, Wittgenstein's *Tractatus*, and Pirandello's play *Henry IV* came out that year. But, as the method of publication of *Ulysses* implied, Paris was becoming the publishing centre of modern writing. New magazines like *Broom* and *Secession* became important outlets for expatriate expression, and many of the most interesting and experimental of the young writers followed their lure. Paris saw the return of Dos Passos, E. E. Cummings, John Peale Bishop; Janet Flanner, Carl Van Vechten and George Antheil joined the expatriate community, which also contained many American painters and musicians. Stein became the great literary hostess; the ever-bohemian Ezra Pound lounged in his studio, learned the bassoon, studied sculpture with Brancusi, worked on an opera about François Villon, and taught younger writers how to read as well as how to write.

It was an international era, with many outside energies supporting the more radical trends of French culture. American, Irish and British writers were becoming a key part of Paris *avant-garde* life, their links with French writers and movements growing. When, that year of 1922, Sydney Schiff gave a party for Diaghilev and friends from the Ballets Russes, he offered to invite the four modern "geniuses" they most admired. They proved an interesting mixture: Picasso, Stravinsky, Joyce and Proust. The two leading writers of modern fiction met for the first time; Joyce complained of his eyes, Proust of his stomach, and each claimed they had not read the other. By the year's end Proust was dead, writing to the last. At his great funeral, with full military honours, in November, huge crowds gathered, and this was not only to honour the greatest modern French novelist, but to ponder the *avant-garde* succession. Ford Madox Ford, formerly Ford Madox Hueffer, friend of Conrad and Crane and James, now disappointed with London, ceremonially turned up for the obsequies, and resolved to pick up the baton and write his "Proustian" four-volume novel of the world at war, *Parade's End* (1924–8). But there was really very little doubt who inherited Proust's mantle. It was Joyce who – for most writers, whether they were American, British, Irish or French – most plainly stood for the spirit of the modern, and the current direction of new fiction. It was just as clear that, for the post-war era, Paris itself had taken back its position as the centre of *atelier* experiment from the rival capitals. It was alive with movements and tendencies, with demonstrations and manifestos. It was filled with salons and galleries and *cénacles*, crowded with rival fiefdoms, where various princes and princesses – Stein, Pound, Ford and Barney, Monnier, Aragon, Cocteau and Gide – ran their own various literary or artistic baronies, all in the interest of creating or claiming title on the drama of the new.

Hemingway had arrived in Paris as another literary novice, though he was just beginning to acquire a rising reputation as a journalist – the chief profession he would follow for the next two years. He was unknown as novelist or story-writer, and had yet to find his "one true sentence," the goal, he said, of the writer. He worked at fiction between major journalistic assignments; in the course of that year he covered the terrible Graeco-Turkish war, returning with malaria, and the Lausanne Peace Conference that followed. But there were four short stories and an unfinished novel in his baggage, and his literary aims were high. It was not desire for wealth or fame but the search for art that drove him, and the value of Paris, he later claimed, was that there you could live very poorly but very well. In fact Hadley's inheritance of $3,000 a year, in a city where their workers' cold-water apartment cost $18 a month, was plenty, and they were able to travel extensively over the next years, to Switzerland, Spain, Austria, Germany, Italy, widening their map of experience. He was soon to become famously informed and informative about the right terrain, the right sports, the right spots (the best fishing rivers, the finest ski-slopes, the ideal cafés and bars); special knowingness was part of the Hemingway style. Above all he had an instinct for the right relationships. He had Anderson's useful introductions to the Paris expatriate community, and his great gift for friendship served him well. He was personable, modest, intelligent, helpful, eager to learn. And Paris was unquestionably the great creative writing class of the day, the great university he had never attended. He soon had access to the best of the gurus who were now passing on the spirit of the pre-war modern experiment to those of the young who would listen, as he did. In February he met Pound and began to show him his work. Pound cut his adjectives, and helped place early writings in little magazines; in return Hemingway taught him to box. In March he met Sylvia Beach and through her Joyce, who also generously, and unusually, read his manuscripts. He soon called on Gertrude Stein, who liked him greatly, at least at first ("He was an extraordinarily good-looking man, twenty-three years old. It was not long after that that everybody was twenty-six. It became the period of being twenty-six"). She dispensed tea, kindness, and some sage if gnomic advice on his fiction: "There is a good deal of description in this, and not particularly useful description. Begin over again and concentrate." In April he met William Bird and Robert McAlmon, who soon competed to publish him in their rival presses, the Three Mountains Press and Contact Editions. He would soon come to know Ford Madox Ford – later to make him assistant editor of his *transatlantic review* – and Jean Rhys, Wyndham Lewis, Lincoln Steffens, Max Eastman, Archibald MacLeish, and a number of French writers.

He did begin over again and concentrate, unwittingly aided by the fact that in December 1922 Hadley lost a suitcase containing some of his earlier and more romantic manuscripts, carbons and all, when catching a train at the Gare de Lyon. This had a near-disastrous impact on their marriage, and marked a crisis in his writing life. But it surely helped to create the distinctive unity of his early stories and sketches, with their unique sharpness of vision. Hence it was over the Paris years, through the Paris experiences, that he learned his serious profession, refined his style, deepened his vision, and became what he called "a true writer." The style he developed over the coming months and years – it was to become one of the dominant styles of modern fiction, far more widely imitated than the complex mannerist methods of Joyce or Stein – was deceptively innocent, seemingly self-made. In fact it owed much to the clarities, confusions and aesthetic self-consciousness of Twenties Modernism, with its codes of concentration and compression, instantaneousness and impersonality, distilled hardness and precise definition. Meantime his work was losing its romantic innocence. His experiences as a journalist covering the terrible Greek flight from Smyrna (Izmir) and across Anatolia, his visits to Italy to meet Mussolini and report the rising tide of Fascism, darkened his awareness of the world, increased his sense of chaos and brutality, enlarged his consciousness of new political danger. His writing acquired the tone of cultural disillusion, the darkened Waste Land vision of a time when Spengler's *Decline of the West* (published in English in 1922) increased the general foreboding, which was central to post-war experimental writing – with its note of historical and linguistic dislocation, of living in a culture displaced and rotten, of war as an outrage perpetrated against the self, the self as victim-subject exposed to meaningless historical violence.

Writing about this later, Hemingway romantically encouraged the idea that he came to writing full-born, and learned his craft working in solitude at the café tables of Montparnasse, until he did finally achieve his "one true sentence" – that authentic under-code that every writer must find, which makes the vision fresh, and lets each image or story be born from a single pure emotion, emerge from felt experience, so creating "the real thing, the sequence of motion and fact which made the emotion . . ." It is true enough that the crafted, object-like, seemingly impersonal stories he started writing had their roots in autobiographical experience and observation: growing up and encountering life and death in the Michigan woods, feeling the wound of war in Italy, seeing the endless spectacle of slaughter and suffering in the Graeco-Turkish conflict, depicting the lives of the emotionally, morally or spiritually wounded in the hotels and cafés of Europe. He always regarded writing as a controlled skill, like boxing or fishing or bullfighting, and saw it as distinctively personal, born from an integrity and wholeness ("grace under pressure," his definition of courage), a distinctive way of living, a controlled personal mythology. His work always had a hard-edged clarity and understated narrative economy that made it accessible and readable, and there seems little in it of those complex strategies that depict the flow, the confusion, the automatic writing that displayed the modern consciousness in the writing of many of his contemporaries. Yet we do know them *as* works of modern consciousness. Hemingway's fiction, more or less from the start, was a clean, well-lighted place, a world of the hard and clearly registered minimum. It had its own distinctive tonality, its own distinctive terrain, and later on it would have its distinctive tenant, the stoic strong Hemingway hero. It was a world, as Edmund Wilson said, pure yet suffused with "the undruggable consciousness of something wrong." It was simple, yet modern, in part because we know that somehow it is filled with the pain and suffering of modern life; one reason why we find the style modern is that the experience it draws on is modern too.

Yet, if the stories Hemingway was writing – a number based round the figure of Nick Adams, his own near-autobiographical portrait of the artist – are notable for their distinctive stylistic precision, their sense of life as crisis, their ever-suggestive stoic note of suppressed modern pain, they are also highly technical pieces, firmly forged in the climate of the Paris *avant-garde*. It was here in the ideal atmosphere he listened, learned, found his manner. It was here that, over the years 1923–4, he published in various experimental and ill-paying expatriate magazines the early stories and sketches, many near to poems, which remain amongst the finest work he ever did. It was here his first two collections – *Three Stories and Ten Poems* (1923) and *in our time* (1924) – appeared from two small presses, Bird's Three Mountains Press and McAlmon's Contact Editions, in the slimmest of volumes and the tiniest of printings (only 300 copies of the first, 170 of the second), but to the acclaim of his experimental peers. Hemingway was a writer forged in the Paris context, which shaped both his art-style and his life-style. Even his adventurous physicality owed much to the atmosphere. It seemed, for instance, that everyone boxed. Hemingway did himself, of course, even organizing a bout on the ship coming over. Later there was a famous bout with the Canadian writer Morley Callaghan, with Scott Fitzgerald as the careless referee; it seems from reports that both of them won, if not all three of them. But Ezra Pound boxed, and Lewis Galántière; even Stein boxed to keep herself in condition. Similarly the expatriates were avid European tourists, travelling everywhere. There was the Alpine skiing; Hemingway became an early promoter of this newly popular winter sport. There were the fishing trips, above all the bullfights: the province of the Paris expatriates covered France, Spain, and Italy, but Spain had a special fascination. Stein felt Spain and America shared much in common, both being brutal and abstract; this was why they were the two Western nations that could comprehend Cubism. She had many fascinating encounters herself there, especially when her hair was cut short and she was mistaken for a priest; in one village where she was taken for a bishop, people queued up to kiss her ring. She too went to bullfights, telling Alice Toklas, now look, now don't, until finally, she reported, she was able to look all the time. Hemingway looked all the time, even going to the Spanish bullfights when his son was about to be born to gather the right foetal atmosphere. There were to be eight Spanish trips over the Paris years, for the fishing and bullfights, in ever larger expatriate groups that came to include most of the leading writers. And it was this wide social and physical geography that would afford the background when he came to write the great expatriate story in his first real novel, *The Sun Also Rises* (1926).

From the start Hemingway was an expatriate writer, and he would always remain one. Most of his life would be spent outside the United States, and very little of his work, that mostly about his Michigan childhood, would be firmly set there. Nearly all the rest would be about the various foreign landscapes and settings he lived in, travelled through, physically appropriated. His initial reputation was born in the art-world of Paris, where he proved himself a serious student. It was not until 1925, when an American publisher, Boni and Liveright, took up a collection of his early work, that he really began to be known in the United States. The volume was called, appropriately enough, *In Our Time* (the title was in capitals this time), and reprinted most of the stories, sketches and vignettes he had produced in Paris over the previous three years, though now he was able to revise them and make them a clear unity. All at once there was a Hemingway theme, a Hemingway style, a Hemingway legend. The volume, hailed by critics for its modern sensibility, had the symbolist wholeness of Joyce's *Dubliners* or Anderson's *Winesburg, Ohio*. It was his first mature book, tight, exact, with all the vivid presentness of journalism, all the reined-in emotion of a strong sensibility, all the control of Modernist method. The stories are set in a period of tragic history, in which glimpses of extreme situations, encounters with death as nullity and heroism as necessary illusion, lead to the realization that those wounded by war or experience can only make a separate peace. They not only created an entire world but a style for addressing it: a style of stoic recessiveness, focused not so much in human consciousness but in things and moods, and the things implied by those moods. The hard methods of Modernism – the flat surfaces, modes of grammatical repetition, the sense of things unspoken, the use of indirect signification – appeared not just an experimental technique but a moral and historical emotion. Certainly the stories had none of the obscurities or angularities of most Modernist writing. Hemingway made no claim to be learned but experienced, so his stories were always easy to reach and grasp – even though, when examined with care, they unlocked their deeper stylistic secrets. Here the spirit of the *avant-garde* transferred readily into mainstream modern style, which effectively became the basic manner of Twenties writing, influencing writers everywhere. But, like so much from the Twenties, it came from the intermingling of French and American energies that took place in Paris.

5.

But the days of his fame and high presence were yet to come. In the summer of 1923, Hemingway not only had two books but a baby on the way, and his expatriate era seemed to reach its end. Hadley wanted the baby born in North America, and in August they sailed for Canada, where he resumed work as a reporter on the *Toronto Star*. From the beginning newsroom work depressed him, and he yearned to get back to Paris. At the year's end, he resigned his job, determined to live as a full-time writer. In January 1924 the enlarged family returned to Montparnasse, taking a larger apartment, over a sawmill at 23 Rue Nôtre-Dame-des-Champs, near the Closerie des Lilas and the Luxembourg Gardens, round the corner from Joyce and Stein. Even over the few months of absence Paris had changed. The American contingent had expanded. Various friends, new and old, were appearing in the city, including Margaret Anderson, the editor of the *Little Review*, which had attempted to serialize *Ulysses* in the USA, and which now moved its attention to Paris. She has come as sexual companion to Georgette Leblanc, deciding that "life in France would be what life should be, or at least that I could live life there as it should be lived."[12] The list of magazines, small presses and publications grew longer; so did the roll-call of artistic names in the city. "By 1922 or 1923 there were quantities of Americans who had settled in France, to stay indefinitely, either in Paris or at houses which they had rented in the small towns nearby," McAlmon would report. "Never a week passed without one or more cocktail parties . . . George Biddle, John Storrs, John Carol, Ford Madox Ford, Sisley Huddleston, George Slocombe, Clotilde Vail, and Laurence Vail with his then wife, Peggy Guggenheim, Jane Heap, Mina Loy, Kathleen Cannel, the Arthur Mosses, Mme Champcommunal (who hadn't then opened her couturier shop), William and Sally Bird, and many others were about and most of them entertained fairly often."[13] Rich American hostesses like Lady Mendl, Elsa Maxwell and Ilka Chase began to preside.[14]

[12] Margaret Anderson, *The Fiery Fountains* (London, Rider and Co., 1953).
[13] Robert McAlmon, *Being Geniuses Together*, cited below, p. 331.
[14] Janet Flanner noted in *An American in Paris* (New York, Simon and Schuster; London, Hamish Hamilton, 1940): "Frankly formed on post-war profits, and assembled well before the day of the depression and the forgotten man, the international smart set introduced what seemed to France the unforgettable woman – the very rich American woman with money which no man could control and which she was free to spend."

Even the French bars and cafés were beginning to Americanize, redecorating, adding a jazz band, multiplying the price of drinks. There were nightclubs like Hilaire Hiler's "The Jockey," "Le Boeuf Sur Le Toit," "Bricktop's," and the "Dingo," and the famous Left Bank cafés, the Rotonde, the Select, the Dôme, the Flore, the Deux Magots, which became central meeting places. Parisian life was now regularly reported in the American press, not always favourably, and over the next years there were attacks on the expatriates from H. L. Mencken, Sinclair Lewis, indeed from Hemingway himself.

1924 was another remarkable Modernist year. Breton's review *La Révolution surréaliste* was founded, and Surrealism, which also published its manifesto that year, proclaiming a new revolution of consciousness, replaced Dada as the spirit of the new. It was a season of transition: Conrad, Anatole France and Franz Kafka all died that year. But Cocteau had published his *Poésie, 1916–1923*, Mann *The Magic Mountain*, Kafka *The Hunger Artist*; and Hemingway himself was now a published writer with *in our time*, which won him small sales but much local attention. He was also developing a more combative style and strategy. Ford Madox Ford had now started his magazine, the *transatlantic review* (Paris was a lower-case city). "It seemed to me that it would be a good thing if someone would start a centre for the more modern and youthful of the art movements, with which, by 1923, the city, like an immense seething cauldron, bubbled and overflowed," Ford noted[15]) though he was hardly alone in the idea; and he took on Hemingway as his assistant editor. This, like many of his relationships, was to end in bitterness and recrimination, mostly on Hemingway's side; Ford was a generous patron to all young writers. But work on the magazine enabled him to bring some of Stein's *The Making of Americans* into print (as Stein said, he learned a lot from reading her proofs), and some of his own poetry and fiction. He was working with other editors bringing out magazines in Paris, like Harold Loeb, and developing new friendships with a fresh generation of writers coming in, like Archibald MacLeish. The franc was falling, the liner-fares dropping, the boats had never been fuller. In January 1924 William Carlos Williams began the six-month visit to "pagan" experimental Paris that formed the basis of his novel *Voyage to Pagany* (1928). He noted: "The Paris of the expatriate artist was our only world – day and night – and if bread is the staff of

[15] Ford Madox Ford, *It Was the Nightingale* (London, Heinemann, 1934).

life, whisky, as Bob [McAlmon] was fond of saying, is the staff of night life, both products of the same grain. *Everyone* was in Paris – if you wanted to see them. But there were grades too of that cream."[16] Williams, indeed, was quick to tire of the cream, coming to believe that Paris was drawing American writers away from their own culture.

But Paris had that year a yet more crucial visitor who was to play a big part in Hemingway's life. In April 1924, Scott and Zelda Fitzgerald came back to Europe on the *Minnewaska* – trying, Scott explained, to escape from "extravagance and clamor and from all the wild extremes among which we had dwelt for five hectic years . . . We were going to the Old World to find a new rhythm for our lives, with a true conviction that we had left our old selves behind forever – and with a capital of just over seven thousand dollars." What they meant to leave behind they actually brought with them. Despite all his books and highly paid magazine stories, he, and especially Zelda, had overspent, and hoped to leave their debts behind. Remembering Wilson's lesson, the twenty-eight-year-old Fitzgerald was trying to write a truly serious novel, the book where he wanted to "tread slowly and carefully," to produce "a conscious literary achievement." That spring they were in Paris only briefly, staying at the Hôtel des Deux Mondes near the Opéra, and meeting new friends, the Murphys, as well as an old one, John Peale Bishop, before travelling south to Hyères, then renting a villa at Saint Raphaël ("We've come to Europe to economize"). Here Scott worked well on the "serious" book, which he intended to call *Under the Red White and Blue*, and would appear as *The Great Gatsby*, and Zelda had an affair with a French aviator (her version would appear in her novel *Save Me the Waltz*, 1932). It was in this troubled marital climate that he completed his most powerful and remarkable novel, one of the great works of the century. It was the archetypal modern American story, a symbolist fable of wealth and waste, a tale of New World dreams and wasteland

[16] William Carlos Williams, *The Autobiography of William Carlos Williams* (New York, Random House, 1951). Williams also recalls the visit in *In the American Grain* (New York, New Directions, 1956): "Picasso (turning to look back, with a smile), Braque (brown cotton), Gertrude Stein (opening the doors of a cabinet of MSS.), Tzara (grinning), André Germain (blocking the door), Van der Pyl (speaking of St. Cloud), Bob Chandler (prodding Marcel), Marcel (shouting), Salmon (in a corner), and my good friends Philip and Madam Soupault; the Prince of Dahomi, Clive Bell (dressed), Nancy, Sylvia, Clothilde, Sally, Kitty, Mina and her two lovely daughters; James and Norah Joyce (in a taxi at the Place de l'Etoile), McAlmon, Antheil, Bryher, H.D. and dear Ezra who took me to talk with Léger; and finally Adrienne Monnier – these were my six weeks in Paris."

actualities, of the East seen from the West, the West from the East, of idealism and illusion, corruption and betrayal. Writing it, he came via Edmund Wilson across a copy of Hemingway's *in our time*, and wrote his publisher, Maxwell Perkins at Scribners, warmly recommending its author, whom he had not yet met: "He's the real thing," he told him. The Fitzgeralds then went for the winter to Rome, which they disliked, and where several disastrous incidents displaying their common tension and destructiveness occurred. In April 1925, they returned to Paris, where they rented an apartment not on the Left Bank but at 14 Rue de Tilsitt, a fine street elegantly placed close to the Arc de Triomphe and the Champs Elysées, among the *hôtels particuliers* and in the heart of social Paris.

1925 was the key year, for Hemingway, Fitzgerald, and the whole enterprise of the modern. A new spirit, radical and aesthetic, was flourishing in American fiction, and would continue to do so for the rest of the decade, as more remarkable and innovative writers, including William Faulkner, another visitor to Twenties Paris, appeared. It was the year of *The Great Gatsby*, which appeared to great critical acclaim and disappointing sales, and of Hemingway's American début with *In Our Time*. With Hemingway's aid, Gertrude Stein finished off her Cubist text *The Making of Americans*, which appeared in Paris from McAlmon's Contact Editions. Dos Passos published his vast Expressionist city novel *Manhattan Transfer*, and Sherwood Anderson his most experimental fiction, *Dark Laughter* (Hemingway promptly parodied it in *The Torrents of Spring*). The great American novelist of Naturalism, Theodore Dreiser, returned to the fray with *An American Tragedy*, another tale of a life fatally led astray by the American dream. American writing was now taking on a new dominance in world literature, as Adrienne Monnier acknowledged when she published a special American number of her French review. Indeed for Parisians this was an American year, when, as Fitzgerald observed later, "something subtle passed to America, the style of man." There was economic crisis and the franc fell severely, multiplying the hordes of American visitors, most now not artists but tourists seeking artistic sensations, which mostly meant cafés, drink, and sexual freedom. The sensation that year was the nude dance of Josephine Baker and her black company at the Revue des Nègres, tempted over by Fernand Léger; among other things it intensified the vogue for African rhythms, jazz and the Charleston. There was a vogue for American cinema;

Chaplin was showing in *The Gold Rush*. In Montparnasse, where the quarter had grown vastly and the cafés had been restyled, Americans dominated. Here were the hotels, bright well-lighted cafés and zinc bars where writers, artists and musicians met, talked, drank, fought, sometimes even wrote every day. It was possible to visit without even meeting the French, write without ever bothering to speak to a French writer. There were several English-language newspapers, magazines, bookstores, and if the writers constantly came and went, these stayed, at least for a time, and provided an elusive continuity. Tastes were changing in Paris; this was the year of the Art Deco Exposition, which put on its great show on both banks of the Seine. In the objects of Lalique, the paintings of Lhote and Delaunay and Tamara de Lempicka, the dress design of Lanvin and Coco Chanel, it was possible to see cubist and futurist forms returning as modern designer style, the expression of a transformed taste that constituted a general Twenties mannerism, of as much influence and importance as the *fin-de-siècle*, *art-nouveau* spirit of thirty years before.

Hemingway and Fitzgerald lived in two different kinds of Paris: Hemingway in the relative bohemian poverty of Montparnasse, Fitzgerald in the greater luxury of the Right Bank, where he met socialites rather than writers, and which over time became the scene of a number of his stories ("Babylon Revisited," "One Trip Abroad," "The Rough Crossing," "News of Paris – Fifteen Years Ago"). Not surprisingly, in the social and artistic excitement of Paris, all Fitzgerald's intentions of living on "practically nothing a year" quickly withered. The domestic crisis continued, and Fitzgerald was drinking hard. But it was now, in May, in the Dingo bar, on the Rue Delambre in Montparnasse, that he first met Hemingway (and in the course of the evening passed out from alcohol). A crucial, much-recorded, much-contested relationship began. To all impressions, Fitzgerald was the famous, wealthy writer who had captured his generation, and whose greatest novel had just appeared; Hemingway was the admired novice whose first American publication was still six months away. But their roles quickly reversed. Fitzgerald was guilty about his earlier writing, and had developed a great admiration for the newcomer. The ever more confident Hemingway, ever quick to sense a weakness in others, saw in Fitzgerald a writer already badly damaged, by drink, over-production, Zelda's jealousy, obsession with failure. In time the complicated relationship would dissolve into jealousy, especially on

Hemingway's part. He was naturally competitive, possibly felt threatened on his own literary territory (Fitzgerald revealed he planned a novel set in expatriate Europe), and he felt he was rising and Fitzgerald was falling. The relationship became crucial for both of them, and would be played out for the rest of both of their lifetimes, and into the critical debates that followed. To this day it divides readers who see in them two different versions of the writer, two different cycles of literary success and failure, two distinctively different versions of the modern and Modernist novel.[17] Between them they would become the essential chroniclers of their generation, time and place, the two dominant American writers of the Twenties.

In fact the two men met just as their lives were dissolving. Fitzgerald's marriage was in trouble, Hemingway's was about to be. An era, too, was dissolving: the first half of the Twenties, which so much shaped the life and writing of each of them. Paris had turned into a place of excitement and exile, amusement and bitter disillusion, wild gaiety mixed with drunken depresssion, continuously lit by the publication of various great works: the later volumes of Proust's great novel, Valéry's *Cimetière Marin*, Gide's *Les Faux-Monnayeurs*. American, Irish, British as well as French writers crowded the city, and many key works emerged from the climate: Stein's growing body of pieces and plays, Pound's early *Cantos* and Williams' *The Great American Novel*, the Twenties fiction of Ford, Jean Rhys, then later Henry Miller, Nathanael West, Samuel Beckett, Lawrence Durrell. Paris by now had become a complete, heavily populated expatriate culture. "When I got to Montparnasse, all the obvious roles had been dropped or were being played by experts," wrote one newcomer, Nathanael West, in a typically satirical tale. "But I made a lucky hit. Instead of trying for strangeness, I formalized and exaggerated the customs of a bond salesman ... I was asked to all the parties."[18] Meantime as new crowds came in, the already established expatriates from the earlier phase were beginning to scatter. Pound moved to Rapallo in 1924, and in the summer of 1925 Hemingway and Fitzgerald were both on the move, and both were planning to write expatriate novels. Off went the

---

[17] The best record is Matthew J. Bruccoli, *Scott and Ernest* (London, Bodley Head, 1978).
[18] Nathanael West, "L'Affaire Beano." West arrived in Paris late in 1924 and stayed two years; his first novel, *The Dream Life of Balso Snell*, was published by Contact Editions in 1931.

Fitzgeralds down to Antibes, where the charming and sociable Murphys were creating their new Riviera "season." It was a summer of "1,000 parties and no work," Scott said, but he was planning his expatriate novel, variously titled *The World's Fair* and *Our Type*, explaining to his publisher "it is about Zelda and me and the hysteria of last May and June in Paris," though it would also take in American life on the Riviera. The Hemingways went off to Pamplona again for the *feria*, in a party that included Harold Loeb, Bill Smith and Lady Duff Twysden. These trips had become a kind of expatriate convention, at which Hemingway showed off his sporting proficiency, on one occasion entering the bullring, catching hold of the bull's horns and wrestling him rodeo-style, to the cheers of the crowd. He had just discarded a novel about Nick Adams and the war in Italy, *Along With Youth*, after thirty pages, but he now drew on his summer experiences and began work in Madrid on what would be his first real novel, completing it in six weeks. As Fitzgerald's book dealt with his social world, Hemingway's dealt with his: with expatriate Montparnasse, the trip to Spain for fishing and bullfighting, the whole troubled expatriate climate ("You're an expatriate. You've lost touch with the soil. You get precious. Fake European standards have ruined you. You drink yourself to death. You become obsessed by sex. You spend all your time talking, not working. You're an expatriate, see? You hang around in cafés"). The book appeared the next year, under two titles; it came from Fitzgerald's publishers, Scribner, in New York as *The Sun Also Rises*, and from Cape in England as *Fiesta*.

That year, 1926, things grew more complicated for them all. Hemingways and Fitzgeralds went skiing together at Schruns in the Austrian Alps. But Hemingway was beginning an affair with Pauline Pfeiffer, who worked for *Vogue*, and would become his second wife. In the summer he went again to Spain, but left Hadley in Antibes with the Murphys. The Fitzgeralds were there again too, their lease in Paris having run out, and were renting a villa at Saint-Juan-les-Pins. Scott reported to Perkins he was happy and the novel was going well. In fact he was struggling with the book, which went, said Zelda, "so slowly it ought to be serialized in the Encyclopedia Britannica." He was drinking heavily, Zelda was suicidal. When Hemingway arrived with Pauline and was welcomed by the Murphys, Scott, feeling he had been ousted, behaved outrageously in public. But at last he read the manuscript of *The Sun Also Rises*, about to be published, and made invaluable suggestions about cutting dross from the opening which Hemingway adopted. It seemed, though, that in one fashion or another the entire American expatriate community was disintegrating. The drinking and display intensified, the domestic and sexual crises worsened; it was, as Fitzgerald came to see it, the beginning of "the crack-up," which, from the eyeline of the Marxizing Thirties, he would acknowledge not just as a moral, psychic and sexual crisis, but as part of the larger breakdown of an entire social and economic era. Antibes itself, a quiet summer resort only two years earlier, had turned into a grotesque carnival, a garish Gatsby-like party, as Fitzgerald reported in a notable and ill-spelt letter to Bishop: "There was no one at Antibes this summer except me, Zelda, the Valentinos, the Murphys, Mistinguet, Rex Ingram, Dos Passos, Alice Terry, the MacLeishes, Charles Bracket, Maude Kahn, Esther Murphy, Maguerite Namara, E. Philips Oppenheim, Mannes the violinist, Floyd Dell, Max and Crystal Eastman, ex-Premier Orlando, Etienne de Beaumont – just a real place to rough it and escape from the world."[19]

The frenzy and disintegration grew as the year continued. The Fitzgeralds stayed on in the South of France: "We've had a fine summer – and now all the gay decorative people have left taking with them the sense of carnival and impending disaster," Scott assured Perkins, even though signs of Zelda's incipient madness were becoming more apparent. In December they decided to go home: "God, how much I've learned in those two and a half years in Europe," Fitzgerald wrote. "It seems like a decade & I feel pretty old but I wouldn't have missed it, even in its most unpleasant and painful aspects." But the novel was still unfinished, and when, after another, much bleaker return to Europe, he did at last publish it in 1934 as *Tender Is the Night*, he had come to think that the whole expatriation had been spent in a tragic and destructive self-indulgence; it is this view that gives the shape and vision to the book. Meanwhile in autumn 1926 Hemingway reported to Fitzgerald: "Our life has gone all to hell." He and Hadley had separated, and divorce proceedings started just as *The Sun Also Rises* appeared in October. This was the book that won Hemingway the reputation of a major writer (some still think it his best novel), and also the voice of his generation – the role Fitzgerald had occupied five years earlier. It was soon followed in 1927 by the brilliant story collection *Men*

[19] Letter of 21 September 1925: in Andrew Turnbull (ed.), *Letters*, and in *The Crack-Up* (see below).

Without Women, pained tales of dislocated male lives, filled with bitter sterility, gender isolation, displaced romantic emotion, the stoic suffering and sleeplessness of those war and life have wounded. A year later Hemingway, now married to Pauline, moved to Key West. His time in Paris, where, with many travels and interruptions, he had spent the previous five years, was over, but it stayed permanently in his mind as the ideal location of writing, the place of all his literary nostalgia.

Ironically enough, *The Sun Also Rises* did more than most things to abolish the Paris he knew. The book had a profound influence on the expatriate scene, as new American hordes rushed to Paris and Spain to visit the bars, drink the drinks, take part in the *ferias*, fish the rivers, talk and make love in the clipped controlled manner of the central characters, and perceive themselves as bookless writers. In fact the book, reported one long-term resident, Samuel Putnam, marked "the point of cleavage between the earlier and the later batches of 'exiles,' by embalming in a work of fiction which was to become a modern classic the spirit that animated those who came in 1921 or shortly thereafter. It was a literary post-mortem. Many of the original *émigrés* had been in the war or at least had fought and lost the battle of America that followed; whereas those who arrived in the late 'twenties were, frequently, of a still younger, unscarred generation . . . These latter had no great disillusionment to drown, they were not rebels, and often they were not genuine writers or artists."[20] In fact it was generally agreed, by those who read the signs (and these days who didn't?), that a great change happened to expatriate Parisian culture around the time of the novel, if not because of it. As Putnam said, Paris had now ceased to be the capital of France, and become an international city or world thorough-fare, a borrowing capital hungry for new style and sensation from any foreign source. Its garrets and studios attracted an unending flow of artistic visitors, tourists, socialites; now the bulk of the expatriation occurred, though it was mostly short-term and seasonal. Even more English-language magazines and publishing houses emerged to print what was called *avant-garde* work – though the writers who published small volumes of free verse or anti-representational fiction in Paris often reverted to familiar realism or journalism when they went home to the USA. Standards, it seemed, were slipping, the expatriate tribes

---

[20] Samuel Putnam, *Paris Was Our Mistress: Memoirs of a Lost and Found Generation* (New York, Viking, 1947).

making the city into a simple extension of American life and wealth. Distressing phenomena were noted; American drinks and their American drinkers grew ever more common, strange American breakfast foods were served on the *terrasse* of the Dôme, and the air of bohemian frenzy increased.

Each generation of expatriates always reports its successors inferior; successors always are. Sherwood Anderson, returning in 1927, noted: "The Americans in Paris are terrible. Such a shuffling lot." Revisiting in 1928 after a year's absence (on a trip that saw him twice put in jail), Fitzgerald said it was now populated with American "Neanderthals." And in an essay he observed a new era had now begun, of Americans wandering wildly and growing ever more extreme in their behaviour: "friends seemed eternally bound for Russia, Persia, Abyssinia and Central Africa. And by 1928 Paris had grown suffocating. With each new shipment of Americans spawned up by the boom the quality fell off, until toward the end there was something sinister about the crazy boatloads."[21] In 1928 Hart Crane came, spent his time with the set round Harry Crosby, famously smashed up the bar of the Select, and was asked to leave the country; just after, Crosby committed suicide. Sisley Huddleston, long-resident Paris correspondent of the London *Times*, reported on the deteriorating standard of American bohemianism: "There is a release of inhibitions which check them in the United States, and in consequence there is much noise and drinking and unpleasant behaviour . . . Bohemianism does not mean rowdiness, and does not mean objectionable conduct."[22] Hemingway himself went on to distinguish two eras of expatriation: the early "serious" period, dominated by real experiment, and the wild era after 1926, composed largely of Americans in flight from "repressive" America. In truth there was a notable second artistic era at the decade's end, considerably influenced by the middle work of Stein and the publication of Joyce's "Work in Progress" in *transition* – the international magazine of the "Revolution of the Word," with its revolt against the rule of syntactical law, its campaign for "vertigralism," its endeavour through linguistic experiment to reach "the collective unconscious of the universe." But the notion of a great decline became a central part of the whole post-war myth. "You are all a lost generation," Stein was supposed to have told

[21] Scott Fitzgerald, "Echoes of the Jazz Age," in *The Crack-Up with Other Pieces and Stories* (New York, New Directions, 1945; London, Penguin, 1965).
[22] Sisley Huddleston, *In and About Paris* (London, Methuen, 1927).

Hemingway, and he used the phrase as one of the two tags of *The Sun Also Rises* (the other, from Ecclesiastes, reminds us that generations are short, but the earth abideth for ever). Stein denied saying it and attributed it to a French garage mechanic, who meant something different; Hemingway partly disavowed it later. But it was evocative, it stuck, for the time it seemed completely appropriate. A sense of sterility and disillusion runs through much modern literature; Hemingway now seemed to have given it a place, a setting, and a name. Here was an entire generation of Americans, post-war, disillusioned, rootless, trying to create a new style of art and life in a new stylish age, and often destroying themselves or their innocent hopes in the process. Perhaps they and their contemporaries were lost, robbed of cultural tradition and moral and psychic security, the victims of historical and economic malaise. But there seemed to be no doubt that, if you wanted to find them, you had only to go to Paris.

6.

What was so remarkable about this great Paris episode? To this day it is seen as one of the most remarkable events in the history of literary mass-migration. Expatriation itself was not new, and there had certainly been large-scale movements of writers before: the drift of Russians to the European capitals in the nineteenth century as the soul of Russia (European or Slavic?) was disputed, even the constant movement of British writers to the sun, sea and vines of Italy from the late eighteenth century on. And American writers especially had been given to European expatriation: so much so that, as Harry Levin has said, "It is a salient fact of American fiction that much of it has been set in foreign parts." Yet, both in sheer human quantity and in long-term artistic consequences, the event of the Twenties, when it seemed that nearly all that was new and exciting in the American arts had upped, taken ship and gone to Paris, remains distinctive in the annals. For one thing, few such episodes have been so vividly remembered and so well-recorded, both in the reports of the time – the stories, novels, poems, plays, essays, magazines, manifestos that came from it – and the memoirs and reminiscences of the many participants, witnesses, survivors. Though Hemingway's account is likely to stay the most famous, it is one of hundreds that build up a portrait in chiaroscuro of a complex world of personalities, salons, cafés, exhibitions, performances, magazines, presses, artistic meetings, drinking bouts and suicides, which happens also to be the great forcing-ground of modern artistic experience, modern American literature. Paris is a story-telling city, strong on remembrance of things past, and most of those involved would sooner or later write their account, to establish their own version or to contradict another.[23] Many of those involved became famous enough to merit a biography, in some cases four or five. And since the spectacle was international, transatlantic and collective, and involved a massive change in the entire spirit of all the modern arts, incorporating

---

[23] Some of the key memoirs are: Margaret Anderson, *My Thirty Years' War: An Autobiography* (New York and London, Knopf, 1930); Sherwood Anderson, *A Story Teller's Story* (cited above); Sylvia Beach, *Shakespeare and Company* (cited above); Morley Callaghan, *That Summer in Paris* (New York, Coward McCann, and London, McGibbon and Kee, 1963); (Jimmy Charters) "Jimmy the Barman," *This Must Be the Place: Memoirs of Montparnasse*, ed. Merrill Cody with an introd. by Ernest Hemingway (London, Herbert Joseph, 1934); Caresse Crosby, *The Passionate Years* (New York, Dial Press, 1953; London, Redman, 1955); Robert M. Coates, *The View from Here* (New York, Harcourt Brace, 1960); John Dos Passos, *The Best Times: An Informal Memoir* (New York, New American Library, 1966); Janet Flanner ("Genet" of the *New Yorker*), *An American in Paris: Profile of an Interlude Between Two Wars* (London, Hamish Hamilton, 1940); Ford Madox Ford, *It Was the Nightingale* (London, Heinemann, 1934); John Glassco, *Memoirs of Montparnasse* (Toronto, Oxford University Press, 1970); Nina Hamnett, *Laughing Torso: Reminiscences* (London, Constable, 1932); Ernest Hemingway, *A Moveable Feast* (New York, Scribner, 1964); Sisley Huddleston, *Back to Montparnasse: Glimpses of Broadway in Bohemia* (London, Harrap, 1931); Bravig Imbs, *Confessions of Another Young Man* (New York, Henkle-Yewdale House, 1936); Eugene Jolas, *I Have Seen Monsters and Angels* (Paris, Transition Press, 1938); Matthew Josephson, *Life Among the Surrealists* (New York, Holt, Rinehart and Winston, 1962); "Kiki," *Kiki's Memoirs* (Paris, Black Manikin Press, 1930); Alfred Kreymbourg, *Troubador: An Autobiography* (New York, Boni and Liveright, 1925); Ludwig Lewisohn, *Mid-Channel: An American Chronicle* (New York and London, Harper, 1939); Harold A. Loeb, *The Way It Was* (New York, Criterion, 1959); Robert McAlmon, *Being Geniuses Together, An Autobiography* (London, Secker and Warburg, 1938; republished as *Being Geniuses Together, 1920–1930, Revised with Additional Material by Kay Boyle* (Garden City, N.Y., Doubleday, 1968; London, Michael Joseph, 1970)); Samuel Putnam, *Paris Was Our Mistress: Memoirs of a Lost and Found Generation* (New York, Viking, 1947); Man Ray, *Self-Portrait* (Boston, Little Brown, 1963); Harold E. Stearns, *The Street I Know* (New York, Lee Furman, 1935); Gertrude Stein, *The Autobiography of Alice B. Toklas* (New York, Harcourt Brace, 1933), and *Everybody's Autobiography* (New York, Random House, 1937; London, Heinemann, 1938); Carl Van Vechten, *Fragments from an Unwritten Autobiography* (New Haven, Yale University Press Library, 2 vols, 1955), and *Sacred and Profane Memories* (New York, Knopf, 1932); William Carlos Williams, *The Autobiography of William Carlos Williams* (New York, Random House, n.d. (1951)), Edmund Wilson, *The Shores of Light* (New York, Farrar, Strauss and Young, 1952).

painting, architecture, design, music, ballet, couture, film, popular theatre, in fact everything that is culture and style, the broader story of the era – in its groupings, movements and aesthetic tendencies – has been repeatedly retold.

On the other hand, obscured perhaps by a more romantic and stylish history of events, serious analysis has been a good deal thinner. However, there are a few useful versions inviting us to look at how and why it happened, and what the consequences were. R. P. Blackmur's seminal essay "The American Literary Expatriate" (1944) argues the episode revealed a fundamental fact about America: it made a point of keeping its cultural capitals a continent away from its political one. Matthew Josephson, himself an expatriate, observes in his *Portrait of the Artist as American* (1930) that, from the Civil War on, expatriation exposed the fact that, in the mass democratic society, American artistic activity was increasingly isolated, aestheticized, and privatized. Edmund Wilson's brilliant *Axel's Castle* (1931), the first great study of international literary modernism, sees the Twenties as a culminating stage in a vast cosmopolitan revolution developing from the 1870s on; "writers such as W. B. Yeats, James Joyce, T. S. Eliot, Gertrude Stein, Marcel Proust and Paul Valéry represent the culmination of a self-conscious and very important literary movement," he notes. In his vividly reminiscent account from the Thirties, *Exile's Return* (first published 1934, later revised), Malcolm Cowley saw the era of expatriation as a defining period in American literature: a time when a new generation who shared an experience, the war, in common followed out the religion of art, and created a literature that also had much in common, the spirit of modern artistic revolution. It was, he says, an apolitical revolution, based on the financial situation of a class, and these exiles were, he says, *valuta* expatriates, following the dollar as the franc and mark declined, seeking the best rate of cultural and monetary exchange. Then everything changed when this privileged economic system collapsed with the Great Crash; so the exiles returned, to bring home their skills to encounter social reality, and the need for political engagement. And in his book *The Twenties: American Writing in the Postwar Decade* (1949), Frederick J. Hoffman stresses perhaps the most familiar aspect of all – expatriation as protest, as an entire generation chose to reject the provincial, puritanical, backward-looking America of Harding and Coolidge, and set off down the path of art and freedom, which took so many of them out of the country altogether.[24]

Every one of these elements was certainly in play. Historians say that any migration needs a push factor and a pull factor. One clear push factor was the mood of cultural disillusion that had emerged in America ever since the excitements of 1912–13. In *America's Coming of Age* (1915), and then in *Letters and Leadership* (1918), the influential Van Wyck Brooks announced that a new artistic maturity was coming to America, but diagnosed that something ("Puritanism") in the culture rejected it ("Human nature in America exists on two irreconcilable planes, the plane of stark intellectuality and the plane of stark business"). Other cultural critics like Randolph Bourne, Harold Stearns and H. L. Mencken, the irrepressible scourge of the American "booboisie," equally assaulted the commercial, anti-progressive, anti-artistic climate of a nation that now had a claim to historical power; and by the start of the economic, commercial American Twenties this had become a dominant theme. The Twenties were, the historians tell us, a time when "there was a marked retreat from politics and public values toward the private and personal sphere, and even in those with a strong impulse toward dissent, bohemianism triumphed over radicalism," and when "never before in American history had artists and writers felt so impotent in relation to American society."[25] A no less important issue was the still-powerful influence of Anglo-Saxon culture over an increasingly plural America; this too was associated with "Puritanism." To this also, Francophilia became a solution. Hence Randolph Bourne, who was Anglophobic, explained that he now looked first to France for "an intellectual vitality, a sincerity and a candor, a tendency to think emotions and feel ideas, that integrated the spiritual world." "Ours is the first generation of Americans consciously engaged in spiritual pioneering," Waldo Frank likewise explained in

[24] R. P. Blackmur, "The American Literary Expatriate," in D. F. Bowers (ed.), *Foreign Influences in American Life: Essays and Critical Bibliographies* (Princeton, Princeton University Press, 1994), also reprinted in Blackmur's *The Lion and the Honeycomb: Essays in Solicitude and Critique* (London, Methuen, 1950); Matthew Josephson, *Portrait of the Artist as American* (New York, Harcourt Brace, 1930); Edmund Wilson, *Axel's Castle* (New York, Scribner, 1931); Malcolm Cowley, *Exile's Return: A Literary Odyssey of the 1920s* (New York, 1934: revised edition, New York, Viking, 1954; and London, Bodley Head, 1951); Frederick J. Hoffman, *The Twenties: American Writing in the Postwar Decade* (New York, Viking, 1955).

[25] Richard Hofstadter, *The Age of Reform: From Bryan to FDR* (New York, Knopf, 1955); and Arthur M. Schlesinger, Jr, *The Age of Roosevelt: Vol. 1: The Crisis of the Old Order, 1919–1933* (London, Heinemann, 1957).

The New America (1922). "The reaction against English domination in American cultural life is not an attack on England," he added. "It is a plea for America . . . Now one way to loose the hold of English literature is to stress the literature of other European centres. The other is to stress our own." One symbol of the disillusion with "Anglo-Saxon" civilization, and the celebration of Gallic civilization, was Ezra Pound's move to Paris in 1921. It was the modern "laboratory of ideas": "it is there poisons can be tested, new modes of sanity discovered," he explained in his essay "Rémy de Gourmont." "It is there the antiseptic conditions of the laboratory exist. That is the function of Paris."[26] The attraction of Paris was not just French "civilization." In fact, it was quite frequently the active rejection of that historic civilization, expressed by many of its most radical artists. In books like *The Sun Also Rises*, it is clear that the Europe of Henry James – elusive, experienced, dangerous, but always a centre of "civilization" – no longer survives, has been transformed into a shattered place, of disorder, conflict, decadence and sexual permissiveness.

But there were other factors, and over time the explanations and interpretations of the various push and pull factors have been many, various, and contradictory. The expatriates went to Paris to reject puritan, repressive America; they went simply to gather up the modern arts and bring them back safely home where they belonged. They went there, as Americans long had, to experience "experience," though the experience in question varied greatly (it meant anything from acquiring the great European cultural heritage to getting drunk); or they went to carry forth the new experience of Americans to the innocent and benighted Europeans. They went to acquire the modernist arts from their elders, and join the great master-class that was Montparnasse; they went for no such thing, but because life in Paris was easy and cheap. They went because they were rejecting the provincial backgrounds they came from; they went the better to understand their backgrounds and transform them into the sufficient material of literary art. They went to immerse themselves in the new French tendencies of the period, like Dada and Surrealism; they went to become even more distinctively American, and spent nearly all their time with compatriots of their own kind. They went because expatriation was an

[26] Ezra Pound, "Rémy de Gourmont," in *Pavannes and Divisions* (New York, Knopf, 1918).

American tradition, and the cultural capitals had always been abroad; they went to witness the disorder and breakdown of European culture, and see how much better things were at home.

It is unsurprising that, when the expatriate magazine *transition* ran an enquiry in Fall 1928, asking the expatriates "Why do you live outside America?", the answers were strikingly varied. Stein wrote of the impossibility of doing serious work in the USA, McAlmon wrote of the writer's utter dependence on deracination. Others noted the joys of wandering and the freedoms of Paris, and some noted these were sexual quite as much as aesthetic. When I interviewed a number of Paris alumni for a BBC Third Programme feature, the same wide variety of motive was clear. To quote one of the writers, Robert Coates:

> the reasons why I went were quite uncomplicated. I went partly because so many of my friends were going and also because I wanted to write, and the climate was such that rightly or wrongly one felt one could write better abroad. But I didn't know I was part of a mass movement until long after, and I doubt if the Kalmuks knew that they were part of a mass movement by that time.[27]

In truth no single explanation will ever sum up the issue; but what is clear is that these writers were part of a vast transformation not just in artistic history but in the very balance of cultural power, a change that was only half-sensed at the time. Paris was the meeting place of two potent forces. One was the peaking of European Modernism, an artistic movement born of a transformation of consciousness in a volatile, troubled Europe. The other was the new stirring of American Modernity, a fundamental process of technological and social change. And what helped bring about the meeting was the inward transformation of an American culture that was becoming morally and behaviourally far less culturally stable, far more experimental, and so responsive to *avant-garde* sentiment. The new in all things, it seemed, was necessary to the spirit of the new America. Until the Twenties, the "bohemian" movement had been almost entirely a European affair – a quarrel between the European social and political establishments and the world of its artistic *refusés*. On the other hand, when American writers talked of experiment, they generally thought they experimented not against but in behalf of the spirit of the nation (as Whitman had put

[27] Robert M. Coates, recorded interview with the author, New York, 1960. Broadcast in *Paris France* by Malcolm Bradbury, produced by Christopher Holme: BBC Third Programme, 19 February 1960.

it, "For all these new and evolutionary facts, meanings, purposes, new poetic messages, new forms and expressions, are inevitable"). But, toward the end of the nineteenth century, increasing signs of deracination and disaffiliation appeared in American culture, and from the "Wilde era" on bohemianism began to prosper. "Bohemia" is usually a revolt of the bourgeoisie against itself: parents prosper economically, but their children demand a yet higher liberation.

By 1913, the year of the Armory Show, American bohemia was already well endowed with devotees, patrons, and publicity. By the Twenties it was becoming victim to its own success. New social freedoms, growing sexual emancipation, a general cultural urbanization, and increasing wealth all combined to make art a desirable activity, radical chic a valued life-style, Greenwich Village an intensely fashionable venue. Style was consumed ever more avidly, old cold-water studios became desirable residences, rents downtown rose alarmingly.[28] And just at the moment when America seemed inclined to grow more conservative and more expensive, Paris was growing more radical and cheap. So what sailed abroad in the Twenties was American bohemia itself: the new youth culture, the radical life-style, the experimental attitude, the artist, the would-be artist and the swinger all rose and boarded the large liners that nowadays shuttled so often and so comfortably between the Manhattan Piers and Cherbourg. With them went many of their supporting networks and institutions: bookshops and publishers, magazines and presses, galleries and salons and patrons, on which the whole experiment depended. In Paris they found a Greenwich Village improved. There were cafés, there was no Volstead Act, a radical tradition of experiment in art-style and life-style, a chance to pose as an artist amongst a group of those doing likewise. Moreover, they found a France ever more responsive to American styles, manners and *mores*, delighted to honour the very fact of their Americanness as part of the spirit of the modern.

Hence, though much of what happened next was trivial and indulgent, part only of the history of modern amusement (for, as Ford Madox Ford said, "there was never any day so gay for the Arts as any twenty-four hours of the early Twenties in Paris"), the episode stays remarkable, first for its sheer scale, then for its ultimate achievement.

[28] See Caroline Ware, *Greenwich Village, 1920–1930: A Comment on American Civilization in the Postwar Years* (Boston, Houghton Mifflin, 1935).

Many writers went, into the several hundreds (McAlmon estimated some 250 writers settled in Paris), some to spend the rest of their lives there, some as temporary visitors. The interwar "long week-end" saw a colony of some 25,000 Americans in the capital.[29] When Frederick Hoffman did a survey of some 85 writers amongst them, he noted a number of common factors. Most were in their twenties, a third were from the Midwest, often from small towns. Many were college graduates, a significant number had seen war service in Europe. Some had private incomes or academic scholarships. About a third were dependent on editing, writing, or daily journalism (six, like Hemingway, were correspondents for American newspapers, twelve contributed regular features to American magazines, eight founded magazines in Paris under sponsorship). About half stayed less than five years, and most arrived before 1925, with a marked second wave in the latter half of the decade. Most were deliberately taking advantage of the favourable exchange rate (though other European cities were cheaper than Paris, but less artistically exciting). Most saw Paris as a place where they could write experimentally and non-commercially, as well as live a freer personal existence.[30] The sheer size and collectivity of the group is one important feature of it. The other is the radical quality and artistic impact of what was then produced. Many of these writers published extensively, and often first with the small presses of Paris. In fact it can fairly be claimed that it was here that the largest proportion of what was new, discovering and radical in modern American literature first expressed and established itself. The overall list would include not just the writing of Stein, Hemingway and Fitzgerald, but work by McAlmon, Djuna Barnes, William Carlos Williams, E. E. Cummings, Kay Boyle, Katherine Anne Porter, Louis Bromfield, Glenway Wescott, Robert Coates, Elliott Paul, Nathanael West, Henry Miller, Anaïs Nin. There was a no less significant contribution in poetry (Pound, Williams, Crane, Benét, MacLeish, etc.), and painting, photography, film, music, dance, and criticism. In fact, there was scarcely a significant artist of the generation who did not in some way respond to the clarion call of the cafés, parties, salons, studios and presses of Paris.[31]

[29] According to Joseph A. Barry, *Left Bank, Right Bank: Paris and Parisians* (London, Kimber, 1952).
[30] Frederick J. Hoffman, *The Twenties: American Writing and the Postwar Decade*, cited above.
[31] For a useful record of this, see Hugh Ford's excellent and detailed *Published in Paris:*

Hence, for one crucial decade, Paris became the chief setting for what Pound liked to call "the American Risorgimento": which would "make the Italian Renaissance look like a tempest in a teapot." But this meant that the "American Risorgimento" became simply one part of a yet larger transformation, part of a Western cosmopolitanization of the arts. There is little doubt that this was the time when the Modern was realized as an aesthetic idea, and that Paris was the chief venue. The migrant cultures it attracted were essential to this process. The city was a multi-lingual art-community; writers Russian and American, British and German, Romanian and Italian, Spanish and Latin American (the young Borges was there, for example) found a common focus in a radical idea of modern style, and through a sequence of international modern movements: Symbolism, Futurism, Expressionism, Dadaism, Surrealism, Art Deco, Vertigralism. The American expatriates were in effect expatriates to expatriation itself. Expatriation, exile, had created its own culture, founded its own institutions, developed its own vision of art and history, its own ways of life, even its own streets, settings, cafés and meeting places. It was an aesthetic melting-pot, dependent on a transatlantic multiplicity of styles. It was also wide open to the American promise; and American writing and arts, the work of a new power in the world, quickly won the acceptance of the advanced spirits of Europe. Indeed they incorporated them into their view of the modern method – just at the point when that writing, with the work of Stein, Hemingway, Faulkner, Pound, Williams, Stevens, West, Miller and Nin, assumed a cosmopolitan spirit it had never yet possessed. Thus the Paris exchanges of the Twenties represented, we can see in retrospect, a triumphant peak of the transatlantic drama of Old World and New that had been affecting and shaping the arts since the moment of American Independence. Many of the key books of the modern age, the books that defined its revolution of style and its aura both of innovation and crisis, came from Paris or its radiation. And they included a growing number of American titles. From now on, works of fiction like Joyce's *Ulysses*, Mann's *The Magic Mountain*, Proust's *Remembrance of Things Past*, Kafka's *The Trial*, Virginia Woolf's *Mrs Dalloway*, André Gide's *The Counterfeiters*, Ford's *Parade's End*, the early

American and British Writers, Printers, and Publishers in Paris, 1920–1939 (London, Garnstone Press, 1975), and Noel Riley Fitch's thorough *Sylvia Beach and the Lost Generation: A History of Literary Paris in the Twenties and Thirties* (New York, Norton, and London, Condor, 1983).

work of Samuel Beckett and Lawrence Durrell, would live naturally alongside Stein's *The Making of Americans*, Cummings' *The Enormous Room*, Dos Passos' *USA*, Hemingway's *In Our Time*, Faulkner's *The Sound and the Fury*, Williams' *The Great American Novel* or Henry Miller's *Tropic of Cancer*. By the decade's end, American literature was acknowledged as a modern world literature. Its acceptance was perhaps signalled by the award of the Nobel Prize for Literature to Sinclair Lewis in 1930, the first American to be honoured. But by 1930, though, everything had changed. The Depression had come, the bank drafts stopped, the exiles returned, to discover their writing had won its own American audience. The transatlantic experiment in writing, as in painting, dance and music, had actually succeeded. American writing was no longer a sub-branch of English literature. It was an active component of a far larger international experiment, acknowledged abroad and increasingly at home. That, in the end, is why the Twenties episode remains so influential, and so important.

7.

What happened in the Twenties in Paris, then, was nothing less than a vast, radical international flowering of every one of the modern arts: architecture and interior design, music and ballet, painting and drama, photography and film. But one of the major beneficiaries was fiction. It was at this time, and especially in this place, that the modern novel and the modern short story finally and confidently took on a new technical, linguistic and imaginative freedom. Both deeply changed in their basic fictional economy. The modern was visibly a new style, hard, clean, spatial, poetic. It meant a new concept of representation, a changed way of denoting space and time, feeling and consciousness. But the modern was also a new subject-matter; and in that too America played a new and novel part. As never before, American themes became motifs of international fiction, as Kafka's novel *Amerika* suggests. Meanwhile American writers themselves celebrated their own time and space with a new and experimental vigour, displaying America to the world as the existential timelessness of Hemingway's Michigan woods, the culture-less modernity of Sinclair Lewis' midwestern *Main Street*, the high-speed skyscraper metropolis of Dos Passos' *Manhattan Transfer*, the dying South of Faulkner's fiction. Working in Paris, American writers and painters looked back, with an expatriate, experimental gaze, on a simpler nation they had left behind, and perhaps America was now leaving behind too: the fading wilderness of the old South, the natural world of the Midwestern lakes and plains, the simple frontier of the Middle Border, all of them now yielding to mechanical and commercial transformation. Inevitably enough, though (and perhaps not least because many of their works were published and read in Paris), the subject-matter of their writings also incorporated the great new international adventure itself. Thus a significant number of their works of fiction were stories of the encounter between a new generation of Americans and a new and more troubled Europe. Robert McAlmon's tales in *A Companion Volume* (1923), the Berlin stories in his *Distinguished Air* (1925) and various other pieces, Glenway Wescott's *The Grandmothers* (1927) and *Goodbye, Wisconsin* (1928), William Carlos Williams' European novel *A Voyage to Pagany* (1928), Elliot Paul's *A Narrow Street* (1942), and the writings of Louis Bromfield, Djuna Barnes, Kay Boyle, Katherine Anne Porter and Henry Miller, and so on, all dealt with the theme.

These were no longer tales of Jamesian encounters between American innocence and European experience. Arriving Americans were no longer naïve spirits from a safe simple world, but critical bearers of the message of change. Likewise the Europeans here depicted no longer carry the weight of social density and moral complexity, but the flavour of crisis, defeat or corruption. Nor were they manipulators of history, but its victims. The whole spirit of transatlantic encounter had changed, reflecting not just the collapse that had taken place in European civilization around the war, but the fast-changing balance of cultural and moral power. For the American visitors themselves, Europe seemed an appropriate echo to their own cultural and historical confusion. Often their stories seemed to be placed ambiguously between here and there, future and past, innocence and corruption, modernity and simplicity, America and Europe, looking both ways for an answer, and often finding nothing but ambiguity. These were, as Robert McAlmon put it in his stories, "deracinated encounters."[32] Or, as Glenway Wescott expressed it, in his story "Goodbye, Wisconsin": "Never live in Paris: everyone there

[32] There is a good record of McAlmon's experience and his autobiographical and fictional treatments of it in Robert E. Knoll (ed.), *McAlmon and the Lost Generation: A Self-Portrait* (Lincoln, Nebraska, University of Nebraska Press, 1962).

has done some harm to everyone else; the heart must be kept in fashion, there was the influence of Henry James, so it is no longer elegant to quarrel; they go dining together, a malicious intimacy with a lump in its throat . . . Never live in New York either: a town in which 'it is essential to wear one's heart on one's sleeve and one's tongue in one's cheek.' New York is half-way between the south of France and Wisconsin, always half-way between any two such places . . ."[33] The half-way house, the rootless centre, became the common residence of the age.

There were two kinds of novel in particular, intricately related to each other, which best seemed to sum up the whole encounter and the climate in which it flourished. One of them was the war novel, the other the post-war novel, and both reflected the new American encounter with Europe. Initially the war novel was not a particularly American form – just as the war was, first and foremost, a European experience. What happened to young soldiers at the front or in the trenches, whether French or Italian, German or Austrian, British or American, was, after all, much the same. Patriotic and sentimental myth shattered, life became simply futile and cheap, culture and history no longer gave good reason for what was happening, language itself seemed to collapse before horror, and silence fell; meanwhile all that was taking place in the field seemed meaningless and inexplicable to those at home. The war novel itself became an international form that emerged from the trenches and the combatants on both sides of the conflict. Henri Barbusse's *Le Feu* (1915), set naturalistically on the Somme and the Marne, and telling the story of a front where the ground was so filled with corpses that the earth itself grew corpse-like, was a prototype. Translated into English in 1917, it became the exemplary work of an age when, said the British writer H. M. Tomlinson in 1915, "the parapet, the wire, the mud" had now become "permanent features of human existence." Writers like the German Ernst Jünger and the Czech Jaroslav Hašek, author of *The Good Soldier Schweik* (1922), would tell similar tales from other sides of the wire.[34] Entering the war late, Americans, it seemed, were left only to record what others

---

[33] Glenway Wescott, "Goodbye, Wisconsin," in *Goodbye, Wisconsin* (New York and London, Harper and Brothers, 1928). His work is discussed in detail in Ira D. Johnson, *Glenway Wescott: The Paradox of Voice* (Port Washington, N.Y., Kennicat Press, 1971).
[34] The international nature of war fiction and its interconnections is especially well explored in Holger Klein (ed.), *The First World War in Fiction* (London, Macmillan, 1976).

had already recorded. But it was with American entry that a European war became a "World War," and for Americans it was a war fought abroad, on foreign soil, so that it was the fate of other cities, empires and political systems, most of them remote from the American, that was at stake. Moreover, though two million Americans served as soldiers, many of those who wrote about the experience were serving in the ambulance services, in some cases because of their pacifist convictions. All this induced into American treatments what Malcolm Cowley has called a "spectatorial attitude," and a somewhat different view of the crisis. War was an intense experience, destructive of illusions, but it was also a parable: of the end of civilization itself, of the loss of certainties and ideals, of the emergence of a new age of machinery and violence. Not just the nations of Europe but many of the fundamental ideals of religion or humanism seemed to be blasting themselves to pieces in the trenches and the mud. The war, as horrific fact, as parable or metaphor, came to play quite as large a part in American fiction as it did in any other. Many of the most powerful novels of the Great War were to come from American writers, and not least from Hemingway himself. The novel of European war entered the mainstream of American fiction as powerfully and influentially as it did the fictional traditions of Europe, and it no less changed fiction's whole form and sensibility.

But for American writers many of these were tales of a double initiation: to war, and to Europe. A variety of striking and often highly experimental books came from the experience. E. E. Cummings had, for instance, left Harvard to become a Cubist painter in New York; then, as soon as America entered the war, and despite his pacifist sympathies, he joined the Norton-Harjes Ambulance Corps. The sense of Cubist playfulness found its way into his anarchistic novel *The Enormous Room* (1922) – the story of his incarceration in the French military prison at La Ferté Macé, along with his friend William Slater Brown, after they had both offended the French censorship by referring to French troop mutinies in their letters home. The book is a prose experiment, with typographical play and stream-of-consciousness episodes; above all it is a satirical comedy about war and the military mind itself. Yet more ambitious and experimental is the war fiction of John Dos Passos, Cummings' friend and a fellow-pacifist – who, over the course of his writings, constantly widened his technical and historical perspective on a war-experience that fundamentally shaped his youth, and stayed with him through the rest of his writing life. The war and its consequences are constantly seen as the emblem of modern outrage, the turning-point of the age, the reason, perhaps, for a sense of cultural ambiguity that has left the world in fragments. Though he had left Harvard opposing American involvement in the conflict, and regarded the war as a conspiracy by international bankers and capitalists, Dos Passos begged his father to be allowed to enlist. When he was refused, he moved to Madrid to be closer to the conflict. On his father's death, he too promptly joined the Norton-Harjes Ambulance brigade, along with Cummings, Brown, Edmund Wilson and Robert Hillyer. As he explained to friends, he had not "gone militarist," but "merely wanted to see a little of the war personally." In letters, diaries, and a novel he began with Robert Hillyer, he persistently assaulted "the mountain of lies," the "suicidal madness," the "merry parade that is stifling in brutishness all the things of the world." He condemned the war as a vast offence against "all the things of art and mind," a senseless corruption of language, a "gibber" of politicians, "the shells of truth putrid and fake." But, he added, "I want to be able to express, later – all of this – all the tragedy and hideous excitement of it. I have seen so little I must experience more of it, & more. The grey crooked fingers of the dead, the dark look of dirty mangled bodies . . ."

When he wrote his first work of fiction, *One Man's Initiation: 1917* (1920), it was to explore these contradictory feelings. As the title says, this book is the very immediate story of one man's experience, about a sensitive American soldier, Martin Howe, through whose highly aesthetic eyes the battlefields are seen. War is a destruction of culture and art, though it is also the symbol of a past civilization trying to crush the spirit of the radical present. But this evidently seemed too narrow a theme, and in further novels Dos Passos returned to the subject, clearly seeking a more epic and political vision of events. In *Three Soldiers* (1921), he explored the theme from the standpoints of three very different American soldiers, from different social backgrounds, with different experiences and expectations; the book has rightly been called a work of cultural crisis, its theme less the war itself than the encounter between individualism and mass mobilization. His next major book, *Manhattan Transfer* (1925), was not about war; it is a vast Expressionist portrait of New York as the exemplary mass modern city, a metropolitan battlefield in itself. But by *USA* (1930–6) the theme of war and history had turned into the stuff of an experimental modern epic. He tried over the work's three volumes – *The 42nd Parallel, 1919*, and *The Big Money* – to give, through a variety of experimental techniques, from newspaper collage to what he called "the camera eye," a vast account of his nation in the world over the first thirty years of the century. The war is at the centre; in various ways the many characters, some real figures, others invented fictions, are drawn into some aspect of its crisis, turmoil and corruption. And war also explains the fragmentary nature of the modern method, the breaking up of the old narrative and reportage of fiction, indeed the moral and linguistic disorientation of the USA itself.

There is little wonder that the Great War came to dominate the spirit of fiction during the Twenties on both sides of the Atlantic. Not only did it represent the crucial experience of a generation, the rite of passage that had made them modern and cut them off from their past and their parenthood. It was also a challenge to writing's very power to confront reality and experience, to encounter the horrific and naked truth of contemporary life. Thus it became a primary source of the modern experiment itself, explaining its need to revolt against traditional representation. For the task of the writer was surely not simply to report the war, as participant or observer, or even to debunk it. It was to grasp its enormous truth, and the crisis for history, culture and representation it signified. For these reasons it is sometimes claimed that war was the prime cause of the Modernist method itself (thus it was the Great War that "smashed all the Stendhalian mirrors," and pushed literature away from report and representation toward radical form, says John McCormick in his *American Literature, 1919–1932*, 1971). But this under-estimates the extent to which a new experimental method had already developed in the fiction of the immediately pre-war years, where the modern novel has its chief foundations. Even so, it cannot be doubted that the encounter with war and battle made many of the Modernist forms and devices – spatialization of form, the use of hard techniques of expression, impression and fragmentation, the mechanization of the human figure, the loss of narrative coherence or moral conviction – seem in effect natural and normal. War and all that went with it – a sense of disorder, dehumanization, meaninglessness, futility – became a prime atmospheric condition of the modern way in writing. It is clearly significant that many of the most experimental novels to appear in the early Twenties – Proust's *A la recherche du temps perdu* and Lawrence's *Women in Love*, Joyce's *Ulysses* and Mann's *The Magic*

Mountain, even Kafka's *The Trial* – were written over wartime, and were deeply affected by its apocalyptic implications. For many younger writers, the war marked not only their first profound experience but the precise moment of their initiation into modernity, the one experience from which all else flowed – just as everything in Hemingway flowed from the single moment at Fossalta.[35]

Thus the war novel translated into the post-war novel, the tale of young lives lived under and transformed, directly or indirectly, by the war's compelling shadow. Scott Fitzgerald explained of his first, youthful novel, *This Side of Paradise,* that it was a story of the young people who thought they would be killed in the war, and claimed the book had won its success "simply for telling people that I felt as they did, that something had to be done with all the nervous energy stored up and unexpended in the war." Faulkner's novels persistently drew on the image of the war-wounded coming back into the world of a post-war decadence. The bright fiction of Michael Arlen (*The Green Hat,* 1924) or Anita Loos (*Gentlemen Prefer Blondes,* 1925) caught the brittle, cynical spirit of a war-changed generation trying to make a style out of a crisis. "I got hurt in the war," explains Jake Barnes, the genitally wounded hero-narrator of Hemingway's expatriate novel *The Sun Also Rises* (1926); and this half-symbolic fate he shares with most of the "herd" of young American, British and European wanderers who make up the cast of the novel. In fact there is no doubt that the remarkable impact Hemingway's fiction had on his generation owed nearly everything to the fact that all took place in the shadow of the war and the wound; hence it captured the tone and intimate style of a generation that felt castrated not just by external violence but by a new general sterility and Spenglerian despair that influenced all behaviour. Throughout

---

[35] So, in *The Great War and Modern Memory* (New York and London, Oxford University Press, 1975), Paul Fussell remarks on the way the accounts of the war memoirists changed in spirit and style: "The passage of . . . literary characters from prewar freedom to wartime bondage, frustration and absurdity signals just as surely as does the experience of Joyce's Bloom, Hemingway's Frederic Henry and Kafka's Joseph K. the passage of modern writing from one mode to another, from the low mimetic of the plausible and the social to the ironic of the outrageous, the ridiculous, and the murderous." Another important study of this matter is Frederick J. Hoffman, *The Mortal No: Death and the Modern Imagination* (Princeton, Princeton University Press, 1964). Also see Sam Hynes, *A War Imagined: The First World War and English Culture* London, Bodley Head, 1990). A valuable study of American war fiction in particular is Stanley Cooperman, *World War I and the American Novel* (Baltimore, Johns Hopkins University Press, 1967).

Hemingway's writing, the theme of war and the generation coincided – creating a distinctive sense of life as tragedy and futility, a mood of stoic despair coupled with the need to discover a new courage that would allow this post-war condition to be borne. Hemingway's world is one where war, violence and brutal death are pervasive, and this is seen both as a new historical fact and as a "natural" and eternal condition, as the rituals of the bullfight or the big-game hunt display. In his stories, descriptions of wartime situations, taken from the experience of "Nick Adams" or from his reportage of the Graeco-Turkish conflict, and sad sterile stories of post-war expatriate life ("Hills Like White Elephants," "A Cat in the Rain") sit naturally side by side, one world illuminating the other.

Part of the great success and influence of *The Sun Also Rises* thus comes from the fact that it is both an exemplary novel of post-war life, or a post-war way of trying to live, and a central expatriate text. Despite the usual unreliable disclaimer ("No character in this book is the portrait of an actual person"), it is, of course, a record of Hemingway's own experience and a picture of many of his friends and ex-friends in the Paris and Spain of the mid-Twenties. It is also the story of a new herd, of a self-conscious generation for whom the style of all things – living, loving, fishing, fighting, drinking, writing, reading and sleeping – has been changed by the shadow now cast everywhere, except over those who foolishly fail, like Robert Cohn, to see it, and are therefore not "one of us." Post-war life and expatriate life are one and the same. Thus the bars of Paris and the bullrings of Spain provide a new stylish Waste Land, where new fashions get started, and new manners and *mores* flourish, but where fertility is everywhere cursed. As the hero Jake Barnes notes, "You paid some way for everything that was any good." Jake has been wounded flying on the Italian front; as the liaison colonel tells him, " 'You, a foreigner, an Englishman' (any foreigner was an Englishman) 'have given more than your life.' " He is thus unable to fulfil a sexual relationship with Lady Brett Ashley, the mannish British aristocrat and near-bitch, whose own promiscuous and androgynous sexuality is another aspect of the same problem. The wound is the resonant symbol – intolerable intrusion and penetration, ultimate exposure – and it is those who in one way or another bear its trauma who carry the weight of the book's action. Meantime male things – the natural joy of a fishing trip, the clean performance of Romero in his bullfights – provide the vivid, existential experiences that compensate for the universal futility. The problem is to find a right manner of living: "I did not care what it was all about," Jake explains. "All I wanted to know was how to live in it. Maybe if you found out how to live in it you learned what it was all about." "It" here is evidently the pervasive condition of the new post-war existence; "how to live" means acquiring the necessary rituals, of stoicism, courage, enjoyment and self-restraint, that *afición* that Jake now possesses, and in which he gives his friends and his readers constant lessons, even down to the correct reading of novels and the proper writing of prose. So the book had a double appeal. On the one hand it was a complete Baedeker of post-war social, geographical, moral, emotional and stylistic knowledge, a handy compendium for travelling abroad and finding out how to drink the right drinks in the right places, acquire the right tone, display the right sensibility, read the right books and say the right lines; it was a lesson in *afición*. On the other hand it was an exemplary and often satirical portrait of a pained, highly self-aware and destructive modern élite, hunting through this particular social and geographical terrain because it is entirely consistent with the condition of their souls. *The Sun Also Rises* is Hemingway's most social novel, and his most fashionable one, a guidebook to an expatriate scene where the life lived was that of a new class of stylists. But all real hope for survival and endurance lies somewhere beyond the social scene of the book. It is seen in the glimpses of somewhere more fundamental, found in Spain and the world of nature, where some new existential contact between the world and the individual can occur, the integrity of event confronting some equal integrity of self. And this is the real heart of the famous Hemingway "style."

Hemingway was thus to be the great recorder of a complex encounter: between war and post-war, between Europe and the sense of modernity. He extended this a year later, in the story-collection *Men Without Women* (1927), probably the best single volume he ever achieved. The stories range widely in subject, though they always share the same exactitude of style. The world of war and then of post-war Europe are again the main settings. "In the fall the war was always there, but we did not go to it any more": so begins "In Another Country," a short tale about wounded soldiers together in a Milan military hospital, "held together by there being something that has happened that they, the people who disliked us, did not understand." Meanwhile other stories – "Che Ti Dice La Patria," "A Simple

Enquiry" – explore something of the fate of Italy after the conflict, and deal with the rising tide of Italian Fascism. Others link with the stories of the earlier volume *In Our Time*, in one of which Nick Adams makes a "separate peace," another where an affair develops between a wounded soldier and a nurse. All this perhaps pointed an inevitable direction for Hemingway to go next. He had already attempted a novel about war on the Italian front, *Along with Youth*, which would follow Nick Adams' adventures on the Italian front, but discarded it after thirty pages. But he still had yet to write his war novel; and war, he told Scott Fitzgerald, was the ideal literary subject: "War groups the maximum of material and speeds up the action and brings out all sorts of stuff you normally have to wait a lifetime to get." When, following his marriage to Pauline, Hemingway left Paris for America in 1928, he therefore carried with him the notion of a book that over the next difficult year he was to develop into his most famous work. There was the experience of soldiering, the discovery of war, its courage and vanity, the emptiness of the peace that followed it. There was the experience of the front, the hospital in Milan, the pain and the sleeplessness, the affair with a nurse. Over the year in which he wrote the book, Pauline had a child by Caesarian section, and his father, worried by illness, shot himself. The book he wrote, and lightly described as "my long tale of transatlantic fornication including the war in Italy," was written on the move as he in effect gave up Paris, except for a few further brief visits. Hemingway finished it just before his thirtieth birthday, and it was published as *A Farewell to Arms* – its title a pun on love and war – in 1929.

Hemingway's treatment of the theme could well have seemed a very late entrant in the war-novel stakes – since his book was well pre-dated by works by Cummings, Dos Passos, and Thomas Boyd, who published the interesting *Through the Wheat* in 1923. But by now the climate around war fiction had greatly changed. The war was seen to have solved nothing, and crisis, economic and political, was growing again throughout Europe; indeed there were now widespread fears of another coming European conflict. The Twenties thus closed on a fresh, warning, international wave of war fiction. 1929 alone saw a spate of war novels and memoirs, works of larger scope and longer retrospect: Erich Maria Remarque's *All Quiet on the Western Front*, Richard Aldington's *Death of a Hero*, Robert Graves' *Goodbye to All That*. At first sight Hemingway's novel seems more much romantic and more personal than the others, and simpler in conception, though not in execution. But his "tale of transatlantic fornication including the war in Italy," dealing chiefly with the story of a finally tragic wartime romance between an American army lieutenant, Frederic Henry, and a British nurse, Catherine Barkley, conducted on the seemingly almost pastoral setting of the Italian front, is far more than a bleak love story that happens to be set in wartime. It is a vision of the historical failure, the psychological and sexual crisis, the war had deposited across a generation, and it summed up not just the experience of war but the experience of the dying Twenties. It was a tragic tale for a time that increasingly felt a new sense of malaise, and despite several notable works to follow remains surely his finest novel, a striking work of felt modernity. It is also not, quite, the story of the young Ernest Hemingway. Frederic Henry, the book's hero and narrator, is not the author, nor quite his surrogate, as Nick Adams would have been in the earlier version. He is older, sexually more experienced, politically wiser, linguistically more adept, and with an irony of observation Hemingway himself only acquired much later. He has lived for a time in Italy, trained as an architect, and now has enlisted in the Italian army, working, obscurely, as an armed officer in an ambulance section. The key events of the novel take place in 1917, when Hemingway himself was still at school in Oak Park; that is because the main story is set around the horrific retreat from Caporetto, when the Austrians and Germans broke through the front line and put the Italian army to flight. As for the book's fundamental theme – disillusion with the heroics, adventure and propaganda of war, and a search beyond the war for a "separate peace" – that is something remote from the Hemingway of 1918.

The book starts brilliantly, with Hemingway's usual deceptive simplicity, which is quickly qualified. "In the late summer of that year we lived in a house in a village that looked across the river and the plain to the mountains," it begins, as if we are about to enter a reassuring, familiar world of nature and pastoral. But the summer is a summer of critical war offensives, those who live in the house are soldiers, the terrain is military, the river is a front, the mountains where lightning seems to flash are in fact lit up by artillery. The trees are caked with dust, the fall comes strangely early, bringing the rains which then bring the cholera ("it was checked and in the end only seven thousand died of it in the army"). From this moment on, the novel concentrates on the intersection of love and war. The mountains, lakes and rivers, the summers and winters, the rains and snows, are metonyms, but also controlling metaphors. As narrator, Henry is cut off from the linguistic funds of the past ("I was always embarrassed by the words sacred, glorious, and sacrifice and the expression in vain . . . Abstract words such as glory, honour, courage or hallow were obscene beside the concrete names of villages, the numbers of roads, the names of rivers, the numbers of regiments and the dates"). The simple style functions clearly and luminously, yet vividly displays the quality Edmund Wilson so memorably defined: "an undruggable consciousness of something wrong." The feeling suppressed leaks out everywhere as tragic symbolism, as the narrative follows the long sequence of nihilistic events: the wounding, the social absurdity of life in Milan, the names of villages, the record of corpses, the courage and the cowardice of fighting men. Henry's controlled response is put at risk when he receives his wound and then falls in love with Catherine, the British VAD nurse with whom he had intended only a brief affair. Throughout the five books of the tragic story, war and love run symbolically parallel, counterpointing each other, and pointing the way through love and their "separate peace" to disaster.

The book's strong opening is echoed in its close, after Henry and Catherine have made their flight by boat to neutral Switzerland, and are together ("We could be alone when we were together, alone against the others"). But, with an ominous reprise, the last act begins at another house in the mountains, over Montreux. "That fall the snow came very late. We lived in a brown wooden house in the pine trees on the side of the mountain and at night there was frost so that there was thin ice over the water in the two pitchers on the dresser in the morning." The "we" is now Henry and Catherine, and "The war seemed very far away. But I knew from the papers that they were still fighting in the mountains because the snow would not come." But love finally ends just where it began, in the hospital ward, where Catherine and the baby die during a Caesarian section. This leads to the final lesson, that in peace as well as war the same rules prevail. There is no innocence, but only more experience: "That was what you did. You died . . . You did not know what it was all about. You never had time to learn. They threw you in and told you the rules and the first time they caught you off base they killed you," Henry reflects, and ends the story alone, in the eternal rain. Even disillusion with the heroics of war, the search for the separate peace, ends in the same futility. Hemingway reaches the opposite of his youthful heroic vision of war in 1918, and the book is a reading of the grim lesson of the Twenties: a war *and* a post-war novel. *A Farewell to Arms* came out in September 1929, to warm reviews. A month later, Wall Street crashed, and the bright, bitter, post-war decade of the Twenties was very plainly over.

8.

1929 proved, in fact, a year of Modernist monuments. Besides Hemingway's highly successful novel, the book that lifted him out of the experimental *avant-garde* and into the literary mainstream, Faulkner's *The Sound and the Fury* appeared; Cocteau published *Les Enfants terribles*, and the Nobel Prize was awarded to Thomas Mann. That same year, satisfying a dream which had started in 1920, in the climate of Dada, and with Man Ray, Duchamp and Katherine Dreier, the Museum of Modern Art (MOMA) opened its doors in New York, with an exhibition of Post-Impressionist paintings. What was happening was that Modernism was now being institutionalized, indeed becoming historical. Instead of being the modern outrage, it was now becoming the modern style. What is more, it was also, increasingly, becoming an American style. In American design, architecture, technology, in the look of the newest skyscrapers, the shape of the newest automobiles, as well as in the magazines, the clothes, the body-shapes and the film-star images of the now busily talking pictures, the modern was a flourishing project. As Scott Fitzgerald, along with Hemingway the great recorder of the time when the modern turned from being a futuristic principle into a habit, wisely put it, during the Twenties "something subtle passed to America, the style of man." Even the French acknowledged it; it was the style of what was called, again with Fitzgerald's help, "the jazz age," and for a time it seemed as if it would go on forever. In September 1929, just as *A Farewell to Arms* appeared, stock prices were 400 per cent over their 1924 level. A month later, on 24 October, the stock market broke. Herbert Hoover blamed the international balance of payments problem and the unmanageable weakness of the European economies. Europeans, with just as much reason, blamed America and its easy credit and careless fiscal policies, which had allowed the bubble of boom to float freely. Whatever the key reason, the consequences on both sides of the water were equally terrible. The European economies, aided by American help during the Twenties, plunged back into disaster. The American economy did likewise, and America's sufferings became very much those of Europe ("We were cheated of our uniqueness," Daniel Boorstin observed). The change in the historical climate was swift. World currencies went out of control, as the now dominant American economy began running backwards and forwards like an absurd machine. And, as Fitzgerald, who observed this as closely as everything that went before, said, "it didn't take long for the whole flimsy structure to settle earthward." What he named "the greatest, gaudiest spree in history" was over.

The Twenties died quickly, and so did the artistic climate they had constructed. The age of leisure, travel and super-wealth was finished, and realities in all their unpleasantness began to take over. Visitors to Germany and Austria now reported they were saying "Heil Hitler" in the streets, while in Italy the Fascism of Mussolini (whom Hemingway twice interviewed) was in full control. As economic and political disorder spread, and the real instability of the post-war order and the failure of the Versailles settlement grew ever more apparent, the cheques that had supported bohemia, and paid for the small presses, the cheap drinks and the easy travels of Americans in Europe stopped flowing. The Modern revolution, it seemed, had been largely paid for by American capital itself. Now the capital was withdrawn, and the patrons and customers no longer around. A "lost generation" which might well have lost itself for good, in the cafés of Paris, the enlarging resorts of the Riviera, the Alpine ski-slopes and the bullfights of Spain, saw its funds begin to dry up, and its institutions start to disappear. Not all the people went. A significant group of American expatriates remained in Paris; some of them, like Stein and Beach, were to be there into the next war, which already began to threaten; and new visitors kept coming, though in a very different mood. But most of the exiles now returned home. With the nation and the world in trouble, even Depression America seemed a better place to be. "Those of brief culture and unsteady fortunes went first," was how Malcolm Cowley put it in his *Exile's Return*, "then the richer ones, then the bank clerks and portrait painters and reporters for American newspapers who had depended on the presence of expatriated wealth." So too had the experimentalists of Europe, who also began to see the world in a different light, as on both sides of the Atlantic the aesthetic Twenties turned into the Marxizing Thirties.

It was again left to Scott Fitzgerald, who had always seen himself as the herald of his age, to chronicle what happened. All his books, he said, had had "a touch of disaster in them," and even as he chronicled the interlocked worlds of beauty and wealth over the Twenties he had seen something glorious but also corrupt. When the Crash came, and the gilded edifice settled earthward, he and his world collapsed too, like a "cracked plate." In that summer of 1929 the Fitzgeralds had returned to Europe on a fresh two-year visit, renting a villa in Cannes while he struggled with his long-unfinished book. "I am working night and day on novel from a new angle that I think will solve all previous difficulties," he reported back to base. And he had changed his Riviera novel drastically, to include recent events and such material as the making of a movie. But this whole new European episode seemed doomed from the start. It turned into two years of decline and disaster, during which he damaged many friendships and was imprisoned twice for his drunken escapades. If he was "cracking," Zelda was cracking even more. She had hoped to become a ballerina with Diaghilev, but was offered only a dancing role with the Folies Bergères; now her breakdown became acute, and she had to be hospitalized, in various sanatoria that clustered around Lake Geneva; she would spend most of the rest of her life in expensive clinics and rest homes that had to be paid for. Fitzgerald's novel now became an exploration not of the dream but the nightmare of the Twenties. Written in drink, financial anxiety, pain and despair, it struggled its way into existence. Starting as a tale about a movie technician working on the Riviera who wishes to murder his possessive mother, the book took on new characters, went through draft after draft and title after title. Characters kept changing sex and function, and the world changed so fast now that new material had constantly to go in. The work finally went through seventeen revisions; the stack of manuscript now held in the Princeton Library is at least a foot high. At last, in 1934, in the middle of the Depression, the book appeared, as *Tender Is the Night*. But even this published version did not satisfy Fitzgerald. "It's amazing how excellent much of it is," Hemingway acknowledged, "much of it better than anything else he ever wrote. How I wish he would have kept on writing. Is it really over or will he write again?" It was a fair question. Fitzgerald, disappointed by the book's poor sales (it sold only 12,000 copies), and feeling he had not solved all of its structural problems, went back to it again, recasting the narrative line, changing the focus. When he died in 1940, this new text was unfinished, as was the only novel he started after it, his story of Hollywood, *The Last Tycoon*.

It was left to Fitzgerald's friend Malcolm Cowley to complete the exercise, turning a chapter of accidents into an accident of chapters. For a long time this revision remained, at least in Britain, the standard version, and the textual confusion did nothing to help critical views of the novel. This was a literary tragedy, for of all the versions of the expatriate experience of the Twenties, *Tender Is the Night* is the most remarkable. And, though the newer version was to have its own merits, the book's original plan and time-scheme, which Fitzgerald thought had contributed to its failure, does actually make perfect sense. (The book's failure had more to do with the speed with which the Thirties discarded the Twenties.) First came the glittering scenes on the summer Riviera in 1925, when expatriate culture has come to luxurious fulfilment. Then the story went back to 1917, when Europe was still in shellshocked wartime. Then came the final phase, which is set amid the psychic and economic tremors of 1930, the year of Zelda's breakdown, when the old decade and the world that went with it are dying. This shape follows out the curve of its author's high sense of European possibilities and his dreams of the American decade, taking us from Dick's very American sense of life's eternal possibilities, and his fascination with the glowing wonders of wealth, backwards into the sources of psychic and economic trauma, which start in wartime, and then bringing us to the final degradation and defeat. The hero, Dick Diver, who is that modern figure the psychologist, starts out innocent and "intact," but "the price of his intactness is incompleteness." He has always wanted to dive into history, to serve. Jotting down his plan in his notebook, Fitzgerald had observed: "The novel should do this: Show a man who is a natural idealist, a spoiled priest, giving in for various causes to the ideas of the haute Burgeoise [*sic*], and in his rise to the top of the social world losing his idealism, his talent and turning to drink and dissipation. Background is one in which the liesure [*sic*] class is at their truly most brilliant & glamorous, such as Murphys." Dick Diver is a "spoiled priest," who has been sent under military orders to study psychiatry in wartime Zürich, but then applies his skills not just to the victims of war but of peace, and who attempts to assume responsibility for others by using all his social charms as well as his psychological wisdom. The chief background is socialite Europe, the place where rich Americans gather, and art, money, amusement and instability converge. Here the great gaudy spree exceeds its season, when the post-war generation attempts to resume its privileged existence after the war has shelled the old order to death. Here cause is divorced from effect, as money is divorced from its origins in labour, or the French Riviera is divorced from the Swiss sanatoria, where the price for everything is paid.

As Hemingway was for once generous enough to see, *Tender Is the Night* is a remarkable novel: a striking work of psycho-history, a sharp view taken from the Marxist Thirties over the gaudy Twenties. In *The Sun Also Rises*, Hemingway had observed the psychic and social crisis in and for itself, and sought to find out "how to live in it." But Fitzgerald sees it all externally, critically, in relation to the processes of history. The signals of Marxist revisionism are apparent: "At that moment, the Divers represented externally the exact furthermost evolution of a class," he comments at one point, giving us the benefit of his reading of *Das Kapital*. But no less powerful is his vision of what the Divers – Dick and his wife Nicole Warren, the daughter of a Chicago tycoon who comes under his treatment after she has been molested by her father – represent internally, psychologically: a world of inner crisis, growing violence and despair. Dick Diver, the initially innocent and intact young doctor who considers the price of his intactness is incompleteness, is evidently a surrogate for Fitzgerald himself – as Nicole, the damaged rich girl who is both lover and patient, is a figure for Zelda. It is Dick who tries to sustain and bless the romance of life in Europe, protect the illusions of others, and sustain his patient and the post-war world together under the umbrella of his care and love. For a time Dick and Nicole do hold things together, becoming a magical couple, wonderful in their charm. They are intelligent, and they belong willingly enough to history, which, as Fitzgerald aptly says, manifests itself day-to-day, as style: "Although the Divers were honestly apathetic to organized fashion, they were nevertheless too acute to abandon its contemporaneous rhythm and beat." Thus they live, like the Fitzgeralds themselves, by history's daily workings, through styles and images, this week's haunting jazz songs and this summer's new resorts. Amongst other things, the book is splendid about the wonder of personal styles, which seduce Rosemary Hoyt, the film actress, and indeed everyone else who come into the Divers' orbit. But the point

Fitzgerald has come to acknowledge by now is that history works more largely. Nicole is the product of wealth and the victim of both its sexual and financial insecurities. And Dick himself is simply a commodity, bought first as healer and then as husband. "So many smart men go to pieces nowadays," says Nicole innocently. Both of them do, trying to hold together what is already split, the flaws being not just in the mental life of a few patients but in the entire system.

Meantime Europe is where Americans, the century's great new capitalists, confidently exploit what is now a declining continent, in order to shore up their own exhausted moral accounts. What Dick is immersing himself in is nothing less than the psychopathology of a post-war Western culture in its later, and transatlantic, decline. American wealth and sexuality has created both the intense glamour and the destructive moral chaos. Europe in turn offers up its beaches and mountains, its hotels and bars, along with its spas, clinics and sanatoria, to the visitors from the new empire. Here spirit is squandered, dissipation grows, bankruptcy financial and moral is encountered, treatment secured. In his novel *The Good Soldier* (1915), to which Fitzgerald's book surely owes much, Ford Madox Ford had depicted his narrator as an innocent American perplexed by the labyrinthine complexes of European adulterous sexuality at a European spa, Bad Neuheim. In *The Magic Mountain* (1925), another great psycho-historical portrait of the age, Thomas Mann had shown a Davos sanatorium as a world of impending death, comparable to the coming death of Europe. Fitzgerald changes the equation again. This is a novel of American wealth in Europe – but what it brings is no longer a splendid innocence, but damaged psyches, a deeply corrupted wealth. In return, Europe offers not cultural wisdom, but the battlefields where the dead were left "like a million bloody rugs," a hotel civilization, expensive indulgence and psychoanalysis, that new apparatus for the supposed recuperation of those damaged by wealth, or war, or history. At the end of the journey lies a crisis for both wealth and psyche. The Wall Street Crash renders the capital base absurd, and the psychic fragility even more fragile. Published when it was all over, but written as both the glow and the pain were still there, the novel draws a lesson many in the Thirties were beginning to draw. It was all a dangerous spree; now it was over. And it died not only because the Depression now summoned all Americans home to face the national problems, but because of the moral, psychic and fiscal carelessness that had run through the decade itself. *Tender Is the Night*, the most vivid account and analysis of the expatriate Twenties we have in fiction, is both a self-dramatization and a self-dismissal. The accusation is plain, so is the regret. For, as Fitzgerald said, "it all seems so rosy and romantic to us who were young then, because we will never feel quite so intensely about our surroundings any more."[36]

In the event, the Wall Street Crash and the withdrawal into nationalisms that followed was a crisis in transatlantic images and relations; the two continents now seemed to pull apart into their own profound difficulties. But it was by no means the end of the relationship. American writers, like Thomas Wolfe and Henry Miller, continued to come to a Europe moving ever deeper into crisis. And Europeans, forced out of their present lives by that crisis, also increasingly turned to America – and not just the future home of the Modern spirit, but of freedom itself. But the great change of 1929 did mark a redrawing of the transatlantic map. For a good many decades, American writers and artists had been fleeing their powerful but provincial nation for a Europe that proved, in the event, to be in the course of a fundamental change, and eventually a major crisis. Out of the change and crisis, the Modern movement had in effect been born. By the Twenties, Paris had become the great destination, the post-war city – the city of artists and writers who felt radicals by temperament, exiles by nature, displaced out of history (often *by* history), and into the realm of art. Alienated by change at home, Americans had been exiles too, and in the course of the episode they created much of the "Risorgimento" of the modern arts they so desired. They found an ambiguous Europe which seemed even more ambiguous in retrospect: a Europe where there was uneasy disorder, where the excitements of Americanization were actually proceeding apace, where the speeded, jazzed-up American way itself seemed a principle of modernity. But the modern was no less a crisis than the old disorder it seemed to replace. And, however much had happened (and much had), a good deal of it was over by the decade's end. It had all depended on a complex mixture of styles, personalities, nationalities, on a search for the new, on a great surge of movements and aesthetic revolutions, on the self-conscious forging of a "modern" generation, even on the rate of exchange. Now

---

[36] References are to Edmund Wilson (ed.), *F. Scott Fitzgerald: The Crack-Up* (New York, New Directions, 1956).

the rate had shifted; and the tide of exchange turned. The Americans went back, and to many Europeans it seemed they had taken much of the spirit of the Modern with them, even though the place they had taken it to was Depression America. Meantime the Modern movement itself was coming to seem too aesthetic, too apolitical, too separated from the hard underlying realities, to grasp at the disorder that now afflicted the Western world or the greater disaster that might now lie ahead. America, it seemed, was now withdrawing into isolation, and leaving Europe behind. But the disorders and rising crises of Europe themselves sustained the transatlantic connection. European modernists and radicals, from Brecht and Mann to Auden and Isherwood, began to flee the disorder and persecution and cross the Atlantic for America. The exiles went home – but much in the Modern movement followed them over. So the great transatlantic transaction continued, as it still does.

NINE

Down and Out in Paris and Mexico:
Miller, Lowry and the low dishonest decade

1.

In March 1930, as world Depression bit and the Jazz Age ended, a very different kind of expatriate sailed over the Atlantic on a ship named with what was now wild incongruity *The American Banker* (who these days would sail with her?). He was thirty-eight, balding, poor, and alone; his name was Henry Miller. According to his own later claim, he had left New York with only ten dollars in his pocket, and would return home with exactly the same amount just nine years later, as the Thirties closed on the tragedy of a new world war. All he had were two trunks, a valise, and some vague promises of handouts from his wife June, an exotic Greenwich Village taxi-dancer with literary and acting ambitions and lesbian inclinations. His intended destination was Spain, but he stopped off in Paris, which he had visited two years earlier, on an extended European tour taken with June. Paris then had excited him wildly, but a trip that started with the usual exhilaration had ended up in a familiar misery. There had been a complicated, adventurous zigzag tour across Central Europe, back toward their immigrant roots, but at the Russian border they had been refused entry. Returning to Paris, they decided to make a cycling tour down the Rhône to Provence and the Riviera. But here, as usual, their funds ran dry, and there had been a hasty return to the USA. It was one more crisis in their tempestuous open marriage – not greatly helped by the fact that Miller, who had given up casual work for writing, was mostly dependent for survival on his wife's sexual tips. What's more, they were also arguing about a near-pornographic novel he was writing about her, to be titled *Crazy Cock*, a text whose contents he would endlessly mine and re-mine later. Now, with the marriage virtually in ruins, and no present source of income, Miller was back in Paris, alone, and hoping for support-cheques from June via American Express. He had been writing away for years, working on four novels, and producing cheap stories and essays for the pulps, sometimes under his wife's name. He knew scarcely anyone at all in Paris, and his work was totally unknown. Still, here he was, down and out, merry and bright – and hoping, as ever, to make his literary fame and fortune.

It was entirely typical of Henry Miller that he should drift into Paris just at the moment when most other American expatriate writers – upset both by European political events and the Depression now becoming endemic in the USA – were packing up their things and going home. What's more, despite all that was distressing about an America now less notable for its inventions and styles than its breadlines and dustbowl, many of those who had left ignorant, commercial America in disgust ten or so years earlier were coming home with a renewed patriotism, to sing its praises. Some were moving left in politics, and looking to find in the USA a new American Marxist or Trotskyist utopia. But nearly all, including the most radical, had tempered their quarrel with the nation as a culture, and were shifting in their writing to deal with life at home. By 1930 it was clear a literary corner had been turned. The mannered literary titles of the Twenties were dropping from the publishers' lists: the new novels of troubled times now had stark manifesto titles: *Jews Without Money, Bottom Dogs, Strike!* But they were American novels, about American society; the American novel had come home. In 1930, too, John Dos Passos began publishing his three-volume experimental fictional history of the American century, telling the nation's story from the hopes of 1900 for "an American century" to the executions of the anarchists Sacco and Vanzetti in the late Twenties, seen by radicals as the ultimate attempt to suppress the progressive spirit. The book, experimental certainly, but also political in impulse, meant to assess the modern nation to date. Over three volumes it would explore its distinctive, noble continental geography (*The 42nd Parallel*), its year of betrayal (*1919*), and the corrupt, capitalist system that had brought it to present collapse (*The Big Money*). But if, as Dos Passos suggested, America was now not one but two nations – not just capitalists and progressives, businessmen and artists, farmers and metropolitans, moneymen and workers, but two different, unreconciled communities with two different languages – then it was time for words, deeds, the nation as a whole to be brought together again. There might be one America, put into a modern book in all its collage and variety; hence the work as a whole would have the all-encompassing title *USA*. Dos Passos' new outreach to the nation was typical. As Harvey Swados has pointed out, the Thirties was a time when nation and land returned as subject. America was back in all the titles: "Poets, novelists, journalists, critics, essayists, produced books throughout the 1930s with such titles as: *My America, Puzzled America, Tragic America, Some American People, America Was Promises, America Now, America: A Reappraisal, An American Exodus, The American Earthquake*..." And, he adds, though the Thirties may have been a divided, bitter decade, for the first time writers of the modern generation presumed to speak of the nation at large *to* the nation at large.[1]

This climactic change – in fact a new kind of American literary neutrality, if not isolationism – meant that the recent age of inter-national artistic experiment was quickly slipping into the past. In darkened times, American fiction was turning social, realistic, political, nationalistic. Its writers now travelled not across the battle-scarred wonderlands of mainland Europe, but across the wide American continent, recording the bitter, yet strangely powerful, landscape of a Depression that was stifling the entire nation and the American Dream, yet bringing everyone together to face the new American challenge. After Roosevelt came to office in 1932, and the spirit of the New Deal came in, the government actually aided its writers, financing them to write guidebooks and regional histories. As never before, America appeared to need, to welcome, the ministrations of its artists. Even the strange, emblematic Harold Stearns, now losing his sight, left behind the cafés and race-tracks of Paris to sail home steerage, to "rediscover America," "my own country, from which I have been away too long." As usual, Stearns had his cultural arguments at the ready. Artistic America had finally passed the borrowing stage: "nowadays, we are beginning to exchange music for music, art for art, architecture for architecture, poetry for poetry, religion for religion" with the rest of the world. It had lost its "derivative, apologetic attitude toward Europe, not by deliberate repudiation but by increasing interest and concern with our own life and our own problems ... We have long ceased to be perturbed about what Europeans do in the arts."[2] From the evan-gelistic leader of expatriate flight, this was significant; but there was

[1] Harvey Swados (ed.), *The American Writer and the Great Depression* (Indianapolis, Bobbs-Merrill, 1966).
[2] Harold E. Stearns, *Rediscovering America* (New York, Boni and Liveright, 1934).

more. By 1937, as Europe moved closer to disaster, Stearns had taken his confident cultural isolationism even further, reflecting the ever-widening gap between European crises and American prospects of recovery. "Culture, like history, has its strange revenges, and I do not think that most of us are yet sufficiently aware that, despite all the weight of centuries of tradition against it, in our world of 1937 it is – from a purely literary point of view – Europe which seems naïve and ourselves sophisticated," he wrote in *America: A Re-Appraisal*. "Europe is dying, but the best of what it once had may still be nurtured and grow in new and lovely ways in America."[3]

Stearns did not speak for all. There were a good many American intellectuals who believed in the power of European ideas and ideologies, tried to keep alive the international Modernist spirit, and continued to sustain public awareness of the dangerous implications of the events unfolding in Europe. Many of the cultural and political magazines carried articles by troubled European intellectuals (Malraux, Chamson, Gide, Orwell, Koestler) that alerted Americans to the terrors now building across the Atlantic. But an instinct for retrenchment, along with a fresh confidence in the American arts, kept attention focused on what Alfred Kazin, in his fine and influential study of modern American fiction in 1942, would dub literature "on native grounds" – which meant not just the progressive Americanization of American writing, but the acceptance of America as itself the essential subject. First, Kazin said, there had been a paralysis, as Americans confronted world economic collapse; then had come a Rooseveltian faith that the nation could weather a world crisis that seemed destined to leave disaster everywhere else, and American writers turned to the artistic rebuilding of the nation. *You Can't Go Home Again*, announced the novelist Thomas Wolfe in one of his titles, telling the expansive story of a romantic American wanderer through what was now a much gloomier and sinister European world, darkened by a Fascism that first interested and then dismayed him. But the underlying message of Wolfe's book was that you could, and you should. Ironically enough, it had taken a double disaster – the Depression at home, followed by a dangerous collapse of democracy and progressive reform in many parts of Europe – to bring writers home to a new confidence in America.[4] But

---

[3] Harold E. Stearns, *America: A Re-Appraisal* (New York, Hillman-Curl, 1937).
[4] See the later chapters of Alfred Kazin, *On Native Grounds: An Interpretation of Modern American Prose Literature* (New York, Reynal & Hitchcock, 1942).

all this was understandable enough. The new world problems – collapse of liberal democracies, pervasive economic insecurity, the failure of European nations to rebuild the social orders that had existed before the Great War, or control events at home or anywhere else in the world – suggested that Western society faced a major breakdown. To many on both sides of the Ocean, it seemed the European era was over at last, the day of historic Western culture and its era of humanism coming to a tragic and self-destructive close. The rising instability, the appearance of mobs and their dictators, the gathering of armies and weapons, the constant tensions, prefigured a new age of war, and social orders of a new and totalitarian type. Each nation in Europe was going its own way, trying to solve its economic and political crisis, give promise to its peoples, define its destiny in a shapeless and collapsing world. America had its own profound difficulties, was a major source of the crisis. But there was an ocean between it and the worst of the troubles, which gave it the chance to come through.

And if the progressive decay of Western humanist culture seemed plain enough in the political world, it also seemed manifest in the arts. The Modern movement now looked less of a great experimental adventure in new space and time; it more resembled, especially if you read it with neo-Marxist eyes, a sign of Western cultural disintegration, a witness to collapsed empires, defeated bourgeois values, dying myths. New post-liberal ideologies – from Communism to Freudianism – argued that old cultural orders and hierarchies, old versions of civilization, were now ready to yield to revolutionary forces of class and mass, consciousness and the unconscious. Meantime America, burdened with its own crisis, and facing rising problems in the Pacific, looked inward, argued the case for neutrality, and had less and less time for the troubles of others. Europe and America, whose shared liberal capitalist destiny had a few years earlier appeared to be bringing them ever closer, seemed a world away from each other. The three thousand miles of ocean that lay between them, now easily spanned not just by the great liner palaces of the steamship lines but by transatlantic flight, marked the space between different political geographies and historical destinies. With the rise of Fascism in Europe, it came to appear that Old World and New had opposite futures in store. For many Europeans, America not only lay in a different space and lived on a different time-scale, but was fundamentally remote from the new forces that were either in process of transforming Europe or tearing it to pieces. To some it was American myths of progress and development that were leading the world to disaster, and the European future lay in its own prospects for revolutionary change, a view of especial appeal to European Marxists, but was no less common among the new Totalitarians.[5] Meantime for many Americans what was happening in Europe displayed the futility of American intervention in 1917, the collapse of Wilsonian idealism, the folly of "foreign entanglements," the uselessness of the attempt to intervene in Europe's endless difficulties. Americans were quick to see through the "new barbarism" of Hitler and Mussolini, though many were slower to see through the infinite corruptions of Stalin. But, with the exception of what was happening in Russia, it seemed Europe had dangers not solutions to offer, and the best way to keep the world safe for democracy or what some hoped would replace it, a revolution of the proletariat, was to confine matters within the continental space of the USA.[6]

The fact remained that many of the issues confronting the American writers and intellectuals of the Thirties (a time when the very word intellectual was elevated into currency) came from the Thirties upheavals of Europe, and European speculation about the ideologies of modernity. The Twenties had been a radical era, a major episode not just in artistic experiment but in the modernization of the Western world. But the energy of radicalism had come from production, consumption, technology and commerce, rather than ideology or

---

[5] In 1930 Bertolt Brecht wrote a derisive poem about America:
  "What men they were! Their boxers the strongest!
  Their inventors the most adept!
  Their trains the swiftest!
  So we imitated this renowned race of men
  Who seemed destined
  To rule the world by helping it to progress.

  It all looked like lasting a thousand
  But it endured a bare eight years."
By the end of the decade Brecht was himself in the United States as a refugee from Hitler's Germany. Poem quoted in William E. Leuchtenberg, "Looking Inward, Looking Backward, Looking Outward: The Europeanization of America, 1929–1950," in Steve Ickringill (ed.), *Looking Inward, Looking Outward: From the 1930s through the 1940s* (Amsterdam, VU University Press, 1990), a valuable collection of essays on the decade.
[6] An evocative documentary record of the decade in America, illustrating its main preoccupations, is Daniel Aaron and Robert Bendiner (eds), *The Strenuous Decade: A Social and Intellectual Record of the 1930s* (Garden City, N.Y., Anchor, 1970).

public action. By the Thirties, politics was back, and intellectuals felt it necessary to address modern history directly. Liberal and more than liberal thoughts – socialism, communism, Marxism, Trotskyism – moved to the forefront of discussion, the modern came under analysis, and it was clearly not just national depression but a structural world crisis in a time of fundamental change that shaped the thoughts of many Americans. Ideas of exceptionalism and isolationism, strongly felt by many Americans, and expressed in Roosevelt's neutrality acts, were more an impulse for survival than a secure political reality. That became ever more obvious as the events of the Thirties unrolled, with crises on every side; the economic and political troubles of the decade were open proof of the interconnectedness of modern history. To many of sense and conscience it grew ever plainer that the United States could not stand permanently apart – intellectually, politically, morally, even perhaps militarily. What started as a sequence of national crises pointed with ever-growing inevitability to a conflict of modern ideologies, hence to a major war. Out of economic despair, political crisis, class, racial and ethnic hostility, disputed frontiers, the crowd frenzies of the age of frightened masses, international conflict was brewing, re-armament surging. Europe was falling into a fresh abyss of its own creation, as modern history rubbed on old sores. A state of crisis perhaps seventy years in the making was pushing, in the aftermath of an already cataclysmic war, toward dictatorship, totalitarianism, disaster. From all this America, for all its continental land mass, could not stay totally remote.

The first great test came in 1936, with the civil war in Spain. To many Americans the conflict was further proof that Europe was an eternal battleground, and America was expected to sort out its troubles. As Elliot Paul put it in his novel *The Life and Death of a Spanish Town* (1937), the prevailing view was "Their land is dying. Mine is not." Still, like many of their European counterparts, American writers and intellectuals were quick on the scene. Like them, they found it hard to decide whether this was a conflict of good and evil, totalitarianism and republicanism, or a war of two dangerous "isms"; but what was clear was that it was an emblematic modern war. Appropriately enough, the novel that opened the American Forties was once more by that specialist in the wounds of war, Ernest Hemingway. His *For Whom the Bell Tolls* (1940) was born from his dramatic return to Spain in 1937–9, when he appeared on the scene not as *aficionado* but as a proactive war correspondent – a role he would continue to fill, to the point of extravagance, over the battle-torn years to come.[7] And the book, like the play he wrote about the experience, *The Fifth Column*, also showed a great transition had taken place in his writing. Instead of the existential separatism of *A Farewell to Arms*, the new theme, as the title says (". . . never send to know for whom the bell tolls; it tolls for thee"), was common interdependence; his hero Robert Jordan, joining the Republican campaign, is brought to social consciousness and finally to sacrificial death in the good cause. Like a good deal of American writing of the late Thirties, the book also displayed a return to the international dimension, a fresh recognition that modern history was now edging toward world crisis.[8] From this point onwards, all events would go to confirm the view. As the reports of fresh European tragedies, the invasion of small nations, the persecution of minorities, the silencing of dissent, the burning of books grew, it was plain that a global crisis would have to be confronted. When, in 1938, the Munich crisis came, T. S. Eliot warned it showed we are all "deeply implicated and responsible." Roosevelt too had already warned the nation that "If those things [the crushing of Western cultures] come to pass in other parts of the world, let no one imagine America will escape." The flight of European intellectuals to America as the decade closed reinforced the lesson. It took a Japanese attack on Pearl Harbor to drive it home, but by 1941 the likelihood that America would be once again involved in the crisis of Europe was great. Ironically, American entry into the war that December at once relieved the Depression. The inward-looking America of the past decade entered the World War it had feared; in fact it was about to take on a world-power status it had never had, and scarcely aspired to. A decade later, Europe along with much else of the world found itself Americanized, or faced by the choice of allegiance with the liberal capitalist West and the communist East. Likewise the United States found itself suddenly internationalized, in ways quite new in its history.

[7] Also see Ernest Hemingway, *By-Line: Selected Articles and Despatches of Four Decades* (London, Collins, 1968), and *The Fifth Column: And Four Unpublished Stories of the Spanish Civil War* (New York, Scribner, 1969).

[8] Hemingway's was by no means the only version. John Dos Passos, who defected from supporting the Communists after they had executed a friend, wrote his anti-Communist view of the conflict in *The Adventures of a Young Man* (1939). And see Stanley Weintraub, *The Last Great Cause: The Intellectuals and the Spanish Civil War* (London, W. H. Allen, 1968), for the intellectual conflict the war generated.

2.

None of this great transformation, though, seemed to matter much to Henry Miller. In setting out for Paris as the Thirties started, he was going in the opposite direction to the cultural tide – and that was just how he meant it to be. If other writers were now getting ready to make their critical peace with America, he was just getting ready to make war with it. He was not interested in politics, only in surviving amidst the chaos they created. If Europe was dying, he was happy to be in at the death. To him America summoned no special loyalty; it had always been, he said, "an air-conditioned nightmare," a deathly mechanical horror from which he had always longed to escape. Born in New York City in the Yorkville section near the East River, to a family of German immigrant stock who then moved on to a depressed but respectable life of tailoring in Brooklyn, he had, he said, begun life hating the place he was born in, and grown up despising everything his parents ever approved of or endorsed. His very earliest impulses had been to break away from his German-speaking family, a New York he detested, and a country with which he had absolutely nothing in common. He explained this in a book, *The Time of the Assassins: A Study of Rimbaud* (1956), which, like most of the books he would write, is ostensibly about one subject but really about another, the great subject, Henry Miller himself. He explained it too in the works of fiction he wrote, books that were not books but anarchist prophecies, the works of an enraged poet and visionary. Miller may have been, right through his life, a streetwise New York panhandler, always looking for the next dime for a meal, or planning a new campaign to raise cash for the next project, usually survival. But he was well enough read, and enough given to romantic self-dramatization, to see himself as that other classic urban figure, the *poète maudit*. He was the "Rimbaud type," as also the Whitman type, the Dostoevsky type, the Lawrence type, the Nietzsche type. He belonged, he said, in the great tradition of the literary "gangsters," the writers from underground – yet another abnormal, psychotic, artistic individual who is maladapted only because the rest of the world has adapted too easily, and who like all the serious artists "lived like scarecrows, amid the abundant riches of our cultural world."

A college drop-out who worked for a while at numerous odd jobs, Miller was always to be an avid if self-instructed reader, a wide-open vehicle for the endless outpouring ideas and mysticisms of the world.

He early on developed radical and anarchist attitudes, admired Jack London and Emma Goldman, Dostoevsky and Spengler, read European philosophy, was drawn to theosophy, and later on astrology, psychoanalysis, cosmology, and many of the things that make California (where he ended his days) what it is now. All this made him "contemptuous of everything that surrounded me, alienating me gradually from my friends and imposing on me that solitary, eccentric nature that causes one to be styled a 'bizarre' individual." So he turned to senseless manual labour and vagabondage, trying to make his living with his hands and his wits, meantime taking his revenge on a hostile society wherever he could. "I had no principles, no loyalty, no code whatsoever," he reported, "I usually repaid kindness with insult and injury. I was insolent, arrogant, intolerant, violently prejudiced, relentlessly obstinate." During the Twenties, as other writers went to the artistic haven of Paris, he bummed around America rather like the writers of the Thirties – trying to live by borrowing, exploiting, scavenging off the riches of the world. He worked for a spell as messenger employment manager of Western Union, a job he got as a result of a trick, and here he wildly hired and fired, exploiting his position and making his protest against "the whole system of American labor, which is rotten at both ends." "I was born in New York City, where there is every opportunity to succeed, as the world imagines," he wrote. "The only job I ever seemed capable of getting in those days was that of a dishwasher. And then I was always too late." Meantime he wrote, partly at the prompting of June, his second wife, who liked to show stories to her sexual patrons. In fact to Miller the writer was always the vagrant, the professional down-and-outer, the smouldering adversary, the *clochard*, the scarecrow amid the riches of the world.

The Paris that attracted him was much the same. It was the vagrant city of would-be artists, the perfect place for the writer on the bum. He was not averse to calamities, and this was, he realized, a place where one could live "on only grief and anguish," along with the other tramps and grotesques who populated the city, and pick up from its disorder a life of sorts worth living. From the moment of arrival, then, he was a different kind of expatriate from most of those who had lived and written in Paris over the decade just coming to its unhappy close. He was no wounded and stoical Jake Barnes, living on his rigorous self-control, his firm style and his literary earnings in a sterile world; he was certainly no Dick Diver, taking the burdens of the wealthy Americans onto his moral shoulders. Like the British George Orwell, who had explored the world of Parisian poverty a year or so earlier, when he became a *plongeur* in French hotels (he would publish the story in *Down and Out in Paris and London*, 1933), Miller was a deliberate expatriate to the underside; but this did not bring him to the reforming political thoughts that shaped Orwell's development as a writer. He belonged naturally in the lower world of literature, always a well-populated space. He had arrived in Paris with no source of income, and only a few vague hopes of cheques that almost never came. His financial and emotional situation was worse than it had ever been. Perhaps he was sinking, not rising. But France at 22 francs to the dollar, and Paris, with its air of literary romance, sexual corruption, and moral extremity, excited him afresh. "All my life I have felt a great kinship with the madman and the criminal," he would later explain in his essay "The Brooklyn Bridge." "To me the city is crime personified. I feel at home." Paris was the place for his way of life, if he could survive in it; it was a classic, or rather romantic, bridge-city between art, sex and crime. At first, in fact, it was the pure romance of Paris that captured him. The streets rang with famous literary associations, the small hotels all round him were where great writers of the past had lived and, frequently, died in poverty, the cafés and galleries beckoned. He found his way to the usual run-down hotel, the Hôtel Saint-Germain-des-Prés in the Rue Bonaparte on the famous Left Bank, where the dollars he didn't have would go as far as possible. He still had an education to complete, and he became an avid and avaricious literary tourist.

Directed by a couple of useful if exotic guidebooks, Arthur B. Maurice's *The Paris of the Novelist* and Francis Carco's *Bohemia*, he made the rounds of the artistic streets and literary *quartiers*, the libraries, the galleries, and, inevitably, American Express on the Rue Scribe, where he hoped against hope for cheques from June or some other friend, who could spare a little cash to save the day and finance his vast, vague but ever-growing literary ambitions. The fellow expatriates he encountered at the Dôme or the Coupole were, he said, "insufferable idiots." But that did not mean he was above going there, offering his amusing, passionate, philosophical conversation in exchange for drinks or a handout. Indeed on the great Parisian stage-set he made a point of sitting on the *terrasse* of the Deux Magots, reading to himself the manuscript of the novel about June he was still busily writing. Meantime, though, he was writing no less furiously about Paris itself, writing sketches for innumerable prospective articles, or maybe a guidebook to the city like Paul Morand's famous French guidebook to New York. These were portraits of a different but no less exotic Paris, the Paris of the pissoirs, the abattoirs, the cheap whores, the zinc cafés, the homosexuals in the Luxembourg Gardens, the *clochards*, the night walks through workers' neighbourhoods. He poured out endless vivid observations, new literary ideas and fantasies, in long letters to friends back home. "I will write here," he announced, "I will live quietly and quite alone. And each day I will see a little more of Paris, study it, learn it as I would a book . . . The streets sing, the stones talk. The houses drip history, glory, romance."

Paris was a book, but it was also a book quite different from the more familiar text of New York City, which he now rejected. "To return to New York . . . was a frightening thought," he was to announce in *The Time of the Assassins*. "The city whose every street I know like a book, where I have so many friends, remains the last place on earth I would turn to. I would rather die than be forced to spend the rest of my days in the place of my birth. I can only visualize myself returning to New York as utterly destitute, as a cripple, as a man who has given up the ghost."[9] Paris not only demanded a new book; it required a new allegiance. "Europe is my homeland – not America," he would finally acknowledge, now under the influence of wartime. "I am with Europe always . . . I think some day the tide of migration will turn and all those hordes who poured over to America to work in the soil and the mills, to erect the great ghastly empty edifice of Work and Progress over there, I think that bloody crew of ghosts and cadavers will return to Europe again and refecundate the soil of Europe." But for the moment the task was to define the process of deracination he felt at work in him. "Is it good here in France? It's wonderful. Marvellous. For me it's marvellous, because it's the only place in the world I know of where I can go on with my murder-and-suicide business – until I strike a new zodiacal realm. For

---

[9] Details of Miller's life in Paris are to be found throughout his own works, and in Alfred Perles, *My Friend Henry Miller* (London, Spearman, 1955); George Wickes (ed.), *Lawrence Durrell and Henry Miller: A Private Correspondence* (New York, Dutton, 1963); Gunther Stuhlmann (ed.), *Henry Miller: Letters to Anaïs Nin* (New York, Putnam, 1965); Gunther Stuhlmann (ed.), *The Diary of Anaïs Nin* (New York, Harcourt Brace, 1966, etc.); and George Wickes, *Americans in Paris* (New York, Doubleday, 1969). Also see Jay Martin's slightly eccentric but highly vivid and informative "unauthorized biography" *Always Merry and Bright: The Life of Henry Miller* (Santa Barbara, Capra Press, 1978; London, Sheldon Press, 1979).

a French writer it may be bad here, but then I am not a French writer
. . . I am a cosmological writer." What did that mean? "I had two
beginnings really, one here in America, which was abortive, and the
other in Europe," he explained in *The World of Sex* (1940), after war had
forced him back home to America again. "How was I able to begin
again, you may well ask? I should answer truthfully – by dying. In the
first year or so in Paris I literally died, was literally annihilated – and
resurrected as a new man."[10]

3.

As for the city where Miller had come to pursue this drama of
annihilation and resurrection – this was to remain the basic trope of his
entire life and writing – it was once more in a time of profound change.
With present unrest, it had quickly begun to lose a good deal of the
artistic confidence and stylish glow that marked its heyday in the
Twenties. "By the Thirties, the Left Bank had changed," Sylvia Beach
was to report. "The so-called 'lost generation' – I can't think of a
generation less deserving of the name – had grown up and become
famous. Many of my friends had gone home . . . It had been pleasanter
emerging from a war than going toward another one."[11] The
Shakespeare bookshop itself was now running into financial difficulties;
the tourist hordes had nearly disappeared, the number of American
residents in the city decreased by half. If writers still travelled – and
they certainly did a great deal in the Thirties – they were looking less for
cities of art than for more threatening frontiers, more unstable borders,
like the Weimar Berlin that Christopher Isherwood was even now
observing in its growing violence and crisis. As George Orwell observed
in his brilliant essay on Miller, "Inside the Whale" (1940), written as
the Second World War began, in going to Paris, Miller was going to a
world of aesthetic exile just at the time when almost every other serious
artist felt forced into political awareness and allegiance. Hence the real
centres of history now lay elsewhere: "The intellectual foci of the world
were now Rome, Moscow, and Berlin."[12] The Modern movement was

10 Quotations are from "A Death Letter to Emil," in *Sunday After the War* (London,
Editions Poetry, 1945); "Peace! It's Wonderful," in *The Cosmological Eye* (London,
Editions Poetry, 1946); and *The World of Sex* (USA, privately printed, 1940).

11 Sylvia Beach, *Shakespeare and Company* (London, Faber, 1960).

12 George Orwell, "Inside the Whale," in *George Orwell: Selected Essays* (Harmondsworth, Penguin, 1957).

itself on the wane, forced to confront the darker face of modernity; Miller's idealization of the romantic and self-conscious artist was thus the opposite to the neutral or politically committed style that was nowadays preferred. Paris, like most of the European capitals, had largely accepted its decadent status, the gloom of Europe in self-acknowledged decline. As for the Parisian experimental movements of the previous decade, they had grown grimmer, more extreme, more certain than ever of the decline of European civilization, the meaninglessness of the world as it was. Surrealism was now the one dominant tendency, and it was growing both more subjectively psychoanalytical and more political and Marxist, offering its life-changing illusionist services to some great revolution of consciousness and desire. It published its review *Le Surréalisme au service de la révolution* from 1930 to 1933, emphasizing its radical elements: fetishism, eroticism, desire, blasphemy, dream, revolt, the power of the occult. The new mood was best expressed in the fiction of Céline, or the surrealist films of Cocteau and Buñuel. Miller saw these almost as soon as he arrived in Paris, wrote about them, and imbibed them into his newly stimulated, increasingly surrealized imagination.

The expatriate scene had changed greatly too. Many of the earlier expatriate magazines and presses had died now, gone broke or followed their editors homeward. But some old hands stayed to enjoy darker days, and magazines old and new flourished: Edward Titus' *This Quarter*, and Samuel Putnam's *New Review*, both of which would play their part in Miller's future fortunes. So did the experimental magazine *transition*, edited by Eugene Jolas, who wrote for the *Chicago Tribune*, and his American wife. It had lapsed a while, but resumed publication in 1932, to play an important part in the Thirties climate, devoting itself ever more passionately and obscurely to Vertigralism, the Surrealist campaign and the great Revolution of the Word, and printing writers who included Franz Kafka, Samuel Beckett, Dylan Thomas, and eventually Miller itself. American books, especially those unacceptable at home, were still published in Paris. Despite the suicide of Harry Crosby, the Black Sun Press went on, and turned into Crosby Continental Editions. There were Edward Titus' Black Manikin Press, and Jack Kahane's new Obelisk Press, both of which would eventually have important dealings with Miller. As for the expatriate group itself, Stein had by now become a distant and imperious guru and, with *The Autobiography of Alice B. Toklas*, an unreliable reminiscer about past artistic battles lost and won; her American tour would make her the nation's exemplary modernist. Joyce was struggling painfully with the book that would finally become *Finnegans Wake*, and seriously thinking of moving to London. Pound was in Rapallo, growing obsessed by economics and impresssed by Mussolini, Ford Madox Ford had gone to teach in the USA. But other younger writers continued to arrive: Samuel Beckett went back and forth between Ireland and Paris, and began to write and publish (his *Murphy* appeared in Paris in 1938). Malcolm Lowry tried the expatriate life; Lawrence Durrell, attracted by Miller, arrived later in the decade. But the newer arrivals were increasingly made up of those who were moving in from disordered Eastern Europe, or Germany and Austria, and were trying to scratch some form of living, artistic or otherwise.

There were still a fair number of Americans who had various reasons, generally professional but sometimes sexual, for being in a still artistic Paris. Miller, ever sociable and constantly wandering the city, soon met a number of them. There was the Czech-born Alfred Perles, who might well have been June's lover on a previous visit, worked on the staff of the *Chicago Tribune*'s Paris edition, and now proved a good friend, letting Miller live in his flat in the working-class area of Clichy, and getting some of Miller's pieces into the paper under his own by-line, for useful dollars. There was the American newspaperman Wambly Bald, a no less helpful gossip columnist on the same paper. Other supportive friends appeared as his network of acquaintance grew: the Hungarian photographer and artist Brassaï, whose photographs of the "forbidden" Paris – its cesspools, brothels, gay and lesbian clubs – appeared as *Paris de Nuit* in 1933; the French writer Blaise Cendrars; the American writer Walter Lowenfels; in time Lawrence Durrell. Two of these in particular were to have a powerful impact on Miller. One was Michael Fraenkel, a naturalized American of Russian stock who had taught literature, done well in New York property, and come to Paris to live at the Villa Seurat, develop a post-Nietzschean philosophy of "creative suicide," and establish his own press, the Carrefour Press, devoted to what he called "the avant garde of death." These two talked incessantly, and Fraenkel fed Miller his mystic philosophy of art, anonymity and death, and the dream of writing "the last book," the latter-day Bible that would "exhaust the age." The other was Anaïs (Guiler) Nin, Paris born of Spanish stock, but educated in the USA. The discontented wife of an American banker and film-maker living wealthily just outside Paris, she was just setting out on the self-recording erotic quest that would make her an explorer of what she called "the future of the novel," and an eventual heroine of feminism. When they met (Nin at first as interested in Miller's wife June as in the man she would later praise as "an artist who re-establishes the potency of illusion by gaping at the open wounds, by courting the stern, psychological reality which man seeks to avoid through recourse to the oblique symbolism of art"), Nin was just in process of publishing her first book, *D. H. Lawrence: An Unprofessional Study* (1932), with the Black Manikin Press – a paean of praise to Lawrence's visionary fecundity, which she had written to help her escape her "prison." Now, like Lawrence, Miller struck her as creating a philosophy of values "vivified and fecundated by instincts and passions." She became guide, lover, educator, analyst and invaluable patron – a central force in Miller's gradually improving Parisian fortunes and surrealist self-discovery.

4.

In fact Miller coincided with what Harold Rosenburg once, in an essay, "The Fall of Paris," calls a time of modern rootlessness, when "the lone individual, stripped yet supported on every side by the vitality of other outcasts, with whom it was necessary to form no permanent ties, could experiment with everything that man today has with him of health or monstrousness . . ." "Because the Modern was often inhuman, modern humanity could interpret itself in its terms," Rosenburg adds, proposing that the extremity of this inhuman modernism was just what transferred itself to European politics by the end of the decade. But even for the inhuman outcast, for Miller the omens at the start looked bleak. The low point came in Miller's first winter: the money ran out, his writing was, as usual, ignored, unpublished, unpublishable, he was in emotional despair over the collapsing relationship with June, and even if he wanted to go home he hadn't the money to pay the fare. Still – and this all became part of the great Miller mythology, a piece of the eternal voyage of the Miller soul – the dark corner was turned, the renewal began. Soon he started to command the situation. He found new places to sleep, sometimes dodging from hotel to hotel, but mostly at the apartments of friends, above all Perles' Clichy flat and Fraenkel's comfortable apartment at the Villa Seurat (the Villa Borghese of *Tropic of Cancer*). He devised a careful schedule of acquaintances (many of whom he despised) to buy him a meal every single day of the week. He gave English lessons to Russian *émigrés*, wrote advertisements for clubs and brothels, read proofs for the *Chicago Tribune*, and took a brief teaching job at a school in Dijon. Meantime he was reading widely (books stolen from the American Library), writing furiously (most notably a story, "Mademoiselle Claude," about a Paris prostitute, a field in which he had grown expert, which duly appeared in Putnam's *New Review*), finally planning a new book in the surreal, the Parisian, way. The experiences of this phase – also mythologically recorded and re-recorded in his own *Quiet Days in Clichy*, Perles' *My Friend Henry Miller*, Miller's letters to his American friend Emil Schnellock and Anaïs Nin, and Nin's *Diary* – were to be the primary material for the new novel he now determined to write. In August 1931 he began it, deciding to call it *Anonymous*; Fraenkel had told him all literature would be anonymous from now on (the idea of the death of the author is by no means new). But nothing could have been further from the truth: the book was a first-person song of myself, covering his recent Paris experiences, literary, philosophical, sexual: "I start tomorrow on the Paris book: first person, uncensored, formless, fuck everything," he noted. It was a book written, he believed, beyond literature ("with every line I write I kill off the 'artist' in me") and he opened it autobiographically – "I am living in the Villa Seurat, the guest of Michael Fraenkel. There is not a crumb of dirt anywhere, not a chair misplaced. We are all alone here and we are dead." It was a book intended to contain everything: "It's like a big, public, garbage can," he explained. "Only the mangy cats are missing. But I'll get them in yet."

This was a first, outpouring draft; and it went through three revisions before it appeared in print. The creative influences were clear, not least that of Surrealism, with its celebration of desire, the distorted body transformed into *objet d'art*, the use of blasphemy, outrage, dream, revolt, and the romantic debased city, Paris itself. Most of his friends were in it too; this was an extremist fiction based on fact. He showed the manuscript to Nin, who in turn showed him her own novel *House of Incest* (1936) and her erotic journals. She led him to further literary guides, even had him read Proust, and also helped steer the book's direction toward the goal of romantic resurrection. Miller was a magpie of styles and ideas, avariciously assimilating everything that came his way in a still vivid artistic environment. But above all this was a book about felt extremity, and his own priapic interests and inclinations; in fact, as he said himself, a work of "obscenity." By 1932 a version was finished and shown to Jack Kahane, the Manchester-born publisher of Frank Harris, Radclyffe Hall and other English writers, at his Obelisk Press, which specialized in banned eroticism in English. Kahane agreed to publish it, but cautiously proposed Miller should temper its publication with a study of D. H. Lawrence (Kahane also published the French edition of *Lady Chatterley's Lover*) to dress himself in some intellectual respectability. In fact Lawrence seemed to be dominating the whole situation (though, had he been alive and in a position to know, he could hardly have been delighted by much of the inheritance). Nin had written her own idiosyncratic and self-engrossed book on him, her attempt at a female freedom, and seen Miller in the tradition. He at first resented the comparison, but increasingly came to believe in it, and the value of Lawrence's apocalyptic vision and influence. He struggled for a year with the book, which became a kind of philosophical credo, but failed to complete it. In any case he was beginning to see himself increasingly in another line, that of the French and European literary "gangsters": the tradition of Rabelais, Sade, Dostoevsky, Lautréamont, Rimbaud, Maeterlinck, and more recently J-F. Céline, whom he now read. *Tropic of Cancer*, now heavily revised, did not appear until 1934, and then mainly thanks to the aid of Nin, who offered money to support its publication. It came out with a hyper-seductive preface, ostensibly by Nin, in fact concocted by Nin and Miller together. It was, it said, a new kind of book, a "naked book," beyond Lawrence or all the antecedent writers: "let us look at it with the eyes of a Patagonian for whom all that is sacred and taboo in our world is meaningless . . . If there is here revealed a capacity to shock, to startle the lifeless ones from their profound slumber, let us congratulate ourselves . . ."

This was familiar surrealist lore, and not surprisingly the book quickly did well in Paris circles, despite or because of the publisher's warning that it should not be displayed in the bookshop windows. Like *Ulysses*, it was helped in sales and reputation by the fact that it was banned in Britain and America (though perhaps for better reason). It was, in its way, a very French book, but it showed America now possessed its own idiosyncratic surrealist (though others no less important also worked in Paris, including Djuna Barnes and Nathanael West); certainly it won Miller credibility and the esteem of other writers. But by now it was ready to become part of an ever-running stream of Miller publication, one piece of a lifetime song of myself. A return to America in pursuit of Anaïs Nin, who had progressed from being a patient of the psychoanalyst Otto Rank to becoming a fellow analyst, produced a brief period when Miller too set out his psychiatristic shingle in Manhattan, leading to another book, called *Aller Retour New York* (1935). Reworking stories, sketches, even some of the Lawrence material, he completed another novel, his most "surreal" and open work, *Black Spring* (1936). This bore a dedication to Nin, who helped him write it, and took credit for the fact that the book shared something of her "feminine revolution." And he was also at work on the next work in the sequence, his American book, *Tropic of Capricorn*, which reverted to the New York of his despair, ten years before *Tropic of Cancer*, and dealt with his Western Union employment, his sexual adventures, his relationship with June. This finally appeared in 1939, the same year Nin published her next novel, *Winter of Artifice*. In fact the two writers were greatly influencing each other. Miller's artistic and indeed astrological education at her hands proceeded apace; his sexualized vigour made its mark on her writing. What's more, by now they were publishing together too. Nin financed the Siana Press back at the Villa Seurat, where she installed Miller in a comfortable apartment and encouraged him to work as the series editor. This was the most fruitful period of Miller's life, a time when he became, as he declared in *transition*, a "cosmological" artist, and attracted many others around him. These included Lawrence Durrell, who produced *The Black Book*, arguably his finest work, heavily influenced by Miller, for the press. George Orwell, a warm admirer, met him then, at the end of 1936, when along with much of his generation Orwell was en route for the Spanish Civil War, which seemed to him the prefiguration of the coming crisis: Miller showed no interest at all. He was living, thought Orwell, "inside the whale," "a writer out of the ordinary . . . a completely negative, unconstructive, amoral writer, a mere Jonah, a passive acceptor of evil, a sort of Whitman among the corpses" – and yet, he felt, worth far more than most of his generation.

In fact the war clouds were already gathering. By the Munich crisis of 1938, it was clear Europe was a threatening place, and Miller considered leaving. This was the other great time of exodus; *transition*, for instance, had closed down and the Jolases gone to the States. Perhaps only the foolhardy remained, but Miller really had no desire to return home. Likewise 1939, the year of *Tropic of Capricorn*, was no time to publish a novel in Europe. It was also the year of the last real work of Modernism, *Finnegans Wake*, but, inevitably enough, neither book won much attention as a bigger crisis of the modern unfolded. That spring Miller accepted an invitation from Durrell to visit Greece; it turned into another profound experience of a rooted and ancient Europe, and gave him the material of another notable book, *The Colossus of Maroussi* (1941). As war broke out, the American consul in Athens arranged his unwilling passage back to the USA, Miller promising to return to Europe "the first Sunday after the war." He arrived in New York, "back in the rat-trap," with, he claimed, ten dollars in his pocket – the royalties from his books, published in Paris, were trapped in occupied France – and had to borrow the money for the cabman from the hotel clerk. Trying to start over again, he travelled America for a year, collecting material for a critical, bitter, and vividly written view of the country, *The Air-Conditioned Nightmare*. It was finished just as the Japanese raided Pearl Harbor in December 1941. Americans were at once in the war too, and it was no time for a critical, expatriate view of the nation that tested its forms and institutions against those of Europe; the book did not appear until 1945. There was a new period of struggle, when he lived largely by painting. But in time he settled, in his Pacific paradise at Big Sur, California, and continued to write in the same visionary way, re-working, in the "Rosy Crucifixion" sequence (*Sexus, Plexus, Nexus*, 1945–60), the same autobiographical materials he had used in the "Tropics" books from a more benign, more celebratory, and at times more pornographic standpoint. These books, again published in Paris, where his fame was growing and his royalties building (alas, they were not always reachable, because of exchange regulations and the fast-falling franc), did not add greatly to his reputation, but they multiplied his sales. By the 1950s, when he celebrated his Californian existence in *Big Sur and the Oranges of Hieronymus Bosch* (1957), he was becoming increasingly accepted – increasingly accepting himself – as a major American writer, continuing to sing his Whitmanesque, apocalyptic song of myself. Even so, it would take until the Sixties, when, in a new era of liberationist freedom, his Paris books from the Thirties appeared in the USA, a quarter of a century after first publication. By now, the expatriate pornographer had become the American liberationist, a guru of Beat Generation sensibility and the voice of visionary romantic anarchism. No longer the exiled, corrupted, scabrous prophet of a dying world, he had become an American transcendental optimist, reforming the nation's consciousness.

5.

Tropic of Cancer (Paris, 1934; New York, 1961) and *Tropic of Capricorn* (Paris, 1939; New York, 1962) are the two large pillars of Miller's work, two versions of the *fourmillante cité* of the inter-war apocalypse. *Tropic of Cancer* – the first written of the sequence, but the later part of the story – is the tale (more fictionalized than it looks, but based on real events and people) of Miller's first two years as poverty-stricken "genius" in Paris, priapically walking the streets, scouring the bars, scrounging meals and handouts, writing and stealing, hunting for beds and girls, arguing with other writers and pseudo-writers, finding whores, picking up as much sex as he can find, or watching as his friends do the same, in a city remarkable amongst other things "for varieties of sexual provender." As the preface says, it is a "naked book," but this means it is as remarkable for its artistic bareness and its degree of self-exposure as for its sexual frankness. It carries no familiar baggage of culture. There is, in the substantive sense, no story. As in much surrealist writing, the overwhelming city, Paris, and its secret places become more important than the characters, central participants in the narrative (as Miller says in the semi-sequel, *Black Spring*: "What is not in the open street is false, derived, that is to say, *literature*"). He has been sent to the city "for a reason I have not been able to fathom." But one thing is certain; Paris is not America, the ashen-grey corpse over the horizon. "America three thousand miles away," he cries, "I never want to see it again." Both Paris and New York are cities dying in a time of crisis and corruption, and Paris is eaten up with cancer, disease, corruption, excremental flow (everywhere in Miller disease is the startling referent, the pervasive metaphor). But it is not defeated in spirit in an age of breakdown, and it still permits the self that is more than a self, the art that is more than art: "One can live in Paris – I discovered that – on just grief and anguish." For the plain-speaking George Orwell, giving a realist's reading, this was an outsider's story of an expatriate's Paris, rendered with a tourist's observant lyricism ("Twilight hour. Indian blue, water of glass, trees glistening and liquescent"), but still an unsocial tale of worthless social types, intellectual deadbeats, sexual opportunists, the *lumpenproletariat* fringe, and all written with no moral or political purpose. Yet, he adds, there is a telling directness to the prose, a new imagination, and everything is "handled with a feeling for character and mastery of technique that are unapproached in any at all recent novel."

But Miller, of course, claimed he meant it as much more than this: nothing less than the new kind of book in a new language. "The poetic is discovered by stripping away the vestiture of art; by descending to what might be styled 'a pre-artistic level,' the durable skeleton of form which is hidden in the phenomena of disintegration reappears to be transfigured again in the ever-changing flesh of emotion," the preface claims grandly. It was not an expatriate report, nor a sexual memoir, but a moral book, a metaphysical book, a philosophical book, a visionary book: the last book, the Bible of death and rebirth for the inter-war apocalypse – a story of the state of life, love and death in the last days, at the end of Western consciousness and the self-destruction of the world. The task of the creator is to reveal "the mystery of his pilgrimages, the flight which the poet makes over the face of the earth and then, as if he had been ordained to re-enact a lost drama, the heroic descent into the very bowels of the earth . . ." It was certainly not literature. "This then? This is not a book," says an early peroration. "This is libel, slander, defamation of character. This is not a book, in the ordinary sense of the word. No, this is a prolonged insult, a gob of spit in the face of Art, a kick in the pants to God, Man, Destiny, Time, Love, Beauty . . . what you will. I am going to sing for you, a little off key perhaps, but I will sing. I will sing while you croak, I will sing over your dirty corpse . . ." In fact the novel, conceived as an outrage or abuse, is permeated with many dominant Thirties ideas: of contemporary Spenglerian decline, historical debasement and sterility, the Waste Land and the Dead City, now corrupted by economic as well as political apocalypse, the need for sexual salvation and the saving reality of the obscene. So the need for an anarchistic surrealism that works toward personal liberation, all conceived in terms of a psycho-history that owes a great deal to Groddeck and, especially, Otto Rank, and encapsulated in the image of the double womb: the womb toward which we regress, avoiding rebirth; the world as womb, permitting the rebirth of individual being and consciousness. Culture, American especially, has broken down, the ecstatic man has disappeared, the false womb spawns corruption, "The world is pooped out." The apocalyptic world, "used up and polished like a leper's skull," calls for an obscene resurrection, a mystery created round the vaginal hole: "If anyone knew what it meant to read the riddle of that thing which today is called a 'crack' or 'hole,' if anyone had the least feeling of mystery about the phenomena which are labelled 'obscene,' the world would crack asunder . . . If there is only a gaping hole left then it must gush forth though it produces nothing but toads and bats and homunculi." In fact what does gush forth from Miller's account of the mystery is not just a confessional shout but a comic farce, a wild vision, a surrealist prophecy, in which the flow from the womb and the city alike pour out images of sex and death, sterility and birth, flowers and excrement.

For this surreal Paris provides the essential setting. It is an ideal city for a time when "the weather will not change," when "It's in the blood now – misfortune, ennui, grief, suicide." Like T. S. Eliot's London in "The Waste Land", it is the city of cities, "simply an artificial stage, a revolving stage that permits the spectator to glimpse all the phases of the conflict. Of itself Paris initiates no dreams, dramas. They are begun elsewhere. Paris is simply an obstetrical instrument that tears the living embryo from the womb and puts it in the incubator. Paris is simply the cradle of artificial births. Rocking here in the cradle one slips back into his soil: one dreams back to Berlin, New York, Chicago, Vienna, Minsk. Vienna is never more Vienna than in Paris." It's a city of the great European decay, acknowledging its own disorder, the cosmopolitan capital of contemporary exposure and inhumanity. And Miller himself delights in his collapsed humanity, rejoices in calling himself inhuman: "I am crying for more and more disasters, for bigger calamities, for grander failures. I want the whole world to be out of whack, I want everyone to scratch himself to death." Yet it is also the rooted setting for a long-lived humanity that modernized America lacks, as he acknowledges in the closing vision: "Suddenly it occurred to me that if I wanted I could go to America myself. It was the first time the opportunity had ever presented itself. I asked myself – 'do you want to go?' There was no answer. My thoughts drifted out, towards the other side where, taking a last look back, I had seen the skyscrapers fading out in a flurry of snowflakes," he writes, then adds: "After everything had quietly sifted through my mind, a great peace came over me. Here, where the river gently winds through the girdle of hills, lies a soil so saturated with the past that however far the human mind roams one can never detach it from its human background."

Tropic of Capricorn then goes back ten years earlier, to the New York City of his working and sexual life before he reaches Paris, to the years before he becomes himself, or rather realizes that he has. "I was perhaps the unique Dadaist in America, and I didn't know it," Miller says. "Nobody understood what I was writing about or why I wrote that way. I was so lucid they said I was daffy. I was describing the New World – unfortunately a little too soon because it had not yet been discovered and nobody could be persuaded it existed. It was an ovarian world . . ."[13] More formless and random than *Tropic of Cancer* (one reason, perhaps, why Miller wanted to rework the matter more intensively in "The Rosy Crucifixion"), the book loosely incorporates the glut of material Miller had built up over twenty years of writing. It is also a good deal more despairing. It starts from the existential premise: "Once you have given up the ghost, everything follows with dead certainty, even in the midst of chaos." It is filled with rage against the American system, which is exemplified by the "Cosmodemonic Telegraph Company of North America," where he works as a corrupt employer, providing the book with some of its most comic scenes (Miller was ever the comedian of corruption and anarchy). This corruption is as much sexual as economic. The dominant image is that of "The Ovarian Trolley," focused around the diseased ovaries of Hymie's wife and the vaginal wound that spawns the paradoxes of "The Land of Fuck," where the flow of life that should be one, continuous and promising is inevitably diseased and tainted. It was an extremist's version of the decade's most anxious image; in the age of the unconscious in crisis, and of fantasies of death, corruption and rebirth, the womb was to be the most troubled metaphor of much of the art of the Thirties. Throughout the book runs an urgent rage for annihilation ("in the bottom of my heart there was murder: I wanted to see America destroyed, razed from top to bottom"). And this is the story of a world of dancing skeletons, relieved by the bitter comedy of his own

13 In another key passage (pp. 302–3 in *Tropic of Capricorn*, Obelisk Press version) Miller intensively celebrates the writers of Dada and Surrealism, quoting the Dadaist manifesto in his own justification: "Every page must explode, either with the profoundly serious and heavy, the whirlwind, dizziness, the new, the eternal, with the overwhelming hoax, with an enthusiasm for principles or with the mode of typography. On the one hand a staggering fleeing world, affianced to the jinglebells of the infernal gamut, on the other hand: *new beings* . . ."

demanding existence. Starting out of rage, disgust, exploitative cunning, Miller is always on the outside, unable to find the flow and only able to link himself to the thing, any one random element or item on which he can make an imprint, or to which he can attach his signature. He learns to look on everything that is happening to him in America as if he were a spectator from another planet, picking up a cabbage-leaf from the gutter to hold it in his hand and see it as a distinct universe, meantime finding the city insane, and envisioning himself as a great eye witnessing it from above.

The structure is free, loose, associative; narrative persistently gives way to the grotesque dream. The aim is clear, the hunger for new, unspeakable languages and for the creation of a new life, where "Equilibrium is no longer the goal – the scales must be destroyed." Nin's astrological preoccupations are there too, so Capricorn, "renaissance in death," balances Cancer, "the extreme point of realization along the wrong path." Meantime America is effacing itself, motheaten by the new, leaving another terrifying hole: "Even a war does not bring this kind of destruction . . . Death is fecundating, for the soil as well as the spirit. In America the destruction is complete, annihilating. There is no rebirth, only a cancerous growth, layer upon layer of new, poisonous tissue, each one uglier than the previous one." But, he adds, "At the point from which this book is written I am the man who has baptized himself anew." The book finally explodes in a huge rhetorical fury; Miller may have discarded the idea of the book as art, but he was always to insist on remaining the prophetic artist. And if New York had given him his sense of metropolitan extremity, it was the Paris of Dada and Surrealism that gave him his sense of a place in the arts and a final conviction of rebirth. Here he had discovered his visionary self, his nature as yet another literary assassin, above all his real identity in the world of Dada. "Do you recognize me, lads?" he asks at the close of *Tropic of Capricorn*, declaring his Dada commitment. "Just a Brooklyn boy communicating with the red-haired albinos of the Zuni region. Making ready, with feet on the desk, to write 'strong works, works forever incomprehensible,' as my dead comrades [the early Dadaists] were promising." In fact, writing here in retrospect, he realizes he has discovered his place in a whole new movement of consciousness, and – or so the critics have confirmed since – become a central figure in the late modern, or postmodern, spirit of literature.[14]

[14] A good critical study of this is Ihab Hassan, *The Literature of Silence: Henry Miller and Samuel Beckett* (New York, Knopf, 1967).

But if Paris gave much to Miller, the chance to realize himself not simply as a writing anarchist but as an artist in tune with other artists of revolt, Miller also left behind a tradition in Paris – an alignment between his American radical vagrancy and the despairs that forged the next new climate, Existentialism, itself a child of the Thirties crisis and of the new war and the German Occupation. For post-war Americans, grim but intellectually active Paris was to become a second capital, a place of angst and anguish, of consciousness in transformation, of radical vagrancy. And Miller's "Tropics" books, available in a cover that said *Jane Eyre*, so that they could pass through American and British customs, became a familiar English-language Bible. Meantime the publishing tradition continued too; Paris remained the city of the American book of exile, visionary extremity and radical outrage. When William S. Burroughs, scion of the distinguished American adding-machine family, found his way from sober Saint Louis to a fifteen-year life of gay drug addiction in Tangier, close to other expatriates like Paul and Jane Bowles, he published the sequence of books that came from that addiction – *The Naked Lunch* (Paris, 1959; New York, 1962), *The Soft Machine* (Paris, 1961; New York, 1966), *The Ticket That Exploded* (Paris, 1962; New York, 1967) – with the Olympia Press in Paris: the post-war descendant of the Obelisk Press, run by Kahane's son, Maurice Girodias. It also published Vladimir Nabokov's *Lolita* (Paris, 1955; New York, 1958), the book that represented its Russian-born author's erotic encounter with the mythology of a youthful and nubile America, where he, like Humbert Humbert in the book, had gone to settle in exile, and J. P. Donleavy's *The Ginger Man* (Paris, 1955; London, 1956; New York, 1958, complete edition, 1965), the tale of another radical American expatriate, Sebastian Dangerfield, who this time chooses James Joyce's other city, Dublin, as his erotic destination. But in this new transatlantic transaction, the familiar roles were already beginning to reverse. In 1964 in Paris, Girodias was sentenced to a year in prison for publishing Miller's acknowledgedly "scabrous" *Sexus*, as well as other works, while the American edition went through unassailed by the courts. By the time Miller died in 1980, he was seen as another benign American philosopher, a latter-day Whitman in the age of the new body hyper-electric. It was as if he had never left the United States at all.

6.

As we can see now, in viewing the Thirties writer as a vagrant in a charnel-house, looking for inhumanity, death and rebirth, Miller was actually very far from alone. This was a season for travelling through disaster. As Paul Fussell has said, the Thirties was a time when "the diaspora . . . of literary modernism" occurred, when the Twenties spirit of experiment dissolved into something else, and many writers sought "abroad."[15] Fussell is chiefly concerned with British ones, and certainly young English writers – perhaps because of the world climate, also because Modernism and exile had so often been paired – began travelling, as perhaps never before, to distant outposts, unreliable frontiers and seedy margins, inspecting the flavour of international crisis as well as pursuing their own need for artistic and sexual adventure amid the new disorder. English writers had always wandered, in a sequence of diaspora that had somehow never really alarmed the political or the public culture; it was, after all, an old literary habit that made even more sense in a stuffy bourgeois country caught in an anxious age. But now the destinations changed: not just artistic, decadent, liberated France, sunny and now Fascist Italy, or the wide reaches of the increasingly troubled Empire, but Weimar Berlin, with its political and sexual corruption, the badlands of Eastern Europe, Morocco, China, Mexico and South America, the Hindu Kush, and, for the most intensely political, the Soviet Union. If most American books of the Thirties had America in their titles (and they were travel books too), many British ones had the opposite in theirs: strange cities, the names of trains and ships, words like "border" or "frontier." Movement itself became a preoccupation; the foreign correspondent turned into folk-hero; writing in transit became a norm; half the books appearing were about the places where the unsettlement of the world was proceeding. Writers like Graham Greene, Evelyn Waugh, Aldous Huxley, Rose Macaulay, Peter Fleming, became avid travellers, at first recording their own wandering adventures, but increasingly selecting the ominous sites of contemporary history, and creating a new global landscape for the imaginaton. "For myself," Evelyn Waugh explained, adventuring in South America, "and many

---

[15] Paul Fussell, *Abroad: British Literary Travelling Between the Wars* (Oxford and New York, Oxford University Press, 1980).

better than me, there is a fascination in distant and barbarous places, and particularly in the borderlands of conflicting cultures and states of development, where ideas, uprooted from their traditions, become oddly changed in transplantation. It is there that I find the experiences vivid enough to demand translation into literary form."[16] But they were also becoming ever more politically involved. The great change came with the Spanish Civil War in 1936 – another highly literary war, and one whose horrors, paid on both sides, emphasized to writers all over Europe the crisis nature of their times and the urgency of political engagement. By the end of the decade, the amusing early diaspora had turned into a time of grim exile. In the wake of Hitler's and Stalin's purges, the burning and banning of books, the imprisonment or murder of their authors, the totalitarian silencing of argument, the controlling of thought and art, writers were not travelling but fleeing – and as often as not across the Atlantic, to the United States.[17]

Some had scouted the journey already. Not the least of these was Malcolm Lowry, a rebel in motion who had early begun on a voyage that never ends. Born in 1909 in New Brighton, Cheshire, the son of a rich cotton-broker, he had grown up in the Wirral, close to the house where Hawthorne had lived during his British consulship, and overlooking the Mersey and the city of Liverpool, where Melville had come as a common sailor, setting down the experience in *Redburn*, described as the "sailor-boy confessions and reminiscences of the Son-of-a-Gentleman." From his schooldays on, Lowry felt the same restless, rebellious feelings, and in 1927, following a Melvillean course, he shipped off as an eighteen-year-old deckhand on the freighter the SS *Pyrrhus*, bound for Yokohama. This would provide him with the material for his first, youthful novel, *Ultramarine* (1933), an elaborate and highly allusive record of the long and disconcerting voyage. At the time of its publication, the book seemed yet another typical Thirties story of a

[16] Evelyn Waugh, *Ninety-Two Days: The Account of a Tropical Journey through British Guiana and Part of Brazil* (London, Duckworth, 1934). Waugh made a later journey to Mexico to see for himself the revolutionary regime of General Cardenas, recorded in *Robbery Under Law: The Mexican Object Lesson* (London, Chapman and Hall, 1939). It sees Mexico as "a waste land, part of a dead or, at any rate, a dying planet," and its revolution, also observed by Malcolm Lowry, as evidence that there is a will to barbarism and "we are all potential recruits for anarchy."

[17] All this is brilliantly discussed in detail in the later chapters of Valentine Cunningham's *British Writers of the Thirties* (Oxford and New York, Oxford University Press, 1989).

middle-class young man's identification with the proletariat. In fact it is essentially the story of a young man's harbourless dispossession, a tale of the spirit outward bound. It was also shaped by several powerful international literary influences. In 1929, just before going up to Cambridge, and right before the Great Crash, Lowry sailed off again, this time via the Caribbean, to Cambridge, Massachusetts, for a summer of tutoring by the American poet and novelist Conrad Aiken, whose own Modernist novel of voyage from America to Liverpool, *Blue Voyage* (1928), he had just admiringly read. Aiken, a friend of T. S. Eliot, was a myth-making, sometimes rather airy Modernist writer, and also an alcoholic. Both these qualities made a strong impression on the rebellious Lowry. Aiken's influence was to increase; during the Twenties Aiken, encouraged by T. S. Eliot, and drawn by the trace of Henry James, had lived at Jeake's House in Mermaid Street in Rye, East Sussex. Financially stricken by the Great Crash and a complicated divorce, he returned there in the early Thirties, staying there for much of the decade, and once attempting suicide – an ominous hint of things to come.[18]

Meantime Lowry went to Cambridge over 1930–3 and took the English tripos, not doing well. But the university provided him with many new and powerful influences. The English Faculty was in a vital critical period, with I. A. Richards, William Empson, T. R. Henn and F. R. Leavis active on the scene, and Lowry met up with a group of young fellow-writers who would support him and his work through difficult times later on. To this early personal mythology, Lowry also added the Norwegian writer Nordahl Greig, whose seafaring novel *The Ship Sails On* (1924) he read returning from the USA. In his first summer vacation, he dramatically signed as fireman on a Norwegian tramp ship in ballast for the White Sea, in order to go in pursuit of his new hero, whom he found in Oslo and befriended. This trip was also to provide material for a novel, *In Ballast for the White Sea*, an ambitious manuscript he worked on for many years until it was sadly lost in a fire (Lowry's manuscripts were to suffer a regular, indeed remarkable sequence of misfortunes). There were other influences very unusual in a young English writer. He was, for instance, reading "B. Traven," the German radical who had disappeared into Mexico, and whose early Mexican books, *The Death Ship* (1926), *The Cotton-Pickers* (1927) and *The*

[18] Aiken tells his story in his autobiography, *Ushant: An Essay* (New York, Duell-Little Brown, 1952; repub. New York, Oxford University Press, 1971).

Treasure of the Sierra Madre (1927), had already appeared in Germany (Lowry had also had a pre-university spell in Berlin, and picked up on Expressionism).[19] He left Cambridge with a third-class degree, a ukelele, a love of jazz, a real drinking problem, and a lifetime guilt about the suicide of a friend. He also left with the manuscript of *Ultramarine*, which was accepted by a publisher, lost by them, reconstructed, and published in 1933. The voyage that never ends had begun.[20]

That year Lowry went to Spain with the Aikens. Aiken, to whom *Ultramarine* is dedicated, and to whom it has a large debt, had become a substitute father to Lowry as his break with his own family worsened, not least over his rebellious behaviour, heavy drinking, heavy spending. In Granada – where, ever reading the literary hieroglyphs, he noted the shade of Washington Irving – Lowry met an American girl, Jan Gabrial, a would-be actress and writer on a European Grand Tour, and began a drunken pursuit of her which eventually led to their marriage. This happened in January 1934 in Paris, where the couple settled for a while, living as expatriates, and appropriately haunting the Shakespeare bookshop. The experience yielded Lowry several short stories, intended as part of a book of tales set in Spain and Paris; he was already constantly conceiving new books and large literary projects. But Jan then went back to America, and showed small sign of returning. After various drunken difficulties Lowry returned to Britain and talked his father into financing a voyage to the USA to retrieve the marriage. For his passage he selected the *Aquitania*, because it was the ship Lawrence and Dorothy Brett had sailed on to establish Rananim in New Mexico. Lowry was always a great reader of literary signals, and he had already some ideas of emulating their savage and dangerous pilgrimage. There were several other crucial literary myths in his mind as he now began what was to prove a twenty-year expatriation to the

---

[19] On Traven's remarkable story and the mystery that still surrounds him see Will Wyatt, *The Man Who Was B. Traven* (London, Cape, 1980).
[20] The two chief biographies of Lowry are Douglas Day's rather psychoanalytical *Malcolm Lowry: A Biography* (New York, Oxford University Press, 1973; London, Oxford University Press, 1974), and Gordon Bowker's much fuller and more detached *Pursued by Furies: A Life of Malcolm Lowry* (London, HarperCollins, 1993). On the Cambridge period, an invaluable book is M. C. Bradbrook, *Malcolm Lowry: His Art and Early Life* (London, Cambridge University Press, 1974). Tony Kilgallin, *Lowry* (Erin, Ont., Porcopio Press, 1973), is an interesting study, and the best brief book is Ronald Binns, *Malcolm Lowry* (London and New York, Methuen, 1984).

American continent; coming through New York Customs, it was said, his trunk contained one football boot and a copy of Melville's *Moby-Dick*. Melville now obsessed him, and, when he met up with Jan, he announced he was in pursuit of his "white whale," and wanted to visit New Bedford, the seaport of *Moby-Dick*, by sea. New Bedford, in its modern state, proved a bitter disappointment, but he and Jan settled on Cape Cod for the summer, then moved on to Greenwich Village. With *Ultramarine* apparently about to appear in the US, he now hoped to establish himself as a writer in New York. Living together in bohemian chaos, Jane wrote short stories of Paris, while he worked away on *In Ballast to the White Sea*. But New York now began to turn into a Henry Miller-ish nightmare. The marriage was in trouble again; Jan, indeed, was gathering "experience" as a taxi-dancer, Lowry chasing round Harlem after the jazz he loved, and drinking seriously. By May 1934, he was in what was to become a familiar state of disintegration, and spent a couple of weeks as a voluntary patient in the psychiatric ward of Bellevue Hospital. Soon he was well or sober enough to start taking notes for a story, or perhaps a novella, based on the experience, and which at this stage he called *Delirium on the East River*. Regularly revised over the years 1935–41, it acquired new titles – *The Last Address, Swinging the Maelstrom* – and at one point was almost published. It was his first American work, his one real story of New York and the United States. It finally appeared in book form in 1968, after his death, as *Lunar Caustic*.

7.

"It sure was a funny way to see America," says Dr Claggart (we can be quite sure the name's grim echo from *Billy Budd* is quite deliberate) to Bill Plantagenet, an Englishman who has lately crossed the Atlantic, in the best rescued but amalgamated version we have of *Lunar Caustic*. In this version the story has been moved on, and it is now emblematically set in 1936; the Spanish Civil War has just broken out in a "mischievous world over which merely more subtle lunatics exerted almost supreme hegemony." Bill has crossed the Atlantic for three mythic reasons: to find his missing wife, to bring his jazz band to its spiritual home in Harlem, and to visit Melville's home at New Bedford, the place from which the quest for the great white whale began. But now, like the story's author, Plantagenet is down, out, and hospitalized in the Bellevue Mental Hospital in Lower Manhattan, undergoing Dr Claggart's treatment for his chronic alcoholism. Lowry once said the book was "about a man's hysterical identification with Melville." The identification is, of course, Lowry's own; like so much of his fiction, this is a tale coded through with complicated intertextual references. The book is heavily packed with Melvillean allusions (in one version Claggart is actually told where his name comes from), and plainly Lowry was trying to mirror in modern form the spirit of a novelist whose chief theme was not only voyage but indecipherability, who had known obscurity in every sense and had also seen the demonic aspects of the world. Lawrence too is here; like Lawrence's, Lowry's journey starts off in American literature, and his hero arrives like a Melvillean hero in reverse, crossing the Atlantic to find the apocalyptic city. Both the *Pequod* and the *Titanic* are recalled; Plantagenet also remembers that the quest for the white whale was actually a quest that ended in destruction. Meantime the world he finds himself in more resembles the dark Manhattan chapters of *Redburn* – the book where Melville linked Liverpool and New York City. Bellevue hospital lies close to the spot where, at the beginning of *Moby-Dick*, Ishmael stands on the waterfront looking at the sea, and realizes he is an inveterate wanderer. Now in Bellevue, Bill and all his disturbed fellow-patients are modern Ishmaelites, always staring out at the transatlantic sea-lanes beyond the windows. Destruction, or self-destruction, is the book's theme, and the ships beyond the windows are failed messengers of wholeness: the patients respond with a sound, "partly a cheer and partly a wailing shriek, like some cry of the imprisoned spirit haunting the abyss between Europe and America and brooding like futurity over the Western Ocean."

Lunar Caustic may be in an imperfect version, but it is an important if neglected book (as Lowry is still an important and neglected writer) – a fresh vision of America, a remarkable Expressionist fable. Lowry knows well he is adapting an old transatlantic myth in order to create a new one. Explaining the myths of his voyage, Plantagenet tells Claggart, speaking of his elusive wife: "She only brought me back as a sort of souvenir from Europe. Perhaps it was America I was in love with. You know, you people get sentimental over England from time to time with your guff about sweetest Shakespeare. Well, this was the other way round. Only it was Eddie Lang and Joe Venuti and the death of Bix . . . And I wanted to see where Melville lived." What he is seeking in New York is the "last frontier," though what he finds instead is the modern Dantean inferno; this is a portrait of New York as a lunatic city, a city of modern despair. The turmoil is reinforced by the cataclysmic visions of the other patients – who dream of the fall of Pompeii or the destruction of the metropolis, that abiding image of the Thirties – as well as the haunting sound of the blues. But it is as a "city of dreadful night without splendour" that New York enters Plantagenet's soul. In the various different versions of the story, the hero has different names (in one he is Sigbjørn Lawhill, taking his name from a ship, and he sometimes thinks he is one) and he is variously a reforming journalist, a musician, and a committed left-winger. In all the versions, though, he is he figure for the *poète maudit* (the resemblances to Miller are apparent), and the theme is essentially infernal. He is led on his way past signs conveying chaos and exposure – *The Best For Less, Romeo and Juliet, the greatest love story in the world, No cover at any time, When Pain Threatens, Strikes* – to the imprisoning hospital door. A very Thirties work, it contains all the period concerns with mechanism, urbanism, social collapse, and with inner psychic breakdown, hallucination, nightmare. It's also a book in the spirit of Expressionism: images of dereliction and imprisonment, and the machine-like rhythms of work and hospital routine dominate. Though there is social concern for others, it is coupled with a total sense of impotence, retreat into the ever-deepening tunnel of neurosis, pain and personal symbolism. Plantagenet is a prophet who sees "disaster encompassing not only himself but the hospital, this land, the whole world." In the final thunderstorm, he has a brief, storm-induced vision of a paradisial world. But it is withdrawn, and the storm confirms New York as the apocalyptic city of misery and destruction:

> An iceberg hurled northward through the clouds and as it poised in its onrush, tilted, he saw his dream of New York crystallized there for an instant, glittering, illuminated by a celestial brilliance, only to be reclaimed by dark, by the pandemonium of an avalanche of falling coal, which, mingled with the cries of the insane speeding the *Providence* on her way, coalesced in his brain with what it conjured of the whole mechanic calamity of the rocking city, with the screaming of suicides, of girls tortured in hotels for transients, of people burning to death in vice dens, through all of which a thousand ambulances were screeching like trumpets.

Lowry's modernistic waste-land vision in this metropolitan fable – Plantagenet thinks he has "voyaged downward to the foul core of his world; here was the true meaning underneath all the loud inflamed words, the squealing headlines, the arrogant years" – was by no means the end of the matter. As Douglas Day explains in his biography, in going through its subsequent versions, the book was ever more intended as part of a sequence: "Apparently, if Lowry had lived long enough to give *Lunar Caustic* the full symbolic treatment, a journey from New York, and then to the rest of America – with Mexico and Canada – would have been something like a journey from Inferno to Purgatory to Paradise. But Lowry, one is sure, would never have made it that simple; journeys for him are never only geographical, and hell never in one place." From the beginning Lowry had had it in his mind to go to Mexico, following the Lawrence trail. The idea was now ominously encouraged by a meeting, in New York, with Waldo Frank, the radical American writer who had edited the poems of Hart Crane – another alcoholic, who had committed suicide by throwing himself off a ship on a return voyage from Mexico. In September 1936 he and Jan set out for Mexico, going first to California and stopping en route at the Lawrence ranch near Taos. They then visited Hollywood (where both would return) and then took a ship, the SS *Pennsylvania*, to Acapulco – arriving there on, Lowry claimed, the Day of the Dead, another sign or cipher for the great mythic record. "Like Columbus I have torn through one reality and discovered another," he would write, as they settled in the country. Following the revolution of General Cárdenas, Mexico was in considerable turmoil, and attracting the attention of other authors. Aldous Huxley came in the wake of Lawrence; Evelyn Waugh and Graham Greene, both Catholics, visited to record their experiences of this borderland. Indeed, in *The Power and the Glory* (1940), Mexico and its secular revolution entered the distinctive world of Greeneland. The Lowrys made their way to Cuernavaca, the pleasant and historic town fifty miles south of Mexico City, in the Sierra Madre, where Maximilian had had his palace, and where many artistic and political expatriates had now settled. They rented a house at 62 Calle Humboldt, "under the volcano" – or rather under two great Mexican volcanoes, Popocatepetl and Ixtaccihuatl.

By the end of the year, another book was brewing, set in the region in this era of political disorder; over time, struggle, many more pains, crises, journeys and textual revisions it would become his best-known and finest novel, *Under the Volcano* (1947). Meantime Lowry was soon drinking his way through the *cantinas* and advancing his own personal disintegration. The visits of friends, including the increasingly destructive Aiken, did not help matters; soon the marriage was in collapse. Jan took trips elsewhere to escape Lowry's benders with friends, and this advanced his sexual suspicions of her. At the end of 1937 the marriage dissolved, Jan going back to Hollywood to work there. Lowry refused to follow, and moved to Oaxaca, where Lawrence had finished *The Plumed Serpent*, and fallen near-fatally ill. Aldous Huxley, who had trod this way already, documenting the experience in *Beyond the Mexique Bay* (1934), had come increasingly to distrust Lawrentian dreams of political renewal and ecstatic mass life, and reported the decline of Indian culture after a volcanic eruption. Now Lowry arrived, and was evidently on a self-destructive quest himself. He was, he wrote friends as his troubles mounted, "sinking fast by the bow and stern," and on his "last Tooloose-Lo(us)wrytrek." There were drunken scenes in the *cantinas* that crossed over with political difficulties; he was three times imprisoned by the authorities for expressing pro-Communist opinions among the Franco sympathizers. General Cárdenas, who had expropriated foreign oil interests and was suppressing the church, was trying to tighten his grip on the country and eliminate foreign influence; the landowners, militia and the church were resisting, and the country was in worse political chaos than that Lawrence had thought to redeem with his new religion fifteen years earlier. Evelyn Waugh, inspecting the Cárdenas "socialist" revolution of land reform and political corruption a year later, found the country in barbaric chaos, serving as an object-lesson for those at home who believed that progress was the normal human condition, while Graham Greene, visiting around the same time, noted in *The Lawless Roads* (1939) the repression of foreigners with dangerous political opinions and the murderous persecution of opponents of the regime. If Lowry was looking for disorder, he had found it. Meantime he was wandering the country, drinking suicidally, acting violently, running deeper into debt, leaving unpaid hotel and bar bills. He had also failed to renew his visa, and only aid summoned up by his distant father, and the help of British and American consular officials, got him safely out of the country in mid-1938.

By now Lowry was something of a specialist in creating disorder. He went to Los Angeles hoping to renew the marriage with Jan, who was now working in the film industry. It dissolved into a sequence of violent scenes and small dishonesties, making him an unpopular immigrant. He met an aspiring film star and writer, Margerie Bonner, and, trying to avoid Jan's divorce papers, moved to Vancouver, British Columbia, only to find he could not get readmitted to the USA. Here, just before war in Europe started, Margerie joined him, and they acquired a squatter's shack on the foreshore of Burrard Inlet, opposite an oil company terminal that flashed the word HELL. In fact the spot, on the Pacific, and right on the US border, became his paradise in exile. Just enough out of touch with American literary culture to confirm him in his lonely originality, but close enough to the magazines and books, it became his third America, an essential landscape for his writing, and his homeless home for fourteen years. He came to see himself as a writer apart from his own generation, and from English culture, and, by the end, he had written of the adventures, the divine comedy, of the suffering modern artist – himself, or a version of himself – in all three of his different American wildernesses.[21] *The Last Address* (later *Lunar Caustic*) was the Manhattan Inferno (or perhaps Purgatorio); *Under the Volcano*, which he now worked over and over, was the Mexican Purgatorio (or perhaps Inferno); the various books that were to follow, mostly left unfinished and then published posthumously, were the Canadian Paradiso. The mythological plan varied from time to time, but then everything varied, for the artist's voyage was never over. It was this longer distance, this ever-fracturing and transforming artistic self, indeed this constantly shifting image of America, that made it difficult for Lowry to bring any of his works to completion. And just as difficult was persuading publishers to publish them, admired though his talents and creative vitality were. The plan was vast, for six or seven volumes of the work that, this interlocking with that, would be the voyage of the modern creative soul, the voyage that never ends. The writing would not stop, revision followed revision, manuscripts were

---

[21] In the interesting, fragmentary story "Through the Panama," written in the 1950s, and amongst other things a speculation on the impact of Europe on the New World, he reflects on his cultural identity, here giving himself the name of Martin Trumbaugh: "Though an Englishman perhaps, in reality he belongs to an older tradition of writers, not English at all, but American, the tradition of Jamesian integrity and chivalry, of which Faulkner and Aiken – though both Southerners, which raises other questions – are about the lasting living exponents, albeit their subject matter might sometimes have scared their elders." See *Hear Us O Lord from Heaven Thy Dwelling Place & Lunar Caustic* (Harmondsworth, Penguin Modern Classics, 1979).

lost or burned in a fire at the shack. But in the end one book would stand out above the others, the book that made his fame and remains a twentieth-century classic. That book was the Mexican story, *Under the Volcano*.

8.

Under the Volcano – the novel Lowry started at Cuernavaca in 1936, though it now tells a story set on the Day of the Dead in 1938, right after the signing of the Munich agreement, and is seen from the perspective of the French consul Laruelle one year further on still, when Europe is already at war – was not to appear in print until 1947. Lowry had submitted a flat version of it to publishers in 1941; it was widely rejected. He then persistently rewrote it, far more densely and mythologically, taking in the influence of William Faulkner and drawing in a wide range of ideas. This was the version accepted both in Britain and the USA in 1946, and warmly hailed when it appeared the next year. By now the book was a post-war novel, very different from the book originally planned in Mexico. No longer a novel of purely personal crisis, it had become a vast retrospect on the Thirties. It was also a symbolic novel, about the journey from paradise to damnation, which paralleled the political and moral crisis which was plunging the world into war. A famous letter Lowry wrote to his British publishers, Jonathan Cape, in 1946 displays how largely the ideas had developed, how much the stylistic mode had changed. The original story of an individual's self-destructing breakdown in a chaotic and mysterious land had become a fable of an age of corruption, suspicion and treachery, and the world's wartime crisis is casting its shadow before. Geoffrey Firmin, the British consul at the end of his tether, had first been a surrogate figure for Lowry himself; now he embodies the crisis of modern man, and he is the victim not only of drink, sexual suspicion and a failing marriage but of a history itself held in stasis. He is the shattered "Faustian gent," caught in his own inner turmoil of innocence and guilt, remorse and sin as well as in some fatal Law of Series. First and foremost this is a novel of romantic extremity, the tragedy of the self-absorbed cuckold drunk as a hero of the modern spirit, a man who finds signs and symbols everywhere via the fantasies of his own drinking and mental frenzy, and is expelled from the paradisial garden (he associates it with Granada) into a destructive and volcanic world, another borderland where the grim if misread signals prove to be true and fatal, and the world really is ready to explode. A history of the world and consciousness unfolds, as in *Ulysses*, in one day; time in the book is "circumfluent again too, mescal-drugged." The extremity is a collusion, a meeting of the subjective and the objective, mirrored in a style of surreal and experimental energy. Places in Lowry become strange equivalents of a state of mind, as if the world has turned into the fiction one has created already. Once again the book is deeply coded: in fact it is an intertextual minefield, so much so that Lowry thought of providing it with the convenience of footnotes, just like Eliot's "The Waste Land." It is riddled with systems, series, labyrinths, verbal puns and ambiguities, allusions to many texts, from Dante and Marlowe to Melville and Joyce, and from the Tarot and the Cabbala to Lawrence and B. Traven, as well as to popular culture and film.

In this sense it is a Modernist work which, somehow surviving its season, was to become one of the greatest and most remarkable of post-war British novels, the story of a crisis world now seen in retrospect. It is, quite appropriately, an expatriate work, a book in which the displaced troubles of Europe cast both their jetsam and their influence over a Mexico ever rendered with the drunkard's chaotic vividness, a labyrinth of foreign signs and mysteries, constantly estranging to the senses. Politically Mexico is an appropriate backdrop, a place where in transfigured form the crises of Europe are indeed played out in the strange mirror of the New World. Cuernavaca – Quauhnahuac in the novel – is another expatriate society, filled with translated Europeans, varied political sympathizers, artists successful and failed, French film-makers, escapees from an ambiguous past. It is also a place where you encounter "every sort of landscape at once," where, crossing a highway, you can meet three civilizations, and which has "the beauty of the Earthly Paradise itself." In the Cape letter Lowry jokingly explains the setting as "the meeting place, according to some, of mankind itself, pyre of Bierce and springboard of Hart Crane, the age-old arena of racial and political conflicts of every nature, and where a colorful people of genius have a religion that we can roughly describe as one of death, so that it is a good place, at least as good as Lancashire or Yorkshire, to set our drama of a man's struggle between the powers of darkness and light." Here (where Trotsky took refuge) the ideologies of

Europe still shape the arguments, and the Spanish Civil War has its direct echoes in the ambiguous, violent local politics. There is a Nazi headquarters in town, a universal climate of suspicion and espionage ("You are de espider, and we shoota de espiders in Mejixo"), a corrupted bureaucracy, a consul who may not be all he seems: the pervasive aroma of the Thirties is everywhere. But Mexico is more than a backdrop, a setting for one man's guilty crisis. Lowry captures it in depth, registering the complex political climate, and the dramatic and extreme spirituality of a world where death is ever-present and the soul is ever haunted. The landscape, first seen in a long gaze, watched over by its two volcanoes, and riven by the *barranca* where all ends up, even the body of Geoffrey Firmin, is an eternal presence; in Lowry's writing landscape is always a literary essence. Mexico's dark history, its history of first encounter, of the bitter transactions of Old World and New, intrudes constantly – a long sequence of political betrayals that continue to the present, a world of political and moral mysteries going back to the ruined Eden of the murdered Emperor Maximilian and Carlotta, "two lonely empurpled exiles," and beyond that to the Aztecs. This is a land where the Day of the Dead is a national emblem, where the Earthly Paradise from which we are all evicted an eternal myth, and the distant Pacific promise of British Columbia, to which Firmin's wife Yvonne is heading, and where Lowry was living when he rewrote the book, an eternal contrast.

Once he had been to Mexico, Lowry could never really be done with it. In the winter of 1945–6, after settling and writing well in his paradisial Canada, he set off back there again, now with Margerie Bonner. Inevitably enough, the journey turned into a new chapter of accidents and conflicts with the authorities, no less complex than before. There was the matter of an unpaid fine left over from the earlier visit, and the fact that he had a file with the authorities; Lowry was evicted from the troubled garden for a second time, the Mexican reality both disputing what he wanted to make of it and proving the truth of his case. Out of this came his second Mexican novel, the story of just such a writer on just such a return visit, *Dark As the Grave Wherein My Friend Is Laid* (post. 1968,). The central character is called Sigbjørn Wilderness – a writer who has already written a still unpublished, probably unpublishable Mexican novel, *The Valley of the Shadow of Death* (this is just what *Under the Volcano* seemed to be at this date), and is now writing a second book called *Dark As the Grave Wherein My Friend Is Laid*, a "real" as opposed to a romantic story about the country. The second novel seems to be an undermining of many of the romantic principles on which the previous book has been built – and Lowry's own new tale, for all its apparatus, is largely a realistic commentary on his own present life and situation. The volcanoes are dead and extinct, the landscape is drab and meaningless, the political meanings have faded, old friends have died, and Mexico has become simply a land that drags the drunk toward drunkenness. But by now Lowry was presenting all of his writing in a complex and ever-changing web of his own construction. The process of mirroring one story in another had now begun. Every new work perspectivized what had gone before; no piece of writing could ever be stable or final, no text fixed, no version of the author the ultimate author. Wilderness has turned into the author of *Under the Volcano*; but he was just one of several author-surrogates who now populated the Lowry world, all authoring each other. *Under the Volcano* was now both its own book and a part of a sequence, psychic and mythic, self-discovering and self-dissolving. If Lowry was intricately permutating the textual status of his book, he was also reshaping its mythological meaning to construct the ever-enlarging adventure of his work, the interlinked sequence he called *The Voyage That Never Ends*.

The endless voyage was still being constantly reshaped when, in 1954, the Lowrys found themselves suddenly evicted from their Dollarton "garden." They decided to return to Europe, living first in Italy and Sicily, where, again, Lawrence had lived. Then they came to London, where Lowry – who was still pining for his Pacific paradise – was treated for severe depression and alcohol addiction. In February 1956 they moved to Ripe in Sussex, near to Lewes and not so far from Rye, where many of his adventures had begun. Here Lowry worked on his last novel, *October Ferry to Gabriola* ("It deals with the theme of eviction, which is related to man's dispossession, but this theme is universalized," he explained). It was yet another part of the voyage that could never end, because it now seemed to him nothing was ever completely written, just as the hidden codes that shaped the chaos of creative life could never be completely read. In June 1957, Lowry died suddenly, at the age of forty-seven, following a new drinking binge he complicated with sleeping tablets. It was called misadventure, but was almost certainly suicide. The voyage that never ends had ended at last.

9.

Eviction, dispossession, exile from paradise: the chords that Lowry struck, and Miller too, showed them as quintessential writers of the Thirties, when so many gardens were lost and so many homelands perished. In 1929 Thomas Mann was the great German novelist, winner of that year's Nobel Prize for Literature. Four years later, Adolf Hitler was the German chancellor, and Mann was in exile at Küsnacht in Switzerland, watching over the border as his books were condemned, his property confiscated, his person excommunicated. He was one of the many writers, teachers, and intellectuals – they included his brother Heinrich, Bertolt Brecht, Josef Albers, Albert Einstein and Walter Benjamin – who found themselves threatened and expelled in or around 1933. For the rest of the decade exile was the story: liberals, radicals, Jews from Germany and Austria, began the pilgrimage to safety, which led them sometimes to Switzerland, frequently to France or Britain, but as often as not finally to the USA. By 1938, the year in which Lowry set his story, Hitler had assumed the powers of War Minister, and marched his troops into Austria to annex it for his thousand-year Reich. Another new age of flight began. Mussolini had likewise annexed Ethiopia, and even won international support for it. In Spain Franco had now begun to win against the Republicans – events that were, as Lowry showed, to cast their shadows in Mexico too. Many liberal Spanish writers emigrated to Latin and South America, where they cosmopolitanized the literary scene. In the USSR that same spring, Stalin's show trials showed those who watched how he was exercising his dictatorial powers. It was everywhere clear that the dictators and the generalissimos, the jackboots and the strutting armies, the rolling tanks and overflying bombers, were dominating the fragile landscape of Europe and much of the Pacific world. By the autumn of Lowry's Day of the Dead, the ranting had grown louder, the marching increased, and everywhere armies were mobilizing, and Chamberlain had come home with the famous piece of paper that let Hitler march into the Sudetenland, precipitate the Czech crisis, and so begin the war. As Laruelle reflects at the beginning of *Under the Volcano*, in a kind of justification for the whole book: "Though tragedy was in the process of becoming unreal and meaningless it seemed one was still permitted to remember the days when an individual life held some value and was not a mere misprint in a communiqué."

In 1938 in America, much of this seemed, at least for the moment, a whole world away. The film of the year was Walt Disney's *Snow White and the Seven Dwarfs*, about seven small people who did succeed in finding work to whistle to during the Depression. The play of the year was Thornton Wilder's nostalgia piece of Americana *Our Town*; the opera of the year was another national celebration, Aaron Copland's Western *Billy the Kid*. Painting was dominated by regionalism, writers were writing travel books about their different parts of the nation under the sponsorship of the Federal Writers' Project, Dos Passos had just completed *USA*. However, the radio event of the year was Orson Welles' version of H. G. Wells' *War of the Worlds*, which caused national hysteria not just because of its subject, but because Orson Welles used just the same broadcasting methods as the remarkable coverage CBS had given the Munich crisis, which brought the noise of the Fascist threat to the American fireside. In the event, it was not a war of the worlds but a world war that was brewing, as many Americans were just beginning to see. In Europe air-raid shelters were being dug, gas-masks issued, the term "concentration camp" was heard, and the refugees were everywhere on the move. It was in 1938 that Mann issued a sombre warning to the German people, then travelled to the United States, first to Princeton, and in 1941 to California, where a community of exiles was gathering. Brecht, Stravinsky, Vladimir Nabokov, a second time exiled, and many others also travelled, bringing much that was central to European culture, thought and historical anxiety across the ocean to the USA. This migration – carrying thousands of European writers, artists, scientists, film-makers and intellectuals to the arts and universities of the USA – was, as H. Stuart Hughes once aptly said, "the most important cultural event . . . of the second quarter of the twentieth century," and it certainly marked a new and fundamental moment in transatlantic relations. If Europe was indeed in terminal disorder, much of what Europe had stood for in art and ideas was now in process of transplantation to the USA.

In the tide that carried many across the Atlantic near the close of the decade, various British writers were included. Some were pacifists, others were escapers from what now seemed to be the totalitarian engulfing of the European world. In 1937 Aldous Huxley, once the bitter satirist of the bright if calamitous intellectual world of the Twenties, had become ever more certain the modern world was spinning out of control. Now, worried by the failure of peace plans, by his own failing eyesight, and married to a Belgian refugee, he set off for the Brave New World, finally going to Hollywood as a screenwriter. He had already prefigured his visit by various travels in America, and by the writing of his remarkable *Brave New World* (1932), a dystopian tale set in a new world state in the seventh century AF (After Ford), which takes its hero to a New Mexico reservation to collect a sample savage for inspection by the scientific caste who now run the brave new world. One of the attractions of California – which became, partly because of the film-industry, a major destination for those departing Europe – was the proximity of his British friend, the prophetic Gerald Heard; Huxley was convinced that only in mysticism and pacifism would the movement toward dehumanization and totalitarianism be reversed. He also hoped to make "tons of money" quickly, so that he could return to an art "in which I can do all the work by myself." A successful screenplay of *Pride and Prejudice* in 1940 secured his reputation, and he remained in California to his death in 1963, writing novels and essays, exploring the drug mescaline, and doing occasional screenplays.[22] Others followed him there, including Christopher Isherwood, who left Britain with his friend W. H. Auden in early 1939, convinced that Europe was finished. Though these departures were much criticized, they had the effect of creating new links between the European and the American imagination, as anti-Fascists on both sides of the water found themselves in common cause. The images of America that such writers sent home to Europe also proved remarkably influential. British readers read of Heard's, Huxley's and Isherwood's California, a curious compound of synthetic gloss, cybernetic mechanism, and spiritual renewal; or of Auden's New York, a city of rootlessness and existential anxiety. In books like *After Many a Summer* (1939), a satire on the Californian myth of eternal life, based on experiences with William Randolph Hearst, *Ape and Essence* (1949), and *The Genius and the Goddess* (1955), Huxley expressed much of the European terror of an America dehumanized and scientized, putting its skills into the making of a system-based future where dreams of perpetual youth turn human beings into ciphers. But there is a visionary element in this too; the land of lunatic and cinematic modernity is also a land of promise, of new

---

[22] The story is told in David King Dunaway, *Huxley in Hollywood* (New York, Harper & Row, 1989). And also see Ian Hamilton's interesting *Writers in Hollywood, 1915–1951* (New York and London, HarperCollins, 1990), which records the screenwriting experience of other European writers, including P. G. Wodehouse.

modes of perception and redeemed inner insight. In America Huxley was able to renew himself, and felt his experiments with hallucinogenic drugs gave a new dimension to his writing and its growing mysticism. Isherwood at first wrote of Europe in America, but he was already exploring a new and filmic world where all is provisional and nothing quite real. His tales of Californian renewal came rather later, in *Down There On a Visit* (1962) and, especially, *A Single Man* (1964) – where the central figure lives in an instantaneous, self-renewing, present-tense world which is also a state of despair, as he recognizes his pathos, loss of connection, and the touch of darkness he has brought with him.[23]

One effect of this great transplantation was to end the separation that had begun to divide European and American writers during the problems of the early Thirties. Many of the European *émigrés* learned to look at America in a new way, as the land of freedom's prospects. Indeed they wanted America to be different, exceptional, apart from the crisis in Europe that seemed to presage an age of totalitarian disaster, its civilizations falling once more into the abyss toward which, it now appeared, everything had been pointing ever since the fatal August of 1914. But at the same time they had brought their history with them, and alerted Americans to the scale and horror of the crisis over the Ocean. They also brought with them their cosmopolitan arts and sciences: the experimentalism of Einstein, the radical humanism of Mann, the political consciousness of the Frankfurt School, the architecture of Bauhaus, the radical Expressionism of German cinema, the early existentialism of Paris, producing a new texture in the nature of the American arts. But the real moment of change came suddenly, when Japanese planes attacked Pearl Harbor on 7 December 1941, and four days later America was at war on both the Atlantic and Pacific fronts. This was one of the most profound transformations in American and world history; it plunged the nation into a war they were not really expecting, with an enemy it had hardly confronted. Like American engagement in the Great War, it produced inner conflict that took time to resolve. But Roosevelt and many intellectuals had seen where events were pointing, and uncertainties were mastered with remarkable speed. The war economy boomed; the Depression ended instantly, the Thirties were history – and history itself, in its larger world sense, was

[23] Peter Conrad offers an interesting, if hyperbolic, reading of both Huxley's and Isherwood's American experience in *Imagining America* (London, Routledge, 1980).

what America now entered. The inward-looking nation preoccupied with its own economic anxieties and its national identity was in process of becoming a world superpower, its anxieties no longer economic but atomic, its identity a model for world identity. A new age not just of transatlantic but of world relations had begun.

TEN

Life Among the Ruins:
Wilson, Waugh and the great Pax Americana

1.

In the spring and summer of 1945, just as the Second World War in Europe was coming toward its shattering and morally horrifying end, the famous American critic Edmund Wilson came back over the Atlantic on assignment for *The New Yorker*, the magazine where in recent years a good deal of his work had appeared. Wilson was now fifty, big and balding, burly and surly. He was also a formidable intellectual figure, in fact the one real "man of letters" America could claim. He had frequently been in Europe before. In the Great War he had served with the American ambulance services in France; this led to the writing of an important journal, and two fine European short stories. In the early Twenties he was one of the first to take up the great Modernist love affair with Paris, and he had written, knowingly and enthusiastically, of its spirit of experiment. He celebrated Cocteau and Milhaud and Stein, the Americanization of French experimental culture, the Francophilia of the new American arts; he had tried to draw his friend Scott Fitzgerald over the water to the better place. An avid reader and language-learner, he had become by the Thirties probably America's most important critic of modern European literature. When in 1931 he published his famous book, *Axel's Castle: A Study in the Imaginative Literature of 1870 to 1930*, he gave us the most important early study we have of European Modernism – the book you really had to read to understand the whole curve of the modern movement. Following the turn of American opinion leftward, he travelled in 1936 to Stalin's Russia, recording what for many Western intellectuals was the decade's most fabulous experience in the revealingly-titled *Travels in Two Democracies* (1936). His considered analytic study of the rise of revolutionary communism and the

Bolshevik Revolution, *To the Finland Station* (1940), became the standard account of modern history in the making. Editor of Fitzgerald's manuscripts after his death in 1941, and the leading American critic, Wilson had also become the maker of the current historical record, the reader of the American jitters, the great artistic journal-keeper of his day. Who could better note the changed cultural climate, account for the vast historical and cultural consequences of another World War, judge what had become of it all?

Wilson started off his trip in London, where the V2 rockets were still falling. He walked the shattered streets, and made a good many literary contacts, finding that most of the writers he knew or admired were somehow holding hosepipes for the voluntary Fire Brigade. But – as is plain not only from the *New Yorker* reports but from his more unbuttoned journal of his journey (reprinted in the volume *The Forties*, post., 1983) – the visit did not go well. Unlike the famed reporting of the broadcaster Ed Murrow from London during the Blitz, Wilson's shrewd sharp notes depict wartime London as an unpleasant, mean-minded austerity city. Little of what he saw or felt helped reinforce the spirit of the much-promoted "Special Relationship" that had supposedly brought British and Americans together as joint defenders of the free world in its fight against Fascism. Wilson found the English snobbish, condescending, and unpleasantly obsessed with their chief national sport: class-consciousness. Always more Francophile than Anglophile, he clearly felt snubbed in Britain, and tried hard to define what snubbed him. He could understand the irritation and unease of a nation that had been battered through the Blitz, thought it had been left to stand too long alone, at times come very close to defeat. But the British were, he judged, anti-American, stung by the greater privileges American troops had in Europe, by America's growing world power, and by a much-resented dependence on American aid and equipment. Moreover, an older cultural war had still not run its course. Just like Mrs Trollope or Charles Dickens, modern British writers still seemed to condescend from high over their American contemporaries. There can be little doubt Wilson was over-touchy; in truth over the wartime period most British writers had become highly Americophile. As cultural links with Europe snapped, and those with the USA improved, they had grown ever more interested in American writing, and constantly looked across the Atlantic – their attention further encouraged by the reports that flowed back from Auden, Isherwood,

Huxley and others, like Benjamin Britten and Peter Pears, who had gone to the USA at the start of the war. One of those he met, Cyril Connolly, editor of the key magazine *Horizon*, seriously proposed in his June 1941 issue that, given the recent deaths of Virginia Woolf, James Joyce and Sigmund Freud, a new "literary renaissance" needed starting in Britain. And the best way to do it was, with T. S. Eliot's advice, to ferry over from the States "about a hundred representative American writers, painters, photographers, editors and artistic directors" who would restore the spark to British intellectual life. To a degree, this redemptive influx actually occurred. Many American writers and reporters, like Hemingway and Steinbeck, appeared in wartime London, bringing the poles of the transatlantic literary world closer together – or sometimes, like Wilson, pushing them further apart.

For, if some saw promise in this fresh transatlantic contact, Wilson saw only disillusion and disappointment. Nothing pleased; indeed a new stage in the transatlantic comedy began. Everywhere Wilson found grimness. The strains of war, he reported, had made the British bitter and unfriendly. The class-system was rigid, the eggs powdered, the sausages a form of bread. He tells an odd, improbable, Graham Greene-like story of eating a deeply suspect roast duck in a London restaurant, then passing a shop that sold only dead crows. He resents British politeness and good manners; it all seems to him bad manners. Everywhere he finds contempt for foreigners, not least Americans, "Yanks." The British are, he observes, a strange people, orderly, superior, yet oddly submissive and culturally narrow, the price of being an island race: "The Englishman sits tight in his island and makes forays into the outside world which are adventurous or predatory but does not establish friendly relations." To confirm his darkest suspicions, he re-reads Dickens and Thackeray, finding in their works what he calls "the basic English qualities . . . the passion for social privilege, the rapacious appetite for property, the egoism that damns one's neighbour, the dependence on inherited advantages, and the almost equally deep-fibered instinct, often not deliberate or conscious, to make all these seem forms of virtue." Nothing has changed; the British stay mean, hypocritical. They hate yielding their world-role to Americans, but are willing victims of Americanization, attending American movies, imitating American speech, chewing American gum, yet never acquiring American friendliness, good-heartedness or gusto. And this was only the beginning; the bitterness increases as Wilson travels on, mostly under military auspices, through shattered, war-torn Italy and freshly liberated Greece. He is offended equally by the climate of European defeat and the fact that British influence seems to be growing in victory. In fact much of his niggling hostility comes from the role the British have seized in occupied Europe; they seem to think themselves a victor nation, when in Wilson's eyes they are among the vanquished, rescued only by American aid. This was in part an argument over the division of the spoils, but Wilson wanted to emphasize that the ruin of Europe was universal. It started in Britain, then spread across the rest of the continent.

When Wilson's reports came out in book form in 1947, they bore the telling title *Europe Without Baedeker: Sketches Among the Ruins of Italy, Greece and England.*[1] In every sense this was a title meant to be taken literally. Here was a report on a Europe that was finished; all the old cultural guidebooks might as well be thrown away. This was an anti-guide book, a grim story of travel among total breakdown and chaotic disillusion. Wilson met writers from George Santayana to Ignazio Silone, and was impressed by their sense of the disaster that had befallen humanism. But everywhere it is above all the war damage, the political chaos, and the universal climate of moral decline that strikes him. Every single thing about the continent is dismaying and unpleasant. Approaching Delphi, he concludes that "the monotony of ruin in Europe becomes sickening and exasperating," and a sense of sickened exasperation is the note of the entire book. The Europe he passes through has shattered its Baedeker heritage, smashing its great cities, blitzing its museums, blasting its history to pieces in six years of brutal war. The trip dispelled most of Wilson's own former European sympathies: the man who had told Fitzgerald that Europe was "the ideal place to live" now finds nothing but damage and waste, which simply provoke a sense of disgust. Everything in Italy has the stench of a new decay. The famous Campagna is derelict with fighting, even the ruins of Rome are ruined: "When you explore the stripped carcases of these structures, with their entrails laid open and their naked ribs, you find them ugly and rather repellent . . . Descending into the dark

---

[1] See Edmund Wilson, *Europe Without Baedeker: Sketches Among the Ruins of Italy, Greece and England, together with Notes from a European Diary: 1963–1964*, reissued London, the Hogarth Press, 1988, with an interesting introduction by Jonathan Raban.

vaulted chambers, you find nothing but human excrement." Milan looks "like a slice of Hell," and "Over the whole city hung the stink of the killing of Mussolini and his followers . . ." When European hostilities finally ceased and Wilson went back to the "central clime," Rome, it appeared "more foetid and corrupt than ever . . . a great brothel."

The ruins Wilson had found everywhere on his journey were, of course, real, terrible and universal – even more so in the middle parts of the continent, which he did not visit. Everywhere whole populations were on the move, communications broken, cities smashed to rubble, economies in ruins, the infra-structure collapsed. What had visibly happened in Europe, and the darker secrets that were now to come out, the horrific news of Belsen and Buchenwald, the extermination camps and the Holocaust, was to provoke everywhere a sense of human outrage, terror and disgrace, a shattering of the most profound assumptions of Western humanism. Yet, for Wilson, visiting the European ruins is also something of a literary trope, another stage in a tradition. American writers had come to see the European ruins before: Irving and Hawthorne and Longfellow and James had made it an imaginative custom. But what they had written of were the ancient sites that excited romantic feeling, "the ruined castle," "the falling tower," the deposits of art and history that provoked a metaphysics of decay and reflections on mutability, and which in fact let the imagination and poetry grow. The new ruins were a self-created and contemporary historical fact, a willed shattering of the meaning of Europe. They depressed and defeated the imagination, stifled poetry, destroyed the sense of history.

There is, in fact, something excessively bitter about Wilson's reaction, which takes the form of a withdrawal of sympathies, an angry detachment from the agonies of the scene. Europe has not just destroyed but disgraced itself, and history too, leaving a mess for Americans to clear up. And, though his report is filled with close and intimate details, it is ever focused on larger things. Saul Bellow once nicely summed up Wilson's style as that of the American aristocrat, and remarked that it was "a pity to waste Mr Wilson's fine rumblings on a lousy republic and that his eccentricities deserved at least an imperial setting." His concern was finally with the nature of new hegemony – "the phenomenon of Anglo-Saxon, Germanic, Russian soviet civilization that is taking over the world." Like any serious observer, he knew well that the end of war in Europe and the Pacific, marked by the death of Hitler and then the dropping of the atomic bomb, signalled the start of a new order in world affairs. What was now at stake was American hegemony: this was the age of the "Pax Americana." Hence his condescension toward the British, who still seemed to condescend to him. Of course his historical instinct was largely right. Though many Britons may not have realized, America, through the management of its Lend-Lease programme, had throughout the war been able to define, determine and control Britain's future economy, world-role and destiny. And if this was true of its chief European ally, it was even truer of the nations that now lay vanquished or were struggling to recover from wartime occupation. The power of America in western Europe would become the basic fact of the post-war world. These European ruins were indeed different. If, for the second time in the century, Europe was to be reconstructed, it would require the entire power of the American economy, and the re-engagement of the American imagination. The remaking of Europe, as not only Americans but many long-sighted Europeans like Jean Monnet realized, was dependent as it had never been before on the whole transatlantic refraction.

2.

Just around the time the uneasy post-atomic peace began, Wilson went home to the States, reflecting in his journals on the moral crisis of the times, the widespread corruption of humanity, the problem of whether America could or should restore human hopes in a time of evil and create a progressive future for a ruined world. Today his observant book also reads like a gloomy period piece. It is a work about a time when Europe is vested not just with physical but with moral corruption, and when America may well risk damaging its own virtue and innocence by taking up the burden of what has gone wrong. It is also the story of a victor's progress, written with the underlying certainty that America does now have the world, or much of it, in its hands. As a result, Wilson comes home observing "how much better off we were at home." And his book concludes with a new reconciliation with America itself; "my optimistic opinion is that the United States is more politically advanced than any other part of the world, because we have been through the worst of our careerist phase and are coming out the other side. We have seen a revival of the democratic creativeness which presided at the birth of the Republic and flourished up through the Civil War.'' In this Wilson prefigured the opinion of many of the left-leaning American intellectuals of the Thirties, who were departing from their former dissent to come to terms with the new state of the nation, and discarding the old critique of the country and the culture. For this was the period of a new and chastened liberalism – "the new liberalism" – which acknowledged that Americans had inherited the burden of history and the task of facing the contemporary reality. It was a time when intellectuals grew benign, when writers left Greenwich Village and Montparnasse for the university campus, when quarrels at home felt settled, America found a world-historical purpose – and the globe out there became a problem, a duty, a sphere for American deeds and American imaginings.[2]

And, as Wilson said, back in the USA things were very different – different not just from the ruinous mess that Europe had become, but from the way they had been in America right the way through the Thirties. Once again American forces had been massively engaged, this time on battlefronts right across the world; 322,000 had lost their lives in battle. But these losses were amazingly light when contrasted with what had happened to other peoples (forty million died in Europe). Apart from the incident at Pearl Harbor, the American continent had never for a moment seemed seriously threatened. Above all, the war

[2] In 1952 *Partisan Review*, which had been a Marxist and Trotskyist cultural journal in the Thirties, polled many American intellectuals on their attitudes to their country and its culture, asking whether their attitudes had changed significantly since the 1920s and 1930s. An "Editorial Statement" drew a clear conclusion: "The American artist and intellectual no longer feels 'disinherited' as Henry James did, or 'astray' as Ezra Pound did in 1913 ... We have obviously come a long way from the earlier rejection of America as spiritually barren, from the attacks of Mencken on the 'booboisie,' or the Marxist picture of America in the thirties as a land of capitalist reaction." And it added: "For more than a hundred years, America was culturally dependent on Europe; now Europe is economically dependent on America. And America is no longer the raw and unformed land of promise from which James, Santayana, and Eliot departed, seeking in Europe what they found lacking in America. Europe is no longer regarded as a sanctuary; it no longer assures that rich experience of culture which inspired and justified a criticism of American life. The wheel has come full circle, and now America has become the protector of Western civilization, at least in a military and economic sense." "Our Country and Our Culture: A Symposium," *Partisan Review*, XIX, 3 (May–June 1952).

had put paid to Depression, and all its workless works. It generated a miracle of American production, organization, invention, scientific development and discovery. As Paul Kennedy observes, by putting its seriously under-utilized resources into war production, the United States had suddenly become the most powerful military state in the world. The sleeping giant had awoken, as so many predicted it would.[3] All this restored a sense of pride, energy, opportunity, growth, even intellectual and artistic confidence to American life in the immediate post-war years. According to John Kenneth Galbraith, the war had been not just a relief from economic crisis, but had given Americans excitements they had never before experienced, new lives they never expected.[4] From the century's second great conflict of ideology and modernity, America had emerged the one outright victor, the one nation to find itself vastly richer rather than poorer as a result of the conflict. It possessed the bulk of the world's resources, had direct influence over the destiny of many nations, and, apart from the Soviet challenge, which was just beginning to show, it dominated the geo-political future.

The United States had, in fact, regained its role as modern technological and political Utopia, the Brave New World. The national mood had changed, grown bullish: "American experience is the key to the future," *Life* magazine announced. Many now thought it best to leave ruined Europe to its fate, and get on with living American lives, but others believed what the post-war world now demanded was the American way. At this moment, America really was the land of the future, a nation shaping the direction of history, a people of un-precedented power and plenty. Its war veterans were coming home to a new nation, a land that was, for most, a land of economic growth, consumption, development, renewed abundance. By the 1950s America, with one-sixth of the world's population, was producing over

3 Paul Kennedy, *The Rise and Fall of the Great Powers: Economic Change and Military Conflict from 1500 to 2000* (New York, Random House, 1987). Kennedy quotes the following American policy statement: "The successful termination of the war against our present enemies will find a world profoundly changed in respect of relative national military strengths, a change more comparable indeed with that occasioned by the fall of Rome than with any other change occurring during the succeeding fifteen hundred years . . . After the defeat of Japan, the United States and the Soviet Union will be the only military powers of the first magnitude. This is due in each case to a combination of geographical position and extent, and vast munitioning potential."
4 J. K. Galbraith, *The Liberal Hour* (Harmondsworth, Pelican, 1963).

a third of the world's goods, half its manufacture. It was consuming 40 per cent of its energy, had 70 per cent of its telephones, 80 per cent of its motor vehicles and refrigerators, nearly 100 per cent of its television sets. Material rewards weren't new to Americans, but up to now their development had been regularly interrupted by cycles of decline and economic depression. Now, part-backed by continued military production, America had evolved a new type of consumer society – and it all seemed the natural outcome of the American system, proof of the rightness of the American way. Democracy, freedom and capitalism had triumphed, and it was America's task to sustain this new international order. It now became natural to speak, as David Riesman did, of America's "age of abundance," to define Americans, as David Potter did, as a "people of plenty," or presume as a matter of course that the American way was now the way of the world.[5]

This new American equilibrium may actually have been (as many of the American novels of the day suggest to us) a time of anxious comfort, utopian irony and half-expressed alienation. But the new age of affluence was in starkest contrast to the poverty, despair, ruin and defeat that marked the European zone – where homeless refugees wandered from country to country, starved prisoners staggered out of camps where millions had died, repatriated soldiers were shipped back to countries they had fled from, often to their deaths, women and children traded their bodies for cigarettes or medicinal drugs. After the war the European ruination and starvation continued and worsened. In 1947, such was the chaos, disorder and disease, Winston Churchill called Europe "a rubble-heap, a charnel house, a breeding ground of pestilence and hate." All this drew Americans, at first doubtingly, into the Marshall Plan that brought American economic aid to much of western Europe, and the "Truman Doctrine," which ensured a long-standing political involvement in its future. So began the period of high American hegemony, in which Europe increasingly became less its historical self than a new Europe of the American mind. In the West, the next two decades were to be American decades, resulting in a new structure of "blocs" and "spheres of influence" that came to be known simply as "West" and "East," one American, the other Soviet-dominated. America was a radiating centre of influence – a vast

[5] See David Riesman, *Individualism Reconsidered* (Glencoe, Ill., Free Press, 1954), and David M. Potter, *People of Plenty: Economic Abundance and the American Character* (Chicago, Chicago University Press, 1954).

modern metaphor for the peoples of western Europe, and many other parts of the world, who found themselves in the American orbit, and whose societies now developed, under American guidance, through patterns of political, social and economic modernization that linked them ever more to American myths, ideologies and values. The country that kept an army smaller than Bulgaria's after the Great War was now a vast military power. Its companies and corporations dominated world trade and markets. Meantime American opportunities and facilities increasingly lured the intellectuals, scientists, writers and artists of Europe across the Atlantic to what now seemed for many nothing less than the new Rome, the cultural capital of the world. America ceased to be a net importer, became a net exporter of modern arts and cultural goods. Likewise American sciences, commodities and technologies spread through other countries, so it now became virtually impossible to distinguish "modernization" from "Americanization." American experience in the Fifties and Sixties was not just a national but a world experience – which, for Americans themselves, meant accepting a new, often threatening internationalism, requiring a different vision of the nation. It also meant a rediscovery of Americanism itself, an endeavour to restate past American values and ideas and explore contemporary ones, defining a changed nation in which old notions of democracy and new experiences of consumerism and materialism, collectivism and psychological individualism had to be united.

Wilson was perfectly right to sense the entire mythological basis of transatlantic relations was changing, and new kinds of guidebook would have to be written about the shifting balance of New World and Old. In 1963–4 he made a fresh visit to Europe, going to a now heavily Americanized Paris (it had become "almost a provincial city") and Rome (which seemed more cosmopolitan), then on to Iron Curtain Budapest. Once again he kept a record, and in 1966 reprinted his European book – adding his new impressions of the continent, reconsidering his previous interpretation. As his new trip showed him, in less than twenty years things had changed greatly. A large European recovery had taken place, chiefly thanks to American intervention. American aid, goods, corporations, advertising, and variants of American political institutions, were now to be found everywhere: "After the war, one felt Europe had been wrecked, and this gave it a certain tragic interest, but now a country that has to any extent recovered is inevitably seen as belonging to a more and more standardized, a more and more Americanized world." Hilton hotels were rising over the European capitals (even Budapest), dominating the urban skylines, high-rise symbols of the American hegemony. The imperial tasks for which Wilson had formerly attacked the British had now been assumed by Americans. In fact he now feels compelled to confess: "Our talk about bringing to backward peoples the processes of democratic government and of defending the 'free world' against Communism is as much an exploit of Anglo-Saxon hypocrisy as anything ever perpetrated by the English."

There is a further interesting dimension to Wilson's revised edition of his vision of Europe without Baedeker. In the new preface, he looks back also on the special offence his book had caused in Britain. It compared, he thinks, only to the reception of Hawthorne's *Our Old Home*, and so deserved Hawthorne's response: "they do me great injustice in supposing that I hate them. I would as soon hate my own people." But this is disingenuous. There can be no doubt that on his visit Wilson had liked neither England, nor the role the British claimed in Europe and history. He had deliberately written a vindictive book, as his more private remarks in *The Forties* make clear ("Perfide Albion, *la morgue anglaise*, international reputation as hypocrite," he notes). Everywhere on his trip he had found British social and military influence feudal, colonial, pervasive (as he shows in an interesting, bitter short story "Through the Abruzzi With Mattie and Harriet"). The same applied to British writing. British writers appeared to him social and snobbish, rather than intellectual; in the course of his tour he regularly contrasts them with European writers like Silone and Malraux, who show "a seriousness, an undulled perspicuity, about the largest problems of human destiny, which has become the rarest thing in the world." The truth is that, in its first version, his book displays the odd, edgy flavour that had begun growing in Anglo-American literary relations when British imperial, moral and cultural power began to decline just as American hegemony rose. This was an anglophone abrasion that – despite the much-vaunted "Special Relationship" that, forged in wartime, and cemented with common work on the atomic bomb, continued through the Cold War years, bringing the USA and Britain closer together than they had been at almost any time, except possibly in the Jamesian era around the turn of the century – would quite often resurface in the post-war years.[6] It was not easy for everyone in Britain

6 A classic study of these developments in Anglo-American relations is H. C. Allen,

to accept the shift in power relations and what followed it – the massive impact of America not just on Europe in general, but on the mythic role of a Britain that saw itself as the mother of democracy, the land of freedom, the longest-lasting European nation-state.

But there was more to it still. As his journals make clear, there were some very interesting personal reasons why Wilson's British visit had not gone as well as it might. It didn't help that a British girl he had been pursuing preferred to marry Arthur Koestler, nor that he really *was* snubbed in London – and by that prince of snubbers, Evelyn Waugh. For Waugh was in fact the British author he most wanted to meet. In a highly sympathetic essay of 1943, "Never Apologize, Never Explain: The Art of Evelyn Waugh," he had acclaimed Waugh's work as a classic of Englishness, describing him as "the only first-class comic genius that had appeared in Britain since Bernard Shaw." Waugh was equally an admirer of *Axel's Castle*. At a party of Cyril Connolly's in April 1945, the two stalwarts met. Waugh had served bravely in the military, and parachuted for the SAS into Yugoslavia, where his attacks on British policy favouring Tito brought him near to court-martial. He was now testy, bitter, and just in the process of publishing his highly romantic and aristocratic novel *Brideshead Revisited* (1945), which looked back on the "better" England of the past, now falling into the hands of the all too common man. The two fell out at once. Wilson found Waugh insufferably rude and anti- American; Waugh in turn found Wilson insufferably rude and anti- British. The result is displayed in Waugh's diary entry for 12 April 1945: "Hangover. Sent flowers to Angie, chucked appointment to show London to an insignificant Yank named Edmund Wilson, critic; spent afternoon at White's with Connolly; dined there, drank bottle of champagne and felt better, and went to Connolly's where I met E. Wilson mentioned above. It was the next day I chucked him. Augustus John, Elizabeth Bowen, Bohemian girls."[7]

Great Britain and the United States, 1783–1952 (London, Odhams, 1954). Also see D. C. Watt, *Succeeding John Bull: America in Britain's Place, 1900–1975* (Cambridge, Cambridge University Press, 1984); W. R. Louis and Hedley Bull (eds), *The "Special Relationship": Anglo-American Relations Since 1945* (Oxford, Clarendon Press, 1986), and Daniel Snowman, *Kissing Cousins: An Interpretation of British and American Culture, 1945–1975* (London, Temple Smith, 1977). For a highly readable study of the history of the Anglo-American relationship, see David Dimbleby and David Reynolds, *An Ocean Apart: The Relationship Between Britain and America in the Twentieth Century* (London, Hodder and Stoughton, 1988).
7 Michael Davie (ed.), *The Diaries of Evelyn Waugh* (London, Weidenfeld and Nicolson, 1976).

If Waugh had taken a gentleman's revenge on invasive America, Wilson took his, reviewing *Brideshead Revisted* in *The New Yorker* in January 1946. Waugh had now lost his literary virtue; the book was, he said, "snobbish," "disastrous," and "a bitter blow to this critic."[8] The truth of the matter was that Waugh and Wilson had forged a very distinctive Anglo-American *entente anti-cordiale* – which would have interesting literary consequences later. On Waugh's side there was exactly that self-mocking British gentlemanly blimpishness and idiosyncracy Wilson himself had seen as the basis of his comedy, which followed Jowett's rule to gentlemen: "Never apologize, never explain." On Wilson's, there was a remnant of the long-lasting resentment of British paternal condescension that had never quite left Anglo-American literary relations. Sydney Smith's "Who reads an American book?" was not quite forgotten, the great Dickens not quite forgiven, the Trollopes still thought unkind, Wilde – who said America had not been discovered but merely been detected – still regarded with suspicion. This went on. As American confidence and power increased, British writers looked with a growing but often sceptical interest at America and Americans; in fact they had to. Meantime across the Atlantic critics attributed ever less noble motives to their views of America and Americans. When in 1955 Graham Greene published his novel *The Quiet American*, about naïve American intervention in the Far East, another *New Yorker* critic, A. J. Liebling, reviewed the novel. Greene was unsympathetic to the American hegemony, and though he wrote little directly about post-war America, he wrote extensively in fiction of its influence elsewhere, in Central America, the Caribbean, South-East Asia, in ways that might have been hostile to State Department policies but were deeply shrewd and observant. But Liebling saw the novel as yet another work of the great British condescension, which

> made me realize that Mr Greene . . . trapped on the moving staircase of history, was registering a classic reaction familiar to me and Spengler. When England, a French cultural colony, outstripped the homeland after Waterloo and the Industrial Revolution, all that remained for the French to say was, 'Nevertheless, you remain nasty, overgrown children.' The Italians of the Renaissance said it to the French, and I

8 Wilson's two articles on Waugh are collected in *Classics and Commercials: A Literary Chronicle of the Forties* (New York, 1950; London, W. H. Allen, 1951). There is a detailed and funny account of the "Edmund Wilson affair" in Christopher Sykes, *Evelyn Waugh: A Biography* (London, Collins, 1975).

suppose the Greeks said it to the Romans. It is part of the ritual of handing over.

3.

Wilson, of course, was right to read a vast change taking place in the balance of the transatlantic world after 1945, and his powerful reporting marks a great turning, a deep transformation of myths and relations. But the "ritual of handing over" was ever a complicated matter, and there were many more observers than Edmund Wilson. In May 1944, just ahead of D-Day, Hemingway returned to Europe as a war correspondent, determined to give the combatants the benefit of his wisdom. He had already done his bit fighting the German U-boat menace off Cuba, and he thought the British had been guilty of appeasing Hitler and Mussolini in the Spanish Civil War. In London he drank, partied, and acquired a well-deserved reputation for arrogance; then a severe car accident in the blackout gave him a head-wound and concussion, and he was momentarily reported dead (not the first time this would happen). France after the D-Day landings now became a battlefield for the reconstruction of all his grandest military imaginings: "re-taking France and especially Paris made me feel the best I had ever felt." He gave his advice to generals, illegally armed himself and formed his own militia, killed German soldiers, and had to be restrained from fighting the war single-handed. A latter-day D'Annunzio, he ran ahead of the advance, and famously liberated two prime logistical sites from the literary Twenties, the Shakespeare Bookshop and the Paris Ritz ("I had never known how winning can make you feel"). At the Ritz, bars and drinks are named after him to this day. At the Scribe there was a famous encounter with George Orwell, a fellow Spanish Civil War hand who was now a war correspondent for the London *Observer*, and the author of perhaps the first novel of the Cold War world, *Animal Farm*, which appeared in the week the war ended in 1945. British and American literature was meeting again.[9]

Hemingway was just one of many established or to-be-established

[9] According to Paul Potts, Orwell wandered into the room when Hemingway was packing, and the exchange went like this: Hem (addressing the gaunt figure who has just introduced himself as Eric Blair): "Well what the hell do you want?" Or: "I'm George Orwell." Hem (extracting a bottle of Scotch from case): "Then why didn't you f***ing say so?"

American writers who attended the war as correspondents or combatants, and who wrote it into the record. John Steinbeck reported from Europe and Africa; John Dos Passos was a war correspondent with American forces in the Pacific. Far more Americans served in the Second World War than the First, and inevitably the conflict left a powerful imprint on new American fiction. The war novel came back, its works set in war-torn Europe, at sea, in the Pacific: John Hersey's *A Bell for Adano* (1944), Gore Vidal's *Williwaw* (1946), John Horne Burns' *The Gallery* (1947), Irwin Shaw's *The Young Lions* (1948), which tells the story of Hemingway in London, James Gould Cozzens' *Guard of Honor* (1948), Norman Mailer's powerful *The Naked and the Dead* (1948). In many of these books, the story is of a darkening age when liberalism gives way to a new era of system, alienation, universal military organization – "authority and nihilism stalking one another in the orgiastic hollow of this century," as Mailer puts it in his novel ("You can consider the army as a preview of the future," says General Cummings). John Hawkes in *The Cannibal* (1949), set in wartime Germany, and *The Beetle Leg* (1951), set in bombed wartime Britain, depicts a Europe Hawkes had not even visited, except in imagination, under the gaze of Gothic horror and extremity – the stuff of a new form of myth. Such books exposed not just a shift in transatlantic relations and perceptions, but a fundamental change in the mood of post-war American fiction. The image of wartime Europe in these novels is bleak and depressing. Moreover, war is no longer a sphere for individual heroism, as in Hemingway's version, but for depressing militarism, which begins in the field, then spreads into peacetime. The atmosphere of moral chaos and humanist defeat generates anxiety and existential despair, a vision of a world fallen into nihilism; and this formed the pervasive literary climate of the early post-war years.

These new writers had begun to dispense with both the Modernist and experimental spirit of the Twenties and the naïve political radicalism of the Thirties. An entire literary generation was now departing, another rising. Many leading writers died over the wartime period, or just at the end of it: Scott Fitzgerald, Nathanael West, Sherwood Anderson. Gertrude Stein just survived the war, staying in France throughout, but died in 1946, asking, as she always had, "What is the answer?" and then "What is the question?" The younger writers possessed not just a different sense of art but a different sense of history, showing a more international, a more bloodied, a more anxious view of time and the world. They saw themselves writing in a climate of crisis, historical, political and moral, the climate that now afflicted and made desperate the post-war, post-nuclear world. It was a world in which the physical and moral ruination of Europe became a familiar symbol. Several significant Jewish-American novelists emerged, to write, directly or indirectly, of the massive price of the Holocaust, not just to six million human lives but to fundamental ideas of humanism and moral responsibility. Others, like J. D. Salinger – who served in the armed forces in Europe – depicted an age of extremity, where love was overwhelmed by historical and moral squalor. Moral pain was the order of the day: in Jewish-American fiction, in Southern fiction, in black fiction. Like the nation itself, American writing was being drawn into a vastly more cosmopolitan spirit, and the troubles of a wider history. As one critic, R. W. B. Lewis, was to put it: "It is as though these novelists, and the characters they create, have been shaken loose by the amount and the violence of the history America had passed through (America, it must be remembered, has until late been unaccustomed to history)."

Beyond the images lay a new juxtaposition of cultural relations and contacts. For the great change came not just from the war itself, and the massive physical and moral devastation it left across Europe. It also came from the new political order that quickly came into shape, as the Iron Curtain snaked from the Baltic to the Adriatic down the European continent, dividing it physically and ideologically in two, and as the USA became ever more embroiled in Western European affairs, political, economic and cultural. Wilson was one of many who would travel the battered, fast-changing world as correspondent or cultural emissary, wondering over the fortunes of Europe and America and the consequent fate of the rest of the world. And, after the six-year interruption, literary relations soon started to develop again. They were now on a new cultural footing – Europe, dependent on American intentions and support, was now the debtor culture, not America, and the mythologization, or demonization, of America was an urgent matter. At first it was difficult for non-military Americans to travel to post-war Europe as visitors or expatriates. But the tide was soon flowing again, as various agencies – American State Department programmes, scholarships like the Fulbright or the Guggenheim, academic centres like the Salzburg Seminar for American Studies – began to surround political and economic activity with new literary and cultural links. Like Wilson's, a good many of the earliest reports were not just depressing but depressed, fatalistic. William Barrett, an early American explorer of post-war French Existentialism, and one of the editors of *Partisan Review*, which began carefully reporting European events in a series of foreign letters, returned from Italy in 1946 quoting Trotsky's phrase about the Great War – "the victory of America over Europe" – and arguing that the Second World War should be called "the victory of America and Russia over Europe."[10] Absurdist, Existentialist Paris became a particular centre of attraction, writers being drawn there not just, as before, by the cheapness of the franc but, very often, by a sense of dissent from the rise of American power and what still looked like a pervasive spirit of Puritanism, racism and sexual oppressiveness, as well as a new wave of McCarthyite witch-hunting.[11]

Other notable figures came in enquiring waves. In April 1946 the black American writer Richard Wright, a former Chicago Communist, and author of the novel *Native Son* (1940) and the memoir of a Mississippi childhood, *Black Boy* (1945), appeared in Paris. It marked the fulfilment of a long-standing ambition, a dream of escape to freedom. He was an admirer of Gertrude Stein, and she of him; though now in the last year of her life, she had kept up her interest in new American writing, welcomed the "doughboys" who came to see her after the Liberation, and now persuaded the French authorities to issue Wright an official invitation, when the American State Department expressed their suspicions of this former Communist's "loyalty" and made difficulties about awarding him a visa. As a black American, and therefore inevitably a victim of American racism, a literary equivalent of Paul Robeson or the many black jazz musicians who made their base in Paris, Wright was warmly welcomed in France, as a figure of *négritude*, from the moment of arrival. He was made an honorary citizen of the city of Paris, taken up by the French intelligentsia, especially the Deux Magots circle around *Les Temps Modernes*, and befriended and written about by Jean-Paul Sartre and Simone de Beauvoir. Wright

[10] William Barrett, "Reflections on Returning from Italy," *Partisan Review*, XIII, 1 (Winter 1946). He adds: "All Europe is now in the position of a backward nation."
[11] For an interesting study of this, see James Campbell, *Paris Interzone: Richard Wright, Lolita, Boris Vian and Others on the Left Bank, 1946–1960* (London, Secker and Warburg, 1994). And also see John de St Jorre, *The Good Ship Venus: The Erotic Voyage of the Olympia Press* (London, Hutchinson, 1994).

eventually settled in the Rue Monsieur le Prince, near the Jardin du Luxembourg, where he and his American Oldsmobile became a familiar sight, and became a good friend of Sylvia Beach. Like other American writers of the day, expatriate and otherwise, he took great interest in the philosophy of Existentialism (Saul Bellow, who came to Paris a little later, reported him reading Husserl in cafés), though it is said he did not get far with Sartre's dense 500-page key text of Existentialist *angst*, *Being and Nothingness* (1943). Still there is profound Existentialist influence on his important novel of black experience, *The Outsider*, written in Paris and published in 1953. A little later another black American writer, James Baldwin, arrived in Paris, in November 1948, claiming "I didn't go to Paris, I left New York." Baldwin and Wright started out as friends; Baldwin, though, was not only black but streetwise and actively homosexual, and the two eventually became bitter rivals for sympathetic French attentions. Baldwin set his second novel, *Giovanni's Room* (1956), the story of a love affair between two white men, in the gay scene of Paris. In new, post-war form, it deals with a familiar theme, the escape from puritanic America into a world of liberation and desire. "Americans should never come to Europe," the central character reflects, "it means they can never be happy again. What's the good of an American who isn't happy? Happiness is all we had." Baldwin himself went home in 1957, to continue his campaign for black rights. Wright stayed, and died in Paris in 1960, in what many still think were suspicious circumstances, connected either with black rivalries, or else with the FBI or the CIA. What is clear is that, with Wright, Baldwin and others expatriates like the crime-writer Chester Himes, the black American novel, which became so important a form over the next years, owes an enormous amount to the climate of post-war Paris.[12]

And in fact Paris was reviving rapidly, with the support of massive American aid, and was once more a powerful lure to members of dissident groups, writers excited by Existentialism and its sultry bohemia, or those who were now travelling freely on the GI Bill or various scholarships. In 1948–50, Saul Bellow – whose brilliant first

[12] I am indebted here to James Campbell, *Paris Interzone*, cited above, and to his study *Talking at the Gates: A Life of James Baldwin* (London, Faber, 1991); and also see Michel Fabre, *The Unfinished Quest of Richard Wright* (New York, 1973). On Paris in the period see Janet Flanner, *Paris Journal: 1944-65*, ed. William Shawn (New York, Athenaeum, 1965).

novel, *Dangling Man* (1944), can be read as a central fable of the way the age of left-leaning Thirties liberalism yielded to the age of war and military regimentation, and who was to become one of the most remarkable interpreters of the intellectual tenor of the times – spent two years there on a Guggenheim, and also travelled and recorded in Spain and Italy. "I was among those who came to investigate, part of the first wave," he recounts. "The blasts of war had no sooner ended than thousands of Americans packed their bags to go abroad. Eager Francophile travelers, poets, painters and philosophers were vastly outnumbered by the restless young – students of art history, cathedral lovers, refugees from the South and the Midwest, ex-soldiers on the GI Bill, sentimental pilgrims – as well as by people no less imaginative, with schemes for getting rich ... Adventurers, black-marketeers, smugglers, would-be *bon vivants*, bargain-hunters, bubbleheads – tens of thousands crossed on old troop ships, seeking business opportunities or sexual opportunities, or just for the hell of it."[13] But, as he notes, the Paris he found was no longer exactly the city of Modernism, or the capital of the great artistic redemption. It was a place embittered and riven by Occupation and collaboration, and darkened by Existentialism. Henry Miller's nihilism was more like it: "I was aware also of a seldom-mentioned force visible in Europe to anyone who has eyes – the force of a nihilism that had destroyed most of its cities and millions of lives in a war of six long years," Bellow reports. "Céline had spelled it out ... Americans of my generation crossed the Atlantic to size up the challenge, to look upon this human, warm, beautiful, and also proud, morbid, cynical and treacherous setting." Paris, he wrily notes, is a city of melancholy – "the seat of a highly developed humanity, and one thus witnesses highly developed forms of suffering there." Apart from coal and food shortages, this included Existentialism, pro-Communism and a suspicious anti-Americanism. He observes Wright learning *angst* by studying Husserl in restaurants, the *flics* reading Racine. These experiences play their part in several of Bellow's novels, where European and later on Eastern European intellectual life (*The Dean's December*) become important scenes in his moral and mental landscape. In the late pages of *The Adventures of Augie March* (1953), Augie, a latter-day Columbus from Chicago, and now just another finagler trying to

---

[13] Saul Bellow, "My Paris," in *It All Adds Up: From the Dim Past to the Uncertain Future* (London, Secker & Warburg, 1994); and also see other essays in the collection.

get rich, goes to immediately post-war Italy, "making a lot of dough" in war-surplus goods. He ends up gazing at a war-battered immoral Europe from the English Channel, whose waves are "like eternity opening up beside destructions of the modern world, hoary and grumbling."

Others American literary visitors went elsewhere, to Britain and France, Ireland and Italy and Scandinavia, cultural missionaries exploring Europe, writing, teaching American literature, meeting European writers, testing the older historical and expatriate myths. Whatever the destination, their reports were generally much the same. The American writer was a guilty tourist in a moral hell, and everywhere he or she went, what was found was a universal atmosphere of innocence lost, human sensibilities corrupted, anxiety rampant. "For shipboard reading en route to Italy, I took along with me *The Marble Faun*," reported another Guggenheim visitor, the critic and storywriter Leslie Fiedler, recording his 1952 Italian experience in *An End to Innocence* (1955): "It was a toss-up between that and *Innocents Abroad*. There seemed no use in trying to kid myself – no American just goes to Italy; he makes willy-nilly a literary journey, and his only choice is between melodrama and comedy. Hawthorne or Mark Twain? . . . a Pilgrimage to the shrines of an idea of man . . . and a Descent into Hell." What Fiedler discovers in Rome is both melodrama and comedy, and a double end to innocence. In the age of American power, Cold War politics, McCarthyism, the Rosenberg case, Americans can no longer travel to Europe in Jamesian naïveté, or even suppose Europe will provide them with some deep historical experience missing at home. And Europeans are no longer innocent about America, or consider its intentions generous, simple or naïve. American styles, customs, goods and mass culture are everywhere imported, *Life* magazine and Mickey Mouse, Indians, outlaws and gangsters, driving out folk culture. The price of the Pax Americana is inexorable Americanization, an economic and political process that scarcely provokes gratitude, rather irony, cultural outrage, and intellectual anti-Americanism. "America has become the hell of its own favourite hell," he nicely says. The worlds of Europe and America now mirror each other almost exactly; neither is the cultural or moral superior of the other. Visiting Americans have no moral claim to their classic innocence: "whoever admits his complicity in the existent America, even down to the crassest Philistine, avows a sense of guilt." Meantime, like many writers and thinkers across Europe, Italian intellectuals are devouring American literature. But what pleases them are the writings of Poe, Melville, Hawthorne, Hemingway, Faulkner, the darker fictions that speak of the corruption of the pastoral utopia (appropriately it was on such "Gothic" literature Fiedler would write his best criticism). "The end of the American artist's pilgrimage to Europe is always the discovery of America," Fiedler concludes, to come home understanding that in the eyes of Europe there are now two Americas: the America of militarism, mass culture and commercial vulgarization, the America of the romantic imagination, now tainted and pushed to the "tragic margin" by its flaws and crimes. "The new American abroad," he says, "finds a Europe racked by self-pity and nostalgia (except where sustained by the manufactured enthusiasms of Stalinism), and as alienated from its own traditions as Sauk City; he finds a Europe reading in its ruins *Moby-Dick*, a Europe haunted by the idea of America." Meanwhile the America he returns to is itself haunted by European crisis, and anti-Communist witchhunts. The Age of Innocence everywhere seemed to have come to a grim end.[14]

4.

So, as the years passed, ever more American writers began to take the pathway back to Europe – often to discover, like Fiedler, the ambiguities of their own history and their present economic and moral empire. The tourists returned, prime investors in the uncertain European economy, and by the mid-1950s it was reported that Americans had never before travelled in such numbers; 1 per cent of the population now lived and worked abroad, another million and a half travelled each year. The European capitals began to fill again, writers resettled abroad, expatriate magazines and presses revived. In Paris a new *transition* appeared, along with other new magazines like *Merlin*. The *Paris Review* came out in France and New York, J. F. McCrindle's *Transatlantic Review* in London. A pattern of expatriation resumed, a good many of the new wanderings based, like those of Richard Wright, James Baldwin and Chester Himes, on convictions of racial, sexual or political exclusion. Paris still offered radical freedoms and political alternatives, and the lively attractions of post-war Parisian intellectual

[14] See Leslie Fiedler, "Italian Pilgrimage: The Discovery of America," in *An End to Innocence: Essays on Culture and Politics* (Boston, Beacon Press, 1955), and other essays in the same volume.

life – Sartre, Beckett, Arthur Adamov, Ionesco, Existentialism and Absurdism – also played their powerful part. By the beginning of the 1960s, Paris, which now had a significant role in the development of American black writing, was also becoming a capital for the American "Beat" generation that would dominate the cultural mood of the decade. Paul and Jane Bowles had moved to Tangier; meantime Bowles himself moved from musical composition to become a remarkable short-story writer and novelist, as also was Jane.[15] Tangier also became a central point on the American art-and-drug trail, and in the 1950s William Burroughs went there, later on moving to Paris. This, indeed, was where many of these radical, experimental, liberationist writers were first published, quite often by Maurice Girodias' Olympia Press. One was J. P. Donleavy, who went to Dublin as an art student, befriended Irish writers like Brendan Behan, then moved to London. In his ribald novel *The Ginger Man* (1955) he spendidly dramatized Dublin's bars and bohemia as a place of anarchistic romp for the displaced and dissenting American. Ironically, the book, which Girodias published in a pornographic series, would bring about his downfall, and the press eventually ended up in Donleavy's hands. All this suggested the nature of American expatriation to Europe had changed yet again, representing the undercurrent of racial, sexual, moral, and political dissent that was in revolt against the culture of American "conformity." It drew on the tolerance Europe granted to American dissent and radicalism, to what came to be called the "counter-culture," which in the Sixties found its way home again – though, at the same time, it remained an international phenomenon, part of a generational politics that would shape sensibility right across the West. If Europe was often seen less as an artistic haven than as a place of disillusion to contrast with the American dream, it also provided a useful base from which to challenge it – as Gore Vidal, that American president *manqué*, did with Olympian grandeur from his base in Ravello, Italy, where, made an honorary citizen of the town, he preferred to see himself as an intellectual, political and sexual exile, a new Henry Adams ironically surveying the great American scene, past and present, rather than as an expatriate writer.[16]

---

[15] See the interesting essay on his work in Gore Vidal, *Armageddon: Essays 1983–1987* (London, André Deutsch, 1987).

[16] Mary McCarthy, who herself went to Paris, noted that the day of the expatriate had somehow faded away: "Today the expatriate writer is mainly a memory. In Paris, so far as I know, there are only Graham Greene, Beckett (unless he counts as French), James

As contacts renewed, American fiction was soon recording not just a grim war but a grim peace: a world where war could no longer be seen as an idealistic struggle to save civilization, or where American political emissaries served as moral redeemers. Unlike the fiction that followed the Great War, most of this writing told tales of wartime violence, soul-defeating occupation, American self-doubt. In the new tales of war and post-war, Gothic pain is everywhere, and guilt afflicts those on both sides, as military systems struggled with chaos only to create more chaos, the methods used to defeat totalitarianism are themselves seen as totalitarian. "I saw that we could prate of the evils of Fascism, yet be just as ruthless as Fascists with people who'd already been pushed around," notes John Horne Burns in the Italian sketches of *The Gallery* (1947). "Fathers and teachers, I ponder 'What is hell?' I maintain it is the suffering of being unable to love," scribbles Sergeant X, who has come through the war in Europe with not all his faculties intact, in J. D. Salinger's "For Esmé – With Love and Squalor" (*Nine Stories*, 1954). With American innocence itself corrupted into a form of violence, a familiar contrast was now between European decadence and American absurdity – the theme of Joseph Heller's remarkable anti-war novel *Catch-22* (1961), which sees Rome as a dark Purgatorio, a place of "tragic vexation," and the war itself as an absurd and malevolent system, exploited by an American war-machine that imposes on the old geography lunatic modern systems of bureaucracy, exploitation and mass destruction; his hero finally flees the American airforce for neutral Sweden. In Bernard Malamud's *Pictures of Fidelman* (1969), Fidelman, the Jew following in the wake of Hawthorne and James, comes to Italy to make art out of decadence, but finds far more decadence than art. In Thomas Pynchon's *V.* (1963) Europe provides a meaningless excess of history, and America an entropic contemporaneity; in his *Gravity's Rainbow* (1973), a London blitzed by the V-rockets becomes a surreal territory for an elaborate speculation about modern technological

Jones, Nancy Mitford, Leslie Blanch, Italo Calvino, though there is a rumour that Lawrence Durrell is around. S. J. Perelman is in England. A few live in Tangiers, a few still in Athens; in Rome, Gore Vidal and Muriel Spark. James Baldwin, in the south of France and before that in Turkey, is more of an exile than an expatriate. That is true of Burroughs too.

"Expatriate writing, a potpourri of the avant-garde and the decadent, has almost faded away. Henry James had set the themes once and for all ..." See Mary McCarthy, "A Guide to Exiles, Expatriates and Internal Emigrés" (1972), in *Occasional Prose* (London, Weidenfeld and Nicolson, 1985).

chaos. In all these the old motifs still have a secret existence, feeding back into a challenge both to Europe and America. The old Gothic fable still goes on – a story of, as it were, the Jamesian underside, psychic corruption tainting both innocence and experience.

5.

The fact was that, with greater ease of travel, increased economic contact, a growing overlapping of experiences and cultures, old expatriate dramas were fading, but transatlantic literary links increasing, indeed flourishing as never before. There was no doubt the centre of cultural gravity was shifting across the Atlantic. In Europe, that led to growing interest in both current and past American writing, more than ever seen as a report on the condition of the world. American titles filled the European bookstores, new American fiction won huge attention, its writers being rapidly translated into European languages. Behind this American Renaissance lay several profound reasons. One was that Europeans felt the need to discover much more about the New World; after all, it was now the shaping influence on the Old. Another, though, was a sense of crisis that pervaded European writing itself. Along with almost every other institution and structure, that of literature had largely collapsed in much of continental Europe. Censorship and the persecution of writers on the one hand, official propaganda and collaboration on the other, had tainted the nature of the word. Under Nazism, German literature had been almost entirely oppressed and silenced. Writers had been imprisoned, murdered, driven into exile or suicide; those who now took up the task of writing had to begin again. To a lesser degree, something similar had happened in Italy, though a significant number of resistance writers, like Silone and Pavese, were there to pick up the line. In Occupied France, some writers had collaborated, others had written obscurely, some had done both, others had grown silent, or gone underground. The whole horrific experience of the totalitarianization of Europe was an unwritten story, one that would take a long time to understand and to tell – though some notable figures, Orwell in Britain, Sartre, Camus and Beckett in France, Günter Grass and Heinrich Böll in Germany, emerged to tell it. More, the enormity of events like the Holocaust and the atomic slaughter of Hiroshima seemed to many to silence expression itself.

Words were tainted, perhaps silence was all that was left: as Theodor Adorno put it, "No poetry after Auschwitz."[17] Tradition had broken, the arts had been discredited, the task of literary reconstruction seemed formidable. When in 1947 Jean-Paul Sartre asked, in his book of this title, *What Is Literature?*, he claimed the European writers of the time were a "third generation" who had inherited a failed or corrupted tradition. One solution he gave was what he named "the American approach," a turn toward American literature. His notable, enthusiastic essays on Faulkner and Dos Passos ("I regard Dos Passos as the greatest writer of our times") suggested why; they had found a new language of clarity, a writing at degree zero. Sartre was not alone in his opinion. During the Fascist period in Italy, writers and intellectuals had turned to American literature in political protest. Much the same thing began to happen in the occupied countries of Eastern Europe, even in Stalin's Russia itself. If writing was to survive in freedom, it needed the American way. American writing, vivid, inventive, often frankly critical of its own nation, offered a vision of both the crisis and the escape that many European authors could recognize.

Later on, Saul Bellow would offer some barbed comments on the fascination American writers had for post-war European intellectuals. They presented them, he suggested, with a new vision of the extremity of modern reality in terms they could understand, drawing on the spirit of alienation and moral crisis that had come down the generations from the European writing of Dostoevsky, Mann and Kafka. New American writers, Bellow noted, seemed to share a common awareness of crisis with the great European writers of modern dehumanization, like Gide, Sartre, Beckett and Sarraute. But the Europeans were "writers whose novels and plays are derived from definite theories which make a historical reckoning of the human condition and are peculiarly responsive to new physical, psychological, and philosophical theories." Exploring their mass society, alien cities, lonely identities, American writers showed their anguish intuitively: "American writers, when they are moved by a similar spirit to reject and despise the Self, are seldom encumbered by such intellectual baggage, and this fact pleases their European contemporaries, who find in them a natural, that is, a brutal or violent acceptance of the new universal truth by minds free from intellectual preconceptions."[18] They had in short instinctively

[17] The most striking study of this is George Steiner, *Language and Silence* (London, Faber, 1967).

[18] Saul Bellow, "Some Notes on Recent American Fiction" (1963), reprinted in

inherited much of the Modernist spirit, the anxieties of contemporary liberalism, the crisis of human complexity. Certainly fascination with American fiction, American literature, American anything, became a dominant phenomenon of the post-war European world. It peaked over the Fifties and Sixties, when a remarkable new generation – Bellow, Mailer, Salinger, Updike, Baldwin, Malamud, Roth, Mary McCarthy, followed by Pynchon, Heller, Vonnegut and Barth – emerged in the American novel. Writing in a spirit very different from the social realism and inward-looking Americanism of the Thirties, they were part of a generation that had cosmopolitanized itself. It showed in the magazines, in their curiosity, even in their intellectualism. It also drew on the fact that many of them had been to post-war Europe, picked up on the crisis of the Western intellectual tradition, drawn on European, Eastern European and Russian influences, and acquired, as many of the subjects of their books showed, a travelling imagination not a little stimulated by the spirit of international and indeed East-West cultural exchange.[19]

Gore Vidal once wrily observed that writers in powerful countries get more recognition than they deserve, because their writing is supported by the simple facts and systems of cultural power. Certainly American writing past and present was promoted in Europe by various agencies, including the Congress for Cultural Freedom, which founded magazines like *Encounter* in Britain, *Preuves* in France, and *Der Monat* in Germany at the beginning of the 1950s, and eventually proved to have been assisted by the CIA. (Data from the CIA and FBI files shows how attempts at the political manipulation of writers, including Richard Wright, were part of American policy at the time.) Then in 1952 there appeared the international magazine *Perspectives*, funded by the Ford Foundation: "It will be the main function . . . to show that the spiritual and artistic elements in American life have not been sterile," its first

Malcolm Bradbury (ed.), *The Novel Today: Contemporary Writers on Modern Fiction* (London, Fontana, rev. ed., 1990).
19 Wonderfully well caught in John Updike's *Bech: A Book* (New York, Knopf, 1970), the tale of a Jewish-American writer's wanderings in an Eastern Europe in the belief that "There seemed no overweening reason why Russia and America, those lovable paranoid giants, could not happily share a globe so big and blue; there certainly seemed no reason why Henry Bech, the recherché but amiable novelist, artistically blocked but socially fluent, should not be flown into Moscow at the expense of our State Department for a month of that mostly imaginary activity termed 'cultural exchange.' "

editorial said. "The United States has poets and novelists, painters and musicians, thinkers and scholars, critics and architects, who have gifts of the first order to give the world. America, if judged merely by second-rate motion pictures, may appear to be a land of gilded barbarians; but America judged also by the poems of a Marianne Moore, the paintings of a Ben Shahn [and other contributors to the volumes] . . . becomes something different: a culture that exhibits an exciting and rounded vitality." Other American intellectual magazines – *Partisan Review*, *The Kenyon Review*, *The Hudson Review*, even the redoubtable *The American Scholar* – were distributed throughout the European libraries by the Rockefeller Foundation; as a schoolboy and student reader, I gained much of my own early intellectual education and world-view from their pages. The funding sources didn't really matter; what they showed was a changed axis of intellectual engagement, a revised Western perspective that was emerging in post-war, post-atomic culture. The fresh interest in American literature, the new collaboration between American and European writers, that shaped the post-war atmosphere finally owed rather little to sinister political conspiracies. It came out of the compelling and critical energy of much American writing, the vigour of its imagination, the anxious exploration of the anxieties and truths of the changing Western condition and culture, the examination of the crises of liberalism and humanism, the vivid imagery of the tempting, alienating postmodern world, the general need for a new understanding and cultural renewal. Something like a common transatlantic culture was beginning to emerge, most easily in Britain, where there was a shared linguistic and cultural link, but also in most of the other western European countries.

6.

The new relations were not entirely easy. "Americanization" was becoming an inevitable fact not just of political, economic and mass cultural life, but also of Western intellectual and artistic experience. It was a source of profound reinvigoration, but also of potential danger, threatening to previous national traditions and cultural institutions. So, unsurprisingly, it provoked in many European intellectuals and writers a bitter sense of cultural supersession, and a profound anxiety about cultural identity and independence. Indeed, right across wearied, ideologically divided western Europe, writers and commentators began exploring the new, overwhelming influence of *le défi américaine*, the American challenge. "America is affecting Europe in so many ways, and at so many different levels, that it is difficult to know where to begin, or what kind of influence to regard as the more important": so Bertrand Russell, opening the argument in a book of British and Irish reflections, *The Impact of America on European Culture*, in 1951.[20] This book was one of a good number of works around this date that explored a deep-seated historic and ideological unease in Europe, not least about the new dominance in Europe of American mass culture. Hence Americophilia was readily balanced by Americophobia, "anti-Americanism." A significant part of the intelligentsia, distrusting or resenting the "American challenge," distinctly came to prefer the radiation from Moscow to the radiation from Washington, Madison Avenue or Hollywood, and the communist and corporate way to the capitalist and individualist way. The larger concern was the omnipresent process of "Americanization" – the term, and the anxiety, went right back to the 1850s – that was visibly overwhelming European cultures, as Wilson noted, displacing past institutions and habits and replacing them with a new model of late twentieth-century society: mass consumers, mass culture, unremitting material aspiration, conformity, inner alienation. This was the future America appeared to stand for, a rolling process of global capitalism, imperialism and Coca-colonization. And American power made it appear an unstoppable process – the process, no less, of late capitalism itself in its post-technological and postmodern phase.[21]

20 Bertrand Russell *et al.*, *The Impact of America on European Culture* (Boston, Beacon Press, 1951). Also see Lewis Galantière (ed.), *America and the Mind of Europe* (London, Hamish Hamilton, 1951), with essays by Arthur Koestler, Raymond Aron, etc. A later highly influential book was Jean-Jacques Servan-Schreiber, *The American Challenge*, trans. Ronald Steel (New York, Avon, 1969), while two similarly important books from Britain were Francis Williams, *The American Invasion* (London, Anthony Blond, 1962), and James McMillan and Bernard Harris, *The American Take-Over of Britain* (London, Leslie Frewin, 1968). It is worth noting that many of these debates were mutual – that is to say, they were occurring on both sides of the Atlantic. And many of the most severe criticisms of American military or economic policy abroad came from commentators within the USA.
21 Important studies of this are Max Beloff, *The United States and the Unity of Europe* (London, Faber, 1963), Coral Bell, *The Debatable Alliance: An Essay in Anglo-American Relations* (London, Oxford University Press, 1964), and Lionel Gelber, *The Alliance of Necessity: Britain's Crisis, The New Europe and American Interests* (London, Robert Hale, 1969). An important study of the impact of American popular culture on Europe is C.

So, even as European conditions improved, as Germany became not a defeated and ruined site but an economic miracle, as new political orders were put into place and began to flourish, as growth, personal aspiration and material security began to improve, it seemed ever plainer that, just as once it had appeared that the Old World had invented the destiny of the New one, now it was the New World that was inventing the character and destiny of the Old. Europe appeared culturally supine, unable to revive its traditions or construct its future. It was part of the American sphere of influence, a unit in the great American marketplace; it was even becoming, said some, the forty-ninth American state. It lacked its own cultural energies, and its near-inevitable prospects lay in the growth of mass democracies on the American model, which pointed inevitably to an order of global uniformity, cultural standardization, disorienting alienation: Super-culture, Post-culture. High culture would yield to mass, folkways would yield to Hollywood, American cultural phenomena – from the "teenager," that strange American pseudo-concept, to mass higher education to the superhighway and the high-rise functionalist office block towering over the urban skylines – would overwhelm the moral and physical landscape of Europe. And if Europe felt threatened culturally by le défi américaine, it felt no less threatened militarily. For now, with the continental land-mass split in two by the iron wall from Stettin in the Baltic to Trieste in the Adriatic, it was permanently placed on the dangerous faultline, between two aggressive and competing superpowers who meant to divide the world between them. It was not only marketplace, but landing-strip, battlefield, slaughter-house, the point of potential atomic confrontation in the age of total annihilation. One invitable consequence was the rise of a variety of powerful forms of anti-Americanism, some of it Marxist and ideological, some instinctive and self-protective, the result of the endeavour to preserve a distinct European cultural identity, a sense of national selfhood, or a political and strategic independence. In the event, the most powerful long-term consequence of this was an unexpected one: the gradual and to this day still incomplete construc-tion of a new European identity, based on the desire not to repeat the nationalistic and tribal conflicts and the territorial desires that had

W. E. Bigsby (ed.), *Superculture: American Popular Culture and Europe* (London, Elek, 1975).

brought about the double collapse of Europe in the two greatest wars of the twentieth century.[22]

Yet, beyond all these debates, the fact remained that, both because of the need for political and financial resuscitation and the nature of late modern technological and economic development, the Old World and the New were coming ever closer together. Sometimes this was in ways some of the parties disliked; but not all. Young people in Europe had grown up, either since wartime itself or the occupation period just after, in the American orbit. The teenager and the skyscraper, Sergeant Bilko and Dallas, the McDonald hamburger and the hula-hoop, the iconography of American popular culture, came into European lives. West Berlin became a showplace of Euro-American commodity culture, a radiating image of the new Western way in the heart of Marxist East Germany. The cultural debate itself was mutual, shaped by arguments coming from both sides of the Atlantic; American radical movements critical of American ways and policies and the European Left forged their transatlantic alliances. It seemed American culture was telling Europeans something about themselves, not just about America. Meantime the same cultural agencies and contacts, the same shared youth culture, the same boom in transatlantic travel which brought American travellers and corporations into Europe likewise carried Europeans, in ever-increasing numbers, across the Atlantic to America. The attractions were many, the cultural pull enormous; for a twenty-year period, America was to stay visibly in advance of any part of struggling Europe. Its great superhighways unfolded across an amazing open continent. Its houses and apartments were crammed with unbelievable technologies. Its music sounded with the voice of a pluricultural age, its universities were alive with experiments and discoveries, its space programme was the amazement of the world. America provided many of the popular mythological funds of the era,

---

[22] For an excellent discussion of European anti-Americanism, see some of the later essays in Marcus Cunliffe, *In Search of America: Transatlantic Essays, 1951–1990* (New York, Westport, London, Greenwood Press, 1991). As Cunliffe rightly points out, a large part of this debate was historical, founded on the accumulation of Old World and New World images and dialectics that had grown up over the centuries, and it is also to be seen as part of the process of "triangulation," the way people define their own identities by measuring their own (ever-shifting) identities against otherness. The process has existed on both sides of the Atlantic, each side holding both honorific and diabolic images of the other. The important thing is the historical power of the whole dialectic, and its part in the making of the modern world.

but in the arts – in architecture, music, painting, perhaps in writing too – it was no less radical and exciting. New York, or so the claim was increasingly made, was the new forum of modern consciousness and expression, nothing less than the artistic and cultural capital of the world.[23]

7.

After 1945, it was largely by looking at the refraction from America that most Europeans, living amid the ruins, saw the changed character of their continent and its history. In time that changed Europe would itself become an idea or an argued concept, a concept of nothing less than a United States of Europe itself. But that lay ahead: to begin with, it was essential to define the institutions, the systems, the ideologies that might point a way out of chaos. The process started even before the war ended. In 1944, after the Liberation of Paris, and the freeing of the Ritz, Jean-Paul Sartre and Simone de Beauvoir were judging the impact of the occupation in a Paris "experienced in shame and despair," planning a review, *Les Temps Modernes*, that would "construct an ideology for the post-war age," and announcing the importance of an "American approach" to the novel. In January 1945, before the European fighting finished, Sartre set off on a two-day flight to the USA, part of a delegation of French intellectuals and journalists invited by the State Department. It marked a new journey, but it was founded on old excitement; French intellectuals from Cocteau, Gide and Blaise Cendrars had been taking America as the supreme example of pure modernity for half a century, and Sartre was already high on the American myths and dreams. "When we were twenty, around 1925, we had heard of skyscrapers," Sartre explained. "In our mind, they symbolized the fabulous wealth of America. We had discovered them with wonder in movies. They were the architecture of the future and jazz the music of the future." He travelled with the stuff of his New World mythology in mind: not just skyscrapers and new cities, but immigrants, the melting-pot, behaviourism, the objective method of writing, "man seen from outside," blacks, the proletariat, the

[23] On this, see for example Irving Sandler, *The Triumph of American Painting: A History of Abstract Expressionism* (New York, Praeger, 1970).

underdog, the America imbibed from the novels of Dos Passos, Faulkner, Erskine Caldwell, all of whom he and his generation admired. Even before the war, in the fiction of Céline, for example, French writers had already been taking up the key motifs: the redskin, the gangster and the drugstore, the Deep South and the Far Ouest, gun-law and crime, *l'amérique noire*. Raymond Chandler (an American writer, he had been schooled in England, and his work always carried something of the European fascination with the mean streets of the American cities), Dashiell Hammett and gangster and crime movies, Faulkner and the suspended piney-winey time-zone of Southern life: all played their part in the mythology that shaped his two-month tour.

The delegation arrived, in cardboard-soled shoes, from the land of occupation and grim rationing to an America where the overwhelming first impression was of freedom, wealth and scale. "Those guys who had just landed in New York were so eager to possess America, and us with it! They were starved!" reported one of their hostesses. An unremitting excitement with America's gigantism and its basic form of "national celebration," jazz, as well as a lively love affair, invigorated Sartre's visit: "I love New York," he reported, "I have learned to love it. I have gotten used to its massive blocks, its large perspectives . . ." Meantime he crisscrossed the entire country on a State Department B-29 bomber, found himself caught in political scandal as he commented on America's role in French wartime events, indicated some pro-communist sympathies, met President Roosevelt, and sent home his reports for Camus' left-wing daily, *Combat*, on America's excitements, sadness and racial problems. Thereafter the American motif began to occur regularly in his writing: his play *La Putaine respectueuse* (1946), for example, influenced by Richard Wright and Faulkner, is about black experience and set in America's "Deep South." Perhaps most importantly, he emphasized the importance of the American way of writing fiction. In talking of the future of the novel, he had already affirmed the model role of American modes of discourse: "All you have to do is narrate a life in the style of American journalism, and the life becomes a social text," he had said back in 1938.[24] Sartre's relations with the USA would sour considerably later, as his Marxist sympathies grew, and his concern with European intellectual identity increased. But the links continued; thus he returned again in 1947, to lecture on

[24] For Sartre's American experiences, and the source of the quotations, see Annie Cohen-Solal, *Sartre: A Life* (London, Heinemann, 1987).

Existentialism at Yale, and find himself hailed as the greatest philosopher of the Age of Anxiety.

There now began a fundamental transaction that continues to this day – in which French philosophy became, rather like Perrier water, a far more potent and elegant commodity in the New World than it seemed in its country of origin, even while America itself became a fundamental mythic landscape for French thinkers, as they tested the alienating, sign-emptying disunity of the late modern world ("America *is* deconstruction," Jacques Derrida, that post-Existentialist shaper of much contemporary American thought, was to declare). For the new contact that had begun in wartime excitement continued into the post-war years: Paris and America indeed still had affairs to settle. In January 1947 Simone de Beauvoir went to the USA on a similar, four-month, coast-to-coast cultural tour, this time to lecture in American universities and colleges, as France's "Number Two Existentialist." The formidable Parisian intellectual soon had Americans enthralled by the insistent rationality of her conversation, her preoccupation with the hyper-urban America, and her insistent desire to read and interpret every single American thing she saw ("I found much poetry in the drug stores and the ten cent stores"). Like Sartre, she evidently felt it was important to know the New World sexually, and she began an affair with the very Chicagoan, streetwise novelist Nelson Algren, who showed her round a good part of the American underside ("I introduced her to stickup men, pimps, baggage thieves, whores and heroin addicts . . . I took her on a tour of the County Jail and showed her the electric chair"). Each found the other an exotic example of another culture, a way into understanding another way of writing and being. Each wrote up the affair, a famous transatlantic near-marriage which continued on a shuttling basis for many years, until it faded into a sense of literary betrayal on Algren's part. The chief record is to be found in de Beauvoir's book on America, *L'Amérique au jour de jour* (*America Day By Day*, 1953), an eroticized text of the mythology of America, a close portrait both of the Algren relationship itself, and of a body of French intellectual certainties constantly encountering American confusions; she also returned to the affair in her novel *The Mandarins* (1954), the book which caused Algren so much offence.[25]

[25] For a detailed account of de Beauvoir's American visits and the complex relationship with Nelson Algren, see Deirdre Bair, *Simone de Beauvoir: A Biography* (London, Jonathan Cape, 1990).

By now this was all part of a familiar trope, as French writers turned again to the American subject in its modern (and strangely erotic) aspect. In France more than in most countries, American myths and dreams had a certain abstract essence, an element of symbolic fantasy that preceded any actual arrival. This went back through generations, to Jules Verne and Villiers de l'Isle Adam and many more, indeed back to Chateaubriand and de Tocqueville. So post-war French writers repeatedly made the New World voyage, and attempted the representation which others had already imaginatively pioneered – in the American episodes in Céline's *Voyage au bout de la nuit* (1932), for instance, or Max Jacob's surrealist *Cinématoma* (1919). The land of extreme modern technology (not unlike that Kafka had explored in *Amerika* and Lowry in *Lunar Caustic*) and modern violence and estrangement appeared in many French novels. From the 1960s, they became a presiding theme in the explorations of the *nouveau roman* – for instance, in Michel Butor's kaleidoscopic *Mobile* (1963), subtitled "Etude pour une représentation des Etats-Unis," Alain Robbe-Grillet's *Projet pour une révolution à New York* (1970), a story of a Manhattan in ruins, or Claude Simon's highly experimental novel of American urban life *Les Corps conducteurs* (1971).[26] America *was* a *nouveau roman*, as is made clear in fascinating experimental manipulation of the French transatlantic myth, by a French writer who expatriated to America and began to write in English: Raymond Federman's *Double or Nothing* (1972). But by now the America myth was Europe-wide, part of the Americanization of the imagination itself. Italian writers (from Cesare Pavese, in *The Moon and the Bonfire* (1953), to Italo Calvino), looking beyond neo-realism to a fiction of desire and fantasy, similarly explored the strangeness of the New World. German writers, Spanish writers and Nordic writers also turned increasingly to the American mythology, often as a result of American visits, but also because of the massive penetration of American images in Europe through the medium of film. Europe, of course, had every reason for seeing a "fantastic" America in the way it did. America tested out ideology and the sense of history; it represented the utopia or dystopia of modernity itself. For much of the writing of the "American age," America remained the great dream or destination, the image of the shape of ever

26 There are some valuable comments on this in John Fletcher, "Comparing the Literatures: Or, What Happens When the American Dream is Celebrated on Opposite Sides of the Fence," in *Comparative Literature Studies*, XIII, 2 (June 1976).

newer things to come. It was a new world waiting to be mythologically constructed – or, as the next generation of French mythologists said, deconstructed. And, though Britain was a different case, it was even true there too.

8.

"What a strange irony of history that Europe should search for its lost secrets in an American mirror," observed John Lehmann in 1951, in his essay in *The Impact of America on European Culture*, remarking on the way European writers, reversing the old Jamesian equation, were turning away from their native traditions toward American influences, and were even setting off westward, in growing numbers, to inspect the half-comprehensible and half-alien culture of contemporary America in its age of superpower confidence and affluent boom. Lehmann was particularly struck by the way the European literary magazines of the post-war period (they included his own influential *Penguin New Writing*) had given themselves over to criticism and interviews from what he termed "the transatlantic realist Parnassus." One result of this, he observed, was a new spirit of cultural interweaving: European writers showed a growing influence from America, American writers seemed increasingly influenced by European. Yet, he acknowledged, the situation in Britain was somewhat different from that in continental Europe. Britain had been neither defeated nor occupied, and the continuity of its literary tradition had not been interrupted to the same degree. Its literary confidence, its freedoms and its liberal spirit had not been broken by the war. In any case, British writers shared with Americans (almost) a common language, and many elements of a common tradition. Writers moved across the Atlantic with greater ease; T. S. Eliot had become, in effect, a British poet, W. H. Auden an American one. But, as Lehmann rightly said, something had changed in the old Jamesian encounter. America was becoming not just increasingly influential but increasingly attractive, especially when compared with the austerity at home. Thus for British writers as well as those in other parts of Europe the American trip became almost an obligatory affair – a journey to the political realities and economic promises of the post-war world. In Britain after 1945, traditional cultural relations with the European continent actually diminished, partly in consequence of travel and currency restrictions. But those with America suddenly vastly increased. Fulbright grants and cheap charter flights, the benison of American patronage and the booming consumer economy, drew many across the water, where the goods and pleasures, the excitements and liberations denied in Attlee's austerity Britain were to be found amidst the American plenty. During the war, Americans, based in Britain, had become a familiar part of the social landscape. Now a new mythology of Western quest developed. As austerity persisted and rationing continued, America offered up the life-styles, the excitements, the music, the intellectual adventures the young felt so much in need of. It also offered educational opportunities, literary outlets, cultural energy, as, certainly up to the mid-Fifties, impoverished, shrinking Britain could not. It was no surprise that the mythology of America began to change, and fables of American voyage started to multiply – Henry James in reverse, post-war European innocence out to encounter American experience.

One of the odder ironies is that an early and powerful pioneer in this post-war enterprise was none other than Edmund Wilson's adversary, Evelyn Waugh. He had travelled greatly in his youth; but, especially since the Socialist transformation of 1945, he was no great lover of the common man's modern world. And, as the episode with Wilson seemed to indicate, he was no great lover of Americans either. But it so happened *Brideshead Revisited* (1945), that richly nostalgic story of the British Catholic aristocracy in the years between the wars (this was the book Wilson so disliked), was actually an enormous success in the United States. It sold three-quarters of a million copies, and earned its author a very large sum – which, he told American readers, had promptly been taken from him by the British tax authorities. The novel that was meant to gluttonize British readers in their bleak age of austerity equally pleased Americans in their new age of abundance. It was not too hard to understand its American appeal. After all, it mythologized a Britain of ancient dreaming spires and wonderful if declining great houses: an England noble, ancestral, aristocratic and Irvingesque, an image gratifying to those who were glad to know that Wilson was wrong, and all that was English in England was not entirely lost. And no less historically English was its author himself, who in the post-war years mythologized himself as an extreme version of the English landed gentleman: eccentric, testy, private, impoverished, suffering no fools gladly, grudgingly yet bravely opening up the ancestral pile to the massed hordes of uncomprehending common visitors. Thus the book stirred a huge correspondence from American readers, who demanded to know more of the British aristocracy and of Waugh himself. Observing that a true gentleman did not believe in leaving letters unanswered, Waugh replied collectively to his American readers in a *Life* magazine article. "I have momentarily become an object of curiosity to Americans and I find that they believe that my friendship and confidence are included in the price of the book," he gently explained.

But this was only the beginning of his transatlantic adventure. In late 1946, MGM took out a film option on the book, showed interest in the rights of others of his novels, and invited its author to Hollywood to discuss a movie version. Despite the warnings of his agent ("I know nobody who would hate Hollywood as intensely as you"), Waugh, no doubt perversely, decided to oblige, tempted among other things by the thought of making a good deal of money that the tax-man might find hard to reach. "I mean to do business with the Californian savages if it is possible," he announced; and in January 1947 the forty-three-year-old Waugh, still suffering badly from an operation for piles, which he had had done for what he described as "cosmetic" reasons, sailed with his wife Laura on the *America* for New York. On shipboard, if his half-fanciful account is correct, he found himself surrounded by impoverished British gentry travelling tourist and GI brides travelling first class. He stayed in New York, where he encountered editors who tried to re-write his works for him, usefully taught him how to deal with the static electricity in the carpets, and appeared amazingly free with their contracts and advances. He travelled pleasantly by super-train across the continent, smuggling liquor with him for safety in a country all too inclined to Prohibition. In February he arrived in sun-drenched Los Angeles: "The sun was shining, tropical flowers were in bloom, all the young people were dressed in shorts and slacks and open shirts and there was Evelyn in a stiff white collar and a bowler hat, carrying a rolled umbrella," his brother Alec reported home. Hollywood – Tinseltown – was where so many modern American writers had ended up, drifting among the backlots of the studios and staring narcissistically at the Pacific Ocean, on the further edge, where modernity stopped. Faulkner had written and drunk here, Fitzgerald had, more destructively, done likewise. Nathanael West had recorded the destruction of the apocalyptic city of fantasists "tired of sunshine and oranges" in *The Day of the Locust* (1939), Fitzgerald had recorded its gift for corrupted illusion in *The Last Tycoon* (post., 1941). Aldous Huxley had from Britain come as a screenwriter, and recorded some of the story in *After Many a Summer* (1939) – a book about a Hollywood magnate who is seeking eternal life amid the mansions of the stars, which are built like cemeteries, and owns his own burial plot at a site based on Glendale's famous cemetery Forest Lawn, where, along with the smiling, sexy embalmed corpses, European works of art have themselves been salvaged from the ravages of time. Christopher Isherwood, reporting on the city in the same year as Waugh's visit, likewise remarks on its two-dimensional nature, its flimsy impermanence and abolition of all human privacy. Bertolt Brecht, who joined the *émigré* community there in 1941, after several exiles, found Hollywood "Tahiti in metropolitan form," and described himself as "a chrysanthemum in a coal-mine." Hollywood was perhaps the writer's strangest fate, something between a graveyard and an extreme form of salvation.

To Waugh, the American trip itself represented almost exactly the reverse of Wilson's European journey. It was the passage from his ancient and comfortless Europe to the lush American ruins: a voyage from civilization to post-civilization or savagery, into a landscape where everything was grotesque, falsified, unreal, made of shards, many of them stolen from Europe and strangely altered in the light of a fantastical, lunatic Gothic imagination. Such were Waugh's ironic but already highly excited expectations it seemed even Hollywood could hardly live up to them; but it did. The city was "quarter built, empty building-lots everywhere and vast distances," and covered over with noxious fog. At the hotel, the excellent suite reserved for them was unavailable, because someone was dying in it of rheumatic fever, "a prevalent local affliction." Waugh soon encountered many strange and barbaric American customs, for instance the inquisitive friendliness of waiters: "There is here the exact opposite of the English custom by which the upper classes are expected to ask personal questions of the lower." There were studio executives who seemed to come fresh-minted from his own earlier fiction, while the screenwriter, an Englishman who had chosen to dress in native costume, told Waugh the book its author considered a serious religious story was here seen as a love story – though an awkward one, since it seemed to favour adultery over conventional matrimony. They did not get on, and in another article Waugh later explained the Hollywood system: it purchased for adaptation a book that had something remarkable about it, whereupon "It is the work of a staff of 'writers' to distinguish this quality, separate it and obliterate it." The negotiations unsurprisingly collapsed, as with Waugh they frequently did. Still, to Waugh's creative delight, Hollywood and the movie industry, which had been glimpsed before in several of his satirical comedies, lived entirely up to type. More importantly still, so did California. In the course of the visit, he too was taken (by an enthusiastic Lady Milbanke) to see Forest Lawn Memorial Park – the great theme-park cemetery created by the undertaker-salvationist Dr Eaton, crowded with improved versions of the treasures of Europe (The Wee Kirk O' The Heather, Michelangelo's David, Leonardo's Last Supper, enlarged and cleaned so that even Mark Twain would like it, and so on). Huxley had already written about it in fiction, reflecting on the strange assumptions about death involved. Waugh too was entranced, and visited it several times a week, had lunch with Dr Eaton himself, and even made friends with the chief embalmer ("It is an entirely unique place, the *only* thing in California that is not a copy of something else," he announced in delight). He wrote another article, for *Life*, about death, considering the reactions of a future archaeologist to Californian burial customs after Los Angeles had been destroyed – most probably, he surmised, by drought. It would prove, he suggests, an unusual necropolis, for here all the traditional religious meanings of burial have been exactly reversed. The body is prevented from decaying, the cemetery is earthquake-proofed to avoid the Apocalypse, the soul goes straight from Slumber Room to Paradise, while Dr Eaton himself is, says Waugh, "the first man to offer eternal salvation at an inclusive charge as part of his undertaking service." It was, Waugh said, wonderful. Cemeteries were the only real thing he had encountered in Hollywood, "a deep mine of literary gold."[27]

9.

For Waugh, California proved one of those strange and wonderful

---

[27] See *The Diaries of Evelyn Waugh*, cited above, and Christopher Sykes, *Evelyn Waugh: A Biography* (London, Collins, 1975). There are fuller details of Waugh's American experiences in Martin Stannard's exemplary life *Evelyn Waugh: No Abiding City, 1939–1966* (London, Dent, 1992), called in the USA *Evelyn Waugh: The Later Years, 1939–1966* (New York, Norton, 1992).

borderlands between civilization and barbarity, faith and materialism, style and vulgarity which provided the settings for most of his best comic fiction. In March he returned home, apparently leaving a trail of exasperated Americans behind him, and soon set to work to mine for his Californian gold. By September he had completed a short novel, *The Loved One: An Anglo-American Tragedy* (1948), about the American Way of Death. It was his return to the true spirit of black comedy, and surely his most accomplished post-war book. The tale was first published in Connolly's *Horizon*, a magazine which had paid much attention to the new love-hate relation of British and American writing. Here Waugh explained, by way of introduction, that the story came from a double impulse: "Quite predominantly, over-excitement with the scene," and "The Anglo-American impasse – 'never the twain shall meet.' " America had brought out all his anarchic decadent's delight in modernity's glossy pleasures and absurdities. In yet another review, Edmund Wilson would complain that Waugh was again patronizing America. So he was; but he was no less patronizing in his fiction to contemporary Britain, while never reaching this degree of comic delight and enthusiasm. And in his enthusiastic mining of the world of American *kitsch* Waugh would prove remarkably prescient: when, four decades later, European theorists began exploring postmodern America, the realm of culture as pastiche, it was to just such sites as Forest Lawn-Glendales they turned.[28] But this was also a very English treatment. If, for the French, the United States frequently represented

---

[28] Thus Umberto Eco in "Travels in Hyperreality," in his *Faith in Fakes: Essays* (London, Secker & Warburg, 1986): "But to understand the Last Beach theme we must go back to California and to the Forest Lawn-Glendales cemetery. The founder's idea was that Forest Lawn, at its various sites, should be a place not of grief but of serenity, and there is nothing like Nature and Art for conveying this feeling. So Mr Eaton, inventor of the new philosophy, peopled Forest Lawn with copies of the great masterpieces of the past, David and Moses, the St George of Donatello, a marble reproduction of Raphael's Sistine Madonna, complementing it all with authentic declarations from Italian Government fine arts authorities, certifying that the Forest Lawn founders really did visit all the Italian museums to commission 'authentic' copies of the real masterpieces of the Renaissance.

To see the Last Supper, admitted at fixed times as if for a theatre performance, you have to take your seat, facing a curtain, with the Pietà on your left and the Medici Tombs sculptures on your right. Before the curtain rises, you have to hear a long speech that explains how in fact this crypt is the new Westminster Abbey and contains the graves of Gutzon Borglum, Jan Styka, Carrie Jacobs Bond, and Robert Andrews Millikan . . . In the construction of Immortal Fame you need first of all a cosmic shamelessness."

a futuristic fantasy, for the British, more or less since Dickens on, they had generally represented a comedy, a perfect example of extremity exotically developed under hothouse conditions. Where else were the follies of the human mind and body, the wildest extravagances of urban life and nature, ideally to be found?

Waugh aptly opens his book on the edge of some unnamed arid desert on the borderlands of the world. Three gentlemanly English travellers are talking, the cicadas sound, there is an endless pulse of music from nearby native huts, and dire warnings are offered about the dangers to the Englishman of going native. After three pages we realize that the settlement in the desert is Los Angeles, and the Englishmen are not colonial officials but film actors, bringing their perfect British manners to the Hollywood movies. Going native is what the story is all about; the central British character, Dennis Barlow, poet, screenwriter, decadent, and rogue-hero, working on a bio-pic on Shelley, decides he is bored with "the monotonous and the makeshift" and chooses to survive amid the native culture and customs. "Through no wish of my own I have become the protagonist of a Jamesian problem," he reflects, realizing that he will have to use all his European experience if he is going to last in the world of American innocence. In Waugh's world, there are no Utopias, the happy outcome of human progress; the myth he prefers is that of Arcadia, with its classic sense of *memento mori* ("*Et in Arcadia ego* . . ."). *The Loved One* is about modernity, barbarism and death. Dennis himself is a decadent poet, "half in love with easeful death"; he is also a reminder of the gross facts of mortality in a land that seeks perfection and eternal serenity even for its corpses. The novel is set almost entirely in cemeteries. The main location is Whispering Glades, based on Forest Lawn, where eternal salvation is included in the charge, and bodies are carefully segregated according to wealth and status. Since America has ruins too, mostly European ones, European culture has been plundered to provide the décor (there is the Wee Kirk O' Auld Lang Syne, and The Lake Isle of Innisfree, complete with nine bean-rows and mechanical bees). In fact Whispering Glades is nothing more or less than American Arcadia itself – and, like Dickens, Waugh is fully and classically acquainted with the literary mythologies appropriate to the subject. The great cemetery is the sinless pastoral Utopia long familiar in American fiction, in Cooper's frontier or Hawthorne's Blithedale; like most Utopias, as seen by the ever-ironic English imagination, it is corrupt. It also has its doggie or four-legged

equivalent the Happier Hunting Ground Pet Cemetery, where Dennis
has a part-time job, consigning terminal pets to the ovens ("Your little
Arthur is thinking of you in heaven today and wagging his tail") – until
the suicide of a compatriot takes him on a visit to Death's true Eden,
Whispering Glades.

"Behold, I dreamed a dream and I saw a New Earth sacred to
HAPPINESS," declares the inscription on the gates, signed by the
founder, Wilbur Kenworthy, The Dreamer. In the New Eden, death
has no dominion, and heaven no hell or purgatory. Corpses are
cosmetically redeemed, turned to "painted and smirking obscene
travesty," by Mr Joyboy, the pious, mom-fixated Senior Mortician,
formerly of the Undertaking Faculty of an historic Eastern university.
This is a place where sin, decay, animality, and fleshly corruption have
apparently never entered; for Dennis, the decadent romantic and agent
of mortality, it is perfect. He soon becomes "over-excited by the scene,"
as Waugh had been himself: "In that zone of insecurity in the mind
where none but the artist dare trespass, the tribes were mustering.
Dennis, the frontiersman, could read the signs." The Muse of
Whispering Glades has him in thrall, and soon she appears in the flesh.
Dennis dislikes the cosmetic standardization of American women: he
comes from "an earlier civilization with sharper needs . . . He did not
covet the spoils of this rich continent, the sprawling limbs of the
swimming pool, the wide-open painted eyes and mouths under the
arc-lights." But he meets a junior cosmetician at the cemetery, Aimée
Thanatagenos – her origins atavistically Greek, her name nicely
uniting love and death – who strikes him as different: "the appropriate
distinguishing epithet leapt to Dennis's mind the moment he saw her:
sole Eve in a bustling hygienic Eden, this girl was a decadent." Soon he
is wooing her away from her fiancé, Mr Joyboy, offering as his own the
seductive verse of Romantic poets like Keats and Poe, until his rival
unmasks him, when he explains, "in the dying world I come from
quotation is a national vice."

And so it is. *The Loved One* has a very parodic literary plot, and closes
in an elaborate parody of the Jamesian myth. "All his stories are about
the same thing – American innocence and European experience,"
Dennis says, recommending the works of James to Mr Schultz, his
employer at the Happier Hunting Ground. "Thinks he can outsmart
us, does he?" asks Mr Schultz. "James was the innocent American,"
Dennis explains, and adds that all his stories were tragedies one way or

another. Waugh's story too is a tragedy, one way or another, or rather a tragi-comedy, a heartless comedy of tragic misfortunes. Tugged between the conflicting claims of the dull, ethical Mr Joyboy and the interesting, "unethical" Dennis, Aimée takes advice from her Delphic oracle, a newspaper advice columnist, the "Guru Brahmin." He proves as incapable as his predecessor in that other brilliant black comedy of Los Angeles life, Nathanael West's *The Day of the Locust*, and, fired from his job, advises her to jump from a high window. Aimée kills herself in Mr Joyboy's room, and Dennis undertakes to dispose of her body according to his own primitive rites, in the oven of the pet cemetery ("Your little Aimée is wagging her tail in heaven tonight, thinking of you"). The novel ends in an emotional loss, but a cultural victory. By blackmailing Mr Joyboy, Dennis makes his lost American love affair serve him well. He can now return to England first-class on the Cunarder, in a stateroom with bath. In a final parody of the familiar American ending, he sets off home, rejecting not art for innocence, but innocence for art. On his final night in Los Angeles he knows he is a favourite of fortune, bearing home the spoils. "Others, better men than he, had foundered here and perished . . . He was leaving it not only unravished but enriched. He was adding his bit to the wreckage, something that had long irked him, his young heart, and was carrying back instead the artist's load, a great, shapeless chunk of experience; bearing it home to his ancient and comfortless shore; to work on it hard and long, for God knew how long. For that moment of vision a lifetime is often too short." Like his author, he has found in California a mine of literary gold.

10.

The Loved One can be taken as a very British comic novel, another story of European experience lording it over American innocence, bitter British irony distrusting American hope, a Catholic anger challenging the American refusal to believe in tragedy. Certainly, like his hero, Waugh sees himself coming from a continent that knows "sharper needs," plainly prefers his own "ancient and comfortless shore," and believes that between Europe and America exists a "cultural impasse." Waugh's *memento mori* is a satire of America as it was often to be seen in the transatlantic gaze – as a sterilized, hygienic, bland culture, drawing not on the fullness of the past but the emptiness of the future. Yet such is Waugh's delight in his absurdist subject that the work surely finds its place along with the best tradition of American black humour – which goes back to Twain, and has its modern expression in the work of Nathanael West, Kurt Vonnegut, Terry Southern and Stanley Elkin, telling their own fables of an eternal American innocence stained by Gothic decadence. In the event, as perhaps might be expected, the book was an enormous success in the United States, solved some of his financial problems, and indeed helped Waugh change his opinion of America, to which he returned in 1948 and 1950. In due time he came to think it might even be the salvation of Europe, if it could only strengthen its Catholic tradition. Waugh's impression of the American utopia/dystopia was shared by other British writers of his generation, though their interpretations were rather more ambiguous. Aldous Huxley chose to settle in California; reading his later, American novels, like *After Many a Summer* (1939) or *Ape and Essence* (1948), which is set after a nuclear war, it remains hard to tell whether they are satires or celebrations of a scientized, mechanical, drug-oriented future, in which the shape of things to come has turned everyone into ciphers. Christopher Isherwood, who also settled there, presents, in *The World in the Evening* (1954), *Down There On a Visit* (1962), and *A Single Man* (1964), an America where there is hope, freedom and a franker sexuality out in the bright sun. But the world is narcissistic, perhaps it is the end of humanism, perhaps a camp paradise. In *A Single Man*, George, the central character, exists self-reflectingly in a present-tense, historyless world, made of neon, plastic, "Have a nice day." Yet his freedom is also a state of despair, and, as a foreigner and homosexual, he recognizes his alienation and feels vacancy, a late-modern, perfectly acceptable pathos and grief.[29]

Waugh, Huxley and Isherwood were all from the Thirties generation. But the British writers who came after them, and started their careers after the war, presented in most of their work an image of America that was significantly different. These were writers who came from a much-changed, vastly more egalitarian society, the world of the Welfare State that drove the older Waugh into depression. For them, the age of the common man was a matter of fact, the end of empire an inevitability, American influence a pervasive condition of life. America

[29] For more on this, see Peter Conrad, *Imagining America*, cited above, p. 402.

447

was no futurist dystopia, rather a new cultural opportunity; and improving contacts and expanding travel made the journey across the Atlantic, previously largely confined to the emigrant or the wealthy, more readily available. With apparently similar language, and an apparently similar tradition of liberal democracy, America seemed a natural second country. Moreover it was a place of new academic and intellectual, and indeed sexual and emotional, opportunities. For these newer writers, it stood less for standardization than variety, less for vulgarity than classlessness, less for the failure of culture than a new popular culture, less for Wall Street than Beale Street. Where the most probable destination of the travelling British writer of the Thirties was to Hollywood, now it was more likely the American campus, which in an age of educational boom had replaced bohemia as the home or meeting place of writers. One such academic traveller was Kingsley Amis, the novelist and then university teacher whose first comic novel, *Lucky Jim* (1954), had seemed to capture the social and intellectual note of post-war, egalitarian, commonplace Britain. In truth Amis, no less than Waugh, a significant influence on his work, had his own Anglocentric prejudices (as is clear from his early novel *I Like It Here*, 1958). But if Amis liked it at home in Britain, and if the aesthetic associations of a Bloomsburified Europe only excited his satirical hostility, the United States was a different matter. After all, it had invented jazz (he shared Sartre's admiration) and produced good writers. In 1958–9 Amis visited the USA in the role of a writer-academic, travelling on a sabbatical from his post in Britain to teach literature and a more mysterious, oddly American subject, "creative writing," at Princeton University. He brought his young family with him, including his son, the young Martin Amis, who later recalled the mysterious sensation of being the only schoolboy in short trousers in town. Amis was enjoying the fame of being a much admired author of the new British fictional generation ("the Angry Young Men"), was well received and entertained, and the visit went so pleasantly that Amis thought of remaining in the country; a return visit to Vanderbilt University, in the South, during the 1960s was to prove a good deal less successful.[30] It was true he did not like discovering that the British "angry young men," with whom he was rather unwillingly identified, were thought by Americans to be the equivalent of the Beat

[30] Amis records his two visits in Kingsley Amis, *Memoirs* (London, Hutchinson, 1991).

Generation, or that he had to share a New York platform with Jack Kerouac as he undertook his mystical, drug-soaked meanderings.

Amis's Princeton visit had an inevitable fictional result. In 1963 he published *One Fat Englishman*, a comedy of Anglo-American misunderstandings, very much in the British tradition. This is yet another tale of a British rogue hero, the corpulent British publisher Roger Micheldene, who descends on the American literary and academic scene attempting to take advantage of his British origins and accent, and happily exploiting his sense of cultural superiority. As usual, Amis is marvellously funny on the linguistic and cultural confusions that occur when two apparently similar languages and cultures turn out to be quite different. And, in line with a British comic tradition going back through Waugh to Dickens, Amis has a good deal of pleasure to take in English outrageousness, and its various triumphs over American boasts and vulgarities. But he is no less committed to the defeats, verbal and otherwise, the freer and more open Americans in turn administer to British pretensions. In fact Roger finally suffers one of the harshest verbal put-downs to emerge from the long tale of fictional Anglo-American relations: "I sometimes get the impression that you think some of the people in this country don't like you because you're British," he is told. "That isn't so . . . It isn't your nationality we don't like, it's you." With Amis's book, the tone of the exchanges was definitely changing from the high-handed spirit of Waugh. And it would change a good deal more in the many new Anglo-American fictions that would appear from this new transatlantic age.

11.

Still, there could be little doubt about which was the most powerful fictional myth to come from post-war European-American relations. In May 1940, Vladimir Nabokov, ever the *émigré*, had to flee from Paris, as he had fled first the Bolshevik Revolution in his native Russia in 1917, and more recently from the Berlin of Nazism in the later 1930s (his wife Véra was Jewish). By this date, Nabokov – born in cultured Saint Petersburg in 1899, and widely travelled as a child – was already a well-established writer in at least two languages, Russian and German, writing since the 1920s, and had established a formidable European reputation. He had already written one novel in English, *The Real Life of*

Sebastian Knight (1941), in 1938–9 while still in Paris. Now, at the age of forty, a European symbolist, he would have to begin all over again, in an America he hardly knew, and which hardly knew him. On a Nansen passport he crossed the Atlantic on the last ship out of France, the *Champlain*, and arrived in New York to financial insecurity. The person who aided him most was Edmund Wilson, who already knew his reputation. In the difficult American publishing scene, in which Nabokov was virtually unknown, Wilson helped place his writings, and steered him toward the *New Yorker*, where a good many pieces began to appear. (This important friendship would, alas, turn into a bitter and famous feud later on.) Like many survivors of the *émigré* modern movement, Nabokov was essentially a polyglot writer. As George Steiner said, the polylinguistic matrix was the forming fact both of his life and art, part of a grid of constant translation, re-translation, and linguistic crossover.[31] He came to describe himself as "an American writer raised in Russia, educated in England, imbued with the cultures of Western Europe"; at other times he said he was a writer who did not "seem to belong to any clearcut continent." Sartre once said his work displayed the *émigré*'s desire to knock down any edifice he had constructed; he observed himself he composed his novels "for the sake of the difficulty." In 1945 he took out American citizenship, and began to acquire a more than *émigré*, an American, reputation. In 1948 he published his second English-language novel, *Bend Sinister*, in 1951 an autobiography, *Inconclusive Evidence*, also written in English, and later revised as *Speak, Memory* (1967). There then followed two remarkable "American" novels. One, *Pnin* (1957), was the splendidly comic tale of a disoriented Russian *émigré* teaching in American colleges and trying to comprehend American ways. The other – written in 1953–4, when he was teaching Russian and European literature at Cornell – was *Lolita*.

Lolita appeared in 1955 back in tolerant Paris, from Girodias' Olympia Press, and it was not risked for American publication until 1958. It promptly became a best-seller; the book's notorious erotic theme, which had required its initial Paris publication, now secured an American *succès de scandale*. For its obsessive and very unreliable narrator, the ageing, educated European *émigré* Humbert Humbert, famously suffers the desires and guilts of the disease of "nympholepsy"

31 See George Steiner, *Extra-Territorial: Papers on Literature and the Language Revolution* (New York, Athenaeum; London, Faber, 1972).

– is erotically attracted only to "nymphets," or pubescent girls just on the cusp of adult life. Humbert is essentially the *fin-de-siècle* decadent, fascinated by the ephemeral and the unobtainable, his guilty taste formed in the unstable, shifting Europe of his youth. The nymphet – as others like Edgar Allan Poe and Lewis Carroll knew – is the decadent's ideal obscure object of desire, representing experience masquerading as innocence, innocence taking on the first flush of experience. However, not all girl-children are potential nymphets. It takes one to know one: "You have to be an artist and a madman, a creature of infinite melancholy, with a bubble of hot poison in your loins and a super-voluptuous flame permanently aglow in your subtle spine . . . , in order to discern at once, by ineffable signs – the slightly feline outline of a cheekbone, the slenderness of a downy limb, and other indices which despair and shame and tears of tenderness forbid me to tabulate – the little deadly demon among the wholesome children; she stands unrecognized by them and unconscious herself of her fantastic power." A crucial fact is that Humbert's nymphet is a decadent version of a figure already well known in transatlantic fiction, the young American girl, Daisy Miller, or Maisie Beale, in her late twentieth-century, gum-chewing condition, as the American teenager. Now she is Dolores Haze – otherwise Lo, Lo-Lo, Lola, Dolly, Lolita. The novel is a self-conscious fable about the European love affair with America – the forms, myths and dreams it contains, the language in which it is written. And, at first famous as an erotic novel, *Lolita* soon won its way as a literary one – a late modernist distillation of the whole crucial mythology.

As Nabokov said in his famous postface to the novel, the book represented his love affair with the English language, or, as George Steiner once put it, the love affair between a speaker and his speech. Nabokov defines the whole adventure of the book as a formidable transatlantic struggle. "It had taken me some forty years to invent Russia and western Europe, and now I was faced with the task of inventing America," he says. He tells us how he did it: "The obtaining of such local ingredients as would allow me to inject a modicum of average 'reality' (one of the few words that mean nothing without quotes) into the brew of individual fancy, proved a much more difficult process than it had been in the Europe of my youth . . ." With both America and a change of literary tongue to deal with, the problems were indeed considerable, not least because Nabokov's own fiction was already rich in the lore of European symbolism, but he had yet to digest the symbols and myths of fictional and "real" America. It was the problem he returned to again in *Ada: A Family Chronicle* (1968), though there he opts for the solution of inventing an alternative world with a quite different history, so America and Russia have merged together in a placeless utopia, and it is perfectly natural to speak Russian and find Russian landscapes on the American continent. In *Lolita* it helps that he confers on Humbert Humbert some of his own symbolist impulses (though Nabokov's own nympholeptic tastes lay with butterflies) and some of his modernist credentials. Humbert is born from "a salad of racial genes," the son of a Swiss hotelier on the Riviera. He has lived in expatriate Paris: "I switched to English literature, where so many frustrated poets end as pipe-smoking teachers with tweeds . . . I discussed Soviet movies with expatriates. I sat with uranists in the Deux Magots. I published tortuous essays in obscure journals." Leaving a failed marriage to a Russian behind him in Paris, he descends on New York at the start of the war, carrying with him, as George Steiner nicely puts it (of Nabokov), "the whole stance of the amateur/*amatore* of genius, fastidiously at ease in a dozen branches of arcane learning, always turning toward the golden afternoons and vintages of the past . . ." In New York he takes "the soft job fate offered me: it consisted mainly of thinking up and editing perfume ads." The reader, he says, can imagine "how hot and dusty I got, trying to catch a glimpse of nymphets (alas, always remote) playing in Central Park, and how repulsed I was by the glitter of deodorized career girls that a gay dog in one of the offices kept unloading on me." (Like Dennis Barlow, he comes from a more ancient civilization with sharper needs.) He gets a job in the Arctic as a "recorder of psychic reactions," has a breakdown, and comes to rest in New England ("elms, white church"). His desire is for an "enigmatic nymphet I would coach in French and fondle in Humbertish." It does not work out as meant.

The core of the book is the story of Humbert's chase across America with, and then after, his obscure object of desire – which proves to be not only the hazy Dolores but the fleeting, symbolist, butterfly nature of art and language themselves. Meantime Humbert himself is being chased by and then is chasing his rival, the American playwright Quilty, that Dostoevskian double, whom he finally murders, so becoming "guilty of killing Quilty." The whole book is a complex system of codes, lists, puns, acrostics, and extensive allusions to other literatures – European and Russian, Lewis Carroll, Gogol and Pushkin, but also American, above all Edgar Allan Poe's poem "Annabel Lee," which is based on similar longings for the girl in the kingdom by the sea. The journey across America from motel to motel, from (symbolic) register to (symbolic) register, is a series of mysteries that constitute hints or clues in the labyrinthine chase, which is also for the signs and signals, the "local ingredients," of the American "reality." Humbert stands here for European experience, which contains within it an eternal search, aesthetic and erotic, for innocence. Lolita stands for a supposed American innocence, actually a smart, knowing form of teenage experience. Humbert tries to define her as in effect his own invention, a construct of his highly European imagination ("My own creation, another, fanciful Lolita"). But Lolita, his supposed American "invention," is constantly eluding and escaping her inventor. "You can always count on a murderer for a fancy prose style," Humbert tells us at the start. There is no doubt that Humbert's (Nabokov's) style is an attempt to impose a rich European baroque onto a much plainer American subject. As Humbert explains: "Oh, my Lolita, I only have words to play with!" But Lolita ("the ideal consumer . . . to whom ads were dedicated") has her own distinctive vernacular to reply with, a vernacular his fancy prose style then has to incorporate. She constantly upsets his linguistic dominance ("You dumb bulb," she calls him) and is far from easy to coach in French and fondle in Humbertish ("Do you mind very much cutting out the French? It annoys everybody"). And his literary double Quilty is no less in a state of linguistic and artistic revolt, ever mocking Humbert's speech and writing ("You are some foreign literary agent"). If the English language is not the graceful literary language of Nabokov's Russian, it has the power to strike back with great linguistic vigour.

Even so, America never quite matches up to Europe, the present to memory, the reality to erotic illusion, the new erotic relationship to the first innocent love Humbert is trying to recreate. The beaches of the Atlantic, the Pacific, the Gulf are never quite as wonderful as the first ancient kingdom by the sea. Throughout this wonderful, self-teasing narrative, we are always aware that Humbert is not just trying to write America, but is also arduously having to learn how to read and listen to it. *Lolita* is a detective story told from the standpoint of the European criminal who never quite understands the offence of his sin. His crimes are not even clearly committed, the clues never quite solved, justice never really done, and so the moral is never brought into the ascendent over the aesthetic – as is perhaps the essential point in any fictive, decadent or symbolist work. But the greater point was that this is not just Nabokov's most famous but his most American book: a visionary, fictive, ever playful European decadent text playing with the endless refractions of the obscure American symbol. It was almost ironic that its success allowed him to cease teaching, and this meant he no longer needed to live in America. In 1961 he moved back to the hotel world of Montreux in Switzerland, from which Humbert himself had come. Here, amid Humbert's "lacquered, toy-bright Swiss villages and exhaustively lauded Alps," he became once more a European symbolist, until he died there in 1977, at the age of seventy-seven. But for twenty years he had indeed been an American novelist, and his impact on American fiction and fictionality was great. When, just after the American publication of *Lolita*, the spirit of fictive postmodernism, black humour, reflexiveness and what John Barth called "the literature of exhaustion" became dominant in Sixties American fiction, in Heller, Barth, Barthelme and Gass, there were perhaps three fundamental influences, and all from elsewhere: the Franco-Irish Samuel Beckett, the Euro-Argentinian Jorge Luis Borges and Vladimir Nabokov.[32]

12.

Myths pass into more myths, stories build on and interrogate earlier stories. In the summer of 1955 – the year *Lolita* was published in Paris – I sailed the Atlantic myself, tourist class on the *Queen Mary*, part of a new student generation for whom the trip to America was the experience of a lifetime. I left behind an England, still in the last throes of rationing, that was just in process of losing an empire and had not yet found a washing machine. England was grim, moral and depressing, and Fifties America – the America of Arthur Miller and Marilyn Monroe, J. D. Salinger and Dave Brubeck, shark-toothed Buicks and

[32] The two chief sources for Nabokov's life are Andrew Field, *VN: The Life and Art of Vladimir Nabokov* (New York, Crown, 1986; London, Macdonald, 1987), and Brian Boyd's *Vladimir Nabokov: The Russian Years* and *Vladimir Nabokov: The American Years* (Princeton, Princeton University Press; London, Chatto and Windus, 1990, 1991). Quite the best recent study of the much-studied Nabokov is Michael Wood, *The Magician's Doubts: Nabokov and the Risks of Fiction* (London, Chatto and Windus, 1994).

meat-filled hamburgers, jeans and tee-shirts – had deeply imprinted itself on nearly all of British youth. It was where all that was freest and most novel came from: the best movies, the best clothes, the best ice-cream, the best gum, the best cars, the best comics, the best jazz, even the best books. America had long stood for the myth of liberation, but at no recent time had the old myth seemed newer than it did in the mid-Fifties, when adventurous journeys out of old limitations and into new possibilities were just what were being looked for. I was a new graduate, a young researcher and would-be novelist, going off to teach freshman composition and study American literature on a midwestern American campus, at Indiana University. I belonged in fact to the Sabbatical Generation, the brand-new breed of scholars, students, critics, journalists, poets and novelists who used to gather on each side of the Atlantic every late summer to exchange themselves for their counterparts on the other, passing each other in midatlantic. A solemn, thesis-carrying generation, ever discussing whether *Hard Times* was truly Dickens' one mature novel, or whether the ending of *The Great Gatsby* was ironic or no, we went on Fulbrights, Harknesses, Commonwealth Funds, Jane Eliza Procters, Henry Fellowships, the new huddled masses of the travel-grant age. We gathered four to an underwater cabin in the bowels of the Cunard liners, or took the strange, difficult fifteen-hour flight by Loftleidir, which stopped mysteriously in the tundra, at Shannon and Reykjavik and Gander, before descending on skyscrapered New York. We arrived in New York at Idlewild or Cunard Pier 92 – the New York of the Rockettes and ice-skating at the Rockefeller Center, Circle Line tours and Sam Goody's record store, eggs any side up you wanted them, free coffee refills with a 25c breakfast. Stalin was dead, Eisenhower was the (then ailing) President of a wealthy and hospitable America; the Korean War had ended, but now not just America but the Soviet Union had the hydrogen bomb, and the spectre of McCarthyism and the House Un-American Activities Committee had not departed the scene.

This was the season of the liberal imagination, anxious Existentialism, the Jewish-American novel. The Beat Generation had emerged in America as Angry Young Men had in Britain, and everywhere there were poets in dark glasses reading to jazz in cellars. But the campus mood was cautious, and even before I left Britain I had had to sign a loyalty oath, swearing not to overthrow the American government by force – as, to my credit, I never have. Teaching, writing and living in

455

America for most of the rest of the Fifties, like a good many British contemporaries, I began reflecting on the fictions of the Anglo-American and the Euro-American relationship – and so started work on this book. I also started, as you might well expect, a novel about transatlantic relationships and fictions, *Stepping Westward* (1965). Other fictions were very much in my mind, and I saw my own book as a fable of reversal – a semi-parodic rewriting of the older, familiar images of Anglo-American intercourse. For Henry James, America was aspiring innocence, Europe the banquet of initiation. For Edith Wharton, America was vulgar wealth, Europe the place to spend it; the playfield of its dreams, the promise of a deeper experience. For D. H. Lawrence, America was the land of mechanistic modern experience that led back to the primitive. For Waugh, the "Jamesian" problem had begun to reverse; America provided the European writer with a shapeless load of experience to bring home to his classic shore. For Nabokov, American innocence proves to be crucial experience: Humbert's labyrinthine story ends in his defeat and death: he fails to find in Lolita the incarnation of the first love he has always sought. British writers – from Dickens and Trollope to Waugh and Amis – had mostly preferred a comic and sometimes suspicious version of the fable, allowing British historical experience and social realism to smile down on American innocence. *Stepping Westward* was meant as a tale of a time when it was the turn of British historical and social innocence to meet American experience, and new British liberalism to meet its American counterpart, and risk its moral anxieties against liberating excitement.

This time it was to be the travelling Englishman – James Walker, the ineffective British provincial writer who has failed at most things, from leading a successful daily life in very realistic and ordinary Britain to being a sufficiently angry Angry Young Man, but who has preserved an amiable moral simplicity – who ships over the Atlantic by Cunard as a visiting teacher of creative writing, and arrives in a world that is far more experienced, politically, historically, emotionally, sexually, than he is himself. The tale is a moral comedy of the meeting of two cultures, two different ideas of freedom, two kinds of writer, two different post-war liberalisms: British liberalism, anxious and moral, and American liberalism, world-weary, tough-minded, imperial and political. It's also about two kinds of writing: the social and moral realism of the British fictional tradition, the spacious, fantastic freedoms of the American way. For my new Briton, America is liberation: the dream in

456

the story is of the moment when the chains that hold the British personality so firmly in place finally break. Since the meeting of Europe and America was always to some degree a sexual encounter, this was to be with the aid, again, of the young American girl (Julie Snowflake); since it was also a moral and political one, Walker is also cast into the hands of a half-benign but half-calculating saviour, Bernard Froelich, who has a serious use for him. Walker makes his way to Party, Colorado, on the edge of the east and the start of the west, a place where westering dreams have either begun or else expired. Like many other heroes in this age of educational exchange and bohemia on campus, he goes to an American university, Benedict Arnold. Here Walker's old plots meet new ones; Froelich, the new American plotter, tries to draw Walker's British moral conscience into the complex world of the politics of McCarthyite times. America is engaging, but in its modern political and moral life it's a good deal less than innocent. Walker, the plodding moral hero, cannot decide to which of his two countries he should sign his Loyalty Oath. He has made all the correct rites of transatlantic passage; he even makes the fantastic journey across the continent, trying to slough off his bloated British skin. But he fails to seize his moment of release and the utopia of self. By, you might say, the classic comic rule, he lets the new self slip from his grasp, and comes back to the old one, the familiar British sniffle, the cold, coddling claims of British domesticity. Though he knows he probably should, he cannot defeat his own national innocence.

As things turned out, this was one of a fair number of novels of the fast-revising American myth to come from British writers of my own particular generation, and tales of American travels increasingly became a staple of British fictional myth. There was Wilfred Sheed's *A Middle Class Education* (1960) and *Transatlantic Blues* (1978), Anthony Bailey's *The Mother Tongue* (1963); there was Julian Mitchell's peripatetic *As Far As You Can Go* (1963) and Andrew Sinclair's *The Hallelujah Bum* (1963), titled in the USA *The Paradise Bum*. Later there was Thomas Hinde's *High* (1968), Anthony Burgess's experimental *MF* (1971), which owes much to the anthropology of Claude Lévi-Strauss, and his half-autobiographical *The Clockwork Testament* (1974), and David Lodge's *Changing Places* (1975). A number of these were, unsurprisingly, university novels – for this was a time when bohemia was exchanged for the campus, and the American college became the new version of Arcadia, the Eldorado of a tribal student community in some ideal world beyond guilt or shame, getting off and getting high. Over time, the plots began to complicate and grow more fictional, as plots tend to do. In Thomas Hinde's *High*, the story is doubled by a novel within a novel: the visiting novelist Maurice Peterson writes a novel about the visiting novelist Peter Morrison. In both versions the hero brings British guilt to American drug-high innocence; Morrison, in the fictional version, reverts to "an old world, lousy with rural value-judgements," and commits murder and then suicide, while ordinary Peterson simply retreats back from the new American dream, of getting high and going higher, by returning to the guilty world of Europe. Anthony Burgess was much preoccupied by the American theme, and in *The Clockwork Testament*, his well-known, bodily anxious Catholic writer Mr Enderby, his ironic surrogate in two previous novels, turns up in New York to teach, of course, as well as face the reputation he's won as the screenplay-author of Gerard Manley Hopkins' "The Wreck of the *Deutschland*." Enderby is not much used to innocence. But the perverse Catholic images he has indulged in his script go on to invest the Manhattan he visits: a place of threatening classrooms, students who frankly offer themselves sexually, violent subways, lonely apartments, constant Anglo-American baiting. Enderby, conservative, prejudiced, sexually tired, anti-American, sinful and ready for death, knows his role in the fiction. And America finally gives Enderby his end. A gun assault by an American admirer turns into a sexual encounter; the result is a heart attack. His corpse lies on the bed at the end for historical inspection, a test of the Euro-American difference.

Since then, the famous two-way plot has enjoyed further variation. David Lodge's *Changing Places* has what is described as a "duplex plot," as a university lecturer from the British Midlands University of Rummidge, Philip Swallow, exchanges posts with an American scholar from the statutory Euphoria State, Morris Zapp. The two men, who leave their spouses behind, indeed change places, taking over each other's offices, apartments, lives, and eventually wives. One man is looking for more, the other for less. America suits the modest, repressed Swallow, who joins the inevitable campus riot, gets arrested, and becomes a one-day hero. And, though the heating never works, the lavatories resemble cathedrals, and British orgasms resemble not an earth-moving experience but "a hissing sigh, rather like the sound of air escaping from a Li-lo," plain Rummidge suits the exhausted whizzkid

Deconstructionist, Zapp. The tales parallel and parody each other; meantime, as in a number of these novels, the book explores the crossover of two different fictional traditions – British social and moral realism, American experimental fantasy. The crunch comes when at the year's end the fictional exchange has to be resolved. The author is left between two modern modes: should the novel be a liberal-realist English fiction about the solid self and society, or an experimental text of American postmodernism? In fact the book, written with elements of both registers, is left literally in mid-air, its fable in suspension: neither Europe nor America, realism or experiment, wins or loses. Whether in life or literary tradition, the best place to be, it seems, is somewhere between the two, a novelist at the crossroads, found midway between Rummidge (or Nottingham, or Manchester, or London) and Euphoria (or Party, or Eden, or Whispering Glades and the snakeless pastoral) – and midway between the British and American novel traditions.

Through the Sixties and Seventies, the "duplex plot" or interrogatory story turned into a familiar convention of transatlantic fiction: not least, we may suspect, because of the powerful influence of Nabokov – whose endlessly dualistic *Ada* is set, he tells us, not just in an alternative Euro-American world, but at the "romantic mansion" of Ardis Hall, which "appeared on the gentle eminence of old novels." John Barth's massive novel *Giles Goat-Boy* (1966) is a "duplex" dialogue of two competing international computers, EASAC and WESAC. His *Letters* (1979), described as an "old-time epistolary novel," contains a fascinating transatlantic interrogation between an ageing English muse, Lady Germaine Amherst ("I am *not* the Great Tradition! I am *not* the ageing Muse of the British Novel!"), and the American author John Barth, to whom she offers the honorary degree of "Doctor of Letters" – which is precisely what he is. Kurt Vonnegut's *Slaughterhouse-Five* (1969) divides its duplex world between the hard historical reality of his own life in the prisoner's slaughterhouse in Dresden, "the Florence of the Elbe," during the hideous firebombing of the city in 1945, and the alternative world of the planet Tralfamadore – where the plots of novels are eternally reversed, and good comes out of evil, innocence out of pain. Thomas Pynchon's *Gravity's Rainbow* (1973) is a novel that incorporates the massive detail of recent European history – experiments in modern rocketry, the arbitrary destructions they produce in the London of 1945 – to dissolve history into cyber-fantasy. Walter Abish's extraordinary novel *How German Is It* (1981) is a story of a post-war, economic-miracle Germany the author had at this date never visited; set in a philosopher's city built on the ruins of a concentration camp, it asks what words can be written, what images can be made, what maps can be drawn of a world of surfaces and economic miracle which hides a historical crime. Abish's experiment in inventing an imaginary Europe is matched by the activities of a number of European authors – Michel Butor, Alain Robbe-Grillet, Peter Handke – who were testing the nature and image of a fictional America with the technologies of the *nouveau roman*. Indeed by now the old transatlantic transaction was increasingly raised up on "the gentle eminence of old novels," and the mythic fable that had begun as a crisis of cultural identities, myths, historical meanings had now transformed into a postmodern fictional paradox. At least, that is, until another generation of writers on both sides (now ever more frequent flyers) began to mythicize and complicate yet further their own new journeys and transactions across the ever-hospitable, story-laden Ocean between the two ever-shifting continents.

ELEVEN

Frequent Flyers:
Transatlantic fictions today

I.

At the end of the Eighties, just around the time the Berlin Wall was being chipped down, Jonathan Raban – an English writer who earlier on in his career had followed Chateaubriand and Twain on a long literary journey down the Mississippi River – again decided to sail across the Atlantic, "looking for Mister Heartbreak." His "Mister Heartbreak" was none other than Hector St John de Crèvecoeur, that ambiguous eighteenth-century writer whose *Letters of an American Farmer* so influentially put into print the mythic idea of the New Man, and his New Start in the New World. Now, with the Old World recession-hit again, and things at home in bad shape, Raban, an old Americanist, thinks he too will take migrant passage for the New. He wishes to ship from the old migrant port of Liverpool, though now it too is a port in decline. Unemployment reigns over the streets where Melville and Hawthorne once walked, the docks where great liners and steamers, the flying national ensigns and the British migrants were to be found, and where Henry James' Lambert Strether had disembarked to the "first note" of Europe. Still, courtesy of Cunard Ellerman, Raban does make his migrant's passage, comfortable in an officer's cabin of the vast container ship *Atlantic Conveyor*, "a custom-built marine pantechnicon" for today's transatlantic trade in consumer commodities, Mercedes and Jaguars, French perfume and Scotch, a half mile of deck with a Hilton Hotel for the crew raised up at one end. He travels, of course, with his pile of useful literature, his guidebooks, past stories of the migrant experience: "I'd brought Irving Howe's *World of Our Fathers* and Moses Rischin's *The Promised City*, for their descriptions of Jewish peasants in steerage; Henry Roth's *Call It Sleep* for the arrival in New York Harbour; Robert Louis Stevenson's *The Amateur Emigrant*;

461

Charles Dickens' *American Notes for General Circulation*." But in our easy times things are different. When he puts a film on the video in his warm officer's cabin, and turns up the air conditioning, he imagines that "the emigrants booed and whistled from behind their covers."

Finally, by aid of radar, Nantucket light is passed, the Statue of Liberty shows, the bright-lit, ritzy, high Manhattan skyline shines out of a storm, American landfall is made. The New World is found and entered, and sure enough it remains a land of new identities, good and bad, real and imagined; there are plenty of fresh human prospects still on offer for the no less abundant migrants of the contemporary world. In fact they are there in postmodern abundance, skewed toward the extremity of illusion. The great New York department store Macy's, which once dressed migrants as new and standard Americans from the ready-made wares of the East Side garment trade, now offers the Euro-golfcourse chic of Ralph Lauren, the rugged woodsy self of Timberland shoes, and a hundred more designer-label identities. The new life is today enjoyed in the condos of Palm Beach or the high-rise apartments of Miami. Today's new migrants ship in drugs through the Florida Keys, or come from the Pacific to settle the West Coast boom-city of Seattle, where a fresh generation of aspiring Koreans and Japanese reconstruct the New World myth all over again ("What did 'America' mean?" "America? It was a place in novels I'd read, and films I'd seen . . ."). "I thought: if I were seeking a fresh start in America, I'd go to Seattle," writes Raban – which is just what he eventually did. More than ever before, America is a land of smart new selves ("I needed another name – a fast, sawn-off American name," Raban reflects) and free trade in fantasies, dreamy or violent; it's a crazy emporium of styles, a multi-ethnic, multi-cultural, multi-image utopia/dystopia. Vast and incomprehensible cities swim up suddenly from the cloud cover as you traverse the so-called friendly skies. The images flickering on the motel television are of vaginas and penises. The self-made men of Wall Street today are insider traders, just being carted off to jail on the evening news. Everyone you meet has a story to tell, a book they've read, and another they want to write. The old migrant mythologies breed a fresh crop of myths and identities, dreams and nightmares, images and illusions, of fame or desire or extremity. Perhaps it will all produce some new story, some remarkable new literary genre, maybe generate "some miraculous transfiguration in the character of the writer"? As Raban puts it, hopefully:

"There was an inherent *plottiness* about Seattle now . . . it would fit inside the covers of a book."[1]

For, like so many of those who went on before him, including the old huddled migrants and Melville's Wellingborough Redburn, Raban travels with books, the old guidebooks he is reading (but: "Guidebooks, Wellingborough, are the least reliable books in all literature; and nearly all literature, in one sense, is made of guide-books"), and the new books he is already planning if not commissioned to write. And, over again, old stories prove no longer to fit the new and extravagant realities. The continent he tours – looking over his shoulder at old fictions in order to sketch out his new one – is, quite unmistakably, postmodern America. It's vast, technological, multiple, over-imaged and over-accumulated, heterodox alike in its material rewards and in the fantasies it produces or provokes. It is filled with instant signals, the icons and badges and style-signs of an endlessly variegated human identity. Culture piles on culture, but the old migrant melting-pot no longer melts. This is the continent of the Americanization of modernity, and of the Americanization of modernism: the two have now merged into one. Modernity has passed beyond itself into a spirit of excess; meanwhile modernism is no longer an *avant-garde* adventure, but the daily state of the experiment of modern life, an habitual style for an age of general bohemianization. Into the random, eclectic energies of American change, into the melting-pot of avid American style-hunger, everything, old and new, nostalgic and futuristic, European and Asian, African and Latin, male and female, straight and gay, religious or criminal, has been incorporated. Life seems insistently plural, parodic, fictional, and without benefit of substance. Culture is any history that empowers, style anything that catches attention, art any object that confers self-esteem on its creator, value is what sells. But if this is it, the late modern way, to the contemporary stranger it no longer appears distant, strange, exceptional, or simply the product of only one continent. Such is the power of the modernizing and Americanizing progress that it simply reflects the world as the world, in its form as a global equivalence of all cultures. Once more it is possible to go to America in order to see more than America, to travel in hyper-reality. And once more America is not so much different as exemplary – the

[1] Jonathan Raban, *Hunting for Mister Heartbreak* (London, Collins Harvill, 1990). And also see his *Old Glory: An American Voyage* (London, Collins, 1981).

ultimate case of that state of multiplied simulacra, semiotic excess, virtual reality, extravagant fantasy in which much of the world thinks it now lives.

"Travels in Hyperreality" is exactly what Umberto Eco – the Italian semiologist whose playful postmodern novel *The Name of the Rose* (1980) somehow turned into an easy-to-read American seller – calls his record of his own American journey. It's an account of the deliberate adventure of a contemporary European intellectual into "furious hyperreality," looking for "instances where the American imagination demands the real thing and, to attain it, must fabricate the absolute fake; where the boundaries between game and illusion are blurred, the art museum is contaminated by the freak show, and falsehood is enjoyed in a condition of absolute 'fullness,' of *horror vacui*." Eco is one of a good number of such travellers: in line with the older voyages of Crèvecoeur and Chateaubriand, Volney and Condorcet, de Tocqueville and Trollope, crossing the Atlantic to see more than America has returned as a familiar European custom. As the twentieth century begins to slip into history (or its current substitute, nostalgia), as older explanations of modernity and its progressive energies start to fade, as modernism itself migrates and turns into something else called daily life ("For the last quarter-century it has been obvious that the idea of an *avant-garde* corresponds to no cultural reality in America . . . Why? Because new art has formed our official culture ever since we can remember"[2]), as Marxism collapses in Europe and America becomes the sole model of contemporary progress, as Existentialism ("existence precedes essence") yields to Deconstruction ("existence has no essence") – so the journey to the New World, the place where borders and categories fragment, has come back in all its anxious excitement. Today it is no longer a journey to the utopian community, the communal Eden, or the Arcadian campus that matters. Indeed the higher expressions of culture – art, ideas, architecture, universities – are themselves aspects of a post-culture without élites, layers or hier-archies. So the sites Eco and his fellow European travellers, seeking the contemporary or the postmodern, now explore and excavate are those that offer some historyless expression of the age. They are Disneyland and the Wax Museum, theme-parked Las Vegas and the Westin Bonaventura

[2] Robert Hughes, *Culture of Complaint: The Fraying of America* (London, Oxford University Press, 1993).

Hotel in Los Angeles, the Getty Museum and Knott's Berry Farm, the Ringling Museum of Art and Forest Lawn-Glendales (Waugh, it seems, was just an old postmodern after all).

It is here we find the new and exemplary America. It is a wraparound hologram, a randomization of culture, a "masterpiece of bricolage." Everything is here, including the masterpieces of European art and culture, which sit side by side with the fake or the new. America is a strange and futuristic parody of Western civilization, though also perhaps its last salvation – for, as Eco puts it, there is now an "ideology of preservation, in the New World, of the treasures that the folly and intransigence of the Old World are causing to disappear into the void." The museums are filled to abundance, the wasted surpluses of Europe are brushed off, cleaned up and given new meanings and uses; it indeed is no accident that London Bridge now stands in the Arizona desert, linking nothing with nothing, the *Queen Mary* of my blessed memory is now a hotel at Long Beach on the Pacific. Likewise noted Italian operatic performers open the World Cup soccer season, and Forest Lawn proudly displays Italian certificates proving the "authenticity" of its copies of the masterpieces of Renaissance art – and indeed, as Eco acknowledges, "once the fetishistic idea of originality has been forgotten, these copies are perfect." America sustains European culture, but in a condition of dislocation – as part of what the American writer Donald Barthelme once named "the Tolstoy Museum," where what was once seen as an art of reality and realism is part of a sentimental homage to what is now the purely aesthetic or the nostalgic.[3] In Walter Benjamin's "age of mechanical reproduction," the work of art loses its "aura"; so it does in America, where European high culture becomes an aspect of American popular culture. Bereft of their theological, historical and hierarchical meanings, the items of what were once called "civilization," the golden treasures of the Old World, ancient and modern, turn into *émigré* style-objects or art-icons, another commodity in the great shopping mall of the postmodern – that epochal bazaar which contains, at a level of equal value, every history, every tradition, every theology, every artist, every art-object, every style, every source and every age of style.[4]

[3] Donald Barthelme, "At the Tolstoy Museum," in *City Life* (New York, Farrar, Strauss, 1970). "At the Tolstoy Museum we sat and wept. Paper streamers came out of our eyes," the story, a parody of ideas of a secure realism or a secure reality, begins.
[4] Umberto Eco, "Travels in Hyperreality," in *Faith in Fakes: Essays*, trans. William Weaver (London, Secker & Warburg, 1986).

2.

It is no wonder that in consequence even the very act of European travel to America itself has grown far more complex and fictional. "What you have to do is enter the fiction of America, enter America as fiction," advises the high-flying French "intellectual terrorist" and Post-Structuralist philosopher Jean Baudrillard, providing the Baedeker code of the late modern transatlantic adventure – now conducted in a latter-day era when the old anti-American assaults of the French Maoist Left have given way to a new era of Americomaniac exhilarations.[5] However, Baudrillard reminds us, America is not simply *any* fiction. It is nothing less than a postmodern text, a "hall of mirrors," a simulacrum, a place where "meaning is born out of erosion." And, like any other such text, it is simply waiting to be deconstructed. Baudrillard explains how to do it. "While others spend their time in libraries, I spend mine on the deserts and on the roads," he reports adventurously in his account, quite simply called *America* (1986). "This country is naive, so you have to be naive. Everything here still bears the marks of a primitive society: technologies, media, total stimulation . . . are developing in a wild state, in their original state." With no past to resist the process, America is now the "achieved utopia," the place where old dreams have come fantastically true. It's the museum of the future, "the original version of *modernity*: we [Europeans] are the dubbed version, even the one with the sub-titles." This is a land where fiction rules, and all the major icons of world history and culture have been assimilated, erasing the referent from

5 For an interesting analysis of the phenomenon in France, see Denis Lacorne and Jacques Rupnik, "Introduction: France Bewitched by America," in Denis Lacorne, Jacques Rupnik and Marie-France Toinet, *The Rise and Fall of Anti-Americanism: A Century of French Perception*, trans. Gerald Turner (London, Macmillan, 1990 (French ed., 1986)). Lacorne and Rupnik see the mood changing with Edgar Morin's book *Journal de Californie* (Paris, Seuil, 1970): "I feel an enormous elation to find myself in California . . . It is also an intense excitement to feel myself inside the homing device of spaceship earth, to be a living witness of this crucial *hic et nunc* of the anthropological adventure . . . I am in my element here where new possible worlds are being forged . . ." The authors contrast this with the wave of anti-American books that appeared at the end of the 1920s, when Americans refused to compromise over the French debt and the French felt the victims of American economic power, or in the debates about Coca-colonization in the 1950s and American world hegemony in the 1960s. They also note the counter-argument about the destruction of French cultural identity, recently renewed in the attempt to purge French of new "Anglo-Saxonisms," especially in the commercial and hi-tech realms.

every image. The crucial sites for the French Baudrillard are similar to those of the Italian Eco: the wilderness, where "meaning is born out of erosion," the funeral home, the body-builder culture that transforms the human figure, the great World Trade Center in New York, and, sure enough, Disneyland – a postmodern place, "spaceship earth," intentionally and deliberately constructed to "reverse the fiction of the real," and so provide "a perfect model of all the entangled orders of simulation" postmodern America offers. History – which for the American Founding Fathers was a great progress, for Karl Marx a vast inevitability – is now a theme-park. Art and architecture, parks and cemeteries, even the desert itself, are now grand parodies of what was once, perhaps falsely, thought real. Meantime in the wider futuristic American culture, the individual surrenders to the universe of signs, communications technologies transmit endless pseudo-meanings, and the film or the TV screen becomes life's refraction, the image of its illusion. America itself deconstructs everything; it's become the home of "virtual reality." And the "achieved utopia" is the ultimate truth – for isn't virtual reality our enveloping condition, the nature of world-life in a time of self-alienation, simulation and simulacra?

But perhaps it is worth deconstructing Baudrillard and his fellow-deconstructors themselves just a little. For, entering the fiction of *their* fiction, we can read them, too, as fast-travelling, culturally-shifting signs of another aspect of the postmodern condition: the process by which the American continent and culture becomes the perfect emblem, the ideal slipping subject, of Europe's own post-realist and post-humanist philosophies. What is more, America is not simply the major subject of the great analysis, but also the chief marketplace for its speculations. For the truth is that no culture, or post-culture, has ever more willingly laid itself open to the gaze of the foreign observer. And, if European philosophers long to deconstruct, America no less longs to be deconstructed. As we have seen, the tradition here is an old one – part of a long and historic French speculation on reason, progress and history that started with or before the Enlightenment. Thus Voltaire enlightened Frederick the Great of Prussia, Diderot carried his deistical wisdom to the Petersburg court of Catherine the Great of Russia, Descartes died under the intense intellectual solicitations of Queen Christina of Sweden. As they created their enlightened Utopia, the First New Nation, the American Founding Fathers no less regularly consulted the *philosophes* of Paris. Rousseau, the Abbé Reynel, de Pauw gave their best advice on the nature of America without ever going there. Chateaubriand, Condorcet, Volney and de Tocqueville ("In order to learn what we have to fear or to hope from its progress . . . I have turned my thoughts to the Future") travelled across the Atlantic to see more than America. So it has gone on. Where the British have always been peculiarly empirical travellers, the French have travelled to philosophize. Jules Verne looked to America to see nothing less than the exotic techno-shape of things to come. Jean-Paul Sartre went to find the glittering, existential, dark-crimed continent he was hunting – a land, he said, of pleasure and sadness, comfort and anguish, an Existentialist's paradise. Simone de Beauvoir came not just to see the skyscraper, classless democracy and the gender-war but the drugstore, the heroin addict and the electric chair, the thrills of actuality. Now the process continues. Even while America does, Paris thinks about the doing. It remains not just something, but an extreme, idealized, hyper-modernized instance of something. As Jacques Derrida, founding father of the intellectual movement that started in Paris and became, from the beginning of the 1970s, powerful first in American and then in popular circles, put it: "America *is* Deconstruction." Should this judgement seem a little too rash, he has gone on, of course, to deconstruct it. "No, 'deconstruction' is not a proper name, nor is America the proper name of deconstruction," he has elaborated. "Let us say instead: deconstruction and America are two open sets which intersect partially according to an allegorico-metonymic figure. In this fiction of truth 'America' would be the title of a new novel on the history of deconstruction and the deconstruction of history." Thus we now have this clear. And even if we do not, what is apparent is that "America," the fiction of truth that might make a new novel, has been an invention not simply of its own eclectic and multicultural self, but of a certain French philosophy that has found its own best home not in Paris but in the United States. America has indeed been an eternal, ever-changing fiction to itself. But to this day it also remains a primary, speculative fiction of Europe.[6]

6 Jean Baudrillard, *Amérique* (Paris, Grasset, 1986), translated by Chris Turner as *America* (London/New York, Verso, 1988). Also see his *Simulacra and Simulations* (1981), trans. Paul Foss *et al.* (New York, Semiotext(e), 1983). For Derrida's comments on Deconstruction and America, see Derrida, *Mémoires: For Paul de Man,* trans. Cecile Lindsay (New York, Columbia University Press, 1986), and for a wider account of its impact on American culture ("Shoplifters will be deconstructed," etc.) see David Lehmann's *Signs of the Times: Deconstruction and the Fall of Paul de Man* (New York,

We may, of course, fairly take it that a postmodern condition exists: if it did not, many very distinguished cultural commentators on both sides of the Atlantic would quickly be out of a job.[7] But it would also be fair to admit that the nature of the historical, social and cultural condition the term seeks to identify – and generally to identify with America – is by no means clear. A notion that started out primarily as an aesthetic definition (of art after modernism) and as an historical one (Western society after the advent of technological modernity) has in recent argument been transformed into an epochal one – that is, it defines not just a style or a process, but a complete and overarching condition of life and culture in the West at the end of the twentieth century. So artistic, philosophical and political commentators on both sides of the Atlantic have come together to develop an ever-growing body of concepts and definitions which, in ever larger order, attempt to measure the contemporary scene, its cultural condition, and its political direction.[8] "Postmodernism" now describes . . . well, plurality, or in other words almost everything: Pop Art and Abstract Expressionism, glitz architecture and body art, shopping fever and cyberpunk, Madonna and laser-packed Las Vegas. It signifies culture without hierarchy, expression without substance, history without process, life without shadows, open stylistic abundance, life as glamour, identity as presentation. It names a chaotic, futuristic, fantastic time of artistic, cultural and stylistic eclecticism, when more and more new groups, genders and regional sub-cultures grow expressive, articulate, self-empowering (just as they do in Raban's polyglot Seattle). It is the sum of an age when, just as 90 per cent of the scientists who ever lived are alive today, so are 90 per cent of the artists, the style-makers, and most of the styles, from past and present, near and far. It is Benjamin's filmic "age of

Poseidon Press; London, André Deutsch, 1991). I am greatly indebted here to an unpublished essay by Mario Klarer (University of Innsbruck) called "Jean Baudrillard's *America*: Deconstruction of America and America as Deconstruction."
[7] Among the large number of studies now in print, three of the most notable are David Harvey, *The Condition of Postmodernity* (Oxford, Basil Blackwell, 1980; rev ed., 1989); Steven Connor, *Postmodernist Culture: An Introduction to Theories of the Contemporary* (Oxford, Basil Blackwell, 1989); and Fredric Jameson, *Postmodernism: Or The Cultural Logic of Late Capitalism* (Durham, N.C., Duke University Press, 1991). One work on the topic notes: "This book is dedicated to a thoroughly postmodern couple," suggesting how close the term has got to daily life.
[8] A useful analysis of the many usages and definitions surrounding the term is Margaret A. Rose, *The Post-Modern and the Post-Industrial* (Cambridge, Cambridge University Press, 1991).

mechanical reproduction," when the fast-developing technologies of image-making, vast new terrestrial and satellite information and communication superhighways, accelerate the transmission of images everywhere. It is a technology functioning almost irrespective of its content, and engulfing much of life and its fantasies within its action. In this process America has been central, but "America" is once again more than America. For one thing, its radiation falls everywhere, and the image and fantasy are themselves primary American products. After all, America makes 90 per cent of the world's movies, 70 per cent of its television programmes, and a great many of the hi-tech commodities, systems and multinational corporations that develop this global traffic in the sign. And no less important in its ever-growing radiation is the global spread of another equally powerful sign-system: the English language, which, energized by American power, spoken by over a billion people on all six continents as a first, second or third language, becomes the *lingua franca* of the world.

Yet the very scale and scope of this international radiation alters the system. Just as the future development of the English language is no longer chiefly shaped and commanded by its native speakers but by its new users, so the nature of "America" and its images is today shaped quite as much by those who consume or copy as those who produce them. As one observer has said, it may no longer even be apt to define this spread of cultural energy and imagery as Americanization, but as Superculture – which has now become a generalized form of world culture. "Changing shape at every cultural interface, [American popular culture] becomes, in effect, a Superculture, a reservoir of shifting values and images splashed like primary colours on the consciousness of the late twentieth century . . . part of the process of communication, part of the cosmology of symbols, with which we seek to make sense of ourselves and our environment," observes Christopher Bigsby.[9] Growing ever more global and pluricultural, it can no longer exactly be defined as a purely American phenomenon, but as an add-on international process of cultural change. Superculture is more than culture, or less than it. Cars in the American style are made in Japan, American Westerns are manufactured in Italian studios, Jean Baudrillard no longer needs risk the American desert to see Disneyland: spaceship earth is waiting for him just outside Paris.

[9] C. W. E. Bigsby, "Europe, America and the Cultural Debate," in C. W. E. Bigsby (ed.), *Superculture: American Popular Culture and Europe* (London, Elek, 1975).

Superculture does not simply spread out all over the world; it also becomes the world, making most of its transactions very much the same. Yet the fact remains that deep in the mythologies of Superculture are the transatlantic themes from which it was born – the European fictions of America, the American fictions of Europe, which, transformed by the intense refraction of their mutual images, are now spreading right across the globe.[10]

3.

For, if it has long been true that Europe's most powerful and commanding fiction has been America, there is little doubt that one of America's most influential fictions has been Europe. And if contemporary America has, in the imagination at least, changed profoundly over the last half of the twentieth century, then this is surely even truer of Europe. In 1945 Western Europe was largely a defeated space, a collapsed order, which was retrieved from the ruins, largely supported by American aid, reshaped by American influence. Since then it has started, in a quite new sense, to be European. Though past ideas of Europe have been important to many, the essential fact of its history is that large tribal regions and racial and religious groupings on the migratory and ever-shifting half-continent have defined themselves by separating themselves from, and often waging war against, some other part of Europe. Throughout its history, major empires and political orders have risen and fallen, and two twentieth-century European wars that turned into world wars made that history into a dangerous global crisis. It is only since 1945, when most of its former political systems and twentieth-century ideologies collapsed, that it has become commonly agreed that, if an effective European order was to survive at all, it depended on the formation of a new, a different, a wider identity. Various super-national projects formed for just this purpose – though at first all they seemed to prove was that there had been and

[10] As Jameson, cited above, acknowledges: "non-North American readers will inevitably deplore the Americocentrism of my own particular account, which is justified only to the degree that it was the brief "American Century" (1945–73) that constituted the hothouse, or forcing ground, of the new system, while the development of the cultural forms of postmodernism may be said to be the first specifically North American global style."

would always be many Europes. In 1947 came the Organization of European Economic Cooperation, formed to administer Marshall Aid; in 1948 came the Western European Union, designed for collective self-defence against the Soviet threat. But as growth resumed, and aspirations multiplied, so did the Europes. Some proposed a new "Atlantic Community," which would include the Superpower USA as a member. There was the Monnet-Schuman plan of 1950, which grew into the European Coal and Steel Community of 1952, and formed the foundation of the European Economic Community of 1957, the beginnings of the "Common Market."[11] There was equally its free-trade rival EFTA, a loose bonding that in part aimed to counter de Gaulle's "grand design" of a great new Europe that stretched "from the Atlantic to the Urals." In their different forms, all these shared some notion of transcending the old framework of the European nation-states, and the dangers of nationalism and territorial competition with which they were now associated.

But what at last began to emerge from the European mists was the notion of some kind of super-state. It was a response to two centuries of European crisis, a fundamental ideological reconstruction, but no less a reflection of the processes of economic globalization that had become characteristic of the modern industrial and commercial system. What first began chiefly as an economic and a defensive policy turned into the dream of a political linkage that would bind together the key European nation-states, and move them beyond their statehoods to forge common institutions – a common system of liberal democracy, a shared system of laws and regulations, common tariffs, a common currency, a common banking system, a common parliament, and an eventual removal of frontiers. Nationalism would give way to supra-nationalism, the ideological differences between states to an interlinked and shared new European political system.[12] What was in mind was

[11] Schuman's Declaration of 9 May 1950 which launched the proposal read in part: "In taking upon herself for more than twenty years the role of champion of a united Europe, France had always as her essential aim the service of peace. A united Europe was not achieved: and we had war. Europe will not be made at once or according to a single general plan. It will be built through concrete achievements, which first create a *de facto* solidity. The gathering together of the nations of Europe requires the elimination of the age-old opposition of France and Germany . . ."

[12] Among the many interesting studies of nationalism, in Europe or in general, see Ernest Gellner, *Nations and Nationalism* (Oxford, Basil Blackwell, 1983), Eric Hobsbawn, *Nations and Nationalism Since 1780: Programme, Myth, Reality* (Cambridge, Cambridge University Press, 1990), and Leah Greenfield, *Nationalism: Five Roads to*

nothing less than a United States of Europe. Many powerful forces encouraged this new process of the Europeanization of Europe. One, unquestionably, was the territorial and military ambitions of the Third Reich of Adolf Hitler, which had brought together under German occupation a significant part of the land area of the present European Community. No less potent was the persistent and fearful presence of a Soviet threat in the East, and the strategic threat of the Warsaw Pact, the dangerous alliance to the East. Another was the great economic potential of a sharing of production, technology, and markets. But what seems certain is that none of this would have happened had it not been for the refraction from America. It came out of the impact of American aid and economic intervention in the post-war years, the powerful influence exerted by the American government over European politics, its pressure toward the formation of capitalist democracies, above all, perhaps, the sheer impact of the process of "Americanization" itself on the damaged culture and ideology of nearly all the Western European nations.

In the reconstruction of a new version of Europe, the lesson of the First New Nation, both as agent and model, was direct, profound and influential. The lesson is worth reflecting on a little further, for the creation of the First New Nation, as it grew from thirteen colonies into an imperial continental power, was hardly as simple as it sometimes seems in retrospect. Indeed the present problems of "Europe" in many ways strangely resemble those of "America" as it took shape two hundred or so years ago, in the years after the Continental Congress, in which its destiny was first formed. It is sometimes hard to recall now that the union of the United States of America came into being only with great conflict and difficulty – and would probably not have done so at all if the first Thirteen Colonies had not been commonly British, with related institutions, a shared language, and limited territorial ambitions. Even so, the conflicts that then followed as the nation became a continental unity of states have many curious parallels to the recent problems in the formation of the idea of "Europe." There was, naturally, a bitter argument about where the capital should be (New York or Philadelphia; Brussels or Strasbourg, etc.), and whether there

Modernity (Cambridge, Mass., Harvard University Press, 1992). On Britain in particular, see Linda Colley, *Britons: Forging the Nation, 1707–1837* (New Haven and London, Yale University Press, 1992). There are important comments by Salman Rushdie in *Imaginary Homelands* (London, Granta Books, 1992).

should be a shared national currency (the Almighty Dollar; the not yet almighty Ecu) or a national "Monster Bank." There was a row about whether this original New Nation should be simply a free market in goods, or should swear allegiance to common Enlightenment principles (life, liberty and the pursuit of shopping). There was another major internecine row about the rules and obligations of membership and the rights of secession (the War Between the States). There were disputes about whether the new nation should be broad or deep: rows about who should be admitted, and whether some should be half-admitted (the American territories). There was a row about which laws belonged to the federation and which to the region (Utah, for instance, wanted to retain the right of polygamy, which in its serial form did in fact become the custom of the entire nation). There was a row about frontiers, and where the rule of America and Americanness started and stopped (the Oregon Crisis, the Mexican War). There was a row about the social chapter, which included the question of whether and where you could hold slaves or not (so the Missouri Compromise). There was a row about the hyphenation of identity (Italian-Americans, German-Americans) which continues to this day, in the ever-pluralizing American identities and ethnicities of the era of multi-culturalism. In fact – with European help, and not a little hindrance – Americans were, for much of the nineteenth century, inventing America as a new kind of nation-state, a united mega-state, with various degrees of success and failure, and many structural contradictions which persist to this day.

But, as I have been aiming to show in the course of this book, over the same time the new Americans were also busily inventing Europe. It was an invention it took most Europeans a good long time to recognize, though the commentary started early, and continues into our present travels into hyper-reality. It was not too long after Condorcet, Chateaubriand and others began travelling to America to see more than America – indeed to begin the establishment of a romantic notion of the "New World" that would serve as a lesson in history and a myth of the future – that Americans began regularly to journey in the other direction, inventing a romantic myth of the "Old World" that became synonymous with Europe. What Washington Irving came to see in Europe in 1815 was, of course, more than Europe – and, looking at things "poetically rather than politically," he sketched an ideal European Greece to go along with the new American Rome. What he constructed was nothing less than the American Grand Tour, and the sights and treasures that made sense of its new mythic function. He found storied associations and classic and eternal landscapes: the ruined castle, the falling tower. He creatively invented England (Westminster Abbey, Stratford-upon-Avon, the snowy English Christmas, the forelock-touching peasant), a land of eternal stasis, fixed in time. Guided by Walter Scott (who for his own reasons had already invented Scotland), he then went and invented Germany: a folkloric land born out of the Rhineland forests, Nordic myths and strange legends, some of which he celebrated for their ancient associations, others of which he stole and Americanized. In Spain, living in the Alhambra, he invented the Iberian picturesque: the mysterious Moors, the world of lace and mantillas, above all the great voyagers and Christopher Columbus. All of this collectively formed an old, picturesque and poetic Europe, which developed its wandering Aeneas in the form of Columbus – who sailed to the New World, founded the new empire in the West, and brought the myth of promise back to America again. It was a striking romanticization not just of European but of American history, of the greatest importance in the formation of an American mythic identity.

Yet the trace it left behind was no less important. Assigned to history, Europeans increasingly came to relish the role they had been offered. Each nation Irving visited and "sketched" felt he had somehow done them quite a favour. Stratford-upon-Avon and Westminster Abbey would certainly not be the places they are today without Irving, and Dickens would not have been quite the novelist he was – just as Cooper would not have seen the international significance of his own mythic materials if it had not been for Chateaubriand and Balzac. For the benefit of Americans, Irving had invented an Old World that would live long (that is, to this very day) in the American imagination: a Europe born of kings and princes, peasants and forests, ancestral English castles and baroque Spanish palaces, the seafaring adventures of the bold Columbus and his brave companions. But the same romantic history acquired its own meanings for the peoples of Europe, the "Old World," too. True, it has taken a long time for what Irving and other Americans were offering, a generalized spirit of "Europe" as one place, to develop in the European imagination. In Europe itself, "Europe" was only the ghost of an idea. Europe, after all, was always the sum of its disunities. Its landscape was dense and variegated, its peoples many, its tribes and languages multiplied. It was a balance of powers, a mix of contending and often warring city-states, principalities, kingdoms and bishoprics, which could be united from time to time only under the idea of "Christendom," which distinguished and protected the old Holy Roman Empire from all that lay to the east of it, the ever-threatening "Orient." It was the American discoveries that helped to distil the idea of Europe, making the centre of the continent its western, seaboard flank. Once the new cartography began after the western *terra incognita* started to be explored, and the Moors had been expelled from the Iberian peninsula, the idea of a distinctive European continent began to be set onto the new map of the world. But Europe's powers, faiths and allegiances, its nationhoods, its frontiers and its eastern limits remained obscure and ever-shifting – in fact they have never ceased being so to this moment. Europe was a continent that lacked any fixed or comprehensible borders or limits, a firm eastern perimeter. It had no acknowledged common existence, and no single nation could ever achieve mastery of this continent.[13] Hence Europe was an idea less of peoples than of élites, monarchs and archbishops, theologians and humanists: Julius Caesar and Charlemagne and Charles V, Erasmus, Montaigne and Bacon, Napoleon, Metternich and Hitler. Maybe there was something that could be called "the European mind," a Graeco-Roman, Christian and humanist heritage, a body of cosmopolitan ideas on which many of the strongest ideas of civilization, reason and progress depended, many of which were translated to America and became emblemized by it. There was a certain community of faiths, doctrines and ideas, and, for its wandering courts, diplomats and scholars, there was even a *lingua franca*: Latin. From time to time the chief principalities, bishoprics, city-states were linked together, by conquest or alliance, matrimony or the papacy; but they were as often unlinked again, by new conquests, treaties, marriages, or wars of economic interest, class or religion. But the larger European ideas and aspirations rarely meant much to the common people, faced as they were with a constant and shifting succession of religious and temporal rulers, and constant changes of allegiance. They generally remained stubbornly regional; the limits of their small community were the limits of their world. It is only in recent times, and largely as a result of industrialization, migration to cities, the transformation of travel and

---

[13] There is an excellent discussion of the reasons for this, above all the fact that each state had the power to buy its own military equivalence with others, in Paul Kennedy, *The Rise and Fall of the Great Powers* (New York, Random House, 1987).

human mobility, the global infrastructure of economic activity, that this has greatly changed, allowing a larger conception of Europe, both personal and communal, to emerge.[14]

Today "Europe" does exist, *de facto*, and not least as a result of steady American pressure toward European unity (curiously, the grand old Pennsylvania Quaker William Penn proposed a European Parliament in the 1650s). It's a strange and fascinating mega-country – with its own flag, its anthem, its court-of-law, its parliament. It has three capitals, nine languages (and a tenth, Acronymic), many beautiful mountains and lakes (mostly made of beef and wine), a currency (but rarely used), a burgundy passport, and bureaucracy and budget each of formidable proportions. But for the moment it remains something of a Euro-fiction, an aspiration or a struggle towards a personal and collective identity, rather than an identity in itself. The old order of the nation-state, itself often stimulated by the success of the American model, is changing, strengthening both the wider concept of Europe and the values of regionality. Even so, its character and its very borders remain obscure. Few would consider that, even now, as the number of member states has risen from six to nine to twelve and now fifteen, very probably rising to twenty-five by the millennium, that this is the total European sum (after all, thirty-five "European" states signed the Helsinki agreement of 1975). Meantime there is a fast-track Europe and a slow-track Europe. Britain, ever with a different sense of history, and still half-aspiring to the older Atlantic Alliance it helped forge, has built the Channel Tunnel, but not decided firmly to go through it; and other states have their own distinctive doubts. On the eastern borders Europe slips away into confused fragmentation. The key fact remains that the great nineteenth-century mainstay of Europe, the new-forming nation-state (Germany was founded as a nation only in 1871, one year after the unification of Italy), has diminished in power, first through it capacity for disastrous conflict, and now through the new endeavour for a more powerful and peaceable supra-national cooperation. And, though since 1989 European history has started to roll back again to its former sites of conflict, its frontiers of crisis, Europe has become a significant new economic and political entity, or at least a sufficient

[14] Of the innumerable books on the subject, Flora Lewis, *Europe: A Tapestry of Nations* (London, Unwin Hyman, 1988), and Richard Hoggart and Douglas Johnson, *An Idea of Europe* (London, Chatto and Windus, 1987), can be especially recommended.

fiction to live in and aspire to (as Gorbachev said, "our common European home"), and so not unlike the United States itself.[15]

Yet this Europe, too, is in a condition of postmodern pluralism. It may be a powerful economic and industrial world-force, but it shares still a very uncertain common culture, which is itself to a large degree a recent refraction from America (as Jean Monnet said, "If I were to start again, I would begin by culture"). It has no distinctive mother tongue (Jacques Delors, former President of the European Commission, said once that the worst crisis that could afflict contemporary Europe was a strike of the interpreters at the Berlaymont building in Brussels). In its official sense, "Europe" for the moment is a babble of languages, a burgeoning of budgets, a polyphony of policies, a confusion of capitals, a turmoil of translators, a shammy of chauffeurs. Its hopeful new goals are based on the ruins of many collapsed aspirations. Some want to see it wide, some want to see it deep. No one is sure where its perimeters lie, where its boundaries start or stop. In his superb book *Danube* (1986), Claudio Magris describes the sensation of travelling eastward across Europe, from the world of the Rhine to the world of the Danube, from Europe to non-Europe, down the twisting Danube river from Pannonia to Transylvania and down to its outcome on the Black Sea. His tale of travel takes in Freud and Wittgenstein, Kafka and Canetti and Lukács, the great European modernist thinkers of the difficult way down the river, and it likewise takes in the great and confused cities of Modernism – Vienna, Budapest, and not too far away Prague – where the modern thinking was done. In a striking passage about the Hungarian Marxist philosopher György Lukács – the "modern thinker *par excellence*" – Magris reflects on his time in Vienna, observing how he had used humanistic reason and intelligence to impose an ideology of order on the world diversity that flowed downstream past his windows. It was an attempt, he notes, to construct a modern order in a postmodern city – for, he says, Vienna today is "the city of the post-modern, in which reality yields to the depiction of itself and of appearances, the strong categories weaken, and the universal comes true in the transcendental or dissolves into the ephemeral, while the mechanisms of necessity engulf all values." Magris wrote his words in the Eighties, just before the eastern frontiers of Europe began shifting

[15] Two useful studies of the EC are Christopher Tugendhat, *Making Sense of Europe* (New York, Columbia University Press, 1988), and John Palmer, *Trading Places: The Future of the European Community* (London, Radius, 1988).

again. But his book is already predictive of a time of reconstructed ideologies, identities, nationalities, psychologies, philosophies and frontiers – the time of Francis Fukuyama's "End of History," which in actuality is nothing less than its twenty-first-century beginning.[16]

The truth today, surely, is that, as ever, each side of the Atlantic observes its own condition in the other. Postmodern Europe gazes across the Ocean at postmodern America; postmodern America looks in turn at the ever-changing form of Europe. For Europe – recovered, rebuilt, revived, a major industrial, economic and inventive force – has become, has perhaps always been, no less eclectic, polyglot and pluricultural than contemporary America is itself. Seen from the Eastern flank, from Central Europe or Russia, it is, just for the moment, not too hard to know what Europe is. It's the West, the free market – which in fact comes quite expensive. It is Berlin and Milan and Vienna bursting with European, American and Japanese consumer goods. It is the Mercedes and the Fiat, the icebox and the CD player, the ecology movement and gender wars, the Beatles and Madonna. Its currency seems to be not the Ecu but the dollar; its culture is prosperous, yet highly migrant. It is those vivid European cities that have restored their historic past with a clinical cultural nostalgia, yet have not failed to take on McDonald's, the shopping mall, and all the high-rise, business skyscraper *chic* of the future. It is the common European home, a focus of security. And, like America itself, Europe is also a network of signs, satellite systems and communications, multiplying electronic images and electronic rates of exchange. Ever since Marxism failed in Eastern Europe, any clear ideological alternative to these particular (American?) patterns and means of modernization, any different account of social progress or evolutionary history, has for the moment died. No more than their American counterparts do European intellectuals today have a distinctive "culture" or a "history" – and like their American counterparts they generally celebrate eclecticism and pluralism as the one late modern "style." One hundred years after the French Revolution, the French celebrated

---

[16] Claudio Magris, *Danube: A Sentimental Journey from the Source to the Black Sea*, trans. Patrick Creagh (London, Collins Harvill, 1990). His wonderful and meditative study reminds us that many of the most remarkable fictions on modern geography and identity, many of the most striking versions of an age of obscure nationalities, identities and borders, have come from the writers of Central Europe, who today include Milan Kundera, Peter Esterhazy, Georgi Conrad, and more.

the Centennial with a flamboyant assertion of their own modernity – the elevation of the Eiffel Tower. Two hundred years after, they celebrated the event with a polyglot global parade, with a black American diva singing the *Marseillaise* to a world television audience. At the Louvre – where, just about a hundred years before, Henry James' Christopher Newman met his cunning little copyist, and, looking at the great art-works of European culture, felt suddenly inspired with "a vague self-mistrust" – the Japanese-American architect I. M. Pei constructed a postmodern crystal pyramid, to open the medieval foundations to public display. An American architect adds a new wing to London's National Gallery; a British architect constructs a striking new wing to the Staatsgalerie in Stuttgart, and another is redesigning the Berlin Reichstag. Architects have always toured their wares, and dispersed new international conventions of form. Still, as one critic has put it, all this represents a new dimension to architectural dissemination and play: "the fictionalization of architecture," he calls it. Or, in other words, the postmodern style.[17]

4.

It would seem just as appropriate to speak of the fictionalization of fiction. For today, too, the novelist works in a world of cultural variety and stylistic play. And, in a time when stylistic plenitude has become the ambient condition of all the arts, and when confident ideas of national traditions, histories and identities have grown ever more unstable, he or she writes in a multiply refracted world. But in this process the reflection across the Atlantic – each continent seeing some sort of mirror in the other – remains crucial. "My mother lived in America for years, and many of my expatriate friends live in America now. My wife is American. Our infant son is half-American. I feel fractionally American myself," explains the British novelist Martin Amis, in his introduction to *The Moronic Inferno* (1986) – a knowing collection of essays on a wide variety of American subjects, many written on assignment and reflecting his own streetwise knowledge of the American beat. The title, Amis explains, comes from Saul Bellow,

[17] For a striking manifesto of the case for cultural pluralism and the "ad hoc" revolution, see Charles Jencks and Nathan Silver, *Adhocism: The Case for Improvisation* (Garden City, N.Y., Anchor, 1973).

who took it from Wyndham Lewis – and it is intended, he explains, to describe what is probably not just an American but a global, maybe an eternal, condition.[18] A similar transatlantic cosmopolitan affords much of the material, voice, and worldly self-knowledge that is the note of many of his best novels. *Money: A Suicide Note* (1984) is a tale of two cities, set equally in London and New York, two disaster-ridden transatlantic conurbations locked together by a common culture of airport lounges, in-flight movies, videos, pornography, fast food, limos, office blocks, hotel rooms, sex, drugs soft and hard. "I'm a thing made up of time-lag, culture-shock, zone-shift," explains the wearily knowing narrator, John Self, himself a frequent flyer to deals in film and business currency on either side of the ocean. Self's life on one side is reflected and refracted on the other, leaving him without a fixed identity, or in other words a Self. Other Amis novels show the same refractive spirit; *London Fields* (1989) has both British and American narrators competing for the story. And Amis's own fictional voice and vital style is itself a midatlantic one, filled with street-talk, wise-crack, American easy speaking, mixed in with the elegances and mannerisms of British literary style. Finally, perhaps, Amis's work is distinguishable as British only by the pervasive irony that suggests that this placeless, identityless modern world we live in does not have to be this way. It's a self-created moronic inferno.

This is the age of the frequent flyer, and the frequent flying of the Atlantic has become a dominant characteristic and motif of contemporary British fiction. Over recent years, as ease and speed of travel have made all places nearer, as everywhere comes to seem an intimate parody of the place you have just left, the novel has again become progressively more international, an instinctively cosmopolitan and wandering form. Feeling "fractionally American," too, is a familiar mood, as more recent writers, influenced quite as much by their American contemporaries as by some past tradition of the English novel, and by their own travelling lives as much as by their particular place of origin, have started to write with a far less clear imprint of nationality. The science-fiction fantasies of J. G. Ballard – *The Atrocity Exhibition* (1970), *Crash* (1973), *Concrete Island* (1974), *High-Rise* (1975), *Hello America* (1981) – are set in refractive landscapes of extreme and

18 See Martin Amis, *The Moronic Inferno and Other Visits to America* (London, Cape, 1986), and also *Visiting Mrs Nabokov and Other Excursions* (London, Cape, 1993).

hostile modernity, of a kind which can nowadays be found on either side of the ocean. Alan Burns' *Dreamerika* (1972) is a bitter and experimental satire of cultural and political interpenetration. Angela Carter's *The Passion of the New Eve* (1977), a latter-day feminist version of Villiers de l'Isle Adam's *L'Eve future*, is an elaborate assemblage of forms drawn from the mythologies of American science fiction and with an American setting. Her later volume of stories, *American Ghosts & Old World Wonders* (post., 1993), twists and turns this Gothic American mythology further, as the title suggests. Examples can multiply: the stories of Clive Sinclair, the fiction of William Boyd and Ian McEwan, Vikram Seth and Gordon Wilkins and Jonathan Holland. French, Italian and German writers have shown, from their own different transatlantic perspectives, just the same fascination. "Is it then so surprising that a change of place should contribute so much to making us forget what we don't like to think of as real, as though it were a dream?" asks the epigraph of the Austrian Peter Handke's *Short Letter, Long Farewell* (1972), the disturbing, alienating tale of an Austrian visitor who has been bombed by the Americans and then returns to what seems a land of terror, oddity and Kafkaesque estrangement ("When I had finished eating, I kept looking through the menu and read the names of dishes as insatiably as I had once read the lives of saints in my prayer book. A steak Alamo, a Louisiana pullet, a bear hock *à la* Daniel Boone, a cutlet *à la* Uncle Tom"). Midatlantic fictions, like midatlantic films, are familiar fare, and the interaction works both ways: American and Canadian writers like John Hawkes, Thomas Pynchon, Walter Abish or Margaret Atwood freely avail themselves of the real or fantastic landscapes of Europe. When genres multiply, styles grow communal, types, plots, settings become freely available, any landscape or mythology, especially one laden with a dense literary or popular imagery, becomes usable material, and a common myth-base emerges. And, as the fictions intersect, so do the lives and worlds of their writers – travellers by warrant, exiles by nature, migrants wandering the world exchanging their fictions. American writers like Russell Hoban, Rachel Ingalls, Paul Theroux, Bill Bryson and Bill Buford, Jerome Charyn and Edmund White regularly, or irregularly, make their homes in Europe; British, Irish and European writers like Brian Moore, Jonathan Raban, Christopher Hitchens, Patrick McGrath, Lawrence Norfolk and Raymond Federman make their homes in that other central trading post of modern literature, the United States of America.

But if the fictive landscapes of Europe and America have increasingly begun to merge and overlap, they have also grown a good deal bigger, more confusing and more varied. Vaster, stranger and more heterodox Europes are taking their place on the printed page, as the once marginal regions, nations or groupings on the continent find an increasing expression and desire for expression. The same is just as true of an America where once-hidden voices have begun to sound very strongly, changing our sense of the history and story of the continent. Wider and wider Americas find their vivid place on the shifting map of late twentieth-century writing. One crucial factor has undoubtedly been the development, over the course of this century, of a major tradition of Hispanic-American fiction, which has had very significant consequences for our ideas of the novel. The discovery and settlement of America led, in due time, to the emergence of a native North American literature that first mirrored, then began to transform, the myths and genres of European writing. More recently, much the same has been true of the modern development of Latin-American literature – a writing that has both drawn on and upturned the fictional traditions of Europe in the interests of telling an original New World story. A crucial figure in this was Jorge Luis Borges, the Argentine writer who lived in Paris and Spain during the ferments of Modernism, and whose main influences were, as he liked to say, the tradition of European and British literature, and the influence of the Argentinian gaucho. Borges was a remarkable collector and hoarder of interesting and obscure artistic influences, and his forty or so brief stories, his "games with infinity," turned the encounter between the labyrinths of modern fiction and the South American landscape into an extraordinary contact point of writing.

Borges' sense that Latin America – from the first conquests onward, one of the great places of encounter between familiarity and strangeness – was a field of play for a new kind of fiction has been inherited by many remarkable successors: Alejo Carpentier, Julio Cortázar, Guillermo Cabrera Infante, Mario Vargas Llosa, Manuel Puig. Each offers some different glimpse of the struggle of modern fiction to master a still only part-written continent, a hidden New World the Western imagination has never fully grasped. Latin-American "magical realism" has been described as a revolt of the imagination against the prison of a limited history, a fictional utopia where not simply tales but the facts and things they encompass break free of historical reality to become a magical part of the historical life. Most of Márquez' stories are set in a Colombia which is itself displayed to us as an exemplary fiction – "a country of mirrors (or mirages)," as he calls it. They show the novel breaking out from its European limits, into a world of strange new histories and multiple identities, a world where time is cyclical and myth and fantasy natural. This process has been echoed in much Latin-American and Caribbean writing – in the writings, say, of V. S. Naipaul, or the Guyanan novels of Wilson Harris, telling self-consciously post-colonial fables of a margin where old stories dissolve, narrative still has to be given a shape, the imagination located in its own landscape, a new myth and history written. Naipaul sets his stories, sometimes fictional, sometimes non-fictional, at innumerable points of cultural intersection, where different cultures and narratives meet, take on shape, fade again, and then are replaced by a new formation. Today such ways of writing have become a crucial part of contemporary fictional culture, as writers from South America, the Caribbean or other places from the shifting post-colonial world come to New York, or London, or Paris, creating a new spirit of imaginative invention where fiction seems in a state of ceaseless refraction and multiplication. The changing climate of the novel still owes much to the impulse that comes from these new imaginative refractions and revisions – which, as such encounters always have, challenge our very idea of fictionality itself. As Carlos Fuentes has said, the novel has always been the book of imaginary new worlds: the form that has most succeeded in carrying our imagination forward through space, time and geography, into new configurations we have yet to understand. Or, as V. S. Naipaul puts it, the task of the novel has always been the making of new maps of the world. What we now see is a widening of the worlds in encounter, and a new kind of story that comes from the point of contact and collision.

5.

As I said at the beginning, this is a book about fictions: the strange surpluses that myth and the imagination add to history. For creative culture has its own geography, which persistently reaches beyond familiar realities or the known historical boundaries. And fictions are self-conscious and complex versions of the diverse and oblique means we use when we try to order and apprehend reality, name the world into existence or give our own space and time sense and significance. As Edmundo O'Gorman put it, the "invention of America" was a great instance of this process, a supreme instance of the fact that "the being of things is not something that they contain in themselves but something that is assigned or granted to them." Needing to be named and ordered by the European imagination, America shattered the frame of the classical and Christian world-view, forced people to recognize that the world was not all there, God-given, but was something that could be named, shaped and discovered by human initiatives, ideas and technologies. The idea that the "invention of America" helped define a first task of modern art, the task of relating a world almost too great to be imagined, has been one of the great sources of our modern notion of the fictional itself. When Europe invented America, and then America in turn invented Europe, a major and risky adventure of the modern imagination began. With the travels, real or imaginary, of Raleigh and Chateaubriand, Irving and Hawthorne, Dickens and James, Kafka and Hemingway, a great new mythology of the fictional imagination grew. Image generated image, and myth generated myth. The myths and images shuttled back and forth, flourishing on each other, and producing their own increasing sense of the power of the fictional. The fictionality of America, the fictionality of Europe, themselves became part of the game, and created a common and infinitely expandible imaginative community. And between the splendid and revealing fictions shuttled the pilgrims, in fact and in fiction: expatriate artists lured to the other shore by something, a dream, an idea of culture, a hunger for experience; fictional voyagers who were drawn by this grand need or that great fantasy, migrant minds passing in both directions. "There's no romance here but what you might have brought with you," Ralph Touchett had said to Isabel Archer, just come to Europe, in Henry James' *The Portrait of a Lady* (1881). "I've brought a great deal, but it seems to me I've brought it to the right place," she replies. It was always a double romance that was at stake, a romance of Europe, a romance of America; and it became nothing less than a myth, if myth is the place where history and the imagination intersect. Meantime the worlds that the writers explored, bringing their romances with them, increasingly came to resemble the identities that had been invented for them – and so provoked new imaginings in their turn.

This complex trade and barter the Atlantic Ocean has summoned into being has, of course, been a trade in commodities, the systems of modern development, the dialectics of history. But it has also been a trade in imaginative operations, and generated some of the most essential dialectics of our modern art. If, in history, we owe much of our experience of the modernizing process and the shaping of our present condition to this transatlantic traffic, so, in literature, we owe much of our sense of the modernities and the styles of art to the great barter of forms, images, dreams of the mind which has travelled across the same geographical space. "America is my country and Paris is my home town," said Gertrude Stein – explaining, among other things, her sense of the international sources of the modern spirit in the arts. And out of these fictive and aesthetic transactions came one of the most striking of products – our very idea of fiction, the novel, itself. The novel, the form that was born in picaresque adventure, has been one of the most striking productions to come from the entire enterprise. The novel, as Carlos Fuentes has said, has always been the book of imaginary new worlds, the equivalent of a voyage of discovery. No doubt it would have existed without the Atlantic Ocean; the fact remains that, at almost every stage in the traffic from the eighteenth century on, the novel has been present. It captured the early utopian imaginings, and it was there in the age of romanticisms and revolutions, at a time when other worlds were still rich in othernesss. It was there during the growth of the modern historical process, as fantastic utopias rose on the western horizon, and in the even more fantastic pages of fiction. It grasped at the rise of modernity, and the new claims and dislocations it created in art. It now explores with us the plural, ever-shifting forms of our time of postmodernity. It has told a story not so much of history, but of how, within the case of history, the fictive mind grasps in its own ways at the new borders and frontiers of the imagination.

Today, we are often told, America and Europe are decisively pulling apart. Since the end of the Cold War in 1989, Americans have been disengaging, militarily and to a lesser degree politically, from Europe, and are now busy exploring their own continent and their distinctive identity on the active Pacific rim, while attending to the quickly changing ethnic mix of their own complex nation. The Columbus year of 1992 saw fresh doubts about the Columbian mythology from those who felt that what it really marked was a long history of colonialism, repression and genocide. Meantime Europe, freed from the omni-present threat of Cold War terror, was turning to pay attention to the labyrinthine mysteries of its own confused Euro-identity. But this supposed break in transatlantic relations seems to me very unlikely in the world of fact (the inter-penetration is far too deep), and even more so in the world of fictions. The stories of America and Europe, historically and mythically, have always been in change, and have constantly opened out to what has been repressed, hidden or falsified. The older stories have long since dissolved into new versions, changed maps of the world, and the process actively continues. The canon dissolves, the multi-culturalists try to dispense with the Dead White European Males and the old stories. But the great fictions themselves, being neither quite true nor utterly false – since they are not simply facts of power but principles of the imagination – are not so easily dispensed with. Too much history and too much art have gone into their making; they are part of our essential record of human under-standing. Meantime, of course, the myths remain for our constant experimental inspection, our deconstructions and our reconstructions.

As for the novel itself, that is too often thought to be under threat from the age of the Death of the Author and the End of the Book. This funereal notion seems to me equally improbable. Our age is one haunted, and perhaps more than any other, by genres and myths and images and narratives. On page and screen, it consumes fictions in ever greater quantities, because narrative – and the novel itself – are amongst our most fundamental ways of exploring space and time, culture, identity, dream and the future. At the close of Italo Calvino's marvellous book *Invisible Cities* (1972), his narrator, Marco Polo, having told innumerable tales of strange and improbable cities seen on his travels, thinks of the new tales he has yet to tell, and the ultimate city "towards which my journey tends": "The catalogue of forms is endless: until every shape has found its city, new cities will continue to be born." The new cities of fiction, born of as yet unimaginable travels into what Marco Polo calls the cities of the future – cities as yet without shape or form – will continue to engage us. They will be stories of different Europes, and different Americas. But our imaginations have always travelled through fact and fiction, and, as I have tried to show, the Atlantic has been one of the chief seas of their voyage.

One of the great fantasies cultivated by various novelists from Jules Verne to Bernard Kellerman has been the idea of building a great bridge or tunnel across the Atlantic, with various dramatic conse-quences. Such are our modern technologies that one of these days we will doubtless have it. But the bridges and tunnels have been constructed already, through the forms of the fictional imagination. America was a myth itself; the American Dream and the American Nightmare, the Golden Shore and the Wonders of the West, the New Start and the Great American Adventure are testaments to our drive to order and explain the world as a romance and a metaphor. No less important was the American romance of Europe, the imagination attaching itself to what had been otherwise discarded. If America was a promise, Europe was a dark and disturbing secret, an aesthetic but also a fallen experience. Stepping westward, stepping eastward, became part of the great story of art. It was an emblematic journey, on which life turned into art or literature. It posed a mystery about the relation of history to form, of material to aesthetic culture, of fact to splendid deception and deceit. Two continents imagined and challenged each other; from it came a universal fable, as well as a changed and original conception of literary art. There is every good reason to suppose that, in ever-changing shapes and forms, and as part of the expanding world-narrative, with its growing web of refractions and human interlockings, such myths and fables will go on being told in the future.

Index

Index

Ballet Suèdois, 313
Ballets Russes, 305n., 314
Balzac, Honoré de, 49, 50, 84, 112, 194, 199
Bancroft, George, 74
Barbusse, Henri
  Feu, Le (Under Fire), 298, 341
Barlow, Joel, 41, 49
  works: Columbiad, The, 76
Barnes, Djuna, 312, 337, 340, 377
Barney, Natalie, 252, 310, 315
Barr, Frederic, 234, 243
Barr, Robert, 234, 238, 242
Barrett, William, 420 and n.
Barrie, J. M., 234
Barry, Joseph A., 337n.
Barth, John, 454
  works: Giles Goat-Boy, 459; Letters, 459
Barth, Karl, 429
Barthelme, Donald, 465 and n.
Bartram, William
  Travels in East and West Florida, 28 and n.
Baudrillard, Jean, 466–8 and n., 470
  works: America, 466
Bauhaus school, 5, 280
Beach, Sylvia, 301, 305, 310–11 and n., 312,
  315, 331n., 371, 421
  works: Shakespeare and Company, 310n.,
  331n., 371n.
Beadle Dime novels, 51
Beardsley, Aubrey, 226
"Beat" generation, 425
Beckett, Samuel, 325, 339, 372–3, 424 and n.,
  427, 428, 454 works: Murphy, 373
Beecher, Rev. Henry Ward, 163
Beerbohm, Max, 206, 226
Behan, Brendan, 425
Behrman, S. N., 182n.
Bell, Alexander Graham, 159
Bell, Clive, 259 and n.
Bell, Coral, 431n.
Bellamy, Edward, 214
  Looking Backward, 276–7
belle époque, 251, 268
Bellow, Saul, 408, 421, 428 and n., 429, 480
  in post-war Paris, 422–3 and n.
  works: Adventures of Augie March, The, 422–
  3; Dangling Man, 421–2; Dean's December,
  The, 422; Humboldt's Gift, 219
Beloff, Max, 431n.
Bendiner, Robert, 364n.

Benét, Stephen Vincent, 310–11, 337
Benfey, Christopher, 238n.
Benjamin, Walter, 465
Bennett, James Gordon, 102
Benson, A. C., 196
Benson, F. E., 201
Berenson, Bernard
  art authenticator, 182–3, 209
  Florence years, 149, 182–3, 209, 256, 258
  Harvard aesthete, 256
  works: Sketch for a Self Portrait, 183
Berger, Max, 87n.
Bergonzi, Bernard, 278 and n.
Berryman, John, 238n.
Besant, Annie, 203
Beveridge, Albert J., 249
Bewley, Marius, 196n.
Biddle, George, 320
Bierce, Ambrose, 184, 223, 229, 230
  works: Tales of Soldiers and Civilians, 230
Bigsby, C. W. E., 431n., 470 and n.
Binns, Ronald, 388n.
Bird, Sally, 320
Bird, William, 316, 320
Bishop, John Peale, 314, 322
Black Manikin Press, 374
Black Sun Press, 372
Blackmur, R. P.
  "American Literary Expatriate," 332
Blackwood's Magazine, 88
Blake, William, 30, 86 works: "America", 30
Blanch, Leslie, 425n.
Blast (magazine), 265
Blind Man (Dada magazine), 270
Bloomsbury Group, 245, 272
Boeuf Sur Le Toit, Le (masked spectacle-
  concert), 304
Bohemianism
  Chicago, 215
  encouraged by Wilde's American visit,
  208–10 and n., 224–5
  New York, 227–8, 233
  see also Paris
Böll, Heinrich, 427
Boni and Liveright (publishers), 319
Bonner, Margerie, 394, 397
Bookman (journal), 234
Borges, Jorge Luis, 454, 483
Boston, 97–8, 114, 115, 181, 189, 212, 277
Bourne, Randolph, 333

Index

Index

READ MORE IN PENGUIN

In every corner of the world, on every subject under the sun, Penguin represents quality and variety – the very best in publishing today.

For complete information about books available from Penguin – including Puffins, Penguin Classics and Arkana – and how to order them, write to us at the appropriate address below. Please note that for copyright reasons the selection of books varies from country to country.

In the United Kingdom: Please write to *Dept. EP, Penguin Books Ltd, Bath Road, Harmondsworth, West Drayton, Middlesex UB7 ODA*

In the United States: Please write to *Consumer Sales, Penguin USA, P.O. Box 999, Dept. 17109, Bergenfield, New Jersey 07621-0120*. VISA and MasterCard holders call 1-800-253-6476 to order Penguin titles

In Canada: Please write to *Penguin Books Canada Ltd, 10 Alcorn Avenue, Suite 300, Toronto, Ontario M4V 3B2*

In Australia: Please write to *Penguin Books Australia Ltd, P.O. Box 257, Ringwood, Victoria 3134*

In New Zealand: Please write to *Penguin Books (NZ) Ltd, Private Bag 102902, North Shore Mail Centre, Auckland 10*

In India: Please write to *Penguin Books India Pvt Ltd, 706 Eros Apartments, 56 Nehru Place, New Delhi 110 019*

In the Netherlands: Please write to *Penguin Books Netherlands bv, Postbus 3507, NL-1001 AH Amsterdam*

In Germany: Please write to *Penguin Books Deutschland GmbH, Metzlerstrasse 26, 60594 Frankfurt am Main*

In Spain: Please write to *Penguin Books S. A., Bravo Murillo 19, 1° B, 28015 Madrid*

In Italy: Please write to *Penguin Italia s.r.l., Via Felice Casati 20, I–20124 Milano*

In France: Please write to *Penguin France S. A., 17 rue Lejeune, F–31000 Toulouse*

In Japan: Please write to *Penguin Books Japan, Ishikiribashi Building, 2–5–4, Suido, Bunkyo-ku, Tokyo 112*

In South Africa: Please write to *Longman Penguin Southern Africa (Pty) Ltd, Private Bag X08, Bertsham 2013*

BY THE SAME AUTHOR

Unsent Letters

The postbag of Malcolm Bradbury – academic, author, lecturer, thinker – is crammed with requests for help and advice. 'Please help me with my thesis on the campus novel', 'Please come and talk to my faculty in a remote area of the Scottish Highlands', 'Please adapt a classic novel for television', and so on.

In reply, Malcolm Bradbury has prepared a book of imaginary letters to cover any request he may receive. There is a letter of thanks for his invitation to talk to three hostile students and pass the night in a barn; a reply to the European student who wishes to know if he is the same person as David Lodge and which of the two stole his supervisor's umbrella; and scathingly funny letters on structuralism, education and a great deal more.

'One of the few genuinely witty books of the decade' – *Observer*

The Modern British Novel

In this stimulating and enjoyable book Malcolm Bradbury assesses a century of the modern Bristish novel from 1878 to the present. The major names are well represented but one of the many pleasures of Malcolm Bradbury's approach is the inclusion of writers that are less well known and read yet deserve some place in a history of twentieth-century fiction. Another is his discussion of recent novelists he admires and the book includes a new afterword on the nineties.

also published:

The Modern World
Modernism: A Guide to European Literature 1890–1930 (edited with James McFarlane)

and:

Cuts	**The Penguin Book of Modern**
Doctor Criminale	**British Short Stories** (ed.)
Eating People is Wrong	**Rates of Exchange**
The History Man	**Stepping Westward**
Mensonge	**Who Do You Think You Are?**
	Why Come to Slaka?